Women and the Criminal Justice System

SECOND EDITION

Women and the Criminal Justice System

Katherine Stuart van Wormer
University of Northern Iowa

Clemens Bartollas
University of Northern Iowa

PEARSON

Boston   New York   San Francisco
Mexico City   Montreal   Toronto   London   Madrid   Munich   Paris
Hong Kong   Singapore   Tokyo   Cape Town   Sydney

Series Editor: *Dave Repetto*
Editorial Assistant: *Liz DiMenno*
Marketing Manager: *Kelly May*
Senior Production Administrator: *Donna Simons*
Cover Administrator: *Kristina Mose-Libon*
Composition Buyer: *Linda Cox*
Manufacturing Buyer: *Megan Cochran*
Editorial Production Service: *Nesbitt Graphics, Inc.*
Electronic Composition: *Nesbitt Graphics, Inc.*

For related titles and support materials, visit our online catalog at www.ablongman.com.

Between the time website information is gathered and then published, it is not unusual for some sites to have closed. Also, the transcription of URLs can result in typographical errors. The publisher would appreciate notification where these errors occur so that they may be corrected in subsequent editions.

Library of Congress Cataloging-in-Publication Data

Van Wormer, Katherine S.
    Women and the criminal justice system / Katherine Stuart van Wormer, Clemens Bartollas. -- 2nd ed.
        p. cm.
        Includes bibliographical references and index.
        Contents: Women criminals -- Women as victims and survivors—Women as professionals.
        ISBN 0-205-48218-X
        1. Sex discrimination in criminal justice administration—United States. 2. Female offenders—United States. 3. Women prisoners—United States. 4. Women criminal justice personnel—United States. I. Bartollas, Clemens. II. Title.

HV9950.V38 2007
364.082—dc22   2006042860

Printed in the United States of America

10 9 8 7 6 5 4 3 2 1   10 09 08 07 06

Dedicated to
Flora Templeton Stuart and Natalie Stuart,
the sister and niece of Katherine van Wormer,
two woman lawyers in Bowling Green, Kentucky,
fighting for social justice.

CONTENTS

PREFACE

The world has changed in many ways since *Women and the Criminal Justice System* was published in 2000. While 9/11 militarized the society and led to reprioritizing of economic spending, hurricane Katrina opened the eyes of the world to the face of poverty in inner-city America. Globalization, or the interconnectedness of nations, perhaps has changed our daily lives most of all, first, in terms of the communications revolution (bestowing the gifts of email and the Internet), and, secondly, in terms of the global market, which has led to downsizing, economic restructuring of social services, and mass migration from the Global South to the Global North.

The impact on the criminal justice system and on professionals who work in that system has been profound. Since the concern of this book is girls and women, consider welfare reform and the many women forced to live at the margins. Economic conditions determine which kinds of crimes will be committed and opportunities for self-fulfillment. At the global level, consider the increasing gap between the rich and the poor, a fact making women from impoverished regions of the world vulnerable to recruitment into the prostitution and sex trafficking industry. Meanwhile, the market in illegal drugs pulls immigrant women into its vortex while the war on drugs continues to be a war against women and minorities.

It is in this context of globalization and the increasing feminization of poverty that the second edition of *Women and the Criminal Justice System* was shaped. Persons familiar with the first edition will soon note that we have made major changes including adding five new chapters, highlighting key terms in bold throughout the text, and listing key terms and relevant Web destinations at the end of every chapter. We have also added new updated boxed readings.

The most distinguishing change in this revised edition are the five new chapters on feminist theory and research; delinquency across the life course; substance abuse; restorative justice programs; and victimization of women globally, which explores in some depth human rights violations against women and takes us into the realms of sex trafficking, genital mutilation, and rape as a policy and product of war. We have much to learn from other nations, not only in terms of the mistreatment of women but also regarding innovations in the prevention and treatment of victimization. This new edition also includes a companion volume of personal narratives written by women inmates, survivors of crime, and professionals who have worked in the fields of the law, policing, and corrections.

The second edition continues to emphasize an empowerment perspective. Empowerment as conceptualized here starts from an understanding of power and powerlessness. Relevant to the criminal justice system, we focus on who makes the laws, who gets punished for which kind of crimes or for which drugs of choice—in short, who gets victimized by the system. Empowerment is a multidimensional construct that applies to the climate of social structures as well as to treatment of individuals. Person-centered, gender-specific initiatives, for example, can help girls and women in trouble with the law tap into their inner strengths to restore (or discover) a sense of well-being. From the victim's perspective, empowerment is about healing the wounds of crime and coming to see oneself not as a victim but as a survivor. Women professionals in the fields of criminal justice—law enforcement, law, and corrections, all of which are male-dominated, patriarchal fields—seek and often find empowerment when their voices are heard.

Plan of the Book

The book is divided into five parts. Part One, Introduction, lays out the theoretical framework: the empowerment perspective for understanding gender, patriarchy, and social control and how these three elements interact. Part Two, Women Criminals, is concerned with girls and women who have been arrested and convicted of crime. Chapter 2 examines current research on crime and delinquency while Chapter 3 is devoted to feminist criminological theory and research. Chapter 4 examines delinquency across the life course.

Part Three, Drug Addiction, Prison, and Restoration, takes us through women's pathway to crime when substance abuse is a factor, as it most often is. Personal and policy considerations are discussed. The final chapter in this section examines innovative processes that restore justice and promote healing, and describes victim-offender conferencing as a form of restorative justice with much relevance.

Part Four, Women as Victims and Survivors, brings an empowerment perspective to the subjects of rape, partner abuse, and the victimization of women internationally. Recent statistics and research findings help reveal the extent and magnitude of the battering, rape, and sexual exploitation of women worldwide.

Part Five, Women as Professionals, takes us into the realm of women as they promote social justice and engage in empowerment of other women (and men). Women's contributions to policing and legal fields have been significant, the more so in recent years. However, corrections is an area in which women have moved from the helm of the profession to the periphery; prison privatization and emphasis on security over counseling are two contributing factors. Even here, however, women's contributions have been and still are substantial, including inside the prison system. In humanizing these areas of criminal justice, women often have had to confront organizational structures that were oppressive and unsuitable for their needs. Women of color have made inroads professionally but often only after challenging institutional racism and sexism simultaneously. Empowerment for women in these legally based fields has come in the form of participating in the formulation of social policy as an avenue for constructive social change, change often directed toward the empowerment of marginalized persons—the offenders and victims with whom and for whom the police officers, lawyers, and correctional staff work. The final chapter presents a summary of the book's themes and prospects of future directions.

Acknowledgments

Many individuals have contributed to the writing of this book. The authors are profoundly grateful to our spouses. Robert van Wormer edited and typed materials throughout the manuscript. Linda Dippold Bartollas was a constant source of support and encouragement throughout the many phases involved in the publication of this text.

The authors are very grateful to those victims, offenders, and professionals in the justice system who were willing to be interviewed, both for the text and for *Voices of Women and the Criminal Justice System*. Special thanks to Lynn Rutz for typing and proofreading and Renese Latoya Wynn for typing, photocopying, and helping get the manuscript ready for submission. To Christopher Mullins, criminologist, we extend thanks for his help in reviewing the manuscript. We are also grateful to Michael Trimble for editing and typing *Voices of Women and the Criminal Justice System*. We want to acknowledge our appreciation to Jennifer Jacobson and Dave Repetto, our editors at Allyn & Bacon, and to Liz DiMenno, the editorial assistant at Allyn & Bacon who helped us in a variety of ways.

We would also like to thank the following reviewers, whose comments helped shape this book: Marion Cockey, Towson University; Kimberly DeTardo-Bora, Marshall University; Martha Karin Dudash, Cameron University; JoAnne Lecci, Nassau Community College; Joseph Keith Price, West Texas A & M University; Debra Ross, Grand Valley State University; and L. Susan Williams, Kansas State University.

Women and the Criminal Justice System

PART ONE

Introduction

This introductory chapter provides the social context necessary to examine the "setting in time" of women who are victims of crime, women who are convicted and sentenced for their crimes, and women who work in various agencies of the criminal justice system. This social context is the patriarchal society in which males are dominant and females experience oppression in a variety of ways. An examination of sexism, racism, ethnicity, classism, sexual orientation, and age is especially helpful in expressing the **multiple marginality** that women face in this society and elsewhere.

Feminists are not united in how women are affected by the oppressions they suffer. Indeed, as Chapter 1 suggests, there are at least six main expressions of feminist theory—liberal feminism, socialist feminism, Marxist feminism, radical feminism, third-wave feminism, and post-modern feminism. Dorie Klein (2000) defined three primary features of feminism, which draw acceptance among various expressions of feminism: (1) An interest in the well-being and empowerment of women victims, offenders, and professionals who work in the field; (2) a focus on gender in explaining individual and institutional behaviors related to crime and crime control; and (3) an understanding that gender relations are socially constructed, rather than being a natural fact, in placing women in statuses and positions subordinate to those of men.

1 Gender, Patriarchy, and Social Control

Two major goals of this text are to understand the sources of gender inequality and to advocate changes to empower women (Williams, 2000, p. 9). Feminist criminology, committed to understanding the status of women in society, will be a helpful guide in our inquiry. Employing interdisciplinary theoretical frameworks, feminist criminology examines gender and gender inequality as well as the intersections of race, ethnicity, class, gender, and age (Miller and Mullins, 2006, p. 204).

In examining the challenges and obstacles faced by women offenders, victims, and workers in the justice system, this book has developed five underlying feminist themes. First, women offenders, victims, and practitioners experience sexism, racism, and classism on an ongoing basis, and these forms of oppression contribute to the feelings of "multiple marginality" (Chesney-Lind, 1997, p. 4). Second, the effects of the multiple oppressions of gender, class, and race are not merely arithmetic; that is, they are not simply interlocking and piled on each other (Spelman, 1989, p. 123). Thus, "how one form of oppression is experienced is influenced by and influences how another form is experienced" (Spelman, 1989, p. 123). Third, this examination focuses on the social construction of knowledge and how it is typically male oriented. The study of crime itself, as the following discussion reveals, has been written by males about males. The myths concerning female offenders, victims, and practitioners are vivid examples of this social construction of knowledge. Fourth, this examination of women in the justice system heavily emphasizes the importance of social context. In this social context, which is a patriarchal society, women discover how they are expected to think, feel, and act (Spelman, 1989, p. 14). Subcultures within society have varying definitions and expectations of what it means to be a woman, and these norms and values can influence a woman to become a lawyer or a criminal. Finally, the chapters of this text nearly always end with a theme of empowerment. They provide a means or a direction for how women, whether offenders, victims, or practitioners, can move from oppression to empowerment.

Beginning with how the study of crime has been dominated by males and the main feminist theories of criminology, this chapter examines the oppressions that females experience in the social context of the United States and elsewhere. These oppressions take place in a patriarchal society and are reflected in the laws defining women's place; the sexual harassments of women in criminal justice institutions; and the expressions of sexism, racism, and class bias as they affect women offenders, victims, and practitioners.

The Study of Crime and the Male Perspective

Men commit the majority of crimes. Arrest, self-report, and victimization data all reveal that men and boys commit more frequent and serious crimes than do women and girls. Men also have a virtual monopoly on the commission of corporate, organized, and political crimes (Beirne and Messerschmidt, 1991, pp. 547–548). It is for this reason that "gender has consistently been advanced by criminologists as the strongest predictor of criminal involvement" (Messerschmidt, 1993, p. 1). Yet, as Heidensohn has aptly observed, "most criminologists have resisted this obvious insight with an energy comparable to that of Medieval churchmen denying Galileo or Victorian bishops attacking Darwin" (Heidensohn, 1987, p. 22).

Heidensohn's emphasis on resistance may be somewhat overstated, but it is apparent that major theoretical works written by male criminologists about men and boys have been alarmingly gender-blind (Messerschmidt, 1993, p. 1). Meda Chesney-Lind (2006) has expressed this viewpoint well:

> In my view, the study of crime has been an incontrovertibly male, even "macho," field. Male criminologists have studied other younger men in conflict with an admittedly unequal society and found in their behavior something repellent but also something compelling—witness a major theorist in the area calling the delinquent a "rogue male." Let's face it, male delinquency, particularly gang behavior, is a dramatic form of defiance. Perhaps for that reason, it has been thought of, at least by some criminologists, as the ultimate form of masculinity.
>
> A quick review of the classics in the area will show that my characterization is not all that extreme and that the study of delinquency was almost always the study of male delinquency. In one early work, for example, male delinquency rates were referred to as "delinquency rates"; another 600-page book on gangs spent only one page on the female gangs found by the researcher. Girls were often not even mentioned and occasionally explicitly eliminated. Delinquency theories, then, stress male experience and male problems. (pp. 195–196)

Chesney-Lind's thesis is that delinquency theories are preoccupied with why males commit delinquent acts. Kathleen Daly and Chesney-Lind also stated that the study of crime and the justice process is shaped by male experiences and understanding of the social world (Daly and Chesney-Lind, 1988). Daly and Chesney-Lind (1988) further listed five aspects of feminist thought that distinguish it from the majority of criminological inquiry:

- Gender is not a natural fact but a complex social, historical, and cultural product; it is related to, but not simply derived from, biological sex difference and reproductive capacities.

- Gender and gender relations order social life and social institutions in fundamental ways.
- Gender relations and constructs of masculinity and femininity are not symmetrical but are based on an organizing principle of men's superiority and social and political–economic dominance over women.
- Systems of knowledge reflect men's views of the natural and social world: the production of knowledge is gendered.
- Women should be at the center of intellectual inquiry, not peripheral, invisible, or appendages to men. (p. 504)

Importance of Patriarchy

Patriarchy can be defined in a number of ways. Walby proposes that patriarchy is a "system of social structures and practices in which men dominate, oppress and exploit women" (1990, p. 20). Anderson contends that patriarchy is "a hierarchical system of social relations among men that creates and maintains the domination of women" (2000, p. 15). Sheryl J. Grana, in expanding the definition of patriarchy, adds that "patriarchy is a social structural arrangement whereby males, just by virtue of being males, have more privilege than women do in society. Moreover, this privilege often leads to greater power, access to opportunity, and better rewards for men" (2002, p. 2).

Grana alerts her readers to a typical problem of most definitions of patriarchy: They tend to lean toward **essentialism,** the idea that all members of one group can be lumped together under one label. Obviously, some men—white, middle to upper class, heterosexual, and Christian—have more privilege than do other men. Yet Grana (2002) points out that the existence of patriarchy benefits men who lack these features because of the sheer virtue of their maleness. She articulates the characteristics of patriarchy as "violence, power, control, linearity, polarization, stereotyping, ideology, phallocentrism, and misogyny" and contends that these characteristics can be felt at the psychological, social, familial, and institutional levels. (p. 3)

Florynce Kennedy (1972) defines four different kinds of **oppression:**

1. Personal/psychological oppression that comes about when a person believes she or he is nothing because society says she or he is nothing;
2. Private oppression in a private situation that could be illustrated by a woman's boss trying to persuade her to have sexual intercourse;
3. Public oppression that involves large-scale situations in which society makes blanket decisions harming individuals' lives, such as when the government spends a female tax payer's money on war even though she needs it far more for child care;
4. Cultural oppression that takes place when an aspect of the culture distorts, omits, or trivializes the energy, input, and ideas of entire groups of people. An example of this is found in history books that attribute everything to white men (cited in Grana, 2002, pp. 6–7).

Grana asserts that these notions of oppression are a reminder that oppression occurs on many levels and takes numerous forms. Oppression not only goes hand in hand with patriarchy, but is also a major force fuelling patriarchy.

Feminist Theories

There have been three waves of feminism. The first feminist movement was born in 1848 at the Seneca Falls Convention when women demanded the right to vote. Its suffrage emphasis culminated when the Nineteenth Amendment to the Constitution was ratified in 1919. The second feminist movement began in the 1960s. It was sparked by the Equal Pay Act of 1963, which required equal pay for equal work, and Title VII of the Civil Rights Act of 1964, which applied to wages as well as hiring and promotions. Another major influence in the birth of the second feminist movement was the publication of Betty Friedan's *The Feminine Mystique* (1983). Friedan issued a call for housewives to seek their own identity through the development of themselves as full human beings. Emerging in the 1980s and 1990s, the third wave of the women's movement challenged the idea that poor women, women of color, and lesbians share the same problems as white middle-class women or similarly located poor men, men of color, or gay men (Price and Sokoloff, 2005, p. 3). These feminist movements, especially the second and third, have resulted in at least six main expressions of feminist theory: liberal feminism, socialist feminism, Marxist feminism, radical feminism, third-wave feminism, and post-modern feminism.

Liberal Feminism

Liberal feminism, or egalitarianism, calls for women's equality of opportunity and freedom of choice. Proponents of this theory do not believe that the system is inherently unequal or that discrimination is systematic. Liberal feminists hold that affirmative action, the equal rights amendment, and other opportunity laws or policies provide evidence that men and women can work together to "androgynize" gender roles (blend male and female traits and characteristics) and eliminate discriminatory policies and practices (Simpson, 1989).

Jaggar and Rothenberg (1984) trace liberal feminism to the eighteenth- and nineteenth-century social ideals of liberty and equality (pp. 83–84). Liberal feminists contend that a major reason for the discrimination against women and female adolescents is gender-role socialization. Conventional family patterns, according to this position, structure masculine and feminine identities (Beirne and Messerschmidt, 1991, p. 518).

In 1972, Congress passed the Equal Rights Amendment (ERA). In the campaign to ratify it, many women were mobilized into feminism, and liberal feminists were introduced to the political mainstream. Liberal feminists argued that the physiological differences between men and women fail to justify providing women and men with unequal opportunities. The National Organization for

Women (NOW) soon represented what has come to be called liberal feminism or egalitarianism (Rollins, 1996, p. 3).

Liberal feminism has become a reform social movement that has sought to bring about change within the existing social order. By the end of the 1970s, NOW had broadened its stance to include such social issues as lesbian and gay rights, homemakers' rights, the threat of nuclear energy to the species, and legal and economic equality. However, the defeat of the ERA in 1982 ushered in a conservative backlash during which rights previously won by feminists, including affirmative action and legal abortion, were challenged (Rollins, 1996, p. 3).

Socialist Feminism

Socialist feminists, in contrast to other feminists, give neither class nor gender the highest priority. Instead, socialist feminists view both class and gender relations as equal, as they interact with and co-reproduce each other in society. To understand class, socialist feminists argue, it is necessary to recognize how class is structured by gender, and to understand that gender requires that one see how it is structured by class. Crime results from the interaction of these relationships, because it is the powerful who have more legitimate and illegitimate opportunities to commit crime. Low female crime rates, then, are related to women's powerless position in the United States (Rogers, 1973, pp. 223–246).

Socialist feminists challenge both liberal feminists and Marxist feminists. They contend that liberal feminists are fighting for a world in which women pursue self-interest in a capitalist system. Women, then, are pursuing profits, continues this critique, regardless of the good of society. Socialist feminists claim that Marxist feminists have paid insufficient attention to women's issues, neglecting that women have been oppressed both as women and as workers.

Socialist feminists hold that patriarchy predated capitalism. In patriarchy, in U.S. society as well as others, men maintain power over women and exploit their labor in the home and in the workplace. MacKinnon (1987) even claims that in socialist feminism sexuality is as central to feminism as work is to Marxism. Accordingly, patriarchy expropriates women's bodies, as is illustrated by rape, pornography, and domestic violence.

Marxist Feminism

Marxist feminists argue that as private property evolved, males dominated all social institutions. Consequently, gender and class inequalities result from property relations and the capitalist mode of production (Beirne and Messerschmidt, 1991). Marxist feminism, sometimes called Marxist feminist radicalism, is based on an anticapitalist premise and, as a reflection of Marxist ideology, sees the oppression of women as arising out of a class society based on private property (Rollins, 1996, p. 5).

According to Marxist radicalism, capitalism makes profits from the low-wage work of women in factories and corporations, both in the United States and elsewhere. The family receives the focus as the means that capitalism uses to conserve and pass on private property and to confine women to domestic slavery. What makes sense from the capitalist perspective, state proponents of Marxist feminism, is that keeping women in a subservient role constitutes the least costly means for a capitalist society to take care of its nonproductive members (Donovan, 1985).

Radical Feminism

Radical feminists view masculine power and privilege as the root cause of all social inequality. The most important relations in any society, according to radical feminists, are found in patriarchy, which pertains to masculine control of labor power and sexuality of women (Beirne and Messerschmidt, 1991, p. 519). Jaggar and Rothensberg (1984), two radical feminists, stated that women were the first oppressed group in history, that women's oppression is so widespread that it exists in virtually every known society, and that women's oppression is so deep that it is the hardest form of oppression to eradicate (pp. 83–84). Radical feminists, especially, focus on sexual violence toward women.

Third-Wave Feminism

Third-wave feminists, who are also called women of color feminists, womanists, and critical race feminists, object to white feminists defining "women's issues" from their own standpoint without including women of color and third-world concerns and to antiracist theory presuming that racial and ethnic minority women's experiences are the same as those of their male counterparts. These feminist theorists focus on the significant roles that sexism, racism, class bias, sexual orientation, age, and other forms of socially structured inequality have in women's lives. They introduced the concept of **intersectionalities** to understand the interlocking sites of oppression and to examine how the categories of race, ethnicity, class, gender, sexuality, and age in intersecting systems of domination rely on each other to function. Third-wave feminism helps clarify not only those behaviors of women defined as criminal but also the many crimes against women. This approach makes clear the need to understand issues of social justice in evaluating the criminalization of women (Price and Sokoloff, 2005, p. 3). Furthermore, this form of feminist theory seeks ways for men and women to work together to eliminate racism, sexism, and class privilege (Rollins, 1996, p. 5). bell hooks (1984), in the following quote, attacks the anti-male stance of radical feminists:

> *They were not eager to call attention to the fact that men do not share a common social status; that patriarchy does not negate the existence of class and race privilege or exploitation; that all men do not benefit equally from sexism. They did not want to acknowledge that bourgeois white women, though often victimized by sexism, have more power and privilege, are less likely to be exploited or oppressed, than poor, uneducated, non-white males. (p. 68)*

Post-Modern Feminism

Post-modern feminists criticize other feminists for assuming that women are a "clearly defined and uncontroversially given interest group" (Smart, 1995, p. 10). While positivist feminists, as well as other modernists, claim that the truth can be determined providing all agree on responsible ways of going about it, **post-modern feminism** argues for multiple truths that take contexts into account (Collins, 1998, pp. 196–197; Wonder and Caulfield, 1993). Post-modern feminists also question whether any knowledge is knowable and reject the idea that there is a universal definition of justice true for all people all of the time. They emphasize the importance of alternative discourses and accounts that frequently take the form of examining the effects of language and symbolic representation (Flavin, 2001).

Backlash to the Women's Movement

There continues to be a backlash to the 1960s women's movement in the United States. This backlash can be viewed among the fervent antiabortionists for whom religion and politics are merged. It can also be seen in the sharply increased rate of incarceration of women, especially poor and minority, throughout the 1990s, despite a significant decline in violent offenses committed by women. Furthermore, it can be seen in the passing of laws by various jurisdictions across the United States that define pregnant women on drugs as criminals alleged to be delivering controlled substances to their unborn child. Finally, this ongoing backlash is viewed through the periodic reemergence of the myth that a new and more dangerous type of female criminal has come on the scene as a result of the women's movement (Price and Sokoloff, 2005, p. 5).

Human Agency

Sociology, and research and theory on feminism have "rediscovered" an emphasis on human agency. The term **human agency,** or **agency,** recognizes the importance that women not only are acted on by social influences and structural constraints, but also make choices and decisions based on the alternatives that they see before them. The symbolic interactionist perspective and life history studies have long acknowledged the importance of human agency. The rational choice approach and routine activities more recently have placed an importance on rationality in delinquent and criminal behaviors. The various perspectives on the life course all consider that individuals are "planful" and make choices among options that are available to them. It is these decisions that are so critical in constructing their life course (Elder, Jr., 1994, p. 6; Emirbayer and Mische, 1998, pp. 962–1023).

There has been intensive interest among sociological theorists in the relationship between agency and structure. Margaret Archer has argued that "the problem of structure and agency has rightly come to be seen as the basic issue in modern social theory" (Archer, 1988, p. ix). In 1964, George Homans called for a move "to return to an action theory grounded firmly in the instrumental, calculating, and purposive orientations of individuals" (Homans, 1964, pp. 809–818). In 1990, James S. Coleman's major work, *Foundations of Social Theory*, linked purposive action at the micro level to interdependence at the macro level, showing that action is a complex social and interactive phenomenon (Coleman, 1990).

To understand gender relations, it is necessary to examine both the structures of relationships, which involve the enduring and expected patterns of behavior that constrain practices, and the agency of individuals in learning, accommodating, navigating, and resisting these structures. Agency itself is made up of both social practices and behaviors and the configurations of gender identity that women bring to these activities. In some cases the two correspond, as when women draw from a repertoire of behaviors in order to enact or demonstrate their gender identity; yet the relationship between gendered social practices and gender identities is sometimes much more complex (Miller and Mullins, 2006, p. 11).

Oppression, Patriarchal Society, and the Criminal Justice System

Each society must grapple with the decision about how to distribute its power, wealth, and opportunities. Sometimes the distribution is fairly egalitarian, and in other cases it is dramatically unequal. Less egalitarian societies have apportioned privilege based on various factors, such as age or race. In the United States and elsewhere, gender has been the determinant. Men and women in U.S. society have been viewed as polar opposites with contrasting abilities and capacities. The very personality traits that are regarded as positive in a man were considered signs of dysfunction in a woman (Rothenberg, 1998). Indeed, as Rothenberg noted, "until very recently, introductory psychology textbooks provided a description of neurosis in a woman that was virtually identical with their description of a healthy male personality" (p. 7).

Social scientists traditionally have distinguished between "sex," which is a biologically based category, and "gender," which refers to the socially constructed meanings that are associated with each sex. The meaning of what is masculine or feminine tends to vary over time. In addition, one culture's perception of masculine or feminine behavior may be the exact opposite of that in another culture. For example, strenuous physical activity is typically considered to be more appropriate for men than for women, but in one society in which women are responsible for such labor, the heaviest load is regarded as being "so heavy only a woman can lift it" (Rothenberg, 1998, pp. 8–9).

It can be argued that the notion of difference between male and female is socially constructed. This social construction of gender's position is based on the assumption that the claimed differences between women and men represent a social and political decision rather than a distinction given in nature (Rothenberg, 1998, p. 9). Rubin (1975) explains it this way:

Gender is a socially imposed division of the sexes. . . . Men and women are, of course, differ-ent. But they are not as different as day and night, earth and sky, yin and yang, life and death. In fact from the standpoint of nature, men and women are closer to each other than either is to anything else—for instance mountains, kangaroos, or coconut palms. The idea that men and women are more different from one another than either is from anything else must come from somewhere other than nature. (p. 321)

What is so disturbing about this social construction of gender is that males have assumed the power and control over women in the United States and in most other nations. This is what the term *patriarchial society* means. In their analytic assess-ment of the patriarchal society, Dobash and Dobash maintain it is comprised of both the structure, or the "hierarchical organization of social institutions and social rela-tions," and the ideology, or the belief system that "is supportive of the principle of a hierarchical order" (Dobash and Dobash, 1979, pp. 43–44). Dougherty adds that it is the way these two elements of structure and ideology are dynamically related "that makes the patriarchal organization of society such an effective means of oppressing women" (Dougherty, 1993, p. 95). In Box 1.1, Capra reveals what the consequences are for women who live in patriarchal societies.

BOX **1.1**
Decline of Patriarchy

The first and perhaps most profound transition is due to the slow and reluctant but inevitable decline of patriarchy. The time span associated with patriarchy is at least three thousand years, a period so long that we cannot say whether we are dealing with a cyclical process because the information we have about prepatriarchal eras is far too tenuous. What we do know is that for the past three thousand years Western civiliza-tion and its precursors, as well as most other cultures, have been based on philosophical, social, and political systems in which men—by force, direct pressure, or through ritual, tradi-tion, law and language, customs, etiquette, edu-cation, and the division of labor—determine what part women shall or shall not play, and in which the female is everywhere subsumed under the male.

The power of patriarchy has been ex-tremely difficult to understand because it is all-pervasive. It has influenced our basic ideas about human nature and about our relation to the universe—"man's" nature and "his" rela-

tions to the universe, in physical language. It is the one system which, until recently, had never in recorded history been openly challenged, and whose doctrines were so universally accepted that they seemed to be laws of nature; indeed, they were usually presented as such. Today, however, the disintegration of patriarchy is in sight. The feminist movement is one of the strongest cultural currents of our time and will have a profound effect on further evolution.

Critical Thinking Questions: Do you agree with Capra that "the disintegration of patriarchy is in sight"? Do you agree that "the feminist movement is one of the strongest cultural cur-rents of our time and will have a profound effect on further evolution"? What are possi-ble avenues for feminism to have greater influ-ence on the culture of the United States and other western societies?

Source: Fritjof Capra, *The Turning Point: Science, Soci-ety, and the Rising Culture* (New York: Bantam Books, 1988), pp. 29–30.

Laws Defining Women's Place

The oppression of women under patriarchy is first seen through the laws of that society. Early in the history of this nation, the men who wrote and interpreted the law saw that it was necessary to secure the safety of women to protect the family and the community Leo Kanowitz (1973) aptly expressed this position: "That God designed the sexes to occupy different spheres of action, and that it belonged to men to make, apply, and execute the laws, was regarded as an almost axiomatic truth" (p. 44). The creators of the law, then, made certain that women could enter certain areas of life only under carefully controlled circumstances. This means of protecting womanhood and motherhood sought by legislators and judges actually harmed women by restricting their ability to work and earn a living on an equal basis with men. Such protections, especially, have made having careers in criminal justice difficult for women (Feinman, 1994, p. 7).

This belief that women had to be protected from the sordid nature of life led to their exclusion from jury duty. In 1879 the U.S. Supreme Court lent its support to the common-law exclusion by deciding that states had the constitutional right to limit jury duty to men only. The Civil Rights Act of 1957 gave women the right to serve on federal juries, but some states continued to impose restrictions. Despite the 1975 U.S. Supreme Court decision in *Taylor v. Louisiana* that women could not be excluded from jury duty because of sex, four states continued to provide automatic exemptions for women (Feinman, 1994, pp. 8–9).

The law that was quick to protect the proper woman was equally quick to punish women who were offenders. The Muncy Act of Pennsylvania is an example of discriminatory legislation that was developed to punish women offenders. This act stated that any female pleading guilty to or convicted of a crime punishable by imprisonment of one year or more "must" be sentenced to the state prison for women and that her sentence "shall be merely a general one" and the court "shall not fix or limit the duration thereof" (Kanowitz, 1969, p. 59).

Eventually, as with those prohibiting women on juries, laws similar to the Muncy Act were declared unconstitutional. In *Commonwealth v. Daniel*, Jane Daniel was convicted in Pennsylvania of robbery, an offense that carried a maximum sentence of ten years. After sentencing her to one to four years in the county prison, the judge brought Daniel back to court for resentencing under the Muncy Act, which required an indeterminate term of up to ten years at the state prison for women. Daniel won her appeal to the Pennsylvania Supreme Court in a precedent-setting case, and the Muncy Act was declared unconstitutional (*Commonwealth v. Daniel*).

In *State v. Costello*, Mary A. Costello successfully argued that her constitutional right to equal protection under the Fourteenth Amendment had been violated when she received an indeterminate sentence of not more than five years for pleading guilty to a gambling offense. Under New Jersey law, a man convicted of a similar offense would have received a sentence of not more than two years and not less than one year. The New Jersey Supreme Court ruled: "These distinctions, in essence, form the basis of defendant's claim of denial of equal protection because of discrimination on the basis of sex" (*State v. Costello*, 1971).

Sexual Harassment of Women in Criminal Justice Institutions

The **sexual harassment of women** emerged as a critically important issue in the 1980s and 1990s. Contributing to the attention given sexual harassment is the number of notorious cases catapulting sexual harassment onto the front pages of newspapers and magazines and onto television news programs. Sportswriter Lisa Olsen claimed that she was sexually harassed by players on the New England Patriots football team, who displayed their body parts in close proximity to her face while she attempted to conduct interviews in the players' locker room (Webb, 1994, p. 4). Dr. Frances Conley, a well-known neurosurgeon, left her position at Stanford University because of "ongoing verbal and physical harassment by her fellow surgeons" (Webb, 1994, p. 4). Three months later, the nation watched as law professor Anita Hill accused Supreme Court nominee Clarence Thomas of creating a hostile working environment "laden with inappropriate sexual overtones." The alleged conduct occurred when they both worked for the Equal Employment Opportunity Commission in the 1980s (Webb, 1994, p. 4). Three weeks before the Thomas-Hill hearing, the military's biggest sex scandal unfolded, involving aviators at the Navy's annual Tailhook Association Convention (Rifkind and Harper, 1994, p. 487). The convention generated nearly 150 complaints of harassment (Petrocelli and Repa, 1994). Finally, accusations of harassment continuously hounded Bill Clinton. Sexual harassment clearly became one of the most important employment issues of the 1990s (Lee and Greenlaw, 1995, p. 357).

G. Patrick Gallagher (1996) defines employee harassment as "any explicit or implicit ridicule, mocking, derision, or belittling of any person or sexual harassment . . ." This inappropriate attitude toward sworn and civilian personnel in an agency "in general will lead to and encourage sexual harassment, because both emanate from the same source—an absence of respect for the individual . . ." Gallagher concludes, ". . . any form of harassment imposes tremendous liabilities on the organization." It does this by reducing productivity, mutual respect, departmental values, philosophical bases for the agency's working relationship with the community, officers' safety, and the organizational climate (p. 21).

The National Advisory Council on Women's Education Programs has categorized sexual harassment into five levels:

1. The first level includes generalized sexual remarks and behavior that are directed at a person because of his or her gender, rather than designed to elicit sexual activity. Examples might include comments about women's supposedly lesser cognitive abilities and their mythical propensity to be vindictive, jealous, and seductive.
2. The second level includes situations that make actual sexual references. What distinguishes this level from the first level is the introduction of the request for sexual encounters, which is often accompanied by some sort of touching. These situations do not need to be blatantly offensive, just inappropriate, and take place where the woman is the subordinate and the man is the superior.

3. The third level includes a solicitation for sex and the promise of some reward. Explicit threats may be absent, but the harasser uses some kind of organizational or institutional authority to "make payment" for a sexual favor.

4. In the fourth level the notion of punishment is introduced for failure to comply with the request for sexual favors. This is generally thought of as the quintessential type of sexual harassment and is illustrated by a failing grade in class, a negative job performance review, or dismissal from work.

5. The final type includes such extreme behaviors as indecent exposure, gross sexual imposition, and outright sexual assaults. Probably the least common type of sexual harassment, this behavior is usually the most devastating to victims. (Erez and Tontodonato, 1995, pp. 231–235)

Through interviewing 106 female officers, Connie Fletcher (1995) observed an underlying theme: Women in law enforcement consistently felt that the system failed to protect them against enemies or harassers within the organization, while it views most male officers as neutral or even encouraging to their female counterparts (p. xi). The interviews were not scientific, random samples of the women police officer population but rather officers referred to Fletcher, yet she does provide insightful observations. She continues:

> I was surprised by the almost universal picture of police work that emerged from these very diverse sources: Policing is a club for men . . . the club still operates in a culture of socializing and informal contacts impervious to legislation; people who are not wanted in the club may be harassed, ostracized, denied desired assignments, days off, shifts, or promotion; speaking or "grieving" (filing a grievance) about what happens within the club breaks the code and, thereafter, breaks the officer. This is a club where harassers can get away with virtually anything because no one, male or female, can afford the punishments that follow ratting on a fellow cop. And this is a club where you can get killed if people don't like you. (pp. xix–xx)

Women who are lawyers, as well as those who are probation, parole, or correctional officers, also face discrimination and sexual harassment. It was a long uphill battle for women to be accepted into law school, then to find jobs as lawyers and to be appointed as judges and, more recently, to be employed in the most desirable law firms and legal positions. Even today, women lawyers face various forms of discrimination and harassment. Women who enter corrections also have found discriminatory barriers placed before them and, on overcoming these barriers, have faced sexual harassment in one form or another. It is these forms of sexual harassment that have prevented probation and parole officers from achieving supervisory positions or being appointed directors of agencies and that have limited the upward mobility of women in correctional institutions. The antiwomen sentiment that is sometimes present in correctional institutions for men is revealed in the following quote from a female correctional officer:

> I expected a negative reaction and thought I was prepared for it. But on my very first day, before I had even been assigned to a post, this male guard came up to me and asked what I was doing there. He said that women don't belong in men's prisons and told me that he would do anything he could to make my life miserable and force me to leave. (Zimmer, 1986, p. 94)

Gender, Class, and Race and Women in the Criminal Justice System

Women grow up in a particular social context of domination and control by males. In this patriarchal society, troublesome females are quickly subjected to various forms of discrimination, exploitation, and criminalization. These forms of oppression are expressions of sexism, racism, and classism. The race discussion in this section also includes ethnicity.

Leonard is one of those who argues that the new theoretical efforts to understand women's crime must include analysis of the links among gender, race, class, and culture (Leonard, 1995, p. 54). Spelman accused some feminists of ignoring racial, class, ethnic, religious, and cultural differences among women. It is through examining sexism, racism, and classism, according to Spelman, that oppression against women can be more clearly grasped and understood (Spelman, 1989, p. ix).

Chesney-Lind (1997) further extended this argument when she said that adolescent females and women are victims of "multiple marginality" because their gender, class, and race have placed them at the economic periphery of society (p. 4). To be labeled a delinquent takes place in a world, Cheseny-Lind charges, "where gender still shapes the lives of young people in very powerful ways. This means that gender matters in girls' lives and that the way gender works varies by the community and the culture into which the girl is born" (p. 121). Chesney-Lind also makes the point that the social context of this world is not fair to women and girls, especially to those of color and those with low incomes (p. 133). For a review of the emerging context of class, race, and gender analysis, see Box 1.2 on page 16.

Gender, class, and race receive the focus of attention in this text. Yet sexuality cannot be ignored and, at times, will be included with gender, class, and race. Culture also becomes a critical component of understanding the criminal justice system's resistance to women pursuing a police career, to women lawyers gaining employment at leading law firms, and to women correctional officers finding acceptance in prisons for men.

Also emphasized is that the total of gender, race, and class is greater than its parts. Spelman (1989) states that "it isn't easy to think about gender, race, and class in ways that don't obscure or underplay their effects on one another" (p. 115). The most common approach focuses on gender and sexism and then considers how gender and racism are related to race and racism and to class and classism and "obscures the way in which race and class identity may be intertwined with gender identity" (pp. 112, 115).

Daly (1993) summarized this argument by saying that "unless you consider all the key relations of inequality—class, race, gender (and also age and sexuality)—you have considered none." She added that "unless you consider the inseparability of these relations in the life of one person, you do not understand what we are saying" (p. 65). This perspective suggests that gender, class, and race are interlocking forms of oppression and that the whole is greater than the parts. Thus, women offenders, victims, and workers in the system suffer the consequences of multiple oppression as more than some form of simple additive experience (p. 65).

BOX **1.2**

Historical Context of Class-Race-Gender Analysis

Two sources seem to be largely accountable for the class-race-gender analysis: experiences of African American women in the 1960s and curriculum-integration projects in higher education that were organized by women's studies faculty members.

The actual inspiration for class-race-gender analysis was the experiences of African American women in movement activities in the 1960s. From their experiences came an analysis of sexism in the civil rights and black nationalist movements and of racism in a predominantly white women's feminist movement.

Their first wave of publications in the 1970s focused on black women's experiences in movement politics and their relationships with white women. In the mid to late 1970s, their analyses became more focused on the development of black feminist thought.

The curriculum-integration projects that were largely organized by women's studies faculty members in higher education were what consolidated and popularized class-race-gender analysis. By 1985, at least eighty projects had been launched to examine how women's studies should be "redefined and reconstructed to include us all." It was not long before the class-race-gender construct was being widely articulated in women's studies, African American studies, cultural and multicultural studies, sociology, anthropology, English and American studies, and history. This became a popular and widely used phrase "to signal a way that theory and research ought to be done."

Critical Thinking Questions: What was the reason for the popularity of the class-race-gender analysis in college settings? Why was the original class-race-gender analysis in the 1990s expanded to include sexual orientation, ethnicity, and age? Does this form of theory and research have different meanings for various groups of women (i.e., African American, Latino, Native American, and white)?

Source: Kathleen Daly, "Class-Race-Gender: Sloganeering in Search of Meaning," *Social Justice* 20 (1993): 56–57.

An examination of the gender, class, race, and sexuality literature reveals six common themes. First, gender, race, class, and sexuality are contextual. They undergo change as part of the emergence of new political, economic, and ideological processes, events, and trends. Second, gender, race, class, and sexuality are socially constructed. The meaning of these social constructs develops out of group struggles over socially desired resources. Third, and perhaps most important, gender, class, race, and sexuality are power relationships that are historically specific and socially constructed hierarchies of domination. They are power hierarchies in which one group (males) exerts control over another (females), securing a position of dominance and assuming control over such material and nonmaterial resources as income, wealth, and access to health care and education. Fourth, gender, class, and race have meaning at the micro level of individuals' lives as well as the macro level of community and social institutions. Understanding the significance of the constructs of gender, class, race, and sexuality requires grasping the meaning in both contexts. Fifth, gender, class, race, and sexuality simultaneously exist in every social situation. This fact suggests that almost everyone experiences both dominant and subordinate positions at some time and that, therefore, there are no pure oppressors or oppressed in the United States or other industrial nations. Finally, gender, race, class, and sexuality scholarship consistently emphasizes the interdependence of knowledge and activism. This process is dynamic, continually moving from understanding oppression to seeking social change and social justice (Weber, 1998, pp. 16–25).

The Empowerment Perspective

An understanding of the class-race-gender (see Box 1.2) interactionist configuration is essential to a study of the criminal justice system. The feminist and empowerment perspectives view power and powerlessness related to race, gender, and class as central to the experiences of women in poverty and women of color. Empowerment theory, sometimes called the strengths approach because of its positive approach in helping people, sees individual problems as arising not from personal deficits, but from the failure of society to meet the needs of all the people (Gutiérrez, 1991).

Central to the **empowerment approach** is the concept of power, which is viewed as an attribute with consequences that may be negative or positive. Negative consequences arise from powerlessness, power imbalances in relationships, and an inability to make choices about one's life or livelihood. The subordination of women is a factor that creates violence, whether institutionally (for example, against women in prison) or within the family system. From a positive standpoint, power can be a liberating force. Gaining a sense of personal power can be a first step in assuming personal responsibility for change and in moving, as Gutiérrez states, from apathy and despair to positive social action.

Of special relevance to criminal behavior, and without which change is unlikely, is the taking of personal responsibility for one's actions and for one's life. The counseling relationship can serve as a powerful tool for helping clients change cognitive misconceptions that result in self-destructive thoughts and behavior. Even in a life crushed by circumstances of time and place, there nevertheless exists the potential for actions other than those characteristically taken. This belief in potential is at the core of a healthy, therapeutic relationship.

An empowerment approach focuses on oppression and on those who suffer from its consequences. Oppressed individuals are not devoid of personal or moral strengths or resources. Help in tapping into those resources often is needed. For all of us, a sense of control over our lives and relationships is crucial. Ellen H. McWhirter (1991) captures the essence of empowerment in her inclusive definition:

> *Empowerment is the process by which people, organizations, or groups who are powerless (a) become aware of the power dynamics at work in their life context, (b) develop the skills and capacity for gaining some reasonable control over their lives, (c) exercise this control without infringing upon rights of others, and (d) support the empowerment of others in their community. (p. 224)*

Shoshana Pollack (2000) warns that there is a danger in prioritizing an individualistic or psychological notion of empowerment, while at the same time minimizing the importance of social influences and oppression. When empowerment is viewed as an individual's subjective sense in which she can determine her own life's course, personal struggles tend to become privatized and individualized. This is particularly problematic in addressing the effects of oppression. Individualizing social issues can result in blaming women for problems that arise from being oppressed in various ways and can result in further disempowering them. In addition, an analysis that views empowerment as residing within the individual will lead to services and policies that are thought to enhance feelings of self-worth and autonomy. In contrast, perspectives assuming that an individual's autonomy is largely determined by social relationships and environment will tend to adopt a social or political analysis of empowerment, advocating critical social reflection and social change as methods of obtaining empowerment (pp. 76–77).

Until recently, the empowerment perspective has been absent from the criminal justice literature. A computer search of the criminal justice abstracts index (as of May, 2006) reveals only five listings for articles under the headings *strengths approach* or *strengths perspective*. The word *empowerment* does appear in the computer index as a progressive term for work with juveniles, female victims, and, occasionally, female offenders. Writing about probation, Clark (1998) calls for a new paradigm to focus on offenders' strengths rather than their faults and failures. This perspective, borrowed from social work, is gaining ground, according to Clark. Barajas (1996), similarly, refers to a paradigm shift in corrections, "a quiet, grassroots, seemingly unobtrusive, but truly revolutionary movement" (p. 32) that reflects a renewed emphasis on rehabilitation rather than punishment. A focus on solutions rather than problems is empowering to clients and corrections workers alike.

Empowerment theory, with its focus on personal, social, educational, and political dimensions, offers a useful framework for addressing the needs of women at all the various levels of the criminal justice hierarchy. Just as a woman in prison or on probation can be empowered through understanding that her situation is not just a personal problem but one related to gender, class, and racial oppression, so too can female correctional officers and lawyers be informed by a macro view that explains why affirmative action programs may be a necessary but not sufficient requisite to success.

The personal is political and the political is personal. This, in a nutshell, is the underlying theme of the feminist empowerment approach. The view of humanity underlying this approach is that humans are unique, multifaceted beings with the potential to make a contribution to their community (Kelley, 1996). This contribution can be made quietly or through public consciousness-raising and networking, for example, through membership in various self-help groups or specialized professional associations. Sharing in writing and receiving newsletters is an example of educational empowerment. Political empowerment can occur through activities such as lobbying politicians and mass media campaigns. Issues relevant to women in criminal justice are lobbying for victims' rights, working toward legislative changes to protect women in prison from sexual abuse, and working to enhance affirmative action programs to increase the female-to-male ratio in policing. The empowerment of professional women in the field of criminal justice should have a ricocheting effect on women at every level of the criminal justice system.

Paradigm Shift

A **paradigm shift** is a revolution in the worldview of a social unit. It can take place on the individual, organizational, institutional, systemic, society, and scientific levels. In a paradigm shift, understanding or knowledge is perceived in a new way. This term is associated with the writings of Thomas Kuhn (1970) who suggested that changes in our construction of reality come about through a series of paradigm shifts. In science, for example, new discoveries from astronomy eventually led to an intellectual revolution in our understanding about the universe.

One of the major paradigm shifts today is a movement from the patriarchal and mechanistic Newtonian paradigm to a post-Newtonian society that includes quantum physics, chaos theory, and complexity theory (Zohar, 1991; Schaef, 2000). This quantum society, as Zohar and Marshall (1994, pp. 21–22) have proposed, is emerging and offers a more responsive and less hierarchic society.

The history of social justice is a history of paradigm shifts related to our conception about the nature of crime and the purpose of punishment. In the 1960s and 1970s, rehabilitation was discredited and replaced by a "just deserts" philosophy and standardization of punishment (Zehr, 1995). The "get-tough" on crime model continues to dominate crime policy and has led to draconian punishments in the courts and to sky-rocketing prison populations.

A number of possible paradigm shifts in terms of how women are viewed and treated in the United States and other nations are featured in this book. Focusing on women offenders, victims, and professionals, these paradigm shifts seek to empower individuals, structures, and systems. The restorative model is one attempt to respond to victims and offenders with a more empowering approach.

Summary

bell hooks (1998) states that "we live in a world in crisis—a world governed by politics of domination, one in which the belief in a notion of superior and inferior, and its concomitant ideology—that the superior should rule over the inferior—affects the lives of all people everywhere, whether poor or privileged, literate or illiterate" (p. 579). She reminds us that "systematic dehumanization, worldwide famine, ecological devastation, industrial contamination, and the possibility of nuclear destruction are realities that remind us daily that we are in crisis" (p. 579). The origin of this crisis, according to some feminist thinkers, is sexual politics. bell hooks adds that these feminist thinkers believe that "differentiation of status between females and males globally is an indication that patriarchal domination of the planet is the root of the problem" (p. 579).

This chapter provided an overview of how male domination affects women victims, offenders, and workers in the criminal justice system. Women have experienced the domination of men in terms of such matters as the right to own property; to vote; to serve on a jury; and to be protected from predators, fathers, and husbands. Sexual harassment has been a special problem for women who become police officers, lawyers, and corrections workers. This chapter also briefly examined the categories of gender, class, and race and how they intersect in the lives of women victims and offenders. As one of the six major themes, an analysis of gender, class, and race/ethnicity guides the discussion throughout the remainder of this book.

Moreover, this chapter has proposed that there is consensus among feminist theorists on at least two beliefs. First, social context, especially patriarchal society, is vitally important in understanding the oppression of women. But a contextual analysis, in turn, requires an examination of politics, economics, law, and culture on both macro and micro levels. Second, feminist ethics is guided by two principles: "that it is wrong to hurt anyone, and that it is right to sustain human relationships" (McDermott, 1993, p. 37).

Finally, this chapter has suggested that there is no single feminist perspective on the victimization of women. Feminist theories have been categorized as liberal, radical, socialist, Marxist third-wave, and post-modern. But, even within perspectives, there are differences. These differences may vary in the extent to which feminist theorists advocate for victims, identify with victims, or emphasize offender rights and treatment. Women, adds Bernat (1995), do not make up a homogenous entity. As she aptly puts it, "we have a community of differences which need to be:

> Celebrated,
> Uncovered,
> Legitimated,
> Taught,
> Understood,
> Respected, and
> Embraced." (p. 7)

KEY TERMS

empowerment approach
essentialism
human agency
intersectionalities
liberal feminism

Marxist feminists
multiple marginality
oppression
paradigm shift
patriarchy

post-modern feminism
radical feminists
sexual harassment of women
socialist feminists
third-wave feminists

CRITICAL THINKING QUESTIONS

1. What is the danger of making empowerment too individualistic a perspective?

2. Which form of feminist theory do you find most attractive? Why?

3. What is essentialism? Why is this an important concept in understanding the oppressions of women?

4. Why has patriarchy led to the oppression of women?

5. What are the consequences to women offenders of the backlash to the women's movement?

WEB DESTINATIONS

New websites are being developed while others are disappearing. Check with a search engine such as Google at www.google.com to locate information on feminism, female victims or offenders, individuals who work with women offenders or victims, and other relevant subjects, using a key word or phrase or organization.

Learn more about liberal feminism at this site: http://newmedia.cgu.edu/feminism/webpagesarea.html

Learn more about socialist feminism at this site: www.dsausa.org/archive/Fem/socfem.html

Check out Meda Chesney-Lind's home page at this site: http://home.hawaii.rr.com/chesneylind/

REFERENCES

Anderson, M. A. (2000). *Thinking about women: Sociological perspectives on sex and gender,* 5th ed. Boston: Allyn & Bacon.

Archer, M. S. (1988). *Culture and agency; the place of culture in social theory.* Cambridge, U.K.: Cambridge University Press, 1988.

Barajas, E. (1996). *Community justice: Striving for safe and just communities.* Washington, D.C.: U.S. Institute of Corrections, 1996.

Beirne, P., and Messerschmidt, J. (1991). *Criminology.* San Diego: Harcourt Brace Jovanovich.

Bernat, F. P. (1995). Opening the dialogue: Women's culture and the criminal justice system. *Women and Criminal Justice 7:* 1–7.

Chesney-Lind, M. (2000). Interview in Clemens Bartollas, *Juvenile delinquency,* 5th ed. Needham Heights: Allyn & Bacon, 2000, p. 214.

Chesney-Lind, M. (1987). Girls' crime and woman's place: Toward a feminist model of female delinquency. Paper presented at the Annual Meeting of the American Society of Criminology. Montreal, Canada, November 10–14, 1987.

Chesney-Lind, M. (1997). *The female offender: Girls, women and crime.* Thousand Oaks, Calif.: Sage.

Clark, M. D. (1998, June). Strength-based practice: The ABC's of working with adolescents who don't want to work with you. *Federal Probation 62,* 46–53.

Coleman, J. S. (1990). *Foundations of social theory.* Cambridge: Harvard University Press.

Collins, P. H. (1998). *Black feminist thought.* New York: Routledge, Chapman, Hall.

Commonwealth v. Daniel, Appellant 430 Pa. 642.

Daly, K., and Chesney-Lind, M. (1988). Feminism and criminology. *Justice Quarterly 5:* 497–538.

Daly, K. (1993). Class-race-gender: Sloganeering in search of meaning. *Social Justice 20:* 56–71.

Dobash, R. E., and Dobash, R. (1979). *Violence against wives: A case against the patriarchy.* New York: Free Press.

Donovan, J. (1985). *Feminist theory: The intellectual traditions of American feminism.* New York: Frederick Ungar.

Dougherty, J. (1993). Women's violence against their children: A feminist perspective. *Women and Criminal Justice 42:* 91–114.

Emirbayer, M., and Mische, A. (1998). What is agency? *American Journal of Sociology 103:* 962–1023.

Elder, Jr., G. H. (1994). Time, human agency, and social change: Perspectives on the life course. *Social Psychology Quarterly 57:* 6.

Erez, E., and Tontodonato, P. (1992). Sexual harassment in the criminal justice system. In *The changing roles of women in the criminal justice system: Offenders, victims, and professionals* (pp. 227–252), 2nd ed. Prospect Heights: Waveland Press.

Feinman, C. (1994). *Women in the criminal justice system,* 3rd ed. Westport, Conn.: Praeger Publishers.

Flavin, J. (2001). Feminism for the mainstream criminologist: An invitation. *Journal of Criminal Justice 29:* 271–285.

Fletcher, C. (1995). *Breaking and entering: Women cops talk about life in the ultimate men's club.* New York: HarperCollins.

Friedan, B. (1983). *The feminine mystique.* New York: Norton.

Gallagher, G. P. (1996, November and December). When will the message about harassment be acted upon. *The Law Enforcement Trainer 11.*

Grana, S. J. (2002). *Women and (in)justice: The criminal and civil effects of the common law on women's lives.* Boston: Allyn & Bacon.

Gutiérrez, L. (1991). Empowering women of color: A feminist model. In M. Bricker-Jenkins, N. R. Hooyman, and N. Gottlieb (eds.), *Feminist social work practices in clinical settings* (pp. 271–303). Newbury Park, Calif.: Sage.

Heidensohn, F. (1987). Women and crime: Questions for criminology. In P. Carlen and A. Worrall (eds.), *Gender, crime, and justice* (pp. 16–27). Philadelphia: Open University Press.

Homans, G. C. (1964). Bringing men back in. *American Sociological Review 29:* 809–818.

hooks, b. (1984). *Feminist theory: From margin to center.* Boston: South End Books.

Jaggar, A. M., and Rothenberg, P. (eds.). (1984). *Feminist frameworks.* New York: McGraw-Hill.

Kanowitz, L. (1973). *Sex roles in law and society: Cases and materials.* Albuquerque: University of New Mexico Press.

Kanowitz, L. (1969). *Women and the law: The unfinished revolution.* Albuquerque: University of New Mexico Press.

Kelley, P. (1996). Narrative theory and social work treatment. In F. Turner (ed.), *Social work treatment: Interlocking theoretical approaches* (pp. 461–479). New York: Free Press.

Kennedy, F. (1972). Pathology of oppression. Sounding Recording. University of Iowa Lecture Series.

Klein, D. (2000). Feminist criminology, USA. In N. H. Rafter (ed.), *Encyclopaedia of women and crime* (pp. 80–81). Phoenix, Arizona: Oryx.

Kuhn. T. (1970). *The structure of scientific revolutions.* Chicago: University of Chicago Press.

Lee, R. D., and Greenlaw, P. S. (1995, July). The legal revolution of sexual harassment. *Public Administration Review 55:* 357–364.

Leonard, E. (1995). Theoretical criminology and gender. In B. R. Price and N. J. Sokoloff (eds.), *The criminal justice system and women: Offenders, victims, and workers* (pp. 54–70), 2nd ed. New York: McGraw-Hill.

MacKinnon, C. (1987). *Feminism unmodified: Discourses on life and law.* Cambridge, Mass.: Harvard University Press.

Mann, C. R. (1995). Women of color and the criminal justice system. In B. R. Price and N. J. Sokoloff (eds.), *The criminal justice system and women: Offenders, victims, and workers* (pp. 118–135), 2nd ed. New York: McGraw-Hill.

McWhirter, E. H. (1991). Empowerment in counseling. *Journal of Counseling and Development* 69(3), 222–227.

Messerschmidt, J. W. (1993). *Masculinities and crime: Critique and reconceptualization of theory.* Lantham, Md.: Rowman & Littlefield.

Miller, J., and Mullins, C. W. (2006a). The status of feminist theories in criminology. In press. In F. Adler and W. Laufer (eds.), *Taking stock: The status of criminological theory.* Vol. 15: *Advances in criminological theory* (206–220), New Brunswick, N.J.: Transaction Publishers.

Money, J. (1988). *Gay, straight, and in-between: Sexology of erotic orientation.* New York: Oxford University Press.

Petrocelli, W., and Repa, B. K. (1994). *Sexual harassment on the job,* 2nd ed. Berkeley, Calif.: Nolo.

Pollack, S. (2000). Reconceptualizing women's agency and empowerment: Challenges to self-esteem discourse and women's lawbreaking. *Women and Criminal Justice 12:* 75–89.

Price, B. R., and Sokoloff, N. J. (2004). The criminal law and women. In B. R. Price and N. J. Sokoloff (eds.), *The criminal justice system and women: Offenders, victims, and workers,* 3rd ed. (pp. 11–29). New York: McGraw-Hill.

Rifkind, L., and Harper, L. (1994, September). Conflict management strategies for the equal opportunity difficult person in the sexually. . . . *Personnel Management 23.*

Rogers, K. O. (1973). For her own protection . . . Conditions of incarceration for female juvenile offenders in the state of Connecticut. *Law and Society Review 7:* 223–246.

Rollins, J. H. (1996). *Women's minds, women's bodies: The psychology of women in a biosocial context.* Upper Saddle River, N.J.: Prentice-Hall.

Rothenberg, P. S. (1998). *Race, class, and gender in the United States: An integrated story,* 4th ed. New York: St. Martin's Press.

Rubin, G. (1975). The traffic in women. In R. R. Reither (ed.), *Toward an anthropology of women* (p. 179). New York: Monthly Review Press.

Schaef, A. W. (2000). *Beyond therapy, beyond science.* Lincoln, Nebraska: iUniverse.com, inc.

Simpson, S. S. (1989, November). Feminist theory, crime, and justice. *Criminology 27:* 605–622.

Spelman, E. V. (1989). *Inessential woman.* Boston: Beacon Press.

State v. Costello. New Jersey State Supreme Court 59, 1971.

Walby, S. (1990). *Theorizing patriarchy.* Cambridge: Blackwell.

Webb, S. L. (1994). *Shockwaves: The global impact of sexual harassment.* New York: MasterMedia.

Weber, L. (1998). A conceptual framework for understanding race, class, gender, and sexuality. *Psychology of Women Quarterly 22:* 13–32.

Williams, C. L. (2000). Preface. *The Annals of the American Academy of Political and Social Science* 571: 8–13.

Wonder, N. A., and Caulfield, S. L. (1993). Women's work? The contradictory implications of courses on women and the criminal justice system. *Journal of Criminal Justice Education 4.*

Zimmer, L. (1986). *Women guarding men.* Chicago: University of Chicago Press.

Zohar, D. (1991). *The quantum self.* New York: William Morrow/Quill.

Zohar, D., and Marshall, I. (1994). *The quantum society: Mind, physics, and a new social vision.* New York: William Morrow.

PART TWO

Women Criminals

Racial, ethnic, and class diversity come together in compelling ways in the chapters of this part. Here we concentrate on the female offender, often a drug addict/alcoholic with a long history of sexual and physical abuse. The typical adjudicated female offender is a woman of color and mother of small children. Their stories reveal how social control of already oppressed people is carried out by the state and legitimized through the mass media. The ultimate inequality of U.S. society is revealed in a visit to the nation's prisons.

How do women get caught up in violating the law? Which crimes do they commit? Are women committing more crimes today, or are they being arrested and prosecuted more diligently than in the past? What are contemporary explanations of women's crime? These are among the questions considered in Chapter 2.

Chapter 3 examines both theories among feminists relating to crime, gender, and criminology and to research methods that are being utilized by feminist criminologists. This chapter builds on and expands material in Chapter 2. The focus in Chapter 3 is on gender because its study is what guides feminist theories in criminology. This chapter points out that the best feminist work remains critically engaged with gendered life situations of women and men.

Chapter 4 examines delinquency across the life course, one of the most exciting new developments in the field of juvenile delinquency. Beginning with an examination of risk factors in adolescence, the chapter compares juveniles who are early offenders with those who begin their delinquency offenses in adolescence. These adolescents are followed through part of and sometimes nearly all of their life span. Their social and criminal histories are compared with those of others in their cohort, and particular attention is given to juveniles who persist and those who desist from law-violating behaviors. Researchers want to know what factors contributed to desistance from such activities. Even though the vast majority of the research has been done on male delinquents, more attention is being given to female delinquents across the life course.

2 Women in Crime

In the midst of a great deal of indifference toward women offenders, Freda Adler's *Sisters in Crime* (1975) contended that a new woman criminal had arrived on our social horizons. She argued that the rise in crime among adult women and juvenile females is clearly linked to opportunity. Adolescent girls and adult women, according to Adler, face the plight because they are instilled with almost boundless ambition but lack opportunities to achieve their desired goals. The end result is that female adults and juveniles strive for the same goals as males and adopt male roles to achieve them. Accordingly, they are becoming involved in more aggressive and violent acts. Adler contended that the rise in official rates of female crime reflects the changes brought about by the liberation of women. The rise in female crime, then, is directly related to females becoming more competitive with males, more aggressive, and more "masculine" in general. As she reported:

> *"I know it's happening but I'll be damned if it still doesn't shock me when I see it," explained one exasperated sergeant who was slumped in the chair of a district precinct house in Washington, D.C. He was talking about the new problems which girls have created for police. "Last week, for instance, we got a call of a disturbance at the high school. A fight . . . after school. So we get down there and pull up and here is a hell of a crowd yelling and screaming at the kids in the center, who are fighting. I push my way through the crowd—they're going crazy like it is really a mean fight and when I get to the middle . . . I like to fell over. Here are two husky broads, and they are fighting . . . now I don't mean any hair-pulling face-scratching kind of thing; I mean two broads squared off and duking it out. Throwing jabs and hooking in at each other and handling themselves like a couple of god-damned pro sparring partners. I mean, I got to ask myself, what the hell is going on? What in the name of God is happening to these girls anymore?" (pp. 96–97)*

Laura Crites (1976) was one of many who found fault with Adler's women's **liberation thesis.** She pointed out that female offenders most often come from minority groups. They are frequently unemployed and usually are responsible for their own support and often for that of any children. In addition, their employment potential is limited because more than half have not graduated from high school and their work experience has generally been in low-wage, low-status occupations. Crites reasons that the psychological independence and expanded economic opportunities of the women's rights movement are almost meaningless for this group; instead of being concerned with the ideological constructs of the women's liberation movement, the typical female offender is caught up in a struggle for economic, emotional, and physical survival (pp. 36–39).

Yet, even though Adler's thesis of the women's liberation movement has received little support, it has contributed in a major way to stimulating interest in the extent and nature of women's crime. The vast amount of recent literature on female delinquents and women criminals has also appeared in part because of a desire to offset the preponderance of theories and studies centered on males and in part as a response to the perceived "dramatic increases" in the amount and versatility of involvement in delinquency by juvenile girls and in criminal behavior by adult women.

Beginning with the various explanations of why females commit unlawful activities, this chapter also considers the extent of female crime, the types of crimes females commit, and the processing of female offenders through the criminal justice system.

Explanations of Female Crime

Feminist criminologists are quick to agree that adolescent females have different experiences from adolescent males. They generally support the view that females are more controlled than males, enjoy more social support, are less disposed to crime, and have fewer opportunities to commit certain types of crimes (Office of Juvenile Justice and Delinquency Prevention, 1998). Some evidence also exists that "high self-esteem discourages definitions favorable to risk-taking among females but encourages these definitions among males" (Heimer, 1994, p. 164). Moreover, juvenile justice research tends to support that young women's patterns of offending differ in scope and motivation from those of their male counterparts (Office of Juvenile Justice and Delinquency Prevention, 1998). Finally, Meda Chesney-Lind (1997) argues that female adolescents are frequently the victims of violence and sexual abuse at home and this abuse is a chief reason that they choose to run away (pp. 25–26).

However, among feminist criminologists there are three vastly different opinions about how the commonly accepted male-oriented approach to delinquency and criminology should be handled. One approach focuses on the question of generalizability. In research on samples that include males and females, a routine strategy for those who emphasize cross-gender similarities is to test whether the given theoretical constructs account for the offending of both groups and to pay little attention to how gender itself might intersect with other factors to create different meanings in the lives of males and females. Those who support this **gender-neutral** position have generally examined such subjects as social bonding, delinquent peer relationships, social learning, the family, and deterrence and strain (Miller, 2001, pp. 3–4). These feminist theorists emphasize that feminist research should be presented in textbooks "as a seamless whole rather than as a separate chapter" (Daly, 1995, pp. 447–448). They question the need for separate discussions on female delinquency or women in crime, because little evidence to date suggests that separate theories are needed to account for female and male delinquency and criminality. Moreover, they claim that latent structural analysis shows that female delinquency and women in crime tend to operate through the same factors as male delinquency and male criminality. Empirical studies generally reveal that much more variation exists within each gender than between the sexes (McDonough and Selo, 1980, pp. 333–343; Hagan, Gillis, and Simpson, 1985, pp. 1151–1178; Smith and Paternoster, 1987, pp. 140–172).

In contrast, other feminist theorists argue that new theoretical efforts are needed to understand female delinquency and women's involvement in adult crime. Carol Smart (1976) and Dorie Klein (1973), two early criminologists, suggested that a **feminist criminology** should be formulated because of the neglect of the feminist perspective in classical delinquency theories. Klein's 1973 article ended in a call for "a new kind of research on women and crime—one that has feminist roots and a radical orientation. . . ." (p. 46). In a 1995 update, Klein contributed that the feminist critique of such subjects as women, crime, and justice "has exploded in volume and advanced light-years in depth, and interest. . . ." (p. 48). Daly and Chesney-Lind (1988) defined a feminist perspective as one "in which women's experiences and ways of knowing are brought to the fore, not suppressed" (p. 498).

Eileen Leonard (1995) further questioned whether anomie, labeling, differential association, subculture, and Marxist theories can be used to explain the crime patterns of women. She concluded that these traditional theories do not work and that they are basically flawed. Chesney-Lind's application of the male-oriented theories to female delinquency has determined that existing delinquency theories are inadequate to explain female delinquency. She suggested that there is a need for a feminist model of delinquency, because a patriarchal context has shaped the explanations and handling of female delinquents and status offenders. Therefore adolescent females' sexual and physical victimizations at home and the relationship between these experiences and their crimes have been systematically ignored (1989, pp. 5–29; 1995, pp. 71–88).

This feminist position argues that the structural categories of gender, class, and race are more helpful than individual or sociopsychological explanations in understanding women's involvement in crime. Based on the assumption that gender, class, and race are interlocking forms of oppression, this position suggests that an adequate explanation of why women commit crime requires an examination of the total effects of not only each of these factors but also the combined effect of these forces of oppression on women's lives. This position poses a rhetorical question: How is being viewed as a female delinquent in U.S. society influenced by a particular social context? It answers this question by proposing that the particular social context is patriarchal society and that discrimination, exploitation, and oppression take place on the basis of sex or gender and are critical factors in explaining why females become involved in criminal behavior.

In the face of these two divergent positions—one seeking to explain away gender gaps and to be gender-specific, the other focusing on the importance of gender in understanding delinquency and crime—Darrell Steffensmeier and Emilie Allen have attempted to put the two approaches together. They contend that there "is no need for general-specific theories," although they acknowledge that "qualitative studies reveal major gender differences in the context and nature of offending" (1996, pp. 459–487). These researchers go on to develop "a middle-road position," which has not received much acceptance or support in the literature.

The following section considers the important question of whether females commit delinquency and criminal acts for reasons different from those of males. Early explanations of female delinquency/criminal behavior focused on biological and psychological factors. These explanations viewed females as having certain biological characteristics or psychological tendencies that made them more receptive to crime. However, there is general agreement that the hopelessly flawed biological and psychological explanations of female crime view troublesome adolescent females and adult women in our patriarchal society through the lens of sexism.

More recent explanations of female crime place much greater emphasis on sociological factors, with criminologists coming to vastly different conclusions. Some criminologists challenge whether gender-specific explanations are needed, claiming that existing sociological theories can account for both male and female crime (Mazerolle, 1998, p. 66). These comparisons of how males and females respond to traditional sociological theories are found in this section. Other criminologists still argue for gender-specific explanations because they claim that the traditional sociological theories of delinquent behavior fail to adequately explain the female experience in the United States.

Biological and Constitutional Explanations.   In *The Female Offender*, initially published in 1903, Cesare Lombroso deals with crime as atavism, or the survival of "primitive" traits in female offenders. First, he argued that women are more primitive, or lower on the evolutionary scale, because they are less intelligent and have fewer variations in their mental capacities than men: "even the female criminal is monotonous and uniform compared with her male companion, just as in general women are inferior to men." Second, Lombroso contended that women are unable to feel pain and, therefore, are insensitive to the pain of others and lack moral refinement. He stated:

> Women have many traits in common with children; that their moral sense is deficient; that they are revengeful, jealous. . . . In ordinary cases these defects are neutralized by piety, maternity, want of passion, sexual coldness, weakness, and an undeveloped intelligence. (p. 151)

Third, he argued, women are characterized by a passive and conservative approach to life. Although he admitted that women's traditional sex roles in the family bind them to a more home-centered life, he insisted that women's passivity can be directly traced to the "immobility of the ovule compared with the zoosperm" (p. 109).

Lombroso (1920) contended that because most women are born with "feminine" characteristics, their innate physiological limitations protect them from crime and predispose them to live unimaginative, dull, and conforming lives. But women criminals, he argued, have inherited male characteristics, such as excessive body hair, moles, wrinkles, crow's feet, and abnormal craniums. He added that the female criminal, being doubly exceptional as a woman and as a criminal, is likely to be more vicious than the male criminal (pp. 150–152).

With the recent biosocial revival in criminology, biological or physiological explanations for crime and delinquency have regained some popularity. In a 1968 study, Cowie, Cowie, and Slater (1968) presented data on an English approved school (training school) sample that emphasize genetic factors as the major cause of delinquency. These researchers even proposed that these genetic factors might be specific enough to determine the types of crimes the sexes will commit (p. 17). T. C. N. Gibbens (1971) also reported a high rate of sex chromosomal abnormalities in delinquent girls (pp. 279–286). Furthermore, Cowie and colleagues (1968) noted the above-average weight of their institutional sample and suggested that physical overdevelopment tends to draw a girl's attention to sex earlier in life, resulting in sexual promiscuity. In addition, they claimed that menstruation is a distressing reminder to females that they can never be males and that this distress makes them increasingly prone to delinquent acts.

In sum, the viewpoints of Lombroso and other supporters of biological explanations for female criminality can be regarded as merely a foolish testimony to the historical chauvinism of males. Unfortunately, the study of female criminality has not yet fully recovered from the idea "that the cause of a socially generated phenomenon might be reduced to a genetically transmitted biological unit" (Campbell, 1981, p. 46).

Psychological Explanations. The claimed "innate nature" of women is the basis of much of the literature on psychological explanations of female crime. W. I. Thomas, Sigmund Freud, and Otto Pollak are among those who addressed this "innate" female nature and its relationship to deviant behavior.

Thomas's works marked a transition from physiological explanations to more sophisticated theories embracing physiological, psychological, and social structural factors. In *Sex and Society* (1907), he suggested that there are basic biological differences between the sexes. Maleness, according to Thomas, is "katabolic," from the animal force that involves a destructive release of energy and allows the possibility of creative work through this outward flow, but femaleness is "anabolic"— motionless, lethargic, and conservative. Thomas's underlying assumptions are physiological ones, for he credits men with higher amounts of sexual energy that lead them to pursue women for sexual pleasure. In contrast, he attributes to women maternal feelings devoid of sexuality, so they exchange sex for domesticity.

In his 1923 work *The Unadjusted Girl,* Thomas dealt with female delinquency as a "normal" response under certain social conditions. He argued that a girl is driven by four wishes or ambitions: new experiences, security, response, and recognition. He assumed that the delinquent girl's problem is not criminality but immorality, and he confined himself almost exclusively to a discussion of prostitution. According to Thomas, the major cause of prostitution rested in the girl's need for love, and a secondary factor is her wish for recognition or ambition. Thomas maintained that it is not sexual desire that motivates delinquent girls, because they are no more passionate than nondelinquent girls, but that they are using male desire for sex to achieve their own ultimate needs (Thomas, 1923).

> *The beginning of delinquency in girls is usually an impulse to get amusement, adventure, pretty clothes, favorable notice, distinction, freedom in the larger world. . . . The girls have usually become "wild" before the development of sexual desire, and their casual sex relations do usually awaken sexual feelings. Their sex is used as a condition of the realization of other wishes. It is their capital. (p. 109)*

The sad commentary on the state of theory regarding female criminality is that until recently the psychoanalytic writings of Sigmund Freud have represented the most pervasive theoretical position. The structure of the personality and the psychosexual stages of development of the child are the two major concepts from which most of Freud's theories have evolved.

The most controversial and ridiculous aspects of Freud's theory had to do with his assumption that women's sex organs make them anatomically inferior to men. Freud (1949) contended that a little girl assumes she has lost her penis as punishment and, therefore, feels traumatized and grows up envious and revengeful. A woman becomes a mother to replace the "lost penis" with a baby. The delinquent girl or woman criminal, in the Freudian perspective, is one who is attempting to be a man. Her drive to accomplishment is the expression of her longing for a penis (p. 278).

The Freudian orientation is not limited to penis envy in its explanation of female crime, because it suggested that at any state of psychosexual development, faulty mechanism, fixations, and other problems may occur. Freud also argued that women are inferior because they are concerned with personal matters and have little social sense. Women, according to Freud (1933), have weaker social interests than men and less capacity for the sublimation of their interests (p. 183).

Otto Pollak's *The Criminality of Women* (1950) advanced the theory that women are more criminal than is usually believed, but that their crimes are largely unreported or hidden. Pollak credited the nature of women themselves for the traditionally low official rates of female crime, because women are inherently deceitful and, therefore, act as instigators rather than perpetrators of criminal activity. The roles played by women are a factor in hidden crimes as well because such roles as domestics, nurses, teachers, and housewives enable them to commit undetectable crimes. Pollak further advances the "chivalry factor" as a root cause of hidden crime; that is, the police and the court forgive a girl for the same act for which they would convict a boy (p. 8).

Pollak (1950) also suggested two factors that influence adolescent females to become juvenile delinquents. First, he said, early physical development and sexual maturity allow a female more opportunities to engage in immoral or delinquent behavior. Second, a female's home life, especially one who has criminal parents or grows up in a broken home, may cause her to seek outside substitutes for that poor home life. She is likely to seek the company of other maladjusted females, and they will eventually become involved in a life of petty crimes (pp. 125–139).

In sum, psychological studies of female crime shifted in the 1950s from the psychoanalytical to the familial-social type. Considerable research continues to perpetuate the notion that personal maladjustment characterizes the female criminal: She has a psychological problem, is unable to perform her proper sex role adequately, or suffers from the ill effects of a bad home life (Giordano and Cernkovich, 1979, p. 24).

Sociological Explanations.   Beginning in the late 1970s, several studies proceeded from the assumption that sociological processes traditionally related to males could also affect the antisocial involvement of females. Juvenile delinquency researchers who examined the sociological themes of blocked opportunity theory, social control theory, masculinity hypothesis, power-control theory, and labeling theory found that they offered much more promise than biological or psychological causes. But Leonard, who focused on other sociological theories, was much less convinced of the value of sociological factors in explaining criminality among women offenders.

Sociological Explanations for Female Delinquent Behavior.   The role of blocked or limited opportunity has received considerable attention in the sociological analysis of male delinquency. The usefulness of such variables in studying female delinquency has been largely ignored because males are seen as concerned with achieving short- and long-term status and economic success, whereas juvenile females are commonly viewed as possessing no such aspirations but, instead, as being satisfied to occupy a role dependent on males (Parsons, 1942; Coleman, 1961; Rittenhouse, 1963).

Yet Susan Datesman and colleagues (1975) found that perception of limited opportunity was more strongly related to female delinquency than it was to male delinquency. Both African American and white female delinquents regarded their opportunities less positively than did nondelinquents in their sample. Status offenders also perceived their opportunities as being less favorable than did nondelinquents (p. 120). Josephina Figueira-McDonough and Elaine Selo's (1980) formulation of feminist opportunity theory contended that similar levels of strain (arising from high success aspirations and low legitimate opportunities) lead to similar antisocial patterns by both genders, provided that they are equal in their knowledge of and access to illegitimate means (pp. 333–343).

Proponents of social control theory contend that females are less involved in crime than males because sex-role socializations result in a greater tie to the social bond for females than for males. In addition, females may have less opportunity to engage in delinquent behavior because in general they are more closely supervised by parents. Adolescent females are also more dependent on others, whereas adolescent males are encouraged to be more independent and achievement oriented.

Consequently, differences in sex-role socialization supposedly promote a greater allegiance to the social bond among females, and this allegiance insulates them from delinquency more than it does males. This position infers that females require a greater "push" to become involved in delinquent and criminal acts.

Anderson, Holmes, and Ostresh (1998) found from a survey of adolescent males and females confined in the Wyoming boys' and girls' training schools that there were no differences in males' and females' levels of attachment when parents' attachment and attitude toward school were controlled. Yet some gender differences in the effects of the various attachments on the severity of delinquency were found. Although attachment to parents reduced the severity of males' delinquency, attachment to peers and schools reduced the severity of females' delinquency.

Freda Adler argued in *Sisters in Crime* (1975) that both adult women and adolescent females are imitating males in their desire for the same goals and their adoption of male roles to achieve them. Because of this merging of gender roles, adolescent females, as well as their older counterparts, engage in more violent crime. Adler contended that as females become more male-like and acquire more "masculine" traits, they become more criminal.

Francis Cullen and colleagues (1977) found that the more male and female adolescents possessed "male" personality traits, the more likely they were to become involved in delinquency, but the relationship between masculinity and delinquency was stronger for males than for females (pp. 87–104). Thornton and James (1979) found a moderate degree of association between masculine self-expectations and delinquency but concluded that males were still more likely to be delinquent than females, regardless of their degree of masculinity (pp. 225–241).

John Hagan and colleagues proposed a power-control theory to explain female delinquency (Hagan, Simpson, and Gillis, 1987, pp. 788–816; Hagan, Gillis, and Simpson, 1985, pp. 1151–1178). Using a Marxian framework and data collected in Toronto, Canada, they contended that as mothers gain power relative to their husbands, usually by employment outside the home, daughters and sons alike are encouraged to be more open to risk taking. Parents in egalitarian families, then, redistribute their control efforts so that daughters are subjected to controls more like those imposed on sons.

In contrast, daughters in patriarchal families are taught by their parents to avoid risks (Hagan, Simpson, and Gillis, 1987, pp. 791–792). Hagan and colleagues concluded that "patriarchal families will be characterized by large gender differences in common delinquent behavior while egalitarian families will be characterized by smaller gender differences in delinquency" (p. 793). Power-control theory thus concludes that when daughters are freed from patriarchal family relations, they more frequently become delinquent (pp. 813–814).

In evaluating power-control theory, Singer and Levine (1987) contended that it is unclear in what ways work relationships produce more egalitarian home environments. The balanced class categories of egalitarian households may still reflect unbalanced work situations; the husband and wife may both be managers, but the husband is likely to make a higher income and to have more authority at work. Chesney-Lind (1987), in an even more stinging criticism, stated that power-control theory is a variation of the earlier liberation hypothesis, but it claims that mothers' liberation causes daughters' crime.

Jeglum Bartusch and Ross L. Matsueda (1996), in assessing whether an interactionist model can account for the gender gap in delinquency, used data from the National Youth Survey. Based on a symbolic interactionist model of delinquency, they argued that "delinquency is determined in part by the self as conceived by symbolic interactionists, which in turn is determined by a process of labeling by significant others" (p. 145). They did find some gender interactions. Parental labeling and reflecting appraisals had a larger effect on male delinquency, and parents were more likely to falsely accuse male delinquents.

Other Sociological Theories and Female Criminality. Eileen Leonard (1995) contends that sociological theories in general inadequately explain adult women's involvement in crime. She argues that anomie theory is unworkable in analyzing the crimes that occur among women. It "fails to explain why women deviate the way they do or what type of strain leads to each outcome. The theory applies largely to men and mainly to the goal of financial success" (p. 57). Leonard also finds a number of difficulties in applying labeling theory to women. She claims that labeling theory fails to explain female criminality because it lacks an analysis of why people engage in crime in the first place, does not examine the impact of positive and negative labeling, and fails to analyze the structures of power as they impinge on women. Furthermore, Leonard finds differential association theory inadequate in explaining female criminality. She argues that this theory fails "to explain not only how certain behavior is transmitted but why such patterns exist in the first place and why they vary so much from one group to another" (p. 61). She adds that this theory deemphasizes "wider historical and structural changes and the responses of women to these changes" (p. 61). Moreover, Leonard charges that the male orientation of subcultural theories makes them inapplicable to females. Each of the sociocultural theories "is viewed primarily in terms of male success goals" (p. 64).

Evaluating the Explanations of Female Crime. A discussion of female delinquency and adult criminals readily leads to the conclusion that biological explanations are the least predictive factors. Assumptions of sexual inferiority appear to be tied more to the historical context of male chauvinism than to the reality of female delinquency. Personal maladjustment hypotheses may have some predictive ability in determining the frequency of crime in girls and women, but these variables, too, have been overemphasized in the past. Sociological explanations appear to be far more predictive of female crime. Used much more in explaining female delinquency and crime in adult women, strain theory, social control theory, power-control theory, labeling and symbolic interactionist theory, and feminist theory all have received some support.

Some feminists argue, using the empirical support found in the above studies relating sociological explanations of male and female delinquency, that little evidence to date suggests that separate theories are needed to account for female and male delinquency, that female delinquency tends to operate through the same factors as

male delinquency, and that empirical studies generally reveal much more variation within gender than between the sexes.

However, Leonard (1995) has written an insightful article evaluating the ability of the major sociological theories of crime to explain the crime patterns of
females. She concluded that the traditional theories do not work and therefore are
basically flawed. She made the case, in both her original article published in the
early 1970s, as well as in its 1995 revision, that new theoretical efforts are needed to
understand female crime, efforts that take into account not only gender but also
race, class, and culture.

Gender, Class, and Race

The application of gender, class, and racial analysis to women and crime leads to a
number of findings.

Gender Relations.   The importance of gender among adult women is seen by
their subordinate position in the creation and implementation of law. Conflict theorists have long argued that women, racial/ethnic minorities, and the poor benefit
far less from the law than others in society. The most influential in creating laws,
according to this perspective, is rich white men and those who work in their interests. The intent of framers of the law, as previously suggested, was to protect both
men and their property. Much of the criminal law is written by state legislatures
and the U.S. Congress, both of which are overwhelmingly male. Thus, this conflict
position, which has gained increased acceptance among mainstream political theorists, contends that states, their legal systems, and criminal laws operate in the
interests of the dominant male class in U.S. society (Price and Sokoloff, 1995, p. 14).

Gender is further related to the themes of domination and subordination.
Those who are subordinate in a society experience inequality of many resources
but chiefly of status and power. Women in a patriarchal society, as in the United
States, are placed in subordinate categories. In analyzing the treatment given to
women offenders, victims, and practitioners, it is useful to question what happens
in situations of inequality and what forces are set in motion (Miller, 1998, p. 73).
Wife battering, incestuous attacks on female adolescents by fathers or father substitutes, and rape are crimes of domination against women that take place in situations of inequality (Caputi and Russell, 1995, p. 272).

Influence of Class.   Class oppression is another facet of multiple marginality
experienced by women in U.S. society. In a number of ways, powerful and serious
problems of childhood and adolescence related to poverty set the stage for females'
entry into homelessness, unemployment, drug use, survival sex and prostitution,
and, ultimately, even more serious criminal acts (Chesney-Lind, 1997, p. 4). Even
adolescent females from middle-class homes may be thrust into a situation of economic survival if they choose to run away from abusive environments.

Traditional theories also fail to address the life situations of females on the
economic and political margins, because researchers typically fail to study or talk

with these females. For example, almost all urban females identified by police as gang members have been drawn from low-income groups (Chesney-Lind, 1993, p. 338). Lee Bowker and Malcolm Klein's (1983) examination of data on females in gangs in Los Angeles stated the importance of classism as well as racism:

> We conclude that the overwhelming impact of racism, sexism, poverty, and limited opportunity structures is likely to be so important in determining the gang membership and juvenile delinquency of women and girls in urban ghettos that personality variables, relations with parents, and problems associated with heterosexual behavior play a relatively minor role in determining gang membership and juvenile delinquency. (pp. 750–751)

Social class also affects adult women's contacts with the system. Lower-class women are more likely to be victimized than are middle- and upper-class ones. Part of the reason for this is that middle-class women usually live in better neighborhoods and are less exposed to the violence of street gangs, to drug trafficking, and to armed robbers and house break-ins. In addition, the lower-class woman must deal with greater areas of indefensible space, in which her likelihood of victimization increases dramatically.

Lower-class women are also more likely to be subjected to domestic abuse. Middle- and upper-class women usually have the advantage of greater economic resources, as well as educational credentials, making it easier for them to leave an abusive situation. But for lower-class women, who are both fearful of their husbands and in need of financial assistance to care for their children, leaving an abusive situation can seem much more like an unmanageable problem. Staying in these situations, of course, increases the likelihood that either the wife or the children will experience a fatal injury from the out-of-control husband, or the wife may in desperation kill her husband.

Middle-class women who commit crimes are also more likely to receive the benefits of chivalry than are lower-class lawbreakers. They tend to be treated with more respect at time of arrest, to be given mental health placements more often than are lower-class offenders, to spend less time in jail, to be given probation more frequently, to be sentenced to residential programs less often than lower-class offenders, and, if sentenced to residential facilities, to spend less time in these placements. Moreover, they are sentenced to prison much less frequently than are lower-class offenders.

Many reasons explain this preferential treatment of middle- and upper-class women. They, of course, are able to privately retain attorneys who can provide legal help superior to that of the public defender services offered the poor. They also have the financial resources to seek out counseling, private therapeutic settings, and other diversionary programs that help avoid criminal justice processing. Further, they are less likely to become involved in crimes of violence, drug trafficking, prostitution, and crimes of larceny, including shoplifting.

Racial Discrimination. Because racism and poverty often go hand-in-hand, females from these backgrounds are forced to deal early and on a regular basis with problems of abuse, drugs, and violence. They also are likely to be attracted to gang membership (Chesney-Lind, 1997). H. C. Covey, S. Menard, and R. Franzese (1997) summarized the effect of ethnicity on gang membership:

> *Racial differences in the frequency of gang formation such as the relative scarcity of non-Hispanic, white, ethnic gangs may be explainable in terms of the smaller proportion of the non-Hispanic European American population that live in neighborhoods characterized by high rates of poverty, welfare dependency, single-parent households, and other symptoms that characterize social disorganization. (p. 240)*

Coramae Richey Mann (1995) has documented how the criminal justice system has widened the net for women of color and particularly for African American women and Latinas. In examining the pretrial treatment and sentencing of women of color, Mann found the disproportionality in prison sentencing in California, Florida, and New York by comparing arrest rates with sentencing rates. She also presented data documenting the dramatic increase in jail incarceration rates for minority women, whereas rates for white women decreased slightly (p. 118).

The specific needs and concerns of African American rape victims, including poverty, homelessness, unemployment, violence in the community, difficulties in feeding their children, racism, and fear of the police, have discouraged them from talking about their rapes to crisis centers. For local antirape or crisis centers to intervene successfully in the victimization of these women, their primary needs and problems must be addressed. The extent of these primary concerns makes women of color reluctant to report their rapes and to file charges against those who have violated them (Matthews, 1995, pp. 216–217).

The Total Is Greater Than the Sum of Its Parts

Diane Lewis (1977) has noted that because feminist theories of women's inequality "focused exclusively upon the effects of sexism, they have been of limited applicability to minority women subjected to the constraints of both racism and sexism" (p. 339). Lewis further noted that "black women . . . tended to see racism as a more powerful cause of their subordinate position than sexism and to view the women's liberation movement with considerable mistrust" (ibid.).

The Combahee River Collective's statement in 1977 about African American feminism was also an important contribution. The group stated that it is committed to challenge all forms of "racial, sexual, heterosexual, and class oppression" (p. 365). This group's multifaceted commitments reflected that it viewed these relations as inseparable:

> *We believe that sexual politics under patriarchy is as pervasive in black women's lives as are the politics of class and race. We also often find it difficult to separate race from sex oppression because in our lives they most often are experienced simultaneously. We know that there is such a thing as racial-sexual oppression which is neither solely racial nor solely sexual, e.g., the history of black women by white men as a weapon of political repression. (ibid.)*

Extent and Nature of Female Crime

This section examines the extent and nature of female crime. Beginning with the extent of female crime, this section discusses the trends in violence of women offending and women and drug violations. The importance of drug violations is that they have become the most significant reason that the rates of arrests among women have increased and that more women are being incarcerated.

Is Female Crime Increasing?

Two views have been expressed about the issue of changing patterns of female crime: (1) the perspective, usually based on official statistics, that female participation in crime has increased significantly, particularly in areas that traditionally have been considered "masculine" crimes and (2) the argument that not much has changed.

Official Statistics.   Darrell Steffensmeier and Jennifer Schwartz, in comparing the male and female arrest rates for a 100,000 population for 1965, 1980, 1990, and 2000, found that for both males and females arrest rates were higher for less serious offenses. Over the entire period, female rates were highest for minor property crimes, such as fraud and larceny, for substance abuse (drugs and liquor law violations, and driving under the influence [DUI]), and for misdemeanor assaults. Prostitution continued to be a chief form of female offending, especially by women facing adverse economic circumstances and drug-dependent women (Steffensmeier and Schwartz, 2004, p. 99).

The pattern of change over the period from 1965 to 2000 was generally similar for both males and females, with large increases occurring mainly for fraud, larceny, forgery, drug violations, DUI, and assaults; decreases in arrest rates for males and females occurred for vagrancy, public drunkenness, gambling, and suspicion of crime. What these findings appear to suggest is that similar legal and social forces underlie arrest rates for both males and females, independent of any conditions unique to women (Steffensmeier and Schwartz, 2004, p. 99). Five trends appear to be present when the female percentage of arrests for various offenses is examined (ibid.):

1. When total arrests across all offenses are considered, the female percentage doubled between 1965 (10 percent) and 2000 (20 percent). However, the bulk of this rise was due to sharp increases in the number of women arrested for minor property crimes.
2. In those categories in which the female share of offending increased, the percentage inched upward (about 1 to 2 percent per year). The most notable change occurred between 1990 and 2000.
3. For a number of offenses, the female percentage held steady or slightly declined, including arrests for drug law violations and homicide.
4. The female difference in arrests has narrowed considerably for minor property crimes of larceny-theft, forgery, and fraud.

5. The most notable trend in recent years has been the rise in the female share of persons arrested for the violent crimes of misdemeanor assault and aggravated assault. However, according to Steffensmeier and Schwartz, this largely reflected changes in citizen reporting and law enforcement (pp. 99–101).

Candace Kruttschnitt (1992, p. 227) argues that such statistics do not give an accurate picture of female crime. On one level, she notes that arrest rates represent only a fraction of the crimes known to the police and that the crimes known by the police represent only a fraction of the total volume of crime. In addition, the courts' reliance on plea bargaining may result in conviction data that bear little resemblance to the actual charges brought against criminal defendants. In examining a stratified random sample of females convicted of assault, forgery, petty theft, and drug law violations in northern California in 1976, Kruttschnitt (1992) discovered a wide degree of discrepancy between the offenses for which women were convicted and those for which they were arrested. In this study, women were arrested most frequently for theft, drunkenness, drug law violations, disorderly conduct, and assaults. However, three of the top five offenses for which women were convicted—forgery, fraud, and drunken driving—failed to appear on the most-frequent arrest list. To explain this discrepancy, Kruttschnitt identified visibility of conduct, deviance processing priorities, and the use of plea bargaining. On further analysis, the defendant's race and income bracket, the respectability of her associates, and the nature of the official conduct seemed to be more important characteristics within a crime category than the crimes themselves (p. 92).

There are a number of possible explanations for new trends in women's crime. The most likely are that changes in female arrest rates are due to more efficient official responses rather than to actual changes in criminal behavior among females; that the detachment of many inner-city minorities from mainstream institutions such as education and employment has led to adaptive strategies, including crime; that the reduced supply of male crime partners due to increased incarceration rates as well as the emerging dominance of drug trafficking have augmented the prospects for female involvement; and that drug addiction amplifies income-generating crime for both males and females, but more so for females than males (Steffensmeier and Schwartz, 2004, p. 117).

Crime Patterns and Race. Mann's (1995) examination of official statistics in California, Florida, and New York in 1990 revealed somewhat different crime patterns based on race/ethnicity. Aggravated assault and other assaults were higher for women of color than for white women. White women showed higher rank order for fraud, whereas women of color showed higher rank order for burglary, forgery, and other thefts. White women tended to exceed women of color, except for Native American women, in the rank ordering of alcohol-related offenses: liquor law violations, drunkenness, and DUI. Drug violations and prostitution were the distinguishing arrest offenses within the public order offense category for African Americans. Indeed, Mann found that drug offenses were the second most frequent cause of arrests for African American women in all three states. For Latinas in the three states, arrests for public order crimes were the most frequent, followed by arrests for property offenses and arrests for violent crimes (p. 123).

The Female Chronic Offender. Wolfgang, Figlio, and Sellin's (1972) cohort study in Philadelphia identified that 6 percent of the total sample had been arrested five times or more. In a second cohort study, which included female offenders, Tracy and Figlio (1982) were able to identify only 1 percent of the females as chronic offenders. These female offenders were involved in significantly less serious crimes than the males of the cohort. Yet, similar to males of both cohorts, the more the female offenders were arrested and the more serious their court's disposition, the more likely they were to be arrested again.

Danner, Blount, Silverman, and Vega (1995) examined female chronic offenders from data on file for 1,076 incarcerated female offenders in Florida. They found that female chronics in comparison with female nonchronics were more likely to be younger, of minority status, substance abusers, single, and involved in spouse abuse as well as to have committed the crimes alone. In comparing the female chronics to female nonchronics, it was found "that the process of becoming a female chronic offender appeared to be more complex than for males in that more criminogenic forces were required to overcome the crime-inhibiting effects of female socialization" (pp. 45–46). Furthermore, they found that the core variables that discriminated most strongly between the female chronics and nonchronics were age at first adult arrest, offense seriousness, substance abuse, and minority group status.

Matt DeLisi, in using the criminal records of 500 male and female adult recidivists, applied the concept of career criminality to women and described how this application had specific gendered elements. The average female offender age was 37 years, nearly three years younger than the male chronic offender. Habitual female offenders were also more ethnically diverse than their male counterparts. Chronic female offenders further had a later onset age of arrest, had shorter criminal careers, and were arrested in fewer states than their male peers. In addition, female career offenders were less migratory than men in terms of the accumulation of arrests in multiple jurisdictions (DeLisi, 2002).

Trends in Violent Crimes among Women Offenders

The amount of violence committed by female offenders has attracted a great deal of attention over the past twenty-five years. Many assume that women are committing more violent and aggressive crimes than they have in the past.

Several factors converged in the mid 1970s to convince the public that women were definitely involved in more violent crimes. The activities of the Symbionese Liberation Army brought Patty Hearst, Emily Harris, and other female offenders into the public eye. Television showed news clips of armed women pulling a bank robbery and tough-looking women engaging in guerrilla warfare. Sara Jane Moore and Lynette "Squeaky" Fromme were each charged with attempted assassination of President Gerald Ford. No longer arrested merely for shoplifting or passing bad checks, women now were making the FBI's most-wanted list. Finally, Freda Adler's *Sisters in Crime* (1975) appeared, seemingly in answer to the public's bewilderment over what to make of the new female criminal. In her book, Adler offered a plausible answer: violent, aggressive female criminals were now committing crimes traditionally committed only by males. Adler's appearance on several television programs gave her views nationwide publicity. She stated:

> *Women are no longer behaving like subhuman primates with only one option. Medical, edu-cational, economic, political, and technological advances have freed women from unwanted pregnancies, provided them with male occupational skills, and equalized their strength with weapons. Is it any wonder that, once women were armed with male opportunities, they should strive for status, criminal as well as civil, through established male hierarchical channels? (pp. 10–11)*

Little evidence shows, however, that women in the 1970s were more violent than they had been previously or that they became more violent in the 1980s or 1990s. In a study of crime among women in Washington, D.C., Rita Simon (1975) found that in 1974 and 1975, 82 percent of the women arrested for violent crimes had attacked someone they knew. Slightly more women than men used weapons when they committed violent acts: 79 percent of women arrested for crimes against persons versus 79 percent of men in 1974, and 84 percent of women versus 78 percent of men in 1975. In 1974, 16.7 percent of those arrested for violent crimes in Washington, D.C., were women, compared with 14.1 percent nationally (pp. 69–70). Thus, the typical violent female offender, as she is revealed in this study, arms herself against a known person: her husband, her lover, or a pimp. She differs only slightly from the stereotype of an enraged women stabbing her husband with a carving knife. Such women, Simon argues, are less desperate and more rational in their violence than ever before.

Chesney-Lind (1995), in examining the dramatic rise in the number of women imprisoned (from 12,300 in 1980 to 43,800 in 1990), considers various possible causes: greater amount of crime by women, more dangerous and tougher women offenders, and a change in the response of the criminal justice system to women offenders (pp. 105–117). Chesney-Lind is quick to dismiss the more dangerous or violent female offender. She observes that the percentage of women incarcerated for violent offenses declined during the 1980s from 49 to 41 percent in prisons and from 21 to 13 percent in jails. Instead of a more violent offender, Chesney-Lind argues that the data reflect: (1) that the justice system is imprisoning more women for drug offenses; (2) that mandatory sentencing laws have reduced the amount of discretion available to judges, which has increased the numbers and lengths of sentences for both men and women; and (3) that women are caught up in the societal mood of "getting tough on crime," driven in part by violent male criminals "getting away with murder" (p. 105).

Thus, researchers generally challenge the popular assumption that women are becoming more violent in their crimes. They say, in effect: Women may be hungrier, greedier, or unhappier, but, as a group, they do not appear to be any more violent than they were in the past.

Homicide by Women.   About one of every nine or ten persons arrested for homicide in the United States is a woman. Compared to men, research has revealed that women arrested for homicide are less likely to have previous criminal histories; are more likely to have committed the offense alone; are more likely to have killed an intimate, especially a spouse; and are more likely to have killed as the result of domestic conflict (Brownstein, Spunt, Crimmins, Goldstein, and Langley, 1994). As Simpson aptly expresses it, "The female offender is an anomaly—both in the United States and cross-culturally. . . . On those rare occasions when women are violent, their victims tend to be intimates" (Simpson, 1991, p. 116).

By the 1980s, there was strong support for the finding that women who killed their male partners were likely to have been battered women whose abuse by their partner had influenced, if not resulted in, the killing (Bannister, 1991; Walker, 1989). This research suggested that violent offending by women, especially lethal violent offending, was the response of victims to subordination in a patriarchal society (DeKeseredy and Hinch, 1991). These women had been abused by their partners and, therefore, were responding to the abuse and the patriarchal society that perpetuated it. These victims were not merely mimicking the aggressive criminal behavior of violent men but were responding as violent victims being forced out of their passive states (Brownstein, Spunt, Crimmins, Goldstein, and Langley, 1994, p. 101).

Recent evidence indicates that women involved in familial homicide are involved in other types of homicides as well. That is, they are not only husband killers, but are also killers of other victims (Goetting, 1988). Indeed, "there appears to be a growing proportion of women involved in the killing of strangers, or at least of people with whom they have no known emotional ties" (Brownstein, Spunt, Crimmins, Goldstein, and Langley, 1994, p. 102).

Women's Violence against Their Children.   Feminists have been reluctant to venture into what they define as the problematic waters of child abuse research (Dougherty, 1991). Washburne (1983), a feminist scholar, attempts to clarify what is at stake in formulating a feminist understanding of women's violence against their children:

> *Feminists have recognized that women are on occasion violent toward men and understand that violence as a direct result of societal and interpersonal pressures on women. Women's violence toward children needs to be recognized and discussed in the same context. Women's abuse of children stems directly from their own oppression in society and within the family. (p. 291)*

Dougherty argues that ultimately, if one is serious about unlocking the secrets of maternal child abuse, the key is found in a feminist perspective that reveals needed insight into the lives of women who live in a patriarchical society. The patriarchal nature of society provides the social context for the oppression of women. The toxicity of this oppression is determined largely by how effective the socialization process has been in internalizing a negative self-concept among women. Women are encouraged by the patriarchy to accept the belief that it is inappropriate for them to struggle against their powerlessness. At the same time, the burden of child care is placed nearly solely on women's shoulders. Women's violence against their children, then, represents their rage and their own abuse of power (Dougherty, 1993, pp. 108–109).

Wilczynski (1991) examined the images of women who kill their children, dividing infanticidal women into the "mad" and the "bad." Women who are defined as "mad" are typically perceived as mentally ill. Ms. B. was one such defendant who appeared before an English court in 1988. While she was severely depressed she suffocated her 11-month-old child and then tried to commit suicide. The judge, who gave Ms. B. a three-year probation, said:

> *You are in need of help and not of punishment. It is quite clear to me that no useful purpose would be served by sending you to prison.*
>
> *Yours is a very sad case. . . . You not only loved that child but love all children because one of the ironies of this case is that in your will you left the residue of your estate to N.S.P.C.C. [National Society for the Prevention of Cruelty to Children]. (pp. 78–79)*

"Bad" women, in contrast, are "viewed as ruthless, selfish, cold, callous, neglectful of their children or domestic responsibilities, violent or promiscuous" (p. 78). These women, according to Wilczynski, are viewed as "monsters" who neglect their infants, fail to protect them from harm, show no remorse for what they have done to their children, and are perceived as "whores" who have strong and inappropriate instinctual sexual drives (p. 80).

In the 1990s, pregnant mothers who used drugs were increasingly identified by the state as "bad." Kasinsky (1994) identifies the state's reaction to pregnant, drug-using mothers today as having major continuities with the Progressive Era's response to mothers accused of child abuse. In both historical periods, the child savers have imposed their class, ethnic, and racial biases on immigrant, poor, and African American women. During the Progressive Era, those mothers who did not conform to a cultural ideal of maternal care were labeled as "unfit" and needing state control. In the modern era, physicians have joined with social workers and prosecutors to prosecute pregnant mothers who use drugs through the use of mandatory reporting laws along with drug tests (p. 97).

The medicalization of pregnant women drug users has led to an increasing number of women being sanctioned by the state. Sanctions include having newborn infants taken away and placed in foster homes; the placement of other, older children in foster homes; the loss of such welfare benefits as eligibility for subsidized housing; and being arrested and prosecuted. In 1992, according to the Center for Reproductive Law and Policy, 164 women in twenty-six states were arrested on criminal charges because of their behavior during pregnancy (Kasinsky, 1994, pp. 110–111). Some of the women have been sentenced to short- or long-term confinement in correctional institutions (Callahan and Knight, 1992).

Callahan and Knight (1992) state three objections to the legal sanctions that have been used or are proposed to be used against pregnant women to prevent prenatal harm. First, they define these sanctions as "morally unjustified" even where they might be legal. Second, they argue that these sanctions "are morally and legally unacceptable because they violate important moral values captured in our legal system." Finally, they contend that the sanctions "are morally unacceptable and would make bad law because they would contribute to the harm they would be instituted to prevent" (p. 5).

Women and Drug Offenses

The discussion in this chapter has suggested that as Alida V. Merlo (1995) aptly puts it: "The typical female offender is not a corporate or computer criminal, a terrorist, a burglar, or a murderer. Instead, she is likely to engage in theft, fraud, drug offenses, forgery, embezzlement, and prostitution." Merlo goes on to say that an important dimension in understanding female criminality as we begin the twenty-first century is the female offender's use of drugs. She adds: "Female drug-related activity merits closer scrutiny as an important element in female criminality. It warrants concern and social policy implications (p. 119). See Chapter 5 to explore the subject of the role of substance abuse in women's involvement with the criminal justice system.

Women in the Illegal Drug Economy. Morgan and Joe (1997) compared women's experiences in the illicit drug economy of San Francisco, San Diego, and Honolulu and found that these women had diverse drug-use careers. In this study, female users tended to fall within four categories, and many women shifted from one category to another during different periods of their drug-using careers. First, "social outlaws" were deeply immersed in a deviant and marginal lifestyle. Of this category, one group lived "on the edge" and was on the lowest level of economic and social status, but another group was able to maintain some control over their lives. Second, "welfare moms" were on welfare, living in poor suburban areas and married or had children at a young age. Methamphetamine was used partly as a survival strategy to cope with daily hardships and social disaster. Third, "floaters" were women who went in and out of mainstream life. For a while, they held a regular job, then quit to live with a boyfriend or to engage in full-time drug dealing. They generally maintained a respectable image, managing to escape from long-term participation in deviant or criminal lifestyles. Finally, "citizens" were women who lived within mainstream society. They were able to retain a measure of stability and respectability, as they resided in good neighborhoods and had money and often a husband and family (pp. 93–94).

Dunlap, Johnson, and Maher (1997) examined female crack sellers in New York City. They found that most of their social and occupational roles were confined to low-level sales and distribution activities. These women did move in and out of various roles at the street level in a way similar to male distributors (p. 52). They summarized the experiences of the female crack sellers:

> *Collectively, these women's experiences illustrate the multiplicity of roles by which females currently participate in the drug economy. While they occupy a minority status in the sense of being women in a male-dominated labor market, these women have the capacity to change and shape this world insofar as they can be seen to exhibit considerable innovation, role variation, and a number of different patterns of involvement. (p. 52)*

Processing of Female Offenders

The issue of discrimination within the criminal justice system has long interested social scientists. They have particularly attempted to identify and explain the disparity in sentences imposed on defendants representing various social classes and racial groups. More recently, as they have analyzed the treatment of male and female defendants, social scientists have reached somewhat contradictory conclusions (Spohn and Spears, 1997). Some have found women to be more likely than men to be released on their own recognizance or on bail, to have their cases dismissed before trial, to be less likely than men to be convicted, to receive less severe sentences, or to be incarcerated. However, other researchers have found that females are treated no differently from males, especially with respect to decisions to prosecute, to plea bargain, or to convict (pp. 30–31).

Yet despite these contradictory findings, the bulk of the evidence has indicated more lenient treatment of female defendants, especially at the sentencing stage. It is generally concluded that this preferential treatment reflects paternalism or chivalry. According to this view, women are treated more leniently than men because criminal justice officials feel that women are physically weaker than men and therefore must be protected from the harshness of the justice system or that women are less dangerous, less culpable, or less likely to recidivate than men and, accordingly, deserve less punitive treatment (Spohn and Spears, 1997, p. 31).

In examining the differences in felony court processing, Margaret Farnworth and R. H. C. Teske, Jr. (1995), express the three most frequently claimed hypotheses concerning women offenders and chivalry. First, the "typicality" hypothesis contends that "women are treated with chivalry in criminal processing, but only when their charges are consistent with stereotypes of female offenders." Second, "selective chivalry" argues that "decision makers extend chivalry disproportionately to white females." Third, "differential discretion" views disparity as "most likely in informal decisions such as charge reduction rather than in formal decisions at final sentencing" (p. 23). Farnworth and Teske found from data of 9,966 felony theft cases and 18,176 felony assault cases disposed in California in 1988 that gender disparity was more frequently found with females with no prior record, who were more likely than similar males to receive charge reductions; this, in turn, enhanced females' chances of receiving probation. The only selective chivalry found was a tendency to change charges of assault to nonassault more frequently among white female defendants than among minority females. They further found that pivotal decisions concerning charge reduction provided some support for the notion of differential discretion, but that the findings provided no clear support for the typicality hypothesis (pp. 23–24).

Cathy C. Spohn and Jeffrey W. Spears (1997) used data on male and female defendants charged with violent felonies to examine the effects of gender on case processing decisions (1997). They found that female defendants were more likely than male defendants to have all the charges against them dismissed and that females were sentenced less harshly than males. But, as with other researchers, Spohn and Spears found that gender and race interacted and highlighted the importance of testing an interactive model incorporating the effects of both gender and race (p. 29).

Summary

This chapter presented a basic agreement and several disagreements among feminists concerning crime and women in the United States. The basic area of agreement, among feminists as well as most nonfeminists, is that delinquency/criminology theories are preoccupied with why males commit delinquent acts. A major disagreement among feminists relates to whether separate theories are needed to explain female delinquency/criminality among women. On one hand are those feminists who argue that separate theories are not needed to account for female and male delinquency and female and male criminality. On the other hand, other feminists charge that existing delinquency/criminology theories are inadequate to explain female delinquency and female criminality. These theories, adds this position, represent an androcentric perspective that cannot encompass the empirical results of available research.

We conclude that both positions are essentially correct. Considerable evidence supports the finding that female delinquency and female criminality operate through the same sociological factors as male delinquency and male criminality and that more variation exists within each gender than between the sexes. This position also charges that proposing new, separate theories of female crime and delinquency actually falls into a brand of reductionism by assuming that the experiences of women are universal and distinct from those of men. Yet a sound argument can be made that adolescent females' sexual and physical victimizations at home and the relationship between these experiences and their later adult crimes have been ignored, and that, therefore, new theoretical efforts are needed to deal with these experiences. The second position is also justified; new theoretical efforts are needed to examine the "multiple marginality" of adolescent females and female criminals.

The problems of sexism, racism, and classism and their implications have been generally ignored by criminologists. As a result, writers on female delinquency and female criminality have been more concerned with the adjustment of the adolescent female or adult woman to society than with the extent and consequences of oppression in her life. An examination of how the categories of gender, class, and race are interlocked will lead to needed insight about what the female delinquent and female criminal faces in U.S. society. As Dorie Klein (1995) has indicated, "[T]he road from Lombroso to the present is surprisingly straight" (p. 33).

The progress recently made in understanding female delinquency and female criminality promises that this area of inquiry may be a fruitful one in the future. For example, much more research is needed into sociological explanations, such as blocked opportunity, the influence of peers, and the impact of labeling. In addition, although adult women and adolescent female offenders appear to have much in common, the significant differences between them need further examination. Moreover, cross-cultural comparisons that show similar patterns of female delinquency and female criminality in the United States and in other cultures should be used more fully.

KEY TERMS

feminist criminology   gender-neutral   liberation thesis

CRITICAL THINKING QUESTIONS

1. Which of the theoretical explanations of women and crime do you find most appealing?

2. What is the importance of gender related to adult women and crime?

3. How does social class contribute to class oppression of women in the United States?

4. What does racial discrimination contribute to our understanding of women and crime?

5. What are the most salient trends regarding women and crime?

WEB DESTINATIONS

See the National Consortium on Violence Research for research reports on violence by women and minorities at: www.heinz.cmu.edu/researchers/centers.html

For research on women in the justice system, visit this site: www.ncjrs.org/pdffiles1/nij/189973.pdf

National Institute of Corrections, gender-responsive strategies: www.nicic.org/pubs/2003/018017.pdf

REFERENCES

Acoca, L. (1998). Defusing the time bomb: Understanding and meeting the growing health care needs of incarcerated women in America. *Crime and Delinquency 44*: 49–69.

Adler, F. (1975). *Sisters in crime.* New York: McGraw-Hill.

Anderson, B. J., Holmes, M. D., and Ostresh, R. (1998, March). Males' and females' delinquent attachments and the effects of attachments on severity of self-reported delinquency. Paper presented to the Annual Meeting of Criminal Justice Sciences in Albuquerque, New Mexico.

Bannister, S. A. (1991). The criminalization of women fighting back against male abuse: Imprisoned battered women as political prisoners. *Humanity and Society 15:* 400–416.

Bartusch, D. J., and Matsueda, R. L. (1996, September). Gender, reflected appraisals, and labeling: A cross-group test of an interactionist theory of delinquency. *Social Forces 75:* 145.

Blanchette, K. (1997, January). Classifying female offenders for correctional interventions. *Forum in Corrections 9:* 1–8.

Bowker, L. H., and Klein, M. W. (1983). The etiology of female juvenile delinquency and gang membership: A test of psychological and social structural explanations. *Adolescence 18:* 739–751.

Brownstein, H. H., Spunt, B. J., Crimmins, S., Goldstein, P. J., and Langley, S. (1994). Changing patterns of lethal violence by women: A research note. *Women and Criminal Justice 5:* 99–118.

Bureau of Justice Statistics. (1999). *Substance abuse and treatment, state and federal prisoners, 1997.* Washington, D.C.: U.S. Department of Justice.

Callahan, J. C., and Knight, J. W. (1992). Prenatal harm as child abuse? *Women and Criminal Justice 3:* 5–33.

Campbell, A. (1981). *Girl delinquents.* New York: St. Martin's Press.

Caputi, J., and Russell, D. E. H. (1995). Femicide: Sexist terrorism against women. In B. R. Price and N. J. Sokoloff (eds.), *The criminal justice system and women: Offenders, victims, and workers* (pp. 272–279). New York: McGraw-Hill.

Chesney-Lind, M. (1987, November 10–14). Girls' crime and woman's place: Toward a feminist model of female delinquency. Paper presented at the Annual Meeting of the American Society of Criminology, Montreal, Canada.

Chesney-Lind, M. (1993). Girls, gangs, and violence: Reinventing the liberated female crook. *Humanity and Society 17:* 321–344.

Chesney-Lind, M. (1997). *The female offender: Girls, women, and crime.* Thousand Oaks, Calif.: Sage Publications.

Chesney-Lind, M. (1995). Rethinking women's imprisonment: A critical examination of trends in female incarceration. In B. R. Price and N. J. Sokoloff (eds.), *The criminal justice system and women: Offenders, victims, and workers* (pp. 89–104). New York: McGraw-Hill.

Coleman, J. S. (1961). *The adolescent society.* New York: Free Press.

Combahee River Collective. (1979). The Combahee River Collective statement. In Z. Eistenstein (ed.), *Capitalist patriarch and the case for socialist feminism* (pp. 362–372). New York: Monthly Review Press.

Corrections Today. (1997, August). U.S. prison population rises. *Corrections Today,* p. 12.

Covey, H. C., Menard, S., and Franzese, R. (1997). *Juvenile gangs,* 2nd ed. Springfield, Ill.: Charles C Thomas.

Cowie, J., Cowie, B., and Slater, E. (1968). *Delinquency in girls.* London: Heinemann.

Crites, L. (1976). Women offenders: Myth vs. reality. In Laura Crites (ed.), *The female offender* (pp. 36–39). Lexington, Mass.: Lexington Books.

Cullen, F. T., Golden, K. M., and Cullen, J. B. (1977). Sex and delinquency: A partial test of the masculinity hypothesis. *Criminology 15:* 87–104.

Daly, K. (1995). Looking back, looking forward: The promise of feminist transformation. In B. R. Price and N. J. Sokoloff (eds.), *The criminal justice system and women: Offenders, victims, and workers* (pp. 447–448). New York: McGraw-Hill.

Daly, K., and Chesney-Lind, M. (1988). Feminism and criminology. *Justice Quarterly 5:* 497–538.

Danner, T. A., Blount, W. R., Silverman, I. J., and Vega, M. (1995). The female chronic offender: Exploring life contingency and offense history dimensions for incarcerated female offenders. *Women and Criminal Justice 6:* 45–66.

Datesman, S. K., Scarpitti, F. R., and Stephenson, R. M. (1975). Truancy: An application of self and opportunity theories. *Journal of Research in Crime and Delinquency 12:* 120.

DeKeseredy, W. S., and Hinch, R. (1991). *Woman abuse—Sociological perspectives.* Toronto: Thompson Educational Publishing.

DeLisi, M. (2002). Not just a boy's club: An empirical assessment of female career criminals. *Women & Criminal Justice 13:* 27–45.

Dougherty, J. (1993). Women's violence against their children: A feminist perspective. *Women and Criminal Justice 4:* 91–114.

Dunlap, E., Johnson, B. D., and Maher, L. (1997). Female crack sellers in New York City: Who they are and what they do. *Women and Criminal Justice 8:* 25–55.

Farnworth, M., and Teske, R. H. C. Jr. (1995). Gender differences in felony court processing: Three hypotheses of disparity. *Women and Criminal Justice 6:* 23–44.

Federal Bureau of Investigation. (1998). *Crime in the United States: Uniform crime reports 1997.* Washington, D.C.: U.S. Government Printing Office.

Feinman, C. (1994). *Women in the criminal justice system,* 3rd ed. Westport, Conn.: Praeger Publishers.

Fields, G. (1998, January 9). Study links drugs to 80% of incarcerations. *USA Today,* p. 2A.

Figueira-McDonough, J., and Selo, E. (1980). A reformulation of the equal opportunity explanation of female delinquency. *Crime and Delinquency 26:* 333–334.

Freud, S. (1949). *An outline of psychoanalysis,* trans. James Strachey. New York: Norton.

Freud, S. (1933). *New introductory lectures on psychoanalysis.* New York: Norton.

Gibbens, T. C. N. (1971). Female offenders. *British Journal of Hospital Medicine 6:* 279–286.

Giordano, P. C. (1978). Girls, guys and gangs: The changing social context of female delinquency. *Journal of Criminal Law and Criminology 69.*

Giordano, P. C., and Cernkovich, S. A. (1979, February 28). Changing patterns of female delinquency. A research proposal submitted to the National Institutes of Mental Health.

Goetting, A. (1988). Patterns of homicide among women. *Journal of Interpersonal Violence 3:* 3–20.

Hagan, J., Simpson, J., and Gillis, A. R. (1987, January). Class in the household: A power-control theory of gender and delinquency. *American Journal of Sociology 92:* 788–816.

Hagan, J., Gillis, A. R., and Simpson, J. (1985). The class structure of gender and delinquency: Toward a power-control theory of common delinquent behavior. *American Journal of Sociology 90:* 1151–1178.

Heimer, K. (1994). Gender, race, and the pathways to delinquency. In J. Hagan and R. Peterson (eds.), *Crime and inequality* (p. 164). Stanford, California: Stanford University Press.

Hirschi, T. (1969). *Causes of delinquency.* Berkeley: University of California Press.

Juvenile female offenders: A status of the states report. (1998). Washington, D.C.: Office of Juvenile Justice Delinquency Prevention.

Kaplan, M. S., and Sasser, J. E. (1996). Women behind bars: Trends and policy issues. *Journal of Sociology and Social Welfare 23:* 43–46.

Kasinsky, R., and Goldsmith. (1994). Child neglect and "unfit" mothers: Child savers in the progressive era and today. *Women and Criminal Justice 6:* 97–129.

Klein, D. (1995). The etiology of female crime: A review of the literature. In B. R. Price and N. J. Sokoloff (eds.), *The criminal justice system and women: Offenders, victims, and workers* (pp. 30–53). New York: McGraw-Hill.

Kruttschnitt, C. (1985). "Female crimes" or legal labels? Are statistics about women offenders representative of their crimes? In I. L. Moyer (ed.), *The changing roles of women in the criminal justice system* (pp. 81–97), 2nd ed. Prospect Heights, Ill.: Waveland Press.

Leonard, E. (1995). Theoretical criminology and gender. In B. R. Price and N. J. Sokoloff (eds.), *The criminal justice system and women: Offenders, victims, and workers* (pp. 54–70). New York: McGraw-Hill.

Lewis, D. K. (1977). A response to inequality: Black women, racism, and sexism. *Signs: Journal of Women in Culture and Society 3:* 339–361.

Lombroso, C. (1920). *The female offender.* New York: Appleton.

Mann, C. R. (1990). Female homicide and substance abuse: Is there a connection? *Women and Criminal Justice 1:* 87–109.

Mann, C. R. (1995). Women of color and the criminal justice system. In B. R. Price and N. J. Sokoloff (eds.), *The criminal justice system and women: Offenders, victims, and workers* (pp. 118–135). New York: McGraw-Hill.

Marron, K. (1996). *The slammer: The crisis in Canada's prison system.* Toronto: Doubleday Canada.

Matthews, N. A. (1995). Surmounting a legacy: The expansion of racial diversity in a local anti-rape movement. In B. R. Price and N. J. Sokoloff (eds.), *The criminal justice system and women: Offenders, victims, and workers* (pp. 216–227). New York: McGraw-Hill.

Mazerolle, P. (1998). Gender, general strain, and delinquency: An empirical examination. *Justice Quarterly 15:* 65–91.

Merlo, A. V. (1995). Female criminality in the 1990s. In A. V. Merlo and J. M. Pollock (eds.), *Women, law, and social control* (pp. 119–134). Boston: Allyn and Bacon.

Miller, J. B. (1998). Domination and subordination. In P. S. Rothenberg (ed.), *Race, class, and gender in the United States* (pp. 73–89), 4th ed. New York: St. Martin's Press.

Morgan, P., and Joe, K. A. (1997). Uncharted terrain: Contexts of experience among women in the illicit drug economy. *Women and Criminal Justice 8:* 85–109.

Norland, S., and Shover, N. (1977). Gender roles and female criminality: Some critical comments. *Criminology 15:* 87–104.

Office of Juvenile Justice and Delinquency Prevention. (1998). Addressing female development in treatment. In *Juvenile female offenders: A status of the states report* (pp. 1–3). Washington, D.C.: U.S. Justice Department.

Parsons, T. (1942, October). Age and sex in the social structure of the United States. *American Sociological Review 7.*

Pollak, O. (1950). *The criminality of women.* Philadelphia: University of Pennsylvania Press.

Price, B. R., and Sokoloff, N. J. (1995). The criminal law and women. In B. R. Price and N. J. Sokoloff (eds.), *The criminal justice system and women: Offenders, victims, and workers* (pp. 11–29). New York: McGraw-Hill.

Rittenhouse, R. (1963). A theory and comparison of male and female delinquency. Ph.D. dissertation, University of Michigan, Ann Arbor.

Rogers, K. O. (1973). For her own protection . . . conditions of incarceration for female juvenile offenders in the state of Connecticut. *Law and Society Review 7:* 223–246.

Sarri, R. C. (1976). Juvenile law: How it penalizes females. In L. Crites (ed.), *The juvenile offender* (pp. 68–69). Lexington, Mass.: Lexington Books.

Simon, R. J. (1995). *Women and crime.* Lexington, Mass.: Heath.

Simpson, S. (1991). Caste, class, and violent crime: Explaining differences in female offending. *Criminology 29:* 115–135.

Singer, S. I., and Levine, M. (1987, November). Re-examining class in the household and a power-control theory of gender and delinquency. A paper presented at the Annual Meeting of the American Society of Criminology.

Smart, C. (1976). *Women, crime and criminology: A feminist critique.* Boston: Routledge and Kegan Paul.

Spohn, C. C., and Spears, J. W. (1997). Gender and case processing decisions: A comparison of case outcomes for male and female defendants charged with violent felonies. *Women and Criminal Justice 8:* 29–59.

Steffensmeier, D., and Allen, E. (1996). Gender and crime: Toward a gendered theory of female offending. *Annual Review of Sociology 22:* 459–487.

Steffensmeier, D., and Schwartz, J. (2004). Trends in female criminality: Is crime still a man's world? In B. R. Price and N. J. Sokoloff (eds.), *The criminal justice system and women: Offenders, victims, and workers* (pp. 95–111). New York: McGraw-Hill.

Terry, R. (1967). Discrimination in the police handling of juvenile offenders by social control agencies. *Journal of Research in Crime and Delinquency 14.*

Thomas, W. I. (1907). *Sex and society.* Boston: Little, Brown.

Thomas, W. I. (1923). *The unadjusted girl.* New York: Harper.

Thornton, W. E., and James, J. (1979, July). Masculinity and delinquency revisited. *British Journal of Criminology 19:* 225–241.

Tracy, P., and Figlio, R. (1982). "Chronic recidivism in the 1958 birth cohort. In L. Shannon (ed.), *Assessing the relationships of adult criminal careers to juvenile careers: A summary* (pp. 742–775). Washington, D.C.: U.S. Department of Justice.

Walker, L. E. (1989). *Terrifying love—Why battered women kill and how society responds.* New York: Harper and Row.

Washburne, C. K. (1983). A feminist analysis of child abuse and neglect. In D. Finkelhor, et al. (eds.), *The dark side of families* (pp. 289–292). Beverly Hills, Calif: Sage Publications.

Wilczynski, A. (1991). Images of women who kill their infants: The mad and the bad. *Women and Criminal Justice 2:* 71–88.

Wolfgang, M. E., Figlio, R. M., and Sellin, T. (1972). *Delinquency in a birth cohort.* Chicago: University of Chicago Press.

3 Feminist Theory and Research

Frances M. Heidensohn is one of those scholars who note that "women and crime" is recognized now as an important topic in criminology texts and readers (Heidensohn, 1996, pp. xiii–xiv). As part of the rapid expansion of the field, authors of many criminology texts not only devote sections to feminist perspectives and theories, but also attempt to differentiate between feminist and nonfeminist analyses (Daly, 1998, p. 86). Expansion has come from two sources: (1) research by nonfeminist scholars who are interested in studies of women and crime or race and gender differences; and (2) research by feminist scholars from a variety of disciplines with diverse political stances. The first source focuses on criminological debates, but its members may not have a grasp of feminist theories and research; the second source focuses on a theoretical and political analysis of women's situations, but its members may fail to grasp the limits of criminalization or be familiar with theories of crime and punishment (Daly, 1998, p. 86).

The purpose of this chapter is to bridge these sources by presenting feminist theory and research within the context of criminology and its theories of crime and punishment. Chapter 2 presented gender differences in lawbreaking, whereas this chapter examines more carefully the patterns of lawbreaking, including gender ratio of crime, gendered crime, gendered pathways, and gendered lives. In addition, this chapter considers feminist epistemologies; epistemology refers to "theories of what knowledge is, what makes it possible, and how to get it" (Harding, 1991, p. 308). Finally, Chapter 3 examines research methodology and methods. Although feminist research employs all of the methods that traditional researchers have used, feminist researchers tend to emphasize the importance of critically examining the nature of the research process itself (Flavin, 2001, p. 277).

Key Features That Distinguish Feminist Theories

The discussion in this chapter begins by highlighting key features that distinguish feminist theories from other theoretical perspectives in criminology. Kathleen Daly and Meda Chesney-Lind (1988) list five aspects of feminist thought that distinguish it from traditional criminological inquiry:

1. Gender is not a natural fact but a complex social, historical, and cultural product; it is related to, but not simply derived from, biological sex difference and reproductive capacities.
2. Gender and gender relations order social life and social institutions in fundamental ways.
3. Gender relations and constructs of masculinity and femininity are not symmetrical but are based on an organizing principle of men's superiority and social and political-economic dominance over women.
4. Systems of knowledge reflect men's views of the natural and social world; the production of knowledge is gendered.
5. Women should be at the center of intellectual inquiry, not peripheral, invisible, or appendages to men. (p. 504)

In addition, as suggested in Chapter 1, feminist theorists investigate the interlocking nature of gender, race/ethnicity, class, sexuality, and age, recognizing that women's experiences of gender may vary according to their position in class and racial/ethnic hierarchies (Simpson, 1991; Daly and Maher, 1998).

Within this broad framework, Jody Miller and Christopher W. Mullins (2006, 218–219) highlight key features that distinguish feminist theories from other theoretical perspectives in criminology. First, feminist scholarship is grounded in the inquiry into the meaning and nature of gender relations. According to this perspective, gender theory is crucial to the study of criminality and crime.

Second, feminist perspectives cut across a broad range of questions within criminology and criminal justice. Feminist research has particularly emphasized juvenile/criminal justice processing, including incarceration and violence against women.

Third, feminist criminologists grapple with what has been referred to as an "intellectual double shift." As Daly and Maher note, gender operates not only within the practices and organizations of social life, but also within "the discursive fields by which women [and men] are constructed or construct themselves" (1998, p. 4). To elaborate, feminist scholars face the challenge not only of examining the impact of gender and gender inequality in "real" life, but also of deconstructing the intertwined ideologies about gender guiding social practices (Miller and Mullins, 2006).

Finally, feminist criminology is best suited to the development of what Daly (1998) refers to as theories of the "middle range." These middle range theories seek to explore how broader structural forces are realized within both organizational contexts and the micro-level interactions of social actors within a specific area. Instead of creating gender theories, feminist criminology requires us to move beyond broad and global analyses. With the starting recognition that society and social life are patterned on the basis of gender, feminist criminology recognizes that **gender order** is complex and shifting.

The Problem of Generalizability

Chapter 2 investigated how much theories of men's crime apply to women. For the most part, these studies have received mixed results (Broidy, 2001). Candace Kruttschnitt aptly summarizes: "It appears that the factors that influence delinquent development differ for males and females in some contexts but not others" (1996, p. 141).

Peggy C. Giordano and colleagues' sample from the Ohio Serious Offender Study led them to conclude "that the either/or dichotomy suggested by the contrast between traditional and feminist frameworks is neither necessary nor helpful to the theory-building process." They suggest that the above study "indicates that the basic tenets of these seemingly opposing viewpoints are not in themselves fundamentally incompatible, and the results show that a comprehensive understanding of girls' delinquency requires a more integrated approach." They found that this was particularly true when the focus is on the small subgroup of girls with serious delinquent histories (Giordano, Deines, and Cernkovich, 2006, p. 18).

Giordano and colleagues' follow-up of their study of this subgroup of serious female offenders suggests that a comprehensive examination of their actions requires that we draw from both classic explanations of delinquency and contemporary perspectives that emphasize uniquely gendered processes. Within the life histories of these girls there is ample evidence of both types of social dynamics. Frequent themes within the narrative include disadvantaged neighborhoods, economic marginality, and "excess of definitions favourable to the violation of law," but, at the same time, parents' criminal involvement and/or severe alcohol and drug problems emerge early on and continue throughout the women's childhood and adolescent years. The adult follow-up further supports the idea that some processes associated with continued crime or desistance seem to be "generic" (that is, they have a good fit with both women and men's life experiences), while others appear to be more heavily gendered (Giordano, Deines, and Cernkovich 2006, p. 36).

One of the major problems with explanations of crime that focus on generalizability is that they cannot account for the gender ratio of offending; that is, men are disproportionately involved in crime. Much of this research also assumes that variables or constructs have the same meaning for males and females. However, recent work reveals that factors have different influences within and across gender. Thus, as a result of the gendered nature of women's and men's lives, factors often take on different meanings and have different consequences for males and females. Thus, feminists insist that while some of the concepts found in presumably gender-neutral theories may be useful for understanding women's offending, those gendered theories that take gender and gender stratification into consideration are preferable to those approaches that assume measures or constructs are gender-neutral. However, instead of assuming that "gender difference is the sole focus of feminist research, feminists question: when, how, and why does gender matter? (Miller and Mullins, 2006, pp. 226–227).

Important questions relate to the vastly different rates of criminal offending by gender: Why are women less likely than men to be involved in crime? Conversely, why are men more crime-prone than women? What explains these gender differences? (Daly and Chesney-Lind, 1988, p. 515). This **gender ratio of crime** issue is typically pursued by inquiring into the factors that block or limit women's involvement in crime. It can be argued that this inquiry "reflects an androcentric perspective that makes men the norm upon which women deviate through their limited offending" (Miller and Mullins, 2006, p. 227).

Feminists tend to propose treating gender as a key element of social organization rather than as an individual trait. This approach permits a more complex examination of the gender gap. For example, data on crime trends reveal that the gender gap is more persistent for some offenses than others, fluctuates over time (Steffensmeier and Schwartz, 2004), and varies by class, race/ethnicity, and age (Sommers and Baskin, 1993). In addition, approaches that simply address a gender gap miss the opportunity to examine how causal factors shape differentially men's and women's offending across cross-cutting social positions. Miller and Mullins illustrate this point by noting that evidence exists of a link between "underclass" conditions and African American women's offending which fails to have explanatory power for women's offending in other contexts (Miller and Mullins, 2006, p. 228).

Karen Heimer and colleagues examine the "economic marginalization thesis" which proposes "that the gender gap in crime decreases and females account for a greater proportion of crime when women's economic well-being declines" (Heimer, Wittrock, and Unal, 2006, p. 115). They found "that the *relative* economic well-being of women and men is the key to understanding the gender gap in offending." "Not only," they add, are "women more likely to live in poverty than men but also that the gender gap in poverty rates for women in the most crime-prone group continues to increase" (Heimer, Wittrock, and Unal, 2006, p. 121). Their conclusion, which is opposite to the liberation argument, is that economic oppression, instead of economic liberation, may be at the root of the narrowing of the gender gap in crime over the previous four decades (Heimer, Wittrock, and Unal, 2006, p. 131).

The most promising avenues for exploring the complexities of the gender ratio of offending are found in Daly's (1995) conceptual scheme of these three areas of inquiry:

- Gendered Pathways: What trajectories bring females and males to offending? What social contexts and factors facilitate entrance to and desistance from offending, and how are they gendered?
- Gendered Crime: What are the ways in which street life, sex and drug markets, crime opportunities, informal economies, and crime groups are ordered by gender and other social relations? What is the variation in the sequencing and contexts of women's and men's lawbreaking?
- Gendered Lives: How does gender affect the daily lives of females and males? How does gender structure courses of identities and action? How do these experiences intersect with lawbreaking? (pp. 96–99)

Gendered Pathways

From the early 1990s, feminist criminologists began to examine what is now referred to as **gendered pathways.** This approach emphasized "biographical elements, life course trajectories and developmental sequences" (Daly, 1998, p. 97). The pathways approach, which will be covered more extensively in the next chapter on life course and delinquency, seeks to map out the life experiences leading girls and women to offending as well as to desistance (Giordano et al., 2002). The recognition of the "blurred boundaries" of victimization and offending is an important underpinning of this research. In a number of publications, and as articulated in her "feminist theory of delinquency," Chesney-Lind has observed how females' earlier victimization set the stage for their entry into homelessness, survival sex and sometimes prostitution, unemployment, drug use, and eventually into other criminal acts (Chesney-Lind and Pasko, 2004, p. 5).

Some feminist scholars, despite the important insights of this "blurred boundaries" approach, contend that it needs to be broadened to recognize the diversity of women's pathways to offending. For example, this exclusive emphasis on victimization as the key pathway to women's offending can overlook other aspects of women's and girls' lives that put them at risk for offending (Miller and Mullins, 2006, p. 18). Gaarder and Belknap's (2002) analysis identified the importance of victimization and violence, but also economic marginality and racial and structural dislocation, school experiences, and drug and alcohol use in explaining adolescent females' delinquency.

Miller and Mullins (2006) also argue that relying only on female samples makes it difficult to specify whether and how such risks influence pathways to offending across gender. One area in which feminist pathways' analysis has been used is the study of youth gangs (Miller, 2001; Moore, 1991). This research has compared males and females in gangs and non-gangs by usually using one of two approaches: (1) an analysis of etiological risk factors from survey research and (2) a qualitative analysis focusing on juvenile females' accounts of why they joined gangs and on their life contexts prior to and at the time of joining (Miller and Mullins, 2006, p. 230).

Gendered Crime

Attention to **gendered crime**—to situational and organizational aspects of crime that relate to gender—emerged in the 1980s with Steffensmeier's (1983) analysis of gender segregation and institutional sexism in criminal networks. As a logical extension of feminist criminology, which views gender as totally relevant to social behavior and recognizes the situational nature of gender accomplishment, some feminist scholars have examined how situational gendered-opportunity structures and gender expectations shape criminal events (Miller and Mullins, 2006, p. 232).

There are at least two ways in which research can be conducted on gendered crime. It is possible to count the frequency of offense elements, such as the role played by and the size of the crime group; awareness exists that this may not be sufficiently nuanced to reveal the extent of crime. A second approach would be to link gender (and race, class, and age) identities to crime as a gendered line of action. Recent research on boys and men reveal ways in which masculine privileges and identities enable certain risk-taking behavior in boys (Cannon, 1991) more so than in girls (Bottcher, 2001). Daly does ask whether it may be better to start "with concrete studies of boys'/men's and girls'/women's lives, rather than with ungrounded, commonsensical assumptions in the professional rush to devise grand theory" (Daly, 1995, p. 99). This approach on gendering crime is found in studies that emphasize how women and men "do gender" in response to those beliefs about femininity and masculinity (Messerschmidt, 1993; Simpson and Ellis, 1995). The importance of this research is its ability to examine both similarities and differences between women's and men's offending.

Gendered Lives

Daly (1998, p. 98) defines the concept of **gendered lives** as the examination of the "significant differences in the ways that women experience society compared with men." Daly argues that "rather than analyze gender as a correlate of crime, one would analyze crime as a correlate of gender" (p. 99). She states that there are several ways to develop the idea of women's gendered lives in criminological research such as by revealing how gender-related conditions of life structure delinquent and nondelinquent identities and actions (Bottcher, 2001). Jean Bottcher's interviews of youths whose brothers had been institutionally confined suggest that the social organization of gender can act as social control. The girls in this study, compared to the boys, were insulated from delinquent interest and activity. Thus, instead of the traditional approach of analyzing gender as a correlate of crime, this approach analyzes crime as a correlate of gender (Bottcher, 2001).

Another approach to the study of gendered lives is to document how methods of income generation over time vary in relation to turning points in women's lives, such as pregnancy and care of children, and to state supports for housing on welfare (Daly, 1995, p. 99). Regina Austin (1992, pp. 1801–1811) shows what can be learned by studying "hustling" as women move between the straight and street worlds. Lisa Maher (1997) also documents the connections among neighborhood conditions, declining value of sex work for women, and drug markets in New York City neighborhoods.

Masculinities and Crime

Early feminist work, as has been stated several times, criticized existing theory and research for focusing on boys' and men's crime at the expense of girls' and women's crime. It was reasoned that given men's overrepresentation as offenders, the study of masculinities and crime could not be ignored. The early work in criminology emphasized subcultural approaches to the study of crime. Walter B. Miller (1958) argued that lower-class boys pursued such focal concerns as toughness, trouble, and independence, which clearly reflect what is now identified as masculine. Elijah Anderson's more recent research (1999) reveals the conceptualization of male identity among persistent offenders. R. Theodore Davidson's (1974) study of Chicano prisoners in San Quentin examined the concept of **machismo,** a Latino hegemonic masculinity, as the organizing principle behind the violence of the inmate world.

James W. Messerschmidt's (1993) broader attempt to situate criminal behavior within gendered social structures highlights intersectionality in examining the criminal behavior of both women and men. Although this approach sees gender norms and definitions as a product of social structure, it is through the micro-level processes of social action/interaction that gender is reproduced. Messerschmidt establishes an analytical framework for understanding the intersection of masculinity and crime. He indicates that "men do masculinity according to the social situation in which they find themselves" (p. 84).

Christopher W. Mullins, Richard Wright, and Bruce A. Jacobs's recent research (2004) revealed that most of men's interpersonal disputes with other men were grounded in the need to build and maintain gendered reputations. They further found that gendered perceptions of appropriate and inappropriate behavior served as the trigger for and the barrier against retaliations. Men viewed retaliation in violent ways as a key street survival strategy that is deeply rooted in their identities as *men*. However, if they were wronged by a woman, the path of action was more complex. Direct action against a woman, who was considered to be physically and emotionally weaker, could be seen as a subordinated masculinity. Yet at the same time, men believed they could not ignore a slight by a woman, another mark of "punkness." A more desirable solution was to enlist women to carry out the retaliation.

Andrew Hochstetler and Heith Copes (2003) provide an analysis of how the situational construction of masculinity frames acts of property crime. Their interviews with convicted property offenders explore how masculine posturing immediately prior to the criminal event frequently "boxes" offenders into a position where backing out of the crime would result in a loss of masculine capital. This study further suggests that such reputation maintenance is more likely to take place with younger than with older men.

Feminist Epistemologies

The feminist epistemology, **feminist empiricism,** basically accepts the value of the scientific method but points out that ignoring women or misrepresenting their experiences is methodologically unsound. This approach attempts to correct so-called bad science through stricter adherence to existing norms of scientific inquiry (Flavin, 2001, pp. 274–275). It has examined the understanding of women victims of crime (especially violence in the home and between inmates), the judicial treatment of offending women and girls, and the experiences of women criminal justice workers (Smart, 1995; Martin and Jurik, 1995).

Feminist standpoint theories go beyond criticizing empirical practice when they challenge mainstream criminology's empirical assumptions. Many feminists consider science and knowledge to be socially situated, and they question how disinterested objectivity is possible in a society that is so deeply stratified by race, gender, and class. Feminist standpoint theories assume that the perspective of the observer influences what can be known. They attempt to construct knowledge from the perspective of those being studied on the grounds that the perspective of the oppressed or marginalized is typically less distorted. It is contended that the powerful have more interest in concealing the conditions that produce their authority and privileges than the dominated groups have in hiding the conditions that produce their situation (Flavin, 2001, p. 274).

Feminist post-modernism, a third epistemological approach, is critical of standpoint feminism because it assumes that women are a "clearly defined and uncontroversially given interest group" (Smart, 1995, p. 10). In opposition to positivists and others, including many feminists, who claim that truth can be determined providing all agree on responsible ways of going about it, post-modern critics argue for multiple truths that take contexts into consideration. Many criminologists recognize that "knowledge" reflects the perspective of those with more power, but post-modernists take this further by questioning whether any knowledge is knowable. They go on to reject the idea that a universal definition of justice exists—one that would be true for all people, all of the time. Thus, post-modernists emphasize the importance of alternative discourses and accounts, which frequently take the approach of examining the effects of symbolic representation and language (Flavin, 2001, p. 274).

Flavin asserts that there are those who charge that post-modernism ultimately results in a "call for inaction" (Tong, 1998, p. 232). According to this charge, if justice is different for everyone depending on one's perspective, then why attempt to pursue it? This position reflects a dismal and somewhat distorted view of the post-modern perspective. Post-modernists, including post-modernist feminists, recognize a responsibility to build bridges across diverse groups in an attempt to work collectively—not with the intent to arrive at a universal understanding of justice, but to make judgments that make the world a good place to be (Flavin, 2001, p. 274).

Flavin pulls this discussion together as she says:

> Regardless of where one falls on the "knowledge is scientifically derived" to "knowledge is socially produced" to "knowledge is power/power is knowledge" continuum, it is hard to imagine a criminal justice enterprise where epistemology is irrelevant. Yet rarely does it receive even passing mention. Given that one routinely encounters "totalitarianism," "bureaucratization," "psychopharmacology," and "heteroskedasticity" in academic publications, it is more than a matter of "epistemology" being a word that does not roll easily off the tongue. (p. 275)

Flavin then concludes that regardless of how unsettling it may be to question how knowledge has been or ought to be produced, or the fact that the process of inquiry might not lead to straightforward and universally accepted answers, nonetheless the recognition of the importance of epistemology and of the biases of the scientific method remains at the core of efforts transform the discipline. The whole process of gaining a better understanding of gender and crime requires not only that gaps in knowledge be filled but also that assumptions on which existing "knowledge" is based be challenged (Flavin, 2001).

Research Methods and Methodology

This chapter has suggested so far that feminists vary in their theoretical orientation and in their views of how knowledge should be acquired. The same is true that there is not a distinctive feminist methodology for the research process, but "rather a feminist perspective on the research process" (Taylor and Rupp, 1991, p. 127).

With this in mind, the following section examines major feminist methodological themes as manifested in criminological research. These themes are concerned with the choice of topic, the choice of research methods; the subjective experiences of doing research, or **reflexivity;** the relationship between the researcher and the research subjects; and the relationships among policy, action, and research. Many of these methodological issues may not be unique to feminism and may be shared by other orientations, especially critical ones, but their close identification with a feminist perspective warrants their inclusion (Flavin, 2001, pp. 277–279).

Choice of Research Topic

Feminist criminological scholarship comprises a substantial and mature body of literature that presents some of the most important questions concerning the nature of criminological knowledge. See Box 3.1 for Jody Miller's study of the difference between males and females in committing robbery. More recently, feminists have conducted new criminological inquiries on the blurred boundaries between victimization and criminalization, the impact of sentencing policies on women, and the media's role in shaping perceptions of crime and justice (Flavin, 2001, p. 277). M. J. McDermott (1992) has observed that feminist research has evolved to the degree that it is "on, by, and for women" while encompassing a larger sphere of inquiry that includes men and masculinity.

Choice of Research Methods and Methodologies

Discussion of the use of qualitative and quantitative research methodologies is one of the most highly debated points of contention. Despite the perception that feminist scholarship is primarily qualitative, feminist researchers use all of the methods that traditional researchers have used. Harding (1987) has summarized this position:

> *Feminist researchers use just about any and all of the methods . . . that traditional androcentric researchers have used. Of course, precisely how they carry out these methods of evidence gathering is often strikingly different . . . it is not by looking at research methods that one will be able to identify the distinctive features of the best of feminist research. (pp. 2–3)*

BOX 3.1
Jody Miller: Robbery as a Case Study

In Miller's secondary analysis of thirty-seven active African American offenders, she compared accounts of why men and women commit robbery. She found that gender influences these crimes in the following ways. Men use physical violence when committing robbery, but women do not. Men target other men, but women do not. Men view robbery as one means to attain their masculinity, a setting in which men complete with each other for status and money through the use of physical contact, guns, and violence. Women, on the other hand, take into consideration the gendered nature of their environment when they rob other women, who are regarded as less likely to be armed and are considered to be easily intimidated and weak. When they do rob men, women typically use their sexuality to manipulate men to be easier targets.

Men and women do share motivations for robbery. What attracts both sexes to robbery is the potential for obtaining money and experiencing excitement. These motives, Miller contends, are reminders that class, race, and gender are important, even critical, to understanding crime. She sees the urban backgrounds as a powerful pathway to street crime. She warns that it is critical to distinguish between motives and causes of crime. She goes on to examine structural elements such as unemployment, poverty, deindustralization, and the underground drug economy in this urban St. Louis neighborhood that provide the context for crime to take place.

In Miller's sample, women described three predominant ways in which they committed robberies: targeting female victims in physical confrontations, targeting male victims by appearing sexually available, and participating with males in street robberies of men. Significantly, most women described participating in two or more of these types of robberies.

Critical Thinking Questions: What do you find surprising about how men and women perceive the act of robbery? If this study were conducted with other racial groups, besides largely an African American sample, do you think the findings would be the same?

Source: Jody Miller, "Up It Up: Gender and the Accomplishment of Street Robbery," *Criminology, 36:* February 1998: 37–65.

For the feminist researcher, quantitative approaches offer a number of advantages in the study of gender and crime. For example, the findings from representative samples may be more generalizable and statistical techniques can handle more contextual variables and allow simultaneous evaluation of interaction terms and complex theoretical models. Quantitative methods have sometimes come under fire because researchers tend to collect and record information thought to be important. However, because most large datasets were originally designed to capture information salient to the treatment and processing of male offenders, characteristics that were particularly salient to women might not be recorded (i.e., childhood victimization experiences and obstetric/gynecological history [Flavin, 2001, p. 278]). See Box 3.2 for an excellent quantitative study by two feminist researchers.

In contrast, qualitative approaches such as interviews, ethnographies, and life histories allow women and men to articulate or conceptualize their experiences in their own terms, potentially providing more valid and accurate information. This is especially important in light of many feminists' interest in examining the situation

BOX 3.2

Karen Heimer and Stacy De Coster: The Gendering of Violent Delinquency

Heimer and De Coster's study reveals the benefits that result from a complex conceptualization of gender. These researchers address two key theoretical problems of interest to feminist criminologists: Within-gender variability in the use of violence, and variability in violence across gender (i.e., the gender-ratio of offending).

Heimer and De Coster's complex theoretical model of violent delinquency is based on the differentials in the experiences of young women and men that result from gender inequality. They focus on the interplay of social structure and culture, arguing that social structural positions based on gender, social class, and race result in variations in the two cultural processes of family controls and peer associations. Heimer and De Coster contend that indirect control derived from emotional bonds to the family are the primary control over adolescent females' behavior, whereas direct controls have a stronger effect on reducing adolescent males' delinquency.

Heimer and De Coster used an analysis of the National Youth Survey to test their theoretical model. They found strong support for its ability to explain variations in adolescent females' and males' use of violence. The data also revealed strong support for variations in the use of violence within gender based on the causal pathways of social structural factors tied to gender, race, and class; the researchers also found that the cultural processes of family controls and peer associations shaped the cultural outcomes of violent definitions and gender definitions. They explain:

> In short, the conclusion of our research is that violent delinquency is "gendered" in significant ways. Adolescence violence can be seen as a product of gendered experiences, gender socialization, and the patriarchal system in which they emerge. Thus, consistent with feminist arguments, gender differences in violence are ultimately rooted in power differences.

Critical Thinking Questions: Are you surprised by the findings of Heimer and De Coster? How would class affect the way that violence is gendered? Why does race appear to be an important variable in the gendering of violence?

Source: Karen Heimer and Stacy De Coster, "The Gendering of Violent Delinquency," *Criminology* 37(1999): 277–317.

---

at hand, "taking real life as the starting point, its subjective consciousness as well as its societal entanglements" (Mies, 1991, p. 66). Many feminist scholars use narrative statements in order to identify important themes with the additional positive outcome of giving their findings a human face (Flavin, 2001, p. 278).

Jody Miller and Christopher W. Mullins's examination of violent crime among girls found that their "involvement in physically aggressive behavior seems to be rather more common than previous research would suggest" (Miller and Mullins, 2006b, p. 41). In a broader qualitative study of violence among African American youths, they examined thirty-four accounts of the situational context of girl-on-girl fights. For girls, they agree with the previous research that found that, "dispute encounters are more about the girl demonstrating the ability to stand up for herself. Violence may only be necessary if the disputants lack a face-saving way out of the aggressive encounter" (Miller and Mullins, 2006b, p. 61).

Qualitative methods are sometimes criticized as unsystematic and politically motivated, therefore overtly biased and unscientific (Jayartne and Stewart, 1991, p. 93). Furthermore, the samples in a qualitative study tend to be small and homogenous because qualitative research is usually very time consuming, requiring intense contact with research subjects (Flavin, 2001, p. 278).

In view of the limitations of both methodologies, some feminists are employing a combination of quantitative and qualitative methods. For example, Barbara Owen's (1998) study of women prisoners includes a quasi-ethnographic study of a women's prison as well as a survey of female inmates and parolees. Kathleen Daly's (1994) study of sentencing disparity uses both a statistical analysis of sentencing disparity as well as a qualitative analysis of forty matched pairs of women and men convicted of similar offenses.

Reflexivity

Reflexivity relates to the importance of critically examining the nature of the research process itself. It involves identifying the assumptions underlying the research endeavor, even including the researcher's reaction to doing the research: Pettiway (1997) explains:

> For the most part, criminology is unreflective. While conscious that researchers should not bring their prejudices to the research table, many criminologists, in their search for neutrality, fail to consider their own identity in their investigative enterprises. Perhaps, this is the aftershock of attempting to impose the strictures and methods of the physical sciences on criminology in our effort to make it more "scientific." (pp. xv–xvi)

This reflecting on the research process involves calling attention to sources of bias introduced as well as providing guidance to future researchers. Reflexivity also involves examination of whether research can ever truly be "objective." The identity of a researcher can even shape an intentional noninterpretive research endeavor—such as presenting transcripts of taped interviews—in that the researcher framed the questions, focused the interviews, and edited the transcripts for publication (Flavin, 2001, p. 279). There are many feminists who consider such subjectivity not only as unavoidable, but also as a possible strength of the study. Barbara Owens, for example (1998), reported that the relationship she had with several inmates enabled her to better understand and appreciate their experiences, but also contributed to a political awareness of their marginalized status.

In sum, reflexivity is able to strengthen the research process because it promotes greater honesty and awareness of the biases and limitations inherent in the research. It also provides a guide to other researchers who may be considering pursuing similar projects. Furthermore, as will be discussed in the next section, reflexivity encourages researchers to think about their relationships with research subjects (Flavin, 2001, p. 279).

Relationship Between Researcher and Subjects.   Feminists have been quite critical of researchers' objectification and exploitation of their subjects, especially when information is gained through surveys or interviews. They view the scientific detachment that is supposedly desired in the research process as one of stripping away the individual humanity of the subjects. Instead, Jeanne Flavin states (2001):

> By contrast, many feminists propose treating interviewees as informants or experts, and using an open-ended format in order to permit new questions to emerge during the course of the interview. A feminist methodological approach tries to minimize hierarchical relationships within the research process. Ideally, the research enterprise will strive for a collaborative and reciprocal association between the researcher and the subject . . . . (p. 279)

Feminists are aware, however, that there are difficulties and some limitations in minimizing the distance between interviewer and subject. The two major limitations are that researchers responsible to funding agencies may lack total control over how their studies are conducted and that the subjects themselves may not be receptive to the idea of collaboration (Flavin, 2001, p. 279).

Policy and Action

Feminists have a long history of placing a premium on policy and action. They are best known for raising awareness of violence against women and of the desirability for creating and enforcing laws and policies regarding marital rape, stalking, acquaintance rape, and other crimes that disproportionately involve victims who are women. They have urged that responses to women victims of crime reflect an appreciation for differences that exist among women (Flavin, 2001, p. 280). Feminists have also been involved in policy evaluation, asking, What is this policy supposed to accomplish? How will it actually be implemented? Who wins and who loses if this policy is adopted? What can we do to improve on this? (Miller, 1998).

Moreover, women's stake in the thirty-year-old "war on crime" is much more important than is traditionally recognized. Although the public notion of the criminal is male, the fact is that the hidden victims of many of these get-tough policies have been women, particularly women of color (Chesney-Lind and Pasko, 2004, p. xi). Feminists have been quick to call attention to the unforeseen consequences of purportedly gender-neutral policies. The newly implemented sentencing policies are designed to treat women and men the same. What in fact has taken place is that women have been increasingly incarcerated; a shift that is often described as "equality with a vengeance" (Flavin, 2001, p. 281).

Another example involves the confiscation of assets from suspected drug offenders. Judges wrongly assume that social and economic power are equally distributed in a marriage or intimate relationship. In addition, judges blame wives for their failure or inability to control their husbands; this ignores not only the gendered power dynamics within intimate relationships, but also the structural limits to women's ability to disentangle themselves from such relationships (Massey, Miller, and Wilhelmi, 1998, p. 29).

Moreover, some policies have been specifically targeted at women, especially for their alleged drug use or other actions during pregnancy. For example, according to a 1996 report by the Center for Reproductive Law and Policy, at least two hundred women in more than thirty states have been arrested for drug use or other actions during pregnancy. The feminist perspective is concerned with the harmful consequences of criminalizing pregnant women's behavior instead of expanding the availability of treatment for pregnant women. One additional concern is that such criminalizing of maternal conduct discourages drug-using women from seeking prenatal care and drug treatment because they fear prosecution (Flavin, 2001, pp. 280–281).

Finally, feminists have challenged the masculine basis of many programs and policies. Feminists have been critical of correctional officers and police training programs for their overemphasis of physical strength, aggressiveness, and intimidation in resolving disputes while at the same time devaluing interpersonal skills. Similarly, feminists have been among those critical of boot camps as demeaning and abusive to inmates. The boot camp model exemplifies a distorted image of masculinity, emphasizing aggressiveness, insensitivity to others' pain, and unquestioned authority, while deemphasizing such "feminine" characteristics as empathy and group cooperation (Flavin, 2001, p. 281).

In summarizing her section on social policy, Flavin states:

> Feminist scholarship has called attention to previously ignored policy issues, evaluated the impact of purportedly "gender-neutral" policies on women, examined the effects of policies targeted specifically at women, and challenged the value of criminal justice policies based on stereotypical ideas of masculinity and femininity. By definition, feminism gives great weight to identifying strategies for social changes and ending domination in all its forms. Feminist perspectives remind one—not only of one's professional responsibilities—but also one's social responsibility to consider the implications of our research and policy for women. (p. 282)

Summary

This chapter has suggested a variety of ways in which feminists do theory and pursue research. One of the major problems of generalization, or investigating how theories of men's crime apply to women, is the failure to account for the gender ratio of offending; that is, the reality that men are disproportionately involved in crime. This gender ratio of crime was explored in this chapter by the conceptual scheme of gendered crime, gendered pathways, and gendered lives. The section on masculinities and crime situated criminal behavior within gendered social structures in highlighting the criminal behavior of both men and women, revealing that it is through the micro-level processes of social action/interaction that gender (re)produced.

Feminist epistemologies, another concern of this chapter, examined feminist empiricism, feminist standpoint theories, and feminist post-modernism. Feminist empiricism basically accepts the value of the scientific method but calls for females and their experiences to be included in the scientific process. Feminist standpoint theories challenge traditional criminology's empirical assumptions. In questioning how disinterested objectivity is possible in a society that is so deeply stratified by race, gender, and class, such theories attempt to construct knowledge from the perspective of those being studied. Feminist post-modernists argue for multiple truths that take context into consideration. They even question whether any knowledge is knowable and emphasize the importance of alternative discourses and accounts.

Moreover, this chapter examined research methods used by feminists. There is no distinct feminist methodology but rather a feminist perspective on the research process. In terms of research topics, feminists have addressed the classical criminological questions as well as new lines of criminological inquiry, including such topics as the blurred boundaries between victimization and criminalization, the impact of sentencing policies on women, and the media's role in shaping perceptions of crime and justice. Qualitative research methods have long been popular with feminist researchers, and, more recently, quantitative research methodologies are increasingly used. Some feminist researchers are beginning to use a combination of quantitative and qualitative methods. Reflexivity involves identifying the assumptions underlying the research endeavor and the researcher's reaction to doing the research. This reflecting on the research process involves calling attention to sources of bias while providing guidance to future researchers.

Finally, this chapter considered policy and action. Feminist scholars' primary interest in examining laws and policies that are in place concerns the protection of women victims; how the "war on crime" has resulted in the increased incarceration of women, in other words, "equality with a vengeance;" and the masculine basis of many programs and policies.

KEY TERMS

feminist empiricism	gendered lives	gender ratio of crime
feminist post-modernism	gendered pathways	machismo
feminist standpoint theories	gender order	reflexivity
gendered crime		

CRITICAL THINKING QUESTIONS

1. Why is this chapter important to a book on women and the criminal justice system?

2. Did this chapter present any paradigm shifts to you? If so, what were they and why are they important?

3. How does this chapter bridge the gap between traditional theory and research in criminology and research done by feminists?

4. What are the various ways that feminists can do research? Evaluate each one.

WEB DESTINATIONS

For a reference on women's studies and issues, see: www.web.gc.cuny.edu/womenstudies/index.html

Gendered justice: a select bibliography: www.criminology.utoronto.ca/library/gender.html

REFERENCES

Anderson, E. (1999). *Code of the street: Decency, violence and the moral life of the inner city.* New York: W. W. Norton.

Austin, R. (1992). The black community, its lawbreakers and a politics of identification. *Southern California Law Review 65:* 1769–1817.

Bottcher, J. (2001). Social practices of gender: How gender relates to delinquency in the everyday lives of high-risk youths. *Criminology 39:* 893–932.

Broidy, L. (2001). A test of general strain theory. *Criminology 39:* 9–32.

Cannon, L. W. W., Higginbotham, E., and Leung, M. L. A. (1991). Race and class bias in qualitative research on women. In M. M. Fonow and J. A. Cook (eds.), *Beyond methodology: feminist scholarship as lived research* (pp. 107–118). Bloomington, Ind.: Indiana University Press.

Chesney-Lind, M., and Pasko, L. (2004). *The female offender,* 2nd ed. Thousand Oaks, Calif.: Sage.

Daly, K. (1998). Gender, crime, and criminology. In M. Tonry (ed.), *The handbook of crime and justice* (pp. 85–108). Oxford: Oxford University Press.

Daly, K. (1994). *Gender, crime and punishment.* New Haven: Yale University Press.

Daly, K., and Chesney-Lind, M. (1988). Feminism and criminology. *Justice Quarterly 5:* 497–538.

Daly, K., and Maher, L. (1998). Women pathways to felony court: Feminist theories of lawbreaking and problems of representation. *Review of Law and Women's Studies 2:* 11–52.

Davidson, R. T. (1974). *Chicano prisoners: The key to San Quentin.* Prospect Heights, Ill.: Waveland.

Flavin, J. (2001). Feminism for the mainstream criminologist: An invitation. *Journal of Criminal Justice 29:* 271–285.

Gaarder, E., and Belknap, J. (2002). Tenuous borders: Girls transferred to adult court. *Criminology 40:* 481–518.

Giordano, P., Cherkovich, S. A., and Rudolf, J. (2002). Gender, crime and desistance: Toward a theory of cognitive transformation. *American Journal of Sociology 107:* 990–1064.

Giordano, P. C., Deines, J. A., and Cernkovich, S. A. (2006). In and out of crime: A life course perspective on girls' delinquency. In K. Heimer and C. Kruttschnitt (eds.), *Gender and crime: Patterns in victimization and offending* (pp. 17–40). New York: New York University Press.

Harding, S. (1991). *Feminism and methodology: Social science issues.* Bloomington, Ind.: Indiana University Press.

Heimer, K., Wittrock, S., and Unal, H. The crimes of poverty: Economic marginalization and the gender gap in crime. In K. Heimer and C. Kruttschnitt (eds), *Gender and crime: Patterns in victimization and offending* (pp. 115–136). New York: New York University Press.

Harding, S. (1991). *Whose science? Whose knowledge?* Ithaca, N.Y.: Cornell University Press.

Heidensohn, F. M. (1996). *Women and crime,* 2nd ed. London: Macmillan.

Hochstetler, A., and Copes, H. (2003). Situational construction of masculinity among male street thieves. *Journal of Contemporary Ethnography 32:* 279–303.

Jayartne, T. E., and Stewart, A. J. (1991). Quantitative and qualitative methods in the social sciences: Current feminist issues and practical strategies. In M. M. Fonow and J. A. Cook (eds.), *Beyond methodology* (pp. 86–106). Bloomington, Ind.: Indiana University Press.

Kruttschnitt, C. (1996). Contributions of quantitative methods to the study of gender and crime, or bootstrapping our way into the theoretical thicket. *Journal of Quantitative Criminology 12:* 135–161.

Martin, S. E., and Junik, N. C. (1995). Doing justice, doing gender. Thousand Oaks, Calif.: Sage Publications.

Maher, L. (1997). *Sexed work: Gender, race and resistance in a Brooklyn drug market.* Oxford: Clarendon Press.

Massey, J., Miller, S. L., Wihelmi, A. (1998). Civil forfeiture of property: The victimization of women as innocent owners and third parties. In S. L. Miller (ed.), *Crime Control and Women.* Thousand Oaks, Calif.: Sage Publications.

McDermott, M. J. (1992). The personal is empirical: Feminism and research methods. *Journal of Criminal Justice Education 3:* 237–249.

Messerschmidt, J. W. (1993). *Masculinities and crime.* Lanham, Md.: Rowman & Littlefield.

Mies, M. (1991). Women's research or feminist research? The debate surrounding feminist science and methodology. In M. Fonow and J. A. Cook (eds.), *Beyond methodology* (pp. 60–84). Bloomington, Ind.: Indiana University Press.

Miller, J. (1998). Up it up: Gender and the accomplishment of street robbery. *Criminology 36:* 37–66.

Miller, J. (2001). *One of the guys: Girls, gangs and gender.* New York: Oxford University Press.

Miller, J., and Mullins, C. W. (2006a). Taking stock: The status of feminist theories in criminology. In F. Cullen, J. P. Wright, and K. Blevins (eds.), F. Adler and W. Laufer (series eds.), *The status of criminological theory. Advances in criminological theory,* 206–230, vol. 15. New Brunswick, N.J.: Transaction. In Press.

Miller, J., and Mullins, C. W. (2006b). Stuck up, telling lies, and talking too much: The gendered context of young women's violence. In K. Heimer and C. Kruttschnitt (eds), *Gender and crime patterns in victimization and offending* (pp. 41–66). New York: New York University Press.

Miller, W. B. (1958). Lower-class culture as a generating milieu of gang delinquency. *Journal of Social Issues 14:* 5–19.

Moore, J. (1991). *Going down to the barrio: Homeboys and homegirls in charge.* Philadelphia: Temple University Press.

Mullins, C. W., Wright, W. R., and Jacobs, B. A. (2004). Gender, streetlife and criminal retaliation. *Criminology 42:* 911–940.

Owen, B. (1998). *In the mix: Struggle and survival in a woman's prison.* Albany, N.Y.: State University of New York Press.

Pettiway, L. E. (1997). *Workin' it: Women living through drugs and crime.* Philadelphia: Temple University Press.

Simpson, S. (1991). Caste, class and violent crime: Explaining differences in female offending. *Criminology 33:* 47–81.

Simpson, S. S., and Ellis, L. Doing gender: Sorting out the case and crime conundrum. *Criminology 33:* 47–81.

Smart, C. (1995). *Law, crime and sexuality: Essays in feminism.* London: Sage.

Sommers, I., and Baskin, D. R. (1993). The situational context of violent female offending. *Journal of Research in Crime and Delinquency 30:* 136–162.

Steffensmeier, D., and Schwartz, J. (2004). Trends in female criminality: Is crime still a man's world? In B. R. Price and N. J. Sokoloff (eds.), *The criminal justice system and women: Offenders, prisoners, victims and workers,* 3rd ed. (pp. 95–111). New York: McGraw-Hill.

Taylor, V. and Rupp, L. J. (1991). Researching the women's movement: We make our own history, but not just as we please. In M. M. Fanow and J. A. Cook (eds.), *Beyond methodology: Feminist scholarship as lived research.* Bloomington, Ind.: Indiana University Press.

Tong, R. (1998). *Feminist thought,* 2nd ed. Boulder, Col.: Westview Press.

4 Delinquency across the Life Span

A major development in the field of juvenile delinquency is the study of delinquency across the life course. Beginning with an examination of risk factors in adolescents, early juvenile offenders are compared with those who begin their delinquency offenses in adolescence. Then, these adolescents are followed through part of and sometimes nearly all of their life span. Their social and criminal histories are compared with those of others in their cohort. Researchers pay particular attention to those who persist and those who desist from law-violating behaviors, as they seek to understand factors that contribute to ending law-violating activities.

It would seem that delinquency across the life course has particular relevance to an examination of women and the criminal justice system. The life-course developmental model focuses on significant life events or transitions, particularly in terms of changes in status, social roles, and relationships. However, this perspective needs to be supplemented by models that address childhood victimization and the ways that discrimination and oppression, based on a juvenile's race or sex, can shape this person's experiences, options, and identity (Gaarder and Belknap, 2004, p. 71). Juvenile female delinquents, often victims of various forms of victimization at home, turn to the use of alcohol and drugs, become involved with youth gangs, and have conflict at home. It is not unusual for these girls to run away from abusive homes and to become involved in various forms of survival on the streets, including prostitution, theft, and drug addiction.

The first half of this chapter examines delinquency across the life course while the second half investigates the relationships among victimization, oppression, and juvenile females' pathways to crime. The task of this chapter is limited in part because there simply has not been the level of research done on females that there has been on males. Beginning with an introduction to the life course, we examine the influence of patriarchy on juvenile females, the effect of human agency on decision making, and the factors dividing those who desist from crime and drug use from those who persist.

The Life Course Perspective

The **life course perspective,** a relatively new but promising theoretical orientation, represents a major change in how we think about and study lives (Elder, Jr., Johnson, and Crosnoe, 2003, p. 3). Until fairly recently, research in both sociology and psychology neglected the life histories and future trajectories of individuals. However, G. H. Elder, Jr., and his colleagues' many publications have done much to stimulate the use of life course theory as an appropriate research base in the study of individuals and groups (Elder, Jr., 1999; Elder, Jr., and Conger, 2000; Elder, 1994).

John Claussen's classic study of children of the Great Depression was one of the earliest attempts to use the life course perspective. He followed members of the Berkeley longitudinal studies for nearly fifty years—from childhood through the later years of the participants' lives. Claussen defined what he called "planful competence" as comprising the dimensions of self-confidence, intellectual investment, and dependability. He found that a youth who demonstrated planful competence was "equipped with an ability to evaluate accurately personal efforts as well as the intentions and responses of others, with an informed knowledge of self, others, and options, and with the self-discipline to pursue chosen goals" (Claussen, 1993, p. 1).

Claussen's research revealed that early competence in study participants meant fewer crises in every decade up to their fifties. Highly competent men were more likely to find the right job and to remain in this rewarding line of work. Highly competent women were more likely to find the right husband and to feel rewarded in family life. Both choice and selection were involved; a choice of attractive options, as well as the ability to be selective, permitted the most competent to take best advantage of their opportunities. Claussen compared the competent individuals with those youngsters who lacked planful competence with far different trajectories or pathways as a result. These youngsters made choices that led to job difficulties, marital breakup, and personal problems with the law and with figures in authority (Claussen, 1993, pp. 512–521).

Researchers are drawing on the increased numbers of longitudinal studies that examine the lives of young children, including their conduct disorders, and following these cohorts sometimes for decades. They are also using the life course perspective in the study of delinquent behavior and how it affects subsequent life experiences (Sampson and Laub, 1993; Laub and Sampson, 2003).

Developmental and life course criminology (DLC) is particularly concerned with documenting and explaining individual changes in offending throughout life. This paradigm has greatly increased knowledge about the measurement of criminal career features such as onset, continuation, and desistance. A major reason for the popularity of DLC during the 1990s was the enormous volume of longitudinal research on offending that was being published (Farrington, 2003, pp. 221–222). Three of the most important contributions were the self-report youth surveys in Denver, Pittsburgh, and Rochester (Browning, Thornberry, and Porter, 1999; Browning and Loeber, 1999; Browning and Huizinga, 1999). Other important longitudinal projects were the Dunedin study in New Zealand (Moffitt et al., 2003), the

Seattle Social Development Project (Hawkins et al., 2001), the Montreal Longitudi-nal-Experimental Study (Tremblay et al., 2003), and further analysis by Robert J. Sampson and John H. Laub (1993 and 2003) of the Gluecks' classic longitudinal study of 1,000 men.

Continuity of Delinquency into Adult Criminality

Sampson and Laub (1993) sought to explain both the continuity of delinquency into adult criminality and noncriminality, or change, in adulthood for those who were delinquent as children. They developed a threefold thesis:

1. Structural context mediated by informal family and school social control explain delinquency in childhood and adolescence.
2. In turn, there is continuity in antisocial behavior from childhood through adulthood in a variety of life domains.
3. Informal social bonds in adulthood to family and employment explain changes in criminality over the life span despite early childhood propensities (p. 7).

Employing life-history data from the Gluecks' longitudinal study, Laub and Sampson found that although adult crime is connected to childhood behavior, both incremental and abrupt changes still take place through changes in adult social bonds. The emergence of strong bonds to work and family among adults appears early, establishing life-long patterns. Laub and Sampson also contend that the events that trigger the formation of strong adult bonds to work and family commonly occur by chance or luck (Laub and Sampson, 1993, pp. 301–320).

The concept of a **turning point** in the life course is one of the fascinating con-tributions of Laub and Sampson's research. A turning point involves a gradual or dramatic change and may lead to "a modification, reshaping, or transition from one state, condition, or phase to another" (Laub and Sampson, 1993, p. 309). In seeking to unravel the mechanisms that operate at key turning points to turn a risk trajec-tory to a more adoptive path, Laub and Sampson found that stable employment and a good marriage, or changing roles and environments, can lead to investment of social capital or relations among persons (Laub and Sampson, 1993, p. 310).

However, not all researchers concur that there is a continuing of behaviors from childhood to adulthood. For example, Raymond Paternoster, Robert Brame, and David Farrington, using data from the Cambridge Study in Delinquent Devel-opment, investigated the relationship between adolescent and adult involvement in criminal behavior. In opposition to Sampson and Laub, Paternoster and colleagues found that adult offending "is not systematically related to events and experiences after adolescence" (Paternoster, Brame, and Farrington, 2001, p. 201). They argue that variation in adult offending is consistent with a random process and, therefore, it is impossible to conclude that relatively simple explanations, such as marriage and employment, can explain complex life course decisions. They propose that much further study is needed to clarify the relationship between adolescent acts and adult criminal behaviors (Paternoster, Brame, and Farrington, 2001, p. 222).

Desistance from Crime

A final piece before moving to the life course and females, as well as the influence of gender, race, and class on women, is the matter of desistance. The age of **desistance,** or the termination of delinquent behavior, has become an important consideration of researchers. One of the problems of establishing desistance is the difficulty of distinguishing between a gap in a delinquent career and true termination. There are bound to be crime-free intervals in the course of delinquent careers (Sampson and Laub, 2001). Long-term follow-up is needed to establish the age of termination. To explain changes in offending over time, or desistance, theorists have proposed several explanations, which follow.

Maturation and Aging Accounts of Desistance. The maturation process appears to be involved in desistance, as youths or adults become aware either of the desirability of pursing a conventional lifestyle or of the undesirability of continuing with unlawful pursuits. Sheldon and Eleanor Glueck drew this conclusion from the follow-up of juvenile delinquent careers: "With the passing of the years there was . . . both a decline in criminality and a decrease in the seriousness of the offences of those who continued to commit crimes" (Glueck and Glueck, 1940, p. 89). James Q. Wilson and Richard Herrnstein contend that the relatively minor gains from crime lose their power to reinforce deviant behavior as juveniles mature and develop increasing ties to conventional society. Another aspect of this maturation process, they add, is the individual's ability to delay gratification and forgo the immediate gains that delinquent or criminal acts bring (Wilson and Herrnstein, 1985, pp. 126–147).

Developmental Accounts of Desistance. One developmental explanation of desistance is that identity changes account for reduction in or cessation of crime. Edward Mulvey and John LaRosa, focusing on the period from age seventeen to twenty—the period they call the time of "natural" recovery—found that desistance was linked to a cognitive process taking place in the late teens when delinquents realized that they were "going nowhere" and that they had better make changes in their lives if they were going to be successful as adults (Mulvey and LaRosa, 1986, pp. 212–214). Peggy C. Giordano and colleagues, in a longitudinal study of serious female offenders, found that desistance took place when there were cognitive shifts in these offenders. Cognitive transformation provided desisters "with a detailed plan of action or a fairly elaborate *cognitive blueprint* for proceeding as a changed individual" (Giordano, Cernkovich, and Rudolph, 2002, p. 1055).

Rational Choice Accounts of Desistance. Theorists who hold to the rational choice framework propose that the decision to give up or continue with crime is based on a person's conscious reappraisal of the costs and benefits of criminal activity. They advance the idea that desisters are seen as "reasoned decisionmakers" (Cornich and Clark, 1986). One of the most important components of the decision to desist is the increased fear of punishment with aging. Barry Glassner and colleagues studied youths in a medium-size city in New York State and found that many youths curtailed involvement in delinquent activities at the age of sixteen because they feared being jailed if they were apprehended as adults (Glassner, Ksander, and Berg, 1983, p. 221).

Social Learning Accounts of Desistance.   According to the social learning framework, the basic variables explaining initiation into crime are essentially the same factors that account for the desistance from crime (Akers, 1998). Michael Warr supports the social learning account of desistance because he found that changing peer relations accounted for the association between marital status and desistance from crime. The transition to marriage was followed by "a dramatic decline in time spent with friends" and "reduced exposure to delinquent peers" (Warr, 1988, pp. 183–216).

Life Course Account of Desistance.   The main objective of the life course perspective on desistance is to link social history and social structure. A central element in the desistance process, according to Laub and Sampson (2004), is any change that "knifes off" individual offenders from their environment and, at the same time, offers them a new script for the future. A new "structured role stability" can emerge across various life domains (for example, marriage, work, and/or community). The men desisting in their study shared a daily routine that provided structure and meaningful activity. Laub and Sampson add that although there are multiple pathways to desistance, they found what seem to be important general processes or mechanisms consistent with the idea of informal social control. In sum, offenders "choose to desist in response to structurally induced turning points that serve as the catalyst for sustaining long-term behavior change" (p. 11).

Female Delinquency across the Life Course

There is both good news and bad news concerning an examination of the female delinquent across the life course. The bad news is that the study of delinquency has long focused on the delinquent male, and the longitudinal studies that have been done or are being done on delinquents across the life course predominantly feature the study of males. The good news is that studies of juvenile females are increasing in number, some of which follow females across the life course.

The study of female delinquents has examined several dimensions of delinquent behavior: females' involvement in offenses; their use of drugs and alcohol; their participation in types of antisocial behaviors, including gangs and prostitution; and their desistance and persistence as offenders.

Relationship Between Male and Female Patterns of Delinquency

The early cohort studies provide some evidence of the relationship between male and female patterns of delinquency. Delinquency cohort studies usually include all people born in a particular year in a city or county and follow this group, or cohort, through part or all of their lives. The second Philadelphia cohort study examined all males and females born in 1958 in Philadelphia. It found that males in this cohort study were two and a half times more likely than females to become involved in delinquent acts. Law-violating females were much more likely to be one-time offenders and less likely to become chronic offenders (Wolfgang, Figlio, and Sellin, 1972). The Racine cohort study examined males and females born in 1942, 1949, and 1955 in Racine, Wisconsin. White females in this study had fewer contacts and less serious involvement with the police than white males or African American males or females (Shannon, 1982). The Columbus cohort study examined all males and females born between 1956 and 1960 in Columbus, Ohio. This study found that males outnumbered females by almost 6 to 1 in the delinquent population. The violent cohort consisted of 84.6 percent boys and 15.7 percent girls (Hamparian et al., 1980).

Terrie E. Moffitt and her colleagues have proposed a developmental taxonomy differentiating a small group of **early-onset, persistent offenders** (LCP) from the much larger category of **adolescence-limited delinquent males** (AL). These researchers found that these two groups differ both in age-related profiles of offending and in patterns of early risk. For persistent offenders, risks center on individual vulnerabilities that were evident early in childhood. In contrast, later-onset, adolescence-limited groups are characterized by more marginal levels of psychosocial and individual risks. Their adolescent difficulties are perceived to be prompted by frustrations associated with an adolescent maturity gap and by coping with the behavior of antisocial peers (Moffitt, 1993, pp. 674–701)

Moffitt, Lynam, and Silva, in their examination of the neuropsychological status of several hundred New Zealand males between the ages of thirteen and eighteen, found that poor neuropsychological scores "were associated with early onset of delinquency" but were "unrelated to delinquency that began in adolescence" (Moffitt, Lynam, and Silva, 1994, p. 277). Moffitt's developmental theory views delinquency as proceeding along two developmental paths. On one path, children develop a lifelong course of delinquency and crime at as early as age three. They may begin to bite and hit at age four, shoplift and be truant at ten, sell drugs and steal cars at sixteen, rob and rape at twenty-two, and commit fraud and child abuse at thirty (Moffitt, 1993; Moffitt et al., 1996, pp. 399–424).

On the other path, the majority of male delinquents begin offending during the adolescent years and desist from delinquent behaviors around the eighteenth birthday. Moffitt refers to these youthful offenders as "adolescence-limited" (AL) delinquents. The early and persistent problems found with members of the LCP group are not found with the AL delinquents. Yet the frequency of offending and even the violence of offending of the AL group during the adolescent years may be as high as with the LCP delinquents. Moffitt notes that AL antisocial behavior is learned from peers and sustained through peer-based rewards and reinforcements. AL delinquents continue in delinquent acts as long as such behaviors appear profitable or rewarding to them, but they have the ability to abandon those behaviors when prosocial styles become more rewarding (Moffitt, 1993; Moffitt et al., 1996, pp. 399–424). See Box 4.1, which followed a sample of 1,000 males and females from age three to age twenty-one.

BOX 4.1

Gender Differences in the Dunedin Longitudinal Study

In *Sex Differences in Antisocial Behavior,* Moffitt and her colleagues report on the findings of the Dunedin Longitudinal Study. The basic findings indicate that youths develop antisocial behavior for two reasons. One form of antisocial behavior may be understood as a disorder with neurodevelopmental origins—a disorder that, like hyperactivity, autism, and dyslexia, shows a strong male preponderance and low prevalence in the population. Extreme gender differences are apparent in this form of antisocial behavior. The other form of antisocial behavior represents the bulk of such behavior, especially by females. This form is best understood as a social phenomenon originating in the context of social relationships, with onset in adolescence and high prevalence across the population. Gender differences in antisocial behaviors, according to this study, are negligible. Males' and females' antisocial behaviors are particularly alike when alcohol and drugs are involved, near the time of female puberty, and when females are yoked with males in intimate relationships. Other important insights were:

- Increasing numbers of symptoms of conduct disorder predict increasingly poor young adult outcomes, regardless of gender.
- Antisocial behavior has disruptive effects on both females and males as they make the transition from adolescence to adulthood.
- The life-course-persistent antisocial female is extremely rare; approximately 1 in 100 females in a birth cohort seem to be on the life-course-persistent path.
- Females and males on the life-course-persistent path share similar risk factors of family adversity, poor discipline, cognitive deficits, hyperactivity, undercontrolled temperament, and rejection by peers.
- Almost all females who engage in antisocial behavior best fit the adolescence-limited type. Among adolescence-limited delinquency, the gender ratio is 1.5 males to 1 female.
- Males on the life-course-persistent path suffer from multiple poor outcomes as young adults, and youth on the adolescence-limited path also have some poor outcomes.

Critical Thinking Questions: Why do you think so few females in this study became life-course-persistent offenders? What predicted offending among male and female offenders? Did you find any of the findings of this study surprising?

Source: Terrie E. Moffitt, Avshalom Caspi, Michael Rutter, and Phil A. Silva, *Sex Differences in Antisocial Behavior* (Cambridge, England: Cambridge University Press, 2001).

Female Use of Drugs and Alcohol

According to the National Survey on Drug Use and Health, 11.6 percent of juveniles aged twelve to seventeen reported current use of illicit drugs in 2002. In the same survey approximately 30 percent of juveniles reported having used an illicit drug at least once during their lifetime, and 22.2 percent reported having used an illicit drug within the past year. The major illicit drug this age group used was marijuana, with 8.2 percent of juveniles being current users (Office of National Drug Control Policy, 2004). The results of this survey were quite similar to those of the Monitoring the Future survey, which found that 24.11 percent of twelfth graders reported using drugs during 2003.

These and other studies have shown a marked decrease in gender differences among drug users. Female high school students are slightly more likely than high school males to smoke cigarettes and to use some illicit drugs, including amphetamines; they use alcohol and marijuana at about the same rates as male high school seniors. Yet male adolescents are more likely to be involved in heavy, or binge, drinking than female adolescents (United States Department of Health and Human Services, 2003).

Gang Behavior among Female Adolescents

Recent decades have brought increased awareness of adolescent girls who are involved in gangs. Lee Bowker and Malcolm Klein studied a group of female African American gang members in Los Angeles in 1980 and reported that they never planned a gang activity. The planning was done by males who usually excluded the females. But the female gang members would participate in violent crimes and drug-related activities (Bowker and Klein, 1980). J. C. Quicker studied Mexican American adolescent female gangs in east Los Angeles in 1983 and drew four conclusions about them. First, he found the gangs always had a connection to a male gang, and they often derived their name from their male counterparts. Second, adolescent females were not coerced into the gang but had to prove their loyalty and undergo an initiation procedure. Third, these females usually operated in a democratic manner. Fourth, loyalty to the gang rivaled loyalty to the family and most friends came from within the gang. The gang offered "warmth, friends, loyalty, and socialization" as it insulated its members from the harsh environment of the barrio (Quicker, 1983).

M. G. Harris's study of the Cholas, a Latina gang in California's San Fernando Valley in the 1980s, revealed that these adolescent females were becoming more independent of male gangs. The gang rejected the traditional image of the Latina as wife and mother and instead supported a more "macha" homegirl role. Gang affiliation also supported members in their estrangement from organized religion, as it substituted a form of familism that served to "provide a strong substitute for weak family and conventional school ties" (Harris, 1988, p. 172).

Esbensen, Deschenes, and Winfree, Jr., found from their analysis of the Denver Youth Survey that girl gang participants committed a wide variety of offenses and at only a slightly lower frequency than boys involved in this survey. Their findings also failed to support the notion that girls involved in gangs were mere sex objects and ancillary members. This study further showed that girls aged out of gangs before boys and that girls received more emotional fulfillment from their involvement with gang activity (Esbensen, Deschenes, and Winfree, Jr., 1998, pp. 20–21).

Lauderback, Hansen, and Waldorf studied the Potrero Hill Posse, an African American girl group in San Francisco in 1992. After sharing the common experiences of being abandoned by the fathers of their children and being abused and controlled by other men, this group of girls began hanging around together. They found that selling crack and organized "boosting" (shoplifting) were among the few resources available for supporting themselves and their children (Lauderback, Hansen, and Waldorf, 1992, pp. 57–72).

In 1993 Beth Bjerregaard and Carolyn Smith, using data from the Rochester Youth Development Study, found that involvement in gangs for both females and males was associated with increased levels of delinquency and substance abuse. For example, female gang members reported a serious delinquency prevalence of 66.8 percent, compared to 6.6 percent for non-gang members. Although there was some similarity in the factors associated with gang membership for both males and females, lack of school success was a particularly important factor for female gang members (Bjerregaard and Smith, 1993, pp. 347–348).

Joan Moore and John Hagedorn's 2001 summary of the research on female gangs reports that the majority of female gang members are involved in delinquent or criminal behaviors (Moore and Hagedorn, 2001). Delinquency rates of female gang members are lower than those of male gang members but higher than those of non-gang females and males. Female gang members are likely to be involved in property crimes and status offenses, but they commit fewer violent crimes than their male counterparts. Female gang members are also heavily involved in drug trafficking. For example, in Los Angeles County, drug offenses were the most frequent cause for the arrest of female gang members (Moore and Hagedorn, 2001).

Jody Miller, in several published papers and in her 2001 book *One of the Guys*, has made a significant contribution to what is known about gender dynamics in gangs (Miller, 1998, pp. 429–453; Miller and Brunson, 2000, pp. 420–447; Miller and Decker, 2001, pp. 115–139; Miller, 2001). Miller found from her research conducted in Columbus, Ohio, and St. Louis, Missouri, that a female in a mixed-gender gang, an environment that supports gender hierarchies and the exploitation of young women, must learn to negotiate to survive in the gang milieu (Miller and Brunson, 2002, pp. 443–445). Gang involvement does expose young women to risks of victimization. Young women can choose to be "one of the guys" and expose themselves to higher risks of being arrested, injured, or even killed in conflicts with rival gangs. Or they can use gender to decrease their risk of being harmed by not participating in "masculine" activities such as fighting and committing crime. However, females who opt out of violence and crime are then viewed as lesser members and may expose themselves to greater risks of victimization within their gangs (Miller, 1998; Miller, 2001).

In sum, most studies have found that girl gangs still serve as adjuncts to boy gangs. Yet an increasing number of studies show that female gangs provide girls with the necessary skills to survive in their harsh communities while allowing them a temporary escape from the dismal future awaiting them. These studies reveal that girls join gangs for the same reasons that boys do and share with boys in their neighborhood the hopelessness and powerlessness of the urban underclass (Joe and Chesney-Lind, 1993, p. 9).

Prostitution

Eleanor M. Miller's *Street Women*, which is based on intensive interviews with sixty-four Milwaukee prostitutes, contends that prostitution evolves out of the profound social and economic problems confronting adolescent females, especially young women of color (Miller, 1986). For African American women, constituting over half of Miller's sample, movement into prostitution took place as a consequence of exposure to deviant street networks. Usually recruited by older African American males with long criminal records, these women organized themselves into "pseudo families" and engaged primarily though not exclusively in prostitution. These women viewed prostitution as an alternative to boring and low-paying jobs and as a means to relieve the burdens of pregnancy and single motherhood. Although they were attracted by the excitement and money involved in prostitution, they soon learned that the life was not nearly as glamorous or remunerative as they had anticipated (Miller, 1986).

For whites, Miller found that street prostitution was not so much a hustle into which one drifted as it was a survival strategy. For this group there was often a direct link between prostitution and difficulties with parents, runaway behavior, and contact with the juvenile justice system. Interviewees described family lives that were characterized by disorganization and extremely high levels of violence and abuse. But running away from these chaotic settings resulted in the girls' arrest and lengthy detention as status offenders (Miller, 1986).

Considerable research supports the conclusion that adolescent female delinquents frequently have histories of abuse and victimization. Mimi Silbert and Ayala M. Pines found that 60 percent of the street prostitutes they interviewed had been sexually abused as juveniles (Silbert and Pines, 1982, p. 476). R. J. Phelps and colleagues' survey of 192 female youths in the Wisconsin juvenile justice system discovered that 79 percent of these youths (most of whom were in the system for petty larceny and status offenses) had been subjected to physical abuse that resulted in some form of injury (cited in Chesney-Lind, 1997). Chesney-Lind and Rodriquez's investigation of the backgrounds of adult women in prison underscored the links between their victimization as children and their later criminal careers. Interviews revealed that virtually all of these women were victims of physical and/or sexual abuse as youngsters; more than 60 percent had been sexually abused and about half had been raped (cited in Chesney-Lind, 1997, p. 19).

Adolescent Females and Violent Behavior

The media, especially in the last few years, have been quick to identify the rise of violence among juvenile girls when reporting increased arrest trends. Between 1992 and 2003, juvenile females' arrests increased 6.4 percent while arrests of adolescent boys decreased by 16.4 percent. While decreases were present across many crimes of violence for both juvenile males and females, the period saw a 7 percent increase in girls' arrests for aggravated assault during a period that showed a 29.1 percent decrease in arrests of juvenile males for this offense. Similarly, arrests of juvenile girls for assault climbed an astonishing 40.9 percent while arrests of juvenile males climbed only 4.3 percent (Federal Bureau of Investigation, 2003). See Box 4.2 for a discussion of the rise of violence among juvenile females.

B O X   4.2

Violence on the Rise among Juvenile Girls

Toledo, Ia. For years, fifteen-year-old Chantal Steeg handled anger by striking and screaming at people. She punched staff members and others at detention centers and foster homes. She threw furniture. She spewed verbal threats on other youths.

"It's a snowball effect—if you're angry at one thing and then another and you don't deal with it, you're going to explode," said Chantal, whose actions caused her to be removed from several foster homes and detention centers.

Violent behavior like Chantal's is on the increase among juvenile females, data from the Iowa Department of Public Safety show.

In 2003, 3,897 females younger than eighteen were arrested, up 19 percent from the 3,283 arrested in 1998. Robbery, aggravated and simple assault, larceny, and vandalism were among the crimes showing increase among female juveniles.

Arrest rates for juvenile males during the same period fell 6 percent.

The numbers don't surprise Deb Hanus, treatment director at the Iowa Juvenile Home and State Training School for Girls in Toledo. An increasing percentage of the home's residents are there for committing violent crimes, she said.

In 2004, 37 percent of the home's residents had been charged with assault, up from 16 percent in 2000, Hanus said. . . .

Two teenage females were arrested this month after a teacher trying to stop a fight was pushed through a plate glass window at Mason City High School. The teacher suffered minor injuries, police said.

Ashley Ashby, 17, and Kedejsia Caples, 16, both students at the Mason City school, were arguing. When the teacher intervened, she was pushed through the window, officials said. . . .

Jamie Gilley, a social worker at Des Moines' East High School, recalls several fights among teenage females that resulted in serious injuries. "These are all-out brawls—I think (females) are more violent in their fighting. It's a level of difference that used to not exist," she said.

Valley High School sophomore Lyndsey Bohall agrees. She said the females she has seen fighting are very physical in their aggression.

"It is really aggressive; they just like, attack each other," she said.

Bohall said she thinks females hit harder and fight longer than boys. She said, males tend to hit each other once, and the fight is over.

"Girls go behind each other's backs— they're more secretive than boys, and that makes girls more angry," she said.

Critical Thinking Questions: According to this article, in what ways has aggressiveness among female offenders recently increased? In this article, how is the media involved in the social construction of knowledge?

Source: Jessica Graham, "Violence on the rise among juvenile girls," *The Register's Iowa Weekly* (March 22, 2005, p. 14).

M. Brown, M. Chesney-Lind, L. Mikel, and Nan Stein in their article, "Patriarchy Matters: Toward a Gendered Theory of Teen Violence and Victimization," challenge this notion of a rise of violence among juvenile females. They claim that self-report data sources reveal that juvenile boys and girls' violence has *decreased* dramatically in the late 1990s. They also refer to the findings of the Youth Risk Behavior Survey, the biennial survey of the Centers for Disease Control (CDC). In 1991, while 34.4 percent of girls surveyed said that they had been in a physical fight in the last year, this figure had dropped to 23.9 percent in 2001, a 30.5 percent decrease in girls' fighting. Furthermore, these researchers are skeptical of arrest data reporting rises in violence among young women, because studies of other systems that monitor injury and mortality do not show dramatic increases in violent victimization. For example, hospital admission data, as well as vital statistics maintained by the health department over the past decades in San Francisco note decreases, rather than increases in girls' injuries and mortality rates. Finally, in considering other forms of violence, such as robbery and murder, there is no trend indicated here that girls are becoming more violent. Instead, arrests of juvenile girls for other crimes of violence, including the most lethal, have shown decreases, rather than increases (Brown et al., 2004, p. 4).

Brown, Chesney-Lind, Mikel, and Stein conclude that "someone's behavior has been changing, but it is likely not the behavior of girls, but rather those that police and monitor youthful behavior, including the behavior of girls" (Brown et al., 2004, p. 6). They believe that three factors are at work in this social construction of crime data for juvenile females' increased rates of violence.

The first is "relabeling," often called "bootstrapping," of female girls' status offense behavior from non-criminal charges like "incorrigibility" to assaultive charges. This practice is taking place, these researchers reason, partly because of parents being advised to do so if they wish their defiant daughters arrested and detained and partly as a result of changing police procedures or practices (Brown et al., 2004, p. 6).

The second factor involves a "rediscovery of girls' violence," especially in the arrests of both girls and women for domestic violence. For example, in California, arrests of girls and women for domestic violence increased from 6 percent of the total in 1988 to 16.5 percent in 1998. Race also appears to be significant here, because African American girls and women had arrest rates for domestic violence about three times that of white girls and women. In citing one study, which assessed 1,000 girls' files from different points in the juvenile justice system, the findings revealed that about one third of these girls were charged with "person offenses," the majority of which involved assault. A closer reading of these files revealed that most of those girls charged with assault were "the result of nonserious, mutual combat, situations with parents" (cited in Brown et al., 2004, p. 6).

The third factor, according to Brown, Chesney-Lind, Mikel, and Stein, is the "upcriming" of minor forms of youth violence (including juvenile females' physical aggression). "Upcriming" refers to policies, such as "zero tolerance policies," which have the effect of increasing the severity of criminal penalties associated with particular offenses, such as minor forms of fighting and school bullying. It was not that long ago that schoolyard fights and other instances of bullying were largely ignored or handled informally by parents and schools But today, with the official concern about youth violence and with the proliferation of "zero tolerance" policies, school principals are increasingly willing to call police onto their campuses (Brown et al., 2004, p. 8).

Brown, Chesney-Lind, Mikel, and Stein conclude:

> In short, criminalizing girls' violence, like the justice system's earlier efforts to criminalize their sexuality, has had an enormous impact on girls. . . . But while the earlier policing of girls was justified by gender difference, today's pattern is masked as gender equity. The results of what might be called "vengeful equity," though, are clearly as disadvantageous to girls as the earlier pattern of inequality. In both systems, girls are the clear losers, and neither affords them the justice promised by a system that purports to seek the "best interest of the child" [italics in the original] (pp. 8–9)

Gender across the Life Course

Jean Bottcher's study of brothers and sisters of incarcerated teenagers conceptualized gender as social practices and used these practices as the unit of analysis. Her study revealed six social factors that intertwined with delinquent activities, limiting female delinquency while at the same time enabling and rewarding male delinquency. These factors included male dominance, differences in routine daily activities, variations in sexual interests and transition to adulthood, and an ideology that defined crime as male activity and child care as female activity (Bottcher, 2001, pp. 905–925).

Longitudinal studies usually reveal that delinquent careers differ by gender. Male careers tend to begin earlier and to extend longer into the adult years. Studies of youth gangs show that female members are more likely than male members to leave the gang if they have a child. Conventional life patterns—especially marriage, parenting, and work—draw both males and females away from gangs and delinquency but do so more completely and quickly for females (Bottcher, 2001, p. 899).

Amy C. D'Unger, Kenneth C. Land, and Patricia L. McCall's follow-up of the second Philadelphia cohort study found both life-course-persistent and adolescence-limited delinquency (see Moffit's classification scheme earlier in the chapter) among the males, with a high and lower category for each group. Among the females in this study, there were comparable adolescence-limited groups, though with lower overall offending levels. The high-rate adolescence-limited female offenders did share marked similarities with low-rate chronic male offenders. Yet the chronic or persistent category of offenders was less prominent among the females (D'Unger, Land, and McCall, 2002, pp. 371–373).

Rebecca S. Katz, using waves 1 and 7 of the National Longitudinal Study of Youth, found that much as in other studies, childhood victimization, sexual discrimination, adult racial discrimination, and the experience of domestic violence largely explained women's involvement in crime and deviance. Katz found some support for revised strain theory as an explanation for female involvement in criminal behavior, but she concluded that female crime may require a unique theoretical model that more directly takes into account females' social and emotional development in a racist and patriarchal society (Katz, 2000, pp. 652–655).

John Hagan and Holly Foster state that American youth experience high levels of violence, and the U.S. public policy response is increasingly to punish the perpetrators of violence through waivers and transfer from juvenile to adult court. Adolescence is a time of expanding vulnerabilities and exposures to violence that can be destructive to self as well as to others. Such violence can involve intimate relationships or strangers. In addition to being perpetrators or victims, juveniles are often bystanders and witnesses to violence. The authors found from an analysis of data from the first two waves of the National Longitudinal Study of Adolescent health that the life course consequences of experiences with violence, especially violence in intimate adolescent relations, results in special difficulties for female juveniles, including depression and teenage pregnancy (Hagan and Foster, 2001, pp. 874–900).

Desistance from Crime

There have been at least three studies that have examined the desistance process among women. Ira Sommers, Debrorah R. Baskin, and John Fagan found that quality marriages led women to desist from crime, with some variation depending on the class and race of the women being studied (Sommers, Baskin, and Fagan, 1994, pp. 125–149). A later study by Sommers and Baskin revealed that the desistance process was quite different for inner-city women of color. These women were more likely to desist as the result of receiving alcohol and drug treatment or because they grew tired or fearful of repeated imprisonments (Sommers and Baskin, 1997, pp. 833–849).

Peggy C. Giordano and her colleagues developed a theory of cognitive transformation to explain desistance in their follow-up of a sample of serious adolescent female delinquents. They found neither marital attachment nor job stability to be strongly related to female desistance. Instead, desisters underwent a cognitive shift, or transformation. These researchers found that four types of cognitive transformations take place as an integral part of the desistance process: (1) There is a shift in the actor's openness to change; (2) the individual is exposed to a hook or set of hooks for change; (3) the individual begins to envision and fashion an appealing and conventional "replacement self"; and (4) a transformation takes place in the way the actor views the former deviant behavior or lifestyle. These various cognitive transformations or shifts not only influence receptivity to one or more hooks of change, but also inspire and direct behavior. These hooks "facilitated the development of an alternative view of self that was seen as fundamentally incompatible with criminal behavior" (Giordano, Cernkovich, and Rudolph, 2002, pp. 1000, 1003; Giordano, Deines, and Cernkovich, 2006, p. 35).

A Feminist Theory of Delinquency

The **feminist theory of delinquency,** an expression of radical feminism, contends that girls' victimization and the relationship between that experience and girls' crime have been systematically ignored. Chesney-Lind, one of the main proponents of this position, stated that it has long been understood that a major reason for girls' presence in juvenile courts is their parents' insistence on their arrest. Researchers, as well as those who work with female status offenders, are discovering today that a substantial number are victims of both physical and sexual abuse (Chesney-Lind, 1989, pp. 5–29).

Chesney-Lind proposed that a feminist perspective on the causes of female delinquency includes the following propositions: First, girls are frequently the victims of violence and sexual abuse (estimates are that three-quarters of sexual-abuse victims are girls); but, unlike boys, girls' victimization and their response to that victimization are shaped by their status as young women. Second, their victimizers (usually fathers or stepfathers) have the ability to invoke official agencies of social control to keep daughters at home and vulnerable. Third, as girls run away from abusive homes characterized by sexual abuse and parental neglect, they are forced into the life of an escaped convict. Unable to enroll in school or take a job to support themselves because they fear detection, female runaways are forced to engage in panhandling, petty theft, and sometimes prostitution to survive. Finally, it is no accident that girls on the run from abusive homes or on the streets because of impoverished homes become involved in criminal activities that exploit their sexuality. Because U.S. society has defined physically "perfect" young women as desirable, girls on the streets, who have little else of value to trade, are encouraged to utilize their bodies as a resource. The criminal subculture also views them from this perspective (Chesney-Lind, 1989, pp. 5–29). In Box 4.3, Chesney-Lind expands on this notion of the feminist theory of delinquency.

Emily Gaarder and Joanne Belknap interviewed twenty-two girls adjudicated and sentenced as adults in a large Midwestern state. They examined their lives before they were imprisoned and their perceptions of being tried and convicted as adults. The interviewees described lives filled with victimization and violence, sexism, racism, and economic marginalization. Significantly, the offending pattern of these girls was found to be similar to that of girls who remained in the juvenile justice system. Status offenses played a major role in this group of girls tried as adults (Gaarder and Belknap, 2004, p. 69).

This article shows the lack of a sound basis and the social construction that takes place in this serious act of transferring girls to the adult court. The researchers titled their chapter "Tenuous Borders" because they found there was a fine line between being retained in the juvenile court and being transferred to the adult court. The authors call for a more complex model of the relationship between victimization, agency, and responsibility, and a greater understanding of the social structural limitations and constraints placed on individual female offenders (Gaarder and Belknap, 2004).

Mary E. Gilfus (1992), in her analysis of life history interviews with incarcerated female offenders, further found that these women's childhoods and adolescence

---

BOX 4.3

Meda Chesney-Lind on the Feminist Theory of Delinquency

The question now is whether the theories of delinquent behavior can be used to understand female crime, delinquency, and victimization. Will the "add women and stir" approach be sufficient to rescue traditional delinquency theories? My research convinces me that it will not work. Gender stratification or the patriarchal context within which both male and female delinquency is lodged has been totally neglected by conventional delinquency theory. This omission means that a total rethinking of delinquency as a social problem is necessary.

The exclusion of girls from delinquency theory might lead one to conclude that girls are almost never delinquent and that they have far fewer problems than boys. Some might even suspect that the juvenile justice system treats the few girls who find their way into it more gently than it does the boys. Both of these assumptions are wrong.

Current work on female delinquency is uncovering the special pains that girls growing up in male-dominated society face. The price one pays for being born female is upped when it is combined with poverty and minority status, but it is always colored by gender. Consequently, sexual abuse is a major theme in girls' lives, and many girls on the run are running away from abusive and violent homes. They run to streets that are themselves sexist, and they are often forced to survive as women—to sell themselves as commodities. All of this is shaped by their gender as well as by their class and their color.

You might ask: How about the system's response to girls' delinquency? First there has been almost no concern about girls' victimization. Instead, large numbers of girls are brought into juvenile courts across America for noncriminal status offenses—running away from home, curfew, truancy, et cetera. Traditionally, no one in the juvenile justice system asked these girls why they were in conflict with their parents, no one looked for reasons why girls might run away from home. They simply tried to force them to return home or sentenced them to training schools. The juvenile justice system, then, has neglected girls' victimization, and it has acted to enforce parental authority over girls, even when the parents were abusive. Clearly, the pattern described above requires an explanation that places girls' delinquent behavior in the context of their lives as girls in a male-dominated society—a feminist model of delinquency if you will. That's what I'm working on these days.

Critical Thinking Questions: Is it as hard for girls to grow up in male-dominated society as Chesney-Lind suggests? What do you think of other feminist theories of delinquency?

Source: Interviewed in 1988 and found in Clemens Bartollas, *Juvenile Delinquency*, 7th ed. (Boston: Allyn & Bacon, 2005, p. 212.)

---

were plagued with neglect and abuse. Many responded by running away from home. Once they were on the streets, they became involved in an onset of drug use, stealing, and truancy, following which a large minority entered into juvenile prostitution as a survival strategy. These offenders participated in this illegal work simply as a survival strategy, but it further enmeshed them in criminal networks. As they transitioned into adulthood, the vast majority experienced continued victimization and many developed drug addictions.

In sum, the research findings of Chesney-Lind, Gaarder and Belknap, and Gilfus reveal that girls can have a different pathway to crime than boys. This means that the life course developmental model examined in the past section is only partly adequate in understanding female delinquency. The life course model focuses on significant life events or transitions, particularly in terms of changes in status, social roles, and relationships. This developmental approach, as identified by Sampson and Laub (1990), makes two hypotheses—first, problems in adult development are a result of childhood antisocial behaviors and, second, changes in offending behavior and development over the life course can be explained by social bonds to family and work in adulthood. However, as Gaarder and Belknap point out, life course developmental models do not adequately address childhood victimizations, such as physical abuse, neglect, and sexual abuse, including those perpetrated by children's parents. Furthermore, the life course perspective does not adequately address how discrimination and oppression, such as those based on a juvenile's race or sex, can shape this person's experiences, options, and identity (Gaarder and Belknap, 2004, p. 71).

The remainder of this chapter places emphasis on gender relations, influence of class, and racial discrimination and how they affect the processing of the female delinquent. It will be seen that delinquency across the life course, as proposed by Gaarder and Belknap, needs to be supplanted by an understanding of the victimizations of young women, as well as the discrimination and oppression they experience, to more fully understand how they process through their life transitions, including juvenile and criminal activities.

How Gender Bias Affects the Processing of the Female Delinquent

The fundamental theme of this section is that adolescent females grow up in a particular social context of domination and control by males (Spelman, 1989, p. 85). In this patriarchal society, troublesome juvenile females are quickly viewed through the lens of discrimination, exploitation, and oppression (Spelman, 1989, p. 51). Sexism, classism, and racism, several forms of oppression girls experience, affect the processing of the female delinquent in the juvenile justice system.

Gender Relations

The oppression of gender on adolescent females can be viewed in several ways. First, adolescent females receive discriminatory treatment because of society's disapproval of sexual activity. Etta A. Anderson provided evidence that society's disapproval of sexual activity on the part of adolescent females has resulted in their discriminatory treatment by the juvenile justice system (Anderson, 1976, pp. 350–357). Krohn, Curry, and Nelson-Kilger's analysis of 10,000 police contacts in a Midwestern city over a thirty-year period found that adolescent females who were suspected of status offenses were more likely than their male counterparts to be referred to juvenile court for such offenses during all three decades (Krohn, Curry, and Nelson-Kilger, 1983, pp. 417–439). Christy A. Visher's study of 785 police-suspect encounters revealed that younger females received harsher punishment than older females. She noted that "police officers adopt a more paternalistic and harsher attitude toward younger females to deter any further violation or inappropriate sex-role behavior" (Visher, 1983, pp. 5–28). Chesney-Lind further found that police in Honolulu, Hawaii, were more likely to arrest females for sexual activity and to ignore the same behavior among males (Chesney-Lind, 1973, pp. 57–59).

Jean Strouse observed that juvenile court judges commonly place adolescent females in confinement for even minor offenses because they assume that these females have engaged in sexual activity and believe that they deserve punishment (Strauss, 1972, p. 84). Yona Cohn's study of the disposition recommendations of juvenile probation officers found that females constituted only one-sixth of her sample of youths in metropolitan courts, yet they constituted one-fifth of the juveniles sentenced to institutional care. She attributed this uneven distribution to the fact that female adolescents frequently "violate" the sexual norms of the middle-class probation officers (Cohn, 1963, pp. 272–275). Furthermore, Kristine O. Rogers's study of a training school for girls in Connecticut found the treatment staff greatly concerned with residents' sexual history and habits (Rogers, 1973, pp. 223–246). Both Rogers and Chesney-Lind also comment on juvenile courts and detention homes' practice of forcing females to undergo pelvic examination and to submit to extensive questioning about their sexual activities, regardless of the offenses with which they are charged (Chesney-Lind, 1973, pp. 57–59; Rogers, 1973, pp. 223–246).

Laurie Schaffner further observed that juvenile females' sexual behavior, orientation, and histories often bring them to the attention of juvenile authorities. However, for many of these girls, rather than being the problem, much of their delinquent behavior actually is a solution to larger life dilemmas. They are taught to be sexy and frequently solve nonsexual problems, such as family and educational troubles, with sexually related romantic solutions. In examining the sexual solutions that juvenile females devise, Schaffner found from her examination of runaway shelters, psychiatric facilities, and juvenile detention centers across the United States that much of the state's response is ultimately a criminalization of young women's survival strategies. Schaffner went on to conclude that "girls' trouble with the law often takes on sexual overtones as the state participates in a gendered sexualizing and criminalizing of female attention, concerns, bodies, desires, and actions" (Schaffner, 1998).

Offering another perspective, Rosemary C. Sarri concluded that juvenile law has long penalized females. She claimed that although the law may not be discriminatory on its face, the attitudes and ideologies of juvenile justice practitioners administering it may result in violations of the equal protection clause of the Fourteenth Amendment, by leading them to commit females to longer sentences than males under the guise of "protecting" the female juveniles (Sarri, 1976, pp. 68–69). She added that "females have a greater probability of being detained and held for longer periods than males, even though the overwhelming majority of females are charged with status offenses" (Sarri, 1976, p. 76).

Randall G. Sheldon and John Horvath further found that adolescent females who were reported to court for status offenses were more likely than their male counterparts to receive formal processing or a court hearing (Sheldon and Horvath, 1986). C. R. Mann's research on runaway youths found that juvenile females were more likely than adolescent males to be detained and to receive harsh sentences (Mann, 1984). Chesney-Lind also concluded that adolescent females are more likely than adolescent males to be held for long periods of time in detention centers (Chesney-Lind, 1988, p. 152).

Randall R. Beger and Harry Hoffman's study of case files of juveniles ordered into detention by an Illinois juvenile court for technical probation violations found that females are confined in detention longer than males for disobeying probation rules (Beger and Hoffman, 1998, p. 173). Probation staff interviews revealed that both personal and contextual factors accounted for the gender-based disparity in the application of detention. Five basic factors were cited as responsible for this disparity: (1) Probation officers perceived female offenders to be more difficult to work with than males; (2) female offenders had more severe family dysfunctions than males; (3) conflicts with parents were an issue, because parents reacted more negatively to minor deviations by daughters; (4) community-based resources were inadequate; and (5) more females than males had had multiple social service interventions before probation (Beger and Hoffman, 1998, pp. 183–184).

Robert Terry's study of 9,000 youths apprehended by police in a Midwestern city found that females were more likely to be referred to the juvenile court than males and, if referred, were more likely to receive an institutional commitment (Terry, 1967, p. 218). K. O. Rogers found that females' average period of confinement in Connecticut was longer than that of males (Rogers, 1973, pp. 243–246). Clemens Bartollas and Christopher M. Sieverdes, in a study of institutionalized youths in North Carolina, found that 80 percent of the confined females had committed status offenses and that they had longer institutional stays than males (Bartollas and Sieverdes, 1985).

According to another perspective, the oppressive treatment of adolescent females is hidden in a couple of ways in the juvenile justice system. Following the decriminalization of status offenses in 1979, Anne R. Mahoney and Carol Fenster reported that many girls appeared in court for criminal-type offenses that had previously been classified as status offenses. They suggested that juvenile justice officials may have redefined these girls to be eligible for the kinds of protectionist sanctions that have been traditionally applied (Mahoney and Fenster, 1982).

Another expression of the gender bias found in this "hidden justice" is that certain provisions of the Juvenile Justice and Delinquency Prevention Act provide that status offenders found in contempt of court for violating a valid court order may be placed in secure detention facilities. This permits juvenile judges to use their contempt power to confine repeat status offenders. If a runaway girl, for example, was ordered by the court to remain at home, and she chose to run away again, she might be found in contempt of court—a criminal-type offense. There is reason to believe that juvenile judges apply their contempt power more often to female status offenders than to their male counterparts (Bishop and Frazier, 1992, p. 1167).

Finally, the early studies, especially, found that police officers, intake personnel, and judges supported a sexual double standard. Female status offenders, as previously indicated, were more likely than their male counterparts to be petitioned to formal court proceedings, to be placed in preadjudicatory detention confinements, and to be confined in juvenile institutions. But at the same time, males who committed delinquent acts frequently received harsher treatment than their female counterparts. Consistent with what is known as the "chivalry" or "paternalism" thesis, police were less likely to arrest females suspected of property or person crimes. If arrested, female delinquents were less likely than male delinquents to be formally charged with criminal offenses, and, if charged, they were less likely than males to be incarcerated for their offenses (Bishop and Frazier, 1992, p. 1164). See Box 4.4 for a critical examination of gender-specific services in the juvenile justice system.

On balance, some evidence does exist that the discriminatory treatment of female status offenders may be declining since passage of the Juvenile and Delinquency Prevention Act (Bishop and Frazier, 1992, p. 1165). No longer do many states send status offenders to training schools with delinquents. But the long tradition of sexism in juvenile justice will be difficult to change. Due process safeguards for female delinquents, as well as for female status offenders, must be established to ensure them greater social justice in the juvenile justice system. The intrusion of extralegal factors into the decision-making process in the juvenile court has led to discrimination against the adolescent female that must become a relic of the past.

Influence of Class

As part of the female delinquent's "multiple marginality," class oppression is another form of exploitation experienced by this young person (Chesney-Lind, 1997, p. 4). In a number of ways, powerful and serious problems of childhood and adolescence related to poverty set the stage for the young person's entry into homelessness, unemployment, drug use, survival sex and prostitution, and, ultimately, even more serious delinquent and criminal acts. Even those adolescents coming from middle-class homes may be thrust into situations of economic survival if they choose to run away from abusive environments.

Traditional theories also fail to address the life situations of girls on the economic and political margins, because researchers typically fail to examine or talk with these girls. For example, almost all urban females identified by police as gang members have been drawn from low-income groups (Bowker and Klein, 1983, pp. 750–751). Lee Bowker and Malcolm Klein's examination of data on girls in gangs in Los Angeles stated the importance of classism as well as racism:

> We conclude that the overwhelming impact of racism, sexism, poverty and limited opportunity structure is likely to be so important in determining the gang membership and juvenile delinquency of women and girls in urban ghettos that personality variables, relations with parents and problems associated with heterosexual behavior play a relatively minor role in determining gang membership and juvenile delinquency. (Bowker and Klein, 1983, pp. 750–751)

BOX 4.4

Sara Goodkind: Gender-Specific Services in the Juvenile Justice System: A Critical Examination

Goodkind refers to the 1992 Juvenile Justice and Delinquency Prevention Appropriations Authorizations (JJDPA) that states that "the term 'gender-specific services' means services designed to address needs unique to the gender of the individual to whom such services are provided." She adds that "the term *gender specific* has been interpreted to mean 'for girls' and that gender-specific programming refers to a comprehensive approach to female delinquency rooted in the experience of girls."

Goodkind found four fundamental critiques of the literature of gender-specific programming for female delinquency.

1. The need for gender-specific services is demonstrated and justified by frequent citations of increased rates of arrest and confinement for girls. However, Goodkind concludes that self-report and other sources have indicated that girls' delinquent behavior may not be on the rise.
2. An essentialized notion of gender is used that serves to reify socially constructed categories and ignore intersections of gender with race, ethnicity, class, sexuality, and other axes of difference.
3. Her third critique is that there is too great a focus on the individual. Interventions focus primarily on changing individuals, with few efforts geared toward institutional or structural change.
4. Her final critique is that girls' delinquency is frequently tied to their victimization, especially physical and sexual abuse. This approach ignores girls' agency and neglects the fact that girls continue to be

punished for behavior that is considered to be acceptable among boys.

Goodkind's concern is to shift the way that treatment agents, such as social workers, think about and engage gender. She is proposing an understanding of gender that is part of a framework for designing services for boys and girls that address their differential social locations without reifying socially constructed gender differences. This framework is based on the following eight principles, which she developed through her critical review:

- Deconstruct and move beyond false dichotomies;
- Adopt an interpretivist or constructionist epistemology that recognizes categories as socially constructed and presents a vision for social change;
- Uncover assumptions and identify interests and goals;
- Attend to the importance of context;
- Balance structure and agency and think in terms of interdependence;
- Focus on progress; and
- Rethink difference.

Critical Thinking Questions: What is your evaluation of Goodkind's article? Do you believe that her recommendations would improve the services for adolescent females involved in the juvenile justice system?

Source: Sara Goodkind, "Gender-Specific Services in the Juvenile Justice System: A Critical Examination," *Affifia 20* (Spring 2005, pp. 52–70).

Class becomes important in shaping the lives of adolescent females in a number of ways: Lower-class adolescent females tend to confront higher risk levels than middle- and upper-class adolescent females. They are more likely to have unsatisfactory experiences at school, to lack educational goals beyond high school, to experience higher rates of physical and sexual abuse, to deal with pregnancy and motherhood, to be involved in drugs and alcohol dependency, to confront the risk of AIDS, and to lack supportive networks at home (Dryfoos, 1990). Although not all adolescent females at risk end up in the juvenile justice system, the likelihood of such a placement is greater for lower-class girls.

Racial Discrimination

Young women of color, as well as other minority girls, often grow up in contexts much different from those of their white counterparts. Signithia Fordeham's article, "Those Loud Black Girls," showed that young African American women resisted accepting the Anglo norm of femininity by being loud or asserting themselves through their voices. Yet this behavior led to negative school experiences, and it does not take long for these juvenile females to discover that it is the quiet ones who do well in school. Some of this population decided to "pass for white" or to adopt more acceptable norms of femininity in order to be successful in the school experience. Others refused to adopt this survival strategy and their tool for liberation contributed to isolating or alienating them from school success (Fordham, 1997, pp. 81–111).

Because racism and poverty often go hand in hand, these girls are forced by their minority status and poverty to deal early and on a regular basis with problems of abuse, drugs, and violence (Chesney-Lind, 1997, p. 23). They also are likely to be attracted to gang membership (Esbensen and Winfree, 1998, p. 510). H. C. Covey, Scott Menard, and R. Franzese summarized the effect of ethnicity on gang membership:

> *Racial difference in the frequency of gang formation such as the relative scarcity of non-Hispanic, white, ethnic gangs may be explainable in terms of the smaller proportion of the non-Hispanic European American population that live in neighborhoods characterized by high rates of poverty, welfare dependency, single-parent households, and other symptoms that characterize social disorganization. (Covey, Menard, and Franzese, 1997, p. 240)*

Minority girls' strategies for coping with the problems of abuse, drugs, violence, and gang membership, as Chesney-Lind has noted, "tend to place them outside the conventional expectations of white girls," and it also increases the likelihood that they will come to the attention of the juvenile justice system (Chesney-Lind, 1997, p. 23).

There is also the belief that girls of color enjoy the benefits of chivalry much less than white girls do. Middle-class white girls, especially those who have committed minor offenses, not sexual ones, may be given greater latitude by the police, court intake officers, and juvenile court officers than their minority counterparts. As with male minority offenders, female minority offenders are likely to be viewed as more dangerous to society and more likely to require long-term institutionalization.

The Whole Is Greater Than the Sum of the Parts

The examination of the experience of African American juvenile girls reveals, as it does with adult women, that it is not as though one form of oppression is piled on another. That is, the effects of the multiple expressions of gender, class, and race are more than mere arithmetic (Spelman, 1989, p. 123). This suggests that gender, class, and race are interlocking forms of oppression and that the whole is greater than the sum of its parts. Thus, female delinquents, like adult women, suffer the consequences of multiple oppressions as more than some form of simple additive experience (Spelman, 1989, p. 123).

Summary

This chapter, in examining the female delinquent across the life course, discussed the ways in which the female delinquent is expected in her culture to think, feel, and act (Spelman, 1989, p. 14). Female delinquency, like all other social behaviors, takes place in a world where gender still shapes the lives of adolescents in powerful ways (Chesney-Lind, 1977, p. 5). The value of feminist theory ultimately is based on accepting the notion that juvenile females are positioned in society in ways that produce vulnerability to victimization by males, including abuse and the negative effects of poverty. This position assumes, then, that behavior is gender-contextualized and that it should be examined from this perspective (Shoemaker, 1996, p. 242). Patriarchal society places a moral chastity belt around the behavior of adolescent females at home, in school, and in the community. Contextual analysis is helpful in understanding females' acceptance or rejection of their expected social norms and roles.

The problems of sexism, racism, and class and their influence on female delinquency have been generally ignored by criminologists. As a result, writers on female delinquency have often been more concerned with the adjustment of the adolescent female to society than with the extent and consequences of oppression in their lives. An examination of how the categories of gender, class, and race are interlocked and influence delinquency across the life course will lead to needed insight about the problems female delinquents face in U.S. society.

KEY TERMS

adolescence-limited
  delinquent males
desistance

early-onset, persistent
  offenders
feminist theory of delinquency

life course perspective
turning point

CRITICAL THINKING QUESTIONS

1. Why is the interlocking nature of gender, class, and race so important in understanding female delinquency?

2. Why has society been so sensitive to the sexual behavior of adolescent girls?

3. What is the relationship between victimization and oppression and the life course of female delinquents?

4. Do you believe that it would be more difficult for males or females to desist from delinquency in their late teens? How about in their mid-thirties? Why do you feel the way you do?

WEB DESTINATIONS

Check out Meda Chesney-Lind's homepage at this site: http://home.hawaii.rr.com/chesneylind/

Girls and gangs: www.knowgangs.com/school_resources/menu_026.htm

Building blocks for youth: www.buildingblocksforyouth.org/issues/girls

Texas youth commission, adolescent girls with co-occurring disorders: www.tyc.state.tx.us/prevention/adolescent_girls.html

American Bar Association, Girls in the juvenile justice system: www.abanet.org/crimjust/juvjus/girls.html

REFERENCES

Akers, R. L. (1998). *Social learning and social structure: A general theory of crime and deviance*. Boston: Northeastern University Press.

Anderson, E. A. (1976). The chivalrous treatment of the female offender in the arms of the criminal justice system: A review of the literature. *Social Problems 23:* 350–357.

Archer, M. S. (1988). *Culture and agency: The place of culture in social theory*. Cambridge, England: Cambridge University Press.

Bartollas, C., and Sieverdes, C. M. (1985). Games juveniles play: How they get their way. Unpublished manuscript.

Beger, R. R., and Hoffman, H. (1998). The role of gender in detention dispositioning of juvenile probation violators. *Journal of Crime and Justice 21:* 173–186.

Bishop, D. M., and Frazier, C. E. (1992). Gender bias in juvenile justice processes: Implications of the JJDP Act. *Journal of Criminal Law and Criminology 82:* 1132–1152.

Bjerregaard, B., and Smith, C. (1993). Gender differences in gang participation, delinquency, and substance abuse. *Journal of Quantitative Criminology 9:* 329–348.

Bottcher, J. (2001). Social practices of gender: How gender relates to delinquency in the everyday lives of high-risk youths. *Criminology 39:* 905–925.

Bowker, L., and Klein, M. W. (1980). Female participation in delinquent gang activities, *Adolescence 15:* 509–519.

Bowker, L., and Klein, M. W. (1983). The etiology of female juvenile delinquency and gang membership: A test of psychological and social structural explanations. *Adolescence 13:* 750–751.

Brown, M., Chesney-Lind, M., Stein, N., and Mikel, L. (2004). *Patriarchy matters: Toward a gendered theory of teen violence and victimization* (Wellesley Centers for Women Working Paper No. 417). Center for Research on Women, Wellesley College, Wellesley, Mass.

Browning, K., and Huizinga, D. (1999). Highlights from the Denver Youth Survey. *OJJDP Fact Sheet.* Washington, D.C.: Office of Juvenile Justice and Delinquency Prevention.

Browning, K., and Loeber, R. (1999). Highlights from the Pittsburgh Youth Study. *OJJDP Fact Sheet.* Washington, D.C.: Office of Juvenile Justice and Delinquency Prevention.

Browning, K., Thornberry, T. P., and Porter, P. K. (1999). Highlights of findings from the Rochester Youth Development Study. *OJJDP Fact Sheet*. Washington, D.C.: Office of Juvenile Justice and Delinquency Prevention.

Centers for Disease Control and Prevention. (2002). *Youth risk behavior surveillance—United States 1991–2001*. Atlanta, Ga.: U.S. Department of Health and Human Services.

Chesney-Lind, M. (1973). Judicial enforcement of the female sex role: The family court and female delinquency. *Issues in Criminology 8:* 57–59.

Chesney-Lind, M. (1988). Girls, crime and women's place. *Crime and Delinquency 35:* 5–29.

Chesney-Lind, M. (1997). *The female offender: Girls, women, and crime*. Thousand Oaks, Calif.: Sage Publications.

Claussen, J. A. (1993). *American lives: Looking back at the children of the Great Depression*. New York: The Free Press.

Cohn, Y. (1963). Criteria for probation officers' recommendations to juvenile court. *Crime and Delinquency 1:* 272–275.

Coleman, J. (1990). *Foundations of social theory*. Cambridge, Mass: Harvard University Press.

Cornich, D. B., and Clark, R. V. (1986). *The reasoning criminal: Rational choice perspectives on offending*. New York: Springer Verlag.

Covey, H. C., Menard, S., and Franzese, R. (1997). *Juvenile gangs,* 2nd ed. Springfield, Ill.: C. C Thomas.

Datesman, S. K., and Aickin, M. (1984). Offense specialization and escalation among status offenders. *Journal of Criminal Law and Criminology 75:* 1260–1273.

Dryfoos, J. G. (1990). *Adolescence at risk: Prevalence and prevention*. New York: Oxford University Press.

D'Unger, A. V., Land, K. C., and McCall, P. L. (2002). Sex differences in age patterns of delinquent/criminal careers: Results from Poisson latent class analyses of the Philadelphia cohort study. *Journal of Quantitative Criminology 18:* 349–375

Elder, G. H., Jr. (1994). Time, human agency, and social change: Perspectives on the life course. *Social Psychology Quarterly 57:* 4–15.

Elder, G. H., Jr., Johnson, M. K. K., and Crosnoe, R. (2003). The emergence and development of life course theory. In J. T. Mortimer and M. J. Shanahan (eds.), *Handbook of the Life Course*, New York: Kluwer Academic/Plenum Publishers.

Elder, G. H., Jr. (1999). *Children of the great depression: Social change in life experience, 25th anniversary edition*. Boulder, Co: Westview Press.

Elder, G. H., Jr. (2000). *Children of the land: Adversity and success in rural America*. Chicago: University of Chicago Press.

Emirbayer, M., and Mische, A. (1998). What is agency? *American Journal of Sociology 103:* 962–1023.

Esbensen, F. A., and Winfree, L. T. (1998). Race and gender differences between gang and non-gang youths: Results from a multisite survey. *Justice Quarterly* 15.

Esbensen, F. A., Deschenes, E. P., and Winfree, Jr., L. T. (1998). *Differences between gang girls and gang boys: Results from a multi-site survey*. Paper presented at the annual meeting of the Academy of Criminal Justice Science in Albuquerque, New Mexico.

Farrington, D. P. (2003). Developmental and life-course criminology: Key theoretical and empirical issues: The 2002 Sutherland Award Address. *Criminology 41:* 221–247.

Federal Bureau of Investigation, (2003). Uniform crime reports. Washington, D.C.: U.S. Government Printing Office.

Fordham, S. (1997). Those loud black girls: (Black) women, silence and gender "passing" in the academy. 81–111. In M. Seller and L. Weis (eds.), *Beyond black and white: New faces and voices in U.S. schools*. Albany: University of New York Press.

Gaarder, E., and Belknap, J. (2004). Tenuous borders: Girls transferred to adult court. *Criminology 40:* 481–517.

Gilfus, M. E. (1992). From victims to survivors to offenders: Women's routes of entry and immersion into street crime. *Women and Criminal Justice 4:* 63–89.

Giordano, P. C., Cernkovich, S. A., and Rudolph, J. L. (2002). Gender, crime, and desistance: toward a theory of cognitive transformation. *American Journal of Sociology 107:* 990–1064.

Giordano, P. C., Deines, J. A., and Cernkovich, S. A. (2006). In and out of crime: A life course perspective on girls' delinquency. *Gender and crime: Patterns in victimization and offending. 17–40.* Eds. Karen Heimer and Candace Kruttschnitt. New York: New York University Press.

Glassner, B., Ksander, M., and Berg, B. (1983). A note on the deterrent effect of juvenile vs. adult jurisdiction. *Social Problems 31:* 219–221.

Glueck, S., and Glueck, E. (1940). *Juvenile delinquents grown up.* New York: Commonwealth Fund.

Hagan, J., and Foster, H. (2001). Youth violence and the end of adolescence. *American Sociological Review 66:* 874–900.

Hamparian, D., Schuster, R., Dinitz, S., and Conrad, J. P. (1980). *A violent few: A study of dangerous juveniles.* Lexington, Mass.: D.C. Heath and Company.

Harms, P. (2002). *Detention and delinquency cases, 1989–1998.* OJJDP Fact Sheet #01. Washington D.C.: U.S. Department of Justice.

Harris, M. G. (1988). *Cholas: Latin girls and gangs.* New York: AMS Press.

Hawkins, D. J., Smith, B. H., Hill, K. G., Kosterman, R., Catalano, R. J., and Abbott, R. D. (2003). Understanding and preventing crime and violence: Findings from the Seattle Social Development Project. In T. P. Thornberry and M. D. Krohn (eds.), *Taking stock of delinquency: An overview of findings from contemporary longitudinal studies* (pp. 255–303) New York: Plenum.

Homans, G. C. (1964). Bring men back in. *American Sociological Review 29:* 809–818.

Joe, K., and Chesney-Lind, M. (1993). *Just every mother's angel: An analysis of gender and ethnic variations in youth gang membership.* Paper presented at the annual meeting of the American Society of Criminology in Phoenix, Arizona.

Johnston, L. D., O'Malley, P. M., Bachman, J. G., and Schulenberg, J. E. (2004). *Monitoring the Future national results on adolescent drug use: Overview of key findings.* Bethesda, Md.: National Institute on Drug Abuse.

Katz, R. S. (2000). Explaining girls' and women's crime and desistance in the context of their victimization experiences. *Violence against Women 6:* 633–660.

Klein, D. (1973). The etiology of female crime: A review of the literature. *Crime and Social Justice: Issues in Criminology 8:* 3–30.

Krohn, M. D., Curry, J. P., and Nelson-Kilger, S. (1983). Is chivalry dead? *Criminology 21:* 417–439.

Laub, J. H., and Sampson, R. J. (2003). *Shared beginnings, divergent lives: Delinquent boys to age 70.* Cambridge, Mass.: Harvard University Press.

Lauderback, D., Hansen, J., and Waldorf, D. (1992). Sisters are doin' it for themselves: Black gang in San Francisco. *Gang Journal 1:* 57–72.

Mahoney, A. R., and Fenster, C. (1982). Family delinquents in a suburban courts. In N. Hahn and E. A. Stanko, (eds.), *Judge, lawyer, victim, thief: Women, gender roles and criminal justice.* Boston: Northeastern University Press.

Mann, C. (1984). *Female crime and delinquency.* University, Al.: University of Alabama Press.

Miller, E. (1986). *Street women.* Philadelphia: Temple University Press.

Miller, J. (1998). Gender and victimization risk among young women in gangs. *The Journal of Research in Crime and Delinquency 35:* 429–454.

Miller, J. (2001). *One of these guys: girls, gangs, and gender.* New York: Oxford University Press.

Miller, J., and Decker, S. (2001). Young women and gang violence: Gender, street offending, and violent victimization in gangs. *Justice Quarterly 18:* 115–139.

Miller, J., and Brunson, R. K. (2000). Gender dynamics in youth gangs: A comparison of males' and females' accounts. *Justice Quarterly 17:* 419–449.

Moffitt, T. E. (1993). Adolescent-limited and life-course persistent antisocial behavior: A developmental taxonomy. *Psychological Review 100:* 674–701.

Moffitt, T. E., Lynam, D. R., and Silva, P. A. (1994). Neuropsychological tests predicted persistent male delinquency. *Criminology 32:* 247–275.

Moffitt, T. E., Caspi, A., Dickson, N., Silva, P. A., and Stanton, W. (1996). Childhood-onset versus adolescent-onset antisocial conduct problems in males: Natural history from ages 3 to 18. *Development and Psychopathology 8:* 399–424.

Moffitt, T. E., Caspi, A., Rutter, M., and Silva, P. A. (2001). *Sex differences in antisocial behavior: Conduct disorder, delinquency, and violence in the Dunedin Longitudinal Study.* Cambridge, England: Cambridge University Press.

Moore, J., and Hagedorn, J. (2001). Female gangs: A focus on research. *Juvenile Justice Bulletin.* Washington, D. C.: Office of Juvenile Justice and Delinquency Prevention.

Mulvey, E., and LaRosa, J. (1986). Delinquency cessation and adolescent development: Preliminary data. *American Journal of Orthopsychiatry 56:* 212–224.

Office of National Drug Control Policy. (2003). *National drug control strategy.* Washington, D.C.: Office of National Drug Control Policy.

Paternoster, R., Brame, R., and Farrington, D. P. (2001). On the relationship between adolescent and adult conviction frequencies. *Journal of Quantitative Criminology 17:* 201–225.

Quicker, J. C. (1983). *Home girls: Characterizing Chicano gangs.* San Pedro, Calif.: International University Press.

Rogers, K. O. (1973). For her own protection: Conditions of incarceration for female juvenile offenders in the state of connecticut. *Law and Society Review 7:* 223–246.

Sampson, R. J., and Laub, J. H. (1990). Crime and deviance over the life course: The salience of adult social bonds. *American Sociological Review 55:* 609–627.

Sampson, R. J., and Laub, J. H. (1993). *Crime in the making: Pathways and turning points through life.* Cambridge, Mass.: Harvard University Press.

Sampson, R. J., and Laub, J. H. (2001). Understanding desistance from crime, In M. Tonry (eds.). *Crime and Justice. 28.* Chicago: University of Chicago Press.

Sampson, R. J., and Laub, J. H. (2004). A general age-graded theory of crime: Lessons learned and the future of the life-course criminology. In David Farrington (ed.), *Advances in criminological theory: Testing integrated developmental/life course theories of offending.* New York: Transaction.

Sarri, R. C. (1976). Juvenile law: How it penalizes females. In Laura Crites (ed.), *The Female Offender.* Lexington, Mass.: Lexington Books.

Schaffner, L. (1998). *Female juvenile delinquency: Sexual solutions and gender bias in juvenile justice.* Paper presented at the annual meeting of the American Society of Criminology in Washington, D.C.

Shannon, L. (1982). *Assessing the relationships of adult criminal careers to juvenile careers: A summary.* Washington, D.C.: U.S. Government Printing Office.

Sheldon, R. G., and Horvath, J. (1986). *Processing offenders in juvenile court: A comparison of males and females.* Paper presented at the annual meeting of the Western Society of Criminology in Newport, Calif.

Shoemaker, D. J. (2005). *Theories of delinquency: An examination of delinquent behavior,* 5th ed. New York: Oxford University Press.

Silbert, M., and Pines, A. M. (1982). Entrance into prostitution. *Youth and Society 13:* 471–500.

Simpson, S. S., and Ellis, L. (1995). Doing gender: Sorting out the case and crime conundrum. *Criminology 33:* 47–81.

Sommers, I., and Baskin, D. R. (1997). Situational or generalized violence in drug dealing networks. *Journal of Drug Issues 27:* 833–849.

Sommers, I., Baskin, D. R., and Fagan, J. (1994). Getting out of the life: Crime desistance by female street offenders. *Deviant Behavior 15:* 125–149.

Spelman, E. (1989). *Inessential woman.* Boston, Mass.: Beacon Press.

Spring, J. H. (2005). Gender-specific services in the juvenile justice system: A critical examination. *Affilia 20:* 52–70.

Sthal, A. (2003). Delinquency cases in juvenile courts. *OJJDP Fact Sheet #31.* Washington D.C.: U.S. Department of Justice.

Strouse, J. (1972). To be a minor and female: The legal rights of women under twenty-one. *Ms. 1: 116,* 70–75.

Terry, R. (1967). Discrimination in the police handling of juvenile offenders by social control agencies. *Journal of Research in Crime and Delinquency 14:* 218–230.

Tremblay, R. E., Vitaro, F., Nagin, D., Pagani, L., and Seguin, J. R. (2003). The Montreal Longitudinal and Experimental Study: Rediscovering the power of description. In T. P. Thornberry and M. D. Krohn (eds.), *Taking stock of delinquency: An overview of findings from contemporary longitudinal studies* (pp. 205–254). New York: Plenum.

United States Department of Health and Human Services (2003). *2002 National Survey on Drug Abuse.* Washington, D.C.: Office of National Drug Control Policy.

United States Department of Health and Human Services (2003). *2002 National household survey of drug abuse.* Washington, D.C.: United States Department of Health and Human Services.

Visher, C. A. (1983). Gender, police arrest decisions, and notion of chivalry. *Criminology 21:* 417–439.

Warr, M. (1998). Life course transitions and desistance from crime. *Criminology 36:* 183–216.

Wilson, J. Q., and Herrnstein, R. (1985). *Crime and human nature.* New York: Simon and Schuster.

Wolfgang, W. E., Figlio, R. M., and Sellin, T. (1972). *Delinquency in a birth cohort.* Chicago: University of Chicago Press.

PART THREE

Drug Addiction, Prison, and Restoration

The title of this section of the book could spell out the journey of one woman, of many women—the journey from drug use to incarceration to redemption. Common to all these chapters is the focus on the female offender. Chapter 5 presents research on the biology, psychology, and sociology of substance use and addiction. The emphasis is on the brain, trauma, and the societal response, respectively. Drugs and alcohol not only are involved in the commission of crime and women's involvement in the criminal justice system in that regard but also in women's victimization and criminal justice involvement.

Chapter 6, The Prison Environment, takes us into the world of the prison. Despite being a small proportion of the U.S. prison population, women and especially women of color have seen their numbers rise drastically over the past decade. Modeled on medium-security prisons for antisocial men, women's prisons are not hospitable places. Research shows that behind bars women's treatment needs—in the areas of substance abuse, mental health, and prior victimization—are not being met. Many of the women in prison could lead productive lives in the community and at tremendous savings to the state if alternative intensive supervision programs were provided.

A promising new development (based on old traditions) is restorative justice. Chapter 7 reveals how the processes that are included under the rubric of restorative justice have special relevance for women, offenders as well as victims. Victim-offender conferencing is a form of peacemaking between the wrongdoer and the victim that is a process of empowerment to offender, the victim, and the community.

5 Women, Substance Abuse, and Criminal Justice

The decision to include a separate chapter on substance abuse problems in female offenders and victims is based on the following considerations:

- The war on drugs and its disproportionate impact on women;
- The extent to which substance abuse is associated with criminal activity of all sorts—for example, prostitution, child abuse, assault, manslaughter, and burglary;
- The considerable extent to which female offenders suffer from addictive tendencies and addiction;
- The implication of drugs and alcohol directly and indirectly in women's victimization.

Exploring the link between female crime and women's involvement with substance abuse is the first and major task of this chapter. This link will be examined through a look at relevant statistics and a description of typical pathways to crime. That the **war on drugs** (and drug users) has drastic repercussions for poor women of color is one of the basic assumptions of this chapter. The effects of this war are seen in the increased rate of arrest and imprisonment of minority women.

To prepare students and staff to work with persons with substance abuse and addictive problems, we have chosen a bio-psycho-social framework. This framework entails a study of the **biology of addiction** and substance abuse, including co-occurring mental disorders. Because so many offenders, especially those who are incarcerated, have both a diagnosable mental disorder and a substance dependency problem, a section is devoted to co-occurring disorders, sometimes known as dual diagnosis. Attention to *psychological* factors traces the pathway through which personal factors, including childhood trauma, can lead to alcohol or other drug use of a harmful nature. *Social* factors in this context encompass the legal response to the drug use or alcohol- or drug-induced behavior; the prosecution can be seen as a form of victimization in itself. The enforcement of anti-drug conspiracy laws and prosecution of mothers who consumed drugs prenatally are among the topics discussed.

A woman does not have to break the law or have a substance abuse problem to find her life controlled by alcohol and other drug use. Her involvement may be indirect, for example, through victimization by a drunken spouse or partner. Her criminal justice involvement might, accordingly, not be as an offender but as a victim of a crime.

Alcoholic- and drug-using women are highly vulnerable to all forms of victimization—robbery, rape, and physical abuse. This is due to their frequenting of dangerous places and their personal involvement with others whose behavior may be out of control. This chapter will consider these multiple dimensions of substance abuse with a special emphasis on gender.

First, the Statistics

Crime rates for both men and women are down and yet because of the war on drugs and this country's punitive sentencing practices, women have been hurt in multiple ways. They have been hurt through incarceration and separation from their families, and through the siphoning of public resources away from health and treatment programs into prison construction and maintenance (Mullings, Pollock, and Crouch, 2002). Let us see what the statistics reveal about the nature of female crime and the extent of drug and alcohol involvement in such crime.

See Table 5.1 for the most recent data available from the Bureau of Justice Statistics (BJS) (2000) on offenses of which female inmates were convicted.

From Table 5.1 we can see that most incarcerated women are serving time or are on probation for nonviolent offenses and that the most frequently committed offenses, especially in the federal prison system, involved drugs. Around 72% of inmates in the federal prison system were convicted of a drug violation. Keep in mind that other crimes for which the women were sentenced, including property crime and public order (DWI, or driving while intoxicated), also might have been

TABLE 5.1   Offenses of Women on Probation or in Jail or Prison

Most Serious Offense*	Percent of Women Offenders			
	Probation	Local Jails	State Prisons	Federal Prisons
Violent offenses	9%	12%	28%	7%
Homicide	1	1	11	1
Property offenses	44%	34%	27%	12%
Larceny	11	15	9	1
Fraud	26	12	10	10
Drug offenses	19%	30%	34%	72%
Public-order offenses	27%	24%	11%	8%
Driving while intoxicated	18	7	2	0
Number of women offenders	721,400	27,900	75,200	9,200

*Based on the offenders' most serious offense. Overall offense categories are shown with selected detail categories containing larger percentages of women offenders.

alcohol/drug related. In her examination of these statistics, Wallace (2005) argues that the extent of alcohol/drug involvement is far more pervasive than the raw statistics indicate. The process of plea bargaining, as she indicates, distorts the picture in that offenders are often sentenced for a lesser non-drug offense to clear the docket. Wallace cites evidence from a New York City study in which urinalysis tests showed that 28 percent of women tested positive for drugs when only 19 percent had been arrested on drug charges.

Substance abuse is a primary cause and contributor to crime for both men and women who were residing in jail at the time of the study: A national interview-survey showed significant alcohol/drug involvement. Table 5.2 provides BJS data that

TABLE 5.2 Substance Dependence or Abuse among Jail Inmates, by Selected Characteristics, 2002

Characteristic	Percent of Jail Inmates		
	All	*Dependence*	*Abuse Only*
All jail inmates	68.0%	45.2%	22.9%
Gender			
Male	67.9%	44.3%	23.6%
Female	69.2	51.8	17.4
Race/Hispanic origin[a]			
White[b]	77.7%	55.4%	22.3%
Black[b]	64.1	40.4	23.7
Hispanic	58.7	35.7	23.0
Other[c]	66.0	45.4	20.7
Age			
24 or younger	66.1%	40.3%	25.8%
25–34	70.5	48.1	22.4
35–44	71.4	50.4	21.0
45–54	61.9	41.7	20.3
55 or older	46.2	23.1	23.1
Most serious offense			
Violent	63.1%	40.8%	22.3%
Property	71.7	50.6	21.1
Drug	72.1	49.6	22.4
Public-order	67.0	41.3	25.7

[a]Excludes inmates who did not specify a race.

[b]Excludes persons of Hispanic origin.

[c]Includes Asians, American Indians, Alaska Natives, Native Hawaiians, other Pacific Islanders, and inmates who specified more than one race.

Source: BJS (2005). *Substance Dependence, Abuse, and Treatment of Jail Inmates* (Washington, D.C.: U.S. Department of Justice, 2002).

Karberg and James (2005) gathered based on interviews that were conducted previously in more than four hundred jails through the Census Bureau. The table also provides a breakdown by gender for substance dependence and abuse. As revealed also in the same research source, although not shown in this table, alcohol or drugs was a factor for both genders (which means predominantly male) in about 67 percent of violent crimes and almost 73 percent of property offenses.

Note in Table 5.2 that approximately 52 percent of female inmates met the criteria for substance dependence. We see from this table that there was little difference in the overall prevalence of substance dependence or abuse between men (68 percent) and women (69 percent) in jails. This means that over half suffered from alcohol or drug addiction (see the next section on biology). Convicted female inmates in jail had a higher rate of previous drug use (61 percent) compared to a comparable male sample (54 percent). In Iowa, and increasingly in other states, **methamphetamine (meth)** is listed as the drug of choice among female but not male inmates. In 2002, for example, 43 percent of women entering prison said meth was their drug of choice (*USA Today*, 2002). Although there is no racial breakdown by gender in tabular form, BJS statisticians Karberg and James (2005) comment that the cohort of white females, like white males, had a slightly higher rate of women who had substance dependence or abuse than did others in the jail population. White females were the minority at 43 percent of women in jail.

We learn further, as stated in the BJS substance dependence report, that convicted women offenders were more likely to have been under the influence of drugs (34 percent) than alcohol (22 percent) at the time of the offense. In contrast, alcohol involvement was more prevalent among the men. Statistics from state prisons are relatively comparable (BJS, 2000). The high incidence of meth use and the tightening of laws intended to deal with this problem are only beginning to be reflected in the statistics. Results from a survey of 500 local officials conducted by the National Association of Counties declared methamphetamine to be the nation's leading law enforcement scourge and blamed it for crowding jails and fueling increases in theft and violence (Zernike, 2005). Meth is associated with Mexicans in terms of its transport and with rural whites in its manufacture and use. Since meth predominantly is a white problem, one could expect an increase in the numbers of white women sentenced for drug use and manufacture.

How about treatment for substance abuse problems? The survey from the National Association of Counties showed that over one third of drug- and alcohol-dependent inmates had received treatment while incarcerated or on probation or parole. (Keep in mind that treatment included attendance at self help groups such as Alcoholics Anonymous [AA] or Narcotics Anonymous [NA].) Female inmates in this category reported more treatment involvement than men, and whites more than persons of other races. Under 10 percent of drug-involved inmates were receiving specialized treatment since entering the jail.

The obvious relationship between substance abuse and crime suggests a strong role for treatment in crime prevention. According to the Substance Abuse and Mental Health Services Administration (SAMHSA, 1999b), the need is far from being met; in fact, while the number of treatment needs among state and federal inmates has risen, the number receiving treatment has actually dropped. We will look at the policy implications under the treatment section of this chapter.

Statistics on prior abuse reported by inmates and persons on probation provide important data in our understanding of the child abuse/substance abuse configuration. BJS tells us, for example, that women in trouble with the law are approximately twice as likely to have been victimized in childhood as were members of the general population. The data show that 89 percent of the women under correctional supervision had used illegal drugs on a regular basis. The highlights are provided in Table 5.3. The facts revealed in this table show a high rape rate for

TABLE 5.3 Prior Abuse of Correctional Populations, by Sex

| | | Percent Experiencing Abuse Before Sentence | | | |
| | | Ever | | Before 18 | |
	Total	*Male*	*Female*	*Male*	*Female*
Ever abused before admission					
State prison inmates	18.7%	16.1%	57.2%	14.4%	36.7%
Federal prison inmates	9.5	7.2	39.9	5.8	23.0
Jail inmates	16.4	12.9	47.6	11.9	36.6
Probationers	15.7	9.3	40.4	8.8	28.2
Physically abused					
State prison inmates	15.4%	13.4%	46.5%	11.9%	25.4%
Federal prison inmates	7.9	6.0	32.3	5.0	14.7
Jail inmates	13.3	10.7	37.3	—	—
Probationers	12.8	7.4	33.5	—	—
Sexually abused					
State prison inmates	7.9%	5.8%	39.0%	5.0%	25.5%
Federal prison inmates	3.7	2.2	22.8	1.9	14.5
Jail inmates	8.8	5.6	37.2	—	—
Probationers	8.4	4.1	25.2	—	—

– Not available.

• A third of women in State prison, a sixth in Federal prison, and a quarter in jail said they had been raped before their sentence. Another 3% to 6% reported that someone had tried unsuccessfully to rape them.

• Over half of the abused women said they were hurt by spouses or boyfriends, and less than a third, by parents or guardians. Over half of the abused men in correctional populations identified parents or guardians as abusers.

• Among State prison inmates 1 in 20 men and 1 in 4 women said they had been sexually abused before age 18; 1 in 10 men and 1 in 4 women, physically abused.

• For State prisoners reporting prior abuse, 89% had ever used illegal drugs: 76% of the men and 89% of the women had used them regularly. Of those not reporting prior abuse, 82% had used illegal drugs: 68% of the men and 65% of the women had used them regularly.

women before they committed their crimes—one in three women in state prison. We see also that abuse of the women had continued into adulthood with partner violence, whereas male inmates were much more likely to have been abused only as children.

To put a human face on these data, read about the compelling case of Amanda Peterson, who was introduced to meth by her father and who became completely hooked on the drug:

> *Following the classic pattern of addiction, she ate or smoked more and more of the drug, gaining less and less effect.*
>
> *She willingly recounts the facts behind the drug charges and assault arrests that littered her teenage years. She speaks more reluctantly about an earlier incident, for which court papers listed her as "victim." Authorities referred to her then as "Jane Doe," because the 1998 crime was so awful. And after all, she was just a kid. In the "defendant" space, the court papers list a man's name. Peterson barely recognizes it, because she only knew him by his nickname, Satan.*
>
> *Satan threw drug parties at his house, and he let kids participate. When Peterson was wasted, he would have sex with her on a couch. Police found out about it, and they arrested him on charges of sex abuse and running a drug house. Peterson didn't understand, at first, what was wrong. She thought he loved her. She was thirteen. He was thirty-two. She sees the truth now. "He didn't love me," she said. "He was just a damned pedophile." (Leys, 2005, p. 2)*

This brief biography of one woman could be a composite drawn from all the stories of meth addiction. The drug-infested household, the predatory sexual abuse, the drug-induced fighting, the drug tolerance leading to demands for more extreme forms of drug ingestion—all are here.

An earlier study by SAMHSA (1997), *Substance Use among Women in the United States*, found the association between drug use and crime is stronger for women than for men, according to self reports. While about a third of the drug-using women reported committing any criminal activity during the past year, only around 5 to 6 percent of women not using drugs did so. Women who were heavy alcohol users had rates of criminal activity as high as those of comparable male drinkers; this included driving while intoxicated offenses. Adult women who used any illicit drugs in the past year were six times as likely as women who had not used any illicit drugs to have been arrested. In a comparison of their sample of more than 1,000 Texas female inmates, Mullings et al. (2002) found that about twice as many women with drug problems committed other crimes (theft, forgery, robbery, prostitution, etc.) in their lifetimes. One drug that may have involved theft but not prostitution was meth. In their survey of sixty-four female offenders in mandated treatment for meth, Strauss and Falkin (2001) found that the women typically had earned money through the dealing and manufacture of the drug and did not resort to prostitution.

More detailed information concerning drug use is available from the Arrestee Drug Abuse Monitoring (ADAM) program *Annual Report* (Taylor, Newton, and

Brownstein, 2003). ADAM conducts extensive interviews at sites throughout the United States and validates results with urinalysis tests.

A summary of their results shows that:

- Of the three drugs analyzed, cocaine was used most frequently followed by marijuana, meth, and the opiates;
- Meth was most prevalent in the western states, at almost half of users in Honolulu;
- Polydrug use was rare;
- Arrestees were 40 percent white, 39.7 percent black, and 4 percent Hispanic, and the rest were "other";
- About one-third had no high school diploma;
- One half of the women and around 18 percent of the women obtained marijuana and crack cocaine, respectively, through non-cash means (usually sex);
- Forty-two percent of the women were at risk of drug dependence.

The Meaning of the Statistics

Many different data sources establish a correlation between drug/alcohol use and other criminal offenses. But correlation does not mean causation. MacCoun, Kilmer, and Reuter (2003), adopting Goldstein's (1985) framework of drug-violence connections, offer a three-part classification scheme. This scheme posits that the connection is (1) psychopharmacological, (2) economic-compulsive, or (3) systemic (territorial fights over drug markets). These explanations can serve to explain the link with property crimes in the economic (stealing to support the habit or embezzlement related to gambling) category. With regard to the violence/drug use link, the psychopharmacological properties of some drugs—especially alcohol and stimulants such as meth and cocaine—may induce violence or bellicosity in certain individuals. As MacCoun, Kilmer, and Reuter explain, such substances can amplify the psychological and situational facilitations of aggression. A combination of suppression of normal inhibitions may lead to impulses that normally are controlled. At the same time, impaired cognitive functioning caused by the influence of the substance on the brain creates a situation ripe for some form of explosive behavior. For example, in a report on violence, suicide, and risky behavior, SAMHSA (2003) reveals a high rate of delinquent behaviors in girls under the influence of alcohol or other drugs. Fighting among girls at school or work, engagement in group-on-group fights, and stealing in older girls were behaviors closely associated with substance abuse. We now turn to a closer look at biological factors relevant to women's substance use.

Biological Factors

Before examining the alcohol/drug crime link, let us examine some of the gender differences in the effect on the body of alcohol/drug consumption. Starting with research on girls, we learn from the National Center on Addiction and Substance Abuse (CASA) at Columbia University (2003) studies that:

- Females have greater smoking-related lung damage than males;
- Females have greater susceptibility to alcohol-induced brain damage, cardiac problems, and liver disease than males;
- Females are more susceptible to Ecstasy-induced brain damage than males;
- Teenage girls are likelier than boys to be hospitalized due to the misuse of medications such as Tylenol, which affects the liver, and antidepressants.

Earlier studies on alcohol abuse from the National Institute on Alcohol Abuse and Alcoholism (NIAAA) (1999) show that, compared to men, women tend to:

- Have a much shorter interval between onset of drinking-related problems and entry into treatment;
- Experience a higher rate of physiological impairment earlier in their drinking careers;
- Become intoxicated after drinking smaller amounts of alcohol, even when compared to men of the same weight (this is due to a diminished activity of the primary enzyme involved in the metabolism of alcohol in the stomach);
- Have a much higher mortality rate from alcohol abuse, with increased death stemming from organ damage, especially of the liver, brain, and heart.

Holly Johnson (2004), a researcher for the Australian government, has delved into the difficult research question of the extent to which pharmaceutical qualities play a key role in criminal behavior in women. Her literature review, which is international in scope, is bolstered by extensive data from interviews with Australian women in the criminal justice system. Women's criminality is apt to be more drug involved than men's, as Johnson reminds us.

Biological effects on human behavior discussed by Johnson include being high, drunk, or craving for drugs at the time of the offense. The process of intoxication is clearly biological; the short-term effects of chemical substances on the brain, liver, and other parts of the body are seen in delayed (or speeded up) reflexes, slurred speech, inability to concentrate, flushed face, or dilated pupils of the eye, and so on. The impact of such a physiological state in combination with situational factors (such as provocation) can be a risk factor for crimes of violence. Johnson found, for example, that 58 percent of women were intoxicated by alcohol when they committed murder. In regard to property and driving offenses, intoxication increases the probability of getting caught.

A few choice descriptions provided by offenders in Johnson's sample are revealing:

> *Drugs, speed made me crazy. You live in an unreal space. I was quite psychotic when I did my armed robbery.*
>
> *Drugs give me courage and I think I can do anything, so I do crime.*

It made me feel good and happy, but my decisions between right and wrong were cloudy. (p. 5).

A second key biological factor emphasized by Johnson is the nature of addiction. The role of addiction is implicated in the motivation for crime—for example, committing burglary or engaging in prostitution to support a habit. Drug dependency was found in Johnson's sample to be highest among sex workers (at 84 percent) and individuals who committed property offenses (74 percent) and lowest for violent offenders (58 percent). The strikingly high dependency rate is no doubt related to the high proportions of aboriginal inmates in the Australian sample. In Australia, 34 percent of the female prison population is aborigine who are 2 percent of the total population (Yehia, 2003). Aboriginal inmates in Australia, like other indigenous populations in Canada and the United States, have a high alcoholism susceptibility and are imprisoned disproportionately to their numbers (Collins and McNair, 2003; van Wormer and Davis, 2003). Women of the Sioux tribe, for example, have drinking rates that match those of the men. Let us digress somewhat to look more closely at the chemistry of alcohol/drug craving and addiction and the particular susceptibility of girls and women to substance dependence. We start with the brain.

The Brain on Drugs

Thanks to advances in technology, namely the development of functional magnetic resonance imaging **(fMRI),** scientists can capture chemical images of the brain at work. They can also observe not only structures but also actual functions of the living brain. Although brain research is in its infancy, new knowledge about the role of **neurotransmitters,** the chemicals that carry messages between nerve cells, have captivated the interest of persons concerned with all forms of substance abuse and addiction. Researchers are now recording brain changes that occur as a person experiences a high or rush from the drug as well as the low associated with craving, as happens with cocaine. The pleasure circuits have been identified. Through the use of fMRI, alterations in the brain register as activity when craving is induced through various means such as showing the individual addict pictures of drug paraphernalia related to his or her addiction. Gamblers who play poker might be shown a deck of cards, for example. Neurotransmitters have been linked to normal emotions and also to mental disorders including substance dependence.

Cocaine's chief biological activity is in preventing the reabsorption of the neurotransmitter dopamine. **Dopamine** is the "feel good" transmitter that triggers a drug user's high. Too much dopamine causes the bizarre thoughts of schizophrenia, and too little is implicated in the tremors of Parkinson's disease. **Serotonin,** associated with sleep and low anxiety, is the neurotransmitter most closely linked with alcohol use. Decreased levels have been linked to depression, anxiety, and aggression.

The fact that addiction runs in families and has been shown to manifest itself disproportionately in the offspring of children put up for adoption who had alcoholic fathers provides some evidence of a hereditary component (Cloninger et al., 1989).

More recent research on brain structure has identified a genetic factor that may predispose young people to harmful drinking habits, as reported by NIAAA (2003). Researchers in the NIAAA study first determined which individuals had long or short versions of the serotonin transporter gene and found that those who carried two copies of the short version were more likely to report excessive drinking. Interestingly, it is also known that the short version is associated with higher levels of anxiety so the implications are that the calming effect of alcohol is an attraction by nature to certain individuals. We know also that alcohol and drug abuse over time depletes the brain of these natural feel-good chemicals. This is what addiction is all about—the compulsion to get back to feeling high or even, when tolerance sets in, to simply feeling good. The individual heavy drug user eventually loses the ability to feel pleasure normally.

Methamphetamine can affect lots of brain structures, but the ones it affects the most are those that contain the chemical dopamine. The reason for this is that the shape, size, and chemical structure of meth and dopamine are similar (NIDA, 2002). (View the photographs of brain injuries at http://nida.nih.com.) Because meth is a high-energy drug that reduces the need for sleep, many of its users began using in order to reduce feelings of exhaustion from the long hours of work necessary in today's competitive job market. Half of the users in a survey by Strauss and Falkin (2001) began using meth to lose weight. A depletion of dopamine following cocaine and meth use probably accounts for the binges, development of tolerance, craving, and the obsessive behavior characteristic of meth users.

Recent research on recovering meth addicts, summarized by Zickler (2004) of the National Institute of Drug Abuse (NIDA) in a small sample of men and women, shows some modest improvement in memory function after nine months of sobriety. Another part of the brain, that related to motivation, future planning, and ability to feel pleasure, however, showed no recovery after abstinence. This fact explains why a long period of in-patient treatment is needed. What we know about meth recovery from anecdotal reports is that a very long time is required for physiological recovery.

What do brain studies show about male/female differences in neurological damage caused by drug/alcohol use? With regard to alcohol abuse, women who drink to excess experience more and earlier brain damage and sooner than males who drink a comparable amount. The effect is a result of the kind of brain shrinkage associated with dementia. Tapert and colleagues (Tapert et al., 2001) found that alcohol-dependent women compared to non-alcoholics showed less activation in the brain areas that are needed for spatial tasks and mathematical calculations. Sohrabji (2003) confirmed this finding in NIAAA research on female susceptibility to brain damage.

New research shows that women process cocaine cues differently than men do (Whitten, 2004). As women listened to a script about cocaine, the blood flow in their brains was measured. In women as with men, the pleasure centers of the brain were activated. During this craving period, however, the brain study showed that part of the emotional response to the craving was inhibited. The significance of this difference requires further study; the findings could have important treatment implications because craving is a key factor in relapse.

Co-occurring Disorders

In the general population, women with substance use disorders are more likely to have mental disorders as compared to their male counterparts. The most common disorders in these women are post-traumatic stress disorder, depression, anxiety, and eating disorders (SAMHSA, 2005). Research indicates that many women who enter the criminal justice system not only have substance abuse problems but also accompanying mental disorders and HIV/AIDS. According to a report on the special needs of female prisoners published by the General Accounting Office (1999), 13 percent of female inmates in federal prisons and 24 percent in state prisons report having a mental disorder or having spent time in a mental hospital (compared to 7 percent and 16 percent of men). A study commissioned by the Canadian government and focused on mental health needs of female inmates reported that federally incarcerated women were three times as likely as men to have received mental health treatment in the community (Laishes, 2002). They were also three times more likely to suffer from depression. Self-mutilation was common among the women but not the men. Compared to community samples, women in the Canadian prison system are about twice as likely to have experienced childhood sexual abuse and two-and-a-half times more likely to have been physically abused as an adult.

Mental disorders are biological in their origins, genetically and constitutionally. Serious mental illnesses are believed to be caused by abnormality of brain chemistry; therefore they can be expected to respond to medication and often do. Evidence of a physical basis of mental disorders such as schizophrenia comes from neuroimaging of the brain, which reveals structural abnormalities. The new technologies also reveal the fact that drugs that block certain dopamine receptors reduce the symptoms of the disease (Ginsberg, Nackerud, and Larrison, 2004). It is a convention in correctional psychiatry to identify as serious mental illness only certain Axis I disorders of the *Diagnostic and Statistical Manual of Mental Disorders-IV-Text Revised* (DSM-IV-TR) (American Psychiatric Association [APA], 2000) such as bipolar disorder, major depression, and schizophrenia, and to limit mental health treatment to prisoners with these disorders only (Human Rights Watch, 2003).

A growing body of evidence from specialized scientific studies implicates common neurological pathways and abnormalities involved in addiction and a number of psychiatric disorders (Brady and Sinha, 2005). Bipolar (manic-depressive) disorder, for example, has a close association with chemical dependency. Friedman and colleagues (Friedman et al., 2005) collected criminal history data on dually diagnosed men and women. The majority of both the men and women in the sample of 132 reported that they had been charged with a crime, and half of those had been incarcerated. The authors concluded that the addition of substance abuse to bipolar disorder has a greater influence on criminal behavior in women than in men, especially when the drug used was cocaine. This research helps explain the overrepresentation of women with bipolar disorder in the corrections system.

In a study of women in prison, Teplin, Abram, and McClelland (1996) found that 56 percent of the women with lifetime substance abuse met the criteria for current post-traumatic stress disorder (PTSD). **PTSD** is listed in the *DSM-IV-TR* as a mental disorder. Whereas with schizophrenia, brain abnormality precedes the development of the disease, with PTSD the mental disorder itself leads to the changes in brain chemistry. The major symptoms of PTDS are denial of event, numbing, flashbacks, intrusive thoughts, guilt feelings, sleep disturbances, jumpiness, and preoccupation. Instead of a diagnosis of PTSD, correctional mental health staff more commonly give female offenders a diagnosis of borderline personality. This diagnosis, which is described in the *DSM* as a personality disorder characterized by volatile behavior is clearly a pejorative one; it is likely to be given to a woman who is considered too difficult for treatment, with the end result that her treatment needs are ignored (Human Rights Watch, 2003).

Neurobiologists, who are pioneering studies using brain imaging to learn how traumatic events are imprinted on the brain through altered brain chemistry, now know there is an organic basis to psychological trauma (Jackson, 2003). In other words, when people who have been victimized by a horrifying event or series of events, such as by rape or combat, experience trauma, the changes in brain chemistry may be long-lasting. These changes are often manifested in depression (probably related to the impact on serotonin levels in the brain). Reduced brain activity of dopamine, a naturally occurring substance that moderates feelings of pleasure, may contribute to obesity as well as to drug addiction. Mathias (2001) reports in *NIDA Notes* of a NIDA-funded study that found dopamine deficiencies in the brains of individuals who were compulsive overeaters. A high incidence of obesity is seen in female prison populations.

The Role of Early Childhood Sexual Abuse

Early childhood sex abuse is widely recognized to be a major factor in the later development of substance abuse problems (Laishes, 2002; Lapham, 2004/2005; Mullings, Marquart, and Hartley, 2003; van Wormer and Davis, 2003). Survivors of such extreme stress who now have depression or anxiety disorder are apt to suffer an abnormal stress response. One of the bridging constructs, in fact, between psychiatric and substance use disorders is the role of stress in the development of substance use disorders (and relapse) and other psychiatric disorders such as PTSD (Brady and Sinha, 2005). This link between trauma and excessive stress reactions was examined by Heim and colleagues (2000) in relation to child abuse.

Published in the *Journal of the American Medical Association*, this article is touted as the first human study to find persistent changes in stress reactivity in adult survivors of early trauma. A comparative study of forty-nine healthy women revealed detectable biochemical abnormalities in those who had been severely abused in childhood. In a laboratory situation women survivors were four times more likely than other women to develop excessive stress response to mild stimuli. Those who were abused and now have anxiety disorder or depression are six times more likely than other women to suffer an abnormal stress response. The significance of this study for our purposes is that it helps explain the drive to self-medicate due to their inability to cope with psychological stress, an inability that derived from early childhood trauma. (We know from animal studies that stress and alcohol consumption levels are highly correlated [Spear, 2001].)

Epidemiological studies report rates of co-occurrence of major depression with nicotine, alcohol, and illicit drug abuse ranging from 32 percent to 54 percent (Brady and Sinha, 2005). Individuals with major depression are more likely to develop substance use disorders, and individuals with substance use disorders are at greater risk for the development of major depression, compared to the general population. Because of the weakened stress response, the stage is set for future psychological problems, especially under conditions of repeated stress. PTSD occurs because of the impact of an extreme stress response on memory. The stress hormones such as cortisol act on the brain, creating a state of heightened alertness and supercharging the circuitry involved in memory formation (Cowley, 2003). Then, even years later, when confronted with stress in adulthood, the adult brain might regress to an infantile state. Fight/flight reactions to stress are common due to the power of the "body memory," as Basham and Miehls (2004) explain. Such memory is often triggered by sights, sounds, touch, or smells. (Recent news reports of extreme overreactions to such stimulus by soldiers recently home from Iraq are relevant here.)

Because memories run on chemicals, they can be altered by chemicals. In an experiment reported by Begley (2005), emergency room patients who were given beta blockers had subdued memories of extremely disturbing events compared to a control group.

These scientific findings concerning the trauma-stress link help explain the close interconnection between women's criminal behavior (often through a link with a drug-involved man) and an earlier history of abuse. Women who have been sexually abused are more likely to engage in behavior placing them at risk for HIV/AIDS infection through such practices as getting intoxicated, trading sex for drugs, and using shared needles in drug use injection (Mullings, Marquart, and Hartley, 2003). According to Mullings and colleagues the rate of HIV infection among female prisoners has increased by almost 90 percent compared to 28 percent for males. It appears that the high prevalence of HIV infections among female inmates is directly related to risky drug activities. The rate is now 3 percent for female inmates in state prisons compared to 1.9 percent for males. This is far higher than the rate for the population as a whole. Most of the inmates with HIV/AIDS are African American and Hispanic (BJS, 2004).

The HIV rate is higher among female than male inmates for a number of reasons (Lanier and Zaitzow, 2007). Women who smoke crack tend to have more sexual partners and are likelier to engage in prostitution than nondrug users. Incarcerated women are more likely than men to be serving time for drug offenses, especially for cocaine. Women who are sexually involved with long-term drug-using men further increase their susceptibility. The high rates of HIV/AIDS in the African American and Latino inner cities are reflected in the prison population.

As we take a closer look at the psychological pathway leading a girl or woman into the criminal justice system, keep in mind the findings from BJS (2000) surveys that nearly six in ten women in state prisons had experienced physical or sexual abuse in the past, that just over a third of imprisoned women had been abused by an intimate in the past, and just under a quarter reported prior abuse by a family member.

Psychological Factors

In this section we focus on victimization. We first look at the situations of women whose problems with the law were related at least in part to their personal background of childhood victimization. Then we consider situations of women whose involvement in the criminal justice system is as witness and victim—a victim of domestic violence, for example. In both types of cases our concern remains with the role of alcohol and other drugs in the victimization. For women, victimization and criminalization typically are intertwined.

Pathways to Crime

In women's lives the connection between addiction and crime is manifest both directly through drug-induced lawbreaking and indirectly through involvement in destructive relationships with people involved in the criminal underworld. Poverty compounds a woman's dependency on drug-abusing, often battering, men. The racial dimension is reflected in the fact that African American women are more likely than white or Latina women to be recruited to deviant street networks through domestic ties, whereas white and Latina women are more likely to be recruited into these networks through running away, drug use, or both—behaviors often associated with physical and sexual abuse in their families of origin (Farr, 2000). The typical pattern or **pathway to crime** is for the girl who runs away from a violent or sexually abusive family to join other runaways on the streets. Once there, she learns how to survive through various illegal means.

Mullings and colleagues (2003) conducted personal interviews with a sample of women prisoners in the Texas system. Their purpose was to study HIV sexual risks and HIV drug risk in terms of the independent variable, which was whether the woman had ever been sexually abused prior to age eighteen. The results echoed those reported elsewhere in the literature. The women who had been victimized in childhood were significantly younger at admission to prison, likely to be white, and from an unstable family background. Overall, the sexually abused groups experienced child neglect at greater frequency than did non-abused women. This fact, of course, explained in part how they became vulnerable to sexual exploitation. Trauma theory that suggests sexually abused girls suffer from low self-esteem and engage in high risk-taking behavior (Downs and Rindels, 2004) is given some support by these findings.

Compared to male offenders, female offenders have a disproportionately high rate of multiple victimization. Chesney-Lind and Pakso (2004) map out the pathway that would lead a girl—desperate to escape the sexual and physical abuse at home—to run away; seek solace in drugs and the company of drug users, gang members, and the like; and survive on the streets through prostitution. This pattern is highlighted in inner-city females for whom prostitution may serve as a means of survival in circumstances of extreme economic hardship. Belknap (2001) and Enos (2001) similarly stress the role of poverty and sexual and physical abuse in women who assist the men in the commission of crime.

Surveys of women in trouble with the law indicate that early childhood victimization—for example, sexual molestation—is highly correlated with later involvement in prostitution (Farley, 2004). Victimization during childhood is associated with feelings of distress and low self-esteem. To dull the pain, the woman may use drugs such as alcohol, cocaine, heroin, or methamphetamines. Sometimes the drugs are introduced to the woman by her boyfriend. Many female addicts report that their drug-using male partners initiated them into drug abuse; and once hooked up with an alcohol- or drug-dependent man, it is very hard for a recovering woman to maintain sobriety (NIDA, 1999).

Enos (2001), who gathered interview data based on fieldwork in a north-eastern women's prison, discusses paths to prison in terms of racial and ethnic differences. For white women, the most typical route to prison was the run-away-to-the-streets path. The white inmate mothers in Enos's study grew up in homes they found dysfunctional and fled as soon as they were able to, often becoming involved in drugs and crime through the influence of a boyfriend or male partner. Most lost contact with their families and were forced to rely on foster care for their children if there was no father in the picture. Looking back, the women characterized their parents as abusive. Sexual abuse was also part of the history, as reported by this inmate:

> My parents were really bad alcoholics. I spent most of my childhood in foster care. I got molested by one of my uncles and nobody wanted to hear about it. (p. 49)

Other white women in Enos's study, however, were from supportive middle-class backgrounds with limited exposure to street crime. While these women spoke highly of their normal upbringings, other white women linked their drug involvement to poor parenting and child neglect.

The pathways for African American women mostly involved introduction to the drug scene through relatives and domestic networks. When the women were arrested, family caretakers often were found to take care of their children if family resources were depleted. The African American women in the study had greater access to help from their mothers than did white women, but less access to help from husbands or boyfriends to care for their children. In the interviews, black women seldom connected their involvement in crime and drugs to bad parenting.

Latina women's paths to prison often exclusively involve drug charges. In Enos's sample, two of the women, recent immigrants, were serving long sentences for drug trafficking and had no prior involvement in the criminal justice system. Two others were serving time for drug-related property crimes. Their pathways to crime were through running away to the streets. In interviews, they attributed the lure of quick money through drug sales as a key factor. Most did not place blame on their parents. They were able to rely on family members, including the children's fathers, for child care.

Partner Violence

We now turn from the topic of pathways to crime to adulthood victimization, still focusing on the alcohol/drug connection. In 2001, there were about 588,490 incidents of partner violence; 1,247 women were killed by an intimate partner in 2000 (compared to 440 men) (BJS, 2003). Alcohol and other drugs consistently have been found to be a major factor in intimate-partner violence. A descriptive study of the types of violence against women and the associated use of alcohol and other drugs by the perpetrators reveals that physical abuse is significantly higher for women in cases of perpetrators who used drugs only in comparison to perpetrators who used alcohol only (Willson et al., 2000). That women who are drug addicted are highly susceptible to partner violence is revealed in a study of heroin-addicted women in methadone maintenance (methadone is a synthetic substitute for heroin that can be legally prescribed by specially qualified physicians). Research at the National Center of Addiction and Substance Abuse at Columbia University (CASA) (1996) found that 70 percent of the women in treatment with methadone reported that they had been beaten. Family violence was associated with alcohol abuse and the use of all other drugs.

The extent of family violence associated with methamphetamine use, as mentioned previously, is a reality highlighted in the media nationwide. A search of www.google.com (recent news for the preceding month) revealed reports from small-town newspapers of a tremendous upsurge in domestic violence related to meth. For example, Harris (2005), a British journalist who visited a small town in Tennessee, wrote of the stranglehold that meth has taken on rural America. The impact he found was substantial as evidenced in the sixty recent "meth orphans" from Cumberland County, in the increase in sexual abuse associated with a drug that gives sex drives a powerful boost, and in the 500 percent increase in domestic violence in this one small county. Significantly, as reported in the article, jails that used to have minority majorities now have white majorities inasmuch as meth is the drug of choice among rural whites. Because women are more likely to use meth than other illegal drugs (many start using it for weight loss), child neglect and abuse are a real part of the scenario (Knickerbocker, 2005).

An earlier scholarly study that examined the history of abuse and violence in more than 1,000 meth users (Cohen et al., 2003) provides validation to the media accounts. In the research on men and women in treatment for meth addiction, the reporting of violence was extensive, with 80 percent of women reporting partner violence. Experiences of early-life violence were commonly recounted as well. Men also experienced violence, more commonly from friends and acquaintances.

The long-term consequences of psychological abuse can include anger and hostility toward others. In their review of the literature, Mullings and colleagues (2003) found "distrust of authority and adults, alienation from others, a negative self-view, substance abuse (for self-medication), emotional volatility (either over-reacting or numb approach to life), inappropriate use of sex and sexuality, and distant or dysfunctional family relationships" (p. 77). The cycle of victimization, substance abuse, unhealthy relationships and victimization goes round and round.

Policies, programs, and services need to respond specifically to women's unique pathways in and out of crime and to the contexts of their lives that support criminal behavior (Bloom, Owen, and Covington, 2004). Instead, public policy through the so-called war on drugs has punished women as victimizers with little consideration of their personal histories of victimization. Female offenders' ties to their children, as Bloom and Chesney-Lind (2007) point out, are often compromised in harsh zero-tolerance policies. Such policies are discussed in the following section under the social aspects of women's involvement in drug/alcohol abuse and dependence.

Social/Societal Factors

We are talking here of responses to women's drug and alcohol use by the criminal justice system. Violence and victimization, as Mullings and colleagues (2003) indicate, carry over into the adult lives of women offenders as they enter the criminal justice system. Once criminalized, women are re-victimized by the state through coercive laws and their "one-size-fits-all" enforcement. Because their involvement with drug dealing, if this is their charge, was typically at a low level with limited involvement with other dealers, their cooperation with prosecutors (in turning in others) is necessarily limited. There may be threats of abuse from a crime partner, or as often happens, the woman may be charged with conspiracy to deliver drugs when her partner or spouse turns her in as the only way he has to reduce his own sentence. This is how the war on drugs is being played out, with the strongest impact inflicted on the poor and vulnerable.

The treatment of substance abuse as a criminal justice rather than a public health problem has led to a situation in which incarceration, instead of a policy of last resort, has become the first-order response for men and women both. Women alcoholics and drug users, especially when they are mothers, minority, and poor, are highly stigmatized in the system. Those who are caught using street-level drugs, and, increasingly, meth, are demonized in ways tied to their drug of choice. Because chivalry (the view that women, especially white women, are weak and need to be protected) was a casualty, as well it should have been, of the women's movement, the judicial system seems to have gone in the opposite direction, and no longer takes into account situational factors related to gender. The lack of attention to the reality of the lives of many women brought before the court of law on drug charges is a part of what Chesney-Lind and Pollack (1994) termed "equality with a vengeance" (see Chapter 1). Gender-neutral (treating men and women the same) laws and standardized treatment now predominate. Policies and procedures developed to subdue potentially violent and highly dangerous male offenders were, in response to gender-equality laws, thrust on women as well. The very architecture of women's prisons was redesigned to stress security over livability. The situation that comes to mind are the reports throughout the correctional system of women forced to give birth in handcuffs and, until the last minute, leg shackles. These facts are explored in more depth in Chapter 6.

Central to understanding the creation of the sentencing guidelines for crimes involving crack cocaine—the cheaper smoked alternative to powder cocaine—are the roles of the media and racism in constructing and presenting the problem of crack. The media focused on three general themes: the claim that crack was more addictive than powder cocaine and a cause of such problems as "crack babies" and exchange of sex for drugs; the strong link to the violent crime world of inner-city gangs; and the low cost and ready supply of the drug. In her content analysis of coverage by the three major TV networks from 1983 to 1994, Humphries (1998) revealed the extremely negative and racially charged image assigned to poor black mothers who had used crack. Although the crack epidemic is over and the media hype has faded, the legacy is still with us, evident in our prisons and in the continuing enforcement of mandatory minimum laws.

In a surprise development, in 2005 the U.S. Supreme Court struck down a part of the mandatory laws to make them advisory but no longer binding on judges. According to the counsel for the Families against Mandatory Minimums Foundation (FAMM Foundation, 2005), however, defendants still have little protection when facing harsh sentencing judges. Time will tell what the impact of the decision will be.

The war on drugs is considered one of the most serious obstacles to achieving racial justice in the United States and internationally. This fact was argued in a petition signed by more than one hundred U.S. civil rights and religious leaders and presented to the U.N. World Conference against Racism. The group cited statistics showing that African Americans constitute 57 percent of the drug offenders in U.S. prisons and Latinos account for 22 percent ("Petition Asks U.N. Racism Conference to Take Up U.S. War on Drugs," 2001).

Black and Latina women started being herded into prison following the passage of the 1986 and 1988 Anti-Drug Abuse Acts, which established harsh mandatory-minimum sentencing guidelines targeting crack cocaine. This is the drug associated in the public mind with inner-city crime. The war on drugs, as stated previously, emerged as a war on minority and poor women, and it is still packing nonviolent women into prison at a record-breaking rate. The 100-to-1 ratio in punishment for crack cocaine compared to powder cocaine has been considered racist and classist by most observers. One of the results of this federal law, which was modeled at the state level, was that the number of black women incarcerated for drug offenses increased 828 percent between 1986 and 1991 (Bush-Baskette, 1998). This increase was more than three times that of white women.

The BJS (2000) report on women offenders provides further evidence of racism ingrained in the system. While nearly two-thirds of women under probation supervision are white, nearly two-thirds of those confined in local jails and prisons are minority.

The interplay of race, class, and gender is at its most pronounced in the prosecution of drug-addicted mothers. Under the rationale of protecting the fetus, poor black, drug-addicted mothers are being hauled into court. This is part of an alarming trend toward greater state intervention into the lives of pregnant women. Poor women of color are the primary targets of government control; they are the least likely to obtain adequate prenatal care, yet the most vulnerable to government monitoring and the least able to conform to the white middle-class standard of motherhood. The prosecution of drug-addicted mothers thus becomes more than an issue of anti-female backlash. Poor black women have been selected for punishment as a result of an inseparable combination of their gender, race, and economic status.

Punishment of Pregnant Drug Addicts

The media hype over "crack babies" that appeared in the early 1990s, later found to be scientifically untenable (Sagatun-Edwards, 2007), was embodied into law due to a landmark case, *Whitner v. South Carolina*, which became law in 1997. This case upheld the prosecution of an African American woman who ingested crack cocaine during the third trimester of her pregnancy. After the baby was found to have cocaine in his bloodstream, the mother was prosecuted under child-abuse and endangerment statutes. On appeal, the South Carolina Supreme Court upheld the conviction based on laws recognizing a viable (defined as past twenty-four weeks of gestation) fetus as a person for the purpose of homicide laws and wrongful death statutes. The implications of the South Carolina decision are far-reaching (Sagatun-Edwards, 2007). Maternal substance abuse during pregnancy has in effect been outlawed, and some women have found themselves shackled to their hospital beds immediately after giving birth.

As of 2004, hundreds of women have been arrested nationwide for their addictive behavior while pregnant (Paltrow, 2004). Many more have lost custody of their children because some states now consider "child neglect" to include prenatal exposure to controlled substances. Mandatory reporting of cases of suspected child abuse and neglect involving drug use are now increasingly common in many states. Since drug testing occurs only in publicly funded health care facilities, such laws, needless to say, fall chiefly on the poor and minority women. There has been no effort to use a newborn's toxicology screen to check for the role of sperm (damaged by drug use) in causing birth defects.

Attorney Lynn Paltrow (2004) who specializes in laws that punish pregnant women for potential harm to the fetus brings to our attention the significance of a new law passed and signed by President Bush in 2004—the Unborn Victims of Violence Act. This law, which was a product of the anti-abortion movement, makes it a crime to cause harm to a "child in utero." More than thirty states have similar laws on the books. Paradoxically, as Paltrow indicates, this federal law does not make it a federal crime to physically attack pregnant women, yet homicide is the number-one killer of pregnant women.

The media hyperbole that played into the crackdown on mothers who used crack while pregnant is now being directed toward meth. In response to the barrage of stories that appeared in the media concerning an epidemic of birth defects caused by meth use in pregnant women, over ninety leading doctors, scientists, and treatment specialists released a public letter calling on the media to stop the use of terms such as "meth babies" (Lewis, 2005). The use of such terms, they said, harms the children to which they are applied and lowers expectations for their academic success and is without scientific basis. The suggestion that treatment will not work for people dependent upon meth, particularly mothers, also lacks any scientific basis. The scientists also fault news reports and policymakers for not consulting experts to obtain information about the effects of prenatal exposure and about the efficacy of treatment. They cite their experience with almost twenty years of research on the chemically related drug cocaine, that "has not identified a recognizable condition, syndrome disorder that should be termed 'crack baby' nor found the degree of harm reported in the media and then used to justify numerous punitive legislative proposals" (p. 2).

Both pregnancy and drug "epidemics" are issues ripe for government exploitation, a way of diverting the people's attention away from the major, structural problems onto issues of "morality" of individuals. Drug wars (whether inner-city blacks and Latinos associated with crack cocaine or poor rural whites involved in meth production) today make excellent scapegoats, and the international war on drugs can be justified on the basis of images of people strung out on drugs. The increase in the prison population and huge expenditures on the prison industrial complex take billions of dollars that otherwise could be spent on housing, health care, and substance abuse treatment on demand.

Treatment Issues

As previously indicated, most of the women incarcerated in the United States are there for drug-related crimes, and most of them have histories of serious long-term substance abuse problems in conjunction with mental health concerns. The latter is related to the fact that prisons have become the dumping grounds for persons with mental illness. Not surprisingly, a review of the literature suggests that most of the women who are released from jail or prison are likely to return to the same difficult conditions that played into their legal problems in the first place (Richie, 2004). When unaccustomed child care responsibilities of children who have their own serious problems and resentments are thrust upon them and with few financial resources to provide proper care, the challenges can be tremendous.

The relapse and recidivism risks are major public health problems that echo the original risks that were the cause of grief to the women and their families in the first place. We are referring to the lack of treatment availability for women (and the men in their lives) due to the lack of nationalized health care in this country. The majority of the women arrestees with drug abuse violations studied in the government's ADAM annual report (Taylor, Newton, and Brownstein, 2003) did not have health care coverage. In their study of the link between the effectiveness of treatment in reducing crime, SAMHSA (1999b) found that at least one potential victim is spared each time that substance abuse treatment is successful. Yet for arrested drug users in many states, there are only a small number of paid-for treatment slots available. Within the prison system very little in the way of professional treatment is provided, this despite the fact that studies show that for every dollar spent per inmate on such treatment, $10 would be saved, a calculation based on the reduction in crime and child welfare costs associated with continued drug use (SAMHSA, 1999b).

Empirical evidence indicates that treatment for drug-abusing women is effective and that its effectiveness is not diminished when women offenders are coerced into treatment by the criminal justice system as a condition of probation or parole (Springer, McNeece, and Arnold, 2003). Within prison walls, women are usually eager for services, and there may be a waiting list to attend. The benefits of group treatment within the prison setting are that the members are eager for an outsider to talk to, absences are rare, and the women often have an extended period of sobriety. On the negative side, there is no family or community involvement, nor is there a chance for women to become independently resourceful. Moreover, there is no testing ground for inmates to learn to resist temptation—there is little or no temptation to resist. The outpatient setting is just the opposite in terms of advantages and disadvantages: clients relapse and disappear, and they may resent being forced to attend when they have pressing family and work demands to attend to. Their support system may still be intact, however, and family members' involvement in the program enhances the addict's chances of recovery. Referral to nearby resources, such as community treatment and self-help groups, can reinforce social skills learned in treatment.

Many prisons (and some jails) subcontract out with substance abuse treatment centers for the provision of counseling services. This approach provides the counseling staff with more professional freedom than would otherwise be the case if their first loyalty were to the correctional authorities. In addition, confidentiality is better maintained by having practitioners answer to their own agencies, not to the correctional system. In any case, inmates—so in need of a friendly professional to talk to, and usually with time on their hands—often are highly motivated for treatment, and they welcome the individual attention to their needs. Mullings and colleagues (2003) agree. Additionally, they make the point that women who were abused as children may require prison-based interventions to reduce their HIV risk and other risk-taking behaviors. But, as such research as that surveyed in Kassebaum (1999) shows, for treatment to be effective in the long term, adequate supervision must be provided to ex-inmates who were abusing substances prior to their arrest. Therefore, extensive services are needed to help a woman during the tough transitional period to the community as she begins to seek work and housing and to regain custody of her children.

Intensive psychological treatment is required for the combination of mental disorders that co-occur with the craving for alcohol and other drugs. Within prisons, substance abuse and psychiatric services tend, as on the outside, to be separate. And yet, inasmuch as we know from brain studies that these disorders co-occur, and often have a common origin in brain chemistry, integrated treatment is best.

The treatment program at Mitchellville women's prison in Iowa is immensely popular with meth addicts, but the waiting list is extremely long. Read Box 5.1 for a glimpse at a successful intensive treatment program. Note the comment by one inmate: "It's really sad that you have to come to prison to get into this kind of program."

BOX 5.1
Addicts Battle Back

The brain damage it causes makes meth hard to kick. But success rates are rising, and long-term recovery prospects are looking better.
—by Tony Leys, *Des Moines Register* staff writer

Inside the razor-wire fences and brick walls of the Mitchellville women's prison, forty inmates sit in a circle, clapping, stomping and singing their way into a new day.

". . . A group of women living right," one of them chants.

"A GROUP OF WOMEN LIVING RIGHT," the rest respond. "That's the way we live our lives."

"THAT'S THE WAY WE LIVE OUR LIVES."

The prisoners are enrolled in an intensive treatment program for addictions. More than half of them were hooked on meth, which led to the crimes that brought them to prison.

The room is full of examples of how difficult the struggle can be. Doctors say meth is even tougher to kick than most other drugs, because it causes such profound damage to the brain. Treatment methods are improving, and new research increases hope that the brains of nearly all addicts can heal over time. But the biggest initial hurdle is that many people trying to recover can't think straight enough to succeed without intense help.

Few of the women here know the scientific details, but they can describe the results. Many went through treatment for a few weeks on the outside, only to return to the pipe or needle. They say being clean left them miserable beyond description. The drug was the only thing that made them feel even close to normal.

Here, they spend at least nine months in the program, constantly surrounded by other women in treatment. They live together in a big, open area. They eat together, work together, take counseling together. They praise each other for becoming more confident and vocal. They criticize each other for slipping back into the anger and self-pity that helped bring them here. They share wishes for strength, which they will need when they return to Iowa neighborhoods riddled with meth.

"It's really sad that you have to come to prison to get into this kind of program," says Rikki Thornton of Des Moines, a thirty-one-year-old serving time for drug trafficking. Thornton has completed the program and now mentors other participants. She acknowledges that few of them would have volunteered for

(continued)

BOX 5.1 Continued

the intensely controlled treatment, even if it had been offered to them before they were arrested.

That fact fits with the reality of the addiction. Counselors say meth users rarely come in for treatment unless they're forced to do so.

Alcoholics and people hooked on many other kinds of drugs are more likely to seek help when they see their habits threatening their marriages, jobs, or children, says John Mathias, who helps run Des Moines' Bridges of Iowa center. Meth quickly strips away such concerns.

"All you want to do is crank up and sleep, crank up and sleep, crank up and sleep," he says. "Nothing else matters."

Iowa's jails and prisons hold plenty of people who have gone back to meth after undergoing treatment on the outside. The successes are plentiful, too, but they're nearly invisible.

A northern Iowa woman explains why. The thirty-eight-year-old mother of four knows that many residents of her hometown are trying to beat the habit, as she did. She would like to step into the spotlight as an example of a person who is making it. She wishes that meth addiction could lose some of its devastating stigma, the way related problems have.

"I know how people are when someone goes into treatment for alcoholism. Everyone thinks they're the greatest for doing it," she says. "But for meth, I don't know. . . ."

Michael Edens is an exception. He will tell you exactly how meth grabbed him, and how he's managing to stay away from it. Edens will only hint at his past during the addiction-information sessions he holds in an Ames conference room. If you're the pony-tailed teenage boy, the college-age guy in the Budweiser T-shirt, the young woman with the squawking toddler son, you've probably come to his class because your probation officer told you to. You don't want to hear why the muscular young man in front of you became an

addictions counselor. So this is what he'll tell you: "Don't think addicts could quit taking drugs if they simply had more willpower."

Scientists know that abuse of alcohol or other drugs damages people's brains, he says, leaving them with an overpowering urge to get more. He poses a challenge to anyone who believes addicts can simply make themselves stop: Take an entire box of Ex-Lax, he says, then tell yourself that you simply won't let the powerful laxative affect you.

"I'm here to tell you," Edens says, "once that chemical change happens in your body, you're going to need to go to the bathroom. I don't care how much willpower you've got."

Edens shows a video, "The Hijacked Brain," explaining the science of addiction. The class members learn how drugs cause brain cells to release huge amounts of dopamine, a chemical that causes pleasurable feelings. They learn how the brain adapts to the drug use by decreasing dopamine production. That leaves addicts feeling dreadful when they're sober.

After a while, they need the drugs just to feel halfway normal. The cycle continues, causing insatiable cravings for the drugs, even though they no longer deliver the euphoria that first pulled in the users.

If you ask him outside the class, Edens will talk about how he first tried meth as a thirteen-year-old in California. He didn't really want to, he says, but he had a crush on the girl who offered it to him, and he didn't want to disappoint her. He describes how the drug gave him energy, helped him finish his homework, and allowed him to open up to other people. By fifteen, he'd become nothing but trouble, and his family sent him to a strict school for boys. As soon as he got out, he went back to tweaking. The habit wound up costing him a marriage and custody of his son. It also led to a stint in prison. "I said, 'Wild horses couldn't drag me back to meth,'" he says.

His father, who lived in Iowa, invited him to move here to make a new start. Edens

(continued)

recalls being stunned at how many Iowans knew how to make meth using anhydrous ammonia, an easily stolen farm chemical. For two years, he resisted the temptation to partake. Then he drank a liter of Black Velvet whiskey at a party one night, and suddenly it didn't seem like such a bad idea to try some of the meth people were passing around.

Eight weeks later, totally hooked again, he was arrested at a farmers co-op, trying to steal anhydrous ammonia. He was too messed up to figure out how to flee. He spent five months in jail, then went to a halfway house and started going to treatment sessions. "I was so ready to do something different," he says. "I swore I was not going to use meth again."

That was three years ago, and he's kept his promise. He's trained as a counselor and is helping others get clean. He says people can succeed, but they must pay a steep price. By the time they quit, many have nothing positive left in their lives. They're broke, unemployed, and friendless. The reality compounds the chemical depression caused by the drug's aftermath. "I learned to expect life to be crappy for the next few months."

Researchers believe that if they could reduce the number of months recovering meth addicts feel crappy, they could greatly increase the chances of success. Des Moines is one of five sites nationally for a study on whether medications could help the brain heal faster and ease the cravings and depression that drive people back to drug use. Dr. Richard Rawson, a California psychologist overseeing the study, is optimistic. Doctors had feared that meth caused permanent devastation inside brain cells, he says. But recent studies on monkeys show that many of the cells repair themselves eventually. Relatively little research has been done on possible medications, because drug manufacturers don't foresee potential profits from helping meth addicts.

"There is not going to be a Xanax or a Prozac or a Viagra for drug abuse," Rawson says. But he predicts at least some benefit from the medications his program is testing— including some already used by people trying to quit smoking cigarettes. A small percentage of meth users suffer permanent psychosis, similar to schizophrenia patients. Years after they stop using the drug, they still hear voices in their heads, and they're paralyzed by feelings of paranoia.

"It's clear that they've done something to their brains that's not going to get better. Those are the most heart-wrenching cases," says Rawson, who works at the University of California-Los Angeles.

Most addicts can recover, however. One key is that they stay away from all addictive drugs—including alcohol. Even for patients who never had serious drinking problems, the odds of relapsing into meth use quintuple if they resume any alcohol use, Rawson says. "That's one of the few things we can tell you for sure."

Another key is to find a treatment program specializing in meth addicts. Older programs designed mainly for alcoholics aren't nearly as effective, he says. Most programs keep patients overnight for the first few days, then help them rebuild their lives in the community. To be effective, treatment must be done several times a week for many months, he says. "You need to be taught how not to use methamphetamine today. Then you need to be taught how not to use it tomorrow."

Dr. Dennis Weis, who runs one of Des Moines' largest treatment programs, says people trying to kick meth have to overcome daunting hurdles. "Rehabilitation" often is an irrelevant concept. The word implies that patients used to have decent lives, which they hope to resume.

Many patients at the Powell Chemical Dependency Center grew up around meth-using parents or even grandparents. They've

(continued)

BOX **5.1** Continued

never known anything else. They've never succeeded at school, worked steady jobs, or maintained healthy friendships.

Weis oversees the Des Moines portion of Rawson's medication study. He is optimistic about the prospects of new medications, and he sees benefits from using current antidepressant drugs with some patients. Those medicines are no cure-all, he says, and they shouldn't be taken until a person is totally off meth. "Taking antidepressants while you're on meth is like building a sand castle with a teaspoon while the waves keep crashing in."

Counselors also must deal with an unusual twist to the addiction: Many patients have become obsessed with making and selling the drug. It fits well with the compulsive behavior meth induces, and it's often one of the only things they've ever succeeded in. The production also gives them a sense of power over other addicts. The temptations will be pervasive throughout their lives. Every time they walk through a store and see batteries, cold medicine, or drain cleaner, they'll be reminded of how easy it was to make money, impress others, and get high.

Even with those complications, Weis and his colleagues stress that success is increasingly possible. Early in the meth epidemic, success rates commonly were reported at 15 percent. Nowadays, carefully tailored programs are seeing 40 percent of their patients stay sober for at least a year, Weis says. Those numbers should continue to climb, and many people who fail at first go on to find success after a second or third try. Society doesn't give up on people who struggle to recover from cancer, heart attacks, or diabetes, counselors say, and it shouldn't give up on people who relapse into addiction. The road to sobriety will always be hard, but never impossible, Weis says. "You don't just walk into treatment and suddenly you're drug-free for life."

Critical Thinking Questions: Consider the statement in this reading that recovery is not about willpower in light of the women meth addicts in prison. How can treatment take into account brain studies on addiction?

Source: Des Moines Register, November 26, 2003. Reprinted with permission of the *Des Moines Register.*

A 172-page report from the U.S. Department of Health and Human Services written by Kassebaum (1999) documents the results of several demonstration programs funded by the Center for Substance Abuse Treatment to address the complex needs of drug-dependent female offenders. These model programs provide intensive all-female in-house therapy geared toward meeting women's special needs with regard to their backgrounds of childhood and partner victimization, low self-esteem and shame, and parenting skills. Examples of exemplary programs described in this research document are: The Forever Free Program at the women's prison at Frontera, California; the six-month pre-release Focus Program at Salem, Oregon; and the Stepping Out in-custody treatment project, with a strong after-care component, at San Diego, California. To this end, the programs modified the male-model, confrontational therapeutic community into a nurturing, family-like setting, and adapted the traditional twelve-step model to suit the needs of women who already felt powerless over most aspects of their lives. In one program, official ceremonies to honor women clients are affirming events to celebrate graduation and follow-up achievements, which serve to bring the community together as a bonding experience.

Preliminary evaluation studies of client retention and abstinence following treatment, as summarized in the Kassebaum report, reveal that women do well only if released from custodial facilities to residential centers for a transitional period, preferably for over five months. Themes common to successful programs are: the provision of a holistic continuum of care built on extensive networking referring women for job placement and sober-living houses (e.g. San Diego County); the avoidance of a move from a woman-specific center (women in Delaware showed that they were not ready for this abrupt transition); continuity in treatment approach so that clients don't get conflicting messages; residential care for pregnant and parenting women and their children; and the presence of a care manager to continue monitoring the women to help keep them from drifting into old patterns.

What we can learn from the compilation of research offered in the Kassebaum document is the key role of a case management system in providing adequate supervision of women who have graduated from treatment to assist them with referrals and track their progress. Case managers need to be able to serve as a linkage among criminal justice, child welfare, and substance abuse agencies. The cost savings to their communities of innovative treatment programs include prevention of the spread of HIV/AIDS and fetal alcohol syndrome, tremendous savings in welfare and foster care costs, and a significant reduction in crime rates.

Stephanie Covington (1999) produced a broad-based treatment curriculum, *Helping Women Recover*, in a special edition for female offenders who are recovering from substance abuse and psychological trauma. This curriculum is widely used in correctional settings and is eclectic in design.

The program that treated Amanda Petersen, the meth addict whose story was described earlier in the chapter, the Sisters Together Achieving Recovery program, is housed in a separate building; treatment lasts for nine months on average. Thanks to a large grant from the federal government each counselor can spend a great deal of time with the fifteen or fewer inmates assigned to her. Fewer than 10 percent of the 220 graduates have been rearrested.

Promising Developments

Increasingly, research is highlighting the superiority of substance abuse programs delivered in the community over those conducted in institutional settings (Weekes, 1997).

Drug Courts and Community Treatment

One of the most promising developments in recent years is the **drug court,** an alternative to prison that was first launched in Florida. These new courts, which divert nonviolent drug offenders from the prison system into treatment, prove that such programs are cost-effective to society and still allow people to obtain treatment and maintain their work and family roles (Springer, McNeece, and Arnold,

2003). Today there are close to 1,621 drug courts across the states. For women, their effectiveness is enhanced because of the continuum of services provided and the close partnerships linking community-based organizations. Federally funded drug courts have been set up in Kentucky, Hawaii, and elsewhere especially to deal with the meth crisis. Intensive case management services are provided, mental health disorders are treated simultaneously with drug treatment, and medication is prescribed where appropriate (Huddleston, 2005). The results have been very favorable both for the offender and the community.

Because many women offenders are mothers (BJS, 2000), correctional programs delivered in the community are particularly important for women who have young children. Community centers that house mothers together with their children are especially valuable, as they can provide counselors who model appropriate parenting skills as issues arise spontaneously in the common living situation. Knowing that jail time awaits them if they begin abusing drugs again can offer women a strong incentive to change. By the same token, without help and the educational and vocational skills necessary to survive on their own, some women seem to deliberately get themselves in trouble in order to return to the safety of the prison environment.

Empowerment and Gender-Responsive Approaches

A gendered policy approach calls for a new vision for the criminal justice system, one that recognizes the behavioral and social differences between female and male offenders that have specific implications for **gender-responsive policy** and practice (Bloom, Owen, and Covington, 2004). Gender-responsive policy provides effective interventions that address the intersecting issues of substance abuse, trauma, mental health, and economic oppression, as Bloom and colleagues indicate. A focus on women's relationships with their family members is paramount as well.

In light of the stigmatizing impact of women's experiences in the criminal justice system, and the relationship between low self-esteem and chemical dependency in the first place, empowerment and consciousness-raising approaches are vital. Programs that use such approaches describe women's success as being linked to their ability to shift their point of view from self-blame to self-responsibility for one's family and neighborhood (Richie, 2004). Since much of consciousness-raising helps women develop critical insight into the structural influences on their lives, as Richie suggests, it is perhaps understandable that prison systems do not very often endorse such programs. Instead, the favored approach, one that was designed for work with male psychopaths, is built around correcting inmates' errors in thinking. The goal of what is appropriately termed a moral-cognitive approach is to encourage inmates' awareness of how they have hurt the people in their lives; the purpose is to arouse feelings of guilt and self-disgust. In Yochelson and Samenow's (1976) influential work on "the criminal personality," narcissism or self-centeredness is taken as the central theme of the criminal's psychological makeup. Environmental factors and structural inequalities are considered irrelevant in the "criminal mind" formulation (Pollack, 2005). Correctional Service of

Canada does not use the psychopathology or antisocial personality diagnosis for women, seeing it as irrelevant to the lives of women (Laishes, 2002). Pollack (2004) cautions that individualizing discourses from psychiatry often dilute a structural analysis. Women's mental health needs, she further argues, should be addressed within a wider social context. Pollack is especially critical of the borderline personality disorder diagnosis, a psychiatric diagnosis given disproportionately to women thought to be manipulative and angry. Models of this sort, argues Pollack, are congruent with notions of criminalized women and consistent with the present conservative political climate. Unfortunately, they encourage women to internalize their oppression rather than to legitimately protest the system.

We present this description of these gender-neutral (as opposed to gender-responsive) frameworks that dominate the substance abuse treatment for offenders as a sharp contrast with what is needed to meet the female offenders' special needs. Key elements of an empowerment gender-specific counseling perspective are: a focus on dialogue and relationships; consciousness-raising to recognize one's own power to change things; motivational work to enhance motivation for change; feeling work to promote healing from earlier victimization; and the instilling of hope (see van Wormer, 2001). Because empowerment methods initially were developed to address the needs and conditions of women and people of color (Gutiérrez, Parsons, and Cox, 1997), this kind of practice has always centered on the experiences of oppressed populations.

Summary

In this chapter, we have examined the key role that biological and psychological aspects of addiction play in women's criminality. Emphasis was placed on the brain and the role of the neurotransmitters, serotonin, and dopamine, both in substance dependency and in one's susceptibility to the development of mental disorders. New developments in neurobiology show the extent to which the brain on drugs is an injured brain; a long period of abstinence may be required before the brain can regenerate itself and healing takes place. The length of treatment needs to parallel the length of time it takes for the "feel-good" brain chemicals to be replenished. This chapter reviewed recent literature on brain and other biologically-based research to help show gender differences in alcohol/drug users' physiological responses to the chemicals they consume.

The psychology of substance use differs by gender as well. Women in the criminal justice system come into the system in ways different from those of men. This is due, in a large part, to a background of early and late victimization as a key factor in the female pathway into drug-related crime. The pathway to crime for a girl or woman, therefore, can be seen to have biological, psychological, and social roots. Addictive or depressive tendencies, magnified by early childhood sexual or physical abuse, and leading to affiliations with abusive and lawbreaking companions—this is the typical pattern. Serious problems related to poverty and perceived lack of opportunity set the stage for the girl or woman's entry into homelessness, unemployment, drug use, fraud, gang life, and prostitution. Drugs are a part of a relationship network, a part of their lifestyle shared with boyfriends and others in their company. Because racism and poverty often go hand in hand, girls from poor, inner-city backgrounds are forced to deal early, and on a regular basis, with problems of abuse, drugs, childhood pregnancy, and rough treatment by the authorities. The intersection of gender, race, and class is thus highly evident in female crime, both in regard to the form that the crime takes and the punishment meted out. The configuration is changed only somewhat with the influx of meth addicts into the system and a shift in media attention from crack cocaine to meth as the most frightening drug on the market.

Within the correctional system, a "one size fits all" philosophy operates to the extent that women's particular circumstances, if they exist, are rarely taken into account. There is little allowance, for example, for the kind of specialized health care needs that accrue to reproduction. Accordingly, the situation of women delivering babies while tied to the bed and in handcuffs has been the logical result. Not only are pregnant inmates mistreated under rules meant for men, but specialized laws are directed at women's reproductive rights: The prosecution of addicts who are pregnant or who have given birth to drug-affected babies is another repressive side effect of the war on drugs.

Ignored by the media is the conundrum of female crime and its relation to social and personal victimization. Virtually absent from the lurid media crime accounts is any serious attempt to connect the dots between the myriad variables involving race, poverty, mental disorders, especially PTSD and mood disorders, and the unhealthy sexual relationships often associated with the heavy drinking and/or other drug use.

Sadly, treatment opportunities often come too late to spare the drug user from family breakups. Much of the substance abuse treatment that women offenders are receiving for addiction problems is taking place through the criminal justice system, offered in highly punitive settings behind prison walls. Yet even in the disempowering environment of prison, effective counseling programs can help women learn healthier ways of coping than using drugs or getting entangled in destructive relationships. To prepare women to make a successful transition into the community and to resume their parenting duties and work roles, halfway houses with professional supervision can be an invaluable aid.

Gender-specific rather than gender-neutral is empowering because it reflects an understanding of the realities of women's lives and their unique needs. Clearly it costs far less money to treat a woman offender for addiction than to incarcerate her. The cost savings of innovative treatment programs are incalculable; they include prevention of the spread of HIV/AIDS and fetal alcohol syndrome, and reduction of crime rates and of extensive welfare and foster care costs. In short, what is good for both mothers and children is good for the society as a whole. Most women who are incarcerated will one day be returned to society. How well they are prepared—psychologically, educationally, and emotionally—for life in the community will depend on the level of investment that our society is willing to make in their care.

KEY TERMS

biology of addiction
dopamine
drug court
fMRI

gender-responsive policy
methamphetamine (meth)
neurotransmitters
pathway to crime

PTSD
serotonin

CRITICAL THINKING QUESTIONS

1. How can the war on drugs be conceived as a war on minorities and women?

2. Describe the empirical findings on the drug-crime link for women.

3. Some people claim addiction is a brain disease. What is the evidence for this claim?

4. How are the media accounts of the crack cocaine crisis and the meth crisis similar?

5. Discuss the link between PTSD and a girl's pathway to crime.

6. Contrast the principles of gender-responsive treatment with gender-neutral approaches used in offender treatment.

WEB DESTINATIONS

Canadian Association of Elizabeth Fry Societies: www.elizabethfry.ca

National Center for Injury Prevention and Control: www.cdc.gov/ncipc/factsheets

National Institute on Drug Abuse: www.nida.nih.gov

National Institute on Alcohol Abuse and Alcoholism: www.niaaa.nih.gov

National Institute of Mental Health: www.nimh.nih.gov

Substance Abuse and Gun Violence Resource: www.jointogether.org

Harm Reduction Coalition: www.harmreduction.org

National Center on Addiction and Substance Abuse at Columbia University: www.casacolumbia.org

Women and Sentencing Policy: www.sentencingproject.org

REFERENCES

American Psychiatric Association (APA) (2000). *Diagnostic and statistical manual of mental disorders* (text revision). Washington, D.C.: APA.

Basham, K., and Miehls, D. (2004). *Transforming the legacy: Couple therapy with survivors of childhood trauma.* New York: Columbia University Press.

Begley, S. (2005, August 19). Science Journal: A spotless mind may ease pain, but erase identity. *Wall Street Journal.* Retrieved from www.post-gazette.com

Belknap, J. (2001). *The invisible woman: Gender, crime, and justice.* Belmont, Calif.: Wadsworth.

Bloom, B., and Chesney-Lind, M. (2007). Women in prison: Vengeful equality. In R. Muraskin (ed.), *It's a crime: Women and justice* (4th ed.) (pp. 542–563). Upper Saddle River, N.J.: Prentice Hall.

Bloom, B., Owen, B., and Covington, S. (2004). Women offenders and the gendered effects of public policy. *Review of Policy Research 21*(1): 31–48.

Brady, K., and Sinha, R. (2005). Co-occurring mental and substance use disorders: The effects of chronic stress. *American Journal of Psychiatry 162*: 1483–1493.

Bureau of Justice Statistics (BJS) (1999). *Prior abuse reported by inmates and probationers.* Washington, D.C.: U.S. Department of Justice.

BJS (2000). *Women offenders.* Washington, D.C.: U.S. Department of Justice.

BJS (2003). Intimate partner violence, 1993–2001. Washington, D.C.: U.S. Department of Justice.

BJS (2004). *HIV in prisons and jails, 2002.* Washington, D.C.: U.S. Department of Justice.

Bush-Baskett, S. (1998). The war on drugs as a war against black women. In S. L. Miller (ed.), *Crime control and women: Feminist implications of criminal justice policy* (pp. 113–129). Thousand Oaks, Calif.: Sage.

Center on Addiction and Substance Abuse (CASA). (1996). Substance abuse and the American woman. Retrieved from www.casacolumbia.org/usr_doc

Chesney-Lind, M., and Pakso, L. (2004). *The female offender: Girls, women, and crime,* 2nd ed. Thousand Oaks, Calif.: Sage.

Chesney-Lind, M., and Pollack, J. (1994). Women's prisons: Equality with a vengeance. In A. Menlo and J. Pollack (eds.), *Women, law, and social control* (pp. 155–177). Boston: Allyn & Bacon.

Cloninger, C. R., Sigvardsson, S., Gilligan, S., van Knorring, A., Reich, T., and Bohman, M. (1989). Genetic heterogeneity and the classification of alcoholism. *Advances in Alcohol and Substance Abuse 7*: 3–16.

Cohen, J., Dickow, A., Horner, K., Zweben, J., Balabis, J., Vandersloot, D., and Reiber, C. (2003). Abuse and violence history of men and women in treatment for methamphetamine dependence. *American Journal on Addictions 12*(5): 377–385.

Collins, R. L., and McNair, L. D. (2003). Minority women and alcohol use. National Institute on Alcohol Abuse and Alcoholism (NIAAA). Retrieved from www.niaaa.nih.gov

Covington, S. (1999). *Helping women recover: A program for teaching substance abuse.* San Francisco: Jossey-Bass.

Cowley, G. (2003, February 24). Our bodies, our fears. *Newsweek:* 43–46.

Downs, W., and Rindels, B. (2004). Adulthood, anxiety, and trauma symptoms: A comparison of women with nonabusive, abusive, and absent father figures in childhood. *Violence and Victims 19*(6): 659–672.

Drug Courts Proliferate Nationally (2005, June 1). Join together. Project of Boston University. Retrieved from www.jointogether.org

Enos, S. (2001). *Mothering from the inside: Parenting in a women's prison.* Albany, N.Y.: State University of New York Press.

Fals-Stewart, W. (2003). The occurrence of partner physical aggression on days of alcohol consumption: a longitudinal diary study. *Journal of Consulting and Clinical Psychology 71*(1): 41–52.

Families against Mandatory Minimums Foundation (FAMM Foundation) (2005, January 12). Sentencing guidelines are not mandatory: Ball now in Congress' court. Retrieved from www.famm.org

Farley, M. (2004). Prostitution is sexual violence. *Psychiatric Times 21*(12). Retrieved from www.psychiatrictimes.com

Farr, K. (2000). Classification for female inmates: Moving forward. *Crime and Delinquency 46*(1): 3–17.

Friedman, S., Shelton, M., Elhaj, O., Youngstrom, E., Rapport, D., Packer, K., Bilali, S., Jackson, K., Sakai, H., Resnick, P., Findling, R., and Calabrese, J. (2005). Gender differences in criminality: Bipolar disorder with co-occurring substance abuse. *The Journal of the American Academy of Psychiatry and the Law 33:* 188–195.

General Accounting Office (GAO) (1999). *Women in prison: Issues and challenges confronting U.S. correctional systems.* Washington, D.C.: GAO.

Ginsberg, L., Nackerud, L., and Larrison, C. (2004). *Human biology for social workers: Development, ecology, genetics, and health.* Boston: Allyn & Bacon.

Gutiérrez, L., Parsons, R., and Cox, E. (1997). *Empowerment in social work practice: A sourcebook.* Belmont, Calif.: Brooks/Cole.

Harris, P. (2005, August 14). Tragedy of US drugs craze orphans. *The Guardian Unlimited.* Retrieved from http://observer.guardian.co.uk

Heim, C., Newport, D., Heit, S., Graham, Y., Wilcox, M., Bonsall, R., Miller, A., and Nemerhoff, C. (2000). Pituitary-adrenal and autonomic responses to stress in women after sexual and physical abuse in childhood. In *Journal of the American Medical Association 284*(5): 592–597.

Huddleston, C. W. III (2005, May). Drug courts: An effective strategy for communities facing methamphetamine. *Bureau of Justice Assistance Bulletin.* Washington, D.C.: U.S. Department of Justice.

Human Rights Watch (2003). *Ill-equipped: U.S. prisons and offenders with mental illness.* New York: Human Rights Watch.

Humphries, D. (1998). Crack mothers at 6. *Violence against Women 6*(1): 45–61.

Jackson, K. (2003, June). Trauma and the national psyche. *Social Work Today:* 20–23.

Johnson, H. (2004). Drugs and crime: A study of incarcerated female offenders. Research and Public Policy Series, Australian government. Canberra, Australia: Australian Institute of Criminology.

Karberg, J., and James, D. (2005). *Substance dependence, abuse, and treatment of jail inmates, 2002.* Bureau of Justice Statistics. Washington, D.C.: U.S. Department of Justice.

Kassebaum, P. A. (1999). *Substance abuse treatment for women offenders: Guide to promising practices.* Rockville, Md.: U.S. Department of Health and Human Services.

Knickerbocker, B. (2005, July 15). Meth's rising US impact. *Christian Science Monitor.* Retrieved from www.csmonitor.com

Laishes, J. (2002). *The 2002 mental health strategy for women offenders.* Ottawa, Canada: Correctional Service of Canada.

Lanier, M., and Zaitzow, B. (2007). Living and dying with HIV/AIDS. In R. Muraskin (ed.), *It's a crime: Women and justice* (pp. 363–391). Upper Saddle River, N.J.: Prentice Hall.

Lapham, S. (2004/2005). Screening and brief intervention in the criminal justice system. *Alcohol Research and Health 28*(2). Retrieved from www.niaaa.nih.gov

Lewis, D. (2005, July 27). Top medical doctors, scientists and specialists urge major media outlets not to create "meth baby" myth. Public letter reprinted by National Advocates for Pregnant Women. Retrieved from www.advocatesforpregnantwomen.org

Leys, T. (2003, November 26). Addicts battle back. *Des Moines Register.* Retrieved from www.desmoinesregister.com.

Leys, T. (2005, January 30). Dad's drug runner. *Des Moines Register,* pp. 1a, 6a.

MacCoun, R., Kilmer, B., and Reuter, P. (2003). *Research on drugs-crime linkages: The next generation.* Washington, D.C.: U.S. Department of Justice. Retrieved from www.ojp.usdoj.gov

Mathias, R. (2001, October). Pathological obesity and drug addiction share common brain characteristics. *NIDA Notes 16*(4). Retrieved from www.drugabuse.gov/NIDA_Notes

Mullings, J., Marquart, J. W., and Hartley, D. J. (2003). Exploring the effects of childhood sexual abuse and its impact on HIV/AIDS risk-taking behavior among women prisoners. *The Prison Journal 83*(4): 442–463.

Mullings, J., Pollock, J., and Crouch, B. (2002). Drugs and criminality: Results from the Texas women inmate study. *Women & Criminal Justice 13*(4): 69–96.

National Center on Addiction and Substance Abuse (CASA) at Columbia University (2003). *The formative years: Pathways to substance abuse among girls and young women ages 8–22.* New York: CASA.

National Institute on Alcohol Abuse and Alcoholism (NIAAA) (1999, December). Are women more vulnerable to alcohol's effects? *Alcohol Alert 10*, 1–4.

NIAAA (2003, August 18). Serotonin transporter gene shown to influence college drinking habits. *News Releases.* NIAAA. Retrieved from www.niaaa.nih.gov

National Institute on Drug Abuse (NIDA) (1999). Infofax: Treatment methods for women. Retrieved from www.drugabuse.gov

National Institute on Drug Abuse (NIDA) (2002). Research report series—Methamphetamine abuse and addiction. *NIDA.* Retrieved from http://nida.nih.com

Paltrow, L. M. (2004, April 5). The pregnancy police. *AlterNet.* Retrieved from www.alternet.org

"Petition Asks U.N. Racism Conference to Take Up U.S. War on Drugs" (2001, August 22). Retrieved from www.drugwarinjustice.org

Pollack, S. (2004). Anti-oppressive social work practice with women in prison: Discursive reconstructions and alternative practices. *British Journal of Social Work 34*: 693–707.

Pollack, S. (2005). Taming the shrew: Regulating prisoners through women-centered mental health programming. *Critical Criminology 13*: 71–87.

Richie, B. E. (2004). Challenges incarcerated women face as they return to their communities. In M. Chesney-Lind and L. Pakso (eds.), *Girls, women, and crime: Selected readings* (pp. 231–245). Thousand Oaks, Calif.: Sage.

Sagatun-Edwards, I. (2007). Legal and social welfare response to substance abuse during pregnancy. In R. Muraskin (ed.), *It's a crime: Women and justice* (4th ed.) (pp. 346–362). Upper Saddle River, N.J.: Prentice Hall.

Strauss, S., and Falkin, G. (2001). Women offenders who use and deal methamphetamine: Implications for mandated drug treatment. *Women & Criminal Justice 12*(4): 77–97.

Substance Abuse and Mental Health Services Administration (SAMHSA) (1997) Substance use among women in the United States. The Center for Substance Abuse Treatment. Retrieved from www.samhsa.gov/csat

SAMHSA (1999a). *Substance abuse in brief.* The Center for Substance Abuse Treatment. Retrieved from www.samhsa.gov/csat

SAMHSA (1999b). *Treatment succeeds in fighting crime.* The Center for Substance Abuse Treatment. Retrieved from www.samhsa.gov/csat

SAMHSA (2003). *Violence, suicide and risky behavior.* Office of Applied Studies. The Center for Substance Abuse Treatment. Retrieved from www.samhsa.gov/csat

SAMHSA (2005). *Substance abuse treatment for persons with co-occurring disorders: A treatment improvement protocol* (TIP) 42. The Center for Substance Abuse Treatment. Retrieved from www.samhsa.gov/csat

Sohrabji, F. (2003). *Neurodegeneration in women.* National Institute on Alcohol Abuse and Alcoholism (NIAAA). Retrieved from www.niaaa.nih.gov

Spear, L. (2000). Modeling adolescent development and alcohol use in animals. *Alcohol Research & Health 24*(2), 115–123.

Springer, D. W., McNeece, C. A., and Arnold, E. M. (2003). *Substance abuse treatment for criminal offenders: An evidence-based guide for practitioners.* Washington, D.C.: American Psychological Association.

Tapert, S., Brown, G., Kinderman, S., et al. (2001). fMRI measurement of brain dysfunction in alcohol dependent young women. *Alcoholism: Clinical and experimental research 25:* 236–245.

Taylor, B., Newton, P., and Brownstein, H. (2003). Drug use among adult female arrestees. *ADAM (Arrestee Drug Abuse Monitoring) 2000 Annual Report.* Washington, D.C.: U.S. Department of Justice.

Teplin, L. A., Abram, K. M., and McClelland, G. (1996). Prevalence of psychiatric disorders among incarcerated women: Pretrial jail detainees. *Archives of General Psychiatry 53:* 505–512.

USA Today (2002, June 10). Meth use among women tough to detect. *USA Today.* Retrieved from www.usatoday.com

van Wormer, K. (2001). *Counseling female offenders and victims: A strengths-restorative approach.* New York: Springer Publishing.

van Wormer, K., and Davis, D. R. (2003). *Addiction treatment: A strengths perspective.* Belmont, Calif.: Brooks/Cole

Wallace, B. (2005). *Making mandated addiction treatment work.* Lanham, Md.: Rowan & Littlefield Publishers.

Weekes, J. R. (1997, July). Substance abuse treatment for offenders. *Corrections Today 59:* 12–16.

Whitten, L. (2004). Men and women process cocaine cues differently. National Institute on Drug Abuse (NIDA). *NIDA Notes 19*(4), retrieved from www.nida.nih.gov

Willson, P., McFarlane, J., Malecha, A., Watson, K., Lemmey, D., Schultz, P., Gist, J., and Fredland, N. (2000). Severity of violence against women by intimate partners and associated use of alcohol and/or illicit drugs by the perpetrator. *Journal of Interpersonal Violence 15*(9): 996–1008.

Yehia, D. (2003, July). Sentencing aboriginal offenders. Law Link. Retrieved from www.lawlink.nsw.gov.au

Yochelson, S., and Samenow, S. (1976). *The criminal personality,* vol. 1. New York: Jason Aronson.

Zernike, K. (2005, July 6). Officials across U.S. describe drug woes. *The New York Times.* Retrieved from www.nytimes.com

Zickler, P. (2004). Long-term abstinence brings partial recovery from methamphetamine damage. *NIDA Notes 19*(4).

CHAPTER

6

The Prison Environment

In the United States, the thrust toward prison reform and rehabilitation is in decline. The public mood, fired up by mass media rabid for stories, cries out for vengeance against people perceived as a threat—specifically, inner-city males engaging in street crime and illegal drug users. Paradoxically, women of color are bearing the brunt of the "lock 'em up and throw away the key" mentality. The war against single mothers on welfare in the "free world" is matched by an increasing severity in the treatment of women within prison walls. This pattern is echoed in Birmingham, England, as well as Birmingham, Alabama; a harshness against women offenders is seen in Tokyo, Japan, as well. Throughout the world, the antifeminist backlash is palpable: If women want to be equal to men, or so the thinking goes, they can be punished like men—put on chain gangs, in boot camps, and even executed. And, at the employee level, if female guards can be assigned to a full range of duties in men's prisons (because of affirmative action mandates), then male guards can operate unrestricted in women's prisons as well.

The major purpose of this chapter is to present the reality and context of life for women in confinement so that budding correctional and social workers and other treatment providers will be prepared, intellectually, at least, for the major challenges awaiting them in this line of work.

We begin to explore the topic of women in prison with a brief history of the imprisonment of women and of theoretical frameworks concerning their criminality. We then construct a profile of the typical female inmate based on statistics involving race, ethnicity, drug involvement, and other demographic criteria available from government sources. Turning our attention to the *internal* dynamics of prison society, we ponder the way in which women of various ages and ethnicities construct a social world that is unique in itself. A related discussion on prison "play" families and sexual role-playing follows. One grim topic—women on death row—and one positive topic—innovative treatment programs—conclude this chapter.

The theme that binds these seemingly disparate topics is that of empowering feminism. *Empowering feminism* is the term we use for a perspective that engenders pride in women through recognition of their unique needs, gifts, and vulnerabilities. Another major theme is the War on Drugs, which has become a war against African American and Latina women. A third major theme, equally disturbing, is the susceptibility of women behind bars to sexual abuse and harassment by male guards.

History of the Women's Prison

To the extent that prisons do indeed represent a social barometer of a nation's health and level of civilization, as Dostoevsky (1864) believed they did, the punishment of female offenders can be viewed as a mirror for the treatment of women in a society. If we view female offenders' treatment historically, as well as culturally, we will realize the connection between the punishment of women who deviated from the norms of society and the patriarchal social structure of the day. In a book written in her prison cell, Jean Harris (1988) (famous for the murder of her unfaithful lover, Dr. Herman Tarnower) summarized the history of women's prison succinctly: "From a woman depraved, to a woman wronged, to a woman who now says she wants to be treated equally with men, we've spanned two hundred years, and we're more ambivalent today than we ever were" (p. 40).

In the early days of prison history, women—like men—suffered in filth, overcrowding, and harsh conditions. They were confined in separate quarters in men's prisons (Kurshan, 1996; Rathbone, 2005). In the 1920s, at Auburn Penitentiary in New York, women were lodged together; they were subject to beating and sexual abuse by the male guards. African American and poor women were, as always, disproportionately incarcerated in all parts of the United States. Following the passage of strict Jim Crow laws in the Southern states, which were designed to keep blacks "in their place," Southern prison populations became almost all black overnight.

Despite retrogressive laws and harsh punishments affecting women as well as men, the roots of feminism lie deep within the prison reform movement. Even before the end of slavery, Quaker abolitionists and suffragists were at the forefront of this movement. Elizabeth Fry of England helped organize the women confined at London's Newgate Gaol in the early 1800s. Her brave and innovative work at Newgate with incarcerated women and their children was testimony to the fact that, with decent treatment, women convicts were redeemable, that a single light could dispel the darkness. She challenged the rampant sexual abuse of institutionalized women, advocated as one of her key principles that women should be under the authority of women and in their own institution, and sought to substitute the Quakers' system of absolute silence with one in which inmates could communicate with each other and help each other reform. Working indefatigably until her death in 1845 to transform the lives of inmate women, Fry managed to instill hope and dignity where there was only despair (American Friends Service Committee, 1971, p. 16). Today, in Canada, the Elizabeth Fry associations play an active role in exposing abuses in prisons for women.

On becoming matron of the woman's prison at Sing Sing in 1844, Eliza Farnham stirred up controversy with the new techniques that she implemented and with her articulate defense of them. Farnham strove in many ways to brighten the tone of inmate life during the period of her tenure (Lewis, 1965, pp. 230–255). But the charge of pampering criminals had already become an easy one to level, and Farnham was finally forced to resign in 1848 (Rathbone, 2005). Across the state, women were sent back to the unsupervised section of men's prisons.

The first separate prison for women, the Indiana Women's Prison was founded by a Quaker couple and opened in 1873. Massachusetts followed four years later with the building of an all-female state reformatory. Another American Quaker cited by Jean Harris (1988) helped found the progressive women's reformatory at Bedford Hills. Gradually, other states followed, until unisexual institutions for men and women became the basic, though not exclusive, pattern. Fry's program, which consisted of women helping women and emphasized rehabilitation, obedience, and religious education, became instituted throughout North America. In the ensuing "matriarchy in corrections," the staffs, architectural designs, and programs reflected the culturally valued norms for women's behavior (Feinman, 1994, p. 44). At the administrative level, the women's prison was to remain, for a considerable time, a domain of female guidance for control and leadership.

Many significant aspects of contemporary corrections were, in fact, pioneered by female administrators in charge of institutions for female offenders (Allen and Simonsen, 1995). Correctional innovations such as educational instruction, work release programs, and vocational activities were initiated in an atmosphere that was female. Women's prisons, as Walker (1980) notes, became a testing ground for the new penology: prison reformers regarded women as good candidates for rehabilitation, probably because they were considered less dangerous than their male counterparts (p. 21).

To speak only of the reformatory tradition in women's prisons and to neglect the existence of harsh, disciplinary institutions, such as the State Prison for Women at Auburn, New York, is to overlook the origins of what is the women's prison as we know it today, a wall built around society's problems. In 1844, New York prison authorities voiced little concern for their charges:

> The opinion seems to have been entertained, that the female convicts were beyond the reach of reformation, and it seems to have been regarded as a sufficient performance of the object of punishment, to turn them loose within the pen of the prison and there leave them to feed upon and destroy each other. (Lewis, 1965, p. 159)

And then there was the racial factor. Chivalry for white women figured into the picture in the form of "cottage-style" reformatories, establishments that proliferated during the Progressive Era as an alternative to the harsh custodial institutions. Whereas the custodial (mainly African American) prisons were characterized by filth and violence inflicted by male guards, "reformatories" were usually staffed by women and stressed correcting women's moral behavior. There were no comparable reformatories for men. Women were sentenced to these prisons for various sexual offenses, including unwed pregnancies and unlawful sexual intercourse (Kurshan, 1996). By 1935, the Progressive Era was over, and the reformatories and custodial prisons were merged. The legacy of the "cottage system" still prevails at the women's federal prison at Alderson, West Virginia, and in many state prisons, such as Bedford Hills in New York State.

The 1960s and 1970s, that period of civil rights awareness and protest by various oppressed groups in the society—minorities, women, gays, and lesbians—was also a time of much feminist reformist zeal concerning women in prison. Although compassion was expressed for women who had killed their husbands in self-defense and were charged with murder, there was also a huge outcry over political prisoners, such as Angela Davis and Joan Little. Davis was charged with abetting a violent prisoner escape, and Little was tried for killing her jailer in the act of rape. Within prison walls, similarly, this period marked the beginning of much prisoner-generated litigation (mostly initiated from men's prisons), protesting inhumane conditions and the violation of human rights.

The period of retrenchment of social services and the **war on drugs,** which got under way in the 1980s and continues at the turn of the century, parallels a mass media campaign dramatizing crimes of violence. As noted in Chapter 5, women of color have been the most adversely affected by the new mandatory drug-sentencing laws, namely, the harsh sentencing for crack cocaine, the drug associated with inner-city drug abuse and violence. In Canada, native women (3 percent of the population) are disproportionately locked up (29 percent of federally sentenced women are aboriginal) (Canadian Human Rights Commission, 2003), as are minorities of African and Latin American origin. A further factor affecting all prisoners, as Chesney-Lind and Pasko (2004) indicate, is the vested interest of major corporations, the **prison industrial complex,** which has become a component of many local communities that depend on the building and maintenance of prisons for economic stability. The new surge in prison privatization has made the operation of prisons, as well as their construction, a typical capitalist venture. It is difficult, therefore, to alter priorities, such as, for example, to put money into substance abuse treatment and subsidized housing to prevent crime, when the dividends of crimes are so profitable to outside interest groups.

According to the 2000 Census of State and Federal Correctional Facilities, a total of 120 privately operated facilities are authorized to house women. Thirty-seven of these facilities are exclusively female. Entries on the 2000 Census range from the Des Moines Women's Residential Center, which has an excellent reputation in Iowa for gender-specific programming, to the notorious correctional center at Florence, Arizona. Operated by the privately owned Corrections Corporation of America, this facility has been the subject of several successful lawsuits on behalf of the sexually violated women (van Wormer, 2003).

The prison privatization movement has enormous implications for female offenders, first with regard to the increase in the number of women being incarcerated, and second, in light of the recent history in private prisons of sexual abuse by male guards. When commercial enterprises take over the hiring and supervision of correctional staff, standards are inevitably lowered. At the same time, as the state relinquishes responsibility for the running of the prisons, public accountability for the abuses inflicted on female inmates has been even further reduced.

In summary, if women at times have been given special consideration throughout correctional history by virtue of their gender, they also have been treated badly. They have been simultaneously protected and punished. A temporal perspective emphasizes that women in society at large, like women in criminal justice, have been thought of in terms of the Madonna/whore duality so aptly spelled out by Feinman (1994).

The **Madonna image** personified women who were faithful and submissive as good women and who, therefore, might be dealt with leniently by the courts. The whore image portrayed women as seductive temptresses of men (Morash and Schram, 2002). Women of color have not historically been placed in these dichotomous categories but rather treated as tough and likely to break the law. (The term "lady" in the old South tellingly was reserved for white women of a certain class.)

The women-centeredness of the early women's prisons no longer exists under the influence of the twin forces of women's equality and the new punitiveness in North American society. In the nation's imagination, a criminal is a criminal, but the strict mandatory penalties are usually set with a hardened male street criminal in mind. Whereas women in prison are significantly less violent than men in prison, women's prisons are constructed on a correctional model based on assumptions about violent men (Muraskin, 2007). Male gangs thrive in prison; women create small families. Men are territorial and fight to maintain positions of power. Women fight because of jealousy, but more often they take out their hostility on themselves through self-mutilation. Men tend to congregate by race; women create their "families" across racial lines. Women relate to each other, too, across security-level lines, whereas men's prisons are divided by classification of dangerousness of crime and criminality. The women are all incarcerated in one location and, for the most part, mix freely.

The Population Profile

The influx of women filling America's prisons significantly eclipses the male incarceration increase. Since 1995, the annual rate of growth in the number of female inmates has averaged 5 percent, higher than the 3.3 percent average increase of male inmates (Bureau of Justice Statistics [BJS], 2005). Whereas women were only 4 percent of the incarcerated population in 1980, today they account for 6.9 percent of all inmates. Women also make up 12.3 percent of the total jail population.

State and county departments of corrections are no longer focused on rehabilitation but are forced to warehouse people and to worry over finding the next cell. Jail and prison construction has become the major expense in counties across the United States. Ironically, the prison building boom is occurring at the same time that the crime rate is steadily decreasing, especially the rates of the crimes of violence so often sensationalized in the news. The more prisons that are built, inevitably the more people will be sentenced to fill them. "Build them and they will convict" is the common refrain. States that once managed with one or no prisons for women now are building several. Bloom, Owen, and Covington (2004) provide documentation to show that in the 1970s, nearly two-thirds of the women convicted of federal felonies were granted probation, but twenty years later only 28 percent were given straight probation.

The repercussions of the upsurge in women's incarceration will be felt well beyond prison walls. Experts point, in particular, to the children of inmates who are far more likely than other children to end up in the juvenile justice system or prison (Gaouette, 1997). Today, two-thirds of the almost 200,000 women behind bars are mothers and most often single parents (BJS, 2005).

A large majority of women prisoners in the United States are serving time for nonviolent offenses—72 percent in state prisons—and 93 percent in federal prisons (BJS, 2000). Mandatory minimum sentences provide the same punishments for conspiracy to commit crimes, such as driving the getaway car, as for the instigator of the crime itself. Accordingly, almost half the women in prison today under these mandatory sentencing laws have been convicted of conspiracy (Siegal, 1998). According to the American Civil Liberties Union (ACLU) (2005), women are increasingly caught up in the ever-widening net cast by current drug laws such as **conspiracy laws** and accomplice liability laws that extend criminal liability to the arrested offender's partners and relatives. Sentencing laws fail to consider the many reasons—including domestic violence, economic dependence, or dependent immigrant status—that may compel women to remain silent. The mandatory minimum laws, despite a recent Supreme Court ruling to give the judge more sentencing leeway, still often subject women to the same, or in some cases, harsher sentences than the principals in the drug trade who are ostensibly the target of those policies (ACLU, 2005). This is an example of what we might call "equality with a vengeance," an equality of punishment meted out to women who violate the law.

In Canada, property crimes bring most women to prison. Canada relies heavily on short sentences for women offenses such as for public intoxication, shoplifting, and theft. Almost 40 percent of the sentences are for fourteen days or less (Shaw, 1994). The lack of alternative sentencing options seems to be a factor in these brief incarcerations. The high percentage of women who have small children is similar to that south of the border (Correctional Service Canada, 2005). Poor women locked in Canadian prisons often have been driven into "underground economies," such as prostitution and drug dealing as a way to make ends meet.

The United States' War on Drugs, combined with the backlash against affirmative action, sometimes is played out in the form of "zero tolerance" for women who violate drug use laws. Mandatory minimum sentencing laws tie the hands of judges who personally might favor probation in sympathetic cases. In the political world, Meda Chesney-Lind (1995) suggests, there seems to be a return to the imagery of depraved women, women whose crimes put them outside the ranks of "true womanhood." The new hostility signaled by the bringing of child-abuse charges against women who use drugs, even before the birth of their children, is a case in point provided by Chesney-Lind. The criminalizing of a pregnancy during which drugs or alcohol were consumed is a fairly recent development that illustrates the power of the political right (see Chapter 5).

Because of the intergenerational costs of locking up mothers and paying for foster care for their children, women are far more expensive to the state to imprison than men. Such a willingness to spend millions of dollars incarcerating women stands, of course, in stark contrast to the paucity of resources made available to other women's programs (Chesney-Lind, 1995).

When a mother is imprisoned, often merely held in jail awaiting trial, the separation from her children can be traumatic for them all. Prisons, and especially women's prisons, generally are located in remote, rural areas far away from home and community. Family ties, over time, are broken. Yet prisoner's family relationships are very important not only for mental health considerations but also in terms of postrelease success (Hairston, 1995). Martin's examination of mothers who were incarcerated in the Minnesota correctional facility at Shakopee in 1985 established that their commitment to parenthood was deeply tenacious (Martin, 1997). When these mothers were followed up five years later, most of them had sustained continuous and primary parenting education from within prison and had reunified with their children when released from prison (p. 1). Nevertheless, internal prison policies as well as traditional public policies, as Hairston indicates, have provided minimal support for the maintenance of family relationships for individuals involved in the criminal justice system.

Mothers in Prison

While the children of imprisoned fathers also experience loss, there is a tremendous difference in the disruption that imprisonment brings to the children of women, as compared to the children of men (Pollock, 2002). A fact to keep in mind is that nine out of ten times, when the father is imprisoned the mother carries on the responsibility of child care alone, but when the mother is incarcerated, only 28 percent of the fathers care for their children (Reed and Reed, 2004). Moreover, a large majority of the children are African American and Latino, so the burden of caring for these "prison orphans" falls disproportionately on families of color. In her research on mothering in a women's prison, Sandra Enos (2001) found that white women, compared to women of color, were less likely to even want their children to be cared for by relatives, first from a belief that these homes were not healthy places, and second from not wanting to feel obligated to reciprocate.

In fact, there are serious risks to children who have to be placed when the mother is sentenced to prison. Sharp and Marcus-Mendoza (2001), in their survey of approximately one hundred female inmates sentenced for drug violations, found that the women's children were often at serious risk of abuse in their placements. Not surprisingly, van Wormer (2001) found, in her nationwide survey of administrators of women's prisons, that practically all of the respondents listed the welfare of children as the primary concern of these mothers. Many such mothers face termination of their legal rights today due to the Adoption and Safe Families Act of 1997 that mandates the termination of parental rights once a child has been in foster care for fifteen or more of the past twenty-two months. The consequences for incarcerated mothers in the loss of their children are obvious.

A key advantage of community correctional programming such as drug courts, as discussed in Chapter 5, is in keeping families intact, providing much needed treatment and supervision, and preventing the next generation from following the pathway to substance abuse, sick relationships, and crime.

When incarceration is a given, family ties can still be maintained through regular contact and restricted home visits. Such maintaining of close family ties during incarceration has been shown to result in decreased recidivism rates and improved mental health of inmates and other family members (Hairston, 1995; Reed and Reed, 2004). Yet surveys show that nearly one third of prison mothers report little or no contact with their children (Reed and Reed, 2004).

An encouraging development is the offering of parenting programs in prison. Such programs have even been helpful in teaching mothers how to handle encounters with difficult teenagers in family visits (Rathbone, 2005). Parenting programs range from parenting classes to prison nurseries. We describe the nursery program at Bedford Hills in a later section of this chapter.

Prisoner and jail inmate profiles can be best revealed through recent studies from the U.S. Bureau of Justice Statistics (BJS) (2000) and (2005) and the American Civil Liberties Union (ACLU) (2005). From these government sources we learn that:

Prisoner Profile

- Black females were two and a half times more likely than Hispanic females and nearly four and a half times more likely than white females to be incarcerated in 2004 (BJS, 2005).
- Approximately 65 percent of women in state prisons have young children; about two-thirds of the women lived with their children before entering prison (BJS, 2000).
- Nearly 60 percent of the women reported they had ever been physically or sexually abused (BJS, 2000).
- About six in ten women in state prison were using drugs in the month before their offense (BJS, 2000).
- In most cases, when a woman is imprisoned, her child is displaced; when the father is incarcerated, the child is more likely to live with the mother and not be displaced (ACLU, 2005).

These statistics, gathered from government services, provide documentation of the racism, sexism, and classism that exists in contemporary society. The racism is revealed in the harsh sentencing practices for involvement with drugs such as crack cocaine, associated in the public mind with inner-city crime. Past mandated minimum sentencing for dealing and conspiring to deal in these kinds of drugs has filled up jail cells with African American and Latina women. Sexism is played out in the harsh sentencing of women and their transportation to prisons far from home. Classism is evidenced in the poor educational backgrounds and high poverty rates of these women.

Approximately 80 percent of women in U.S. prisons and almost two-thirds of women in Canadian prisons have a serious problem with drugs or alcohol, and substance abuse is associated with their crime in some way. Related problems are eating disorders, other mental health problems such as depression and high anxiety, and self-mutilation. The profile of Canadian women in prison is more or less comparable to that of their contemporaries south of the border. Approximately

70 percent of these women have had serious problems with alcohol and other drug-related problems and eating disorders (Canadian Human Rights Commission, 2003). Around 80 percent had a history of abuse.

Reports from the United Kingdom (U.K.) revealed similar problems in British prisons for women, mainly because of overcrowding, the incarceration of juveniles for lack of female juvenile institutions, and the shortage of professionally trained personnel. In recognition of the problems, the U.K. Parliament (2004) in its House of Lords took up the matter of women in prison and presented the following facts:

- There were three times as many women prisoners in 2003 as in 1993, yet the crime rate is not rising;
- Nearly 50 percent of the women are mothers of young children;
- The women increasingly are dependent on medication;
- Many have neurotic disorders and are suicidal;
- Almost half of the women were imprisoned for drug offenses;
- Research from abroad shows that in Germany mothers are housed in nearby units with their children; women in Russia are given suspended sentences until the child is fourteen; women in France are imprisoned far less than in the U.K.
- Some 18 percent of the women in U.K. prisons are foreign, often serving drug sentences for having been used as drug carriers or "mules."

On the positive side, the United Kingdom has set up modern juvenile homes with professionally trained staff and specialized treatment services for the girls. Methadone maintenance programs will be in place in all women's prisons, and extensive mental health and substance abuse treatment will be provided.

Carlen and Tchaikovsky (1996) argue convincingly that women's imprisonment is different from men's and that their special needs have been systematically ignored by prisoner advocates as well as prison administrators. As elsewhere, the major stumbling block in substantial reform is the new punitiveness, which is an outgrowth of a climate of fear and resentment toward the deviant poor and nonworking single mothers living on welfare. Disproportionate numbers of ethnic minorities are members of this group and are especially prominent among those sentenced to prison.

One reason for the increasingly multicultural composition of prison populations is the result of the international War on Drugs. In England, Canada, and elsewhere, women who have been convicted for their work as "mules" in international drug trafficking are being held in countries far from home. Women are forced or talked into doing this work by international drug smugglers. Because they are generally ignorant of the overall operations and criminal justice policies, women often plead guilty and receive extensive mandatory minimum sentences (Pollock, 1998). The sex-neutral Draconian sentences, as Pollock argues, do not take into account that many of the seemingly hardened female criminals may have been acting on behalf of male drug traffickers, who are often their boyfriends and partners.

In conjunction with the high profits in the drug trade, increasing numbers of female drug smugglers are caught while passing through customs in Washington, D.C., New York, and London. In private correspondence, Kim Pate (1998) of the Elizabeth Fry Association of Canada, describes the situation befalling foreign women in Canada:

> We have a few Latina women in prison, but more women from the Caribbean, and increasingly, women from Southeast Asia for drug importation and/or trafficking charges. Most have no contact with their families for fear of repercussions on them if it is known that their sister/mother/daughter/etc. is in prison abroad. They are terribly isolated as a result, all the more so if they do not speak English or French. We used to be able to try to get them early parole for the purposes of deportation, but legislative changes in 1992 stopped this. . . . Now the women have to serve their entire prison sentences prior to deportation.

Prison Structure

Because women are such a small percentage of the U.S. prison population, they inherit a system designed for men who are defined as a high security risk to society. It was for the sake of controlling a population of violent male predators that the whole correctional apparatus, this military-style system of command run by officers given the ranks of lieutenant, captain, and sergeant, originally was set up. This framework, designed for the 93 percent or so inmates who are the majority of (male) prisoners, was superimposed on the female minority, for whom its suitability is questionable. Some allowance is made for women's particular needs, admittedly, such as the establishment of nurseries for inmate children in a few select places; to date no one has argued for placing a nursery in a men's prison.

The formal structure of the women's prison in many ways belies the informal treatment women receive within the prison walls. At the personal level, women are treated not as tough men, but as children; they are infantilized. Harsh punishments are meted out for cursing, disrespect, and other minor violations (Pollock, 1998). Called "girls" by staff or "ladies" as at New Bedford (as the title of Harris's book, *They Always Call Us Ladies* indicates), but never "women," female prisoners are encouraged to display "good" passive behavior by prison officials. Independent thinking, much less grassroots organizing for social change, is severely punished. Appropriately, Watterson (1996) refers to women's prison as "inside the concrete womb," a phrase that serves as the subtitle of her book. On the subject of sex, Watterson comments, "It seems sex for prisoners is considered dessert in our culture—too special and rare a treat for bad children" (p. 285).

The Social World of the Women's Prison

The complex and diverse histories of women incarcerated in prison produce a prison culture that is itself complex and diverse in many ways (Owen, 1998). We now consider three critical dimensions of life that constitute the culture of women's prisons: the social and cultural background of the women themselves, the cliques or families that develop in prison, and prison sexuality.

Any attempt to comprehend the social organization of prisons must address the contemporary prisoner experience in light of what John Irwin (1980) calls the "cultural baggage" that inmates import into the prison setting with them. Much of this cultural baggage today is the end product of the drug wars on the streets and the War on Drugs in society. Caught up in the War on Drugs are minority women involved with male gang members (Latino and African American), foreigners arrested at airports as drug "couriers" for international syndicates, and the usual array of violent and nonviolent offenders arrested for crimes that are indirectly related to drug use. Race and class intersect in predictable ways to ensure that the persons most feared and resented by society will be those who are shut away. Today, as Chesney-Lind (1997) suggests, street crime has become a code word for *race*. And racial tensions in the community lay the groundwork for ethnic differences and resentments behind prison bars.

Sometimes the resentments, as Jean Harris (1988) reports, are taken out on "honkie," or white, correctional officers. Sometimes prisoners take them out on each other. In at least one prison, as reported by Feinman (1994), observers note that overt problems occur more often between African American and Latina women than between white and African American women. More studies are needed to confirm this phenomenon throughout the prison system. Research does tell us that the kind of race wars and gang warfare that characterize the social structure in men's prisons seem to have no counterpart in women's institutions (Pollock, 1998). Two aspects of the social structure with which we are concerned here are prison homosexuality and kinship ties, parts of the female prison culture that, although addressed separately in the literature, are inextricably linked.

Prison Families

Often located in rural areas miles away from their own families, and inaccessible in any case because of financial and legal restrictions, women in prisons tend to develop their own networks for familial ties. In sharp contrast to the male prison society organized around power, women prisoners, at least in the United States, often replicate the family patterns they knew on the outside for life on the inside. "Married" couples may head such families and even occasionally include a father figure. Lesbians often assume the male role within the prison environment. Prison "mamas" keep their "children" in line and provide emotional support (see Giallombardo, 1966; van Wormer, 2001). Although these inmates generally live in a world dominated by pettiness, gossip, and much regressive behavior, a lot of love and nurturing goes on in such a society of women; care and respect for the elderly and mothering of the very young (or retarded) are common themes.

In her study of the Federal Reformatory for Women at Alderson, West Virginia, Giallombardo discovered that the major difference between male and female prisons is that the women's inmate society establishes a substitute world in which women can identify or construct family patterns similar to those in the free world, whereas male prisoners design a social system to combat the social and physical deprivations of imprisonment. Family life—with "mothers and fathers," "grandparents," and "aunts and uncles"—was at the very center of inmate life at Alderson.

Considerable controversy surrounds the viability of these family forms and whether or not they even exist. As Pollock (1998) suggests, "Although it seems clear that women do form affectional ties that have some similarity to familial relationships, it is not clear that the extensive kinship networks were or are anywhere near as defined as one might believe reading the early studies" (p. 38). Faith (1993) concurs in the view that early researchers exaggerated the centrality of family forms.

Among the witnesses to the prison "kinship" scene are Owen (1998), who studied the subculture on the prison yard in a California institution; Jean Harris (1988), who spent eight years in residence at Bedford Hills, New York; and Watterson (1996), a journalist, who reports that she would occasionally be introduced to an inmate's entire prison family, including the wife, son, daughter-in-law, and daughter. In her survey of women's prison's administrators, van Wormer (2001) found that thirty-one of thirty-five respondents said that the women in their prison assumed family roles. Significantly, the administrators did not approve of this role playing, for the most part, and thought the intensity of the relationships interfered with the inmates working on their own issues.

The open expression of affection among women is highly visible, in contrast to relations among men in prison. Dana Britton (2003), who wrote of the prison as a gendered organization, found that correctional officers' views were shaped by heterosexist perceptions of such interactions as "sickening" and saw dealing with them as a serious management problem. A major theme of Britton's book, in fact, was the near-universal disdain especially by male officers for working in a women's institution and dealing with the emotions of women and their unpredictable outbursts.

As long as women are shut away from the outside world and from the close, caring (and scolding) relationships to which they are accustomed, the argument can be made that the familiar relationship pattern of the outside world will be replayed in the prison world with a different cast, that family ties will be created to replace the ties that were lost. From a strengths perspective, we can appreciate women's bonding, their recreation of the life they had known and valued in "the free world." The differences between male and female social organization is revealed most tellingly in the inner social structure of the unisexual environment.

Because there has never been any consensus concerning the percentage of inmates involved in **prison play-families** it is hard to conclude whether they are, in fact, on the decline, as contemporary writers such as Fox (1984), Harris (1988), and Diaz-Cotto (1996) contend. Diaz-Cotto argues that the degree to which family groupings are growing less common may be the result of increasing access to family, friends, and outside volunteers. Her description of the Latina prisoners' active involvement in these adoptive families and of the tremendous emotional investment in these relationships is consistent with descriptions in the classic studies. A difference is the ethnic cliquishness of these bondings. Because Latina inmates come from families with strong extended kinship ties and they are in many cases incarcerated in a foreign country logically increases their need to recreate familiar role relationships.

Far from viewing these family forms and even the homosexual aspects of jail house relationships as negative, we need to view them as a means of psychological survival in a situation that is extreme and abnormal. The functions of prison families are many: They offer mutual support and protection in a strange and often bewildering environment; they provide a mutual aid network in an atmosphere of deprivation; they are often encouraged by the administration for their social control aspect—keeping family members out of trouble; and above all, they create situations for fun and laughter (Hart, 1995).

Pollack (2004), in her research in Canadian prisons, found the close prison relationships to be multifaceted, complex, and in many ways supportive and sustaining. For example, an underground network of peers helped bandage the wounds of inmates who self-injured. Gaarder and Belknap (2004) interviewed juveniles sentenced to a women's prison, finding that although these girls were housed separately from the women, they intermingled all day with women of all ages and, in many cases, were mothered and nurtured by them. Through such relationships, women acquire an increase in self-esteem. The training of peer counselors can build on such nurturing relationships.

Another possible advantage of clearly defined family roles for women who live in close quarters is that relationships can become very intimate and include touching and hugging without taking on sexual connotations. In same-sex institutions, where sexual tensions often are played out as homophobia, a clarification of one's relationship in terms of sister-to-sister and mother-to-daughter ties can serve to legitimize the bonding between unrelated women (see van Wormer, 1987). Pollack (2004) reached the same conclusion that institutional homophobia serves to perpetuate these normative familial ties.

Prison Sexuality

In men's prisons, homophobia is played out in a different way. A men's prison is a world of untempered masculinity where the strong preserve their sense of manhood through sexual conquest of the weak. Sexual threats, taunting, and assault dominate the scene into which the new inmate is initiated. Under a ruthless inmate code that enables carefully executed schemes of smuggling and escape to go undetected, predators subdue their prey. Young men, especially nonstreetwise white males, are especially vulnerable to sexual harassment and physical attack. In the male prison society, rape or the threat of rape serves as a form of peer group social control exerted by the aggressors and leaders in the facility. While the rapist wields power and respect, the victim is shamed and feminized. The aggressor is never considered anything other than heterosexual; his "punk" is a mere woman substitute. Among men, rape is about power and dominance as well as sexual gratification. Once victimized, a man is ranked as a target for sexual exploitation and subject to gang rapes; one escape avenue is to become more or less a prostitute to one "protector" (Donaldson, 1995; *Prison Legal News*, 1995). Interestingly, a similar pattern prevailed among the convict laborers in colonial Australia as described in disturbing detail in the epic history, *The Fatal Shore* (Hughes, 1987).

Behind bars, women recreate a world of the familiar. Many seek out strong types of women with whom to relate and to play their accustomed roles. The father or brother role in the family is usually assumed by the studs or butches; these "players" generally are not lesbians but women playing at being men. Their popularity in a house of femmes exceeds all expectations. Referred to by the pronouns "he" and "him," butches are sought after by male-starved women who provide them with cigarettes and all kinds of other enticements. It is a myth perpetuated in Hollywood B grade movies that butches have to resort to force against unwilling parties.

Hensley, Tewksbury, and Koscheski (2002) conducted a survey of 245 inmates in a southern correctional facility. Their purpose was to study the motivations behind female prison sex. Almost half of the women acknowledged engagement in homosexual activities including kissing and oral sex. White women were less sexually active than were women of other races/ethnicities. Similarly, in her review of the recent literature on women's prisons, Severance (2004) found that estimates are that about one-third of women inmates are sexually active with other inmates. In her own interviews with forty incarcerated women in Ohio, some respondents who were sexually involved saw their involvements as limited to prison while others were questioning their sexual identity and thought they might continue the same or other same-sex relationships on the outside. Reasons given for the prison sexual involvement were a past of abusive relationships with men, loneliness, curiosity, and deprivation of sexual contact. Many were uncertain why they got involved and there was much confusion over their sexual identity as a result of their behavior. Jean Harris (1988) described the role-playing at the New York State facility:

> Many of the butches make a concentrated effort to emulate the behavior of young black males, the hip-walking, cool-talking model of masculinity. Some cut their hair short or shave their heads. . . . I've watched many a woman wash, iron, and cook for her "butch," "dike," "bulldagger," and I've heard one stand outside a cell door, begging forgiveness for some wrongdoing she couldn't identify. Inside, as well as outside, it's the woman who pays. (pp. 136, 139)

In personal correspondence with Katherine van Wormer, Kathy Tyler (1998), who was sentenced to life at the Iowa Correctional Institution for Women at Mitchellville, shares her reactions to the author's earlier research:

> I was rather astonished to learn of the mother/sister/brother/cousin, whatever, that you have researched. I have not seen that at all here. What I have seen, and sadly, lots of it is the

homosexual relationships. I find them sad because they are so counterproductive in many ways. First, the women fight—it is strange relationships, almost like they fight between each other to ease the boredom. Secondly, I think the relationships prevent them from doing things they would otherwise do because they always do things in tandem. And thirdly, they are transient, and each time a breakup occurs and a new one takes the place, I think something is lost within each of them. (pp. 1–2)

The prison sex role-playing, even though it says more about female heterosexuality than about homosexuality, in all probability makes the homophobia that much worse by increasing sexual tensions in crowded institutions. Hence, as we have seen, one finds the tendency throughout the prison system for women to define themselves as kin—as sisters, mainly, or as mother/daughters. As kin, they can maintain a certain closeness while avoiding all the gossip that would flow from a less clearly defined relationship. The prison counselor is well advised to recognize the centrality of family relationships to women and to advocate for strengthening family ties with relatives on the outside. A good example is found at Bedford Hills, one of comparatively few prisons in the United States to permit family visits overnight. Trailers on the prison grounds make such extended visits possible.

In summary, taken together, these dimensions—ethnicity, prison family construction, and sexual relationships—compose the prison culture typical of many U.S. prisons for women. An inmate's participation in this culture is determined by many factors, as Owen (1998) informs us, including time spent in prison, social and cultural background, and commitment to a deviant law-breaking lifestyle.

Attitudes toward Women in Prison

It is now clear to all researchers, as it was always clear to feminist theorists, that the notion that Women's Liberation was associated with a new type of female criminal was false (Crites, 1976; Erez, 1988; Watterson, 1996; Weisheit and Mahan, 1988). The now exponential increase in the numbers of women in prison is a political fact, a result of a societal backlash against poor and minority women who become involved with drugs, often through their men. Typically, these women get caught up in legal violations, through drug possession, drug transporting, or drug trafficking. Far from being liberated, such women are doubly dependent—dependent on drugs and dependent on the men who supply them.

Despite women inmates' relatively low level of criminality (compared to male offenders), female correctional officers are very often biased against their female charges (Lutze, 2003). They see "the girls" they supervise as immature, overemotional, and quarrelsome. It has been van Wormer's experience in her prison study, confirmed by Faith, that female correctional officers overwhelmingly prefer to work with male offenders, who are considered less difficult. The negative attitude is often mutual (Erez, 1988). Women inmates resent female officers enforcing rules, many of them quite petty. Infantilization is enforced in petty sanctions

(Lutze, 2003). Correspondents writing to van Wormer list the following rules, which are especially oppressive:

> Shirts must be tucked in
> No Q Tips
> No lending, borrowing, or trading
> No giving gifts to each other
> No hugging
> No writing to people in other institutions
> No tank tops or sleeveless shirts

In Canada during the 1980s, women's groups succeeded in persuading criminal justice agencies to refer to convicted female lawbreakers as "women in conflict with the law," as a less pejorative term (Faith, 1993). Nevertheless, the prejudice against women offenders persists. Women in Canadian as in U.S. prisons are punished much more readily than men for minor offenses such as disrespect and use of strong language, as Faith indicates.

Prison Health Care

The failure of the state to provide adequate medical care to meet the special needs of female prisoners is highlighted in the report of the General Accounting Office (1999) *Women in Prison: Issues and Challenges Confronting U.S. Correctional Systems.* Focusing on the nation's three largest correctional systems—the federal prisons, the California Department of Corrections, and the Texas Department of Criminal Justice— that together hold more than one-third of the nation's female inmates, the report found serious deficiencies in the areas of treatment for substance abuse, mental health problems, and HIV infection. Compared to men, women in prison have higher rates of illness in all three areas. For mental illness, for example, 13 percent of female inmates in federal prisons and 24 percent in state prisons report having a mental disorder or having spent time in a mental hospital (compared to 7 and 16 percent of men). The 1999 government report revealed that the prisons surveyed provided ready access to female-specific health care services, and that initial physical and pelvic examinations, mammograms, and routine pregnancy screening were done. The lack of substance abuse treatment was cited as the area of most striking deficiency in light of the fact that the majority of the inmates have substance abuse problems. Many of the prisons studied were under close external scrutiny due to lawsuits over neglectful health care in the past.

That little has been done since the 1999 report was published is revealed in the following recent news account: "Third Death in Two Months at Tutwiler Raises More Questions." This recent headline refers to the scandal concerning medical treatment inadequacies at the Julia Tutwiler correctional facility in Wetumpka, Alabama (Associated Press, 2005). The news report provides the results of a federal lawsuit brought against the prison following the death through negligent care of three inmates. Earlier, the prison health services had been privatized. An appointed court monitor cited the lack of a treatment plan and failure to watch vital signs in seriously ill inmates as responsible for unnecessary deaths at the prison. Throughout the prison system, the growing trend toward privatization of prison services with its undeniable profit motive rather than a goal to help inmates receive better health care has exacerbated the problem of poor quality health care. For some women in prison, their ten- and twenty-year sentences become death sentences, as chronic illnesses become terminal.

In their in-depth study of medical care through the eyes of inmates at a detention center in Arizona, Moe and Ferraro (2003) found that although some women were pleased to get any health care available because none had been available to them on the outside, many provided chilling stories of near fatal neglect. Fear of contracting diseases in the enclosed space of the prison was a constant among the women.

With the dismantling of public mental health hospitals in the 1960s and the incarceration boom of the past decade, prisons have become home for alarming numbers of the mentally ill. Jails and prison today have become the poor person's mental hospitals, the dumping grounds for people whose bizarre behavior lands them behind bars. According to Moe and Ferraro (2003) in their Arizona study, it appeared that the only time inmates received treatment for their mental problems was when they threatened suicide. But then they were locked in solitary confinement on "suicide watch."

In a nationwide investigation by the international human rights watch group, Amnesty International (1999), Florida, Virginia, and Washington, D.C. were singled out for their routine medical neglect of female inmates. **Amnesty International** (AI) called attention to the following health care failings:

- Partly because of the explosion in female prison population, there are too few staff to meet physical and mental health needs;
- There are long delays in obtaining medical attention, disrupted and poor quality treatment causing physical deterioration of prisoners with chronic and degenerative diseases, like cancer, and overmedication of prisoners with psychotropic drugs;
- Use of nonmedical staff to screen requests for treatment is common;
- There is a serious lack of mental health staffing;
- Women attempting to access mental health services are routinely given medication without opportunity to undergo psychotherapeutic treatment;
- Women in Security Housing Units (SHU) spend between twenty-two and twenty-four hours a day in small, concrete cells. A large proportion of women in SHU have been diagnosed with mental health problems. One California psychiatrist told AI that harsh conditions there can induce psychosis or exacerbate existing mental illness;
- Shackling of all prisoners including pregnant prisoners is policy in federal prisons and the U.S. Marshall Service and exists in almost all state prisons. Shackling during labor may cause possible complications during delivery, such as hemorrhage or decrease in fetal heart rate. If a caesarean section is

needed, a delay of even five minutes could result in permanent brain damage to the baby;

- Women inmates suffering from treatable diseases such as asthma, diabetes, sickle cell anemia, cancer, late-term miscarriages, and seizures have little or no access to medical attention, sometimes resulting in death or permanent injury;
- There is a failure to deliver lifesaving drugs for inmates with HIV/AIDS;
- In violation of international standards, many prisons/jails charge inmates for medical attention, arguing that the charge deters prisoners from seeking medical attention for minor matters or because they want to avoid work.

Amnesty International made the following recommendations:

- Local, state, and federal authorities should provide resources to ensure identification of the physical and mental health care needs of all inmates upon admission and while in custody and to provide necessary services and treatment;
- Health care should be provided without charge;
- Health care should accord with professionally recognized community standards for services to women;
- Authorities should establish standards of adequacy and appropriateness for prison and jail health services and conduct periodic, independent external reviews of the services;
- People suffering severe mental illness should not be in jails and prisons, but in mental health institutions.

The Bad Mother Image

One of the most painful stigmas attached to imprisonment is that of being a bad mother. Incarcerated mothers are often blamed for their forced separation from their children (Watterson, 1996). For prison mothers as we have seen, visits with children are rare; no touching is generally a rule, and access to the telephone is limited. Whether out of shame or to keep children from "blabbing" about where their mothers are, small children are often told, especially by their grandparents, that the prison they are visiting is a hospital. If the children are in foster care, there is little incentive to take them for what could be a disturbing institutional visit.

Especially in divorce proceedings, women are often declared to be unfit mothers by virtue of their imprisonment. If they retain custody, after they serve their time their role as mother is difficult in every way. Among the major challenges are children who feel abandoned, foster parents or grandparents who may not want to let go, and a society that has little compassion for a woman who took drugs or stole or killed, much less a mother who did these things.

Females convicted of infanticide occupy the lowest status in the female convict world. Because most women in prison are mothers who sincerely miss their children, they have little understanding of a mother who would harm her baby. Women who take the lives of their young are often highly suicidal and act out of extreme hopelessness. In a personal interview, Chaplain Kay Kopatich (1998) of the Iowa Correctional Institution for Women, informs us:

> They [mothers convicted of killing their children] are subject to discrimination and to cruel words. I don't think that they are beaten up in women's prison like they might be in a men's prison, but there is mental cruelty. They might be going through the food line and somebody might, an inmate who is serving her might whisper, "baby killer."

Degrading Practices

The history of women in conflict with the law is the history of male oppression. Society is afraid of both the feminist and the female criminal, for each of them in her own way tests society's established boundaries (Jones, 1980). The interconnectedness of feminist advances and harsh punishment of female criminality noted by Ann Jones in her book, *Women Who Kill* (1980) is even more apparent today than when it was written, because of current sentencing practices. Not surprisingly, the political interests of feminist and criminal, therefore, sometimes coincide. The sexual harassment of women in prison by male guards is clearly a women's political issue, however reluctant women prisoners are to unite their cause with that of "liberated" women on the outside.

Increased sexual harassment of women prisoners has come about, ironically, because of the push for women's equality to work as correctional officers in men's prisons and to engage in body-pat frisks and other close contact searches the same as men do. This has led to a situation in which men are allowed the same responsibilities in female institutions. Because of men's greater proclivity than women to be sexually aroused by visual stimuli, the results are about what one would expect (Moir and Jessel, 1991).

Whether the guard is a man or a woman, loss of control over privacy and the most intimate access to one's body are among the most disturbing aspects of imprisonment for women. So disturbing that they can be defined as sexual abuse are invasive body cavity searches, use of strip searches for punishment, women giving birth in chairs and leg shackles, gynecological medical neglect, gynecological procedures performed with male guards present, and women's susceptibility to sexual abuse by male guards.

What Erving Goffman (1961) said about the functions of degradation ceremonies and mortification of the self in total institutions as a means of establishing control certainly rings true in women's prisons. The prisoner must surrender again and again to degrading rituals in which the state has taken ownership of the body/self (Rathbone, 2005). Prisoners who do not submit readily to body-part searches, which may be performed by male guards, typically are forced to strip for more thorough searches. This is how power is negotiated, how the new prisoner is moved into the status of "nonperson" as a passive recipient of whatever the guards choose to mete out. This is not to impugn the motives of the prison employees but rather to show, in the Goffman tradition, how a total institution keeps its charges in line.

One in six women entering U.S. prisons is pregnant (Bureau of Justice Statistics, 2000). Pregnancy poses special difficulties. Delivery is often an ordeal for women who, if drug addicted, commonly are deprived of sufficient pain medication and who may deliver while shackled to the delivery table and then be whisked back to the prison away from the baby and health care (Watterson, 1996). This shoddy medical care of women in childbirth is duplicated in all areas of health care. Gynecological care, for example, is poor to nonexistent.

Taking into account that about half the women in U.S. and Canadian prisons have been victimized sexually in the past, the forced body searches are especially disturbing. Indeed, as Albor (1997) tells us, for many women, prison literally recalls the arbitrary, self-eroding terror of life in previous violent relationships. Inmates may be stripped naked at any time and made to kneel on all fours for rectal/vaginal searches. Male or female guards are often required by institutional policy to probe inmates' body cavities for contraband.

The public got a rare look at the racist and sexist brutality in the women's federal prison when the Canadian Broadcasting Company aired a videotape of male guards roughing up crying women in a forced strip search. The outcry that ensued and the resulting follow-up investigations have done a lot to force the prison to take remedial action and to get the women removed to regional institutions (Dreidger, 1997). Faith (2004), however, cautions that much of the progressive decarceration rhetoric has not been heeded. The fact that the numbers of women confined to prison has tripled during this "reform" period parallels the conservative political mood of the times even while some improvements have occurred.

Prison Sexual Abuse

All rape is an exercise in power, but some rapists have an edge that is more than physical; they operate within an institutionalized setting (Brownmiller, 1975). Rape in slavery, rape in the military, and rape in prison are three such examples.

The scandal involving sexual harassment of women in the military has been highlighted in the mass media. Relatively little attention has been paid until recently to the sexual assaults on female prisoners by their male guards. In 1996, extensive documentation was provided by the Human Rights Watch Women's Rights Project (1996), an international nongovernmental organization, which revealed that the extent of guard-on-inmate abuse behind the closed doors of prisons is staggering. This 347-page report, drawn from firsthand interviews, court records, and records of guards' disciplinary hearings, is astonishing in its graphic detail of everyday experiences of women in our state prisons. As one would expect of a cross-gender power imbalance such as exists between male guards and female inmates, sexual misconduct has been rampant. Here is a summary of the report's findings:

The custodial sexual misconduct documented in this report takes many forms. We found that male correctional employees have vaginally, anally, and orally raped female prisoners and sexually assaulted and abused them. We found that in the course of committing such gross misconduct, male officers have not only used actual or threatened physical force, but have also used their near total authority to provide or deny goods and privileges to female prisoners to compel them to have sex or, in other cases, to reward them for having done so. In other cases, male officers have violated their most basic professional duty and engaged in sexual contact with female prisoners absent the use of threat of force or any material exchange. In addition to engaging in sexual relations with prisoners, male officers have used mandatory pat-frisks or room searches to grope women's breasts, buttocks, and vaginal areas and to view them inappropriately while in a state of undress in the housing or bathroom areas. Male correctional officers and staff have also engaged in regular verbal degradation and harassment of female prisoners, thus contributing to a custodial environment in the state prisons for women which is often highly sexualized and excessively hostile. (p. 1)

Human Rights Watch (1996) and Amnesty International (1999) took the U.S. government to task for failing to protect the women who are subjected to institutionalized rape by prison authorities. The placing of male officers in contact positions over female prisoners is in violation of the United Nations Standard Minimum Rules for the Treatment of Prisoners.

The persons who are most vulnerable to sexual abuse are first-time offenders, the young or mentally ill, and lesbian and transgendered persons. The gripping prison Hollywood drama *Love Child*, produced in 1982, tells the true story of an inmate who became pregnant by a guard in Florida and fought for her right to keep the baby. Many times female inmates willingly trade sex for favors; male guards who have been involved in sexual relations with inmates are transferred to men's prisons rather than being fired. Prisoners, such as those in Georgia who are not given a stipend for their work, have no means of purchasing the many supplies they need or the cigarettes they so badly crave. This dependency enhances their vulnerability to sexual exploitation (Human Rights Watch, 1996). In many instances, women have been impregnated as a result of sexual misconduct, placed in segregation if they filed a complaint, and sometimes pressured to get an abortion (Human Rights Watch, 1996).

According to psychologist Louis Rothenstein, who worked for six years in the federal prison in Dublin, California, it was not uncommon for guards to go into women's cells and have sex (cited in Stein, 1996). Complaints by women inmates and their advocates were ignored. "You would be blackballed if you were thought of as an advocate for the inmates," he said (p. 24). A code of silence within the prison industry shields it from public scrutiny, he added. In 1998, at the U.S. District Court in San Francisco, a settlement was reached providing $500,000 for three female inmates who filed a grievance after being raped by male inmates while housed at the male facility at Dublin, California (*Prison Legal News*, 1998a). The inmates reportedly had been given access to women after bribing a male officer.

According to Stop Prisoner Rape (2003), the sexual abuse of female inmates at the Ohio Reformatory for Women was widespread and persistent. Reports of such abuse were brought by a therapist and confirmed by a nurse administrator and former inmates at the facility. The extensive investigation conducted by Stop Prisoner Rape, which was bolstered by widespread media coverage in Ohio, further revealed that female inmates who complained were locked in solitary confinement.

Examples from recent news reports highlight the issue of sexual abuse of female inmates by correctional staff:

- "Charges Allege Sex with Inmates," *Casper Star Tribune*, July 29, 2005
- "City to Settle with Thousands over Illegal Strip-Searches," *The New York Times*, July 14, 2005
- "Claims of Jail Sex, Beatings Pile Up," *The Sun Herald*, July 16, 2005

The above reports were all retrieved on www.google.com under the category news and the typed-in heading, "sexual abuse, inmates." The frequency of such reports and of those still emerging from U.S. prisons reveals that rampant abuse of women continues to take place.

Rathbone's (2005) interviews with women confined in the Massachusetts women's prison at Framingham provide details of sexual relationships between inmates and guards, often the trading of sex for small privileges. A further account of prison scandals from the popular literature is provided by Amy Fisher (2004), who at age sixteen shot her lover's wife at his request. In prison, as a celebrity murderer, Fisher was sexually abused by correctional officers. Today, now a free woman, she is active in prison reform.

Official reports both echo those from the scholarly and popular literature and provide additional information. Survey results from the sexual violence report conducted by the U.S. Department of Justice and analyzed by BJS statisticians Beck and Hughes (2005) provide some rather startling information about sexual misconduct in the nation's jails and prisons. Female staff members were frequently reported for sexual misconduct in men's prisons. The statistics are these: with regard to inmate-on-inmate nonconsensual sexual acts in prison and jail, males comprised 90 percent of the victims and perpetrators. In local jails, 70 percent of victims were female, and 65 percent of perpetrators were male. In state prisons, however, 67 percent of those involved in sexual misconduct were female, as perpetrators, and 69 percent of the victims were male. No specific illustrations are given, but one can speculate from other studies in the literature that some female officers who work in men's prisons might be psychologically susceptible to being manipulated by men in their charge.

To understand this phenomenon, we turn to a special report from the U.S. Department of Justice (2005). This inquiry, the first of its kind, was undertaken as a requirement of the Prison Rape Elimination Act passed by Congress and signed into law in 2003. Among the cases it described: a female psychologist overheard discussing her sexual relationship with an inmate; a letter that was intercepted describing a female teacher's sexual relationship with a male inmate; a male officer who raped a male inmate; and a female inmate who reported to authorities that she had had sexual relations twelve times with a guard. What stands out in these cases is that the male inmates were not the ones filing the complaints, whereas we know from other reports many of the women who get sexually involved with their male correctional officers do feel victimized and do complain. Although the female officers who violate the boundaries are clearly behaving in an unprofessional manner and could be expected to be sanctioned by the prison, accordingly, one wonders if criminal prosecution is appropriate for female officers who engage in sexual conduct with their male charges. Gender differences in human sexuality, including who takes the initiative, perhaps should be considered in these cases. Few prosecutors, in fact, prosecute such cases, perhaps in light of an intuitive understanding that sex with a female officer may have a different meaning for a male inmate than sex with a male guard for a female inmate. To our knowledge, there is no discussion in the academic literature on this matter; hopefully, future BJS victim reports will provide further clarification about this behavior.

How about inmate-to-inmate sexual coercion among women? Hensley, Castle, and Tewksbury (2003) explored that issue via questionnaires completed by 245 inmates in a southern correctional facility. Over 4 percent of the 245 inmates reported that they had been sexually coerced by other female inmates and two percent admitted they had sexually coerced another inmate. The incidents included genital touching or attempts at sexual contact. Although African Americans were more heavily represented among perpetrators than as victims, whites were sometimes perpetrators as well. Interestingly, for some, a perceived change in sexual orientation occurred. Over half of the victims and perpetrators stated that they had identified as heterosexual prior to incarceration. However, the sample size of perpetrators was extremely small, only 5 inmates out of the 245 who filled out questionnaires, however, so further research is needed on this subject.

Inmate Litigation

We begin by summarizing litigative events at the notorious women's prison in Georgia. These events have special meaning for van Wormer; she was personally escorted out of the Milledgeville facility in 1973 by a correctional officer speaking on behalf of the warden (this prison had gone through five wardens in that one year), who said, "It has been decided that you cannot consider your [dissertation] study here; you might see some things you don't understand."

The New York Times (1992) described some of the things that might, in truth, have been understood by the investigator only too well: Although women in Georgia's prison sued the prison for sexual abuse in 1984, they had to wait eight years to win their case in November 1992. In the end, fourteen former employees—ten men, including the deputy warden, and four women—were indicted on sexual abuse charges, including rape, sexual assault, and sodomy in "one of the worst episodes of its kind in the history of the nation's women's prisons" (p. 1). The incidents took place in the warden's house, in a prison rest room, and in other areas.

These indictments at the Georgia Penitentiary were only the tip of the iceberg at the penitentiary. Whether brought about through trade-offs or coerced through violence between male guards and female inmates, sexual involvement was not deviant behavior in that setting; it was the norm. Even female staff members were implicated in sexual abusive behavior, according to court records cited in the Human Rights Watch (1996) report. There is no way to begin to estimate the number of inmates involved before the lawsuit was filed in 1992. Between 1992 and 1996 (Human Rights Watch, 1996), when better records were kept owing to the investigations taking place, attorney Bob Cullen told Human Rights Watch that he had learned of approximately 370 reported incidents during this period. Some of the cases have been publicized in the media.

Legislation in the form of the Prison Litigation Reform Act was passed by the U.S. Congress and signed into law in 1996 (Human Rights Watch, 1996). The intent was to stifle the spate of frivolous lawsuits coming from prisons and mainly from men's prisons. Unfortunately, the ability of women inmates and their legal advocates to sue over human rights violations is now drastically curtailed, according to the Human Rights Watch.

Not surprisingly, extensive litigation concerns the sexual mistreatment of female inmates. According to Chesney-Lind and Pasko (2004), scandals have erupted in California, Georgia, Hawaii, Ohio, Louisiana, Michigan, Tennessee, New York, and New Mexico. Most of these scandals have come to light only because of publicity surrounding legal suits. The past decades may portend a new trend in the nature of legal action taken against the criminal justice system. Van Wormer (2001) in her survey of prison administrators asked if media reporting of sexual abuse of inmates was blown out of proportion or reflective of reality. The responses were equally divided on this issue. On the question of whether or not male correctional officers performed all the same tasks as female officers, two left the question blank, two said yes, and twenty-six said no. The exceptions were said to be with regard to routine strip searches. Most indicated that with regard to pat-down searches, shower duties, emergency strip searches, and dorm assignments, men were still unrestricted as before.

These practices, although improved in that some restrictions are imposed on male officers, are still below the standard recommended by Amnesty International (1999). The organization declared that the sexual abuse of women inmates was a form of torture and called for female inmates to be supervised by female staff only in accordance with international standards.

In addition to sexual abuse, female prisoners are raising issues of clemency for battered women who killed in self-defense, drug treatment, prison nurseries, decent dental care, and health care for the aged and for those with HIV/AIDS. Much of the litigation concerns the lack of employment and vocational training opportunities for women, compared to men, in prison. Correctional policy makers often justify the poor training options in light of the numbers of women in prison being too small to provide many options, few of the female inmates have marketable skills, and interest in men's prison programs such as auto mechanics is minimal (Feinman, 1994). Accordingly, most work in prison relates to the everyday running of the prison—washing, cleaning, and cooking.

A major problem with the litigation to equalize employment training opportunities for men and women is that male prisoners are heavily exploited as a source of cheap labor, making only a few dollars per hour, at the most. The extent of this exploitation is revealed in an article in the 1997 summer issue of *Iowa Commerce Magazine:* "Employers pay an hourly wage only. No workers' compensation. No unemployment. No health insurance. No benefits" (cited in Basu, 1998, p. 6). Instead of going to Mexico, many private companies, as Basu (1998) contends, are relying on this state-subsidized program to get inmates to work. The issues are the same as with the exploitation of cheap labor overseas: wages for regular labor can be driven down and work opportunities are provided for persons in no position to bargain. Controversial convict-for-hire agreements have been reached across the United States. The risk of displacement of free-world labor is a real fear in some quarters (Lomax, 1998).

Historically, almost all the legal action for prisoner rights was pursued on behalf of men. Suggested reasons for gender differences in filing litigation are women's general passivity, their prisons' locations far from urban centers and legal aid attorneys, and the scarcity of jailhouse lawyers among them (Feinman, 1994). A unique explanation is that the female inmate tendency to form play-families and to pair off as "married couples" serves inadvertently to suppress troublemakers and absorb women's energies, while having a subduing effect on their activism (see Giallombardo, 1966; van Wormer, 1987).

In other countries, although there has been litigation, corrections reform for women has come more often from highly publicized efforts on their account and a concerned public enlightened by sympathetic press accounts. In Canada, for example, a 1990 task force report on federally sentenced women led to construction of model prisons designed for the offenders' well-being. In 1994, a Canadian federal inquiry into strip searches by a male riot squad at the women's federal prison resulted in a castigating report written by Madam Justice Louise Arbour Faith (2004). A human rights issue desperately in need of litigation, but that seems unlikely to benefit from court action, is the extremely brutal treatment of detained political refugees who, because they are not U.S. citizens, are considered to be outside the jurisdiction of the Constitution. Kassindja's harrowing memoir, *Do They Hear You When You Cry?* (1998), graphically recounts the horrors of her oppression during confinement by the Immigration and Naturalization Service. Kassindja, who arrived in the United States as a refugee from forced genital mutilation in Togo, Africa, was successful only because her story received rare national press coverage.

Women on Death Row

In Europe, in early February 1998, editorial writers called the execution of Karla Fay Tucker a "barbaric act." The *Irish Times,* in contrast to the major papers in the United States, featured the story on page 1 for two consecutive days (Carroll, 1998; *Irish Times,* 1998). Entreaties from all over the world and from the Pope failed to gain clemency for Tucker, the first woman executed in Texas since 1863. Tucker, despite being an admitted axe murderer who had killed strangers in a drug-induced rage, galvanized the sympathy of the world. Like Velma Barfield before her, Tucker was a born-again Christian whose femininity and good works in prison endeared her to people. Following Tucker's execution, but this time without much fanfare, Judias Buenoano, an unrepentant woman prisoner known as the Black Widow, was executed in Florida's electric chair in March 1998. More recently, with Texas preparing to execute the first black woman in the state since the Civil War, the British news carried a story raising questions about her guilt. Frances Newton, forty years old, was convicted for killing her husband and two children. Like other women who are charged with murdering their husbands, Newton, it was claimed, killed him to get his insurance. (Since men often carry life insurance, this charge is commonly made in such cases.) Newton never confessed and always said an intruder committed the murders. New evidence uncovered the existence of a second gun at the scene (Luscombe, 2005). Nevertheless, Newton was executed on September 15, 2005, an act witnessed by her grieving parents (Turner and Ganza, 2005).

The deaths of these women, like all executions, were highly political. The message sent to the public by the state execution of these women is that justice is without mercy and, as for women, that if they want equality of opportunity they can also have equality of punishment. Laster's (1994) astute analysis of women executed in Australia between 1842 and 1967 demonstrates that politics rather than law influences the sentencing outcome for women. Women were hanged in Victoria not for what they did but for what they were. They were not hardened criminals or a threat to society; their crimes were different from those of their male counterparts. Overwhelmingly, their victims were intimates. Execution of women, as Laster argues, is a kind of social control in a society stressing traditional family values. In a twisted irony, in today's world, the insistence of feminists for equal treatment is used as a way of advancing antifeminist political agendas.

As of July 2005 there were 54 women on death row; this constitutes 1.6 percent of the total death row population of about 3,415 persons (Death Penalty Information, 2005). In the past 100 years, over 40 women have been executed in the United States, including ten since 1976. Of these ten, nine were white and one black (Streib, 2005). Of the total of 152 death sentences handed out from 1973 to 2005, around 70 percent were black, 17.7 percent were white, 1 percent were Latino, and .02 percent were American Indian. Around one-fourth killed their husbands or boyfriends, one-fourth killed children or grandchildren, and a few killed multiple family members. The others were in a variety of situations often related to drugs or robbery.

Of all the women who commit murder, only a small fraction end up on death row. The figures give some indication that race played some role in this. We can surmise that all the women were poor. One thing that we probably did not consider though, was how many were lesbian.

Kathryn Ann Farr (2000) argues that the masculinized portrayal of female evil affects sentencing decisions pertaining to an already heinous crime. The unfeminine image of women such as Buenoano, portrayed as a man-hater, the "black widow" reduces any sympathy for such women who are seen as deserving of their fate, in contrast to Karla Fay Tucker, described in the media as pretty and married to her prison chaplain, who aroused national sympathy in her passing. Farr's article relates the experiences of thirty five women who were sent to death row in part because they are lesbians and were seen as being in defiance of appropriate gender roles. Her findings showed that lesbians are over-represented in death sentence cases, and that the playing up of non-feminine personality traits by prosecutors and the media undoubtedly influenced the juries or judges when it came to imposing the maximum penalty. A recent study by the American Civil Liberties Union (2004) confirmed that prosecutors used sexual orientation and images of masculinization to prejudice juries in at least three cases of female death row inmates.

Death row conditions vary from state to state (Thompson, 1997). Some states allow the women to mingle for visits and yard time, but most allow no contact visits (only visits behind glass, by means of a telephone), no work, and solitary confinement for 23 hours per day. Death row inmates have some limited contact with correctional officers, prison chaplains, and treatment staff (Feinman, 1994).

The literature on women on death row has been sparse until recently. Velma Barfield's (1985) autobiography, *Women on Death Row*, mainly concerns her religious conversion and her work in spreading the word to other women to whom she talked through the walls. Thus we learn of her routine at the Raleigh, North Carolina, penitentiary:

> *I was put in an end cell that, like all the others, contained four bunks. "No one else," the officer said, "will ever occupy the cell with you."*
>
> *I didn't realize it then, but for the next four and a half years, my world would consist of a room ten feet by ten feet, with bars for two sides and concrete walls for the other two. Little natural light penetrated the cell. . . . A guard led me out of my cell every day for one hour of exercise. Aside from that daily hour and occasional trips to the administrative building or to the mental health unit or when I was taken to court, I never moved outside my cell. (p. 106)*

Cathy Thompson (1997), an inmate confined on death row in Chowchilla, California, writes to the Irish anti–death penalty organization, Lifelines, "It is known factually that women sentenced to death are usually first-time offenders. The vast majority of these women come from abusive families and easily fall prey to abusive relationships. Other than when their crimes occur or when an execution date is scheduled for one of us, we remain totally invisible to society" (p. 3).

Kathleen O'Shea, a former nun, has made it her life's work to publicize conditions for women sentenced to die. In her absorbing newsletter, *Women on the Row* (1998), O'Shea describes the grim circumstances facing one of these women: "[She] told me they had changed from cuffing her hands to go to the shower from the front to the back, so that it is extremely difficult to carry anything on the way. They have to literally sit down on a filthy floor to pick it up and the male guards just watch, and according to this woman, enjoy it quite a bit" (p. 7). In her book, *Women and the Death Penalty in the United States, 1900–1998*, O'Shea (1999) describes the utter secrecy surrounding how women on death row are treated by the men who supervise them. The prisons, according to this author, try their best to keep conditions in these "prisons within prisons" from coming to light. The book is currently being updated and is forthcoming with Praeger (O'Shea, 2005).

It is impossible to discuss the death penalty as the ultimate cruelty without revealing its curious attraction to suicidal inmates. Elsewhere, van Wormer (1995) has documented twenty cases (nineteen men, one woman) of persons who committed murder as a form of wished-for state-assisted suicide. Some of them were serving life sentences in prison. In personal correspondence with the author, Beverly Seymour (1998) describes her legal suit in Ohio in which she requests the death penalty as a form of euthanasia. "If I don't get it," she writes, "I'm outa here."

Chaplain Kopatich (1998) describes the scene for women inmates in Iowa, a state without the death penalty:

> *I have heard that over and over again, they wish that they could end this agony. And they would like to have the death penalty. But that is probably cyclical too because the urge for life is very strong. So when they first come in I hear that a lot, "I wish that I would have gotten the death penalty." But they haven't faced death row so I'm not sure about that. But I just know it's very harsh to face life in prison. (p. 3)*

Innovative Programs

To move from the grimmest aspect of penal policy—executions—to the brightest, we now briefly review some laudable innovations within the context of women's imprisonment. Some of the innovations are holistic and structural and woman-centered from top to bottom. The others discussed in this section are piecemeal, positive programs operating against a backdrop of punitiveness and antifeminism. We could refer to these as beacons of light. These types of programs are family centered, cultural, specific, and educational.

We start with two international approaches. First, Denmark, a country with a strong social welfare state and a nonpunitive philosophy toward offenders, maintains a state prison at Ringe that is the prototype of progressivism. As described by Feinman (1994) and Krepel (2002), Denmark's prison accommodates young men and young women in totally integrated housing. A man and woman are permitted to be alone in each other's rooms until 10:30 at night; they also may entertain spouses or lovers from the outside in their rooms. All prison activities are completely integrated. There are a few guards, but no heavy fences, no riot equipment, no guns, no uniforms, and certainly no bars (Krepel, 2002). The prisoners are required to attend school or work from 7:30 a.m. to 3 p.m. To maintain family ties even the inmates with the longest sentences can go home once every three weeks. What is the escape rate? One in ten. But most escapees report to the police immediately and ask to be transferred to a different prison due to personal conflicts. Since

Denmark is a small country, inmates can't hide for long. Even if they leave the country, most Danes feel so strongly attached to their homeland that escapees eventually return to finish their sentences. The Denmark example typifies Scandinavian cultural values, values that promote sexual equality and fewer restrictions on sexuality. For our second example, we look north to Canada.

Feminist Empowering Programs

Canadian culture, although having much in common with that in the United States, is generally regarded as having a more humane social welfare system (see Adams, 2003). Canada's prison system is less harsh, but the Canadian Correctional Service has had to answer to a barrage of criticisms from human rights groups, especially concerning the disproportionate confinement of aboriginal women in maximum security prisons and the continued use of male guards in women's prisons (Cordon, 2005). Nevertheless, the correctional service that placed female offenders in small regional, woman-centered facilities to help integrate inmates into the environment has now pledged to make further improvements. The United States has much to learn from Canada's gender-responsive approach. As described by a New Jersey newspaper account (Peet, 2004):

> *Arguably the most progressive corrections system in North America, Canada is the only place that offers a healing lodge for Native American women offenders, nontraditional job training off-site, a certified trade school and, it was announced this month, prison tattoo parlors to lower the risk of spreading hepatitis through self-inflicted jailhouse body art . . . , Unlike U.S. states that are just now developing gender-specific inmate programs, Canada operates under a Strategy for Women Offenders established in 1994. (p. 1)*

The Canadian approach follows a "special-needs" model as opposed to a gender-neutral one. The special-needs approach for women prisoners caters to women's special needs, such as privacy, self-esteem work, and maintenance of family ties. The gender-neutral model, on the other hand, is exemplified in Denmark's prison programming, which emphasizes gender equality. An outgrowth in the United States of feminist-inspired court cases demanding equality of opportunity (in jobs and vocational training) for female inmates, enforcement of the gender-neutral has led to solutions that, in turn, have created new problems. For example, co-correctional (often called coeducational) establishments have subjected women, who are in the minority, to exploitation by male inmates and guards and to special restrictions on their freedom of movement to prevent sexual activity among inmates.

Hannah-Moffat (1994) argues forcefully against the placing of women in male-oriented facilities. For empowerment of women to occur, she suggests, male and female inmates need programs especially geared toward their needs. Ignoring women's reality is not the way to sexual equality, and the whole notion of incarceration for women needs to be carefully evaluated.

At the Amerswiel women's prison in the Netherlands, the authorities attempt to follow the U.N. Standard Minimum Rules for the Treatment of Prisoners. Davis and Martinez (1996) describe the Dutch model honoring the right to life and integrity of the person as well as respect for one's dignity and family life. In the Netherlands, female inmates have private rooms with a bath and a desk; they can rent luxuries such as a CD player with money they earn working 20 hours a week. The importance of alternatives to incarceration is also stressed by the Dutch government (Ortmann, 1998).

Family Programs

There are a few exemplary prison programs for mothers of small children. Bedford Hills in New York State is the one most written about. (See, for example, Boudin, 1998; Pollack, 2004.) The Bedford Hills program provides a nursery where babies up to eighteen months old can live with their mothers. A playroom is available for older children, who are encouraged to come and visit their moms. The mother-child bonding has been excellent in this program; mothers learn child-care skills from child development experts. The theoretical foundations for the program were drawn from feminist consciousness-raising groups, group psychology, and the trauma recovery process. This peer support program is facilitated by the incarcerated mothers themselves. Pollack (2004) describes the philosophy as anti-oppressive in its acknowledgement of structural oppression and its impact on the women, and as empowering in its building on the women's initiative and autonomy. Pollack correctly concludes that the task of progressive mental health services for this population is to counter constructions of women offenders as having personality and thinking disorders. Rather, she says, we need to tap into women's strengths and acknowledge their varied and skillful modes of coping. Women's prisons in Nebraska, Ohio, and Washington let inmates who meet the requirements live with their newborns (Lohn, 2005). The Shakopee program in Minnesota allows for twenty-four-hour visits with mother and child. The child sleeps on a trundle bed that pulls out from under the mother's bed in her cell.

The Nebraska Correctional Center for Women, similarly, has a prison nursery and allows overnight visits for older children to maintain the bonds between mother and child. Children can stay up to five days a month. According to the male warden, the presence of children has a harmonizing effect on the whole population (Lohn, 2005). Advocates say that programs that help mothers behind bars to maintain relationships with children are key to reducing crime over the long run (Lohn, 2005). Cost savings of such nursery programs not only are reflected in reduced foster care expenses, but also in the reduced likelihood that the incarcerated mother's children will be incarcerated themselves (Office of Performance Evaluations, 2003).

Although nothing positive has been said about the California system and its treatment of women in years past, hope is on the horizon as the California Legislative Women's Caucus has made this issue of the treatment of women in prison a top priority (Warren, 2005). Now, new rules are to be applied; in the future, for example, male guards will no longer conduct pat searches of women. The intense focus on security for women, who typically have been convicted of survival crimes, who are little or no security threat, is at last being questioned. This questioning is perhaps a reflection of the realization that equality does not have to mean sameness, that to take into account gender differences is not to belittle women. Attention to the importance of the role of motherhood to most of the women is to be given more attention in the future. The California Department of Corrections is looking to innovative programs in other states as models, to Indiana that keeps women convicts heavily involved in their children's lives, to Missouri that emphasizes a transition to parole, and to Minnesota in its focus on alternatives to prison close to the women's homes.

A European organization, Children of Imprisoned Parents (Eurochips), advocates that attention be paid to the needs of children in maintaining ties with their incarcerated parents. The Swedish Prison and Probation Service ordered the following for all prisons in Sweden:

- Special leave will be granted for important events concerning children.
- Children should be allowed to telephone and speak directly to the parent. (In the past, children could only leave a message and ask the parent to call back, which frequently occurred several hours later.)
- Each new prisoner should be asked about his/her children.
- Flexible visiting hours for children need to be provided (Eurochips, 2005).

In Australia, inmate mothers can usually care for their children until they reach the age of two or three. In western Europe, except for Norway (a country that makes extensive use of long-term foster care), children are kept at the prison for up to several years. Germany has, perhaps, the most outstanding prison nursery system. In this program, described by Harris (1988), teachers and social workers help mothers learn how to be good mothers. According to a BBC broadcast (2001), mothers of small children who have been sentenced to prison can keep their children until the children are six years old. The facility at Frondenberg in northwest Germany has no bars in the windows; the mothers can go outside and play with the children and can visit the town. The mothers go to work after the child is two years old, and they can go on leave from the grounds for twenty one days of vacation per year. The children attend a regular nursery school and kindergarten. It has been found that mothers in this program have a much lower reoffending rate than a comparable group of mothers who do not have their children with them. A California state program allows female prisoners with small children a chance to move to one of seven homes in the state where they can live with their children and take parenting classes. Several hundred women, only a fraction of the mothers in California's prison system, have graduated from the program.

Other family programs involve conjugal rights for prisoners and their spouses. Russian women are entitled to a couple of three-day visits a year with their husbands. In the United States, only eight states allow conjugal visits (Dowling, 1997). At Bedford Hills, families can spend forty-eight-hour periods together in trailers on the campus.

Ethnic-Specific Programs

The Correctional Service of Canada has now endorsed Native Canadians' right to practice Native ceremonies and healing circles. With help from spiritual teachers, Native women have formed healing circles and have revived such practices as fasting; having potlatches; burning sweetgrass, sage, and cedar; and holding medicine bundles (Faith, 1993). Correctional Service of Canada (2005) has incorporated an Elder consultation program to provide personal support to aboriginal women. Native liaison officers also consult with Elders, who are older, respected members of the community, regarding their clients. The Elders not only provide ceremony but also impart ongoing wisdom to the group. They also participate in Elder-assisted parole hearings and the reintroduction of women to the community.

Increasingly, Spanish-language radio and television programming is available for the influx of Hispanic women entering prison for drug-related offenses. A great deal more needs to be done for Latina inmates with culturally specific programming. For African Americans, also, Afrocentric consciousness-raising is helpful in engendering pride. Many of the newly developed substance abuse programs, imported from the outside by substance counselors, offer cultural-sensitive group counseling sessions for inmates. My Sister's Keeper, a Chicago-based program that is a division of the Black on Black Love Organization, is a complete after-care program that helps women who have been released from prison to lead productive lives. This **ethnic-specific program** promotes drug education, life-skills and parenting training, cultural enrichment activities, and help with housing and legal services (Samuel, 2003).

To prevent recidivism, such services are vital. In their investigation of the effects of poverty and state programming on recidivism, Holtfreter, Reisig, and Morash (2004) studied factors leading to re-arrest in a sample of 134 female felony offenders in community corrections in Oregon and Minnesota. They found that poverty status after prison increased the odds of re-arrest by about five times and the odds of supervision violation by about thirteen times. Their recommendation is for policy reforms that provide state-sponsored resources in the areas of childcare, education, health care, and job training, all of which address the causes of economic marginalization associated with crime.

Summary

Today, women make up 6 percent of the prison population, and 10 percent of those are confined in jail cells. Although their percentage of the total is small, the increase in the numbers of female inmates has well exceeded the increase for male prisoners, as a study of the latest U.S. government statistics shows.

Race, gender, and class, as we have seen in this chapter, intersect in the reality, indeed, the tragedy, of women's prisons. Viewed another way, one could easily make the argument that the antifeminist and antiwelfare movements are being played out in the courtrooms and prisons of the United States. The War on Drugs has taken its toll on poor minority women and on their children, who are destined to grow up in foster homes while their mothers serve their time.

The euphemisms known as "sentencing reform" and "welfare reform" are not a threat to rich, white women. The few rich, white women one finds behind prison walls are generally there for murder.

The new antidrug laws bring their effects to bear disproportionately on persons without political and legal leverage in U.S. society.

In this chapter, we have seen the circumstances for women in prison come full circle—from confinement in overcrowded, male-run prisons, to removal into maternal reformatories focusing on inmates' moral development, to confinement once again in overcrowded, punitive prisons run by a predominantly male staff. We have turned our attention to two developments in the administration of women's institutions since the 1970s: the rise of prisoner litigation, and the replacement of matrons with male officers.

Today's scandals, which center around sexual abuse and exploitation of female inmates, echo those days gone by when females were originally placed under male authority. Surprisingly, the media, which in the United States have concentrated on the drug war and harsher sentencing laws, seem to have largely overlooked the shocking developments as revealed in the international investigations conducted by Human Rights Watch. In Canada, in contrast, there has been considerable local media coverage of rough treatment of women by male prison officers. In any case, in both countries current litigation has offered prisoners some protection they might not otherwise have had.

In the 1980s, equality for women was the word. In the field of corrections, the focus was on equality of opportunity for female correctional officers in men's prisons and equality of educational and vocational opportunity for male and female offenders. In light of some unintended consequences of the bid for equality, namely, the widespread sexual harassment of female prisoners by male correctional officers (the counterpart of female officers who work without restriction in men's prisons) and the mandatory harsh minimum sentences for drug possession and dealing, women's advocates today are arguing for an empowering feminist approach geared toward women's special needs.

KEY TERMS

Amnesty International
conspiracy laws
ethnic-specific program

Madonna image
prison industrial complex

prison play-families
war on drugs

CRITICAL THINKING QUESTIONS

1. Consider prison construction and management as a big business enterprise. What are the ramifications for residents? Why are states privatizing? Discuss advantages and disadvantages.

2. Is there such a thing as the "Madonna image"? Discuss this concept with regard to historical racial differences.

3. How do conspiracy laws hurt women? Make up a situation in which a woman who is innocent of drug dealing can get caught up in the criminal justice net as a result of these laws.

4. How is the war on drugs played out as a war against poor women and minorities?

5. The text briefly theorizes that homophobia in prison may cause inmates to declare themselves to be sisters and mother and daughter. Discuss how this process operates.

6. Discuss advantages and disadvantages to female inmates in forming pseudo-family bonds.

7. Compare the expression of sexuality in men's and women's prison institutions.

8. Describe the pathways by which some women in prison come to adopt different sexual identities. How do you think this new identity will or will not affect their homecoming?

9. Discuss how the sexual abuse of women came about due to legal factors. Compare the situation in which male officers sexually abuse female inmates and female officers get into trouble with male inmates. Are these offenses exactly the same in terms of gender factors?

10. How does the case for equality not have to entail sameness?

11. Compare two scenarios, one in which a drug user gets treatment in the community and one in which she is sent to serve a prison term. Consider economic costs and consequences for her and her children's lives.

12. Discuss the death penalty in terms of how it is carried out. Does the death penalty bring about justice in our society?

13. Design a women's prison in which you would like to work. Would the way the women's prison in Denmark is run work in the United States?

14. Do small children belong in prison? If so, up to what age? Discuss advantages and disadvantages of prison nurseries.

WEB DESTINATIONS

Amnesty International: www.amnesty.usa.org

California Coalition for Women Prisoners: www.womenprisoners.org

Canadian Service Canada: www.csc-scc.gc.ca

Children of Incarcerated Parents: www.eurochips.org/uk

Death Penalty Information: www.deathpenaltyinfo.org

Human Rights Watch: www.hrw.org

The November Coalition: www.november.org

Stop Prisoner Rape: www.spr.org/pdf

U.S. Department of Justice: www.usdoj.gov

REFERENCES

Aamot, G. (1998, May 24). Pregnant in S.D.? Don't try drinking. *Daily News, Bowling Green, KY*, p. 13A.

Adams, M. (2003). *Fire and ice: The United States, Canada and the myth of converging values*. Toronto: Penguin Press.

Albor, B. J. (1997, July 18). The women behind bars who could go free. *The Independent* (London), p. 10.

Allen, H. E., & Simonsen, C. E. (1995). *Corrections in America: An introduction*. Englewood Cliffs, N.J.: Prentice-Hall.

American Civil Liberties Union (ACLU) (2004, December). *The forgotten population: A look at death row in the United States through the experiences of women*. Retrieved from www.aclu.org/DeathPenalty

American Civil Liberties Union (ACLU) (2005, May 17). *Caught in the net: The impact of drug policies on women and families*. ACLU. Retrieved from www.civilrights.org

American Friends Service Committee. (1971). *Struggle for justice: A report on crime and punishment in America*. New York: Hill & Wang.

Amnesty International (1999). *Not a part of my sentence—Violation of the human rights of women in custody*. New York: Amnesty International.

Associated Press (2005, May 7). Third death in two months at Tutwiler raises more questions. *Tuscaloosa News*. Retrieved from www.tuscaloosanews.com

Barfield, V. (1985). *Woman on death row*. Minneapolis, Minn.: World Wide Publications.

Basu, R. (1998, March 15). What's at work in Iowa prisons? *Des Moines Register*, p. A6.

Beck, A., and Hughes, T. (2005). *Sexual violence reported by correctional authorities, 2004*. U.S. Department of Justice: Bureau of Justice Statistics.

Bloom, B., Owen, B., and Covington, S. (2004). Women offenders and the gendered effects of public policy. *The Review of Policy Research 21*(1): 31–49.

Boudin, K. (1998). Lessons from a mother's program in prison: A psychosocial approach supports women and their children. *Women and Therapy, 21*(1): 103–125.

British Broadcasting Company (BBC) (2001, November 20). Mothers in prison. Woman's Hour. *BBC*. Retrieved from www.bbc.co.uk/radio4

Britton, D. (2003). *At work in the iron cage: The prison as gendered organization*. New York: New York University Press.

Brownmiller, S. (1975). *Against our will: Men, women, and rape*. New York: Bantam Books.

Bureau of Justice Statistics. (1997a). Capital punishment 1996. Washington, D.C.: U.S. Department of Justice.

Bureau of Justice Statistics. (1998a). Prison and jail inmates at midyear 1997. Washington, D.C.: U.S. Department of Justice.

Bureau of Justice Statistics. (1998b). *Prisoners in 1997*. Washington, D.C.: U.S. Department of Justice.

Bureau of Justice Statistics. (1994). *Women in prison*. Washington, D.C.: U.S. Department of Justice.

Bureau of Justice Statistics (BJS) (2000). *Women offenders*. Washington, D.C.: U.S. Department of Justice.

Bureau of Justice Statistics (BJS) (2005). *Prison and jail inmates at midyear 2004*. Washington, D.C.: U.S. Department of Justice.

Canadian Human Rights Commission (2003, December). *Protecting their rights*. Retrieved from www.web.net/~efryont

Carlen, P., and Tchaikovsky, C. (1996). Women's imprisonment in England at the end of the twentieth century: Legitimacy, realities, and utopias. In R. Matthews and P. Francis (eds.), *Prisons 2000* (pp. 179–200). New York: St. Martin's Press.

Carroll, J. (1998, February 4). Tucker executed by lethal injection. *The Irish Times*, p. 1.

Chesney-Lind, M. (1997). *The female offender: Girls, women, and crime.* Thousand Oaks, Calif.: Sage.

Chesney-Lind, M. (1995). Rethinking women's imprisonment: A critical examination of trends in female incarceration. In B. R. Price and N. J. Sokoloff (eds.), *The criminal justice system and women: Offenders, victims, and workers* (pp. 105–117), 2nd ed. New York: McGraw-Hill.

Chesney-Lind, M., and Pasko, L. (2004). *The female offender: Girls, women, and crime,* 2nd ed. Thousand Oaks, Calif.: Sage.

Children of Imprisoned Parents (Eurochips) (2005, March). News: Sweden. Eurochips. Retrieved from www.eurochips.org/uk

Cordon, S. (2005, February 17). Correctional service promises changes in women's jails. *The Canadian Press.* Retrieved from www.cp.org

Correctional Service Canada (CSC) (2005).*CSC action plan in response to the report of the Canadian human rights commission.* Ottawa, Canada: CSC. Retrieved from www.csc-scc.gc.ca/text/prgrm

Crites, L. (1976). *The female offender.* Lexington, Mass.: Lexington Books.

Davis, A., and Martinez, E. (1996, May 9). *A conversation on women, culture, and politics* (Cassette Recording No. 1). San Francisco: Herbst Theater.

Death Penalty Information (2005). *Women and the death penalty.* Retrieved from www.deathpenaltyinfo.org/article.

Diaz-Cotto, J. (1996). *Gender, ethnicity, and the state: Latina and Latino prison politics.* Albany, N.Y.: New York State University Press.

Donaldson, S. (1995, May). Can we put an end to inmate rape? *USA Today, 123:* 41–42.

Dostoevsky, F. (1969) [1864]. *Notes from the underground.* Washington, D.C.: University Press of America.

Dowling, C. G. (1997, October). Women behind bars. *Life,* 77–90.

Driedger, S. D. (1997, January 27). Showdown of P4W; women are being moved into men's prisons. *Maclean's, 110:* 4.

The Economist (2005, June 4). Sex changes: Women and work. *The Economist,* 55–56.

Enos, S. (2001). *Mothering from the inside: Parenting in a women's prison.* Albany, N.Y.: State University of New York Press.

Erez, E. (1988). The myth of the new female offender: Some evidence from attitudes toward law and justice. *Journal of Criminal Justice, 16:* 499–509.

Faith, K. (1993). *Unruly women: The politics of confinement and resistance.* Vancouver, British Columbia: Press Gang Publishing.

Faith, K. (2004). Progressive rhetoric, regressive policies: Canadian prisons for women. In B. Price and N. Sokoloff (eds.), *The criminal justice system and women: Offenders, victims, and workers* (pp. 281–288). New York: McGraw Hill.

Farr, K. A. (2000). Defeminizing and dehumanizing female murderers: Depictions of lesbians on death row. *Women and Criminal Justice 11*(1): 49–66.

Feinman, C. (1994). *Women in the criminal justice system,* 3rd ed. Westport, Conn.: Praeger.

Fisher, A. (2004). *If I knew then.* Lincoln, Nebraska: iUniverse.

Fox, J. G. (1984, March). Women's prison policy, prisoner activism, and the impact of the contemporary feminist movement: A case study. *The Prison Journal 64:* 25.

Gaarder, E., and Belknap, J. (2004). Little women: Girls in adult prison. *Women and Criminal Justice, 15*(2): 51–80.

Gable, K., and Johnson, D. (1995). Female criminal offenders. In *Encyclopedia of social work* (pp. 1013–1027), 19th ed. Washington, D.C.: NASW Press.

Gaouette, N. (1997, May 19). Prisons grapple with rapid influx of women—and mothers. *Christian Science Monitor:* 1ff.

General Accounting Office (1999). *Women in prison: Issues and challenges confronting U.S. correctional systems.* Washington, D.C.: U.S. Department of Justice.

Giallombardo, R. (1966). *Society of women: A study of a woman's prison.* New York: Wiley.

Goffman, E. (1961). *Asylums: Essays on the social situation of mental patients and other inmates.* Garden City, N.Y.: Doubleday.

Hairston, C. (1995). Family views in correctional programs. In *Encyclopedia of social work,* 19th ed. (pp. 991–996). Washington D.C.: NASW Press.

Hannah-Moffat, K. (1994, January). Unintended consequences of feminism and prison reform. *Forum in Corrections Research, 6*(1): 1–4.

Harris, J. (1988). *They always call us ladies: Stories from prison.* New York: Zebra Books.

Hart, C. B. (1995). Gender differences in social support among inmates. *Women and Criminal Justice 6:* 67–68.

Hensley, C., Castle, T., and Tewksbury, R. (2003). Inmate-to-inmate sexual coercion in a prison for women. *Journal of Offender Rehabilitation 37*(2): 77–87.

Hensley, C., Tewksbury, R., and Koscheski, M. (2002). *Women and Criminal Justice 13*(2/3): 125–139.

Holtfreter, K., Reisig, M., and Morash, M. (2004). Poverty, state capital, and recidivism among women. *Criminology and Public Policy 3*(2): 185–209.

Hughes, R. (1987). *The fatal shore: The epic of Australia's founding.* New York: Alfred A. Knopf.

Human Rights Watch Women's Rights Project (1996). *All too familiar: Sexual abuse of women in U.S. state prisons.* New York: Human Rights Watch.

Irish Times. (1998, February 5). Robinson critical of U.S. execution of double killer.

Irwin, J. (1980). *Prisons in turmoil.* Boston: Little, Brown.

Jones, A. (1980). *Women who kill.* New York: Holt, Rinehart & Winston.

Kassindja, F. (1998). *Do they hear you when you cry?* New York: Delacorte Press.

Knight, B. B. (1992). Women in prison as litigants: Prospects for post-prison futures. *Women and Criminal Justice 4:* 91–116.

Kopatich, K. (1998, May 8). Interviewed by social work student Lynette Keefe at the women's prison in Mitchellville, Iowa.

Krepel, K. (2002, February). Prisons without bars: Guards without guns. *The Protest 3*(1). Retrieved from http://groups.northwestern.edu/protest

Kurshan, N. (1996). Behind the walls: The history and current reality of women's imprisonment. In E. Rosenblatt (ed.), *Criminal injustice: Confronting the prison crisis* (pp. 116–164). Boston: South End Press.

Laster, K. (1994). Arbitrary chivalry: Women and capital punishment in Victoria, Australia 1842–1967. *Women and Criminal Justice, 6*(1): 67–95.

Lewis, W. D. (1965). *From Newgate to Dannemora.* Ithaca, N.Y.: Cornell University Press.

Lohn, M. (2005, October 13). Prisons struggle to meet needs of women. *Washington Post.* Retrieved from www.washingtonpost.com.

Lomax, A. (1998, May). Prison jobs and free world unemployment. *Prison Legal News,* 14.

Luscombe, R. (2005, August 26). Fight to stop Texas woman's execution. *The Guardian*. Retrieved at www.guardian.co.uk

Lutze, F. (2003). Ultramasculine stereotypes and violence in the control of women inmates. In B. Zaitzow and J. Thomas (eds.), *Women in prison: Gender and social control* (pp. 183–203). Boulder, Col.: Lynne Rienner Publishers.

Martin, M. (1997). Connected mothers: A follow-up study of incarcerated women and their children. *Women and Criminal Justice 8*: 1–23.

Moe, A., and Ferraro, K. (2003). Malign neglect or benign respect: Women's health care in a carceral setting. *Women and Criminal Justice 14*(4): 53–80.

Moir, A., and Jessel, D. (1991). *Brain sex: The real difference between men and women*. New York: Delta.

Morash, M., and Schram, P. (2002). *The prison experience: Special issues of women in prison*. Prospect Heights, Ill.: Waveland Press.

National Crime Prevention Council Canada (1995, September). Offender profiles: Prevention and Children Committee.

New York Times. (1992, November 14), pp. 1, 7.

Muraskin, R. (2007). Disparate treatment in correctional facilities: Women incarcerated. In R. Muraskin (ed.), *It's a crime: Women and justice* (4th ed.) (pp. 493–506). Upper Saddle River, N.J.: Prentice Hall.

Office of Performance Evaluations (2003, February). *Programs for incarcerated mothers*. State of Idaho Legislature. Retrieved from www.legislature.idaho.gov/ope

O'Mahony, P. (1994). The Irish psyche imprisoned. *The Irish Journal of Psychology 15*(2/3): 456–468.

Ortmann, D. (1998). Mothers behind the walls. *Social Work Perspectives, 8*(1): 58–62.

O'Shea, K. (1998, May 25). *Women on the Row* (Special issue based on an online discussion): 1–18.

O'Shea, K. (1999). *Women and the death penalty in the United States, 1900–1998*. Westport, Conn.: Greenwood Press.

O'Shea, K. (2005, August). Crozet, Virg.: *Women on the row*. Quarterly newsletter with updates on women on death row.

Owen, B. (1998). *In the mix: Struggle and survival in a women's prison*. Albany, N.Y.: State University of New York Press.

Pate, K. (1998, August 20). E-mail correspondence with Katherine van Wormer, p. 1.

Peet, J. (2004, May 25). Canada's system specializes in unusual solutions. Trenton, N.J.: *The Star-Ledger*. Retrieved from www.starledger.com

Pollack, S. (2004). Anti-oppressive social work practice with women in prison: Discursive reconstructions and alternative practices. *British Journal of Social Work 34*(5): 693–707.

Pollock, J. M. (1998). *Counseling women in prison*. Thousand Oaks, Calif.: Sage.

Pollock, J. M. (2002), Parenting programs in women's prisons. *Women and Criminal Justice 14*(1): 131–148.

Prison Legal News. (1998a, May). Bureau of prisons sexual abuse suit settled for $500,000. *Prison Legal News*, p. 9.

Prison Legal News. (1995). New stateside data show prison rape a widespread problem. *Prison Legal News 6*(11), 17.

Rathbone, C. (2005). *A world apart: Women, prison and life behind bars*. New York: Random House.

Reed, D., and Reed, E. (2004). Mothers in prison and their children. In B. Price and N. Sokoloff (eds.), *The criminal justice system and women: Offenders, victims, and workers*, 3rd ed. (pp. 261–279). New York: McGraw-Hill.

Samuel, L. (2003, October). Nowhere to go. *The Chicago Reporter*. Retrieved from www .chicagoreporter.com

Severance, T. (2004). The prison lesbian revisited. *Journal of Gay and Lesbian Social Services* 17(3): 39–57.

Seymour, B. (1998, June 4). Personal correspondence from Franklin Pre-Release, Columbus, Ohio.

Sharp, S., and Marcus-Mendoza, S. (2001). It's a family affair: Incarcerated women and their families. *Women and Criminal Justice* 12(4): 21–49.

Shaw, M. (1994). Women in prison: A literature review. *Forum in Corrections Research* 6(1): 1–7.

Siegal, N. (1998). Women in prison: The number of women serving time behind bars has increased dramatically. *Ms Magazine* 9(2): 64–73.

Solicitor General of Canada (SGC) (2004). *Women 2003–2004: Corrections and conditional statistical overview*. Public Safety and Emergency Preparedness. SGC. Retrieved from www.sgc.gc.ca/ publications.

Stein, B. (1996, July). Life in prison: Sexual abuse. *The Progressive:* 23–24.

Stop Prisoner Rape (2003, December). *The sexual abuse of female inmates of Ohio*. Stop Prisoner Rape. Retrieved from www.spr.org/pdf/sexabuseohio.

Streib, V. (1973). Death penalty for female offenders, January 1, 1973–June 30, 2005. Ohio Northern University College of Law. Retrieved at www.law.onw.edu/faculty/streib

Thompson, C. (1997, autumn). The invisibility of women on death row: A personal view. *Lifelines Ireland*, 3(3): 3.

Tracy, Smith, and Steurer, S. J. (1998, April). Standing up for education. *Corrections Today:* 144–145, 156.

Turner, A., and Ganza, C. (2005). Newton is executed for slaying her family. *Houston Chronicle*. Retrieved from www.chron.com/cs/CDA

Tyler, K. (1998, June 10). Personal correspondence from Iowa Correctional Institute for Women.

United Kingdom Parliament (2004, October 28). Debate, House of Lords. London. Retrieved from www.publications.parliament.uk

U.S. Department of Justice Office of Inspector General (OIG). (2005, May 13). Sex abuse of federal inmates by guards "a significant problem." OIG. Retrieved from www.november.org

van Wormer, K. (1995). Execution-inspired murder: A form of suicide. *Journal of Offender Rehabilitation*, 23(3/4): 1–10.

van Wormer, K. (1987). Female prison families: How are they dysfunctional? *International Journal of Comparative and Applied Criminal Justice*, 11(2): 263–271.

van Wormer, K. (2001). *Counseling female offenders and victims: A strengths-restorative perspective*. New York: Springer Publishing.

van Wormer, K. (2003). Prison privatization and women. In A. Coyle, A. Campbell, and R. Neufeld (eds.), *Capitalist punishment: Prison privatization and human rights* (pp. 102–113). Atlanta, Ga: Clarity Press.

Walker, S. (1980). *Popular justice: A history of American criminal justice*. New York: Oxford University Press.

Warren, J. (2005, June 19). Rethinking treatment of female prisoners. *Los Angeles Times*. Retrieved from www.latimes.com/news/local

Watterson, K. (1996). *Women in prison: Inside the concrete womb*. Boston: Northeastern University Press.

Weisheit, R., and Mahan, S. (1988). *Women, crime, and criminal justice*. Cincinnati, Ohio: Anderson.

7 Restorative Justice Programs: Innovation and Advocacy

The current rallying cry for a "justice paradigm shift" from retributive to restorative processes of criminal justice (Zehr, 1995a) has set the stage for discussion of restorative justice programs designed to meet the needs of women offenders. The result of this rallying cry has been dramatic, on both the criminal justice system and the more theoretical discussions regarding those intricate and murky interrelationships between religious and philosophical concepts such as justice, mercy, forgiveness, and reconciliation.

In this chapter, we will explore several critical issues related to restorative justice. First, we explore briefly its reliance on native forms of settling disputes, as well as its roots in certain religious traditions that emphasize reparation and reconciliation over retribution. Second, we look at four of its incarnations—community conferencing, family group conferencing, reparative probation, and victim-offender dialogue. We then shift our focus to female offenders and consider ways in which restorative justice model programming can meet their special needs. After a consideration of research findings on program effectiveness, the chapter concludes with a list of guidelines for restorative justice advocacy.

With its roots in the rituals of indigenous populations and traditional religious practices, *restorative justice* is a non-adversarial, three-pronged approach to settling disputes that seeks justice for the individual offender, the victim, and the community. Restorative justice represents a growing international movement with a relatively clear set of values, principles, and guidelines for practice (Umbreit, 1998). Its purpose is to restore the torn fabric of community and wholeness to all those affected by crime, to repair the harm done to the victim and the community, and to make the offender accountable to both.

Humanistic in its treatment of offenders, restorative justice has as its focus the welfare of victims in the aftermath of crime. In bringing criminal and victim together to heal the wounds of violation, the campaign for restorative justice advocates

This chapter was adapted from a book chapter by K. van Wormer and L. Praglin, Restorative Justice Programs to Meet Female Offender Needs: Innovation and Advocacy in A. Roberts (ed.) (2003), *Critical issues in crime and justice* (2nd ed.). (pp. 395–407). Thousand Oaks, CA: Sage, Reprinted with permission of Sage.

alternative methods to incarceration, such as intensive community supervision. The most popular of the restorative strategies are victim–offender conferencing and community restitution. In many states, representatives of the victims' rights movement have been instrumental in setting up programs in which victims/survivors may confront their violators.

On the international stage, the thrust for a restorative vision has been embraced through the role of the United Nations. In consultation with nongovernmental organizations, the U.N. is in the process of drawing up formal standards or guidelines for countries to use in restorative justice programming (Van Ness, 2001). The United States, however, has not officially endorsed these procedures.

Worldwide, restorative justice has come a long way since two probation officers first pushed two tentative offenders toward their victims' homes in 1974 in Ontario (Zehr, 1997). The criminal justice literature is almost exclamatory regarding this new development. Restorative justice has variously been called "a new model for a new century" (van Wormer, 2001), "a paradigm shift" (Zehr, 1997), and "a revolution" (Barajas, 1995, National Institute of Corrections).

For the offender charged with a crime, the goal of conventional justice is to "beat the rap." The process of adjudication typically involves "copping a plea" to a lesser charge through a deal between prosecutor and defense attorney or participation in the adversarial arena, the modern-day equivalent of trial by combat. One party wins; the other party loses. The dominant form of justice in most of the western world is retributive justice. But where is the reconciliation, the mercy, the healing?

Proponents of restorative justice contend that such qualities of reconciliation, mercy, and healing may be preserved alongside accountability in nonadversarial criminal justice approaches found in the restorative justice movement. There are now more than 1,000 such programs operating throughout North America (315) and Europe (707) according to the international survey done by The Center for Restorative Justice and Peacemaking (Umbreit, 2000). Included in this number are many programs operating inside the U.S. prisons. There is also a significant restorative justice focus in the Australian prison system: a search of the keyword "restorative justice" in the Australian Institute of Criminology Database revealed more than 200 references alone from January through March of 2002.

Role Models

Whether inspired by religion or human rights activism, an unusual coalition of idealistic lawyers, religious leaders, and even conservative victims' advocates have been at the helm of this restorative policy movement. Among these movers and shakers are two known to one of the authors personally, Linda Harvey and Mary Roche. Members of the helping professions, their work has special relevance for female offenders and victims.

Linda Harvey

"I have a passion for the restorative justice philosophy because it is about the healing of relationships and harm. I believe that I am doing the ministry of reconciliation to which God is calling all of us." So says Linda Harvey (2001), social worker, devoted Catholic, and founder of Transformation House in Lexington, Kentucky. Transformation House provides assistance to victim survivors who are struggling with the emotional devastation of homicide of a family member. Operating under independent auspices, this program is not derived from the criminal justice system. It does build on personal relationships and relies on the goodwill of public officials such as the prison warden. Harvey's vision for promoting reconciliation includes working closely with incarcerated women, especially those who have killed their abusers (personal correspondence with van Wormer, November 27, 2001). For such women and others at the Pee Wee Valley Correctional Institute, Transformation House provides a series of educational classes and seminars. The dual focus of the classes and seminars is to help women take responsibility for what they have done, as well as to experience catharsis and healing (Transformation House, 2001). During the seminar, a panel of victims and survivors share their stories of grief and loss with the inmates.

Transformation House, for Linda Harvey, was the culmination of her vision to bring death row inmates together with their victims' families. In 1999, Harvey brought together Patsy Smith, whose mother had been murdered, with an inmate at the women's prison who had been convicted as an accomplice in the mother's death. The meeting turned out to be a powerful, experience for both parties according to the newspaper's account:

> For Smith, the meeting challenged her faith and gave her the chance to live it out. It was a time for facing her sorrow and anger. It was what her mother would have wanted her to do, she said. She was also finally able to hear that her mother had died a few minutes after midnight. (Kimbro, 1999, A1)

Mary Roche

Mary Roche's husband died in 1993. A young Iowan who left a two-year-old son, he had been in recovery from alcoholism for seven years and very involved in AA (Alcoholics Anonymous). So the fact that a drunk driver killed him was ironic. As Mary Roche tells it:

> I very much wanted to have a voice at the trial and express my feelings to him [the driver]. People wouldn't feel that way, but to me I needed to see him, to talk to him. He needed to hear it from me.
>
> I called the Department of Corrections. They said, "you're the victim, you can't do that." A few years later in therapy I realized I could run into him at Kwik Star after his release. So I became motivated and [again] called the Department of Corrections. This time I was referred to Betty Brown in Des Moines who is now the administrator of restorative justice for the state. Betty met with Robert Clay (who had killed my husband)

at the prison in Fort Madison. At first he said there was no way. We both went through months of preparation. This was a serious crime, so the meeting was about dialogue, not restitution.

"What do you want?" This was the question I worked on. I wanted him to make amends, to make amends so that he would not drink because of what he had done. I wrote out questions I wanted the answers to so when we met we'd know each other's responses. Arrangements were made through the prison system. The warden was suspicious, however. "I have no idea why you want to do this," he said. The meeting lasted three and a half hours. I was seated first. The security guards looked on. When Robert walked in, I had a strong physical reaction. Betty was with me and Robert's counselor with him. Robert's counselor had not wanted him to participate so Betty had to speak with her. After a period of time, we were dialoguing. I played a tape of my son, Sam, now six, during this meeting. Was it cathartic? Yes. And did Robert open up? Prior to the meeting, Robert was very quiet. This is what his counselor said; he expressed no emotions. This meeting had an effect on him; now he's smiling for the first time.

One day a woman called me to speak on a victim impact panel. I started with MADD (Mothers Against Drunk Drivers). I found this had an impact on offenders, especially juvenile offenders. Then, two years ago I was hired because of my mental health training [Roche has an M.A. in mental health counseling] to become a victim liaison for the Department of Corrections in Waterloo, Iowa.

Today Mary Roche carries the message to students and church groups. She offers seminars on restorative justice for members of the community and conducts classes at the women's prison in Mitchellville.

Principles of Restorative Justice

From the grassroots level to state and local headquarters, restorative justice is rapidly gaining momentum within the United States. In other countries, such as New Zealand, Australia, and South Africa, restorative justice practices have become institutionalized nationally. Victim-offender conferencing (sometimes called mediation) is the oldest and most widely used expression of restorative justice, with more than 1,300 programs in 18 countries (Umbreit, Coates, and Vos, 2001).

Four models of restorative justice pertinent to women offenders are community conferencing (and circle sentencing), family group conferences, community reparation, and victim/offender conferencing. Although derived from Bazemore and Umbreit's (2001) typology, which was developed within the juvenile justice context, the models may easily be adapted to the needs of adult offenders as well. All four models take place within a community-based context and seek to bring victims, offenders, and family, and community members together in a nonadversarial setting so they may come to terms with the dimensions of pain and violation caused by the offender's actions.

While stressing accountability for offenses committed, restorative strategies operate with the goal of repairing injuries to victims and to communities in which these crimes have taken place. Whether these conferences occur before, during, or after adjudication, they promote education and transformation within a context of respect and healing. These models are neither mutually exclusive nor complete in and of themselves. They can be combined or adapted depending on the specific situation at hand. It is, in fact, critical that the implementation of such models be context-specific in order to promote compassionate healing and to do no harm. Following from this logic, we must also be aware of evaluative processes and outcomes (Umbreit and Coates, 1992) including the nature of the harm done to the victim, personality characteristics of the offender, and the existence of any relationship between victim and offender (Peachey, 1992).

Community Conferencing and Circle Sentencing

Community conferences make it possible for victims, offenders, and community members to meet one another to resolve issues raised by the offender's trespass (Swart, 2000). A particularly promising form of community conferencing is termed circle sentencing. Historically, *sentencing circles* may be found in United States native and Canadian aboriginal cultures. These circles were adopted by the criminal justice system in the 1980s as First Nations peoples of the Yukon and local criminal justice officials endeavored to build more constructive ties between the criminal justice system and the grassroots community. In 1991, Judge Barry Stuart of the Yukon Territorial Court introduced circle sentencing in order to empower the community to participate in the justice process (Parker, 2001). One of the most promising developments in sentencing circles, as indicated by Parker, is the Hollow Water First Nations Community Holistic Healing Circle, which simultaneously addressed harm created by the offender, healing the victim, and restoring community goodwill. Circles have been developed most extensively in the western provinces of Canada. They have also experienced a resurgence in modern times among American Indian tribes, for example, in the Navaho courts. Today circles increasingly may be found in more mainstream criminal justice settings. In Minnesota, for example, circles are used in a variety of ways for a variety of crimes and in varied settings (Bazemore and Umbreit, 2001).

How does a sentencing circle work? As Lynette Parker describes the process, participants in healing or sentencing circles typically speak out while passing around a "talking piece." Separate healing circles are initially held for the victim and offender. After the healing circles meet, a sentencing circle (with feedback from family, community, and the justice system) determines a course of action. Other circles then follow up to monitor compliance, whether that involves, for example, restitution or community service (Bazemore and Umbreit, 2001; McCold, 2000). While few studies have been done on the effectiveness of sentencing circles, those few do show generally positive results, despite some concerns over the duration of the process and the need to better prepare circle participants.

Family Group Conferences (FGCs)

This second model of restorative justice grows out of both aboriginal and feminist approaches and practice concerns stemming from the international women's and children's rights movements of the late 1980s and beyond. Evoking the family group decision-making model in order to try to stop family violence, the *family group conference* made its mainstream criminal justice debut in New Zealand in 1989. It also made a stage appearance at about the same time in England and Oregon. This model currently is being tested in Newfoundland and Labrador, as well as in communities in New Zealand, Austria, England and Wales, Canada and the United States (Hudson, Galaway, Morris, and Maxwell, 1996). Currently, FGCs are used in many countries as a preferred sentencing and restorative justice forum for youthful offenders. Despite differences among jurisdictions, one common theme is overriding, as noted by Pennell and Burford (1994): family group conferences are more likely than traditional forms of dispute resolution to give effective voice to those who are traditionally disadvantaged.

Reparation and Restitution

Often referred to as the "Vermont model" of **reparative probation,** this form of restorative justice can be implemented more quickly within existing structures and processes of the criminal justice system (Karp and Walther, 2001). Vermont's radical restructuring of its corrections philosophy and practices stems from influences of the communitarian movement and personalist philosophy generally (Hudson and Galaway, 1990; Thorvaldson, 1990). This model involves a "reparative programs" track designed for offenders who commit nonviolent offenses and who are considered at low risk for re-offense. The reparative programs track mandates that the offender make reparations to both the victim(s) and to the community. A reparative probation program, moreover, directly engages the community in sentencing and monitoring offenders, and depends heavily on small-scale community-based committees to deal with minor crimes (Sinkinson and Broderick, 1998). Reparative agreements are made between perpetrators and these community representatives, while citizen volunteers furnish social support in order to facilitate victim and community reparation.

    Restitution, the most popular model of **restorative justice,** enables in-kind or actual return of what has been lost. Restitution is best viewed within the larger context of "making amends." This includes the provision that the offender offers a sincere apology and promises to change the behavior that caused the initial injury. Ideally, restitution also encourages a move beyond "balancing the scales" toward a true spirit of generosity and forgiveness on both sides (Van Ness and Strong, 2002). Victims identify and then seek redress for their losses, whether identified as material (damage to property); personal (bodily or psychic harm); or communal (injury to the quality of life of an entire community). In many cases, offenders can offer individuals, families, or communities compensation for such losses. Yet, in cases of homicide, for example, what is lost can in no way be restored. Using a community justice focus, Ventura County, California, juvenile justice officials have implemented a successful program that emphasizes restitution as the key element of the reparative process. To compensate for material losses, for instance, youthful offenders in the South Oxnard Challenge Project offer various types of financial or in-kind restitution to victims. The latter have included needed projects for victims, whether individuals or neighborhoods, such as painting a victim's garage, cleaning up graffiti, or working in an office reception area (Karp and Walther, 2001).

Victim-Offender Conferencing

The fourth and final restorative strategy is *victim-offender conferencing*. Introduced formally into the criminal justice arena in the 1980s, this model encourages one-on-one victim-offender reconciliation facilitated through a mediator. Key issues still to be resolved include the utilization of co-mediators; the nature and duration of follow-up victim-offender meetings; the use of victim-offender mediation for more serious and violent offenses; and the implementation of victim-offender mediation in multicultural and prison settings. A growing body of empirical research worldwide reveals that successful victim-offender programs have been implemented in British Columbia and Ontario, Canada; Valparaiso, Indiana; Minneapolis, Minnesota; Quincy, Massachusetts; and Batavia, New York, as well as in Kettering, England, and Glasgow, Scotland (Umbreit, Vos, Coates, and Brown, 2003). While the verdict is still out, initial outcomes research does indicate considerable satisfaction among both victims and offenders, although the question of recidivism looms. It remains to be seen how such programs can begin to be viewed with utmost seriousness by attorneys and judges as a viable alternative to traditional retributive justice procedures.

Female Offender Special Needs

First, let us look at a description of the needs of adult offenders—both male and female—from the point of view of the restorative justice school. Mackey and Shadle (1998) compare the victims' need for healing through the offender's admission of guilt with the offender's need to heal the brokenness in himself or herself. "To be transformed, the offender needs to hear experiences of pain; understand the impact of the crime; [and] develop compassion . . .", write Mackey and Shadle (p. 31).

Like many discussions in the field of restorative and criminal justice, however, such thinking assumes a generic rather than gendered quality, and the special needs of girls and women are not taken into account. When we treat female offenders generically, we often confuse equality with sameness. Gender-blind treatment of girls and women in the criminal justice system subjects them to discipline designed for antisocial men, without allowances either for the role of motherhood or for a history of personal victimization. Addiction and dependency on drug-using and often violent men is another female-specific theme. To help meet the special needs of female offenders, van Wormer (2001) has introduced a strengths-restorative approach, which joins a strengths-based feminist perspective with a restorative framework.

The finding of distinct gender differences in pathways to law-breaking is a focus of contemporary studies on female offenders (Belknap and Holsinger, 1997; Chesney-Lind, 1997). Drawing on the empirical finding that there is a disproportionately high rate of multiple victimization for female compared to male offenders, Chesney-Lind describes the pathway that often leads a girl, desperate to escape sexual and physical abuse at home, to run away, seek solace in drugs and "bad company," and survive on the streets through prostitution. Some end up in prison, mostly as a result of incarceration secondary to drug involvement. In their path, they have victimized others as well—their children and family members, and sometimes strangers—through theft and robbery.

Are restorative justice strategies appropriate for such offenders, given their own histories of victimization and low self-esteem? Some examples follow.

Innovative Programming

As Umbreit and Carey (1995) indicate, restorative justice does not involve a specific program but, rather, a way of thinking. It involves a reorientation of how we think about crime and justice (Zehr, 1997). It involves a call for a new paradigm to heed the cries of victims, offenders, and their parents and children as society shows its increasingly punitive face.

Among the diverse interventions that fall under the umbrella of restorative justice we find common principles: restorative justice condemns the criminal act, not the actor; holds offenders accountable to the victims and to themselves; involves all parties to the crime and their respective support systems; and offers a way for offenders to make amends and, in many cases, be reintegrated into the community.

This section examines strategies designed to meet the particular needs of girls and women in conflict with the law. Central to these strategies is a focus on developing healthy relationships within the context of prior familial abuse and/or neglect. There are few reports of female-focused restorative initiatives for offenders, although there is some attention in the literature on the impact of restorative conferencing techniques on female victims, especially victims of violent crime, as well as on the need for sensitivity to power imbalances. From conferences and personal networking, however, we have discovered several gender-sensitive restorative justice programs.

Restorative justice concepts focus not only on criminal offenses, but also on preventive measures such as education and community awareness. Restorative justice, in its focus on repairing the harm done to people and communities, above all emphasizes communication and reconciliation. The healing circle, for instance, a form of interactive conferencing used in the Toronto and Waterloo, Canada school systems, seems ideally suited to the needs of teenage girls in conflict. Facilitated by a social worker, the healing circle brings offenders and their victims face to face, forcing them to listen to each other and to grasp the impact of their behavior—such as threats, rumor mongering, teasing, and holding grudges. As indicated in the *Toronto*

Star, the use of the circle has been highly effective in healing wounds and reducing animosities ("Healing circle shows offenders their human toll," 2001).

Looking within the juvenile justice system, Miriam DiBiase (2000) makes the case for gender-specific treatment programs to meet girls' developmental needs. Programs such as the Alternative Rehabilitative Communities program at Harrisburg, Pennsylvania, address personal and romantic relationships, abuse issues, victimization, self-esteem, and sexual responsibility. The programs also emphasize victim empathy and community restitution. Since many of the girls have been victimized themselves, they often can come to appreciate the impact of their behavior on others, and the need to move beyond excusing themselves from responsible behaviors due to their own histories of victimization.

Minnesota in particular has infused restorative justice strategies within its Department of Corrections and has also developed gender-specific programming within its juvenile and adult institutions. The Minnesota Department of Corrections furthermore employs restorative justice planners to train people at the county level for diversionary conferencing (to divert offenders from prison) (Pranis, 1999), emphasizing above all a spirit of dialogue and healing.

AMICUS in Minneapolis is an exemplary program for troubled girls for its unique combination of gender-specific concepts with restorative justice principles (Goodenough, 2000). AMICUS has admirably faced the challenge of trying to counter what the girls, hardened by their experiences with the criminal justice system, have learned: Don't trust anyone; don't admit your offenses; the victim is out to get you. The girls are now asked to sit in a circle with victims, family members (their own and the victims'), and their supportive probation officer, and to trust that healing and truth will emerge from the circle. Although the individuals level with the offender about how her behavior has caused them harm, a spirit of empathy, dialogue, and healing prevails. Meanwhile, the AMICUS boys counterpart, JUMP! (Juvenile United with Mentors and Peers), maintains a similar spirit in its outreach to serious and chronic juvenile male offenders who link up with adult mentors, reconnect with family and community, and hopefully develop positive peer relationships.

Adult Corrections

Within prison walls, some powerful encounters are taking place between offenders and their victims. Encounters occur, however, only after the facilitator has provided a great deal of preparation for both parties. Often, as at the Kentucky Correctional Institute for Women, the starting point for offenders is participation in the Impact of Crime on Victims seminar. What is unique in this program is that the focus is on inmates convicted of murder. Preliminary reports from some of the inmates who attended the seminar indicate a reduction in anger and more acceptance of responsibility (Tereshkova, 2000). If inmates later desire a meeting with the homicide victim's family, facilitators act through local victim advocates or through the church to gauge the survivors' desire for such an encounter. If family members so wish, volunteers prepare them for a face-to-face meeting.

Out of such sessions, there will most likely be an apology by the offender. In rare cases, forgiveness from the victim's family may result, although it can never be forced.

Whether or not they are involved in personal meetings with those they have harmed, female inmates are often especially plagued by feelings of grief, loss, and self-denigration. A particularly meaningful class offered by Transformation House professionals and volunteers to inmates deals with shame and self-forgiveness. Among the questions pondered in small group discussion are these:

- How hard are you on yourself?
- What qualities or behaviors do you think are your "gifts to the world"?
- What are some ways you can nurture your growth and well-being? (Harvey, 2002).

In New Zealand and Canada, indigenously based programs are directed toward the needs of Native women in confinement. The Sycamore Tree Project in New Zealand follows the principle of restorative justice in helping female inmates move toward reintegration into the community (Wilmerding, 1999). The Tree of Creation project introduced into the women's prison in Northwestern Canada focuses on the spiritual process of healing (Lambert, 1998). The symbol used for this nature-based program is a large model of a tree, the branches of which take female inmates from the past to the present. The particular focus of that exchange is on healthful practices to prevent the spread of HIV. (Though a small percentage of the Canadian population, First Nations women constitute 20 percent of federally incarcerated women; a much larger proportion is found in the western provinces [Faith, 2000]).

To provide women with the continuum of care they need as they leave prison, transitional programs are essential. Karlene Faith (2000) of the Centre for Restorative Justice of Canada's Simon Fraser University describes the work of the support group, Strength in Sisterhood. Members of this grassroots group of activists befriend women who are newly paroled to help them get reestablished in the community. Many mentors from this group are themselves former prisoners. The only real way to strengthen the women's bonds with the community, as Faith indicates, is to invest in these types of less expensive and non-penal community resources.

A Look at Program Effectiveness

Zehr (1995a) has constructed a theoretical yardstick for measuring the effectiveness of restorative justice practices. The five questions to be considered are:

- Do victims experience justice?
- Do offenders experience justice?
- Is the victim-offender relationship addressed?
- Are community concerns being taken into account?
- Is the future being addressed? (pp. 230–231)

Yet, as Goodenough asks, "[h]ow can we measure the impact of an apology that was ten years in coming, or of an offender visiting a grave site, or of a circle of loving eyes focused on one girl who thought she had no one?" (Goodenough, 2000). The best we can do is to provide subjective documentation of the success or failure of witnessed interventions, or, for more objective measures, collect empirical survey data from the offender-victim mediation efforts. For purposes of generalization, key variables such as gender, race, and class should be delineated.

Given the recent acceptance of restorative strategies in the criminal justice system, there is much research yet to be done that would provide further justification for the proliferation of restorative justice sanctions. In her comprehensive review of empirical data on restorative intervention for juveniles, Schiff (1998) indicates that the kind of data we need on long-term effectiveness of victim impact panels and family group conferencing are lacking. Research on victim offender mediation has been more forthcoming. Results consistently indicate a positive impact on offenders both in terms of compliance rates and the belief by offenders surveyed that they were held appropriately accountable for their actions. Much more is known about restitution compliance due to standardized record-keeping, and success here is widely reported. These interventions, however, are not always tied in to a restorative model.

In their meta-analysis of relevant outcome assessments, Presser and Van Voorhis (2002) call for systematic assessment of recidivism measures as well as follow-up measures of change in attitude as a result of specific interventions. Sophisticated experimental designs are needed so that we can know what works and under what circumstances.

Sophisticated designs must include an experimental and control group, and random assignment of subjects to each. McGarrell (2001) conducted one such recent study that includes a measure of gender differences. A team of trained observers attended 157 restorative conferences involving youthful offenders in Indianapolis. Approximately one-third of the young offenders were female. Findings indicated that almost all the conferences involved apologies by the youth; completion rates of the total program were significantly higher in the experimental than in the control group; and the re-arrest rates were significantly lower. Most significantly for our purposes, the difference in outcome between the comparison groups was greater for females than for males, although there were no racial differences in outcome. Victims and family members alike later reported that they were impressed with the treatment they received in the conferences.

The most extensive and comprehensive studies of the impact of restorative justice interventions to date have been conducted at the Center for Restorative Justice and Peacemaking in Minnesota under the leadership of Mark Umbreit (1996). Data were collected from four Canadian victim-offender mediation programs on 4,445 offenders, mostly adults, who were referred to the programs. Approximately 75 percent of the victims and the offenders who were interviewed reported satisfaction with the process. Ninety percent from both groups felt they had been treated fairly. A comparison group, which did not participate in mediation, was significantly less satisfied with the handling of their case.

Umbreit's summary (1998) reported that for victims, the possibility of receiving restitution appeared to initially motivate them to enter the mediation process. After mediation, however, they reported that meeting the offender and being able to talk about what happened was more satisfying than receiving restitution. Even in cases of extreme violence, victims and offenders often highlighted their participation in mediated dialogue as a powerful and transformative experience that helped them express personal pain, let go of their hatred, and, finally, heal. In a study of arranged and monitored meetings between incarcerated inmates and victims in British Columbia, victims reported seeing the offender for the first time as a person rather than a monster; and thus felt less fear and more at peace. Offenders, conversely, felt more empathy regarding the victim's feelings.

Similar results have emerged from large-scale victim-offender conferencing in Vermont, where the restorative justice model has been institutionalized (Marks, 1999), as well as from a Canadian government evaluation of a restorative project in Winnipeg (Bonta et al., 1998).

What do these research results tell us about the effectiveness of such programming for women? From comprehensive reviews in the rehabilitation literature, we can learn which types of interventions are effective with female offenders. Dowden and Andrews (1999) have conducted a meta-analysis of the rehabilitation literature on treatment effectiveness for female offenders, and singled out a number of key variables correlated with a reduction in the recidivism rate. Human service programs emerged as highly effective; these related to inmates' psychological needs such as targeting issues of victimization and low self-esteem, cognitive work, and intensity of treatment for high-risk offenders with a history of criminality. What we learn from this analysis of the treatment literature is that interventions directed toward the needs of female offenders are significantly positive, especially if they include work in the areas of past trauma and in cognitions (e.g., attitude and irrational thinking). Such an approach is consistent with gender-based restorative justice conferencing programs, although more specific research related to specialized restorative justice interventions is needed to definitively assert these claims.

Advocacy

Vision and leadership are two key ingredients singled out by Umbreit and Carey (1995) for effective restorative justice planning. In an article directed at corrections administrators seeking to move from a standard criminal justice model to a restorative model, the writers recount the journey toward innovative systemic change in one community corrections department in Minnesota. The starting point was a change in thinking from an offender-only concern to a three-dimensional conceptualization involving victims, offenders, and the community. This involved staff education through a variety of presentations and workshops, given that collaboration with staff and administration was critical to the formation of an effective vision and final action plan. Bazemore and Pranis (1997) similarly emphasize partnerships between managers and direct service staff to overcome the stumbling blocks often encountered in inherently rigid bureaucratic structures. Other guidelines for advocacy proposed by Bazemore and Pranis include:

- Seeking input from those most affected by crime: crime victims and their advocates;
- Addressing crime victims' issues first;
- Being careful not to equate restorative justice with victim services or offender/treatment rehabilitation will be overlooked;
- Involving judges, prosecutors, police and public in order to legitimize the program, ensure its effectiveness, and prevent its marginalization;
- Involving the community in the process such as in projects to repair the damage of the offense.

Among corrections administrators, it appears that broadcasting successful strategies implemented in one state can help effect change somewhere else. For example, the policy of requiring inmate restitution (like that of mandatory arrests of batterers) spreads from one jurisdiction to another. State and national agencies can carry out pilot programs to demonstrate applications of principles (Pranis, 1999), and often grant money is available to encourage initiatives, hire personnel, and set up such experimental programs. The Kentucky Department of Justice, for example, awarded Transformation House a small grant for its victim-offender conferencing initiative.

Often such ideas are spread through grassroots organizing. In Minnesota, several community groups and a nonprofit criminal justice agency sponsored a conference on restorative justice and introduced the idea to established criminal justice practitioners. Statewide conferences and involvement of key leaders from all parts of the corrections system followed (Pranis, 1996). Today, the Minnesota Department of Corrections Initiative provides technical assistance throughout the state for designing applications related to the restorative vision.

We can take a lesson from the victim impact panels first initiated by MADD (Mothers Against Drunk Driving). In order to change attitudes about drunk driving so that it could be regarded as serious and preventable, panels of victims' families provided first-hand testimony on the pain and suffering caused by car crashes. The strategy spread and is now used in prison and jail settings as well as in treatment programs.

Advocacy on behalf of female offenders and victims can be especially effective given the strength of the advocacy groups. Faith (2000) largely credits a Canadian feminist task force with the regionalizing and feminizing of women's prisons in Canada. Pranis (1999) offers specific guidelines on steps to take in building community support for restorative justice.

Advocacy on behalf of an individual or a community is an obligation at the very core of the social work profession, and is in fact spelled out in the *NASW Code of Ethics* (1999). Students of criminal justice would therefore do well to refer to one of the many social workbooks on policy practice and advocacy (see, e.g., Schneider and Lester, *Social Work Advocacy* [2000]; Jansson, *Becoming an Effective Policy Advocate* [1999]). Social work students and practitioners, conversely, would do well to turn their attention to some of the dynamic and innovative work being done by criminal justice planners.

Summary

Because crime is a violation of people within a community, the community should be involved in helping to repair the harm. Whereas the usual criminal justice approach focuses almost solely on the individual offender and the offense to the state, restorative justice is three-dimensional. Whether the restorative rituals follow the standard court procedures or are a separate entity, the interconnectedness among victim, offender, and community is integral to the healing process of all three.

Restorative justice, in short, has much to offer female offenders of any given age. In this alternative method of dispensing justice, the importance of human relationships, the opportunity to speak and express feelings, support system involvement, and consensus-style decision making are central to gender-specific programming for female offenders. Empowerment, likewise, is integral to both restorative and gender-specific initiatives.

From grassroots activity to the highest level of government, change is in the wind. With healing the wounds of crime as our goal, there is no end to the imaginative possibilities for advancing social justice and bringing people together for the common good. There is a groundswell of support out there, voiced by a diverse group of dedicated professionals and volunteers striving to foster a form of justice more interested in helping people than in processing them, and more interested in restoration than in retribution.

KEY TERMS

community conferences
family group conference
reparative probation

restitution
restorative justice

sentencing circles
victim-offender conferencing

CRITICAL THINKING QUESTIONS

1. Considering issues such as truth telling and expression of remorse by the offender, discuss the conventional process of criminal justice compared with restorative justice.

2. Discuss the need for restorative strategies from the point of view of the victim.

3. What are some of the difficult issues that might be raised in work in bringing together the murder victim's families with the victim's murderer who is now in prison or on death row?

4. Consider the possible uses and abuses of circle sentencing laws in cases of sexual abuse.

5. Discuss family group conferencing and how such conferencing could be used in situations of family violence.

6. How can restorative strategies address a youthful female offender's background of victimization?

7. What kind of advocacy work could be done in your area to institute or reinforce restorative justice programming?

WEB DESTINATIONS

Center for Justice and Peacebuilding: www.emu.edu/ctp/ctp.html

Center for Restorative Justice and Peacemaking: http://2ssw.che.umn.edu/rjp

Child, Youth and Family, New Zealand: www.cyf.govt.nz

Restorative Justice Consortium: www.restorativejustice.org.uk

Restorative Justice Online: www.restorativejustice.org

For more information on Linda Harvey and other restorative justice pioneers, see: www
.restorativejustice.org

REFERENCES

Barajas, E. (1995). *Moving toward community justice: Topics in community corrections.* Washington, D.C.: National Institute of Corrections.

Bazemore, G., and Umbreit, M. (2001). *A comparison of four restorative conferencing models.* U.S. Department of Justice, Office of Juvenile Justice and Delinquency Prevention. Washington, D.C.: U.S. Department of Justice, National Institute of Corrections.

Bazemore, G., and Pranis, K. (1997). Hazards along the way: Practitioners should stay true to the principles behind restorative justice. *Corrections Today 59*(7): 84–89.

Bannenberg, B. (2000). Victim-offender mediation in Germany. In *Victim-offender mediation in Europe: Making restorative justice work.* First Conference of the European Forum for Victim-Offender Mediation and Restorative Justice, Leuven, Belgium, 1999. Leuven: Leuven University Press, pp. 251–279.

Belknap, J., and Holsinger, K. (1997). Understanding incarcerated girls: The results of a focus. *Prison Journal 77*(4): 381–405.

Bonta, J., Wallace-Capretta, S., and Rooney, J. (1998). *Restorative justice: An evaluation of the restorative resolution project* (Report No.1998-05). Ottawa, Canada: Office of Solicitor General.

Chesney-Lind, M. (1997). *The female offender: Girls, women and crime.* Thousand Oaks, Calif.: Sage.

DiBiase, M. (2000). Psychology and justice working together: Addressing the needs of female juvenile offenders. *Healing Magazine 5*(2): 4–10.

Dowden, C., and Andrews, D. A. (1999). What works for female offenders: A meta-analytic review. *Crime and Delinquency 45*(4): 438–443.

Faith, K. (2000). Reflections on inside/out organizing. *Social Justice 27*(3): 158–168.

Goodenough, K. (2000). AMICUS: Restorative justice for girls. Unpublished manuscript.

Harvey, L. (2001). Leading edge: Linda Harvey. Online at: www.restorativejustice.org/rj3

Harvey, L. (2002, Jan. 12). Personal interview with Katherine van Wormer, Elizabethtown, Ky.

"Healing circle shows offenders their human toll" (2001). *Toronto Star*, NE4.

Hudson, J., and Galaway, B. (1990). Restitution program models with adult offenders. In B. Galaway and J. Hudson (eds.), *Criminal Justice, Restitution, and Reconciliation* (pp. 165–175) Monsey, N.Y.: Criminal Justice Press.

Hudson, J., Galaway, B., Morris, A., and Maxwell, G. (1996). Introduction [to family group conferences]. In J. Hudson et al. (ed.), *Family Group Conferences: Perspectives on Policy and Practice* (pp. 1–16). Monsey, N.Y.: Criminal Justice Press.

Karp, D., and Walther, L. (2001). Community reparative boards in Vermont: Theory and practice. In G. Bazemore and M. Schiff (eds.), Restorative community justice: Repairing harm and transforming communities (pp. 199–217). Cincinnati, Ohio: Anderson.

Kimbro, P. L. (1999, May 30). A profound meeting, a healing bond. *Lexington Herald-Leader:* A1, A16.

Jansson, B. S. (1999). *Becoming an effective policy advocate*. Belmont, Calif.: Wadsworth.

Lambert, D. (1998, June 20). Tree of creation: aboriginal HIV strategy. Poster presentation at the Canadian Association of Social Workers National Social Work Conference, Edmonton, Alberta.

Mackey, V., and Shadle, C. (1998). *Justice or "just deserts"? An adult study of the restorative justice approach*. Louisville, Ky.: Presbyterian Criminal Justice Program.

Marks, A. (1999, September 8). Instead of jail, criminals face victims. *Christian Science Monitor:* 1, 4.

McCold, P. (2000). *Overview of mediation, conferencing and circles*. Paper presented to 10th United Nations Congress on Crime Prevention and Treatment of Offenders. International Institute for Restorative Practices. Vienna: April 10–17.

McGarrell, E. F. (2001). Restorative justice conferences as an early response to young offenders. *Office of Juvenile Justice and Delinquency Prevention Bulletin*. Washington, D.C.: U.S. Department of Justice.

NASW (1999). Code of ethics. Washington, D.C.: NASW Press.

Parker, L. (2001). "Circles." Online at www.restorativejustice.org

Peachey, D. E. (1992). Restitution, reconciliation, retribution: identifying the forms of justice people desire. In H. Messmer and H. Otto (eds.), *Restorative justice on trial: Pitfalls and potentials of victim-offender mediation: International research perspectives* (pp. 551–557). Dordrecht, Netherlands: Kluwer.

Pennell, J., and Burford, G. (1994). Widening the circle: family group decision making. *Journal of Child and Youth Care* 9(1): 1–11.

Pranis, K. (1996). A state initiative toward restorative justice: The Minnesota experience. In B. Galaway and J. Hudson (eds.), *Restorative justice: International perspectives* (pp. 493–504). Monsey, N.Y.: Criminal Justice Press.

Pranis, K. (1999). *Building community support for restorative justice: Principles and strategies*. Online at: www. restortivejustice.org/rj3/A

Presser, L., and Van Voorhis, P. (2002). Values and evaluation: Assessing processes and outcomes of restorative justice programs. *Crime and Delinquency* 48(1): 162–187.

Roche, M. (2001, November 11). Restorative justice. Presentation before graduate social work class. Cedar Falls: University of Northern Iowa.

Schiff, M. F. (1998). Restorative justice interventions for juvenile offenders: a research agenda for the next decade. *Western Criminology Review* 1(1). Online at http://wcr.sonoma.edu/vlnl/schiff.html

Schneider, R. L., and Lester, L. (2000). *Social work advocacy*. Belmont, Calif.: Wadsworth.

Sinkinson, H. D., and Broderick, J. J. (1998). A case study of restorative justice: The Vermont reparative probation program. In L. Walgrave (ed.), *Restorative Justice for Juveniles: Potentialities, Risks, and Problems,* Leuven, Belgium: Leuven University Press.

Swart, S. (2000). Restorative processes: Mediation, conferencing, and circles. Online at www.restorativejustice.org

Tereshkova, Z. (2000, Mar. 15). Lexington-based group brings inmates, their victims together for mutual healing. *Lexington Herald-Leader:* A1.

Thorvaldson, S. (1990). Restitution and victim participation in sentencing: A comparison of two models. In B. Galaway and J. Hudson (eds.), *Criminal Justice, Restitution, and Reconciliation* (pp. 23–26). Monsey, N.Y.: Criminal Justice Press.

Transformation House (2001). L. Harvey. Online at www.restorativejustice.org/rj3

Turpin, J. (1999). Restorative justice challenges corrections. *Corrections Today* 61(6): 60–63.

Umbreit, M. (1985). *Victim offender mediation: Conflict resolution and restitution.* Valparaiso, Ind.: PACT Institute of Justice.

Umbreit, M. (1996). Restorative justice through mediation: The impact of programs in four Canadian provinces. In B. Galaway and J. Hudson (eds.), *Restorative justice: International perspectives* (pp. 373–385). Monsey, New York: Criminal Justice Press.

Umbreit, M. (1998). Restorative justice through victim-offender mediation: a multi-site assessment. *Western Criminology Review* 1(1): 24–30.

Umbreit, M. (2000). *National survey of victim-offender mediation programs in the United States.* Center for Restorative Justice and Peacemaking, St. Paul, Minnesota.

Umbreit, M., and Carey, M. (1995). Restorative justice: implications for organizational change. *Federal Probation* 59(1): 47–54

Umbreit, M., and Coates, R. (1992). *Victim offender mediation: An analysis of programs in four states of the U.S.* Minneapolis, Minn.: Minnesota Citizens Council on Crime and Justice.

Umbreit, M., Coates, R., and Vos, B. (2001). The impact of victim-offender mediation—two decades of research. *Federal Probation* 65(3): 29–36.

Umbreit, M., Vos, B., Coates, R., and Brown, K. (2003). *Facing violence: The path of restorative justice and dialogue.* Monsey, NY: Criminal Justice Press.

Van Ness, D. (2001, Dec.). UN expert meeting recommends declaration of basic principles on restorative justice. Online at: www.restorativejustice.org

Van Ness, D. and Strong, K. H. (2002). *Restoring justice,* 2nd ed. Cincinnati: Anderson.

Van Wormer, K. (2001). *Counseling female offenders and victims: A strengths-restorative approach.* New York: Springer.

Wilmerding, J. V. (1999, July 7). Sycamore tree: A pre-release for victims and offenders. Personal communication with K. van Wormer.

Zehr, H. (1997). Restorative justice: The concept. *Corrections Today* 59(7): 68–71.

Zehr, H. (1995a). *Changing lenses: A new focus for crime and justice.* Waterloo, Ontario: Herald Press.

Zehr, H. (1995b). Justice paradigm shift? Values and visions in the reform process. *Mediation Quarterly* 12(3): 207–216.

PART FOUR

Women as Victims
and Survivors

Whether a woman is subjected to one-time rape by a stranger or to a pattern of brutality by a family member, the emotional scars will be with her always. Although women have more social and legal rights now than at any other time in history, vestiges of the old attitudes still prevail. Given the natural tendency to blame the victim, combined with a backlash against women's advancement, these antiwoman, antivictim attitudes continue to rear their ugly heads.

The victimization of women at the personal level is matched by the oppression of women in the wider society. Chapter 8 focuses on the crime of rape. The very existence of this crime has unique ramifications for all girls and women everywhere. The amount of compassion and respect accorded the victims of this crime is a barometer of a society's regard for women in general. Woman hating is at the heart of both rape and battering; rape can be construed as assault that is sexualized, and partner violence often includes sexual abuse.

Chapter 9 examines victimization closer to home and more enduring—battering or wife (partner) abuse. Both forms of victimization—rape and battering—are about power and humiliation; they are both about male dominance and female subordination. The essence of the male power structure is further reflected in paternalistic courtroom practices concerning these crimes. The criminal justice system itself can be seen as an instrument of control and one that reflects women's economic and political station in society. It is through the great awakening that took place among women of the 1970s, women who had been seasoned through protests for peace and social justice of that era, that we recognize rape and battering for what they are. Before that time women were consistently blamed for causing their own victimization. Many are still blamed and blame themselves for their mistreatment.

Consistent with our awareness of the forces of globalization and the extent to which transnational crime victimizes women, we have included Chapter 10, Women's Victimization: Global Perspectives. This chapter explores domestic violence in terms of the brutalizing and exploitative treatment of women in parts of the world where male privilege is most entrenched. We look at both violence against girls and women in the home and outside the home, as institutionalized by the state. Genital mutilation and the mass rape of the enemy's women in war are examples of the latter. Sex trafficking, a major industry involving the selling of women's bodies, is discussed in some detail as well. The chapter concludes on a brighter note, with a description of innovative practices from across the world to prevent and counter female victimization.

An empowerment approach is crucial to helping such women find their own voices, in the first instance to articulate their pain, and in the second, to share their insights with others. Consistent with feminist tradition, the word *victim* is used to denote a person who has sustained an injury and *survivor* for one who has lived through and is attempting to heal from an assault. Survivorship is a state of empowerment; victimhood is not. Together, these chapters offer a framework for empowerment therapy, a framework for helping people move from a position of "I am a victim" to "I am a survivor" or, better yet, "We are survivors."

CHAPTER

8 Rape

In Chapter 5 we learned of the tremendous overlap between early childhood sexual abuse and the later development of addiction in women. Women under the influence of intoxication are especially vulnerable to sexual exploitation and rape. Chapters 5 and 6 also explored the link between women's victimization in society—sexually, economically, and personally—and their criminality. Then we saw how once in prison many women become retraumatized by the invasive strip searches sometimes performed by male guards that are a part of the prison regime. Direct incidents of guard-inmate violations were described. Now we come to look at rape in the community, a crime that is always antiwoman, even when it is practiced by men against men.

Martha Ramsey (1995) was raped at age thirteen. There was one brief moment of openness between her mother and herself, then nothing. Now after two decades, she has decided to "speak about this hurt that people do not want to hear about" (p. 105). Returning to the police station after all these years, she thanks the detective whose kindness meant so much to her. "I remember you as being very sensitive and gentle," she says (p. 105). They both cry.

Raped thirty-four years ago, Gerry Cummins, a white woman, reluctantly gave the mixed-race baby up. And now, her grown daughter comes looking for her roots, only to discover that she was a child of rape. Still the reunion of mother and daughter is wonderful. "My life is now complete," the mother says (O'Neill, 1996, p. 98).

When Georgetown University student Kate Dieriger was raped by a fellow student she decided to have her case heard by the university disciplinary panel. The light sanction imposed on the rapist did not seem congruent with the harm done by the crime. Moreover, the adjudication process placed all of its interest in protecting the "crystal clean image of the university," Dieriger said, "instead of protecting the well-being and safety of the students" (Security on Campus, 2002). She also decried the use of student privacy laws to keep the information secret.

These incidents, drawn from popular literature, offer just a glimpse of the many ramifications of the crime of rape. In addition to the ones we have mentioned, there are also the risk of AIDS, the intrusive fears and nightmares, and the enduring sexual problems.

The word *rape* comes by way of the Anglo-Norman *raper* from the Latin *rapere,* to seize by force (Ayto, 1990, p. 431). This definition with its emphasis on force is strikingly similar to our understanding today. Legally, the definition of rape varies by state. The National Crime Victimization Survey (Bureau of Justice Statistics [BJS], 2005), the most reliable source of data on this highly unreported crime, defines **rape** as "forced sexual intercourse including both psychological coercion as well as physical force. Forced sexual intercourse means vaginal, anal or oral penetration by the offender(s). . . . Includes attempted rapes, male as well as female victims and both heterosexual and homosexual rape. Attempted rape includes threats of rape" (p. 141). The FBI defines "forcible rape" more specifically as "the carnal knowledge of a female forcibly against her will" (BJS Crime and Justice Data Online, 2004). Some states continue to restrict the definition of rape to crimes against a female. *Sexual assault* includes a wide range of victimizations involving attacks in which unwanted sexual contact occurs between the victim and the offender. Sexual assault includes verbal threats.

Raped as a college freshman, Alice Sebold (2002), who tells her story in the book *Lucky,* did not receive the sensitive treatment she needed immediately following the rape. Instead she was told by the police officer that she was lucky, lucky she wasn't murdered like the girl before her. This, her first sexual experience, was the beginning of a journey that would become a struggle with post-traumatic stress disorder and heroin addiction.

To the victim, rape is a painful violation of the self. The humiliation of the act leads to a secrecy that, in itself, can further maximize a sense of shame in the person violated. To be raped is to enter unwittingly the bizarre sisterhood of the victimized, a sisterhood in which the membership is secret, often even among individual victims. The reality of having been unable to fight the attacker off is haunting. The reality of being physically defiled and sexually scarred may stay with a woman forever. The trial, if there is one, instead of bringing catharsis or even closure, reopens the old wounds and subjects the victim to new wounds of public accusation and labeling. To offset the trauma and promote healing, intensive counseling should be provided to all rape victims, especially in the early period of the aftermath of the crime. Because victims of this type of crime often find the circumstances unmentionable—no one wants to hear about it—survivor self-help groups can be a godsend. Fortunately today, through the work of rape crisis lines and victim assistance programs, the help that is needed, at least for adults, is widely available.

To glimpse how rape victims were treated yesterday versus the way they are treated today, we begin this chapter with a historical overview. Then, the prevalence of rape and the impact of the mass media are discussed. From the victim's standpoint, we look at types of rape, including acquaintance rape, mass rape, and child sexual abuse. The chapter concludes by revealing the criminal justice response and with a discussion of an empowerment approach for work with survivors of this type of crime.

Historical Overview

In terms of official treatment, there has never been a time of greater sensitivity to the needs of rape victims than today. Campaigns by women's groups and rape crisis centers worldwide have resulted in significant changes in the law and legal procedures in relation to sexual offenses against women. To know how much better the climate is now, let us look at how things were before the mid 1970s, when feminist voices began to make themselves heard. After that time, victims of rape still had it rough, but never again would they be so alone.

We begin with the law. The law tends to reflect social values. In our recent past, a rape victim's behavior before the claim of rape, her behavior during the sexual encounter, and her relationship to the perpetrator were often all taken into consideration by legal officials in deciding whether a "real" rape occurred. Until the 1970s, the law in most states recognized that a rape occurred only when a man forced a woman to have sex under the threat of injury, when she had resisted strenuously, and when there was outside corroboration (Maschke, 1997).

To understand these traditions we need to go back centuries to a time when a man who wanted a woman simply raped her and brought her into his tribe (Flowers, 1987). Later, the status of women as property was embodied in custom and law. Rape entered the law as a property crime of man against man; women were the property (Brownmiller, 1975). Indeed, rape has been a part of war in most societies throughout history. Rape within marriage, of course, was considered an oxymoron. Only in recent years, in fact, has marital rape come to be recognized in some places as a crime.

In the decades before Brownmiller (1975), Burgess and Holmstrom (1974), and Griffin (1971) revolutionized the concept of rape by desexualizing it, virtually no research was done on this form of female victimization. In the 1960s, for example, there were a few studies on sexual deviance that focused exclusively on the stranger-rapist. Most theories that attempted to explain rape treated it as a single phenomenon (Sigler, Johnson, and Morgan, 2003). The rapist was characterized as a mentally defective person who was unable to control his urges. The word *rape* was rarely spoken in polite circles. From the earliest age, girls were merely warned in hushed tones against strangers who might try to lure them away with candy to "do terrible things to them." At the same time, virginity in the unmarried female was a requirement for successful marriage; women who were sexually violated were said to be "ruined" and "damaged goods." Compounding the problem, psychoanalytical theory maintained that girls and women unconsciously desired to be raped (Brownmiller, 1975).

African American Women and Rape

Whether they were raped by white men as a legacy of slavery (there was no way a slave could resist a master's advances) or by their black brothers, African American women have learned to be silent about sexual assault. Stereotypes of hypersexual

African Americans grew out of the slavery era ethos (Robinson, 1997). Historian Fay Yarbrough (2005) examined interracial sex in her content analysis of the fascinating interviews of ex-slaves collected by the Works Progress Administration (WPA) in the 1930s. The reminiscences of former slaves revealed that they viewed the relations between slaves and the whites as coercive or exploitative. Relationships between blacks and American Indians, in contrast, were perceived as more equal and consensual. The protection of the white woman's virtue became the rationalization for brutalizing black men and women. The rape of African American women historically has been given little or no attention by the larger society. For a black woman to accuse a black man of raping or sexually harassing her (as Anita Hill did Clarence Thomas) is to risk attack within her own community for speaking out against one of her own kind. As a survivor wanting to end this legacy of silence in the black community, Lori Robinson courageously tells us:

> *I guess more than anything, what I carry with me and walk out of this valley in my life is a commitment to help end the silence. A close male mentor of my family could not bring himself to speak to me about my rape for an entire year. The last time we were both together was at Spelman on my graduation day.*
>
> *I have learned that he cried when told about my rape. I wonder how it would have been if we had cried—and healed—together. (p. 53)*

In a survey of readers of an African American news magazine, 89 percent of respondents perceived that African American females report acts of sexual violence less frequently than do white females (*Emerge*, 1997). The primary reason given is the fear of not being believed. Distrust of the authorities compounds the reluctance to tell (McNair and Neville, 1996).

Reconceptualization of Rape

Until recent times, a woman who engaged in sex outside marriage, even against her will, was considered a "fallen" woman and often was blamed for her own victimization (Donat and D'Emilio, 1992). An unmarried woman who wished to prosecute her rapist had to have a good reputation without any previous sexual experience to get a conviction for the rapist. The victim, not the defendant, was on trial; the typical caution to the jury was that the charge of rape was easy to make and hard to disprove. Few cases were prosecuted, and for those that were, the conviction rate was very low. In 1972, in Chicago, for example, of more than 3,000 reported rapes fewer than 1 percent resulted in jail terms (Deckard, 1983).

Some of the early research on rape, even after 1970, played into victim-blaming. The publication of Menachem Amir's *Patterns in Forcible Rape* (1971) marked the first sociological study of its kind. This investigation of *victim-precipitated* crime was very influential in criminological circles and much studied throughout the next decade.

About the same time, the feminist movement offered a framework for viewing male-on-female violence that was to turn the conceptualization of rape upside-down and to be a complete eye-opener to men and women both. For the first time, sexual assault was redefined from the victim's and society's perspective. Rape was seen as the violence that it is. Through the efforts of the antirape movement, it would soon become clear that such violence against women is one more mechanism for male social control (McPhail, 2002). In a landmark article entitled "Rape—The All American Crime," Susan Griffin (1971) articulated for the movement how rape and the fear of rape work to keep women dependent on men. Rape was recognized in this article, among others, as an act about domination and control, not sex.

The work of well-known feminists such as Brownmiller and Griffin has further helped us to conceive of rape not in either-or terms but as a series of acts along a continuum. Far from being an isolated event that could be rooted out from the society at large, the crime of rape was now seen as only the logical extension of what was there already. Walker and Brodsky (1976), for example, spoke of the forms of sexual harassment that were commonplace, the "little rapes" that ranged from teasing and innuendos to making unwelcome sexual advances. Considered fair game, women were targeted as legitimate objects of sexual aggression. Unless protected by a man, a woman's personal territory could be violated by suggestion and intimidation.

According to the feminist school, the violation to the self caused by everyday whistles and unsolicited greetings on the street is but one aspect of the cultural perspective that defines women as objects and men as possessors (Sigler et al., 2003). And in the spectrum of male behavior, rape violence is the penultimate violent act.

Prevalence

Thanks to recent incentives to gather extensive data on sexual offenses, the Centers for Disease Control and Prevention (CDC) (2004) through the National Center for Injury and Prevention and Control has prepared fact sheets on sexual violence while the Bureau of Justice Statistics (BJS) (2004) has accumulated data on criminal victimization. The former draws on scientific research, and both sources collect data from crimes known to the police as well as reports from the national victimization surveys. Among the CDC's significant findings:

- The National College Women Sexual Victimization Study estimated that between 1 in 4 and 1 in 5 college women experienced completed or attempted rape during their college years;
- More than half of all rapes of women occur before age 18; 22 percent of these rapes occur before age 12;
- According to the National Violence against Women Survey, 1 in 6 women and 1 in 33 men has experienced an attempted or complete rape at some time in their lives.
- According to the youth risk surveys, approximately 12 percent of female students and 6 percent of male students reported they had been forced to have sexual intercourse;

- Between 4 percent and 30 percent of rape victims contract sexually transmitted diseases including HIV; an estimated 32,000 pregnancies result each year from rape in victims age 12 to 45 years.
- Victims of sexual violence are more likely to engage in risky sexual behavior, to smoke, overeat, drink alcohol, and not use seat belts;
- American Indian and Alaskan Native women were significantly more likely (34 percent) to report they had been raped than African American women (19 percent) or white women (18 percent).

In many states, criminal justice systems allow sex offenders to plead guilty to non-sex crimes such as aggravated assault or criminal trespass (see, for example, DeSantis, 2005; Gershman, 2006; and Troxler, 2005). Byington (1995) offers insight into the high number of rape cases plea-bargained to lesser charges: Rape victims understandably are anxious to avoid the humiliation of a public trial, including vigorous cross-examination by the defense attorney, and therefore often do not press for a trial. The relatively low conviction rate for sexual crimes against adult women is a further factor in the prosecutor's willingness to settle such a case through negotiations with the accused's attorney. A figure not given in the BJS report is the percentage of women victimized by rape in their lifetimes. Victimization rates for Asian Americans and Native Americans are also lacking. Until now, empirical data on the relationship between certain types of violence against women, such as childhood victimization and subsequent adult victimization, have been limited.

To further our understanding of violence against women, the National Violence Against Women Survey, under the sponsorship of the federal government, conducted a national survey of 8,000 men and 8,000 women. Among the key findings: 1 out of 6 women and 1 out of 33 men has been raped over his or her lifetime; twice as many girls raped before age 18 were raped after the age of 18 as women who were not raped in childhood; and the typical female rape victim is a child (Tjaden and Thoennes, 2000, pp. 3, 6).

The National Violence Against Women Survey also clarified racial and ethnic differences. American Indians disclosed a higher rate of rape and physical assault than women of other racial/ethnic backgrounds, while Asian/Pacific Islander women were significantly less likely to report rape and physical assault. However, among Asian Americans sexual assault may be underreported because of the sense of shame this crime brings to the victims and their families (Tseuneyoshi, 1996).

Kilpatrick, Saunders, and Smith (2003) report high rates of victimization among African Americans as compared to youth of different ethnicities. Since the official rates from BJS (2004) report rates that are more or less equal across black/white racial lines, one is left to speculate that fewer blacks than whites are willing to report the crime to the police. To get a more detailed study of different types of sexual victimization among young African American women and the link with several background factors, Cecil and Matsen (2005) interviewed 249 patients who received services from an adolescent health care facility and who were sexually active. The background factors consisted of reports of family dysfunction, depression, and substance abuse problems. Results showed that 32 percent of the participants reported that they had been raped, and 11 percent that they had experienced attempted rape. Keep in mind that this sample was of inner-city health care patients, so making generalization difficult. The study does show within this sample that a background of mental health problems and family dysfunction were closely correlated with reported victimization of all kinds. The rape survivors had significantly lower levels of self-esteem than did adolescents who had experienced consensual sex.

Vulnerability factors as spelled out in the statistics presented above are: young age, prior history of sexual violence, multiple sexual partners, and poverty. Poverty, according to CDC (2004), is a high-risk factor that forces study participants into certain high-risk occupations, including prostitution. We would add high-crime neighborhoods, unsafe forms of transportation, and the need to work the night shift.

The World Health Organization (WHO) data presented by Krug and colleagues (2002) single out the following individual risk factors in sexual offending on the part of the perpetrator—substance abuse, coercive sexual fantasies, antisocial tendencies, hostility towards women, history of childhood sexual abuse, witnessing family violence, association with a sexually aggressive peer group, and exposure to societal norms that support male superiority and sexual entitlement.

Hispanic women in the national survey reported a lower rate of rape victimization than did non-Hispanic women. Previous studies have produced contradictory findings on this score. A survey of Mexican Americans in Los Angeles found that Anglos had two and one-half times the rate of sexual assault as Mexican Americans (Sorenson and Siegel, 1992). Reasons given for the lower rate were the greater sense of community as well as the protective restrictions on Mexican American females.

A review of literature reveals that, not surprisingly, more men than women (Crowell and Burgess, 1996) and boys than girls (Cowan and Campbell, 1995) subscribe to rape myths. A number of studies have found a significant association between acceptance of rape myths in men and self-reported sexually aggressive behavior (Koss, Leonard, Beezley, and Oros, 1985; Reilly, Lott, Caldwell, and Deluca, 1992). For a number of rape myths, see Box 8.1.

BOX **8.1**

Rape Myths

What are rape myths? Basically they are false beliefs that are refuted by the statistics provided in this chapter. Typical rape myths are:

- Most rape claims are false; women feel guilty about sex and redefine the situation later.
- Rape happens only to bad women such as prostitutes.
- Unconsciously, women want to be raped.

- Most rape is committed by a stranger in a dark alley.
- When women say no, they mean yes.
- Women's wearing of seductive clothes causes rape.
- Rapes are impulsive acts committed by men unable to control their passions.
- Rapes are black-on-white crimes.
- Rape is caused by male deviance and pathology.

Impact of the Mass Media

The impact of the television drama *Something about Amelia*, first shown on MTV in 1984, is hard to describe. The subject was incest in a middle-class family. Extensive coverage was given to this production in the general mass media and in specialized newsletters for the counseling professions. The interest of professionals was heightened, no doubt because of the central role given to family therapy in the film. In the drama, when the incest is discovered, the father, not the daughter, is removed from the home. Then intensive professional attention is devoted to this family in crisis. Following the broadcast there was a flurry of phone calls to hotlines and children protective services. A few years later when Israeli television aired this startling and well-acted program, the impact was similarly sensational (Oppenheimer, 1998).

When the movie *The Accused* hit the screens in 1988, it was another first of sorts: at last, a portrayal of the difficulty of prosecuting a gang-rape case from the point of view of the victim! Portrayed convincingly by Jodie Foster, the victim meets her fate while she is drinking at a bar. *The Accused* is based on a true story of a working-class Portuguese woman from New Bedford, Massachusetts, who brought criminal charges against Portuguese onlookers who cheered as she was raped. In her heroic fight for justice, the survivor emerges as victor, and the prosecutor learns something about courage and determination. It is a sad commentary that when the movie was first shown, some young men in the audience hooted and cheered at the rape scene (Faludi, 1991). The real victim on which *The Accused* was based was condemned by her community for the negative attention brought on them by the crime. She died of alcoholism several years later.

As Faludi suggested in her book *Backlash* (1991), it is a sad day when a sympathetic portrait of a rape victim is hailed as a daring feminist statement. Yet this portrayal is certainly an improvement over the way Hollywood dealt with rape in the past. In *Gone With the Wind*, which was released in 1939, Rhett Butler forces his attentions on Scarlett, who has been "getting out of hand." Although frightened at the time, the next day she wakes up in her luxurious bed humming. Mammy comments that she looks extra cheerful this morning, and Scarlett grins ear to ear. Contrast this with *A Streetcar Named Desire*, the Tennessee Williams masterpiece that was produced as a movie in 1951. The class and sexual tensions between Stanley (played by Marlon Brando) and Blanche (Vivien Leigh) result in a climactic rape scene. (This scene was watered down for the movie.) Sinking into the chasm of mental illness, the violated sister-in-law is taken away. Perhaps because of his sexual orientation or artistry, Tennessee Williams handled the rape with a rare sensitivity.

Newspaper coverage of rape cases has tended to be sensationalized when they involve celebrities, fraternity members, or athletic teams. In recent years, some women courageously have identified themselves publicly and spoken out, an event practically unheard of before the 1980s. Rape victims, in fact, have been "in the closet" far more than gays and lesbians have been, and male victims remain the most hidden of all. Rape is a crime unlike any other; the sordidness of the crime somehow attaches to the unwilling party as much as to the instigator and sometimes even more so.

Racism is evident not only in the reduced prosecution of cases of African American victimization but also in mass media accounts. Media attention rarely focuses on African American victims of crime (Rollins, 1996). Outrage seems to be reserved for white victims, especially those of high socioeconomic status. Rollins cites the widely publicized case of a white jogger who was raped and set on fire allegedly by a group of black youths. (Note: In 2003, the judge threw out the conviction.) Meanwhile, comparable cases of inner-city victimization were largely ignored.

Paralleling the growth of two revolutionary developments from the late 1970s—feminism and the self-help movement—reports of childhood sexual abuse rose to prominence. A deluge of newspaper articles, books, and television movies appeared in North America and western Europe. Political progress in child welfare has historically been linked to the success of feminism, and the fact that women are disproportionately victims of sexual abuse has cemented the linkage in the modern period (Finkelhor, 1994). When feminists joined forces with child welfare professionals, who tend for the most part to be trained in social work, child protection advocacy got off the ground. Despite a formidable backlash against false accusations in recent years, there is a public and professional awareness of the exploitation of children that did not exist in previous decades. The U.S., Canadian, and Irish press has been inundated with reports of court cases involving child molesters who were in positions of authority, such as priests and teachers.

A promising development in media history occurred several years ago as the cable network Lifetime Television made women's advocacy campaigns a top priority. The network used an online petition drive to help push anti-rape legislation (involving DNA samples) through Congress. "Our lifetime commitment: Stop violence against women" reached millions of people through public service announcements and the Internet. Oxygen Media, another cable outlet for women, has also run its own online and on-air campaigns (Dollarhide, 2002). Unlike other networks, cable TV has the freedom to endorse public policy campaigns, so their potential should not be underestimated.

"Rape in a Small Town: The Florence Holway Story" (HBO, 2005) is a recent TV production, a documentary that chronicles an elderly woman's heroic, twelve-year struggle for justice following an intruder rape in her rural New Hampshire home. Holway, as revealed in the documentary, felt she had been brutalized twice—first by the rapist and then by a flawed legal system that offered the rapist a plea bargain to a lesser sentence without consulting her. Holway, remarkably, launched a solo campaign to force her attacker to trial. When her story was picked up by big-city media, she became a national figure. Eventually, her campaign paid off with the state legislature ushering in reforms to rape law. The TV broadcast incited much interest in Australia when it aired there on a major TV station.

Blaming the Victim

A counterforce to feminist awareness of the personal as political, one related to society's antifeminist backlash, is the societal propensity for victim blaming when it comes to sexual assault (Neame, 2004). Writing a *Time* cover story on the new feminism, Bellafonte (1998) chided the new feminism which "has come to seem divorced from matters of public purpose" and obsessed with celebrity, the body, and image (p. 60). The postfeminists seek to get beyond an ideology of victimhood into an awareness of their sexual power over men; men are simply untamable according to this view. Feminism today, claims Bellafonte, is "wed to the culture of celebrity and self-obsession" (p. 57).

Social theorists Robbins, Chatterjee, and Canda (2006) concede that the new feminism, commonly known as third-wave feminism, has produced a variety of perspectives, many of which are at odds with each other. However, as they further point out, most feminist theory continues to stress the centrality of ideological domination based on the dynamics of patriarchy.

As feminist researchers and scholars have sought to create public awareness about the prevalence of sexual assault in the society, the popular literature has sought to refute it by various means. The very act of launching primary prevention campaigns on disturbing social issues has the capacity, as Neame (2004) indicates, to provoke a backlash. Members of society with vested interests in maintaining the status quo, accordingly, are apt to challenge research indicating, for example, that high rates of rape in dating relationships exist. Roiphe's (1993) *The Morning After: Sex, Fear and Feminism* became a bestseller within this context. The thesis of her book was that if women did not define the forced sex they experienced as rape, then it was not rape but just a misunderstanding. "Someone's rape," she famously claimed, "may be another person's bad night" (p. 54). Karmen (2004), in contrast, argues that to view date rape as a terrible misunderstanding in "he said-she said" terms, is a form of victim blaming.

Denial of the reality of rape crime victimhood can be understood not only in terms of current trends, but also because the natural social-psychological tendency has been always to belittle the load that others carry and to look away from others' pain. We do not want to see the homeless, hear the complaints of those on welfare, and certainly not hear of bad things happening to good people. A concept derived from social psychology, **victim blaming** refers to a fundamental tendency in American culture to hold the downtrodden or underdogs of society responsible for creating their own distress (Zastrow, 2003). Because of the reciprocity involved, the victim tends to internalize the blame attached to his or her condition ("I have failed"), and the negativity may become a self-fulfilling prophecy ("I am a tainted person").

In an article aptly titled "All the World Loathes a Loser," Lerner (1971) indicates our vulnerability to the suffering of other people: We are vulnerable though only to the suffering of a hero. Condemning the victim (of crime, of disease, of a bad relationship) is a process that takes its place in a long series of American ideologies that have rationalized cruelty and injustice (Ryan, 1971). Victim blaming's appeal lies in its apparently reassuring message (to outside observers) that a just world exists (Karmen, 2004). Victim blaming can be conceived as a validation of the offender's point of view because it shifts some of the burden of responsibility from the perpetrator to his or her target.

The fact is that the closer we try to identify ourselves with victims, the more vulnerable we are to their suffering. Although we have a tendency to put ourselves in the place of someone who is suffering, there is also the countertendency to believe that the unfortunate victim in some sense merited his or her fate. In the case of crimes of personal violation, we attach a stigma to the victim almost out of fear of contamination. Accordingly, we may develop an unfavorable perception of a rape victim and are apt to reject her.

In a survey of 200 undergraduate students at Kent State University in the early 1980s, van Wormer found that although the majority of respondents did not blame the rape victim, some students attributed blame to the victims of rape far more than they did victims of non–person-oriented crimes. More negative reaction was expressed by males than females toward sexual offense victims. Male students reacted intensely to two possibilities: their own victimization by a fellow male and knowledge that their mothers had once been raped or were victims of incest. They often had no response to the former possibility (two students wrote in that they'd kill the guy). Regarding knowledge that their mother was sexually abused, over half did not wish to know that this happened. A replication of this study in 1998 with another 200 students at the University of Northern Iowa revealed few gender differences and less victim-blaming, but a strong male reluctance to reveal their own victimization persisted.

Because of the myth that the typical rapist looks like a rapist—rough and disheveled in appearance—blame is transferred to the victim if the accused rapist defies the stereotype. This is what happened in the crime documentary *Our Guys* (Lefkowitz, 1997), a work that stirred up much talk in criminology circles. *Our Guys* stands as an indictment of suburbia where when the high school jocks are charged with sexual crimes, the entire community turns the other way. As Lefkowitz writes:

> *What kind of place was Glen Ridge anyway? A large group of charismatic athletes. A retarded young woman. The silence of the students and adults. The inclination to blame the woman and exonerate the men. These elements seemed to be linked by a familiar theme in my life in journalism. I began to frame Glen Ridge as a story of power and powerlessness: The power of young males and the community that venerated them, and the powerlessness of one marginalized young woman. (pp. 2–3)*

Lefkowitz found in Glen Ridge a microcosm of the affluent small town, a town where girls were labeled in distinct categories and treated accordingly. "Little mothers" provided tea and sympathy; other girls served as party decorations, and still others were targeted for a blend of sexual release and abuse. Girls who were targeted received vulgar nicknames by the boys; such girls were used sexually, then passed on to the boys' friends. The surprising aspect of the rape of the brain-injured girl was that arrests were made and convictions followed. What is not surprising, given our knowledge of victim-blaming, is that the town rallied around the accused jocks, "our guys." Following the arrests, the townspeople spoke of the tragedy that had befallen these boys, a tragedy that would scar them forever: "In the bosom of their hometown, they were greeted like returning warriors who had prevailed in a noble crusade. Or, if you prefer, martyred heroes" (p. 5).

Some have argued that the tremendous effort we put into teaching aggression to athletes leads to an increase in aggressive behavior off the field (Schwartz and DeKeseredy, 1997). In an age of sports hero idolatry, star athletes get the message that they can break the law with impunity and that a certain amount of violence against women will be tolerated. This message protects star athletes from taking responsibility. It sets girls and women up for abuse and denigration. We are, as Schwartz (1998) terms it, a **rape-supportive culture.**

Let us digress briefly to consider the perceived contrast of rape-prone and rape-free culture. Within American society there are enclaves where male dominance reigns. Consider, for example, the male prison, the street gang, sports teams, and fraternities. Here, conditions are conducive to male dominance and sexual violence. In a **rape-prone culture,** dominance and control over women become aspects of achieving and experiencing masculinity to the extent that rape, while not condoned, becomes part of the cultural ethos (Watson-Franke, 2003).

What do cross-cultural data say about the opposite pattern—societies that are **rape free** or relatively so? Watson-Franke, in her survey of anthropological research from matrilineal cultures, did find some instances of societies where rape was unknown. Among the Iroquois, for example, rape was reported by European explorers to be unknown; in several societies such as Apache, a man would have been considered less than human if he attacked a woman in this way. Watson-Franke's explanation for the absence of rape in such matrilineal societies is that biological paternity is not a concern and, typically, the role of maternal uncle is as important as the role of father. Watson-Franke contrasts rape-free culture with that described in Lefkowitz's book *Our Guys*, a culture that was male- rather than female-centered, in which the athletes formed a special, often protected class of adolescents that seemed to give them a sense of entitlement. Criminologists Godenzi, Schwartz, and Dekeseredy (2001) concur with this appraisal. University groups (such as fraternities, sports teams), they suggest, may enforce adherence through homophobia and group pressure, while promising a hypermasculine culture that encourages men to use coercion and force to increase their count of sexual encounters.

Problems on the college campus may be substantial, but they pale in contrast to the extent of sexual abuse of women serving in the military. Recently, the Defense Department identified over 1,000 cases of sexual assault on service members in 2004, only about 100 of which resulted in a court-martial (Martineau, 2005). Because acquaintance rape is not included as an offense under military law, the U.S. Senate is expected to make the necessary changes in the military's Uniform Code of Military Justice to rectify the situation to include varying kinds of sexual assault.

Compounding the victim-blaming ethos is the social-psychological phenomenon called *erotophobia*, or fear and ambivalence concerning sex. Erotophobia is unconsciously conveyed to children so that they will have the socially acceptable inhibitions to keep them from being a source of embarrassment to their parents in polite company. Foremost among the challenging tasks of growing up is to unlearn some of the inhibitions that one so conscientiously has been taught. Even learning the language of sexuality presents difficulties; one must employ a different vocabulary in different circles. In adulthood, a vague feeling that sex is dirty may persist (see van Wormer, Wells, and Boes, 1999). If problems exist in dealing with sex as a part of making love, the problems of dealing with sex under forced and frightening circumstances, sometimes with multiple violators, are insurmountable.

Erotophobia combined with victim-blaming even affects our handling of cases involving children. Our revulsion against sexual contact with children causes us to distance ourselves from child molesters in treatment, those who provide the treatment, and even children who claim to have been sexually abused. The result, according to Baartman (1998), is that almost all who hear of these situations feel an automatic inclination to look for arguments that contradict the accusations.

Types of Rape

The types of rape that occur most frequently are acquaintance rape, mass rape, and child abuse or sexual abuse. (Marital rape is discussed in connection with wife abuse in Chapter 9.)

Acquaintance Rape

Acquaintance rape is any rape in which the parties know one another. Included in this definition are date rape, campus rape, and partner or marital rape. Stranger rape was thought at one time to be the most common form of sexual violence. Yet, thanks to self-report surveys of both men and women, we now know that most victims know their rapists. Acquaintance rape is extremely common on college campuses.

Because practically all the studies of acquaintance rape use college samples, not much is known about this phenomenon, apart from BJS statistics on nonstranger rape. Another major problem in data gathering, as noted by Koss and colleagues (1985), is that so many victims of rape by their dates or boyfriends feel responsible themselves for their own vulnerability and, even in surveys, don't define what happened to them as rape. The statistics therefore vastly underestimate the prevalence of rape/sexual assault.

In one midwestern survey, 100 percent of all rapists knew their victims (Meyer, 1990). *Rape in America,* a report issued by the National Victims Center (1992), found that only 22 percent of all women in the national sample who had been raped were assaulted by strangers. Friends, neighbors, boyfriends, husbands, ex-husbands, and relatives headed the list of perpetrators. In-depth interviews with a random sample of 420 women in Toronto revealed that of those who had been sexually assaulted after age 16, 58 percent were assaulted by husbands, boyfriends, or dates (Randall and Haskell, 1995).

When rape occurs in a dating relationship, it does not necessarily lead to the breakup of the relationship. The likelihood of multiple experiences of forced sex increases substantially if the rapist is a woman's husband or lover (Kelly, 1988). In many women's minds, the boundaries between rape and strong pressure to have sex are unclear. For this reason, rape surveys often ask if respondents were "forced to have sex" instead of "raped" for greater accuracy in results (Koss et al., 1985).

Kelly conducted in-depth interviews with sixty English women volunteers who had experienced sexual violence. Her book, *Surviving Sexual Violence* (1988), is a study of how women cope and survive very bitter experiences with men. Her illustrations of women's reactions to bad experiences across the spectrum of sexual violence are gripping. For instance:

> *"I didn't say no, I didn't dare to . . . you know you don't want to, but you are still doing it. That's why in my eyes now it's rape with consent. It's rape because it's pressurized, but you do it because you don't feel you can say no."*
>
> *"I remember an occasion where he wouldn't let me get up, and he was very strong. He pulled my arms over my head. I didn't put up much of a struggle. I mean I wouldn't have seen that as rape because I associated rape with strangers, night and struggle. I didn't put up much of a struggle, but I didn't want to, so in a sense that was rape, yes." (p. 113)*

Although sexual aggression in dating relationships has been studied for more than thirty years, most U.S. citizens still have problems accepting that rape can occur among friends and especially among intimates (Wallace, 1998). Estrich (1987), in her groundbreaking *Real Rape*, alerted our attention to the seriousness of the form of rape that takes place in a relationship of trust—acquaintance rape. Taking a historical perspective, Estrich shows how this form of rape by a non-stranger frequently has been characterized by the courts and by the general public as not "real rape." The male-dominated system, as Estrich indicates, is reluctant to classify rape as violence because violence is construed as getting beaten up, while rape is viewed in sexual terms. Consider the following case, admittedly extreme, of the badgering that a survivor of date rape endured at the hands of her abusive husband to whom she had confided several years before of the rape by a man who she thought was her friend:

> *I truly believed my husband requested these things because of his pain. However, I soon found out that this was a lie. One day B. asked me to talk about how I had been raped. I tried to explain that the Panamanian man took off my clothes and I told him, "no" as he was doing it, but he refused to listen. B. told me he thought I "wanted it" because, after all, I went in his dorm room when I was visiting my sister (who was attending college at the time and I was in high school). I told B. that I went to this man's room (a dorm room) because I thought we were friends and we could practice Spanish together. This explanation was not sufficient for B. He insisted I give him explicit details about the rape from beginning to end, focusing on details such as "how he went in and out" and "how I liked it." B. would badger me for hours (sometimes up to eight hours at a time) about the rape and would not stop until I convinced him that I really did not want to be raped and that I did not like it. (Confided to van Wormer in private correspondence of October 5, 2005)*

As in the United States, in Britain the public still believes the stereotype of what constitutes "real rape," which is the rape by a stranger of a victim who resists and who reports the crime immediately to the police. The saliency of this belief system is reflected in results from an analysis by criminologist Liz Kelly (cited in a British news release by Sawyer, 2005) who studied relevant court documents. In 1985 there was a 24 percent conviction rate in rape trials; in 2003 only 5 percent of rape allegations ended in a guilty verdict. "Twenty years ago," according to Kelly's report, "if a woman wore a short skirt she was deemed to be 'asking for it.' These days alcohol is the equivalent of that miniskirt" (p. 2). Prosecutors in the United Kingdom, as in the United States, only take a case to court if they have a reasonable chance of winning. Often the prospects of a harsh cross-examination and reliving the trauma over and over are enough to dissuade the victim from pursuing justice. Yet American prosecutors receive special training to prepare them to prosecute rape cases, and their conviction rate is substantially higher than that of their British counterparts (Sawyer).

McDonald and Kline (2004) presented vignettes to 300 college students and had the students recommend appropriate sanctions in cases of date rape. The results showed, as predicted, that women chose harsher sanctions for the violators than did the men.

Cases of forced sex when there have previously been sexual relations are rarely reported and, if they are reported, they are rarely prosecuted. Many campus rapes are handled internally through student conduct board hearings. One advantage of this process is that the perpetrator is forced to admit his bad behavior under threat of otherwise having the matter turned over to the police. This may spare victims the agony of the adversarial process and allow the perpetrator to "come clean." Typical in-house punishments are probation, suspension, and substance abuse counseling. Disadvantages are that the student offender generally remains on campus which puts other women at risk, the offense is not viewed as a crime, and the victim-survivor is apt to be the one to leave the campus, in the end.

In the backlash rhetoric of some of the popular press, **date rape,** as Neame (2004) suggests, is commonly viewed as less serious and less traumatic than rape by a stranger. Yet research shows that date rape has significant consequences for women. Shapiro and Schwartz (1997) determined, in a study of forty-one college women who had been date raped, that when compared to those who had not been victimized, the former showed more trauma symptoms and lower sexual self-esteem than the latter. Similarly, Kowalski (1995) found that the emotional effects of acquaintance rape are profound and that appropriate intervention is crucial.

Who is vulnerable to rape, and how can rape be avoided? In fact, all women are vulnerable to rape. Factors associated with avoiding stranger rape, according to Rollins (1996), are being tall, having been the oldest daughter, and having had major household responsibilities, all factors associated with assertiveness. Based on a survey of studies of women who escaped their attackers, Rollins recommends physical resistance, screaming, and reasoning with the rapist, but not pleading or arguing with him. African American women, she notes, are most likely to avoid rape by having "street smarts" in dangerous situations. Surveys of convicted rapists indicate they stalk potential victims first, noting how women carry themselves as they walk. Those who seem weak and fearful are singled out as likely targets.

One area of much public concern has been the growing use of the drugs Rohypnol ("roofies") and gamma hydroxybutyric acid (GHB) to sedate women in order to take sexual advantage of them. Rohypnol resembles Valium in its properties; sedation occurs twenty to thirty minutes after ingestion. GHB can have intoxicating effects. Both are dangerous when consumed with alcohol. In Las Vegas, use of the so-called date-rape drugs was reported in about 100 cases last year; in the United States, there have been just under 200 fatalities so far with GHB, mostly from deliberate recreational use (Glauber, 2005). Prosecution is difficult because the victim typically suffers from drug-induced amnesia. Actually, alcohol has been used successfully by men for years to achieve similarly disabling results. "Candy is dandy, but liquor is quicker" goes the saying.

The fact that acquaintance rape is rampant on college campuses and that stereotypical stranger rape is relatively rare outside so-called high-crime areas has important implications for prevention. College rape prevention efforts are devoted to blue lights all over the campus, student escort services, and warnings to women about how to avoid rape. Campus authorities pay relatively little attention to date rape (Schwartz and DeKeseredy, 1997). Efforts would be better spent on education and on men educating men about the risks of aggressive masculinity and objectification of women. Because of the alcohol abuse typically present on college campuses, stepped-up substance abuse prevention efforts could be immensely helpful as well.

Mass Rape

Susan Brownmiller's landmark study, *Against Our Will: Men, Women, and Rape* (1975) put the crime in an international and cultural perspective. She defined rape as "a conscious process of intimidation by which all men keep all women in a state of fear" (p. 5). As a collective act, rape can promote male bonding. Among adolescent boys and gangs of bikers, rape is a ritual of manhood. In an anthropological study of fraternity gang rape, Sanday (1990) argues that the sexual and drinking practices of fraternities on American university campuses encourage gang rape. Sorority women therefore are at heightened risk for attack. Gang rape and rape of the enemy's women in war are documented extensively in this study.

In their book, *Sexual Assault on the College Campus* (1997), Schwartz and DeKeseredy probe what they term the "hypererotic subculture" that permeates the college scene. Men socialized into this subculture regard sex in terms of gaining possession of a woman. The more "girls you can have sex with," in fact, the better (p. 35). "Frat" house conformity combined with strong peer-group pressure to "score" leads some to experience a sense of relative deprivation. As Schwartz and DeKeseredy thoughtfully suggest, "the frustration caused by a reference group–anchored sex drive often results in predatory sexual conduct" (p. 35). All-male alliances can reduce sexual intercourse to a violent power game, one that says more about relationships between men and their brothers than between men and women.

Where there is hostility between enemies, women are particularly subject to predatory attack. Although rare, interracial sexual assault can take on political overtones. Such attacks against women can serve to "get at" an entire racial or ethnic group. Writing in his autobiography, *Soul on Ice,* Eldridge Cleaver (1968) showed little respect for his black sisters as he declared:

> *I became a rapist. To refine my technique and* modus operandi, *I started out by practicing on black girls in the ghetto . . . and when I considered myself smooth enough, I crossed the tracks and sought out white prey. (p. 26)*

The dynamics of wartime rape are similar. War rape and sexual violence have a history as long as the practice of war itself (Farwell, 2004). General George Patton is quoted by Brownmiller (1975) as follows, "I then told them that, in spite of my most diligent efforts, there would unquestionably be some raping" (p. 23). General Patton was speaking from experience and from his knowledge of history. Rape is more than an accident of war. Its widespread use under military occupation reflects the special terror it holds for the enemy's women. It also reflects the inequalities and discrimination women face in their everyday lives in peacetime (Amnesty International, 1995).

Mass rape of women by conquering warriors is so much a part of conquest that it is more remarkable in its absence than in its presence. In the battles of ancient Greece, the Crusades, the U.S. Civil War, World Wars I and II, and the Vietnam War, rape was used as a physical and psychological weapon of war (Wing and Merchan, 1993). In the Civil War, Union soldiers were said to have raped former slave women as they plundered towns and plantations (Wyatt, 1997). The rape that accompanies war is both a tremendous act of aggression and humiliation against a conquered people and a reward to soldiers who are encouraged by their officers to loot villages and rape the women at will. Rape is the act of patriotism, misogyny, and lust rolled into one (van Wormer, 1997). In the name of victory and the power of the gun, war provides men with a tacit license to rape (Brownmiller, 1975). In her analysis of rape in warfare, Brownmiller did not mince words:

> *Sexual sadism arises with astonishing rapidity in ground warfare, when the penis becomes justified as a weapon in a logistical reality of unarmed non-combatants, encircled and trapped. Rape of a doubly dehumanized object—as woman, as enemy—carries its own terrible logic. In one act of aggression, the collective spirit of women and of the nation is broken, leaving a reminder long after the troops depart. And if she survives the assault, what does the victim of wartime rape become to her people? Evidence of the enemy's bestiality. Symbol of her nation's defeat. A pariah. Damaged property. A pawn in the subtle wars of international propaganda. (p. 37)*

This is what happened in Haiti, Bosnia, Rwanda, and Sudan. Today, 70 percent of Rwanda's population is female, and the vast majority have lived through rape. "We are the living dead," said one survivor (Flanders, 1998, p. 30). Compounding the injury to the victims, the husbands often transfer their feelings of revulsion from the enemy to the victimized wives. Such rejection of women as defiled beings is consistent with traditional patriarchal ideology that universally demands that women should not allow more than one man to have access to their bodies (Wetzel, 1993).

A descendant of Confederate General Beauregard and one of his slave-mistresses, law professor Adrien Wing draws a gripping parallel between the ethnic cleansing and forced impregnation in Bosnia and the history of rape and miscegenation in the American South (Wing and Merchan, 1993). The early American South and Bosnia share common ground in terms of six key attributes that are all related to "spirit injury" of a people. These traits are:

1. rape as defilement not only of the individual woman but of a whole culture;
2. rape as silence as the women internalize their experience of oppression, rendering them more vulnerable to males within their own group;
3. rape as sexuality in which raped women are seen as promiscuous and impure;
4. rape as emasculation of men due to their sense of helplessness to protect their wives and daughters;
5. rape as trespass on the "property" rights of men, which was most pronounced under slavery in which the women were the property of their white masters, as were the racially mixed offspring; and
6. rape as pollution of the victim and of her children born as the result of non-consensual sex.

Rape as an instrument of war is clearly a violation of international law and its proscriptions against war crimes, taking of hostages, torture, and violation of human dignity (Wing and Merchan, 1993). Deplorably, although torture has been prosecuted as a war crime, only recently was war rape considered anything more than an inevitable by-product of war. Now, at last, women's rights are seen as human rights. Recent decisions, particularly those emanating from the International Criminal Tribunal for Rwanda and for the former Yugoslavia, established legal definitions and precedents for prosecuting perpetrators of war rape and defining war rape as a crime against humanity (Farwell, 2004). (See Chapter 12, this text.)

Changes in the conceptualization of rape have been reflected in significant changes in the treatment of victims. Women's group counseling centers and rape crisis centers were developed by grassroots organizations in local communities, at medical centers, and on college campuses. Numerous magazine and newspaper articles appeared, chronicling the reality of rape and its aftermath and especially the courtroom denigration of the victim's character and insinuations about her sexual history. Federal funding for a time poured into rape crisis centers and other crisis intervention programs for victims. Perhaps the most noteworthy outcome of the rape reform movement was the progress made on the legal front. Law enforcement officers gradually became more sensitized to the feelings of women who had been sexually abused. We consider the criminal justice response to rape later in this chapter.

Child Sexual Abuse

Child sexual abuse was rediscovered in the late 1970s and early 1980s when a deluge of newspaper articles, books, and television movies about this subject appeared in North America and western Europe. The percentage of women in the general population who report having been sexually abused as children varies from study to study. In 1991, researchers concluded that as many as 10–15 percent of boys and 20–25 percent of girls had experienced at least one instance of sexual abuse (Briere, 1992; Finkelhor, 1986). In their review of accumulated data, Freyd and colleagues (2005) produced the estimate of 20 percent of women and 5 to 10 percent of men sexually victimized worldwide. Such surveys, as the authors point out, likely underestimate prevalence because of underreporting and memory failure. Because the overwhelming majority of cases are not known to authorities and national crime statistics do not include crimes against children, the only measures available are small-sample retrospective surveys.

We do have some data based on reports of child abuse and neglect from the U.S. Department of Health and Human Services (DHHS, 2003). (Keep in mind the small percentage of abuse and neglect cases that are reported.) Of all child victims in 2003, around 1.2 percent of children were reported for abuse and neglect, most of which were cases of neglect; around 10 percent were cases of sexual abuse. Most child sexual abuse is committed by a relative or someone known to the child; yet the media focus is on a few rare sexual kidnapping cases (Cheit and Freyd, 2005).

Incest, usually differentiated from other forms of sexual assault, is defined as sexual acts performed within a family by an adult or an older family member against a child (Byington, 1995). Incest is the ultimate violation of a child's trust and love. Because of the child welfare issues involved, these cases are often handled by departments of human services, and prosecution is waived in lieu of treatment and reform. In both clinical and nonclinical American samples, perpetrators are predominantly male. In general population samples, which reflect reality more accurately than samples of persons in treatment, sexual abuse by parent figures constitutes 6 to 16 percent of the cases, abuse by other relatives constitutes 25 percent, abuse by strangers equals 5 to 15 percent, and the rest of the cases involve acquaintances (Berliner, 1995). Boys are more likely than girls to be abused by nonfamily members. All types of sexual acts occur, and attempted or completed intercourse is reported in 20 to 40 percent of the cases. Because of the secrecy and shame attached to incest, its prevalence is hard to determine.

From research we learn that father-daughter incest is associated with social isolation, religiosity, illness in the mother, and a daughter who assumes homemaker roles (Storer, 1992). The presence of a stepfather in the household may be a further precipitating factor (Finkelhor, 1984).

The classic pattern of incest is a progression from fondling of breasts, buttocks, and genitals to mutual masturbation to full intercourse. The ongoing need for secrecy is handled through a combination of threats and bribery. Typically, the pattern continues until the child runs away or otherwise escapes the situation. If the family discovers what is going on, often through a teacher or doctor, there may be disbelief and strong pressure on the child to keep her mouth shut. "It didn't happen and don't tell anyone" is the typical twisted message given. Years later the adult is left to try to pick up the pieces from a stolen childhood.

To survive psychologically, children in a continuing incest situation may dissociate their moods from their bodies during sex. Such altered consciousness can result in clouded memories of the abuse. The unconscious, unresolved trauma may result in symptoms both in childhood and much later, such as phobias, which appear to be meaningless in themselves (Meiselman, 1990).

In the 1990s, a great deal of media attention in North America was given to false reports. The fact that innocent persons actually were sentenced to prison based on flimsy evidence is undeniable. Some false reports were promoted through suggestion by therapists with a fixed agenda. In carefully controlled laboratory experiments, children were shown to be highly suggestible as they try to make sense of their psychological distress. The risk is that because some children were too readily believed in the past, too few will be believed in the future. Cheit and Freyd (2005) discuss the fallout from the handful of highly publicized cases of false memories. Now truly guilty perpetrators, they argue, can be represented by attorneys who present evidence of false accusations that were made in the past. Meanwhile, extended societal denial coupled with the belief that child sexual abuse is rare thwarts the healing process and leaves other children vulnerable to predators. To protect children's welfare, Cheit and Freyd call for the creation of a new Institute of Child Abuse and Interpersonal Violence to exist within the Institute of Health and for research funding to be drastically increased.

The words of Maya Angelou (1969), who, at the age of eight, was raped by her mother's boyfriend, resonate:

> Then there was the pain. A breaking and entering when even the senses are torn apart. The act of rape is a matter of the needle giving because the camel can't. The child gives, because the body can, and the mind of the violator cannot.
>
> I thought I had died—I woke up in a white-walled world, and it had to be heaven. But Mr. Freeman was there and he was washing me. His hands shook, but he held me upright in the tub and washed my legs. "I didn't mean to hurt you, Ritie. I didn't mean it. But don't you tell. . . . Remember, don't tell a soul." (p. 76)

Now we turn our attention to a form of child abuse that was little known to the world until the past decade, the church's dark and shameful secret.

Priest Abuse

Hundreds of Catholic priests have been accused of sexual misconduct with children and youths in incidents that go back to the 1960s. This is referred to in the media as **priest abuse** or clergy abuse. The focus in media accounts and the limited scholarly research on the topic has been on the harm done to boys and young men. Yet there are a large number of cases involving girls and young women as well.

In his random survey of over 7,000 active Catholics in the United States and Canada, Rossetti (1995) found that 1.7 percent of the females and 3.3 percent of the males had been sexually abused in childhood by a priest. His documentation seemed to indicate that about twice as many boys as girls experience such victimization. This figure may be a reflection of the fact that in the past, only boys could serve the priest at the altar so priests had greater access to them than to girls.

The priest holds a position of sacred trust and is generally viewed by Catholics as God's representative on earth (Rossetti, 1995). Sexual abuse by such a trusted figure may lead to low self-esteem and disillusionment in the victim. Rossetti noted that adults who had been sexually abused as children by priests reported less trust in the priesthood than did other Catholics. One interesting finding was that the female survivors reported a greater loss of trust in their relationship to God than did the male survivors. Perhaps, as Rossetti speculated, the women were more rejecting of the male-identified God than were the men. Another interesting finding was that persons who had received treatment for the abuse were more aware of their traumatization than were those who had not received treatment. Whether this is positive or negative is unclear.

Kennedy (2001), a former Catholic priest, wrote a book about priest abuse entitled *The Unhealed Wound*. Catholicism will have a hard time righting its wrongs, wrote Kennedy, because so much of its institutional power depends on keeping its members in a dependent state. The "unhealed wound" in the title of Kennedy's book refers to Catholicism's failure to deal with sexuality in a mature fashion. Kennedy made a strong case for ending the unnatural mandate for celibacy by priests. Such a requirement, he suggested, attracts young men who are psychologically and emotionally immature.

Van Wormer and Berns (2004) conducted an analysis of in-depth interviews of women survivors of priest molestation in their youth. The sample of nine women was available through workshops for survivors of priest sexual misconduct. All the women had been heavily active in church affairs and rituals; all lacked a close relationship with their fathers. Several of the women had experienced earlier sexual violation, a fact that probably increased their vulnerability, as research on childhood sexual trauma has demonstrated (Fieldman and Crespi, 2002). One of the survivors even had gone to her priest for help in coping with her experience of childhood abuse. The sense of pain and personal anguish was considerable. Moreover, because the priest represents the church, and the church represents religion in a devout Catholic family, the child or adolescent who is fondled or otherwise sexually exploited by a priest has nowhere to turn. In addition, if she (or he) successfully exposes the priest as a predator, many church attenders will be disillusioned.

In the media coverage and lawsuits, the plight of the female victims of clergy abuse has largely gone unnoticed. Yet the evidence is that the suffering engendered by their victimization is pronounced. Compared to male victims who have had to wrestle with the homosexuality dimension, women, according to what evidence we have, report that they undergo a major crisis in religious faith. Additionally, as van Wormer and Berns discovered, these girls and young women received little community support when they sought help from their friends and other confidantes; most typically, they were silenced. Such healing as did occur took place through social and therapeutic support, often years later.

A perusal of the narratives provided by these survivors reveals that the aftermath of the sexual victimization involved a second victimization. Instead of the support they needed, their needs were brushed away; often their reputations were besmirched. As we know from studies of rape survivors, a crucial factor in their recovery is the immediate response from significant others and authorities (Schwartz and DeKeseredy, 1997). And if trauma is to be prevented, early intervention is essential.

Criminal Justice Response

Because of the work of the women's movement, the contemporary understanding of rape and the legal response to this crime have undergone significant revision. Most police officers today view rape as a serious crime. A nationwide survey revealed that law enforcement officers who had received training to demolish the myths about rape credited the training with changing their attitudes (Horne, 1993). The entry of increasing numbers of women into this field has further promoted change from within the system. Yet, considering the long cultural tradition of women bearing the guilt for sexual victimization, it is not surprising that the legacy of the past is with us still.

The legacy of antiquated concepts that have been translated into law and custom and an innate distaste for this type of crime by all parties often cause the victim of sexual assault to feel victimized a second time. The woman's problem in confronting the law stems from three sources: attitudes of the police, the difficulty of answering questions of an intensely personal nature, and treatment by the courts. In some prosecutors' offices, rape victims are routinely asked to take lie detector tests.

An investigative report by journalists of the police department practices in the major cities of St. Louis and Philadelphia revealed that a large number of reported rapes were not officially recorded (Kohler, 2005). These cases instead were relegated to informal memos and eventually shredded. These were cases that were believed to be not proven; in other words, the victim had to prove the offense occurred. One woman had her case dismissed, as noted on the memo, because she could not stop crying long enough to answer the detective's questions.

Rape is a unique crime both in the low rate at which it is reported to the police and in the low conviction rate if it is prosecuted. It is the only crime in which the victim, at least in part, is considered guilty until proven innocent. From the first police encounter, the victim is gauged in terms of respectability and believability, and these attributes may be judged on a racial and class basis. Abused hitchhikers or women who went alone to a bar can expect to have marks against them from the start.

Why is rape so rarely reported? More to the point, why is it *ever* reported? In light of the feared mistreatment by justice officials of sexual assault victims and the ordeal of continually reliving the crime, it is remarkable that it is reported at all. Perhaps persons who have experienced crime go to the law for protection as a matter of course. Perhaps a vague sense of responsibility or a determination to get justice guides them. Caring and sensitive treatment by law enforcement officers can instill in the survivor a sense of not wanting to let them down by failing to follow through with prosecution. Sometimes the aim is to expiate the shame by publicly declaring it to have been a crime, the desire of the victim for some sort of vindication. Because what the victim really wants is for someone, an expert in these matters, to tell her, "You handled it well; you were fighting for your life. There was no other way."

Immediately after the attack, the victim approaches the authorities in an extreme state of emotional vulnerability. Because of her heightened awareness, words spoken to her at this time may stay with her forever. Rough treatment during the medical exam can cause physical pain and retraumatize the victim. An article in the popular press takes us through the process from the viewpoint of the good and the bad in criminal justice treatment. From *Glamour*, Karen Houppert (1996), a reporter with *Village Voice*, tells the story of Jeannie Dampf.

It is four months after the rape when the reporter travels to Tulsa to interview Jeannie. As the reporter describes the timing, "The rape has not yet become a manageable part of her personal history; it intrudes on her present, raw and relentless, and talking about it still brings on tears" (p. 274).

Jeannie describes the rape not as an isolated trauma, but as a catalyst—an event that sparked a series of traumas for which she was unprepared. Once the act was over, the repercussions began. Nevertheless, the treatment Jeannie received combined the thoroughness of the legal requirements with the support afforded by a rape crisis volunteer and later treatment at the rape crisis center.

One week later, Jeannie was receiving sensitive and skilled counseling at the rape crisis center. She needed to work through her unarticulated feeling of being dirty and wanting to hide, and the counselor helped her express and normalize her feelings. The preliminary hearing was difficult, but Jeannie got through it by keeping herself angry. In the trial, the rapist was convicted. Today, Jeannie reports, the flashbacks have mostly gone away, and she has tried to resume a normal sex life with her boyfriend. She has been tested twice for AIDS, but this is still a constant worry for both her and her partner.

Because new technologies such as the use of DNA evidence can clearly reveal that the defendant made contact with the accused, defense attorneys are hard put to find a way around the facts. Rather than try to counter this evidence, defense attorneys attempt to frighten witnesses away with threats to reveal personal information drawn from medical and counseling records. Among the personal details presented by O'Malley that served to scare witnesses away was testimony about drinking habits, a prior eating disorder, and revealing clothing worn while jogging (1997).

Many factors go into a high conviction rate, such as the social class and respectability of victims in the area, the ability to speak English, and acceptable behavior at the time of the crime (Hope, 2005). Apart from the fact that special training of nurses and doctors is crucial, the evidence must be properly preserved. The fact is that rape victims are held to a higher standard of proof than victims of other crime, so without strong evidence, a conviction is hard to get. A woman named Mary who was interviewed by Hope for *The New York Sun*, told him it took three years for her case to come to trial; when it did the accused represented himself. He grilled her for hours about the experience. Today she works for the Sexual

Assault Intervention Program at Mount Sinai Hospital to help others get through the ordeal that follows the rape.

Victims' Rights

In the United States, the jury selection process, whereby each opposing side can eliminate a certain number of prospective jurors, is unique. Whole trials can be won or lost on the basis of who occupies the jury seats. In rape trials, in which victim-blaming is a common component, a key question is whether men or women are the most likely to vote to convict an accused rapist. In the past, it was commonly believed that women would be harsher on other women. Three studies, however, indicate that men are more likely than women to excuse the perpetrator in jury trials (Johnson and Jackson, 1988; Kleinke and Meyer, 1990; Clark and Nightingale, 1997). New York Assistant District Attorney Linda Fairstein (1993) contends that getting a conviction in a date rape case is especially difficult. According to Fairstein, people have a fixed image of how a rapist should look. "But he doesn't look like a rapist" is the typical comment of jurors in date rape cases, which Fairstein has tried (p. 155).

Justice F. B. Kelly's Canadian study from the International Centre for Criminal Law Reform and Criminal Justice Policy (1998) compares victims' rights cross-nationally. In the past two or three decades, Kelly observes, an unprecedented international movement has evolved, devoted to the plight of victims of crime. In the United States and Canada one heralded change is the introduction in court proceedings of victim impact statements. In the United States, uniquely, victims play an active role in the plea-bargaining process. In both countries, evidence about the sex life of victims is excluded from sexual offense cases where it could be used to imply consent by the victim. In North America and Britain, more protection is being granted to children in sexual abuse cases by allowing them to testify on videotape or behind a screen away from the accused molester.

A favorable development is the allotment of financial compensation by the government for pain and suffering as a result of crime. Some Canadian provinces cover the maintenance of a child born as a result of rape. In the United States, victims may receive financial assistance from state victims' compensation programs. Victims must, however, demonstrate financial need.

Canadian laws are very strict concerning protection of the assault victim's right to privacy. The witness, if she so desires, can apply for a ban, and her identity will be protected. In the United States, half of the states restrict the publication of victims' names. In the other states, the newspapers usually do not publish the names out of custom. In Britain, the anonymity of rape victims is strictly maintained.

Despite all the obstacles described in North America and Europe, participation in the criminal justice process can be cathartic for the survivor, a way of getting beyond the pain. As Fairstein (1993) describes one woman's experience, "She had courageously faced her attacker and accused him with confidence and dignity. No one had humiliated or debased her, and none of the 'myths' of a complaining witness's ordeal had befallen her" (p. 261).

Hate crime law has the potential to help in the prosecution of cases on the basis of gender bias. Unfortunately, as McPhail (2002) indicates, there is a strong resistance to recognizing violence against women as a hate crime. The fact that many female victims know their attackers precludes some policy makers from fitting rape and domestic violence into a hate crime model. Recently Congressman Maloney (U.S. Congress, 2005) has introduced a bill, the Hate Crimes Statistics Improvement Act, to ensure that hate crimes motivated by gender are accounted for by the FBI and local law enforcement agencies. If a gang only beat up people of a certain race, that would be recognized as a hate crime; targeting a group based on their gender is a hate crime too, according to the Representative. Although nineteen states have included gender-based hate crimes in their hate crimes laws, the Federal Hate Crimes Statistics Act does not require the FBI to collect data on this important category.

Psychological Trauma

In an extensive review of international studies that looked at long-term effects, Finkelhor (1994) found an association between early sexual abuse and adult mental health impairments. Symptoms of anxiety and fear that are consistent with **post-traumatic stress disorder (PTSD)** are found in approximately one-third to one-half of sexually abused children (Berliner, 1995). PTSD includes intrusive, unpleasant recollections of the event and avoidance and numbing symptoms. Guilt feelings and a generalized sense of feeling dirty and damaged are common. Long-term sexual dysfunction is a corollary of childhood abuse. Repressed memories may be associated with phobias of a disabling sort. In short, the destruction of childhoods and the wreckage of adult lives in the wake of child abuse is monumental (Steed, 1995).

Increasing evidence shows that childhood trauma significantly alters the biochemistry of the brain (Ginsberg, Nackereed, and Larrison, 2004). Adaptation to trauma, such as hypervigilance, prepares the victim for fight-or-flight responses and may become biochemically ingrained when triggered again and again (Basham and Miehls, 2004). Cognitive and neurological mechanisms that may underlie the forgetting of abuse have been identified (Cheit and Freyd, 2005). Still we have a great deal to learn about how childhood trauma affects brain chemistry and how the tendency toward depression and addiction figure into the equation.

For women who suffer with addictive problems and with the law, a history of early childhood sexual abuse is almost a given. Ironically, a history of abuse seems to predispose women to adult victimization such as rape or battering. Even the early teenage pregnancy phenomenon so derided by the media and politicians is associated with a history of childhood sexual abuse (*NASW News*, 1995).

Maya Angelou shares with us—in her moving autobiography *I Know Why the Caged Bird Sings* (1969), in speeches, and in interviews—the trauma that rape produced in her life. In the years following the rape, she did not speak. The fact that her family killed the perpetrator made a bad situation worse. Maya was a victim with blood on her hands. Only the efforts of a lovely English teacher who introduced her to the world of literature brought out her gifts of self-expression. Today she is one of America's foremost poets.

In a book on sexual offenders, Tony Parker (1969) captures the sense of a survivor's early pain:

> *Afterwards I was suffering from shock: I had been physically hurt, I was numb, but then the first feelings which began were those of self-questioning—whether I shouldn't have struggled harder, whether in some way I might even at the last have prevented it. (p. 303)*

On top of the normal reaction to what may have been a near-death assault, the person who has been victimized suffers from her involvement in a hideously sordid sexual activity, an involvement that may be known by the entire community. For this reason the victim may have to not only change jobs but leave town as well. Even marriages do not always survive such an attack, because long after the wife is ready to forget (and she *will* want to go on to other things) her husband may not be able to.

Approximately 5 percent of rape victims become pregnant as a result of the rape. Today, some emergency rooms dispense morning-after pills to prevent pregnancy. If the rapist is of a different race from the victim, child-rearing problems and difficulties in explanation abound. A recent award-winning British film, *Secrets and Lies*, portrays the stirring reunion between a white working-class woman and the mixed-race daughter she gave up for adoption years earlier in the aftermath of interracial rape. In this film, a young woman who gave birth to a son as a result of rape describes her feelings, which were exacerbated by thoughtless initial reactions by her family.

The concept of "the rape trauma syndrome" was first identified by Burgess and Holmstrom (1979). This syndrome is now considered a part of PTSD. (See the American Psychiatric Association [APA], 2000.) Based on their emergency room work with rape victims, Burgess and Holmstrom identified two stages of adjustment to rape. The initial or acute stage, lasting approximately two weeks, involves shock and disbelief and some seeming acceptance of what has taken place. A common coping mechanism at this stage is forgetting. In her in-depth interviews with sixty British survivors of rape, Kelly (1988) discovered that forgetting or repression can help in the short term but causes serious problems in the long run. The need to suppress horrible events derives from the threat they represent to the person, as Kelly explains. Typically, part of the experience is remembered and part shut out of the mind. These acute reactions are a normative response. According to a comparison study of 215 assault and sexual assault victims, Valentiner, Riggs, Foa, and Gershung (1996) found that symptom severity decreased significantly after three months.

In the second phase of adjustment to the rape, the survivor may begin to experience physical and emotional turmoil—insomnia, unexpected crying fits, and extreme fear related to the violence of the attack. Kelly's (1988) interviewees spoke of intrusive flashbacks that harked back to the scene of the crime. The fear was compounded if the attacker was an ex-boyfriend or ex-spouse. Such a man, who used rape to punish a woman for the breakup of their relationship, would occasionally strike again. Sometimes the harassment was so bad that the woman, feeling utterly helpless, would return to her abuser.

Many women feel anger during this second stage, anger at the police, the courts, their families, and the offender. Over 90 percent of the women Kelly interviewed felt that their attitudes toward men had been affected by the encounter. Others, with a less healthy reaction, internalize their anger and sense of shame and become suicidal. Valentiner and colleagues (1996), in their large sample of victims, found that women who had severe trauma reactions earlier were likely to develop chronic PTSD later. This was especially true of rape victims. Since one-third of the victims developed enduring problems, it is clear that early intervention is vital, according to these research findings.

Kelly (1988) provides a list of the losses women may experience as a result of sexual violence. Among them are sense of safety, independence, control, self-esteem, memories, trust, positive feelings about sex, support networks, and health. Sexually inexperienced victims experience loss of virginity and a linking in their minds of sex and violence. As research indicates, younger women are more deeply traumatized than are more mature women who have had a positive experience of sex. Those who were sexually assaulted as children were the most likely to develop anxiety and other emotional disorders (Burnam et al., 1988).

Treatment and Empowerment

Recovery from trauma occurs when the child or woman who has been victimized is transformed into a survivor who is able to integrate the catastrophe into her life history and see it as a source of strength. Recovery takes place when the world seems a beautiful and trusting place again and your body feels whole and like yours alone.

Research shows that the initial meeting and relationship between a rape victim and the first person-friend or authority figure who responds has more impact on the victim's eventual recovery than anything else. The initial response by a trusted individual also determines the extent to which the survivor will blame herself and even whether or not she will acknowledge that what happened to her was a crime. A study of college rape victims, cited by Schwartz and DeKeseredy (1997), revealed that if the victims got the message that they were loved no matter what they had undergone, they tended to blame themselves. But if survivors got the message that it was not their fault, they tended to shift the blame to the perpetrator. Society's reaction to a woman's victimization, therefore, has long-term consequences.

The need for expert help is crucial following victimization. To prevent life-long problems, the sooner one gets professional counseling, the better. One study showed that completed rape led to PTSD symptoms in as many as 90 percent of women at four weeks following the assault and remained as high as 47 percent three months later (Rothbaum, Foa, Riggs, Murdock, and Walsh, 1992). In a random sample of 1,007 young members of a large health maintenance organization, a higher prevalence of PTSD was found in women than in men; of the sixteen women who experienced rape, thirteen developed PTSD (reported in *Science News*, 1991).

From van Wormer's experience counseling adult survivors of rape and incest and from the literature, we have filtered out four phases of adjustment to the shock and horror of forced sexual contact. In reality, the stages overlap and many survivors get stuck at one stage or bypass it altogether. This model represents an ideal type, in short, for the purpose of constructing a working intervention scheme. We must always recognize, however, that each survivor experiences a unique crime under unique circumstances and that her constitutional and environmental contingencies will have a strong bearing on her resolution of the crisis. The duration of the abuse, the degree of violence and terror experienced, the age of the victim, and the initial reactions of the authorities and significant others all fall into play in determining the course of the recovery process. These are the four phases: denial-avoidance, guilt and sexualization, reexperience and rage, and finally, healing.

At the political level, empowerment practice helps survivors redefine personal experiences as political. Klaw and colleagues (2005) describe an intensive semester-long rape prevention training for college students to develop acquaintance rape consciousness to parallel feminist consciousness. The authors concluded after completion of the program that such sustained efforts can play a vital role in dismantling rape-supportive culture. For women who had been personally victimized, the course seemed to facilitate the healing process by countering internalized messages of self-blame. Men, for their part, developed an awareness of how a rape experience could affect someone close to them.

Denial-Avoidance

In denying the gravity of the event and minimizing the difficulties ahead—"I'm alive; I'm all right"—the recent victim enables herself to handle as much as she can at that time. **Denial-avoidance** or repression of some of the most disturbing aspects, coupled with dissociation of the self from the act, allows victims to cope with experiences they are not yet ready to absorb into their reality. Feelings of detachment and emotional withdrawal from others are common.

To enhance long-term recovery, referral to crisis counseling services should be made at the earliest possible moment. Much personal tragedy and self-destructiveness can be avoided if the survivor can receive support during the critical early period of trauma. Brief crisis intervention early on may offset the need for intensive in-depth psychotherapy at a later stage. The worst thing that can happen to a child who has been abused is to leave her or him to sort out these experiences alone (Wyatt, 1997). Key elements of counseling during this initial period are psychological support—listening, caring, nurturing the strengths in the survivor as they manifest themselves—and education. Education includes providing information about the criminal justice process if the client chooses to get involved in this system and health care information if the client has not yet received medical care for the attack.

Victim/witness assistance programs, usually situated in local county prosecutors' offices or nearby court buildings, are designed to boost witness cooperation and to provide advocacy for their needs. For victims of rape and domestic violence, however, more specialized treatment is needed. The ideal arrangement is the provision of crisis intervention programs, which may be lodged in police departments, hospitals, or nonprofit agencies and are prepared to act within the first 24 hours after the victimization (Roberts, 1995). Help is given in filling out victim compensation forms, and crisis counseling and referral to extended counseling and psychotherapy are provided. Treatment in both short- and long-term counseling consists of a great deal of reassurance that the victim did not precipitate or deserve the assault. Because, according to a government video on crime victimization (U.S. Department of Justice, 1997), 13 percent of victims develop a plan for suicide, survivors need to be informed about actions to take to save their lives, such as hot-line numbers to call. Above all, as this training video further indicates, it is vital for criminal justice personnel to communicate that they believe the victim and that they are sorry about what has happened. This simple acknowledgment can mean a great deal to a recently traumatized person; it can bring tears of relief. One helpful approach is to ask the victim about her fears and concerns and always to validate and not disregard or dispute her feelings (Zastrow and Kirst-Ashman, 2004).

Guilt and Sexualization

The greatest irony is that the sexual offender often feels no remorse at all, while the victim is left with a sense of uncleanness and even guilt. The guilt feelings that are internalized by the child victim and that may remain with her until adulthood seem to make little sense on the surface. Sexual trauma survivors, however, feel guilty because they have engaged in forbidden sex often under sordid and horrible circumstances.

In adults, **traumatic sexualization** can occur also (see Patten, Gatz, Jones, and Thomas, 1995). Problems can range from negatively charged sexuality or association of all aspects of sex with self-loathing and disgust to inappropriately compulsive eroticism. Often the problems do not emerge until the survivor enters or tries to enter a committed relationship; only then does the seriousness of the trauma become apparent. *Stigmatization,* according to the same source, is associated with shame and guilt feelings that are internalized by the abused individual, especially if this individual is a child. The child may believe she is tainted forever by a bad experience, as we have seen.

The survivor therapy approach utilizes the strengths perspective to help reempower the client. Reestablishing trust in herself and the world and rediscovering her sense of personal control are primary goals in recovery from victimization. Group therapy is an invaluable technique for helping survivors let go of their self-blaming thoughts and regain their self-confidence. As group members, each of whom may unconsciously blame herself for her own suffering, come to share each other's stories of brutalization, a revelation may take place. In conjunction with an emerging sense of *we* instead of *I*, the revelation "We did not deserve this to happen to us" may come to light.

Reexperience and Rage

Adult survivors can benefit from intensive thinking and feeling work at any stage in the recovery process. Implicit in the philosophy of feeling work is the belief that feeling and thinking are in constant interaction with each other, that it is not the *event* itself that is significant but one's view of the event that shapes its impact. Whether a person is a victim or a survivor may be shaped more by the *definition* of the situation than by the situation itself.

The primary goal of treatment for sex trauma survivors is to help them reprocess their trauma and integrate it into their lives so as to resolve symptoms and related issues. A Canadian report of intervention with female survivors of childhood sexual abuse showed excellent results in raising self-esteem and reducing depression among members of thirteen closed-process groups (Richter, Snider, and Gorey, 1997). Group exercises ranged from reading relevant poetry, prose, or a chapter in *The Courage to Heal* (Bass and Davis, 1994). As for the women's sexual abuse experiences, the social workers gently and in a noncoercive way encouraged each woman to talk about what happened to her as a way of relieving the burden of the "secret."

An effective approach toward empowerment is to affirm the resourcefulness and competence of women who managed to use all the wiles at their disposal to survive and who have continued to survive ever since. In recovery, the survivor reviews a situation in which she seemed to have been completely overtaken yet, in fact, used many creative maneuvers for her own protection. In this way, a new meaning can be given to the trauma of rape or childhood sexual abuse. Some individuals, as they discard their sense of a damaged self, embrace instead the belief that the misfortune they endured made them stronger and more compassionate (Harvey and Harney, 1995). Only when safety and self-care are reliably established, as Harvey and Harney indicate, will the survivor be ready for this process of reviewing, reliving, and integrating the traumatic past.

Healing

Healing is simply the inner change, the sense of peace that may result from therapy work on labeling feelings and controlling them through cognitive techniques, reframing troubling events in one's life, and recognizing how past events influence present feelings, thoughts, and behavior. Reclaiming lost and damaged childhood selves may occur through the joint effort of treatment and support group relationships.

The aim of such memory retrieval work, as Harvey and Harney (1995) indicate, is to place the past in the past and to realize the role that past events play in shaping one's present life. Through sharing a painful and conflict-ridden episode in her life with a concerned professional, the survivor begins to perceive events increasingly through the eyes of the listener-observer. bell hooks (1993) speaks eloquently of the joy of reconciliation, the gift of healing. Referring to Alice Walker's (1982) novel, *The Color Purple,* hooks recalls how Celie, the black heroine, begins to recover from her traumatic experiences of incest/rape, domestic violence, and marital rape only when she is able to tell her story, to be open and honest. Telling one's story in any form, giving voice to the unmentionable, is the first step, according to hooks, in releasing the bitterness and in healing the inner wounds that makes reconciliation possible.

Summary

Childhood sexual abuse, incest, and rape are predatory acts that constitute serious problems for society and have long-lasting consequences for victims. In this chapter, we viewed this problem from a feminist/strengths approach; the emphasis was structural, on the power dynamics of a male-dominated society in which the threat of rape can serve, as Brownmiller (1975) suggests, to keep all women in a state of fear. Rape is thus at once both a personal and a political phenomenon. At the personal level, as we have seen, women are not only susceptible to being raped but also to being blamed for their own vulnerability.

To understand the political dimensions of rape, we looked to history, to the European-American heritage. Considered the property of men, of their fathers and husbands, women who were attacked were considered ruined and contaminated; the attack itself was conceived as an attack on their menfolk. In wartime, the victor has access to his enemy's women. Under the institution of slavery, access to slave women was a given.

Today, although rape in war and sexual slavery persist, there is growing international recognition, through the United Nations, of the human rights of women. The right to exercise control over one's sexuality is an important basic right. Without protection from physical and sexual violation in the home or elsewhere, previous guarantees of political and economic equality remain hollow.

The theoretical approach presented in this chapter, consistent with contemporary feminist theory, conceives of sexual aggression and abuse as a continuum or series of behaviors ranging from ordinary harassment to full-blown violent, life-threatening attacks. The common thread of dehumanization is the unifying element. Surveys show that although stranger rape is the prototype of rape, date rape and marital rape are far more common. Self-reports of college males and of women in national victim surveys reveal that sexual aggression by peers on the college campus is commonplace.

Rape victims suffer psychological as well as physical trauma. Because of the stigma attached to this crime, survivors often feel torn between the desire to talk about it, even years later, and a reluctance to tell people what they probably don't want to hear. Society's tendency to blame the victim, especially the victim of a sexual crime, effectively silences the survivor of rape. In cases of stranger rape, the omission of the victim's name from newspaper accounts, although advisable, prevents people from reaching out to the woman who has survived a life-threatening experience. Such an individual may forever wonder who knows and who doesn't know about this unmentionable crime. Shrouded in silence and internalizing society's blame, the survivor desperately needs someone to talk to. The importance of a rape crisis telephone line, rape advocates, and victim assistance programs cannot be underestimated. The choices and problems facing a recently victimized woman will seem insurmountable: whether to report the crime, how to endure the medical procedures, whom to tell, and how to go forward are just a few of the immediate concerns. Victimized children and their families need help most of all. Participation in group counseling sessions can reinforce girls' and women's self-worth and keep any self-destructive tendency that may arise in check.

Personal empowerment of women has its counterpart in political empowerment. We have the feminist movement to thank for both the recognition that violence against women is a public issue and the funding for prevention and intervention efforts to curb the impact of this type of crime. Women's interests and the state's political interests coinciding at this time of heightened attention to victims of crime provides an opportunity that should not be overlooked. To end the widespread rape and sexual harassment of women, we must continue our work toward legislative reform, educational initiatives, improved child-rearing practices, and better-funded advocacy/counseling services.

KEY TERMS

acquaintance rape (also date rape)
child sexual abuse
denial-avoidance
incest

mass rape
priest abuse
post-traumatic stress disorder (PTSD)
rape

rape-prone versus rape-free culture
rape-supportive culture
traumatic sexualization
victim blaming

CRITICAL THINKING QUESTIONS

1. Discuss the historic connection between laws against rape and property laws.

2. Account for the differences in African American reaction to having white versus American Indian ancestors.

3. How has rape victimization been reconceptualized over time?

4. What are "little rapes"? What is their impact on young women?

5. Some say the victimization rates are exaggerated. Discuss Roiphe's arguments on this point.

6. Discuss rape myths and the resistance to treating rape by an acquaintance the same as stranger rape.

7. Discuss the concept of rape-supportive culture.

8. What would rape-free culture be like?

9. Discuss the particular violation and spiritual repercussions of priest abuse.

10. Account for the common occurrence of rape in war. Pick a particular war in history and research the extent and consequences of rape during that period.

11. Compare PTSD with regard to rape trauma and to war trauma.

12. Consider ways that survivors of rape can be empowered.

WEB DESTINATIONS

Bureau of Justice Statistics: http://bjsdata.ojp.usdoj.gov

Family Violence and Sexual Assault Institute: www.fvsai.org

Latina Alliance Against Sexual Aggression: www.arte-sana.com

Rape, Abuse, and Incest National Network: www.rainn.org

Survivors of Incest Anonymous: www.siawso.org

Human Rights Watch: www.hrw.org

Violence Against Women of Color: Incite!: www.incite-national.org

REFERENCES

Allison, D. (1993). *Bastard out of Carolina*. New York: Plume.

American Psychiatric Association (APA) (2000). *Diagnostic and statistical manual of mental disorders,* 4th ed. (DSM-IV-TR) (Text Revision). Arlington, Va.: APA.

Amir, M. (1971). *Patterns in forcible rape*. Chicago: University of Chicago Press.

Amnesty International (1995). *Amnesty International report*. New York: Amnesty International U.S.A.

Angelou, M. (1969). *I know why the caged bird sings*. New York: Random House.

Australian Institute of Family Studies (2004, winter). Revisiting America's "date rape" controversy. *Family Matters 68:* 50–55.

Ayto, J. (1990). *Dictionary of word origins*. New York: Arcade.

Baartman, H. E. (1998). Compassion and scepticism in child sexual abuse: Some historical aspects and explanations. *International Reviews of Victimology 5*(2): 189–202.

Basham, K., and Miehls, D. (2004). *Transforming the legacy: Couple therapy with survivors of childhood trauma*. New York: Columbia University Press.

Bass, E., and Davis, L. (1994). *The courage to heal: A guide for women survivors of child sexual abuse,* 3rd ed. New York: HarperPerennial.

Bellafonte, G. (1998, June 29). Feminism: It's all about me! *Time:* 54–62.

Berliner, L. (1995). Child sexual abuse: Direct practice. *Encyclopedia of Social Work,* 19th ed. (pp. 408–417). Washington, D.C.: NASW Press.

Briere, J. N. (1992). *Child abuse trauma: Theory and treatment of lasting effects*. Newbury Park, Calif.: Sage.

Brownmiller, S. (1975). *Against our will: Men, women and rape*. New York: Bantam.

Bureau of Justice Statistics (1998). *Alcohol and crime.* Washington, D.C.: U.S. Department of Justice.

Bureau of Justice Statistics (1997, February). *Sex offenses and offenders: An analysis of data on rape and sexual assault.* Washington, D.C.: U.S. Department of Justice.

Bureau of Justice Statistics (BJS) (2004). *Criminal victimization, 2003.* Washington, D.C.: U.S. Department of Justice.

Bureau of Justice Statistics (BJS) Crime and Justice Data Online (2004). *Definitions for crime trends from the FBI's Uniform Crime Reports.* Washington, D.C.: U.S. Department of Justice. Retrieved from http://bjsdata.ojp.usdoj.gov.

Burgess, A. W., and Holmstrom, L. L. (1979). Rape trauma syndrome. *American Journal of Psychiatry 131:* 981–986.

Burnham, M. S., Stein, J. A., Golding, J. M., Siegel, J. A., Sorenson, S. B., Forsythe, A. B., and Telles, C. A. (1988). Sexual assault and mental disorders in a community population. *Journal of Consulting and Clinical Psychology 56:* 843–850.

Byington, D. B. (1995). Sexual assault. *The encyclopedia of social work,* 19th ed. (pp. 2136–2141). Washington, D.C.: NASW Press.

Cecil, H., and Matson, S. (2005). Differences in psychological health and family dysfunction by sexual victimization type in a clinical sample of African American adolescent women. *The Journal of Sex Research 42*(3): 203–228.

Centers for Disease Control and Prevention (CDC) (2004). *Sexual violence: Fact sheet.* National Center for Injury Prevention and Control. Retrieved from www.cdc.gov/ncipc/factsheets/svfacts.htm.

Cheit, R., and Freyd, J. (2005). Let's have an honest fight against child sex abuse. *The Brown University Child and Adolescent Behavior Letter 21*(6): 8.

Clark, H. L., and Nightingale, N. N. (1997). When jurors consider recovered memory cases: Effects of victim and juror gender. *Journal of Offender Rehabilitation 25*(3/4): 87–104.

Cleaver, E. (1968). *Soul on ice.* New York: Dell Publishing.

Cowan, G., and Campbell, R. R. (1995). Rape and causal attitudes among adolescents. *The Journal of Sex Research 32*(2): 145–153.

Crowell, N. A., and Burgess, A. W. (eds.) (1996). *Understanding violence against women.* Washington, D.C.: National Academy Press.

Deckard, B. S. (1983). *The woman's movement: Political, socioeconomic, and psychological issues,* 3rd ed. New York: Harper and Row.

DeSantis, J. (2005, June 26). When "no" is not enough. *Star News* (Wilmington, NC), 1A, 4A.

Dollarhide, M. (2002, May 6). Cable network pushes anti-rape legislation. *Women's E News.* Retrieved from www.feminist.com/news.

Donat, P., and D'Emilio, J. (1992). A feminist redefinition of rape and sexual assault: Historical foundations and change. *Journal of Social Issues 48:* 9–2.

Emerge (1997). Sexual assault survey results. *Emerge 8*(9): 512.

Estrich, S. (1987). *Real rape.* Cambridge, Mass.: Harvard University Press.

Fairstein, L. (1993). *Sexual violence: Our war against rape.* New York: Morrow.

Faludi, S. (1991). *Backlash: The undeclared war on American women.* New York: Doubleday.

Farwell, A. (2004). War rape: New conceptualizations and responses. *Affilia 19*(4): 389–403.

Fieldman, J. P., and Crespi, T. D. (2002). Child sexual abuse: Offenders disclosure, and school-based initiative. *Adolescence 37:* 151–160.

Finkelhor, D. (1984). *Child sexual abuse.* New York: Free Press.

Finkelhor, D. (1994). The international epidemiology of child sexual abuse. *Child Abuse and Neglect 18:* 409–417.

Finkelhor, D. (1986). *A sourcebook on child sexual abuse.* Beverly Hills, Calif.: Sage.

Flanders, L. (1998, March/April). Rwanda's living casualties. *Ms:* 27–30.

Flowers, R. B. (1987). Women and criminality: *The woman as victim, offender, and practitioner.* New York: Greenwood Press.

Freyd, J., Putnam, F., Lyon, T., Becker-Blease, K., Chiet, R., Siegel, N., and Pezdek, K. (2005, April 22). The science of child sexual abuse. *Science* (308). Retrieved from www.sciencemag.org.

Gershman, J. (2006, February 10). Putting sex predators in mental facilities may impact plea bargains. *The New York Sun,* 4.

Ginsberg, L., Nackereed, L., and Larrison, C. (2004). *Human biology for social workers: Development, ecology, genetics and health.* Boston: Allyn & Bacon.

Glauber, B. (2005, August 28). Women now practice defensive drinking. *Chicago Tribune.* Retrieved from www.chicagotribune.com.

Godenzi, A., Schwartz, M., Dekeseredy, W. (2001). Toward a gendered social bond/male peer support theory of university woman abuse. In *Critical Criminology Annual 2001 10*(1): 1–17.

Goodwin, J. (1994). *Price of honor.* Boston: Little, Brown.

Griffin, S. (1971). Rape: The all-American crime. *Ramparts 10*(3): 26–35.

The Guardian (2005, July 31). Observer campaign: Justice for rape victims. United Kingdom: *Observer News.* Retrieved from http://web.lexis-nexis.com.

Harvey, M. R., and Harney, P. A. (1995). Individual psychotherapy. In C. Classen (ed.), *Treating women molested in childhood* (pp. 63–93). San Francisco: Jossey-Bass.

Home Box Office (HBO) (2005, May 30). Rape in a small town: The Florence Holway Story. ABC Network, Australia. Retrieved from www.abc.net.au/4corners/content/20.

hooks, b. (1993). *Sisters of the yam: Black women and self-recovery.* Boston: South End Press.

Hope, B. (2005). Treatment, conviction rates vary by borough. *The New York Sun,* 1.

Horne, F. (1993). The issue is rape. In R. Muraskin and T. Alleman (eds.), *It's a crime: women and justice.* Englewood Cliffs, N.J.: Prentice-Hall.

Houppert, K. (1996, April). After the rape. *Glamour 94*(4): 274–277, 298.

Johnson, J. D., and Jackson, L. A. (1988). Assessing effects of factors that might underlie the differential perception of acquaintance and stranger rape. *Sex Roles 19:* 37–45.

Karmen, A. (2004). The victimization of girls and women by boys and men: Competing analytical frameworks. In B. Price and N. Sokoloff (eds.), *The criminal justice system and women offenders: Prisoners, victims, and workers* (pp. 289–301). New York: McGraw-Hill.

Kelly, F. B. (1998). *The unfinished triangle: The criminal justice system, the victim, and the offender.* Ottawa, Canada: International Centre for Criminal Law Reform and Criminal Justice Policy.

Kelly, L. (1988). *Surviving sexual violence.* Minneapolis: University of Minnesota Press.

Kennedy, E. (2001). *The unhealed wound: The church and human sexuality.* New York: St. Martin's.

Kilpatrick, D. G., Saunders, B. E., and Smith, D. W. (2003). Youth victimization: Prevalence and implications. *Research in brief* (NCJ 194972). Washington, D.C.: U.S. Department of Justice, Office of Justice Programs, National Institute of Justice. Retrieved from http://www.ojp.usdoj.gov/nij.

Klaw, E., Lonsway, K., Berg, D., Waldo, C., Kothari, C., Mazurek, C., and Hegeman, K. (2005). Challenging rape culture: Awareness, emotion and action through campus acquaintance rape education. In *Women & Therapy 28*(2): 47–63.

Kleinke, C. L., and Meyer, C. (1990). Evaluation of rape victims by men and women with high and low belief in a just world. *Psychology of Women Quarterly 14.*

Kohler, J. (2005). Abused by the system. *St. Louis Post-Dispatch,* A1.

Koss, M. P., Leonard, K. D., Beezley, D. A., and Oros, C. J. (1985). Nonstranger sexual aggression: A discriminant analysis of the psychological characteristics of undetected offenders. *Sex Roles 12:* 981–992.

Kowalski, L. B. (1995). *School Social Work Journal 20*(1): 1–12.

Krug, E. G., Dahlberg, L., Mercy, J. A., Awi, A., Lozano, R. (eds.) (2004). *World report on health and violence.* World Health Organization. Retrieved from www.who.int/violence_injury_prevention.

Lefkowitz, B. (1997). *Our guys.* Berkeley: University of California Press.

Lerner, M. J. (1971). All the world loathes a loser. *Psychology Today 5:* 51–66.

Maclean's. (1997, March 31). Hanging for rape? *Maclean's 110*(13): 41.

Martineau, P. (2005, May 28). Bill would bolster response to sex assaults in military. *Sacramento Bee,* A1.

Maschke, K. (ed.) (1997). *The legal response to violence against women* (pp. vi–xi). New York: Garland Publishing.

McDonald, T., and Kline, L. (2004, March). Perceptions of appropriate punishment for committing date rape: Male college students recommend lenient punishments. In *College Student Journal 38*(1): 44–57.

McNair, L. D., and Neville, H. A. (1996). African American women survivors of sexual assault: The interaction of race and class. *Women and Therapy 18*(3/4): 107–118.

McPhail, B. (2002, April). Gender-bias hate crimes: A review. In *Trauma, Violence, & Abuse 3*(2): 125–143.

Meiselman, K. C. (1990). *Resolving the trauma of incest: Reintegration therapy with survivors.* San Francisco: Jossey-Bass.

Meyer, T. (1990, December 5). Date rape: A serious campus problem that few talk about. *Chronicle of Higher Education,* p. A15.

Neame, A. (2004, winter). Revisiting America's "date rape" controversy. *Family Matters 68:* 50–55.

NASW News. (1995, October). Teens and age differences. *NASW News:* 13.

National Victims Center (1992). *Rape in America: A report to the nation.* Arlington, Va.: author.

O'Carroll, A. (1997, August 21–23). Defense counsels' response to women who have been raped. Paper presented at the World Congress on Violence, Dublin, Ireland.

O'Malley, S. (1997, August). The new reason rapists are going free. *Redbook:* 16–80, 108.

O'Neill, A. M. (1996, September 2). *People:* 94–98.

Oppenheimer, J. (1998). Politicizing survivors of incest and sexual abuse: Another facet of healing. *Women and Therapy 21*(2): 79–87.

Parker, Tony. (1969). *The twisting lane: The hidden world of sex offenders.* New York: Harrow Books.

Patten, S. B., Gatz, Y. K., Jones, B., and Thomas, D. L. (1995). Posttraumatic stress disorder and the treatment of sexual abuse. In F. Turner (ed.), *Differential diagnosis and treatment in social work* (pp. 456–487). New York: Free Press.

Progressive. (1995). Refuge for women. *Progressive 59*(7): 9.

Ramsey, M. (1995, November). Remembering rape. *Harper's Bazaar:* 104–105.

Rand, M. R. (1997). Violence-related injuries treated in hospital emergency departments. Unpublished report.

Randall, M., and Haskell, L. (1995). Sexual violence in women's lives. *Violence against Women 1*(1): 6–31.

Reilly, M. E., Lott, B., Caldwell, D., and Deluca, L. (1992). Tolerance for sexual harassment related to self-reported sexual victimization. *Gender and Society 6:* 122–138.

Richter, N., Snider, E., and Gorey, K. M. (1997). Group work intervention with female survivors of childhood sexual abuse. *Research on Social Work Practice* 7(1), 53–69.

Robbins, S. P., Chatterjee, P., and Canda, E. R. (2006). *Contemporary human behavior theory: A critical perspective for social work.* Boston: Allyn & Bacon.

Roberts, A. R. (1995). Victim services and victim/witness assistance programs. In *Encyclopedia of Social Work* 19th ed. (pp. 2440–2444). Washington D.C.: NASW Press.

Robinson, L. (1997). "I was raped." *Emerge* 8(7): 42–53.

Roiphe, K. (1994). *The morning after: Sex, fear and feminism.* Boston; Little, Brown & Co.

Rollins, J. H. (1996). *Women's minds, women's bodies: The psychology of women in a biosocial context.* Upper Saddle River, N.J.: Prentice-Hall.

Rossetti, S. (1995). The impact of child sexual abuse on attitudes toward God and the Catholic Church. *Child Abuse and Neglect* 19: 1469–1481.

Rothbaum, B. O., Foa, E. B., Riggs, D. S., Murdock, T., and Walsh, W. (1992). A prospective examination of post-traumatic stress disorder in rape victims. *Journal of Traumatic Stress* 5: 455–475.

Ryan, W. (1971). *Blaming the victim.* New York: Random House.

Sanday, P. R. (1990). *Fraternity gang rape: Sex, brotherhood, and privilege on campus.* New York: New York University Press.

Sawyer, M. (2005, July 31). 50,000 rapes each year but only 600 rapists sent to jail. *The Observer.* Retrieved from http://observer.guardian.co.uk.

Schechter, S. (1982). *Women and male violence.* Boston: South End Press.

Schwartz, M. D. (1998, November 20). The culture of violence among males. Keynote address given at the Violence against Women Conference. Cedar Falls, Iowa.

Schwartz, M. D., and DeKeseredy, W. S. (1997). *Sexual assault on the college campus: The role of male peer support.* Thousand Oaks, Calif.: Sage.

Science News. (1991). Trauma disorder strikes many young adults. *Science News:* 139, 198.

Sebold, A. (2002). *Lucky.* Philadelphia: Bay Books.

Security on Campus (2002). Press release: Parents of student killed on campus, campus rape victim say Georgetown discipline insufficient to deter assaults. Retrieved from www.securityoncampus.org.

Shapiro, B. L., and Schwarz, J. C. (1997, June). Date rape: Its relationship to trauma symptoms and sexual self-esteem. *Journal of Interpersonal Violence* 12(3): 407–419.

Sigler, R., Johnson, I., and Morgan, E. (2003). Forced sexual intercourse: Contemporary views. In R. Muraskin (ed.), *It's a crime: Women and justice,* 3rd ed. (pp. 363–379). Upper Saddle River, N.J.: Prentice-Hall.

Sorenson, S. B., and Siegel, J. M. (1992). Gender, ethnicity, and sexual assault: Findings from a Los Angeles study. *Journal of Social Issues* 48: 93–104.

Steed, J. (1995). *Our little secret: Confronting child sexual abuse in Canada.* Toronto: Vintage Canada.

Storer, J. H. (1992). Gender and kin role transposition as an accommodation to father-daughter incest. In T. L. Whitehead and B. Y. Reid (eds.), *Gender constructs and social issues* (pp. 70–102). Urbana: University of Illinois Press.

Tjaden, P., and Thoennes, N. (2000). *Prevalence, incidence, and consequences of violence against women: Findings from the national violence against women survey.* Washington, D.C.: U.S. Department of Justice.

Troxler, H. (2005, April 19). Tough talk, tough laws, but no easy answers. *St. Petersburg Times,* 1B.

Tseuneyoshi, S. (1996). Rape trauma syndrome: Case illustration of Elizabeth. In F. H. McClure, E. Teyber et al. (eds.), *Child and adolescent therapy: A multicultural-relational approach* (pp. 287–320). Fort Worth, Tex.: Harcourt Brace.

U.S. Congress (2005, March 9). Press release: Rep. Maloney: "Include women in hate crime statistics." Retrieved www.house.gov/maloney/press/109th.

U.S. Department of Human and Health Services (DHHS) (2003). *Child maltreatment 2003.* Administration for Children and Families. Retrieved from www.acf.dhhs.gov.

U.S. Department of Justice (1997). Meeting the mental health needs of crime victims. Video produced by the Office for Victims of Crime. Washington, D.C.: U.S. Department of Justice.

Valentiner, D. P., Riggs, D. S., Foa, E. B., and Gershung, B. S. (1996). Coping strategies and posttraumatic stress disorder in female victims of sexual and nonsexual assault. *Journal of Abnormal Psychology 105*(3): 455–458.

van Wormer, K. (1997). *Social welfare: A world view.* Chicago: Nelson-Hall.

van Wormer, K., and Berns, L. (2004). The impact of priest sexual abuse: Female survivors' narratives. *Affilia 19*(1): 53–67.

van Wormer, K., Wells, J., and Boes, M. (2000). *Social work with lesbians, gays, and bisexuals: A strengths perspective.* Chicago: Nelson-Hall.

Walker, A. (1982). *The color purple.* New York: Harcourt Brace Jovanovich.

Walker, M., and Brodsky, S. (1976). *Sexual assault: The victim and the rapist.* Lexington, Mass.: Lexington Books.

Wallace, H. (1998). *Victimology: Legal, psychological, and social perspectives.* Boston: Allyn and Bacon.

Watson-Franke, M.-B. (2003). A world in which women move freely without fear of men: An anthropological perspective on rape. *Women's Studies International Forum 25*(6): 599–606.

Wetzel, J. (1993). *The world of women.* London: Macmillan.

Wing, A., and Merchan, S. (1993). Rape, ethnicity, and culture: Spirit injury from Bosnia to black America. *Columbia Human Rights Law Review 25*(1): 1–46.

Wyatt, G. E. (1997). *Stolen women: Reclaiming our sexuality, taking back our lives.* New York: John Wiley and Sons.

Yarbrough, F. (2005, August). Power, perception, and interracial sex: Former slaves recall a multiracial south. *Journal of Southern History 71*(3): 559–589.

Zastrow, C. (2003). *Introduction to social work and social welfare,* 8th ed. Belmont, Calif.: Brooks/Cole.

Zastrow, C., and Kirst-Ashman, K. (2004). *Understanding human behavior and the social environment,* 6th ed. Belmont, Calif.: Brooks/Cole.

9

Wife and Partner Abuse

With regard to violence, where is the single most dangerous place for women? The family home. What is the leading cause of death for women at work? Homicide by a spouse or partner. When is the battered woman most likely to get killed? When she leaves the relationship. Who overwhelmingly are the victims of murder-suicides? Women. Evidence for these and other generalizations concerning the intimate victimization of women is provided in this chapter.

This chapter concerns female partner abuse or battering. Such abuse occurs in a marriage or other close relationship and consists of intentional acts to cause injury. *Battering* is physical aggression with a purpose to control, intimidate, and subjugate another human being. It is always accompanied by emotional abuse and normally always causes fear in the battered woman (Jacobson and Gottman, 1998a). *Domestic abuse* is the term that came into common usage in the 1970s; this term is gender neutral and encompasses a wide range of abuse within families.

Stordeur and Stille (1989) state that "there is a continuum of violence against women in our society that includes sexist and degrading language, pornography, wife assault, child sexual assault, rape, sexual mutilation, resource deprivation, and murder" (p. 34). From this perspective, one that is consistent with the perspective found in this chapter, "wife assault is seen as one behavior on a continuum of behaviors that serve the purpose of maintaining the domination and power of a patriarchal society" (pp. 34–35).

Research on partner violence has continued to be provided by the U.S. Department of Justice in recent years and analyzed by scholars, and the mass media have continued to focus attention on this serious problem. In Iowa, for example, a spate of male-on-female murder-suicides has been featured in the regional news, and in Canada the media attention has focused on sexual abuse against women and controversial cutbacks in funding for women's shelters. Meanwhile, throughout North America, the death toll of women at the hands of their partners continues to mount, although at a slower pace than formerly (Rennison, Bureau of Justice Statistics [BJS], 2003).

Our emphasis in this second chapter on female victimization is on the kind of violence that takes place in intimate relationships. The issues of authority and control by men over women, both physically and emotionally, are explored first, with a historical overview and later by an examination of theories of partner abuse. To dispel the myths about partner violence, we consider statistical data from both national police reports and crime victimization surveys. Special attention is devoted to several areas often neglected in the literature: the substance abuse connection, marital rape, suicide-murder, and the relationship between battering and child abuse. In the final sections of these pages we consider the criminal justice response and successful treatment interventions for both the batterer and the battered. Throughout this discussion, variables of race, ethnicity, and class are considered.

See Box 9.1 to learn about an annual ritual performed by women who care.

B O X 9.1

The Tombstone Project

The stories of fifty-two women killed by domestic violence since 1990 are etched on tombstones in front of the lawn at Valley View Baptist Church, Cedar Falls, Iowa. It is a blustery night in late October 1996. Twenty to thirty of us, all women, are holding candles to commemorate those who did not survive partner violence. Each of us, in turn, reads the story of one victim, then places the lit candle before the wooden tombstone. In the eerie quiet, one woman reads:

> "Laura Garrison, 30, of Waterloo, died July 7, 1990. She was shot to death in front of her small children by a man she had dated. The man then shot himself and later died."
>
> She places the candle before the tombstone. Now it is my turn: I read: "Loretta Ellen Foster, 29, of Waterloo, died November 21, 1991. Foster was shot to death by the man she lived with and the father of her children in front of their 5-year-old daughter and 7-year-old son. He then killed himself."

After all fifty-two of the slain women are remembered in this fashion, we all stand in a circle and read in unison a closing poem composed by women's shelter advocates Sharon Spring, Mary Langholz, and Mary Roche:

> *Oh Connectedness of Life*
> *Of that we cannot see*
> *As air we breathe*
> *and wind we feel*
> *Embrace us in this moment*
> *As we stand here to*
> *Remember*
> *Honor*
> *And give name to all women*
> *Whose voices have been silenced.*
> *May we know they are us*
> *And we are them.*
> *In this month of remembering*
> *Affirm us as we*
> *Remember their names*
> *Remember our own*
> *And give voice to both.*

Critical thinking question: What are the functions of an annual ceremony such as this one for victims of domestic violence?

Source: Katherine van Wormer. Poem printed with permission of Mary Langholz, Sharon Spring, and Mary Roche.

Historical Overview

In the United States today men who beat their wives are going against cultural norms and the law. Historically a man's right to chastise his wife was affirmed in church doctrine as well as in early Roman law and English common law. Under English common law, which influenced law on this side of the Atlantic, to be a wife meant becoming the property of one's husband. There was some effort, however, to prevent excessive violence. Men could give their wives "moderate correction" under the doctrine of coverture, the legal doctrine that held that a married woman's identity was subsumed under her husband's (Blackstone, 1979). All through the years, even after physical punishment of one's wife was outlawed (in the late 1800s), domestic violence was considered a private matter, not one for intervention by the state (Presser and Gaarder 2004). One may recall testimony in the O. J. Simpson trial that when Nicole Simpson called the police for help, her husband persuaded the authorities that the problem was "a family matter" (see Ingrassia and Beck, 1994). So the legacy of the past is with us still.

Nevertheless, in the 1970s, when the women's liberation movement took hold, attention was drawn to rape as a crime of power, the very threat of which frightened all women and restricted their movements. Exposing victim-blaming not only produced new theoretical understandings but also laid the groundwork for pushing institutions to change the treatment of victims, especially in the criminal justice system (Smith, 2003). It laid the groundwork as well for collective political action and social support. The efforts of this movement culminated in the landmark **Violence against Women Act (VAWA)** of 1994, federal legislation providing for improved prevention and prosecution of violent crimes against women and children and for the care of victims (Kurz, 1998). The law also provided funding for prevention, shelter services, and legal advocacy. Unfortunately, however, as Kurz indicates, the new welfare "reform" legislation puts poor women who are trying to escape abuse at grave risk. Forcing them to seek child support from violent men puts them in jeopardy; the scarcity of affordable housing means that large numbers of them will end up homeless; restrictions on welfare recipients crossing state lines to receive benefits makes escape from the batterer more difficult. VAWA was reauthorized in 2000, adding important services for immigrant, rural, disabled, and older women (Family Violence Prevention Fund, 2005). In 2006, VAWA was reauthorized and priorities were set for the future.

Nature and Scope of the Problem

Women often experience their greatest risk of violence from their intimate male partners and spouses. Although one of the most underestimated and underreported crimes in the United States and the single most significant cause of injury to women, intimate partner violence has received increased national attention in recent years. Research informs us that about one woman in four will be physically assaulted by a partner or ex-partner in her lifetime (National Institute of Justice

[NIJ] [2004]). Another study suggests that "as many as 37 percent of obstetrics patients are physically abused during pregnancy" (Council on Scientific Affairs, 1992). The Bureau of Justice Statistics special reports *Intimate Partner Violence, 1993–2001* (Rennison, 2003) and *Full Report of the Prevalence, Incidence, and Consequences of Violence Against Women* (Tjaden and Thoennes, 2000) provide the most comprehensive data on reported victimization. From *Intimate Partner Violence*, we learn that:

- Between 1976 and 2000, the number of women murdered by intimates (spouses, partners, or dates) fell 22 percent, from 1,600 to 1,247;
- The number of men murdered by intimates during that period dropped 68 percent, from 1,357 to 440.

These figures are startling in their implications. What they seem to indicate is that the effect of recent efforts to curb domestic violence—the police protection, battered women's advocates, greater hospital sensitivity, and women's shelters—seems to be succeeding more in saving the lives of men than of women. Later in the chapter, we will look at this phenomenon more closely.

From Tjaden and Thoennes's *Full Report*, we learn that:

- Women experience more **intimate partner violence** than do men: 22.1 percent of surveyed women, compared with 7.4 percent of surveyed men, reported they were physically assaulted by a current or former spouse, cohabiting partner, boyfriend, girlfriend, or date in their lifetime; 1.3 percent of surveyed women and 0.9 percent of surveyed men reported experiencing such violence in the previous twelve months. Approximately 1.3 million women and 835,000 men are physically assaulted by an intimate partner annually in the United States;
- Women are significantly more likely than men to be injured during an assault: 31.5 percent of female rape victims, compared with 16.1 percent of male rape victims, reported being injured during their most recent rape; 39.0 percent of female physical assault victims, compared with 24.8 percent of male physical assault victims, reported being injured during their most recent physical assault;
- Stalking is more prevalent than previously thought: 8.1 percent of surveyed women and 2.2 percent of surveyed men reported being stalked at some time in their life;
- Most injuries to women were inflicted in the home; in almost half of the cases the perpetrator and victim had used drugs or alcohol.

From further governmental sources we learn that:

- A woman's attempt to leave a relationship was the precipitating factor in 45 percent of the murders of a woman by a man (Block, 2003);

- Sexual assault or forced sex occurs in approximately 40–45 percent of battering relationships (Campbell et al., 2003).

In one of the largest studies of its kind, a survey of 3,455 women interviewed at rural and urban emergency rooms in California and Pennsylvania found that nearly 14 percent of the women reported sexual and physical abuse at the hands of an intimate partner (Dearwater et al., 1998). Only 2.2 percent of the patients, however, over the preceding year were treated at that time for acute trauma for the abuse. Women who had ended a relationship within the previous year were seven times more likely to report abuse than women who had not. Reports of domestic abuse were more frequent in California than in Pennsylvania; those most at risk were young women with children who had extremely low incomes.

Survey data provided by Straus and Gelles (1986) and widely reported in the mass media indicated that women reported hitting men even slightly more often than men reported they hit women. The instrument used, the Conflict Tactics Scale, as Miller and White (2003) indicate, is problematic because its exclusive focus is on acts performed rather than context and meaning. Data from the National Victimization Survey reveal that women make up 85 percent of all intimate assault victims (Rennison, 2003).

Lesbian and Gay Couples

Women living with female partners experience less partner violence than do women living with male partners. Slightly more than 11 percent of the women who had lived with a woman as part of a couple reported being raped, physically assaulted, and/or stalked by a female cohabitant, but 21.7 percent of the women who had married or lived with a man as part of a couple reported such violence by a husband or male cohabitant (Tjaden and Thoennes, 2000). These findings suggest that lesbian couples experience less intimate partner violence than do heterosexual couples; however, more research is needed to support or refute this conclusion.

Men living with male partners experience more partner violence than do men who live with female partners. Approximately 23 percent of the men who had lived with a man as a couple reported being raped, physically assaulted, and/or stalked by a male cohabitant, while 7.4 percent of the men who had married or lived with a woman as a couple reported such violence by a wife or female cohabitant (Tjaden and Thoennes, 2000). These findings provide further evidence that intimate partner violence is perpetrated primarily by men, whether against male or female intimates.

This same-sex violence is linked to violence in the family of origin, homophobia in the society, and alcohol abuse (West, 1998a). Lesbian batterers tend, like their heterosexual counterparts, to be overly emotionally dependent on their partners (Rollins, 1996).

Rates of Violence among Ethnic Minorities

Women living in cultures that value community over individuality, as well as those that hold women responsible for holding the community together, face enormous barriers when it comes to reporting abuse. This reluctance to bring shame on the community is strongest among Asian Americans. African American and American Indian women also may want to protect their men from law enforcement contact due to a history of discrimination. For these defensive reasons, comprehensive data on ethnic and racial minorities are hard to come by.

Rates of partner violence are higher among African Americans than for their white counterparts (Tjaden and Thoennes, 2000). These data, based on the **National Violence Against Women (NVAW)** survey, also reveal that Asian/Pacific Islander women and men tend to report lower rates of intimate partner violence than do women and men from minority backgrounds, while Indian/Alaska Native women and men report higher rates than all other groups. However, differences among minority groups diminish when other sociodemographic and relationship variables are controlled. Dugan and Apel (2003) enlighten us on the details of incidents of violence in their statistical analysis of the NVAW data. Their analysis reveals that risk factors for all forms of violence against women include moving frequently, living in an urban setting, going out at night, living in a low-income household, having a job, and having little education. Marriage is a protective factor. Significantly, Asian women are at high risk for victimization outside the home and by multiple attackers. They are least likely to report victimization to the police; African American women are most likely to contact the police. This group is also most likely to be victimized by a boyfriend at home and with a weapon. Native American women are most likely to be victimized by someone they know and by a person using drugs or alcohol.

In their in-depth interviews with African American adolescents, Miller and White found that girls' violence was interpreted as out-of-control behavior, but not seen as physically threatening, while boys' violence was seen as dangerous. A further flaw in these survey data is that they fail to report the level of injury incurred.

Concerning Latino/Latina Americans, West (1998b) notes that when face-to-face bilingual interviews are conducted, a more complete picture of the violence among ethnic groups can be discovered. Kaufman-Kantor, Jasinski, and Aldarondo (1994), for example, found that Puerto Rican husbands are approximately two times more likely than Anglo husbands to beat their wives. Cuban Americans were found to have a low rate of wife abuse, only 2.5 percent.

Studies of Mexican-born immigrants indicate that they have significantly lower rates of partner violence than either Anglos or U.S.-born Mexican Americans (Sorenson and Telles, 1991). A strong possibility exists, however, that immigrant women fear reporting incidents of violence because they are insecure. Many South Asian Indian women in America are facing the terror of being trapped in abusive relationships as well, staying with their spouse to protect their immigration status and avoid deportation (Schakowsky, 2005). Data from a household survey in Mexico City show that 38 percent of women had experienced some form of marital violence

(Natera, Tiburcio, and Villatoro, 1997). Partners' drinking and jealousy were found to be significantly associated with violent acts and threats.

A rare study of Chinese battered women in North America conducted by Lee and Au (1998) indicates the tremendous pressures foreign-born battered women experience in trying to break through the abusive cycle within their cultural milieu. Because the family name has to be protected at all costs and because individual well-being should be subordinated to the common good, Chinese women do not admit to the occurrence of abuse. In a survey of directors of women's shelters in cities in the United States and Canada with large Chinese populations, Lee and Au discovered that women of Chinese origin endured much abuse in silence, that they perceived marriage as a license for the man to have sex with his wife whenever or however he desired, and that they did not consider divorce an option to escape physical abuse. Unique to the Chinese culture, gambling, rather than alcohol or drugs, was associated with violence. A second culturally specific aspect of Chinese North American wife abuse is the conjoint physical and emotional abuse by the husband's parents along with the husband.

West (1998b) summarized partner violence research on American Indian groups by indicating that all the studies cited show a very high rate of battering in American Indian couples. He also indicated that the relatively small nonrandom sample sizes make it difficult to reach definitive conclusions. Given that Native Americans have the highest alcoholism rate of all ethnic groups, a high rate of family violence would not be unexpected.

International Research

Following the Beijing Women's Conference in 1995, Japan is one of the nations that has demanded accountability in response to antifemale violence. Despite a slow start due to its legacy of traditionalism, increasing public awareness today is being devoted to violence against women in general and to that by male intimate partners. In her review of research on domestic violence in Japan, Yoshihama (1998) concludes that although some services are available, a high degree of tolerance for domestic violence against women still exists. Japanese college students surveyed, for example, tend to minimize such violence. Similarly, in other research surveys, many believed that the wife abuse was a private matter and that the wife likely had provoked the abuse.

An earlier nationwide survey of domestic violence in Japan in 1992, in which Yoshihama participated, revealed a shockingly high rate of male-on-female violence. In dating, marriage, and separation, 77 percent of the 796 women surveyed revealed that they had experienced some type of violence from their partners. It is not uncommon in Japan, according to this writer, for the man to demand, through threats of violence, that the woman quit her job. Unlike in the United States, where domestic violence is recognized as a serious public health problem, the awareness among health care workers in Japan is extremely low. There is a need, as Yoshihama argues, for reform in the criminal justice system and in civil and family law as well. More recent data confirm the pattern. A nationwide government survey showed that in 2000, 27.5 percent of Japanese wives said they had been beaten by their husbands and 4.6 percent of women in another study said spousal abuse had put them in a life-threatening situation (Kambayashi, 2004). Most perpetrators were habitual drinkers. Comparable U.S. rates are estimated to be between 1 and 3 percent. In 2001, because of the work of grassroots efforts, publicly funded shelters were mandated by Japanese law.

In Britain, as elsewhere, a woman is more vulnerable to violence in her home than in public. Diane Dwyer (1995), in a comparative study of the United States and Britain, highlights the prevalence of domestic assault and the role of the British criminal justice system in processing domestic violence cases. Despite a much lower overall level of violence in British society and despite a much stronger feminist movement, Dwyer found that the prevalence of domestic violence was similar to that in the United States, that the British criminal justice response had been relatively less progressive, and that victims' assistance units were absent from prosecutorial services. Based on her cross-cultural study, Dwyer concludes that woman abuse is gender-based rather than just a reflection of violence in the wider culture.

Statistics Canada (2005) provides a thorough portrait of violence against women in the report, "Family Violence in Canada." Lauritsen and White (2001) bring our attention to the role of socioeconomic disadvantage in increasing the risk for non-lethal violence. Using the NVAW data, these researchers found that controlling for socioeconomic status, the differences between black and white women would no longer be significant and that the rate for Latinos would be somewhat less if all lived in similar communities.

Miller and White (2003), drawing from personal narratives with African American teens, provide a personal dimension to attitudes toward violence that goes beyond the statistical data. Youths described strong norms against male violence, making it likely that many men would be reticent to admit such activity. A number of young men said they were taught by their mothers not to hit girls. But both males and females justified a violent response when a young woman initiated violence or if the young woman seemed to have "forgotten her place." As one young woman explained, "If you be big enough to hit a man, you big enough to take that lick back" and a young man said, "Certain times I feel that if a girl is man enough to hit you she man enough to get hit back" (p. 1237). Male youths also defined females as deserving violence when they "runnin' they mouth" (p. 1239). Young females' violence was typically minor, but seen as posing a threat to the young men. For young women, jealousy and anger over infidelities were key factors.

Based on a national telephone survey, Statistics Canada (2005) found that the rate of partner physical assault over the past five years has remained unchanged from previous reports of 7 percent of women and 6 percent of men. In their lifetimes, 21 percent of females and 16 percent of males had experienced partner violence. Female victims were more than twice as likely as male victims to be injured, also twice as likely to be stalked by a previous partner. Of aboriginal people, 24 percent of the women and 18 percent of the men said they had suffered violence from a current or previous partner. Similar to studies in Mexico, the strongest predictors of wife assault are the young age of the couple, chronic unemployment by male partners, women and men who witnessed parental abuse as children, and the presence of emotional abuse in the relationship. Just over half the violent partners usually drank at the time of the assaults.

Sparked by a series of articles on domestic violence in the *Toronto Star,* an inquest was held to examine the widespread problem. The inquest was held after the death of a woman in a murder-suicide case. Testimony by experts at the inquest revealed that the murderer's behavior was typical—stalking his previous wives and using his children as pawns, a breakup with his present wife followed by a series of death threats. Many Canadian women are safer on the streets than in their own homes, a clinical psychologist told the inquest (Darroch, 1998).

Another Canadian newspaper report (Loomis, 1998) revealed problems for women within Canadian ethnic groups. In the East Indian community, an incident of a woman who was thrown off a balcony by her husband spurred plans for a new women's shelter in the neighborhood. Many of the abused women in this community were part of arranged marriages and cut all family ties when they left India, according to the article. In India if a man hurts a woman, the community will go after the man. But in Canada, such abuse of immigrant women who are culturally isolated and unable to speak the language of the country often goes undetected. Abusive men in all immigrant groups, in fact, can isolate their women by keeping them from learning the language of the adopted country. To enhance services to the East Indian women, several volunteers at the new shelter will speak Punjabi.

Statistics Canada (1998, 2005) reveals that in recent years the rate of male spouses killed by their wives had declined, but the number of women killed by their husbands had stayed about the same. Comparable data from the United States shows a similar trend. One could speculate that the growth in women's shelters is saving *men's* lives more than women's lives by providing a way out for battered women besides murder. The fact that women's professional opportunities and economic independence have increased may give women more confidence to escape domestic violence as well.

To summarize, we can say of ethnic/cultural variations in domestic abuse that essentially, the universal, underlying dynamic in battering is male control and dominance, but that violence also is correlated with stress factors in the environment. Thus, the manifestation of violence in a relationship is influenced by cultural and contextual factors.

Dynamics of Intimate Abuse

Since physical abuse of a woman or a man in a gay battering situation is about power and control, it is accompanied emotionally by psychological abuse. Psychological or emotional abuse, in other words, is the context within which the slaps, hits, kicks, and so forth occur. Emotional abuse can include verbal assaults, ridicule, isolation from family and friends, unwarranted accusations about infidelity, control of finances, damage to property, stealing, torture or killing of pets, and threats to harm children and others. The effect of these acts is to attack the person's sense of self-worth. A kind of brainwashing occurs as the victim internalizes the insinuations and accusations of his or her attacker, gradually coming to believe them. Psychological abuse among lesbians may include the threat of "outing" a partner to her boss or family.

In any country, when psychological abuse moves on to physical abuse, the added element is terror. Women who are beaten know that they are at high risk of being killed if they try to leave. As the director of crime-victim assistance of the Iowa attorney general's office, Marti Anderson suggests that victims of such domestic terror live in perpetual fear of the next attack, of losing their children and their home, of being stalked, of losing their lives. "And yet people ask," she writes, "Why doesn't she leave?" (Anderson, 1997, p. 4AA). Protection orders, safety plans, and divorces do not stop an attack, a bullet, or a knife. These attempts at self-protection, in fact, often precipitate an attack by paranoid individuals with a history of out-of-control violence.

Instead of asking the question so resented by battered women, "Why don't you leave?" we will consider the practical and psychological barriers to escape. This approach is consistent with the empowerment/strengths-based perspective. Angela Browne (1995) summarizes the barriers in terms of practical realities, fear of retaliation, and the shock reactions of victims to constant danger. The practical barriers include such issues as finding a place to live, fear of losing one's children, and difficulty in receiving public assistance while married. The woman who works cannot hide, nor can she protect her children who are in school and day care from being taken for ransom. The woman who does not work has no means of support. Moving into a shelter is only for a brief period of time. If the woman gets a legal separation, her spouse will have visitation rights with the children.

Fear of reprisal is made more compelling by death threats. Browne compared forty-two battered women who killed their abusers with 205 women who did not kill their abusers. In the homicide group, many of the women stayed out of terror of further victimization or because they had tried to escape and were beaten for it. Expecting to get killed, they saw no way out of the danger. In fact, violent men do search out the women after they leave. And as their husbands, they know all the hiding places.

Research on victims of trauma helps explain how women cope in the height of danger by denying the threat, by being extremely suggestible, or by withdrawing emotionally so that they can survive. Chronic fatigue and tension coupled with sleep disturbances keep the victim in a state of confusion. Typically, little anger is shown toward the victimizers who are seen as all-powerful and even admired. Browne's theories are reminiscent of social psychological studies of brainwashed prisoners of war who, over time, submit to their captors and even come to admire them. Referred to as the **Stockholm syndrome,** this phenomenon is named for an incident in Stockholm, Sweden, where four bank employees were held hostage in the bank's vault for four days. Following the ordeal, the women's expressions of gratitude toward the offenders was disturbing to many people (Wallace, 1998).

Dutton and Painter (1993) developed the **traumatic bonding theory** to explain why battered women stay in abusive relationships. Power imbalance in combination with intermittent good–bad treatment was predicted to increase the emotional attachment in an abusive situation, a prediction based on classical social psychological theory (see, for example, Bettelheim, 1943, and Zimbardo, Haney, and Banks, 1972). (Note that we are not talking about gender here. The Bettelheim and Zimbardo et al. studies concerned mostly men.) Dutton and Painter tested this theory empirically with in-depth assessments conducted on seventy-five women who had recently left abusive situations; emotional involvement was strong. Follow-up measures six months later revealed some decrease in the level of attachment but showed that prolonged effects of the abuse were still evident.

An understanding of the dynamics of social psychology is crucial if we are to make sense of situations and reactions that may seem irrational on the surface, especially for victim service counselors who have not experienced such long-term abuse firsthand. Much criminal behavior by accomplices who are forced into it by their abusers, moreover, can be understood in the context of traumatic bonding. The story of Patty Hearst, kidnap victim, a woman locked in a closet and periodically raped over a period of many long months, is well known. Hearst inevitably fell in love with one of her captors and joined their gang—the Symbionese Liberation Front—to commit robberies (Castiglia, 1996). Unfortunately, at her trial the jury was not informed of the phenomenon of psychological traumatizing that can occur in such cases, and Hearst was sentenced to a lengthy prison term for her crimes. The story of teenager Elizabeth Smart, also beaten, raped, and held captive for months, is similar. When the police came to rescue her, she gave a false name. It was later revealed that she had conformed to the lifestyle of her captors (Browning, 2003). There are many women in prison today whose abuse impaired their judgment in a similar vein.

Ulrich (1998) perceives leaving as a process that may involve many attempts to be successful. Stages in the process of breaking loose involve changes in one's level of self-awareness combined with a reevaluation of the relationship as dangerous. During this gradual process of awareness survivors build up their courage to retreat from the danger. In her study of women who have managed to leave, Ulrich found that women with adequate self-esteem to make the break attributed social support as helping them start a new life.

The concept of the **battered woman syndrome** was introduced by Walker (1979). As Rothenberg (2003) correctly indicates, this term, like codependency, is one we might want to avoid in that it puts the stress on women's helplessness rather than on agency and resilience. The model of an active survivor has been embraced by feminists in its emphasis on competent decision making and safety seeking behavior.

Marital Rape

The laws regarding marital rape offer a clear picture of how society has viewed this phenomenon. Historically, following British law, it was decreed that husbands were exempt from any rape laws (Jerin and Moriarty, 1998). After all, the marriage contract stipulated that a wife must submit willingly to her husband. Accordingly, she could not legally refuse him. In the United States, it was not until 1977 that Oregon became the first state to repeal the marital rape exemption. The controversy that arose in Oregon over its first marital rape case prompted a great deal of mass media coverage and public ridicule of the young woman who had the audacity to charge her husband with this crime. Yet by 1990, forty-eight states had marital rape laws. Today, this is a crime in all states, although some states exempt husbands when no force is used (Jerin and Moriarty, 1998). Still about half the states treat spousal rape differently from other types of rape. Arizona recently considered revising its laws in response to a public outcry over the lenient treatment of spousal rapists (*USA Today*, 2005).

In 1983 a Canadian law recognized that any sexual contact without consent within a marriage is sexual assault. But in most other countries, such as Mexico which recently declared rape in marriage legal, wife rape is viewed as an oxymoron.

Because marital rape is rarely differentiated from rape in general in victimization surveys and because victim/survivors of this kind of rape are reluctant to acknowledge its existence even to themselves, the prevalence of marital rape is hard to determine. In the Bureau of Justice Statistics survey (Tjaden and Thoennes, 2000), the term "intimate partner rape" was used. It was found that 7.7 percent of women surveyed and 0.3 percent of men surveyed had experienced this form of abuse. Approximately one-third to one-half of women who are physically abused by their partners are raped by them (Bergen, 1998; Pagelow, 1992).

Statistics Canada (2005) reports that 8 percent of ever-married women in their 1993 national telephone survey were forced into sexual activity against their will. The National Survey of Wives in Great Britain used a quota sample from ten regions in that country (Painter and Farrington, 1998). Interview results showed that 28 percent of wives had been hit by their husbands. Working-class wives and separated or divorced wives were particularly likely to have been assaulted and also raped. Disproportionately high numbers of raped wives were also raped outside the marriage. Marital rape was more common in Scotland than elsewhere.

Whereas a woman raped by a stranger has to live with the bad memory, a women raped by her husband has to live with the rapist. Bergen (1998) conducted in-depth interviews with a sample of forty survivors of wife rape who had contacted a rape crisis center or women's shelter for help. Based on her findings she divided the causes of wife rape into four categories: entitlement to sex attitudes, sexual jealousy, rape as punishment, and rape as a form of control. The majority of rapes were battering rapes in which the woman was beaten and then raped. Nine of the men performed sadistic rapes on the women, often in connection with porno films. Unlike stranger-rape experiences, marital rape occurs frequently to women who are attacked in this way by their husbands. Like battered women, marital rape victims develop strategies of resistance—going to bed late, spending the night out, getting the husband too drunk for sex, physically resisting, and saving enough money to leave. Above all, when rape seemed inevitable, the women tried to manage the violence by giving in to avoid serious injury. Emotionally, many of the women "tuned out" during the rape. Afterward they would bathe and act as if nothing had happened. Yet only one-third of the women in Bergen's sample defined their experience as rape. Emotionally, the word *disgust* came up over and over in the interviews. In the end, all but three of the women were traumatized; over half considered or attempted suicide. Sexual dysfunction and distrust of other men were among the long-term consequences. Although we can't generalize from these findings because the sample was drawn from women who sought help, the interviews do show the seriousness of the crime of marital rape. The numbers of women who go to the police under these circumstances and have their husbands criminally charged is minuscule (Rollins, 1996). The risk of being killed in such situations is real.

Murder-Suicide

Statistically, **murder-suicide** is a rare form of suicide but a more common accompaniment of homicide, according to Marzuk, Tardiff, and Hirsch (1992). In spousal homicide, estimates are that one-third of these homicides in the United States and Canada end in suicide (Easteal, 1994). In Iowa a spate of murder-suicides has occurred over the past few years (Clayworth and Erb, 1998). The significance of this wave of spousal murder-suicide (representing almost one-quarter of the total homicide rate for the year) is that in every case the man did the killing and that the killings seemed to have emerged in conjunction with marital breakup.

From Statistics Canada (2005) we learn that over the past forty years, one in ten solved homicides were cases in which the suspect took his or her own life following the homicide. About three-quarters of these victims were killed by a family member. Virtually all of the incidents (97 percent) involved female victims killed by a male spouse.

In the first epidemiological study of homicide-suicides in England and Wales, Barraclough and Harris (2002) studied death certificates for all murders-suicide over a four-year time span. They found that 3 percent of male, 11 percent of female, and 19 percent of child homicides were of this type. Similarly, of all suicides, 0.8 percent male and 0.4 percent female deaths occurred in homicide-suicide incidents. The typical cases involved families of low socioeconomic status.

Palermo (1994) analyzes the psyche of the jealous, paranoid perpetrator who kills both his partner and himself. The twin nature of murder and suicide are recognized in Palermo's concept, *extended suicide*. Palermo argues that it is plausible to assume that the individual who is dangerously violent and also prone to depression will kill his partner and himself when the relationship goes sour. See Box 9.2 for a closer look at this phenomenon.

BOX **9.2**

Murder-**Suicide** or *Suicide*-**Murder?**
A Psychological Study

By Katherine van Wormer

Anyone who reads or watches local or national news reports is aware that a spate of murder-suicides is taking place. In recent months, in the national news, we have learned of at least one school shooting, numerous teen-family killings, and far more adult partner murders—all ending in suicide or attempted suicide. But most such cases are not reported nationally; they appear in headlines in the local paper.

According to the Violence Policy Center (VPC) (2006), at least 591 people died in murder-suicides in the United States during the six-month period of the study. That averages out to about two per day. Three-fourths of the murder-suicides involved "intimate partner" situations; of these, 94 percent involved male attacks on women.

To determine the recent frequency of reports for the present day, I went to www.google.com, typed in murder suicide and pressed search, then went to news in the row above which gives recent news stories for that item. Indeed, the frequency is high; there are at least two or more reports of these double or triple murders, and we have to keep in mind that all newspaper headlines are not recorded on Google. So we can conclude that even two of these events per day is an underestimate. My search as of June 10, 2005, yielded the following incidents for that week:

Ansonia, CT: A twenty-seven-year-old man strangled his wife, then jumped off the roof to his death. The two were Albanian; theirs was an arranged marriage, one reportedly fraught with difficulty.
Milwaukie, OR: A couple in their 80s who had often been seen strolling arm-in-arm were found dead of gunshot wounds, a case of suspected murder-suicide.

Union, SC: Problems with money and child custody seemed to be precipitating factors in this murder-suicide committed by a husband in his 20s.
Waco, TX: When the wife broke off the relationship and was found with her boyfriend, the husband killed her and her boyfriend. The man's first cousin had killed his wife in an act of murder-suicide fifteen years earlier, under similar circumstances.
New Providence, NJ: An elderly couple was found dead in what authorities called a murder-suicide. The husband's note seemed to confirm this.
Lakewood, WA: A couple in their 20s was found shot to death in an apparent homicide and suicide. Police said the man had broken into his ex-girlfriend's home with a hammer. There was a history of stalking.
Landenberg, PA: A man who shot and killed his wife and two sons before killing himself was said to be suffering from depression.

All of these cases took place in the space of several days. And they are only a sample. As can be seen from these illustrations, this type of suicide is hardly a solitary act. During the six-month period of the VPC study, more people died from murder associated with suicide—369—than from suicide itself—293. Children in the family are orphaned, and others are left in a state of despair.

As reported by the VPC (www.vpc.org), the pattern of the murder-suicide is predictable: a male perpetrator, female victim, decision by the woman to leave the man, and a gun. The typical Florida pattern (Florida had the

(continued)

BOX **9.2** Continued

largest number at 35 of the 2002 total) involved an elderly male caregiver overwhelmed by his inability to care for an infirm wife.

I want to make the case that these killings, in whichever age group, are suicide-driven; hence I refer to them as **suicide-murders**. There are three basic types of suicide-murders. The first is the elderly couple situation; the elderly man is old and feeble and does not want to go to a nursing home. Suffering from depression, he chooses suicide instead and takes his wife with him. Their relationship was typically a healthy, close one. Their children have moved away.

The mass school shooting is a highly publicized but rare event. The usual scenario is this: the boy was teased and bullied at school. He hates himself and is seething with anger. Influenced by media accounts of mass killings about which he obsesses, he gets a gun and goes on a rampage before killing himself.

The third and most common variety of suicide-murder is the case of intimate partner violence. From the dozens of cases I have read about from news reports, a consistent pattern emerges. The intimate couple is usually in the twenty- to thirty-five-years-old age range. The man is abusive, psychologically and/or physically. Obsessed with the woman to the extent he feels he can't live without her, he is fiercely jealous and determined to isolate her. Characteristically, suicidal murderers have little regard for the lives of other people; they would be considered, in mental health jargon, to be antisocial. So dependent are these men on their wives or girlfriends that they would sooner be dead than live without them. But for them, suicide is hard—they can't get the nerve—so they have to find a way to force themselves to do it.

Some choose suicide-by-cop, hoping to get the police officer to end their misery. Some even, in death penalty states, kill some strangers for the sole reason of qualifying for the death penalty (I have recorded twenty such cases elsewhere—see www.katherinevanwormer.com).

In the intimate-partner situation, the girlfriend/wife makes a move to leave. Her partner is absolutely distraught in the belief that he can't live without her. These types of men, when rejected, often have a history of stalking. He either decides to kill himself and take her with him or, in another possible scenario, can't get the nerve to kill himself but realizes that if he commits a homicide first, the suicide will then be the only way out. The pattern here is the notion that after you've killed another, it's easier to get the nerve to kill yourself. In any case, the urge to commit suicide is primary.

A key factor in suicide-murders across the states is the power of suggestion and contagion. When one high-profile case is in the headlines, there is another, and another, and another. Consider the fact that in the two years following the Columbine High massacre there were nineteen incidents of school violence (half of them foiled), that were clearly imitative. So it is with intimate partner suicide-murders. A second key factor is, of course, access to a gun.

Let me differentiate this pattern of suicide from that of the suicide bombers such as Arab terrorists. These terrorist situations are truly *murder*-suicides because the impetus to kill and destroy takes precedence over suicide; suicide is simply the escape or necessity to get the job done or desire for martyrdom. In testimony given before the Senate Armed Services Committee Professor of Psychiatry, Jerrod Post presented the results of his thirty-five interviews with incarcerated terrorists in Israeli prisons (reported on CNNFN, October 1, 2001, "The Mind of a Suicide Bomber"). These individuals were failed suicide bombers whose suicide missions had failed because of unforeseen circumstances. In their interviews, they consistently spoke of the need to defend "the land of their honor," their willingness to become martyrs to a sacrificial act, and the fact that these were not acts of suicide but actions performed in service to Allah.

Are such men weak emotionally; are they sick? "No," declares Post. "Such men are

(continued)

BOX **9.2** Continued

fortified by religion. As a result of ruthless indoctrination, these men have subordinated their own individuality to the group. Emotionally disturbed individuals are expelled from these quasi-military units as a security risk." Unlike solitary terrorists in the United States, the members of these terrorist cells tend to have close relationships with their families who support them in their efforts to kill the Zionist or American enemy.

Post's research on the suicide bombers could be replicated through interviews with

American men convicted of murder whose suicide attempts had failed. Then our analysis of their motivation would be more complete, especially regarding the role of contagion.

Critical Thinking Questions: How is suicide-murder different from murder-suicide, according to van Wormer? What are the psychological factors involved in cases of intimate partner murders that end in suicide of the murderer? Check news sources in your state and analyze situations of this sort.

Women Who Kill Their Husbands/Partners

As we have seen, in about three-fourths of intimate murders in 2000, the woman was the victim (Rennison, 2003). This still leaves a substantial number of cases, approximately 440, in which the woman killed her spouse or boyfriend. Since 1976, the number of male spouses and other intimates killed was cut by around two-thirds while the decline in the number of female victims was cut only by about one-fourth. Pollock (1998) has speculated that the increase in the availability of shelters for battered women has helped to reduce the numbers of women who kill their abusers by removing them from an extremely volatile situation.

Wells and DeLeon-Granados (2004) explain the striking decline in male homicides by their wives/partners in terms of "exposure reduction theory" (p. 233). **Exposure reduction theory** is the notion that the availability of mechanisms that allow a woman to sever ties with an abusive partner will spare her from seeking a violent solution. This theory is based on the body of evidence supporting the view that when women resort to using lethal partner violence, it is most likely a protective mechanism. On the other hand, when the woman does escape, the man may seek revenge, a fact that puts her life at risk following the suicide. About three-quarters of these victims were killed by a family member. Virtually all of the incidents (97 percent) involved female victims killed by a male spouse.

Firearms were the most commonly used weapon in Australia as in the United States (Carcach and Grabosky, 1998). Evidence suggests, according to Carcach and Grabosky, that nations with a high homicide rate have a low proportion of homicides followed by suicide. This relationship is borne out in the states and territories of Australia. As in other countries, in Australia most of these crimes took place in the context of disputes over the termination of a relationship. White males, as in other studies, were the most likely offenders. Carcach and Grabosky recommend tighter gun control as a key prevention measure. The American Violence Policy Center (2002), which has made the most comprehensive study of the issue (see Box 9.2) is a strong advocate of gun control as well. According to their estimates, around 95 percent of murder-suicides are committed with firearms.

An added consideration is that since most females arrested for murder are involved in substance abuse in some way, we can further speculate that removal from the drug scene in the home into the more sober shelter atmosphere gives women the chance to think more clearly about the consequences of their actions and prevents them from taking the law into their own hands.

In a comparison study, which builds on an earlier study by Browne (1995) described previously, Roberts (1996) analyzed data drawn in a sample of 105 women in prison convicted of killing their husbands with a community sample of 105 battered women. Compared to the battered women who did not kill their partners, the prison sample was far more likely to have received death threats from their partners that were specific as to time and place and method. The majority of the convicts were more likely than the community representatives to have dropped out of high school, had a history of sexual abuse and a poor work history, cohabitated with her partner, had a substance abuse problem, attempted suicide, and had access to the batterer's guns. Noteworthy in these findings was the murderer's desperation to escape, first through chemical abuse, then through suicide, and finally through a direct attack on the source of the problem.

An article in the *Des Moines Register* (Roos, 1997) tells the story of Katherine Sallis, an African American battered woman who, while drunk in a bar, contracted to have her husband killed. Today, on parole, she counsels women at a domestic violence shelter. Often she hears the women say, "I want to kill my husband." Sallis knows there are far better options at hand. "I'm helping the community by keeping many women from experiencing the same thing that I went through, by showing them the legal way. There are other ways to express these differences with their spouses" (Roos, 1997, p. 1).

Because battering men are, in all probability, active substance abusers who are not getting the help they need (whether in prison or in the community), their homicide rates against their partners have not declined. The paradox could be expressed in the following imaginary promotion ad: "Save men's lives; increase funding for women's shelters."

Despite occasional well-publicized cases of battered women who kill and are acquitted of murder or manslaughter, the law often shows greater leniency toward men who kill their wives than toward women who kill their husbands (Bannister, 1993; Leonard, 2003). The difference seems to be explained by the fact that battered women who have killed will cooperate with the police, making no attempt to cover up their crime. Men who kill their wives, on the other hand, can often afford a lawyer, and since they did not confess, they are in a position to enter a plea of guilty to a lesser charge. The plea of self-defense for a battered woman is often not believed, since she may kill her spouse while he is asleep or drunk or otherwise vulnerable. A woman who kills during a fight will be convicted because the man being more physically powerful is less likely to use a weapon. It is hard for the jury in such cases, as Bannister indicates, to appreciate the danger the woman may have been in. The court system fails women, Bannister concludes, because it is based on a male model of how to determine fact such as self-defense.

In a politicized battered woman's murder trial, expert witnesses often rely on a battered woman syndrome self-defense argument. According to this argument—derived from Lenore Walker's (1979) theory of "learned helplessness"—repeatedly beaten women lose their faith in themselves and their judgment becomes impaired. They perceive use of force as their only means of escape. Donald Downs (1997) opposes this line of argument in that its success depends on portraying women as passive victims. Rothenberg (2003) concurs. (Such a defense additionally may be used against battered mothers fighting for custody of their children; such women are often seen as incapable of protecting their children in their helplessness.) Downs's recommendation regarding homicide cases is that the law be changed to help women argue realistically that danger need not be immediate to be present, that a woman beaten in her home has no duty to retreat when this is her home, and that what is seen as extreme force used by the victim may be proportionate to a man's long history of abuse.

Canadian law has been revised under a progressive Supreme Court decision. Judges must instruct jurors in battered women's cases that the woman is not required to leave the home. Formal consultations are being conducted with lawyers and women's groups on how the law can be brought into line with new thinking on abusive relationships (Geddes, 1998). The justices were divided, however, over use of the battered woman syndrome concept. The fear is that the claims of self-defense by women who do not seem passive and helpless will not be fairly decided if the concept of "learned helplessness" is set as a standard for every case. The inherent contradiction between a "learned helplessness" argument and a woman who took the direct action of committing murder is likely to leave the jury unconvinced. We must keep in mind that many victims do not survive; they are murdered by their batterers: These are the true victims of a long period of domestic abuse. For the ones who kill their assaulters, a more relevant and empowering defense than learned helplessness must be found.

Theories of Partner Abuse

Consider a battered woman who is catering to her partner's every demand, preoccupied with her partner's needs and moods, consistently covering up for him after outbursts, and alternately protective of her children and neglectful of their needs. Is she a codependent woman who was bred for a self-sacrificial, self-destructive role, or has her seemingly bizarre response developed out of the abnormal demands of the situation? We will not answer this rhetorical question now but will instead look at several broad-based theories to explain domestic violence.

Societal Stress

Roberts and Burman (1998) consider a variety of stresses that can increase the potential for violence by men of women. Among them are the birth of children, fear of job loss and work-related problems, financial instability, and a pattern of alcohol abuse. The use of alcohol on the part of highly stressed men can magnify negative feelings, which may be redirected onto family members as a form of displaced aggression. Research confirms a correlation between stress factors such as unemployment and wife abuse (Rollins, 1996). Although some critics of the stress theory of violence, such as Kurz (1998), criticize this conclusion for not explaining why women are the primary targets of violence, women's vulnerability would seem to make them more likely to be the recipients than the perpetrators of violence.

Family Violence Framework

Some researchers challenge the sexual differentiation notion altogether. Basing their conclusions on data gathered by Straus and Gelles (1986) from the Conflict Tactics Scales, researchers claim that wives are as violent as their husbands. Results are based on women's responses to the Conflict Tactics Scales survey. A British study on dating habits used the scale to indicate that more men than women experienced assault by their date, usually in the form of slapping (Carrado, George, Loxam, Jones, and Templar, 1996). The survey measures a continuum of tactics used in resolving conflict. The continuum is extremely broad, including very low levels of violence, and it fails to differentiate initiated violence from acts of self-defense. Sexual abuse is not considered (Kurz, 1998). One study of male/female differences in response to violence indicated that when women were hit they were afraid, but when men were hit, they often laughed (Muchkenfuss, 1998).

The National Violence Against Women Survey of 8,000 men and 8,000 women, which gathered detailed data on a random sample of the population, found that

> *women experience significantly more partner violence than men do: 25 percent of surveyed women, compared with 8 percent of surveyed men, said they were raped and/or physically assaulted by a current or former spouse, cohabiting partner, or date in their lifetime; 1.5 percent of surveyed women and 0.9 percent of surveyed men said they were raped and/or physically assaulted by such a perpetrator in the previous 12 months. It is important to note that differences between women's and men's rates of physical assault by an intimate partner become greater as the seriousness of the assault increases. . . . They [women] were 7 to 14 times more likely to report that an intimate partner beat them up, choked or tried to drown them, threatened them with a gun, or actually used a gun on them. Eight percent of women and 2 percent of men reported that they had been stalked over their lifetime. (Tjaden and Thoennes, 1998, pp. 2, 7, 12)*

These figures, which were gathered with the most advanced state-of-the-art techniques in terms of sampling and preserving anonymity, should put older, misinterpreted findings to rest. Unfortunately, as Kurz indicates, false claims that levels of abuse between men and women are equal and mutual have been used to cut funding for women's shelters. Such an argument of conjoint violence can also be used to reinforce those family systems therapists who perceive family violence as an outgrowth of faulty communication styles between husband and wife.

Systems Theory

Systems theory offers a multidimensional view of reality. The concept of interactionism, which is central to systems theory, describes the influence of people's feedback on each other simultaneously. Cause and effect under this formulation are viewed as in constant and dynamic interaction with each other.

However useful this framework may be in counseling troubled families and in helping family members improve their skills in communication, when applied to a battering situation, therapy from a systems perspective is fraught with risks. Viewing family pathology as the source of the problem is one step removed from asking questions such as, What is the woman's role in perpetrating the violence? In gender-blind systems theory, each partner is held responsible for his or her contribution to the violence dynamic and for changing his or her behavior accordingly. Within this context, systems theory encourages a denial of the reality of victimization. Under conditions of violence, family counseling can be downright dangerous. Following the sessions, the batterer, in his own insecurity, may attack his wife for revelations made to the therapist.

A concept related to classical systems theory is *codependency*, a term popularized by substance abuse practitioners. The prefix "co-" implies shared responsibility for the behavior of another. So-called codependents are said to have gravitated toward a relationship with an abuser because of an unconscious desire to be enmeshed in an unhealthy relationship. Codependency theory suggests that women remain in an unhealthy situation because of some early deficit in the woman herself (Frank and Golden, 1992). Such a conceptualization overlooks the fact that women who are beaten by a violent man are roughly interchangeable: If one woman manages to extricate herself, she likely will be replaced with another vulnerable woman who will also be beaten. The fact that such a woman may be competent and confident at the beginning of the relationship is no insurance against her subsequent victimization. For example, in their in-depth study of battered mothers presenting children at a hospital for abuse and neglect, Stark and Flitcraft (1998) found no evidence that the mothers were predisposed by their history to be battered. Only the mothers of children suffering from child neglect were found to have had a problematic family history, including disorganization and violence.

Feminist Therapy

Are we looking at a codependent woman, feminists will ask, or are we looking at the results of traditional feminine training? Are we seeing poor communication skills among partners, or are we seeing the effect of severe power imbalance in our society? Because the structure of our patriarchal history has supported the concept of male entitlement vis-à-vis their wives, many men have trampled on their partners for years with relative impunity (Frank and Golden, 1992). Understanding the context of interpersonal violence in women's lives and examining why such violence continues to happen on a massive scale means calling into question the patriarchal structure in our society (Randall and Haskell, 1995). Feminists perceive the violent family as a microcosm of a society that oppresses and keeps women in their place (Davis, 1995). The recent antifeminist backlash in North American society compounds the original tendency to lean over backwards to avoid anything that hints of "male bashing." As they peruse the literature, researchers need to be especially wary of the taboo against defining an issue in gender-specific terms.

The challenge to feminist theorists is how to explain the often irrational attachment of battered women to their abusers. Most writers of the feminist school, such as Frank and Golden, focus on rational aspects (such as economic considerations and death threats) in a battered woman's decision to stay with her man. Dee Graham (1994), in contrast, refers to the Stockholm syndrome as an explanation for why women who are exposed to intermittent kindnesses by the captor—kindnesses that emerge within the context of a life-and-death situation from which there is only limited possibility of escape—may bond with the captor and even testify on his behalf in the eventual court proceedings. Basically, one's identity with powerful individuals who can exact terrible punishments and withhold the necessities of life can be understood as a regression to a dependent, childlike state. Bettelheim (1943) defined this phenomenon in his classic study of concentration camp survivors. Instead of anger, many prisoners identified with the SS troops and tried to emulate them.

McKenzie (1984, p. 219) defines the Stockholm syndrome as a "normal process of bonding, accelerated by severe conditions, coupled with attitude change resulting from an inability to reject arguments." In her book, *Loving to Survive,* Graham (1994) extends the concept to describe what she calls the Societal Stockholm Syndrome. Because male violence so permeates our society, as Graham and her associates argue, this engenders a societal response whereby some women are rendered isolated, powerless, and subject to male domination as a survival tactic. The captive bonds to the captor over time and may even experience love in the midst of fear. This response is viewed in the book as not related to gender but as a normal human response to an abnormal situation.

From the feminist perspective, cultural norms that support and maintain violence against women are the central culprit in partner abuse. Structural change (for example, instituting policies that increase victim safety and personal empowerment) is the focus, along with the re-education of batterers and of other men in their use of power and male privilege.

The Substance Abuse Connection

The relationship between substance abuse and family violence is best conceived of as interactive rather than causative. Persons prone toward violence are also likely to be risk takers, impulsive, and apt to indulge in the use of a variety of substances. At the same time their victims, being in a high state of stress and agitation, are apt to self-medicate with mood-altering substances as well. Research has shown that men (or women) who perpetrate partner violence or are victims are more likely than companion groups to have alcohol problems (Stuart et al., 2004). Heavy drinking and the use of certain drugs such as cocaine and methamphetamine lower one's inhibitions and ability to think rationally and often produce a state of paranoia. So the stage is set for violent outbursts. In Mason City, Iowa, the executive director of Crisis Intervention Services estimates that probably close to 65 percent of their clients in shelters have partners who are using meth or another drug (Buehner and Horgen, 2005). (See Chapter 5.)

In a study comparing 225 women in substance abuse treatment with 222 women at a shelter for domestic violence, William Downs (2000) found that the overlap was considerable. While a majority of the substance abuse treatment participants reported a recent incident of partner violence, a majority of the women at the shelter reported problematic use of substances. Substance abuse treatment can be integrated into a harm reduction model so that women can work on reducing the harm that substance abuse is playing in their lives at the same time that they develop a safety plan to reduce the harm of violence to themselves and their loved ones. Mandated substance abuse treatment for the batterer is also indicated. To the extent that the violence is drug-induced, treatment can be beneficial in curbing it. The correlation between substance use and partner violence is revealed in the following research studies:

- Approximately one-half of clinical spouse batterers have significant alcohol problems. (Tolman and Bennet, 1990)
- One-half to two-thirds of married male alcoholics are physically aggressive toward their partners during the year before alcoholism treatment. (Gondolf and Foster, 1991)
- In men, the combination of blue-collar status, drinking, and approval of violence is significantly associated with a high rate of wife abuse. (Associated Press, 1996)
- Binge drinkers, as opposed to daily drinkers, have an inordinately high rate of reported assault. (Gondolf and Foster, 1991; Murphy and O'Farrell, 1997)
- The female victims of abuse often also have substance abuse problems. (Bennett and Lawson, 1994)
- Sixty percent of female substance abusers have been victims of partner assault, according to estimates by treatment providers. (Bennett and Lawson, 1994; Miller, Downs, and Gondoli, 1989)
- Over one-third of substance abuse patients in a Veterans Administration program survey reported assaulting their wives in the previous year. (Gondolf and Foster, 1991)
- Cocaine, methamphetamine, and alcohol in high doses are all associated with hyperactivity and violence. Marijuana and heroin have not been proven to be associated with violence. (van Wormer and Davis, 2003)
- A study of alcohol consumption in the army revealed that soldiers who drink heavily are likely to abuse their partners both when they drink and when they don't, compared to moderate drinking soldiers. (Bell et al., 2004)

- A study of men in treatment for domestic violence showed that severe physical aggression was eleven times higher on days when the male partners were intoxicated than on other days. (Fals-Stewart, 2003)
- Women in methadone treatment who reported frequent crack cocaine use or frequent marijuana use were likely to be victimized over the next six months; women who were physically assaulted were more likely than other women to indicate frequent heroin use over the next six months. (El-Bassel et al., 2005)

The close correlation between substance abuse and relationship violence appears to be unquestionable. The only doubt is over the interpretation of this relationship. What all researchers and treatment personnel agree on is the crying need to put a stop to the violence and the high-risk substance abuse. Unfortunately, the relationship between the treatment providers at substance abuse and domestic violence programs is problematic (Bennett and Lawson, 1994). At the core of the problem is the tendency to dichotomize problems and to treat various components of antisocial behavior as separate entities. The differences arise not only from differing worldviews—disease model versus feminist approach—but also from a parallel tendency to view reality in terms of linear causation.

In the addictions treatment field, where many of the male clients have been enrolled for treatment for domestic violence offenses, the family is viewed as a system. This viewpoint tends to regard the violence as well as the substance abuse as closely linked and the victim in the family playing a role in enabling these bad behaviors to continue. Moreover, substance abuse counselors see addiction as the primary problem. The focus is therefore on sobriety: Get the chemicals out of the system and many of the other problems will subside.

The addictions focus in the substance abuse treatment field is matched by the male culture determinism of the domestic violence field. Workers in domestic violence programs have no less firm and sincere a commitment to their clients than do substance abuse counselors to theirs. And just as their counterparts in addictions work tend to be recovering addicts/alcoholics, many of those who counsel battered women have themselves been abused. Women's shelter counselors tend to stress individual/cultural responsibility for antisocial behavior. Drug usage is viewed by these workers as merely an excuse for deliberate acts of aggression. The tendency toward antisocial, risk-taking, and impulsive behavior may play a role in the development of both substance abuse and violence. Studies link low serotonin in the brain to both aggression and addiction as well as to a host of other behaviors.

Social factors link substance abuse and violence against women in regard to cultural expectations. In families in which men are expected to beat their wives when drunk, they will be inclined to do so. Gondolf (1995) argues effectively that the key to the link between alcohol abuse and control is in man's craving for power and control, a craving fostered by distortions of masculinity rooted in social upbringing. The effect of alcohol, in turn, contributes to a misreading of social cues through cognitive impairment, and violence may provide some sense of immediate gratification. A woman's substance abuse often parallels her partner's drug usage. "It takes being drunk to be married to a drunk," as one of van Wormer's clients succinctly

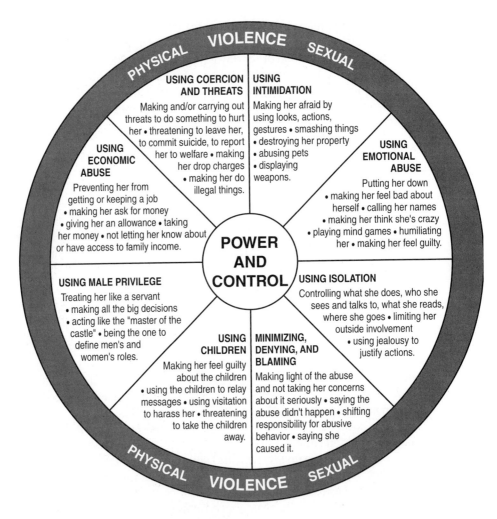

FIGURE 9.1 Power and Control Wheel

Source: Domestic Abuse Violence Project, 202 E. Superior Street, Duluth, MN 55802. Printed with permission of the Domestic Abuse Intervention Project.

put it. Once the man was in recovery, accordingly, his wife's sobriety quickly followed. See Figure 9.1 for a visual representation in the **Power and Control Wheel** of the interplay between power and control in an abusive relationship.

The Psychology of Male Abuse

The question one asks, to a large extent, determines the answer. Instead of asking, Why do they (the women) stay? we should ask, as psychologist Hara Marano (1993), suggests, What makes them (the men) so dependent, so vulnerable? To understand the dynamics of male-on-female violence, we need to consider biological as well as cognitive and social-psychological influences. In his study of battering men, Marano links intrapsychic deficits—a hypersensitivity to abandonment, inability to control negative emotions, and poor impulse control—with biological deficits— low serotonin levels in the brain, high testosterone production, and brain damage from head injury—and with cultural contributions such as traditional gender-role attitudes.

Jacobson and Gottman (1998b) monitored 140 couples with electric sensors while they discussed marital problems. The researchers were surprised to find that the ones they eventually labeled **cobras,** the most violent men who sounded and looked aggressive, were actually internally calm. Those labeled **pit bulls** became internally aroused with heart rates that increased with their anger; they never let up. The wives of pit bulls often took the risk of arguing back. If the women ever left the relationship, such men tended to stalk them. So self-centered were the cobras that, once their women were out of the way, they tended to let go of the relationship. The danger of violence with cobras occurs during the initial separation, whereas pit bulls become more dangerous following separation due to their ambivalent feelings of love. The cobras, about 20 percent of the total of the most violent husbands, are sadistic, prone to death threats, and belong in prison. Because these men have a certain charisma, as Jacobson and Gottman note, their wives tend to find them hard to resist.

A biological proclivity toward rage does not mean control is totally absent in most cases. In analyzing the rationales of eighteen batterers involved in group therapy, Ptacek (1997) found that although most of the men complained of totally losing control, usually in response to their wives' disturbing remarks, their violence was very selective. For example, these men did not attack people outside their family.

Virtually every study of batterers points to their low self-esteem (Stosny, 1997). Afflicted with an inability to compromise with others, they see themselves as powerless victims. Because of their underlying feelings of insecurity, jealousy is an emotion with special meaning for battering men. Marano (1993) summarizes recent research linking wife abuse with difficulty handling jealousy reactions. Violent men were found, in hypothetical jealousy-provoking situations, to consistently misinterpret their wives' motives as intentionally hostile. Nonviolent men in a comparison group did not feel personally threatened by the scenarios presented. Abusive men, according to Marano, may go into a rage when their wives go out with friends. Treatment consists of helping abusers to see that as long as they give their spouses undue power over their emotions and behavior, they will continue to abuse them. Their own overdependence on their spouses causes these men to resent and hate them. This is why murderers may say things like, "I loved my wife so much that I ended up killing her."

Children Witnessing Violence

The harm done to children who witness horrendous scenes of violence cannot be underestimated. Effects are both immediate and long-term. An extensive literature review by Kolbo, Blakely, and Engleman (1996) found that children who witness partner violence are more likely than other children to have problems in all major areas of functioning. Behaviorally, some children who have witnessed violence display aggression, cruelty to animals, and tantrums. Common emotional problems include anxiety, anger, and low self-esteem. Physical problems include sleeping and eating disturbances, bed-wetting, and other regressive behaviors; cognitive difficulties show up in learning and language lags.

In a large sample of predominantly Mexican American female students, the relationship between childhood exposure to parental violence and adult functioning was examined. Davies, DiLillo, and Martinez (2004) found that witnessing such violence was associated with depressive symptoms, low self-esteem, and trauma symptoms, even after controlling for child physical and sexual abuse.

Abused women do worry about their children and about their ability to protect them from experiencing or witnessing abuse. This is not surprising, since children of battered women are at risk for a variety of emotional, cognitive, and behavioral difficulties. Compared with the literature regarding child abuse and abuse of women, little has been published about the children of battered women (Humphreys, 1998). Children's protective services has focused on child abuse and neglect and on the mother's responsibilities in this regard, often overlooking the origin of the mother's helplessness. By the same token, women's shelters where the large majority of women arrive with children have focused on women-battering, with little attention to the long-term psychological consequences that family violence has had on the children. The result is that women's shelters and child welfare agencies are often seeing the same families. Some attention has been paid in recent years to the coexistence of wife abuse and child abuse in the same households.

Unless the child protective worker understands that a battered woman is often more afraid of her abusive partner than even of the loss of her children, he or she cannot be expected to obtain accurate information. Apart from interviewing the mother privately, key indicators are a child who is overprotective of his or her mother and a child who is abusive toward the mother (McKay, 1994).

Competition for funding, overwhelming child welfare caseloads, specialization of training and focus, and different philosophies and mandates have artificially separated the issues of wife and child abuse. The fact that both women and children may be simultaneously victimized and in terror, therefore, may not even be considered. And the fact that domestic violence against a child's mother is in itself a form of child abuse often escapes notice by child protection agencies.

The interrelationship between wife and child abuse is real. Although specialized training programs are being offered in the United States, evaluative research, even in progressive states such as Minnesota, continue to show that child welfare workers fail to investigate the coexistence of child abuse and wife abuse (Shepard and Raschick, 1999). A survey of child welfare cases and of domestic abuse cases conducted by Raschick and Shepard (1997) indicated that approximately one-third of each involved dual incidents of wife and child abuse. In a hospital sample of 116 women whose children were abused, 45 percent of the mothers had a history of probable victimization themselves (Stark and Flitcraft, 1998). Battering men may slap their children around out of sense of jealousy, as a power play, or as a way of sadistically hurting the wife. In a survey of 1,000 women, Bowker, Arbitell, and McFerron (1988) found that 70 percent of battered mothers reported that their children had also been abused. Such research may be biased, however, in relying on mothers' reports, since these do not, for example, indicate whether or not the battered mothers were also abusive themselves.

To what extent do battered women abuse their kids? In Stark and Flitcraft's hospital sample (1998), 50 percent of the children of the at-risk-for-battering women were abused by the batterer, 35 percent by the mother, and the rest by others or both. That abused mothers are often abusive themselves is indicated anecdotally from women's shelter directors and workers. We can even speculate that such violence may reflect a desperation to keep the child "in line" to prevent the batterer from inflicting harsher punishment. The violence could also result from stress, intergenerational tradition, and/or displacement of aggression onto a weaker source.

The paradox facing a battered mother is that if she reports domestic violence in her home, and especially if children are involved, her children may be removed. In order to get her children back, the mother has to demonstrate to the court and the social workers that she could provide a safe environment. The child's welfare understandably comes first.

The fact that foster placement is more likely when a mother is being battered reflects, as Stark and Flitcraft (1998) argue, the dearth of tools available to manage men. In effect, the woman at risk is punished through loss of their children. Once the children are gone, moreover, these women typically lose whatever therapeutic supports they may have had, as the emphasis shifts to the children in the new milieu.

Criminal Justice Process

Through the 1970s in most states, the police did not have the authority to make arrests in misdemeanor cases unless they personally had witnessed the offense. In New York State, as in many states, domestic violence cases were heard in family court, a special nonpunitive court, the function of which was to stabilize the family. Married women thus had no legal protection from battery, and unmarried women beaten by their partners had less protection still (Frisch and Caruso, 1996).

Over the next decades, however, drastic changes in the law occurred. The results from a large research study in the Minneapolis Police Department helped change the police perspective regarding the handling of domestic assault calls. In 1981, the Minneapolis Police Department participated in an experiment that assessed the effectiveness of three responses—mediate, separate, or arrest—in preventing future domestic abuse. Sherman and Berk (1984) concluded from this study that "The arrest treatment is clearly an improvement over sending the suspect away, which produced two and a half times as many repeat incidents as arrest" (p. 261). This finding held "regardless of the race, employment status, educational level, criminal history of the suspect, or how long the suspect was in jail when arrested" (p. 262).

Even though replication of this experiment has failed to achieve similar results (Dunford, Huizinga, and Elliot, 1990; Hirschel, Hutchison, and Dean, 1992), research indicates that this experiment significantly changed the policies of police departments nationwide (Sherman and Cohn, 1989). That early research seemed to silence many of those who doubted the wisdom of a law enforcement-centered approach to the problem of domestic violence (Chesney-Lind, 2002). In response to the Minneapolis domestic violence experiment and an outcry from feminist groups, strict, mandatory arrest policies were instituted (Miller, 2003). In New York State, for example, the police were required to provide victims with information about their rights and community services available. Marital rape was criminalized in 1984; then in 1994 new legislation required that the police make arrests where there is probable cause to believe that a felony or misdemeanor was committed or if an order of protection was violated.

Feder (1997) did find from her examination of a large police jurisdiction in south Florida that "officers with more traditional views of women's roles were less likely to self-report an arrest response when answering domestic assault calls" (p. 93). In addition, she found that a belief in the effectiveness of intervention in such calls turned out "to be positively associated with the likelihood of arresting" (p. 93).

Domestic violence among police officers themselves has gained recent recognition as a major problem. As indicated in two studies cited by Fields (1998) as many as 40 percent of the officers had been violent with their spouses or children in the preceding year. Because of such findings, the International Association of Chiefs of Police, headed by Nancy Turner, has introduced new guidelines to address potentially problematic behavior. According to the guidelines, coworkers will be held responsible for withholding information about troubled officers. Supervisors will be trained to look for trouble signs, including increased controlling behavior, greater amount of alcohol or other drug use, and unwarranted verbal abuse.

A major development that sprang out of Duluth, Minnesota ("the Duluth model") is the "no-drop" policy of prosecutors. This policy is now in place in many jurisdictions in the United States and Canada. Instead of dropping charges of assault and battery, which the victim often requests under duress or a change of heart, prosecutors continue the case based on evidence produced by the police. Batterers are viewed as a menace to other potential victims, including their children, and as potential homicide/suicide risks. Victim-support units attached to the prosecutor's office assist with these cases. Requirements for the perpetrators to enter specialized treatment programs are generally a part of any probation plan. Noncompliance, ideally, results in a lengthy prison term. The use of restraining orders to keep offenders away from the survivors offers protection to women in cases of low-level abuse but offers no security in life-threatening situations (Saunders, 1995). A man who is suicidal as well as violent has a high potential to kill his wife or partner.

Today, the mandatory arrest policy is being reconsidered in a number of quarters. The replication studies have failed to demonstrate convincingly that arrest of batterers deters repeat offenses from occurring in sites other than Minneapolis; arrest may, in fact, as Miller (2003) suggests, make the situation worse. This is the escalation-of-violence effect related to antagonizing the perpetrator when the time served was relatively short. Another potential problem with mandatory arrest policies is with regard to the minority community. Such an arrest policy subjects minorities to what might seem like police harassment. For minorities who are poor and others of low socioeconomic class, other resources are lacking; they cannot simply move into a motel, for example. The economic consequences of arrest of a breadwinner in a low-income family may be devastating.

Chesney-Lind points to a major unintended consequence of pro-arrest policies for women and girls. This is the manner in which the law requiring an arrest has resulted in dual arrest—arrest of both parties to a "fight." If it is not clear who the aggressor is, if the man has a scratch or mark on him, if both partners have been drinking, the police have taken to arresting the man and woman both. This change in policy is reflected in the arrest rate for assault, a fact that has fueled media reports of girls' and women's increasing violence. Studies on arrest rates from Wichita to Sacramento to Baltimore to Winnipeg, Canada, all found that the "zero tolerance" policy has had a dramatic effect on women's arrest patterns. Mothers who are arrested often see their children taken away to foster care; later loss of custody is a real risk. The arrest of girls, as Chesney-Lind documents, is a result most often of mother-daughter conflicts.

One solution, consistent with feminist practice, might be to simply listen to the victim of the assault. In their study of gender differences in police officers' perceptions about violence cases, Stalans and Finn (2000) found that women officers working in situations of marital abuse consulted with the wife and if she wished to settle the matter with the help of the police, the female officer gave consideration to the victim's preference and was more willing than male officers to make an arrest when the victim indicated an unwillingness to otherwise settle the matter.

In divorce cases where there has been domestic violence, the woman may risk loss of custody, now that states (since the 1970s) have adopted an equality or gender-blind system for awarding custody for small children in those rare cases in which the father files a petition for custody. The father can more often afford to hire a lawyer than the mother. The father more often having a job, and a new wife or mother who can care for the child, may appear to be in a better position to take responsibility. Battering, if involved, is often overlooked if the wife has flaws such as a drinking problem or a poor work history. It is common for courts to rule that the father's violence toward the mother has no effect on the children. In Canada, because of a backlash against a rash of claims of father/child incest and the widespread belief that such claims may be false, some lawyers are advising the mothers in custody disputes to be silent about such abuse (S. Charlesworth, personal communication, March 16, 2000).

All these situations show that domestic violence education is a must for child welfare authorities and judicial magistrates. Morrill and colleagues (2005) evaluated hundreds of child custody and visitation orders in cases of father-perpetrated domestic violence. Judges were surveyed as well. Judges who had received specialized education on partner violence gave mothers sole physical custody more often than those without such education yet few structured or restricted the fathers' visitation. The researchers recommend improvement in the education that is provided.

The entry of women into the legal profession and therefore into the ranks of prosecutors and judges has helped reshape the justice meted out to wife abusers and, more important, the process itself. Raleigh, North Carolina's county courtroom is leading the effort to bring police, prosecutors, and judges under one roof to curb the violence (Nifong, 1997). If a victim refuses to testify, police officers who are specially trained to provide the evidence present the case. A special domestic violence court hears the charges. A standard sentence for first-time offenders is to enter a twenty-six-week social service program for batterers. Judge Joyce Hamilton orders such treatment based on research showing that only 12 percent of offenders involved in a similar program reoffend. In the Raleigh program, a parole officer tracks the offender's progress. Supporters of the new approach say that preventing violence will reduce the murder rate. Judge Hamilton says that's not why she's there; she's there for the kids.

At the national level, the advocacy-oriented Violence Against Women Office of the U.S. Justice Department has been designed to bolster police and prosecutorial work on domestic and sexual violence cases. Funding is allocated for prevention and victim services programs as well. A setback for women's protection against violent men came with the Supreme Court decision in the *Castle Rock v. Gonzales* case. In this tragic case, a battered woman, Jessica Gonzales of Colorado, had a protective restraining order against her husband. Her estranged husband drove off with their daughters, and Gonzales pleaded with the police for help but the police ignored her pleas (Richey, 2005). Gonzales's husband then killed the children and had himself killed in a suicide-by-cop shoot-out. Gonzales sued the police, and her case landed at the Supreme Court. The Court ruled in favor of the police department. This ruling leaves victims at the mercy of their police departments. The hiring of more women in policing most likely would give assaulted women a better chance of protection (see Chapter 11).

Human Rights Issues

International law provides for freedom from domestic violence under the 1980 Convention for the Elimination of All Forms of Discrimination Against Women. Former President Jimmy Carter signed the document, which has never been ratified by the U.S. Senate. Every country in Europe has signed. The European Convention for the Protection of Human Rights provides for the same protection against domestic violence. In the 1990s, a complaint was lodged with the European Court on behalf of an Irish woman who sought to separate from her husband due to alleged physical and mental abuse (Barnes, 1998). The complainant was unable to do so because, under the new divorce law in Ireland (divorce was not allowed until 1996), the costs of separation were prohibitive as was the four-year continuous waiting period. The required mediation sessions retraumatize women in forced face-to-face confrontations. Moreover, the nondisclosure stance of the mediation means that if the abused woman is subjected to psychological abuse during mediation, secrecy must prevail. The European Court ruled against the separation fee to make divorce accessible. The extent to which the Irish government will follow this decision is unclear.

This example of reliance on international law to link partner violence with human rights violations has important implications worldwide for women who are subjected to behaviors that could be described as torture, including the element of captivity. Hamby (1998) brings our attention to advocacy efforts to reclassify partner violence as a human rights violation, recognized as such by international organizations such as the United Nations. The significance of such an approach would be in changing societal attitudes and promoting international standards of humanity and equality.

Empowerment

Sometimes you can learn as much from a negative example as from a positive one. In an ethnographic analysis of services that battered women received, Baker (1996) found that the sixteen Iowa women interviewed encountered varying responses to their situations. On the whole, police encounters were conceived of as negative due to the slowness of response and lack of respect for the woman. Contacts with clergy did more harm than good because ministers tended to focus on the woman's behavior as a cause of the violence. Couples counseling was especially destructive in treating the partners as co-acting equals and leading to assaults immediately afterward for something that was said in therapy. On the positive side, participation in women's support groups led to a heightened awareness and camaraderie that helped group members gain control over their own lives. Baker discovered from her interviews that being stronger, more aware, and knowledgeable about social and political aspects of domestic violence was among the ways battered women felt helped by the group therapy experience.

Crisis Intervention

Immediate care for a woman in a potentially harmful or already abusive situation involves the development of a safety plan (Boes, 1998). Through obtaining crisis intervention services, many women are able to regain control of their lives by identifying current options and goals and by working to attain those goals. Typically, the battered woman has been subject to psychological and physical abuse for a long period of time before calling for help. She may be mobilized to call a telephone hotline, the police, or a women's shelter or to go to a hospital emergency room. Effective treatment for battered women and their children includes thorough documentation for the possibility of a later legal complaint.

Roberts's (1997) Seven-Stage Crisis Intervention Model offers a framework that can be applied by hospital staff, social workers, or shelter workers. The stages of the crisis intervention model are:

1. Plan and conduct a thorough assessment (including a level-of-danger assessment); inquire about death threats, suicide threats, weapons present, and so forth and immediate psychosocial needs.
2. Establish rapport and rapidly establish a relationship based on genuineness and respect.
3. Identify the precipitating event that led the client to seek treatment; encourage the client to describe the immediate situation.
4. Deal with feelings and emotions. Open-ended questions are recommended. Some examples: *How are you feeling now? What are some of the options you're thinking about? What is the usual situation at home?* Use verbal counseling skills such as reflection of feelings, reassurance, paraphrasing, and attentive silence.
5. Generate and explore alternatives. Helping the client find a safe place is essential.
6. Develop and formulate an action plan. Help the client face her fears and gain control as a self-empowering act. Assistance in a shift from fatalistic thinking toward an attitude of hope and renewal is essential. A cognitive approach will help redirect destructive thought patterns, such as "I can't live without him" or "I must stay for the sake of the kids," and a redirection to empowering affirmations and beliefs, such as, "If other women have made it, so can I."
7. Follow up. Informal and formal agreements should be reached for another meeting to gauge the client's progress and daily functioning. It is hoped that future moves will be toward healing and growth. (p. 43)

Given the enormity and depth of the problems encountered, battered women need a continuity of supportive networks and helping services. Crisis intervention, as Roberts and Burman (1998) indicate, can be the starting point on a longer journey toward safety and renewal. For the majority of battered women, permanently leaving the batterer, regaining self-esteem, and finding safe housing and a job are all necessary.

Empowerment can come to a survivor of domestic abuse in working closely with a counselor or other helper as she becomes conscious of inner strengths of which she was unaware, even strengths paradoxically that emerged from her history of abuse. Like many other women who have survived trauma and called for help, she may come to recognize her strength in retrospect. Viewed in the context of the abusive situation and the structural oppression of women, all coping strategies can be recognized as valid resourcefulness and resistance in the face of severe stress.

A serious hindrance to adequate long-term treatment for survivors is the unavailability of affordable services. Sadly, mental health providers must compete with other human service agencies for scarce economic resources in a climate that defines non-emergency services as expendable whenever there is a budget crunch. The hope is that, with the current political focus on the needs of crime victims, advocates for prevention of domestic violence and for treatment of its survivors will be heard.

Shelters for Battered Women

Thanks to feminist activism starting in the 1970s, over 1,500 women's shelters have been established as safe havens for women and their children. Shelters offer more than safety and a way out; living in close quarters with other battered women and participating in group counseling provides an opportunity for consciousness-raising. Unfortunately, due to serious underfunding, most shelters can take in only a minority of the women who need their help. The importance of shelters in preventing further battering, in saving lives, and in revealing options other than returning to an abusive situation is widely acknowledged (Dziegielewski and Resnick, 1996).

Before the establishment of shelters, abused women were whispered about and generally regarded as a source of embarrassment. When shelters were opened to provide safety, they ended up providing a whole lot more. Shelters, as Schechter (1982) observed, offered the supportive framework through which thousands of women turned "personal" problems into political ones, rid themselves of self-blame, and called attention to the sexism that left millions of women violently victimized.

Institutionalized racism or the kind of racism that is unintended has been a continuous problem with the shelters. Donnelly, Cook, Ausdale, and Foley (2005) made a study of white privilege in battered women's shelters in the Deep South. The sixty executive directors of the shelter who were interviewed were proud of being "color blind," and as the researchers argue, that is part of the problem. By not noticing race, they ignore cultural diversity and attitude differences in African Americans. For example, the feminist philosophy concerning the causes of male violence often doesn't coincide with black women's understandings. Battered women of color are less likely than whites to seek the services of the shelters. Greater outreach and culturally specific services are needed.

The empowerment philosophy characteristic of women's shelters centers on an awareness of oppression based on race, class, sexual orientation, and gender. Shelter life is woman-centered, chaotic with so much coming and going, emotionally charged, and guided by women who have an agenda and an awareness often different from that of their charges. Threat to life and bodily integrity overwhelms normal adaptive processes. In group sessions, the process of empowerment takes place as women fully acknowledge their vulnerability to male violence. The emphasis on self-protection, on finding one's voice, sharing, and listening to others frees up the mind to contemplate the forbidden and prepares the way for progression from fear to anger to self-expression.

A three-part model of empowerment for women presented by Glen Maye (1998) includes the following:

1. Development of consciousness of self as a woman
2. Reduction of shame and self-blame, and acknowledgment of anger as a catalyst toward change
3. Assumption of personal responsibility for changing self and society. (p. 36)

Overall, about 50 percent of the battered women who get help from shelters or other agencies decide to leave their abusers (Lesser, 1990). The others who return to their abusers have also been frequently changed by their experience. Based on their study of twenty battered Israeli women, Eisikovits, Buchbinder, and Mor (1998) argue that even when a woman decides to stay with the batterer, turning points can still take place. In other words, women may choose to stay in the relationship but never again on the same terms as before. Such a turning point, as these authors indicate, is not sudden but the culmination of a lengthy process in which a woman will actively negotiate, plan, and vow that violence must be stopped. She will confront her partner about her unwillingness to tolerate violence and about her involvement with formal organizations specializing in domestic violence.

A woman who decides to stay, nevertheless, needs a safety plan (Lindhorst, Macey, and Nurius, 2005). Such a plan should include acquiring job skills for personal independence; maintaining and reviving friendships; attending a support group on a regular basis; knowing the phone number of the women's shelter by heart; keeping money on hand for emergencies; working out a signal system with a neighbor; getting rid of all weapons and keeping sharp knives in hard-to-reach places; learning how to anticipate violence so as to slip away while it is still safe; preparing older children to call for help; and, finally, preparing to make an escape with the children rather than leaving them behind. The availability of community resources and the possibility of receiving financial aid without being forced onto the job market for the time being are vital for the safety of battered women who are trying to start a new life. See Box 9.3 for a firsthand description of one day's work at a women's shelter.

Treatment for Batterers

Can batterers change their behavior? This is a major consideration because if all the treatment effort is directed toward rescuing the woman, sooner or later the batterer will find another family to victimize. If the partner's behavior can be changed, however, a far more effective form of crime prevention is available.

In intensive group therapy sessions, such as those offered at the Domestic Abuse Project in Minneapolis, offenders confront each other whenever they rationalize and minimize their behavior. Follow-up studies suggest that two out of three clients in the program have not battered their partners eighteen months following treatment (Cowley, 1994). Unfortunately, only one-fourth of the court-ordered men who are registered in the program actually complete it.

Because aggression is associated with low serotonin levels in the brain, drug treatment, such as with antidepressant therapy, is becoming increasingly common. "I always tell abusers to try antidepressants," says psychologist Roland Maiuro (1998), who has been conducting a controlled study using the antidepressant Paxil. He adds that "anything that increases serotonin will reduce shame," and shame causes anger and aggression (p. 83). Jacobsen and Gottman (1998a) and Bednar (2001) claim excellent results in their harm reduction program for abusive men, which utilizes feeling-regulation techniques to keep them from getting out of control.

BOX **9.3**

Snapshot—A Social Worker's Daily Reality at a Domestic Violence Shelter

On this beautiful day I'm driving to the local hospital to pick up yet another woman and children affected by the crime of domestic violence. Looking out of my window at everyday people going about their business, I would have little awareness that a woman is assaulted and her children traumatized by this crime that happens every six seconds in this country.

I've been manager of this domestic violence shelter for battered women and children for four years. In that time we have had over a thousand women and children pass through our doors. The stories are all unique and yet all the same. We assist some in relocating out of state to hide and escape the violence; some move in with a mother or sister close to home; and others go back to their homes with promises that the abuser would change.

In my mind I'm making mental notes to prepare to meet the caller and her children. My backseat has three brand-new stuffed animals for the children and a carseat for the baby. There are extra diapers and a blanket in my trunk. I must be alert for anyone suspicious in the parking lot, just in case her abuser has followed her here. That must be her in the waiting room trying to juggle the baby in one arm and two more toddlers in the other. "Hi, I'm Janet from the shelter." She looks scared, but relieved that I'm finally here as I scoop up a toddler. Thus begins another journey that I will take alongside this woman and her babies.

I know that she will have many decisions to make and many obstacles to overcome. Later I find out that this mother is only nineteen

years old, uneducated and with few job skills. Her income came totally from her abuser and now is no more. I marvel at her bravery and her desire for a better life.

Another factor complicating this battered woman's life is the fact that she is Caucasian and her children are biracial (African American). I've seen many women come through the shelter under such bicultural circumstances that pose their unique set of problems. In many cases the support systems for these women and, most of all, for the children are lacking. The white world does not embrace biracial children with white mothers. There is a negative stigma in our society attached to a Caucasian woman with biracial children, especially if she has personal problems. Oftentimes her own family has cut her off, disapproving of her choice of partners. The African American community seems more accepting of her and her children, but not when there are accusations of abuse toward one of its members. This leaves her in limbo. Where can she go for help? It is very difficult to find a safe, supportive, nurturing place for her and her children.

Now, we will sit down and begin the process. First come the pain and tears. Then, the harsh reality of figuring out what to do and where to go. I hope we can find some answers.

Critical Thinking Question: How does the intersection of class, race, and gender come into play in the case history described in this reading?

Source: Janet Wood, LBSW. Printed with permission of Janet Wood.

With regard to violence intervention, much more programming is needed, especially at the high school level, to help youths develop healthy relationships. More culturally specific programming is needed as well. Anecdotal evidence from programs designed specifically for African American men suggest that such programs are more successful with African Americans than are other batterers'

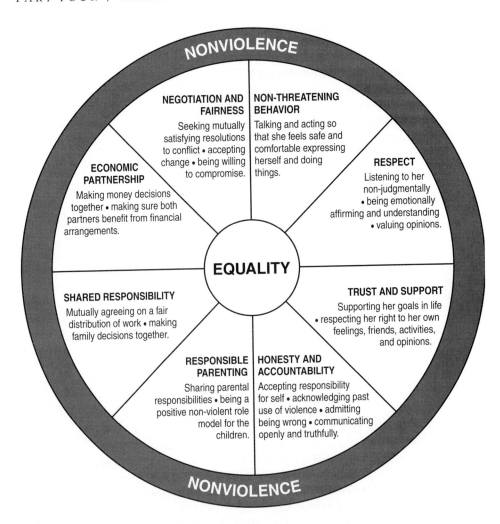

FIGURE 9.2   Equality Wheel

Source: Domestic Abuse Violence Project, 202 E. Superior Street, Duluth, MN 55802. Printed with permission of the Domestic Abuse Intervention Project.

programs (National Research Council, 1996). For an example of the goals of a healthy relationship, see the equality wheel depicted in Figure 9.2, designed by battered women of Duluth, Minnesota.

Martinez (1996) explains that the abuse victim being subjected to her first assault is a very different person from the one who comes to the attention of the authorities years later. Before the assault, the abuser has spent months or years wearing her down psychologically, using minor acts of aggression to control her. The wife or partner is thus undermined psychologically by the time the physical abuse reaches a dangerous level.

A more recent study (Shepard, Falk, and Raschick, 2000) examined recidivism rates and victim reports of improved well-being following their partner's participation in an enhanced domestic abuse intervention program, which included improved coordination between agencies involved. The enhanced program did seem to result in lower recidivism rates in about half of the women while 9 percent reported that it was actually harmful. This is an area in need of further study.

A government study entitled, "Do Batterer Intervention Programs Work?" examined two studies in considerable depth, one from Florida and one from New York, both of which used control groups. Results showed that the one-size-fits-all model does not work; the best predictor of success was whether or not the individual was employed and lived under stable residential circumstances.

In their curriculum description, Pence and Paymar report that voluntary participants complete the batterers' program only 10 percent of the time (Pence and Paymar, 1993). Possible reasons suggested for this dismal statistic are that the program challenges participants' cherished belief systems, that individuals entering the program voluntarily may do so for ulterior motives, such as the possibility of lowering their penalties or manipulating the victim into returning to the relationship, and that voluntary participants are treated in the same manner as court-ordered participants.

Ellen Pence (1999) commented on the changing philosophy of the Duluth Abuse Intervention Program (DAIP) in a recent review of the project's evolution. She described an ideological shift that moved professionals from their early emphasis on psychological explanations for violence towards the notion that power and control were the underlying motivation for battering. According to Pence, the staff believed their analysis to be based on neutral observation, while they in fact remained blind to the discrepancy between their theory and the actual experiences of the men and women with whom they worked. While staff persisted in explaining the underlying power motive, few men seemed to identify with the explanation. In addition, attempts to explain violence by women against men, lesbian violence, and the violence of men who were appalled by their own actions further undermined the theory that violence was solely a tool of control. According to Pence, the DAIP is now coming to acknowledge that violence may come about in many ways. Although male-on-female violence is still seen as a byproduct of dominance and inequality in relationships, attempts are now being made to understand such violence from a more holistic perspective that takes into consideration multiple views of reality.

Summary

Learning to believe in oneself as a woman is a lifelong process in a patriarchal society. Learning the functions that violence and the threat of violence serve for the abuser in quelling all criticism and dialogue is a part of that process. Partner abuse is pervasive and an unrecognized cause of chronic psychological and physical health problems. One of the most underreported crimes in the United States, family violence is the single most significant cause of injury to women. About two million women are victimized in this way each year. In whatever capacity we encounter these victim/survivors, whether we are police officers, court officials, child welfare workers, or shelter advocates, we must recognize and challenge the dominant ideology of victim-blaming, welfare "reform," and anti–affirmative action backlash. Moreover, we must do more to educate our children in nonviolent ways of resolving disputes and teach them how to deal with powerful feelings and about the danger signs of psychological abuse.

We began this chapter with a historical overview of domestic woman violence. During Colonial times and even before that, the man was "the lord and master" of the household; he could physically chastise his wife to correct her behavior. In the twentieth century, physical punishment of wives was outlawed. Nevertheless, one form of violence that was retained was marital rape, which is still legal in some states today. Wife beating was not defined as a significant social problem until the 1970s when, in the wake of the civil rights movement, feminists publicized this issue as one that affected all social classes.

Feminist perspectives on wife and partner abuse have encompassed both a challenge to the presumption that domestic violence is rare—demonstrating that on some levels and in some parts of society wife beating is normative—and a call to public action. Incredible strides have been made; the establishment of thousands of women's shelters across North America is the most obvious example. Despite these advances, much more needs to be done at the societal level to aid women on the road to independence. Welfare reforms are a priority. Public assistance programs need to be responsive to women at risk of being trapped in a situation of abuse and much more flexible regarding workfare requirements. Moreover, allowance must be made for the risks that battered women face in cooperating with child support enforcement efforts. Safe and affordable housing must be provided for families on the run. Finally, to be self-supporting women require access to an array of educational and vocational training opportunities.

Repeated physical and sexual violation are assaults on the integrity and value of the self. Empowerment is critically important so that battered women can recover, heal, and lead lives free from fear and psychological cruelty. Economic and social empowerment are essential to personal survival. Equally essential are institutional and group support to help women subjected to violence to survive and thrive. Substance abuse treatment may be a necessary but not sufficient requirement to end male violence and threatening power plays. What is both necessary and sufficient is to sacrifice a sick relationship for personal wellness, perhaps even embracing a survivor mission as a part of the recovery process. Whichever path is chosen—life within a renewed relationship or apart from it—women released from rigid role stereotypes will be better able to manage their own lives and those of her children.

KEY TERMS

battered woman syndrome
cobras and pit bulls
exposure reduction theory
intimate partner violence
murder-suicide

National Violence Against
    Women (NVAW) Survey
Stockholm syndrome
suicide-murder

systems theory
traumatic bonding theory
Violence Against Women Act
    (VAWA)

CRITICAL THINKING QUESTIONS

1. Why is the home the most dangerous place for women with regard to violence?

2. Discuss the significance of the Violence Against Women Act and the impact of "welfare reform" in protecting women.

3. Consider the plight of immigrant battered women.

4. Check out the controversy that women are as violent as men. Argue pro or con using recent data.

5. Should marital rape be treated the same as stranger or date rape? How is it different and the same?

6. Argue that traumatic bonding or the Stockholm syndrome is not specific to the female gender.

7. Think about the conflict between women's shelters and substance abuse treatment centers in terms of factors in violence.

8. Study the Power and Control Wheel. Why do victims identify with this wheel? How might its use in batterer intervention programs fail to bring about the desired results?

9. Discuss the psychology of men who batter. How can interventions be individualized for men of various personality types?

WEB DESTINATIONS

Bureau of Justice Statistics for victimization data: www.ojp.usdoj.gov/bjs

Family Violence Prevention Fund: http://endabuse.org

Family Violence Statistics: www.ojp.usdoj.gov/bjs/abstract/fvs.htm

Infoplease-information on domestic violence surveys: www.infoplease.com/ipa/A0875303.html

National Coalition against Domestic Violence: www.ncadv.org

National Center for Injury Prevention and Control: www.cdc.gov/ncipc

Violence Policy Center: www.vpc.org

REFERENCES

Anderson, M. (1997, October 26). The family home is the most dangerous place for women. *Des Moines Register*, p. 4AA.

Associated Press (1996, September 23). Violence research brings startling results. *Waterloo/Cedar Falls Courier*, p. A6.

Baker, P. L. (1996). Doin' what it takes to survive: Battered women and the consequences of compliance to a cultural script. *Studies in Symbolic Interaction 20:* 73–90.

Bannister, S. A. (1993). Battered women who kill their abusers: Their courtroom battles. In R. Muraskin and T. Alleman, *It's a crime: Women and justice* (pp. 316–333). Englewood Cliffs, N.J.: Prentice Hall.

Barnes, A. T. (1998). Ireland's divorce bill: Traditional Irish and international norms of equality in a domestic abuse context. *Vanderbilt Journal of Transnational Law 31*(3): 643–670.

Barrachlough, B., and Harris, E. (2002, May). Suicide preceded by murder: The epidemiology of homicide-suicide in England and Wales 1988–92. *Psychological Medicine 32*(2): 577–584.

Bednar, S. (2001). Recovering strengths in batterers. Sidebar in K. van Wormer, *Counseling female offenders and victims: A strengths-restorative approach*. New York: Springer Publishing.

Bell, N., Hartford, T., McCarroll, J., and Senier, L. (2004). Drinking and spouse abuse among U.S. army soldiers. *Alcoholism: Clinical and Experimental Research 28*(12): 1890–1897.

Bennett, L., and Lawson, M. (1994). Barriers to cooperation between domestic-violence and substance-abuse programs. *Families in Society 75:* 277–286.

Bergen, R. K. (1998). The reality of wife rape. In R. K. Beyen (ed.), *Issues in intimate violence*. Thousand Oaks, Calif.: Sage.

Bettleheim, B. (1943). Individual and mass behavior in extreme situations. *Journal of Abnormal and Social Psychology 38:* 417–452.

Blackstone, W. (1979). *Commentaries on the laws of England* (pp. 444–445). Facsimile of the first edition of 1765–1769.

Block, C. R. (2003). How can practitioners help an abused woman lower her risk of death? In Intimate Partner Homicide. *NIJ Journal 250:* 4–7. Washington, D.C.: National Institute of Justice, U.S. Dept. of Justice.

Boes, M. (1998). Battered women in the emergency room: Emerging roles for the ER social worker and clinical nurse specialist. In A. Roberts (ed.), *Battered women and their families*, 2nd ed. (pp. 205–229). New York: Springer.

Bowker, L. H., Arbitell, M., and McFerron, J. R. (1988). On the relationship between wife beating and child abuse. In K. Yllo and M. Bogard (eds.), *Feminist perspectives on wife abuse* (pp. 158–174). Newbury Park, Calif.: Sage.

Browne, A. (1995). Fear and the perception of alternatives: Asking "why battered women don't leave" is the wrong question. In B. R. Price and N. Sokoloff (eds.), *The criminal justice system and women: Offenders, victims, and workers* (pp. 228–245). New York: McGraw-Hill.

Browning, M. (2003, March 14). Brainwashing agitates victims into submission. *Palm Beach Post*. Retrieved from www.rickross.com/brainwashing.

Buehner, K., and Horgen, J. (2005, January 31). Abuse connected to methamphetamine use. Mason City (Iowa) *Globe Gazette*. Retrieved from www.globegazette.com.

Campbell, J. C., Webster, D., Koziol-McLain, J., Block, C. R., Campbell, D., Curry, M. A., Gary, F., McFarlane, J., Sachs, C., Sharps, P., Ulrich, Y., and Wilt, S. A. (2003). Assessing risk factors for intimate partner homicide. In Intimate Partner Homicide, *NIJ Journal 250:* 14–19. Washington, D.C.: National Institute of Justice, U.S. Dept. of Justice.

Carcach, C., and Grabosky, P. (1998, March). Murder-suicide in Australia. *Trends & Issues in Crime and Criminal Justice:* 1–5. Australian Institute of Criminology.

Carrado, M., George, M., Loxam, E., Jones, L., and Templar, D. (1996). Aggression in British heterosexual relationships. *Journal of Aggressive Behavior 22:* 401–415.

Castiglia, C. (1996). *Bound and determined: Captivity, culture-crossing, and white womenhood from Mary Rowlandson to Patty Hearst*. Chicago: University of Chicago Press.

Chesney-Lind, M. (2002, November). Criminalizing victimization: The unintended consequences of pro-arrest policies for girls and women. *Criminology and Public Policy 2*(1): 81–90.

Clayworth, J., and Erb, G. (1998, September 20). Another murder, suicide in Iowa. *Des Moines Register*, p. 1A.

Council on Scientific Affairs, American Medical Association. (1992). Violence against a woman: Relevance for medical practitioners. *Journal of the American Medical Association 267:* 3184–3189.

Cowley, G. (1994, July 4). Stopping abuse: What works. *Newsweek:* 33.

Darroch, W. (1998, February 19). Streets safer than home for women, inquest told. *Toronto Star*, p. 1.

Davies, C., DiLillo, D., and Martinez, I. (2004, December). Isolating adult psychological correlates of witnessing parental violence: Findings from a predominantly Latina sample. *Journal of Family Violence* 19(6): 369–378.

Davis, L. V. (1995). Domestic violence. *Encyclopedia of social work,* 19th ed. Washington, D.C: 780–788.

Dearwater, S. R., Coben, J. H., Campbell, J. C., et al. (1998). Prevalence of intimate partner abuse in women treated at community hospital emergency departments. *Journal of the American Medical Association* 280(5): 433–438.

Donnelly, D., Cook, K., Ausdale, D., and Foley, L. (2005, January). White privilege, color blindness, and services to battered women. *Violence Against Women* 11(1): 6–37.

Downs, D. (1997). *More than victims: Battered women, the syndrome society, and the law.* Chicago: University of Chicago Press.

Downs, W. (2000, February). Paper presentation: Partner violence and substance abuse. Cedar Falls, Iowa: University of Northern Iowa.

Dugan, L., and Apel, R. (2003). An exploratory study of the violent victimization of women: Race/ethnicity and situational context. *Criminology* 41(3): 959–979.

Dunford, F., Huizinga, D., and Elliot, D. (1990). The role of arrest in domestic assault: The Omaha police experiment. *Criminology 28:* 183–206.

Dutton, D. G., and Painter, S. (1993). Emotional attachments in abusive relationships: A test of traumatic bonding theory. *Violence and Victims 8*(2): 105–120.

Dwyer, D. C. (1995). Response to the victims of domestic violence: Analysis and implications of the British experience. *Crime and Delinquency 41*(4): 527–540.

Dziegielewski, S. F., and Resnick, C. (1996). Assessment and intervention: Abused women in the shelter setting. In A. Roberts (ed.), *Crisis management and brief treatment: Theory, technique and application* (pp. 123–141). Belmont, Calif.: Wadsworth.

Easteal, P. (1994). Homicide suicides between adult sexual intimates: An Australian study. *Suicide and Life-Threatening Behavior 24*(2): 140–151.

Eisikovits, Z., Buchbinder, E., and Mor, M. (1998). "What it was won't be anymore": Reaching the turning point in coping with intimate violence. *Affilia 13*(4): 411–434.

El-Bassel, N., Gilbert, L., Wu, E., Go, H., and Hill, J. (2005, March). Relationship between drug abuse and intimate partner violence: A longitudinal study among women receiving methadone. *The American Journal of Public Health 95*(3): 465–471.

Fals-Stewart, W. (2003). The occurrence of partner physical aggression on days of alcohol consumption: A longitudinal diary study. *Journal of Consulting and Clinical Psychology 71:* 41–52.

Family Violence in Canada: A Statistical Profile (2005, July 14). *The Daily.* Retrieved from http://www.statcan.ca/Daily/English/050714/d050714a.htm.

Family Violence Prevention Fund (2005). Violence against women act reauthorization. *Family Violence Prevention Fund.* Retrieved from http://endabuse.org/vawa.

Feder, L. (1997). Domestic violence and police response in a pro-arrest jurisdiction. *Women and Criminal Justice 8:* 79–98.

Fields, G. (1998, October 14). Domestic abuse among cops. *USA Today,* p. 5A.

Frank, P. B., and Golden, K. (1992). Blaming by naming: Battered women and the epidemic of codependence. *Social Work 37*(1): 5–6.

Frish, L. A., and Caruso, J. M. (1996). The criminalization of woman battering: Planned change experiences in New York State. In *Helping battered women: New perspectives and remedies* (pp. 102–131). New York: Oxford University Press.

Geddes, J. (1998, February 23). Victims who kill. *Maclean's*, p. 64.

Glen Maye, L. (1998). Empowerment of women. In L. Gutierrez, R. F. Parsons, and E. O. Cox (eds.), *Empowerment in social work practice: A sourcebook* (pp. 29–51). Pacific Grove, Calif.: Brooks/Cole.

Gondolf, E. W. (1995). Alcohol abuse, wife assault, and power needs. *Social Service Review 69*: 274–284.

Gondolf, E. W., and Foster, R. A. (1991). Wife assault among V.A. alcohol rehabilitation patients. *Hospital and Community Psychiatry 42*: 74–79.

Graham, D. L., with Rawlings, E., and Rigsby, R. K. (1994). *Loving to survive: Sexual terror, men's violence, and women's lives.* New York: University Press.

Hamby, S. (1998). Partner violence: Prevention and intervention. In J. L. Jasinski and L. M. Williams (eds.), *Partner violence* (pp. 210–258). Thousand Oaks, Calif.: Sage.

Hirschel, J. D., Hutchison, I., and Dean, C. (1992). The failure of arrest to deter spouse abuse. *Journal of Research in Crime and Delinquency 29*: 7–33.

Humphreys, J. (1998). Helping battered women take care of their children. In J. C. Campbell (ed.), *Empowering survivors of abuse: Healthcare for battered women and their children* (pp. 121–137). Thousand Oaks, Calif.: Sage.

Ingrassia, M., and Beck, M. (1994, July 4). Patterns of abuse. *Newsweek*, pp. 26–33.

Jacobson, N. S., and Gottman, J. M. (1998a, March). Violent relationship. *Psychology Today*, pp. 60–65, 81–84.

Jacobson, N. S., and Gottman, J. M. (1998b). *When men batter women: New insights into ending abusive relationships.* New York: Simon and Schuster.

Jerin, R. A., and Moriarty, L. J. (1998). *Victims of crime.* Chicago: Nelson-Hall.

Kambayashi, T. (2004, February 24). A defender for Japan's battered women. *Christian Science Monitor.* Retrieved from www.csmonitor.com.

Karmen, A. (2004). The victimization of girls and women by boys and men: Competing analytical frameworks. In B. R. Price and N. J. Solokoff (eds.), *The criminal justice system and women offenders, prisoners, mothers and workers*, 3rd ed. (pp. 289–301). New York: McGraw-Hill.

Kaufman-Kantor, G., Jasinski, J., and Aldarondo, E. (1994). Sociocultural status and incidence of marital violence in Hispanic families. *Violence and Victims 9*(3): 207–222.

Kolbo, J. R., Blakely, E. H., and Engelman, D. (1996). Children who witness domestic violence: A review of empirical literature. *Journal of Interpersonal Violence 11*: 281–294.

Kurz, D. (1998). Old problems and new directions in the study of violence against women. In R. K. Bergen (ed.), *Intimate violence* (pp. 197–208). Thousand Oaks, Calif.: Sage.

Lauritsen, J., and White, N. (2001). Putting violence in its place: The influence of race, ethnicity, gender, and place on the risk for violence. *Criminology & Public Policy 1*(1): 37–59.

Lee, M.-Y., and Au, P. (1998). Chinese battered women in North America: Their experiences and treatment. In A. Roberts (ed.), *Battered women and their families*, 2nd ed. (pp. 448–482). New York: Springer.

Leonard, E. D. (2003). Stages of gendered disadvantage in the lives of convicted battered women. In B. Bloom (ed.), *Gendered justice: Addressing female offenders* (pp. 97–139). Durham, N.C.: Carolina Academic Press.

Lesser, B. (1990). Attachment and situational factors influencing battered women's return to their mate following a shelter program. In K. Pottharst (ed.), *Research explorations in adult attachment* (pp. 81–128). New York: Peter Lang.

Lindhorst, T., Macey, R., and Nurius, P. (2005 Spring/Summer). Contextualized assessment with battered women: Strategic safety planning to cope with multiple harms. *Journal of Social Work Education 41*(2): 331–352.

Loomis, J. (1998). Balcony incident spurs plans for women's shelter. *Edmonton Sun*, p. 1A.

Maiuro, R. (1998, March/April). Interviewed in "Can they stop?" *Psychology Today*, p. 83.

Marano, H. (1993, November/December). Inside the heart of marital violence. *Psychology Today*, pp. 50–53, 76–78, 91.

Martinez, J. (1996). Hostage in the home. In *Pennsylvania coalition against rape. Victim empowerment*. Washington, D.C.: U.S. Department of Justice, pp. 58–73.

Marzuk, P., Tardiff, K., and Hirsch, C. (1992). The epidemiology of murder-suicide. *Journal of the American Medical Association 267*(23): 3179–3183.

McKay, M. M. (1994). The link between domestic violence and child abuse: Assessment and treatment considerations. *Child Welfare 63*(1): 29–39.

McKenzie, I. K. (1984). Hostage-captor relationship: Some behavioral and environmental determinants. *Police Studies 9*(4): 219–223.

Miller, B. A., Downs, W. R., and Gondoli, D. M. (1989). Spousal violence among alcoholic women as compared to a random household sample of women. *Journal of Studies on Alcohol 50:* 533–540.

Miller, J., and White, N. (2003). Gender and adolescent relationship violence: A contextual examination. *Criminology 41*(4): 1207–1245.

Miller, S. (2003). Arrest policies for domestic violence: Their implications for battered women. In R. Muraskin (ed.), *It's a crime: Women and justice*, 3rd ed. (pp. 307–329). Upper Saddle River, N.J.: Prentice Hall.

Morrill, A., Dai, J., Dunor, S., Sung, I., and Smith, K. (2005). Child custody and visitation decisions when the father has perpetrated violence against the mother. In *Violence Against Women 11*(8): 1076–1107.

Muchkenfuss, M. (1998, September 13). Battering in teen relationships, too. *Des Moines Register*, p. 6E.

Murphy, C. M., and O'Farrell, T. J. (1997). Couple communication patterns of maritally aggressive and nonaggressive male alcoholics. *Journal of Studies on Alchohol 15*, 83–90.

Natera, G. R., Tiburcio, M. S., and Villatoro, J. V. (1997). *Contemporary Drug Problems 24*(4): 787–804.

National Institute of Justice (2003, September). *Do battering intervention programs work? Two studies*. Washington, D.C.: U.S. Department of Justice.

National Institute of Justice (2004). *NIJ's violence against women research and evaluation program: Selected results*. Violence against women, and family violence. Retrieved from www.ojp.usdoj.gov/nij/vawprog.

National Research Council. (1996). *Understanding violence against women*. Washington, D.C.: National Academy Press.

Nifong, C. (1997, October 21). A full-court press on domestic abuse. *Christian Science Monitor*, p. 1.

Pagelow, M. (1992). Adult victims of domestic violence. *Journal of Interpersonal Violence 7*: 87–120.

Painter, K., and Farrington, D. P. (1998). Marital violence in Great Britain and its relationship to marital and non-marital rape. *International Review of Victimology 5*: 257–276.

Palermo, G. B. (1994). Murder-suicide—An extended suicide. *International Journal of Offender Therapy and Comparative Criminology 8*(3): 205–216.

Pence, E. (1999). Some thoughts on philosophy. In M. Shepard and E. Pence (eds.), *Coordinating community responses to domestic violence: Lessons from Duluth and beyond* (pp. 25–40). Thousand Oaks, Calif.: Sage.

Pence, E., and Paymar, M. (1993). *Education groups for men who batter*. New York: Springer.

Pollock, J. M. (1998). *Counseling women in prison*. Thousand Oaks, Calif.: Sage.

Presser, L., and Gaarder, E. (2004). Can restorative justice reduce battering? In B. R. Price and N. J. Solokoff (eds.), *The criminal justice system and women offenders, prisoners, mothers and workers,* 3rd ed. (pp. 403–418). New York: McGraw-Hill.

Ptacek, J. (1997). The tactics and strategies of men who batter: Testimony from women seeking restraining orders. *Violence between intimate partners: Patterns, causes, and effects* (pp. 104–123). Boston: Allyn & Bacon.

Randall, M., and Haskell, L. (1995). Sexual violence in women's lives. *Violence against Women 9* (1): 6–31.

Raschick, M., and Shephard, M. (1997, June 20). How child welfare workers assess and intervene around issues of domestic violence. A paper presented at the Fifth International Family Violence Research Conference, Durham, N.H.

Rennison, C. M. (2003). Intimate partner violence 1993–2001. Bureau of Justice Statistics (BJS). Washington, D.C.: U.S. Department of Justice.

Resnick, H., Kilpatrick, D., Walsh, C., and Vernonen, L. (1991). Marital rape. In R. Ammerman and M. Herson (eds.), *Case studies in family violence.* New York: Plenum.

Richey, W. (2005, June 28). Court sides with police in restraining order case. *Christian Science Monitor,* p. 25.

Roberts, A. R. (1996). Battered women who kill: A comparative study of incarcerated participants with a community sample of battered women. *Journal of Family Violence 11*(3): 291–304.

Roberts, A. R. (1997). Epidemiology and definitions of acute crisis in American society. In A. Roberts (ed.), *Crisis management and brief treatment* (pp. 16–33). Chicago: Nelson-Hall.

Roberts, A. R., and Burman, S. (1998). Crisis intervention and cognitive problem-solving therapy with battered women: A national survey and practice model. In A. Roberts (ed.), *Battered women and their families,* 2nd ed. (pp. 3–28). New York: Springer.

Rollins, J. H. (1996). *Women's minds, women's bodies: The psychology of women in a biosocial context.* Upper Saddle River, N.J.: Prentice-Hall.

Roos, J. (1997, June 30). Abuse victim leads battle cry against violence. *Des Moines Register,* p. 1.

Rothenberg, B. (2003, October). "We don't have time for social change": Cultural compromise and the battered woman syndrome. *Gender and Society 17*(5): 771–787.

Sakai-shi. (1995). *The report of the 3rd study of attitudes towards human rights.* Osaka: Author.

Saunders, D. G. (1995). Domestic violence: Legal issues. In *Encyclopedia of social work,* 19th ed. (pp. 789–794). Washington, D.C.: NASW Press.

Schakowsky, J. (2005, September 3). Indian immigrant women in U.S. are trapped in abusive marriages. Retrieved from www.newmindpress.com.

Schechter, S. (1982). *Women and male violence.* New York: Macmillan.

Shepard, M., Falk, D., and Raschick, M. (2000, October). Final report of the evaluation of the enhanced domestic abuse intervention project. Paper presented at the Partner Abuse Intervention 2000 Research, Practice and Criminal Justice Conference. Springfield, Ill.

Shepard, M., and Raschick, M. (1999, March 10–13). Domestic violence training for child welfare workers: Implications for social work and education. Paper presented at the Council on Social Work Education, Orlando, Fla.

Sherman, L. W., and Berk, R. A. (1984). The specific deterrent effects of arrest for domestic assault. *American Sociological Review 49:* 261–272.

Sherman, L. W., and Cohn, E. G. (1989). The impact of research on legal policy: The Minneapolis domestic violence experiment. *Law and Society Review 23:* 117–144.

Smith, A. (2003). Battered women on mandatory arrest laws: A comparison across three states. In R. Muraskin (ed.), *It's a crime: Women and justice* (pp. 380–393). Upper Saddle River, N.J.: Prentice Hall.

Sokoloff, N. (1995). *The criminal justice system and women: Offenders, victims, and workers* (pp. 228–245). New York: McGraw-Hill.

Sorenson, S. B., and Telles, C. A. (1991). Self-reports of spousal violence in a Mexican-American and non-Hispanic white population. *Violence and Victims* 6(1): 3–15.

Stalans, L., and Finn, M. (2000). Gender differences in officers' perceptions and decisions about domestic violence cases. *Women & Criminal Justice* 11(3): 1–24.

Stark, E., and Flitcraft, A. (1998). Women and children at risk. In R. K. Bergen (ed.), *Issues in intimate violence* (pp. 25–41). Thousand Oaks, Calif.: Sage.

Statistics Canada (2005). *Family violence in Canada: A statistical profile 2005*. Ottawa: Statistics Canada.

Stordeur, R. A., and Stille, R. (1989). *Ending men's violence against their partners*. Newbury Park, Calif.: Sage Publications.

Stosny, S. (1997). Group treatment of spouse abusers. In G. L. Greif and P. H. Ephrons (eds.), *Group work with populations at risk* (pp. 147–159). New York: Oxford University Press.

Straus, M., and Gelles, R. (1986). Societal change and change in family violence from 1975 to 1985 as revealed by two national surveys. *Journal of Marriage and the Family* 48: 465–479.

Straus, M. A., and Gelles, R. J. (1990). How violent are American families? Estimates from the National Family Violence Resurvey and other studies. In M. A. Straus and R. J. Gelles (eds.), *Physical violence in American families: Risk factors and adaptations to violence in 8,145 families* (pp. 95–112). New Brunswick, N.J.: Transaction.

Stuart, G., Moore, T., Ramsey, S., and Kahler, C. (2004, January). Hazardous drinking and relationship violence perpetration and victimization in women arrested for domestic violence. *Journal of Studies on Alcohol* 65(1): 46–54.

Swink, S. (2005, Fall). No restraint: A troubling Supreme Court decision weakens women's protection from abusers. *Ms. Magazine*: 63.

Tjaden, P., and Thoennes, N. (2000). *Full report of the prevalence, incidence, and consequences of violence against women: Findings from the national violence against women survey*. Bureau of Justice Statistics. Washington, D.C.: U.S. Department of Justice.

Tolman, R. M., and Bennett, L. W. (1990). A review of quantitative research on men who batter. *Journal of Interpersonal Violence* 5: 87–118.

Ulrich, Y. C. (1998). What helped most in leaving spouse abuse: Implications for interventions. In J. C. Campbell (ed.), *Empowering survivors of abuse: Health care for battered women and their children* (pp. 70–78). Thousand Oaks, Calif.: Sage.

USA Today (2005, February 7). Groups challenge Arizona spousal rape law. *USA Today*. Retrieved from www.usatoday.com/news.

van Wormer, K., and Davis, D. R. (2003). *Addiction treatment: A strengths perspective*. Belmont, Calif.: Brooks/Cole.

Violence Policy Center (VPC). (2006). American roulette: The untold story of murder-suicide in the United States, VPC. Retrieved from www.vpc.org/studyndx.htm.

Vitanza, S., Vogel, L. C., and Marshall, L. L. (1995). *Violence and Victims* 10(1): 23–34.

Wallace, H. (1998). *Victimology: Legal, psychological, and social perspectives*. Boston: Allyn & Bacon.

Walker, L. (1979). *The battered woman*. New York: Harper and Row.

Wells, W., and DeLeon-Granados, W. (2004, June). The intimate partner homicide decline: Disaggregated trends, theoretical explanations, and policy implications. *Criminal Justice Policy Review* 15(2): 229–246.

West, C. M. (1998a). Leaving a second closet: Outing partner violence in same-sex couples. In J. Jasinski and L. Williams (eds.), *Partner violence: A comprehensive review of 20 years of research* (pp. 163–183). Thousand Oaks, Calif.: Sage.

West, C. M. (1998b). Lifting the political gag order: Breaking the silence around partner violence in ethnic minority families. In J. Jasinski and L. Williams (eds.), *Partner violence: A comprehensive review of 20 years of research* (pp. 184–209). Thousand Oaks, Calif.: Sage.

Yoshihama, M. (1998). Domestic violence in Japan: Research program development and emerging movements. In A. Roberts (ed.), *Women and their families* (pp. 405–447). New York: Springer.

Zimbardo, P. G., Haney, C., and Banks, W. C. (1972, April 8). A Pirandellian prison: The mind is a formidable jailer. *New York Times Magazine*, pp. 38–60.

10 Women's Victimization: Global Perspectives

The study of the victimization of women is incomplete without a consideration of the treatment of women worldwide. While we recognize that the offering of such a global view is a first in a book of this kind, we made the decision to write an international chapter for several reasons. The first consideration is the impact of **globalization,** the fact that due to the growth of the global economy and the revolution in communication technologies, the world is growing palpably smaller. This impact of this commercial "flattening" of the world (see Friedman's *The World Is Flat,* 2005) is seen not only in the lowering of trade and political barriers, but also in the nature of crime, the passage and enforcement of transnational laws, and the victimization of women. Feminist theory recognizes that economic factors stemming from global competition play a part in the international exploitation of women's labor and the trade in girls' and women's bodies. The ubiquity of organized crime, terrorism, drug abuse, and the sex trade industry graphically illustrates the interconnectedness of nations in this regard. Attention to such issues and to human rights violations today has catapulted to the forefront of international media concerns.

The second reason for a chapter on global perspectives reflects the increasing numbers of undocumented immigrants and refugees and the concomitant diversification of the U.S. population. The reality of global interdependence, in fact, extends to every profession in the criminal justice field. The case can easily be made, therefore, that to be a culturally competent correctional worker, a familiarity with the values and customs of diversified populations is required.

The third and perhaps most salient argument for including an international chapter in a criminal justice text is that we have so much to learn from other countries. All nations face more or less the same problems, yet the solutions are varied. At the policy-making level, acknowledgment of other nations' approaches to the prevention of crime, the resolution of domestic conflict, the enacting and enforcing of laws, and the protection of vulnerable women can contribute to the resolution of domestic problems. Such comparative study reveals the commonality of social problems across the world and the fact that solutions found to work in one country might be worth a try elsewhere. Comparative criminology, furthermore, introduces the student to creative options of proven feasibility and to ideas that might someday be the inspiration for grant-funded research or be incorporated in state legislation for improved correctional services. From a research standpoint, when a correlation (as between pregnancy and battering by the spouse) is found in one nation, and then the correlation holds in one or more other nations surveyed, this fact helps give credence to the original finding. From the broader perspective, global truths help resolve the issue of whether or not certain behaviors (for example, rape) are culturally specific or whether they are universal in nature.

In summary, a multicultural worldview can direct our attention to new concepts, theoretical frameworks, and approaches that never would have been contemplated otherwise. This is what critical thinking is all about—developing a perspective based on a comprehensive, "no-holds-barred" knowledge base. Through learning about alternative attitudes and programming, for example, we can come to appreciate the uniqueness of American values. Relevant to women's issues is the belief in gender equality (relatively), individualism, the primacy of the nuclear family, and moralism played out as punitiveness (van Wormer, 2004). We can also, through a global view, come to appreciate how prevalent are certain negative cultural characteristics so closely associated in the public mind with the United States—classism, racism, and sexism, for example.

This chapter has as its starting point an examination of international law through relevant human rights documents; such documents provide a template for the study of the mistreatment of women worldwide as well as a universal standard according to which the treatment of women can be measured. The major part of the chapter is devoted to human rights violations that are gendered—for example, the sex trade in women, punishment of women for disobedience of sex-restrictive laws such as not wearing a veil, femicide that includes "honor killings" in places such as Jordan and Pakistan, "dowry deaths" (or killings related to dowry disputes), genital mutilation, rape in war, and the victimization of female refugees. A related issue is the harsh treatment of women prisoners worldwide and of immigrant women who are detained in U.S. detention centers and prisons. The plight of immigrant women married to abusive men is also explored.

The final portion of the chapter is devoted to positive developments across the world from which Americans have much to learn. These are initiatives of empowerment, ideas that have been tested in various parts of the world. In New Zealand, restorative justice conferencing reveals a potential for providing justice in cases of abuse and sexual assault; in Brazil, a women's police station supports female victims of family violence; and an all-women's village in Kenya opens its doors to escapees from male violence. In these and other countries, the role of international nongovernmental organizations (NGOs) has been prominent in opening the eyes of the world to anti-female abuses. NGOs have engaged in social action, for example, in reuniting abducted and sexually abused girls with their families. And more often, they have investigated crimes against humanity, such as the mass raping of women in wartime.

Feminist criminological theory is the underlying theoretical framework for this chapter. A focus on empowerment of women is integral to this perspective. Feminist criminological theory provides an important grounding for the understanding of the treatment of women worldwide in locating sources of women's oppression in social practices of the wider societal structure. This theoretical approach offers an alternative vision of crime in directing our attention to **gender-based violence,** or crimes committed against women because they are women. Feminist writers, increasingly, are turning their attention to events of global import. For an overview of women's victimization in global perspective, see Box 10.1 below.

BOX **10.1**

Women's Victimization: Global Perspectives

Press Release from Worldwatch Institute

Despite the widespread belief that women have "come a long way," International Women's Day will still see millions of women from all parts of the world trapped in lives where they are not allowed to attend schools, own property, vote, earn wages, or control their bodies and where violence is a constant threat.

Unfortunately, statistics point to a much bleaker world where on too many fronts, women are still struggling to gain equal rights.

- Over half a million women die each year from preventable complications during pregnancy and childbirth; another 18 million are left disabled or chronically ill. In other words, more than 1,300 women will die while giving birth on International Women's Day alone.
- Worldwide, AIDS infection rates are now higher for women than men. In sub-Saharan Africa, where AIDS is spreading faster than anywhere else on the planet, women account for 55 percent of all new cases of HIV. Sadly, most of these women lack the sexual autonomy to refuse sex or demand that their "partner" use a condom.
- Twenty to 50 percent of all women have experienced violence from a so-called "loved one." Gender-based violence takes many forms and plagues girls and women throughout their lives. An estimated 60,000 girls are considered "missing" in China and India because of sex-selective abortions,

female infanticide, and neglect. In 2000, more than 5,000 girls were murdered by their parents or other family members because they spoke to boys on the street or "dishonored" the family by becoming a rape victim. More than 2 million women undergo female genital mutilation each year, which leads to a lifetime of suffering.

- Two thirds of the world's 876 million illiterate people are female. In 22 African and 9 Asian nations, school enrollment for girls is less than 80 percent that for boys, and only about half of girls in the least developed nations stay in school after grade 4. In sub-Saharan Africa and South Asia, only between 2 and 7 women per 1,000 attend high school or college.
- In most parts of the world, women-headed households are much more vulnerable to poverty than those headed by males. In the United States, single-mother households are raising one-third of the children living in poverty.
- Throughout most of the world women earn on average two thirds to three fourths as much as men for the same work. In addition, women perform most of the invisible work that keeps families going day to day. However, housekeeping, child care, water fetching, collection of firewood, and other activities mainly performed by women are rarely included

(continued)

B O X   **10.1**   Continued

in economic accounting, although their value is about one third of the world's economic production.

■ Women are still vastly underrepresented in all levels of government and in international institutions despite high-profile leaders like Gloria Macapagal-Arroyoomen, the president of the Philippines, and former First Lady and now Senator Hillary Clinton. At the United Nations, women only made up 21 percent of senior management in 1999. In only 9 countries is the proportion of women national parliament membership at 30 percent or above. And as of mid-2001, at least seven nations—Djibouti, Jordan, Kuwait, Palau, Tonga, Tuvalu, and Vanuatu—did not have a single woman sitting on their legislatures.

"There is ample evidence that when women take political power, issues important to women and their families—such as maternal care, nutrition, and family planning—rise

in priority and are acted upon by those in power," says Worldwatch [Institute] Staff Researcher Danielle Nierenberg.

And providing the resources to keep girls in schools can be more effective than improved sanitation, employment, or higher income in boosting child survival rates. U.N. sources show that the nations with the highest levels of schooling in sub-Saharan Africa—Botswana, Kenya, and Zimbabwe—are also the nations with the lowest levels of child mortality, despite higher levels of poverty than many of their neighbors.

Nierenberg continues, "Ultimately what is good for women, is good for the world. The full participation and full empowerment of the world's women is a keystone for any meaningful sustainable development strategy. But we still have a long way to go before women have the same rights as men."

Source: Worldwatch Institute, 2003. Reprinted with permission of Worldwatch Institute.

The Impact of Globalization

Globalization can be looked at in a number of contexts, both positive and negative, that are relevant to the lives of women. First, as noted by Dominelli (2002), increasing global interconnectedness has resulted in social problems that transcend national boundaries. Among these problems are the plight of women refugees escaping the ravages of war; the mass emigration of immigrants escaping personal and political violence; sex trafficking; and women used as "mules" to transport illegal drugs across borders. The war on drugs is a war of global proportions, and its impact falls sharply on the shoulders of women. A second context, from an economic perspective, is the impact of market-driven measures of capitalism as evidenced in the reduction of social services through cutbacks, the privatization of services, and the deprofessionalization of workers. The loss of welfare benefits and services by the state, in conjunction with deinstitutionalization of mental patients, in turn, has increased the numbers of homeless young people roaming the streets; this fact has intensified the vulnerability of girls and women to sexual victimization, sexual exploitation, and drug use. Consider also the reduction in funding for victim assistance services and women's shelters. Third, global market forces pave the way for agency consolidation and corporate management techniques with the result that men displace women managers (Dominelli, 2000). This fact is seen in connection with the masculinization of correctional services and standardization of treatment philosophies (see Chapter 6). The bulk of the funding here has gone to high-tech security systems and to surveillance rather than to educational and counseling services. The fourth aspect of globalization relates to the clash of civilizations through the communications revolution. The fear in certain quarters across the globe is that if women's consciousness is raised, they will demand their rights. A counter-reaction, therefore, has taken place, a backlash by entrenched forces with a vested interest in the status quo. This backlash is especially pronounced in regions of the world where religious fundamentalism has been used to threaten women and suppress them. Economic competition undoubtedly plays a role in what has been termed the "world's war against women" as well.

Worldwide, as competition for well-paying and secure jobs in a global economy heats up, dangerous right-wing extremist movements are seizing political power. The mistreatment of women globally tends to be expressed in the guise of an attack on modernization, including the threatened liberation of women (van Wormer, 2004).

Economic globalization, or the macroeconomic policies associated with the global economy, has important human rights implications. Such policies require that the non-industrialized nations reduce their indebtedness to the world banks by reducing social welfare spending of the kind that makes life livable. Relevant to economic inequities, women perform two-thirds of the world's work but earn only one-tenth of all income; women own less than one-tenth of the world's property (Human Rights Watch, 2002a). People in a position of economic servitude to others who have control over the resources are generally vulnerable to mistreatment, and they have little recourse for justice. Economic destitution makes a young woman ripe for sexual exploitation, including being tricked into prostitution with the promise of a lucrative job abroad.

It stands to reason that as the economy improves in a country, more girls are educated, birth control is practiced more widely, women move into the work force, and the lives of women improve. The United Nations (U.N.) (2005) in a new report has reversed the proposition that ending poverty is key to ending violence against women by stating instead that stopping violence against women is the key to eliminating poverty. This is because women who are not terrorized by violence, and live in circumstances of gender equality, are free to make decisions concerning family size and to access health care for themselves and for their children, including girls, thereby reducing incidences of harmful traditional practices. Studies show that when women control the family spending, they are more likely than men to invest a higher percentage of their earnings in family needs (U.N., 2005).

The adoption of a human rights framework is increasingly relevant today, given the realities of the global market. A human rights discourse can provide a basis for awareness of, and alternatives to, the global regime that reinforces structures of disadvantage "through blatantly undemocratic processes which result in benefits for the few rather than the many" (Ife, 2001, p. 202). For a study of the human rights of women at three levels—family, community, and state—read criminologist Edna Erez's insightful analysis in Box 10.2.

BOX 10.2

Women as Victims and Survivors in the Context of Transnational Crime

by Edna Erez, LL.B., Ph.D.
Professor, Justice Studies Department
Kent State University

Transnational crime is now recognized as a pressing global problem. With diminishing barriers of language, communication, information, technology transfer, and mobility, and with the ever-increasing globalization of the economy, there has been a growing transnational character of crime (including organized, financial, immigration, computer, and sex-related criminality).

Transnational crime presents intricate problems of victimization for all vulnerable people, but it has had a disproportionately adverse impact on women. For instance, it is well documented that migration exacerbates the gender-linked vulnerability of women; it makes them further dependent on, and at times at the mercy of, husbands, sponsors, or employers, nuclear or extended families, and their own ethnic/racial communities (Erez, 2000). The United Nations Population Division and the U.N. High Commissioner for Refugees (1993) estimate that at a minimum 2 percent of the world's population are migrants. This estimate translates into a large number of women who are affected by migration. Furthermore, the rapid globalization of the world's economies and polities will ensure that the number of migrants, at least half of whom are women (in some countries women actually account for the overwhelming majority of migrants), will increase substantially in all of the world's major geographical regions well into the twenty-first century (Teitelbaum and Russell, 1994).

The victimization of women, however, is one of the most difficult issues to redress because it is related to deep-seated gender ideologies (e.g., prevalent notions that women are inferior to or dependent on men) which often tolerate, and in some instances even encourage, victimization. Poverty, racism, and xenophobia interact with such ideologies and exacerbate women's victimization (e.g., Daly, 1994). Current global economic strategies and the power divide between first- and third-world countries reinforce or heighten these conditions, although their impact on women may differ between regions. For instance, the "democratization" of formerly socialist countries has resulted in huge losses for women at the social, economic, and political levels, evidenced by women's higher unemployment rates, or the elimination of child care options due to the breakdown of socialist infrastructures. These changes have also made women from these countries particularly vulnerable to trafficking and exploitation.[1] Because these phenomena transcend geographical borders, the international community has a shared interest in collectively addressing the problem.

Women's Victimization and Transnational Crime: Definitions and Strategy Issues

No single agreed upon definition of women's victimization exists, but a range of activities is commonly subsumed under this concept. Women's victimization commonly includes violence against women, which is sometimes referred to as gender violence, and sexual exploitation (Kelly, 1999). This victimization is perpetrated by a variety of offenders in the private and public spheres, and encompasses, but is not limited to, physical, sexual, and psychological harm occurring in or inflicted by:

A. The family (for instance, woman battering; sexual abuse of girls in the household; dowry-related violence; marital rape; genital mutilation; honor killings and other

(continued)

BOX **10.2** Continued

traditional practices harmful to women such as sati, nonspousal violence, and violence related to exploitation).

B. The community (for instance, rape; sexual abuse; harassment or intimidation at work, in public, or in educational or other institutions; trafficking in women and forced prostitution).

C. The state (violence perpetrated or condoned by the state, such as rape during armed conflicts or cultural wars; forced abortions or sterilization; custodial rape and sexual harassment by police and prison guards; secondary victimization upon reporting crimes to the police) (ICCLR, 1999).

Sexual exploitation commonly refers to trafficking (quasi-voluntary and involuntary) of women and girls for the international sex industry—prostitution, entertainment, and pornography—and is now increasingly understood to encompass domestic help, forced or arranged marriages, "mail order" brides, temporary wives, or marriages of convenience.

Equally important to reaching a consensus on definitions of victimization is arriving at an agreement on universal standards about acceptable and unacceptable behaviors. The starting point for a discussion of women's victimization must be the protection of women and girls from any form of victimization. Researchers and activists have noted that acts that constitute victimization violate women's integrity and dignity, and result in a reduction in opportunities, quality of life, health, freedom, and autonomy. The 1993 U.N. World Congress on Human Rights has defined some of the facets of women's victimization as a violation of human rights[2] (see also Coalition Against Trafficking in Women, 1999).

Research has also identified multiple practical concerns and barriers to reporting of women's victimization. In addition to difficulties encountered by all abused women, such as threats by abusers, cultural attitudes that minimize or excuse victimization, and

lack of confidence in the justice system, immigrant women experience unique barriers. They include language and communication problems, a lack of information about the legal process or availability of support and assistance, perceived or anticipated racism, xenophobia, discrimination by the justice system, a fear of accessing the system based on historical or prior negative experiences, or of being deported or returned to their home countries (Erez, 2000; Narayan, 1995). For women who are undocumented, or have been forced to engage in illegal activities, including forced prostitution, the barriers to report victimization are compounded. These barriers to reporting crime must be eliminated so that women who manage to overcome their fear of authorities or cultural proscriptions about disclosing abuse and make the difficult decision to report their victimization are supported.

References

Coalition Against Trafficking in Women (1999). Sex: From intimacy to "sexual labor," or Is it a human right to prostitute? CATW: South East Asia.

Daly, K. (1994) Criminal law and justice system practices as racist, white, and racialized. *Washington & Lee Law Review 51*(2):431–464.

Erez, E. (2000). Immigration, culture conflict and domestic violence/woman battering. *Crime Prevention and Community Safety: An International Journal* 2(2):17–21.

ICCLR (International Centre for Criminal Law Reform and Criminal Justice Policy) (1999). *Strategies to eliminate violence against women: A resource manual.* Vancouver, Canada (in conjunction with CICP/ODCCP, HEUNI, and UNALI).

Kelly, L. (1999) *Violence against women.* British Council, London.

Narayan, U. (1995) "Male order" brides: Immigrant women domestic violence and immigration law. *Hypatia 10*(1):104–119.

Teitelbaum, M. S., and Russell S. S. (1994). Fertility, international migration, and development, in Robert Cassen (ed.), *Population and development: Old debates, new conclusions,* pp. 229–252. New Brunswick (U.S.) and Oxford (U.K.): Transaction Publishers.

(continued)

BOX **10.2** Continued

United Nations High Commissioner for Refugees (UNHCR)(1993). *The state of the world's refugees: The challenges of protection.* New York: Penguin Books, p. 153.

Critical Thinking Questions: What is the nature of female victimization worldwide? What are some of the barriers to women's reporting such victimization?

[1]Norma Hotaling of SAGE (Standing Against Global Exploitation) in San Francisco, one of the presenters in the module of "women as victims and survivors," noted in her presentation the increase in the streets of American cities in the numbers of Russian and other eastern European women who were forced into prostitution. The recent *NBC Dateline* program with Maria Shriver that aired on April 28, 2000, also presented the plight of Ukrainian women and the way they were lured by false promises for well-paying domestic help jobs or similar respectable occupations, and then were trafficked to become sex slaves in the Czech Republic, in other European countries, or the United States.

[2]Amnesty International (May 2000) has, for the first time, listed trafficking in women as human rights abuses. Trading in women, along with torture, slavery, and jailing "prisoners of conscience" are considered human rights violations. The Amnesty International report used Israel as a case study to describe and analyze the various factors that shape the extent and methods of trading in women, particularly women from the former Soviet Union and east European countries. It outlines the mechanism by which hundreds of women a year are smuggled, imprisoned, exploited, raped continuously, blackmailed, and physically and sexually abused, and the reasons for the minimal attempts made to combat this human rights violation.

Source: Edna Erez (2000, April 10–17). Women as Victims and Survivors in the Context of Transnational Crime. Paper presented at the 10th U.N. Congress on Crime Prevention and the Treatment of Offenders, Vienna, Austria. Printed with permission of Edna Erez.

Women's Rights Are Human Rights

According to the modern human rights perspective, there are universal principles that transcend individual national practices and cultural norms when these principles are violated. International pressure then can be exerted on the nations involved, often first through nongovernmental organizations, which report to the United Nations at the second and final level; intervention may take place to protect the individuals and groups whose rights are being violated. Over most of the course of human rights history (the starting point was in the 1940s with the passage of the Universal Declaration of Human Rights) issues of gender have been ignored. Much of the reason lay in the philosophy of cultural relativism, the belief that we must respect cultural tradition, even those that seem abhorrent to us because of our own cultural conditioning. This reluctance of social scientists, including feminists, to appear ethnocentric, to judge other people according to principles of Western society, is understandable. But this reluctance has meant that until relatively recently, such abuses as family murders for adultery ("honor killings") and mutilation of girls' genital organs were not investigated and rarely, if ever, mentioned in the literature. And it would have been thought that it is up to the women in the individual countries to bring about the changes they desired without outside interference.

This hands-off attitude has changed drastically in recent years as reformers—feminists and other social activists—in collaboration with indigenous women or women who have become refugees from violence—increasingly look to international law. The focus on human rights is, by definition, international—the belief in higher laws that transcend national laws. This broadening of focus is a legacy of the Nuremburg Trials that followed World War II when Nazi leaders were judged by a world body (albeit one organized by the victors) for crimes against humanity. Even more significant as a legacy was the United Nations Declaration of Human Rights that was adopted in 1948.

The Declaration's significance is that it gave the world, for the first time in history, international principles on the basis of which sovereign nations could be held accountable. This human rights document transcends social justice to civil and political customs, in consideration of the basic life-sustaining needs of all human beings, without distinction (National Association of Social Work, 2003).

The U.N. document consists of two covenants: one for political and civil rights; another for economic, social, and cultural rights. The civil and political rights against the arbitrary powers of the state are the ones that concern us here. The United Nations Declaration of Human Rights had included women as an at-risk population since it was written in 1948. Yet, just as with the Civil Rights Act of 1964, which forbade discrimination on grounds of sex, little heed was paid to gender issues until women organized to demand it. It was largely through their participation in the U.N. world conference that women's groups have brought attention to the United Nations as a key forum for advancing women's rights (Fried, 1997). "Human rights are women's rights" became the motto of the international movement to protect women from abuse. In 1995, women linked up from Austria to Zambia at the United Nations Fourth World Conference on Women. The historic conference was held at Huaira and Beijing, China. Whereas at previous women's conferences, feminists from the westernized nations were reluctant to even appear to criticize traditions from other parts of the world for fear of being accused of lacking cultural sensitivity, this time women's voices were united on behalf of the many who are unable to speak. At the 1995 conference, the debate on health and reproductive rights was led primarily by delegates who were neither Western nor white. In demanding that women's rights should supersede national traditions, the Beijing accord marked a historic breakthrough (Chesler and Dunlop, 1995). It was only after the Beijing conference that Amnesty International, the well-known NGO that has done so much to publicize human rights abuses worldwide, took up the call.

Today feminists and human rights activists unreservedly endorse the human rights of people as a universal value that takes precedence over cultural norms when cultural norms conflict with such values. However much rituals such as the genital mutilation of girls and women or the infanticide of females are integrated with cultural and religious beliefs, such practices are actively opposed and condemned as human rights violations.

According to a conference document of the United Nations Fourth World Conference on Women (Mason, 1995), the cultural origins of this violence are in the historically unequal power relations between men and women. Indeed, the low social and economic status of women can be both a cause and a consequence of violence against women. The dowry bride burnings in India (an illegal custom in which a bride is set on fire by her in-laws if the demands for dowry payment from the bride's family are unmet), which number over five a day, illustrate crass materialism at its extreme. A report by the United Nations International Children's Fund (UNICEF, 2003) calls for international solidarity against anti-female homicides such as the honor killings in Pakistan (to "restore honor" to a family when an unmarried woman lost her virginity whether she had been raped or not), the acid attacks on women in Bangladesh who had displeased men, and the bride deaths in India. Stone and James (1995) studied the phenomenon in India in terms of recent changes in women's roles and sources of female power. Bride burnings occur most often in cases of arranged marriages and among the urban middle class. As India has shifted to a market cash economy, the new consumerism has put more value on the size of the dowry itself than on the woman. Economic discrimination against women and their vulnerability to violence are thus intertwined (van Wormer, 2004).

The United Nations adopted the Convention on the Elimination of All Forms of Discrimination against Women in 1979. The United States stands alone among Western nations in its reluctance to ratify this document. (President Jimmy Carter signed it, but the U.S. Senate has never ratified it; the major concern is about the preservation of the traditional family.) If the United States would join other nations in endorsing this treaty, it would provide a tool for women fighting for their lives across the world; it would strengthen, not weaken, the family. Such human rights laws, as Watkinson (2001) indicates, "provide a valuable theoretical and practical base for assisting in social change" (p. 271). Because Canada was a signatory (unlike the United States) to the Covenant on Economic, Social and Political Rights, human rights activists in that country can turn to international law as a valuable tool for advocacy for social and economic justice within the era of globalization. Their counterparts in the United States are relatively limited in this regard.

Around the globe, death by stoning in Iran and Nigeria, genital mutilation in twenty-eight African nations, rape of young girls in South Africa in the belief that sex with a virgin will cure AIDS, dowry deaths in India and Pakistan, sexual slavery in Thailand, and wife abuse in all countries have shocked the sensibilities of humanists. The savage suppression of women by the Taliban in Afghanistan received enormous media attention in the 1990s. It was only after September 11, however, that the American government, which had previously looked the other way, called for the liberation of these women. Today, under a new regime in Afghanistan, many women are still forced to hide their bodies in the burqa and girls' schools are subject to burning. The treatment of women in the United States, although strikingly better than their treatment in some parts of the world, is not exempt from international concern. According to an Amnesty International (2001) investigation, *Broken Bodies, Shattered Minds*, family violence against women is a common occurrence in the United States. And two years before the writing of this document, the sexual abuse of women in U.S. prisons by male guards was the source of a major investigation (Amnesty International, 1999).

Violations of Women Domestically

Following Erez's (2000) organizational scheme, we begin with the family as the source of victimization. Under this category are included partner violence, dowry-related violence, marital rape, genital mutilation, and honor killing. Ponder the following headlines:

- "Entrenched Epidemic: Wife-Beatings in Africa" (LaFraniere, 2005, *The New York Times*)
- "Female Genital Mutilation a Vote-Winner in Sierra Leone" (*Afrol News*, 2005)
- "Pakistani Women: A Cruel Repression" (Rupert, 2005, *Newsday*)
- "Afghan Women Remain Victims of Hope Unfulfilled" (M. Landsberg, 2002, *Toronto Star*)
- "The Lack of Equal Rights for African Women Is a Central Cause of the Rapid Transmission of HIV/AIDS on the Continent" (UNIFEM, 2003)
- "Sierra Leone: Human Rights Watch Details Sexual Atrocities in Civil War" (United Nations, 2003a)
- "Book Credits Women's Shelters for Saving Men's Lives" (A. Wind, 2000, *Waterloo/Cedar Falls Courier*)

The **World Health Organization's (WHO)** (2002) comprehensive report, *World Report on Violence and Health*, provides data on gender-based violence worldwide. In recognition of the difficulty of making international comparisons, they have developed guidelines to help improve the comparability of data for future use. In the meantime, WHO relies on data from a wide range of national sources; these data suggest that partner violence accounts for a significant number of deaths by murder of women. Studies from Australia, Canada, Israel, South Africa, and the United States, for example, collectively show that 40–70 percent of female murder victims were killed by their boyfriends and husbands, frequently in the context of an ongoing abusive relationship.

In contrast to the American pattern in which the weapon of choice was a gun, in India, a large number of deaths among women, as mentioned above, were "bride burnings" and officially recorded as accidental burns. Indian feminists use the term **femicide** to fit the reality of such female-killing in their country (Russell, 2001b). This term also includes the common practice of elimination of female fetuses through abortion or of female infants through neglect. Such killing of females is considered femicide, according to Russell's definition, inasmuch as it is violence "in the interests of men" (p. 16). In China, the number of "missing females" is the highest in the world. At birth, the sex ratio is 117 boys to 100 girls (Banister, 2004). The Chinese "one-child" policy, coupled with modern technology (ultrasound tests), favors the selection of male over female children because parents, for economic reasons and tradition, favor having sons over daughters.

An especially brutal form of child abuse, one that has involved millions of girls throughout the world is known as **genital mutilation.** Genital mutilation is included by Russell (2001a) as a form of femicide because of the high rate of fatalities due to poor sanitation of instruments used and its indirect association with AIDS. Unknown numbers of girls and women who are butchered in this way contract the AIDS virus, either in the short term due the crude, unsanitary instruments used, or in early adulthood, due to the genital bleeding related to the mutilation when intercourse takes place. When the man is infected, the infection spreads. Russell suggests that this form of female abuse contributes to the massive numbers of women in some African nations who today are HIV positive.

As stated in the United Nations (1989) Convention on the Rights of the Child:

> Children have a right to protection from all forms of physical or mental violence, injury or abuse, negligent treatment, maltreatment, or exploitation, including sexual abuse, while in the care of parents, legal guardians, or any other person who has the care of the child. (Article 19)

International health authorities find the most extensive evidence of such customs on the African continent and Arabian peninsula (Steinem and Morgan, 2002). A high rate of mortality is suspected to occur. DeMause (2002), drawing on indigenous sources, graphically describes the procedure:

> The girl's sexuality is so hated that when she is five or so, the women grab her, pin her down, and chop off her clitoris and often her labia with a razor blade or piece of glass, ignoring her agony and screams for help, because, they say, her clitoris is "dirty," "ugly," "poisonous," "can cause a voracious appetite for promiscuous sex," and "might render men impotent." The area is then often sewn up to prevent intercourse, leaving only a tiny hole for urination. The genital mutilation is excruciatingly painful. (p. 341)

Such practices frequently are erroneously described as "female circumcision," a puberty ritual. Yet the degree of damage, psychological and physical, is not comparable to the African custom of male circumcision. Such male circumcision, although it may be considered abusive in its own right, is not, as Steinem and Morgan (2002) point out, performed for the purpose of destroying its victim's capacity for sexual pleasure.

Although some African countries such as Sudan, Egypt, Ghana, and Guinea have banned genital mutilation, in recognition of Western sensibilities, the laws, generally, are not enforced. Recently, the United Nations General Assembly's Special Session on children set a goal to work to end female genital mutilation (Bellamy, 2003).

Sexual oppression, too, rears its ugly head in the statistical anomaly of the births of far more males than females in parts of Southeast Asia. Griswold (2003), a journalist reporting on life in the Taliban-controlled area of Pakistan, for example, provides this description of an interview he had with a young mother: "How many children does she have now? 'Two,' she says. 'Three if you count the girl'"(p. 62).

In China, as mentioned above, a serious sex ratio disparity exists. One result of this deliberate disparity is that Chinese men are now paying up to $4,000 for kidnapped Vietnamese women to marry (Gittings, 2002). In India, there is a similar shortfall of women, despite a government ban on ultrasound. Young Indian men have difficulty finding wives (the girl/ boy ratio has dropped to 927 per 1,000 and far less in certain regions), so prosperous men are buying girls from poor villagers (Kennedy, 2004). Such children become part of a mass trafficking trade to meet the demand for brides, often to provide sexual favors to the men in an entire family.

Wife Beating

According to a World Health Report based on 48 surveys from around the world, between 10 and 69 percent of women report having been physically assaulted by a partner. In the United States, 22 percent report domestic violence (Lite, 2002).

In traditional societies, wife beating is largely regarded as a consequence of a man's right to inflict physical punishment on his wife—something indicated by studies from Bangladesh, Cambodia, India, Mexico, Nigeria, Pakistan, Papua New Guinea, and Zimbabwe (WHO, 2002). Research from industrialized and nonindustrialized nations alike shows that partner violence is justified by the perpetrator on the following grounds: the woman's arguing back, refusing sex, not having the meal ready, suspected infidelity, and disobedience. In many nations, women who were interviewed agreed that beatings were justified under certain circumstances. According to a *New York Times* report, about half of the women interviewed in a Zambian survey said husbands had a right to beat wives for cause—burning the dinner, for example, or refusing sex. But even where the culture grants men the right to beat their wives, there are limits. Studies reviewed by WHO suggest that women stay in abusive situations because of fear of retribution, lack of means of economic support, concern for the children, and the stigma attached to being unmarried. Research also showed that leaving such a relationship was not a one-time thing, that most women leave and return several times before making the final break (LaFraniere, 2005).

In a comparative study of sixteen societies, Counts, Browns, and Campbell (1992) found that societies with community sanctions against partner violence and support for abused women had the lowest levels of partner violence. Because maintaining shelters is expensive, many poor nations have set up an informal network of "safe houses" to deal with the emergency of domestic abuse. Nongovernmental organizations often offer specialized services for victims of abuse in countries in which they are active (WHO, 2002).

When a woman is pregnant she is at a high risk for physical abuse and loss of the developing fetus as well. Estimates of abuse during pregnancy range from 3 to 15 percent in population-based studies in Canada, Egypt, Nicaragua, Chile, and the United States (WHO, 2002).

Sexual abuse is a common co-occurring component of partner violence. In most countries, in fact, marital rape is considered an oxymoron. In Ethiopia, until recently, a man who wanted to marry a girl or women could kidnap and rape her, then agree to marry her and escape punishment (Women's Action, 2005). Since the girl or woman was defiled, the family had to agree to the arrangement. Recent legal reform removed the exemption for forced marriage from the crime of rape as abduction. So far, the new rape law has not been enforced.

In Pakistan, especially in southern Punjab province, women who are raped typically experience rejection by their family and society. Tribal traditions dictate that a raped woman is dishonored, cannot marry, and should be discarded, if not killed, by her family (Rupert, 2005). Suicide is common. This brings us to the tragic story of Dr. Shazia, a thirty-two-year-old Pakistani physician (Equality Now, 2005). Her story began with rape in her home by an intruder. When she reported the crime to the police, her employers and the government pressured her to keep silent. Her husband was supportive, but her father-in-law declared that she was a stain on the family honor. When she pursued the case, the President announced on television that her life was in danger. Shazia contemplated suicide but then decided to emigrate instead in hopes of getting political asylum somewhere. To date, she has not been granted asylum in any country. Although in this case it was probably not her family members who threatened her life, women in Pakistan who have been raped are at risk of honor killing by a male relative for a perceived violation to the family honor. An estimated 1,000 honor killings take place each year in Pakistan.

Honor Killing

Honor killing is the ancient practice in which men, often brothers, kill female relatives who have disgraced the family through sexual activity, even rape victimization. In Jordan, according to the UNICEF report, there are around 23 such murders per year; another 300 took place in 1997 in Pakistan and Yemen, and 52 in Egypt. Hundreds of women in Bangladesh are subjected to acid attacks while in India more than 5,000 women are killed each year because their in-laws consider their dowries inadequate.

Amnesty International's (2001) report *Broken Bodies, Shattered Minds* was a complement to earlier reports of sexual abuse of women in custody and the use of sexual violence as a weapon of war. In providing the results of investigations of abuses committed by private individuals, of acts of torture against women in the home, this report shows that women at risk of violence require protection, whether through refugee services that grant them the right of political asylum or safe places such as women's shelters in their own countries. Escape through emigration may be the only recourse. This brings us to the topic of immigration and the kind of domestic violence to which immigrants are uniquely subject.

Immigration and Domestic Violence

Many factors, notes Hochschild (2003), contribute to what she calls "the growing feminization of migration" (p. 17). Economic opportunity is one such factor; romantic attachments and the promise of happiness in a land where women have more freedom undoubtedly are others. In her discussion of battered immigrant women, Gilfus (2002) describes how immigration status can be used as a weapon of abuse by husbands who threaten to destroy vital documents and by threats to turn their wives over to the Immigration and Naturalization Service for deportation. A power imbalance takes place here because immigration laws allow men to sponsor their wives and thus to control their wives' immigration status. Many women also fear that the batterer himself, due to his violent behavior, might be deported or leave the country, taking the children with him.

A study of the experience of domestic violence among Cambodian refugees (who met in focus groups) revealed that, according to these women, such violence was often viewed as the woman's fault (Bhuyan et al., 2005). Divorced women faced disapproval within the community. The participants in the focus groups described extensive verbal abuse within their marriages. Some of the women described their husband's affairs with other women as a form of abuse. The women's wish for the future was for support from each other, not to end the marriage.

In her study of Vietnamese immigrants, Bui (2003) stressed the impact of resettlement on the man's sense of control and the impact of exposure to racism and classism in the new society. Downward mobility, changes in gender-role practices, and role reversals may cause family conflict and lead to aggression in immigrant families. Data drawn from interviews with the women in Bui's study showed that wife abuse occurred within the context of adjustment to life in a new and frustrating environment. Loss of status emerged as a key aspect in the men's personal adjustment. Moreover, when Vietnamese American women changed their attitudes toward gender equality while their husbands did not, the men sometimes tried to assert their control through violence.

Foreign wives of military men often have difficulties as well. Erez and Bach (2003) conducted in-depth interviews of ten immigrant women who were intimate partners of U.S. servicemen. Abuse of these "military brides" was a common occurrence, and the women's immigrant status and the military context compounded the abuse. While we know that military men, especially those returning from war, often have problems with violence at home (Zamichow and Perry, 2003), foreign women are especially vulnerable. They may not speak the language, lack familiarity with American cultural norms and the law, and tend to be socially isolated and dependent for their immigration status on the man. Military men who choose to marry foreign women may be atypical Americans in the sense that they may expect that a foreign woman would be submissive as well as extremely grateful for the opportunity to have material comforts not available at home. Such men may be personally insecure, in other words, and therefore prone to overreact when they feel threatened through interpersonal conflicts. Some of the men, if war veterans, may also be suffering the after-effects of warfare. Let us now look more closely at what the experience of combat does to a relationship.

The Legacy of the Iraq War

Unique to the military is the training of men (and women) to kill. In warfare, combat conditions the soldier kills almost as a reflex in a situation of danger. **Military**

socialization "to make a man out of the boy" not only attempts to obliterate all that is feminine but also breeds misogynous heterosexuality in the soldier as well (Farr, 2005). The degradation of traits associated with femininity such as weakness in battle, squeamishness, and compassion—traditionally associated with femininity—helps create or preserve masculine detachment and aggression desirable for battle. Such conditioning can be devastating for later family functioning.

On the homefront, a condition such as post-traumatic stress disorder (PTSD) or a state of intoxication (even being suddenly aroused from sleep) can trigger violence. Depression related to PTSD can lead to suicide. Anderson (2005) studied the seven homicides and three suicides that have taken place in western Washington State by returning soldiers from the war in Iraq. Five wives, one girlfriend, and a child have all been killed. Two of the suicides were committed after murder. These cases and others like them reported across the United States seem to suggest that as an antiwar slogan popular in the sixties said, "War is not good for people or other living things."

Community-Level Victimization: Sex Trafficking

Erez listed sex trafficking as an example of gender-based violence that stemmed from forces in the community—forces related to the big business of transnational organized crime. **Sex trafficking** is defined simply by Kathryn Farr (2005), the author of a book by that title, as "a business venture in which traffickers trade the sexualized bodies of others for money" (p. 2). As defined by WHO (2002), sexual trafficking "encompasses the organized movement of people, usually women, between countries and within countries for sex work" (p. 150). Over one million women and children are trafficked each year, often for vast amounts of money to the industry. Girls and women are bought or kidnapped from poor countries such as Thailand, Nepal, or countries of the former Soviet Union to richer countries such as China, Germany, Japan, or the Netherlands. Israel is a major destination site for Russian and Ukrainian women. The women work for little or no pay while the pimps earn thousands of dollars each week per prostitute.

In *Global Woman: Nannies, Maids, and Sex Workers in the New Economy*, Ehrenreich and Hochschild (2003) write graphically of girls from rural areas of Thailand sold into sexual slavery. The girls are not allowed to use condoms; eventually most will die of AIDS.

Farr (2005) describes the various roles in the trafficking industry that range from recruiter to travel agent to transporter to employer (the employer sells the service to the customer and provides the women with a place to live and work). The recruiter typically puts together the book of photographs and other promotional material for mass distribution. The girls and women generally are recruited for prostitution through coercion or deception (usually regarding the nature of the work). Most of the women are controlled through threats and often severe violence. The majority live under a debt bondage system in which they are held in debt for their transportation and expenses.

As Farr describes it, beatings take place because of rule violations, failure to please customers, indebtedness, or failure to report to the pimp on time.

Documentation of routine abuse of women trafficked in the United States showed that over 70 percent had been abused by their traffickers and/or pimps, often sexually. Violence against the trafficked women serves the purpose first of breaking them in, then of maintaining their submission and obedience. Examples from Nepal and India are especially horrific because they involve children sold to brothels such as one in Bombay, India, where "tens of thousands of young women are displayed in row after row of zoo-like animal cages" (Farr, 2005, p. 39).

The very same forces that lead to the organization of the sex trade and to the male demand for it, as Farr indicates, are rooted in patriarchal constructs about women and men and the relations between them. Wartime prostitution and rape in war occur within the patriarchal structure of the military. This topic that Farr terms "the militarized view of women as both male property and inferior to men" (2005, p. 164) brings us to the third dimension of global victimization of women (the first two of which were victimization within the family and community-level victimization of sex trafficking). This is the level of violence by the state.

Victimization of Women at the State Level

Under the category of **state violence,** Erez (2000) includes violence that is perpetrated or condoned by the state. Included under this rubric is rape committed during armed conflict or cultural wars, forced abortion or sterilization, and custodial rape and sexual harassment by police and prison officers. We start with the sexual defilement of women under the auspices of military structures. To the victors of military conquest, the enemy's property, including women, are seen as legitimate spoils of war, ripe for the taking (Farr, 2005). Sometimes, too, rape of the enemy's women is a deliberate strategy for winning the war.

Rape in War

An important but belated development in recent years was the recognition of rape of the enemy's women—a common occurrence during and after a war—as a war crime. The International War Crimes Tribunal in The Hague took a revolutionary step when three Bosnian soldiers were convicted of rape and sexual enslavement as crimes against humanity. The judgment followed years of lobbying by women's rights groups (Pittaway, 2003). Women's rights activists participated in every major United Nations preparatory meeting on the new International Criminal Court (ICC) (Human Rights Watch, 2002b).

The advantage of an international tribunal is in sending a message worldwide that such violence is widely condemned and in the tribunal's image of impartiality. The "power of shame" can play a role both as an enforcement tool and in helping to impart justice to the victim population. An exciting development today is the establishment of a permanent world criminal tribunal, the ICC, which now has jurisdiction over crimes against humanity committed by ratifying states and nationals of those states. It is to be based in The Hague (Human Rights Watch, 2003). As of August, 2005, ninety-nine countries had ratified the ICC treaty

(Wikipedia, 2005). Unfortunately, the United States under the Bush administration has expressed strong opposition to the existence of the world court and withdrawn the U.S. signature on the treaty (Human Rights Watch, 2003). Moreover, special arrangements were made with the United Nations to protect U.S. "peacekeepers" from accountability to the international body for human rights violations. Despite this U.S. opposition, however, the establishment of such a world court of justice, a dream ever since the United Nations was established, is a major victory for world peace and human rights.

Now, the new ICC, which has replaced the U.N. tribunals that have been convened on strictly an ad-hoc basis, has officially (in statutes seven and eight) declared rape in a conflict situation to be a war crime and a crime against humanity. The ICC provides witness and victim protection and the possibility of redress for the wrongs done. Counseling and other assistance will be provided through the ICC's Victims and Witnesses Unit (Human Rights Watch, 2003).

War rape of the enemy's women is so much a part of war and its aftermath that, under conditions of military occupation, it is more remarkable in its absence than in its presence. The rape that accompanies war involves both a tremendous act of aggression and humiliation against a conquered people and a reward to soldiers who are encouraged by their officers to loot a village and rape the women at will. Rape is the act of patriotism, misogyny, and lust combined. In the name of victory war provides men with a tacit license to rape (Brownmiller, 1975). In her analysis of rape in warfare, Brownmiller (1993) forcefully concludes:

> *Rape of a doubly dehumanized object—as woman, as enemy—carries its own terrible logic. In one act of aggression, the collective spirit of women and of the nation is broken, leaving a reminder long after the troops depart. And if she survives the assault, what does the victim of wartime rape become to her people? Evidence of the enemy's bestiality. Symbol of her nation's defeat. A pariah. Damaged property. A pawn in the subtle wars of international propaganda. (p. 37)*

Notably, in the battles of ancient Greece, the Crusades, the U.S. Civil War, World Wars I and II, and Vietnam, rape was utilized as a physical and psychological weapon of war (Wing and Merchan, 1993). Within this context, it is not surprising to hear of mass rapes by all factions in the Bosnian and Rwandan conflicts. In Haiti, too, military rapists targeted women in terrorism preceding the recent government overthrow. Compounding the injury to the victims, the husbands often transfer their feelings of revulsion from the enemy to their victimized wives. Such rejection of women as defiled beings is consistent with traditional patriarchal ideology that universally demands that women should not allow more than one man to have access to their bodies (Wetzel, 1993).

Wing and Merchan (1993) drew a gripping parallel between the ethnic cleansing and forced impregnation in Bosnia and the history of rape and miscegenation in the American South. On six key attributes related to what Wing and Merchan call "spirit injury" or "the slow death of the psyche, of the soul, and of the identity of the individual" (p. 2) and of the group, the early American South and Bosnia share a common ground. These traits are rape as defilement not only of the individual woman but of a whole culture; rape as silence as the women internalize their experience of oppression, rendering them more vulnerable to males within their own group; rape as sexuality, with raped women seen as promiscuous and impure; rape as emasculation of men due to their sense of helplessness to protect their wives and daughters; rape as trespass on the "property" rights of men most pronounced under slavery where the women were the property of their white masters as were the racially mixed offspring; and rape as pollution of the victim and of her children born as a result of nonconsensual sex.

Rape as an instrument of war is clearly a violation of international law and its proscriptions against war crimes, taking of hostages, torture, and violation of human dignity (Wing and Merchan, 1993). Deplorably, although torture has been prosecuted as a war crime, only recently has war rape been considered anything more than an inevitable byproduct of war. Now, at last, women's rights are seen as human rights. And justice and accountability for past abuses increasingly are seen as bedrock issues for human rights organizations everywhere and a vital protection against future abuses. That the ICC has come into force today as a potentially powerful instrument for protecting women's rights is a testament to the mass networking and courage of women's rights activists throughout the world (Human Rights Watch, 2002b).

In their investigation of the extent of rape in recent wars, the United Nations Office for the Coordination of Humanitarian Affairs (2004) relied on data that women's groups have managed painstakingly to piece together. As summarized by the U.N. office:

> *An estimated half a million women were raped during the 1994 genocide in Rwanda. A staggering 50 percent of all women in Sierra Leone were subjected to sexual violence, including rape, torture and sexual slavery, according to a 2002 report by Physicians for Human Rights. In Liberia, an estimated 40 percent of all girls and women have fallen victim to abuse. During the war in Bosnia-Herzegovina in the 1990s, between 20,000 and 50,000 women were raped.*
>
> *Many researchers feel this is not just the result of violent male opportunism, but rather a weapon of war. This is particularly true of ethnic conflicts, during which systematic rape is commonly used to destabili[z]e populations and destroy community and family bonds. Amnesty International now considers rape a commonly used tool for "ethnic cleansing," including the forced impregnation of girls.*
>
> *Rape is also used to humiliate and demorali[z]e families and communities. In many cases, men are forced to watch the rape of their wives or daughters. In Bosnia-Herzegovina sons and fathers were forced to commit sexual atrocities against each other. (p. 1)*

A contemporary interest in the social and cultural side of war has brought *A Woman in Berlin: Eight Weeks in the Conquered City* (Anonymous, 2005/1945) to the forefront of world consciousness. The anonymous author, a journalist, recorded the horrors of mass rape imposed on German women by Russian "liberators" during World War II. At the time of its original publication, the book was condemned for its shameless immorality in discussing what could not be discussed, not by Germans, and not by people who hated Germans (Dotinga, 2005). Written as an eight-week diary, *A Woman in Berlin* recorded stories of some of the 100,000 women in Berlin who were raped by drunken Russian soldiers. The author herself was raped by two Russians on the first day of the occupation. Later that day she offered to submit to a high-ranking Russian officer to get protection from multiple assailants. He took her up on the offer. The book was ahead of its time when it was first published and has only now with its reissue received the recognition it was due.

The story of the conquered Berlin women is echoed in more recent times in the Democratic Republic of Congo, in Darfur, in Sierra Leone, and in Liberia; whenever there is armed conflict women's bodies become targets of war. So widespread are such attacks on women that gender-based violence accounts for more death and disability worldwide among women aged fifteen to forty years old than cancer, malaria, traffic injuries, and war combined, according to the World Health Organization (U.N. Office for the Coordination of Humanitarian Affairs, 2004).

An academic study of mass war rape in Bosnia-Herzegovina is offered by Snyder and colleagues (2006). This study traces the history of the rise of ethnic nationalism that accompanied a complete rejection of state socialism in what used to be Yugoslavia. Gender equality that had been a hallmark of the communist government then took a backseat as well. The new task of womanhood was now to regenerate the nation through motherhood, not through careers. A strong anti-abortion movement was mobilized as well in Croatia, Slovenia, and Serbia. Meanwhile, the feminist movement fractured along ethnic lines. Serbia's plan to establish a Greater Serbia and drive out the Muslims was thwarted in 1992 when Bosnia declared its independence from Yugoslavia. Within this context then, Serb nationalists launched a war that produced a campaign of killing and mass rape. While rapes were committed by men from all ethnicities, the vast majority were initiated by Serbs who attacked Muslim women during the Bosnian conflict. The Serbs' strategy included rape of women in front of their husbands and fathers, and confinement of women in rape camps for the purpose of impregnation with rape babies. From an ethnic cleansing perspective, the child assumes the nationality of the rapist. Snyder et al. put these events in perspective:

> The Bosnian conflict signaled the end of invisibility of women raped in war. No longer could war rape be viewed as an unfortunate by-product of war. It was now clear that it was being used as an intentional strategy to achieve genocide. (p. 191)

An especially odious development took place in the rape and genocide campaign during the civil war in Rwanda. Within the space of one hundred days over one million people were killed (Hentz, 2005). The calculation of one million, however, does not include those women who were intentionally infected with HIV as a part of a calculated campaign to destroy Tutsi culture. Significantly, before the genocide took place, cartoons were printed depicting Tutsi women as sexual creatures who used their sexuality for political purposes. Testimony before the international tribunal, which in a landmark decision in 1998 declared rape an independent crime under international law, established that virtually every woman who survived the genocide was raped and that the crimes of gang rape, sexual torture and humiliation, and sexual slavery took place. Men who were HIV positive were paid by the Hutu government to rape Tutsi women.

One of the long-term effects of war is the militarization of society. A militarizing society calls on patriarchal values and mechanisms of domination and control that heighten hierarchical relations between men and women (Farwell, 2004).

Women, War, and Peace

The title for this section is taken from a book by Elisabeth Rehn of Finland and Ellen Johnson Sirleaf of Liberia. Commissioned by the United Nations Development Fund for Women (UNIFEM), Rehn and Sirleaf (2002) conducted an independent expert assessment on the gender dimensions of conflict. This effort parallels a new impetus by the U.N. Security Council to attend to the needs of war-affected women. *Women, War and Peace* documents in graphic detail the injustices inflicted on the bodies and lives of women stemming from the horrors of war and its aftermath. Women in war zones throughout the world shared the impact of armed conflict on their families. They told how militarization affected their sons, their husbands, and brothers—turning them into different, often explosive, and violent people. They described the unaccustomed roles they were required to fill as the peacetime infrastructure was destroyed. In the upheaval that follows war, women become especially vulnerable as the social and legal institutions are weakened.

The injury to women and their families can be seen as well in uprootedness; mental trauma; lack of food, potable water, and electricity; health problems stemming from exposure to chemicals such as uranium; violence and sexual assault in refugee camps; and the numbers of women resorting to sex work to feed their children. Eighty percent of the world's refugees are women and children.

Refugees from war in one land become immigrants in another land, often in Europe, the United States, and Canada. Refugee women are especially vulnerable to abuse, both in their travels across the world and in their detention as they seek asylum in circumstances that inevitably are less than hospitable.

Treatment of Immigrants in U.S. Detention

Female immigrants, including refugees in detention, are another group of women who have suffered serious human rights violations. Even before the war on terrorism was declared, brutal treatment of detained political refugees was the norm. Yet because the detainees are not U.S. citizens, they are considered to be outside the jurisdiction of the protections of the U.S. Constitution. They are not, however, outside the scope of international law.

Amnesty International, in its 1999 report *"Not Part of My Sentence": Violations of the Human Rights of Women in Custody,* expressed the following concern with reference to immigrants in detention:

> *Women asylum seekers are often subjected to harsh treatment. While awaiting action on the INS claims, they often languish in penal institutions facing the same human rights violations all women prisoners face. Many times they are placed in cells with hardened criminals. (p. 8, 9)*

New harsh sentencing laws have created a special population of prisoners—immigrant prisoners—whom the federal government segregates from the rest of the prison population and turns over to private companies (Dow, 2004). (Advantages of privatization of prisons include cost savings and exemption of the government from lawsuits.) Since September 11, when U.S. national security became the top priority of the nation, the numbers of immigrants in detention has increased in conjunction with new antiterrorism laws. In a personal interview with a social worker from Elizabeth, New Jersey, where immigrants, including refugees who request political asylum, are kept in lock-up, van Wormer learned that conditions that would qualify as "cruel and unusual" (8th amendment, U.S. Constitution) clearly apply. In the privately run Elizabeth Detention Center, the same prison where many of the terrorist suspects now are being held, women are kept all in one cell; no recreation is offered and telephone calls are priced at $1.00 per minute. One woman has been so detained for five years. To what extent the usual protections offered to Americans under the Bill of Rights applies to these non-citizens is still not completely settled (interview with social work educator Patricia Levy of Elizabeth, New Jersey). A search of the Web reveals numerous reports on the human rights violations, some in connection with facts that have come out in lawsuits.

Global Initiatives for Rights and Justice

Empowerment describes the transformation from individual and collective powerlessness to personal, political, and cultural power (GlenMaye, 1997). Of special relevance to addressing victimization is the gaining of a sense of personal power, assuming responsibility for recovery, and change which may entail helping others. Of special relevance to addressing criminal behavior, and without which change is unlikely, is the taking of personal responsibility for one's actions and one's life.

Rehn and Sirleaf (2002) credit the United Nations for its expression of political commitment to women's special needs in war-torn societies. But women need to be at the forefront of peacemaking and humanitarian relief efforts; the resources allocated to the relief efforts are entirely inadequate, and greater high-level support to effectively address the gender dimensions of war and peace are required.

One model program that could be emulated elsewhere is offered by the International Rescue Committee (IRC) in Sierra Leone to aid the victims of war. Susan Koch (2003), a global health expert, describes the remarkable work performed by this organization. Originally founded by Albert Einstein, the IRC conducts a reunification project in war-torn Sierra Leone to reunite abducted girls and their families or help the girls receive education for a new life if family members can't be found. The matter of reunification is problematic because typically the girls who were kidnapped were sexually abused and used as sex slaves. Some families might refuse to take them back, seeing them as tainted or as changed. IRC works to locate the families. Videotapes are made of the girl talking about how much she wants to come home. The family sees this. Then if they are receptive, family members are videotaped saying how much they miss their daughter. To date, there have been sixty successful reunifications.

Other approaches to empowerment for survivors of war rape are described by Farwell (2004). A Rwandan women's NGO, the Association of Widows of Genocide, includes in its membership survivors who are taking care of orphans of extended family members. In Bosnia-Herzegovina, a center for traumatized displaced women staffed by women physicians and other professionals has treated tens of thousands of women. The team has offered treatment to Kosovan refugees as well.

Women's organizations, as Farwell argues, must go beyond therapy; they need to engage in a range of strategies to combat war rape and address its cause and consequences. One such strategy, which the Women's Rights International uses, is the collection of extensive documentation of human rights violations against women to focus attention on the pervasiveness of sexual crimes in wartime. As feminists with a global perspective, Farwell further suggests we need to examine the causal connections between burgeoning militarism and all forms of violence against women.

Two interesting innovations from abroad are the all-women police stations in Brazil and an all-female village in Kenya. In Brazil, more than 300 **women's police stations** have opened. Women who have been attacked go to these stations where they know they will be heard (Downie, 2005). In the past such crimes long went unreported largely because of Brazil's macho culture and the legal system's leniency for male offenders. This innovation has been modeled now in at least ten nations in Latin America and Asia. The women go to these stations, not to end the relationship but to stop the violence. This process empowers the woman and holds the man accountable. The all-female village of thirty-six women at Umoja, Kenya, was formed ten years ago by a group of homeless women who were abandoned by their husbands after they were raped (Feminist Majority Foundation, 2005). This village continues to serve as a safe haven for women escaping violence, including genital mutilation. The World Health Organization (2002) also brings our attention to active NGO units in Egypt mobilized against genital mutilation and the "One-Stop Crisis Centre" of integrated services for rape victims in Malaysian hospitals.

Restorative Justice

In an aboriginal peacekeeping circle, members of the community open the session with a prayer and reminder that the circle has been convened to discuss the behavior of a young man who assaulted his sister in a drunken rage; an eagle feather is passed around the circle, held by each speaker as he or she expresses feelings about the harmful behavior. This process is about reconciliation and the healing of wounds. It is about restoring the balance or the sense of justice that was lost.

In Canada, perhaps due to the influence of First Nations people, restorative justice principles are well known. In the United States, restorative justice practices have made inroads within the criminal justice field (an October 2005 search of *Criminal Justice Abstracts* reveals 374 relevant articles). The states of Minnesota and Vermont have integrated restorative policies within their departments of corrections.

Restorative justice as we learned in Chapter 7, is a broad term that refers to various strategies to find resolutions to criminal and human rights violations. Both an ideal principle—providing justice to the offender, victim, and community—and a method of dispensing justice when a violation has been committed, restorative justice can be considered a form of social justice because of its fairness to all parties. Reparations is the form of justice most closely linked to human rights and our concern in this chapter.

On the international stage, the thrust for a restorative vision has been embraced through the role of the United Nations. In consultation with nongovernmental organizations, the U.N. sets up formal standards or guidelines for countries to use in restorative justice programming ("U.N. Crime Commission Acts on Basic Principles," 2002). The United States, however, has not officially endorsed these procedures.

There are now more than 1,000 such programs operating throughout North America and Europe, according to the international survey done by the Center of Restorative Justice and Peacemaking (Umbreit, 2000). In Germany alone, there are 400 victim-offender mediation centers. Many programs operate inside the U.S. and Belgian prisons. Belgium now has a restorative justice coordinator in each of its thirty prisons arranging conferences between victims and inmates (McGeorge, 2003). There is also a significant restorative justice focus in the Australian prison system, while in New Zealand most of the criminal justice system, following Maori tradition, utilizes a restorative conferencing format.

Where there has been victimization and possible trauma, rituals are needed to "heal the damaged souls of the people, to help them find ways to transform hatred into sorrow or forgiveness, to be able to move forward with hope rather than wallow in the evil of the past" (Braithwaite, 2002, p. 207). When the state is the culprit, restorative justice means reparations for the human rights violations that occurred. Reparations may take the form of governmental acceptance of responsibility for the wrongs done, often following a national inquiry. The victims may even be later generations; the descendants of the original injured parties may be the actual complainants. The complaint is often filed in court through an attorney. The connection to restorative justice is in the aim of reparation or restoring what is due to victims, also the grassroots movement out of which the impetus for justice is derived.

When reparations were made in 1988 by the U.S. Congress to Japanese Americans for wrongs inflicted on them after war was declared on Japan (including confiscation of their property and confinement in internment camps), a precedent was set for other people to seek compensatory measures. Among them are the Native Americans, seeking redress for treaties broken and brutal forced assimilation practices. In Australia, aboriginal peoples are currently organizing to receive reparations for their "stolen childhoods." The reference is to the forced removal of mixed-race children from aboriginal mothers into orphanages or white homes. In the United States, the African American movement for reparations for the harms done to their ancestors through enslavement has been widely publicized.

A key theme with respect to ending conflict and healing wounds is forgiveness in communities and societies. Russell Daye (2004) introduces the notion of **political forgiveness,** which he describes as a form of deep reconciliation, a kind of social healing. South Africa set the stage for such a process of social healing in the post-apartheid era, especially through the principles and practice of the Truth and Reconciliation Commission. Truth commissions investigate situations of gross human rights violations and serve to validate the experiences of victims and propose ways to repair the harm.

Modeled on the truth-seeking efforts in South Africa, the Peruvian Truth and Reconciliation Commission specifically addressed sexual violence against women that had been inflicted on them by warring factions. This commission issued its final report in 2003. The report, following those investigating war rape in Rwanda and Bosnia, documented that rape was used as a deliberate tactic of war to degrade the population and punish women who were members of subversive groups (Falcón, 2005).

In summary, the restorative process with its peacemaking and reconciliatory powers is a powerful way of handling conflict. Whether in a one-on-one situation or *writ large*, peacemaking is enhanced when amends can be made in a spirit of reconciliation. All of these initiatives (including the women's police stations and women's village) meet the criteria recommended by Erez (2000) of indigenous solutions to women's victimization. At the macro level, establishing gender equality and economically viable options for women is an essential step in reducing victimization, particularly regarding sex trafficking. As Erez concludes:

> *The extent of women's victimization should serve as a barometer for the country's compliance with human rights laws, or conversely, as its record of human rights violations. Visions for international cooperation on ways to reduce women's victimization, empower women and girls, increase their independence and autonomy, and preserve their integrity and dignity, should be top priorities of the international community. (p. 5)*

Summary

This chapter, following Erez's organizational scheme for examining women's victimization globally, what we might term "the world's war against women," has discussed family, community, and state victimization, respectively. The starting point was globalization, a force that enters into the equation, in terms of economically restricting poor women's progress as they live at the bottom end of the market economy, while at the same time making mass organization on their behalf possible through the communications revolution.

Under family violence, we looked at such violations as genital mutilation in Sudan, wife beating in Nigeria, honor killing in Pakistan, and the plight of battered immigrant women married to American soldiers. Sex trafficking was the example of community-level victimization, a phenomenon closely tied to global markets, a transportation of women from struggling nations to richer ones. At the state level, we focused on rape as an act of war, militarization in general, and the mistreatment of female immigrants in U.S. detentions.

This chapter discussed innovative programming to protect women with an emphasis on global restorative justice processes at the societal level. It highlighted restorative justice because of its truth-telling and healing attributes. The South African Truth and Reconciliation Commission served as the model. The chapter also described empowerment strategies from Africa and Latin America.

Central to this chapter was the theme of human rights: rights inscribed in international laws to protect women and other marginalized populations from abuse. The Beijing Fourth World Conference in 1995 marked a milestone in women's rights history as women of the world let go of their cultural differences and stood united against anti-woman violence, whether in the home or community. Still the horror stories persist—the infanticides in China of unwanted girls, the public stoning of rape victims in Pakistan. A promising development is the founding of the International Criminal Court, which will investigate war rape as a war crime and crime against humanity. Meanwhile, NGOs such as Human Rights Watch and Amnesty International inform the media and report to the United Nations on human rights violations across the globe that they have investigated. The days of looking the other way out of respect for cultural practices in the interests of cultural autonomy are over. Change will only come through international unity against the forces of oppression.

United under the banner of a human rights framework, feminists in collaboration with oppressed minorities and other allies are challenging governments to honor the rights of their citizens. Such a global, human rights perspective provides for justification for demands of social justice by drawing on principles from a higher authority. Just as the demands of social justice are new, so we must think anew. And such new thinking is enhanced through the globalization of information through the new communications technologies.

KEY TERMS

economic globalization
femicide
gender-based violence
genital mutilation
globalization

honor killing
military socialization
political forgiveness
restorative justice
sex trafficking

state violence
war rape
women's police stations
World Health Organization
(WHO)

CRITICAL THINKING QUESTIONS

1. How can crime be gender based? How about male victimization?

2. Argue either for cultural relativism or a modern human rights perspective concerning some practices in non-industrialized parts of the world.

3. Consider the jurisdiction of the International Criminal Court and the reluctance of the United States to join this body. Consider also the unofficial role of the United States as the world's primary policing structure. Is this arrogance or altruism?

4. What are some parallels of mistreatment of women globally discussed in this chapter and within the United States as revealed in early chapters?

5. Research rape in one war of interest. Is war rape simply collateral damage of war or a deliberate use of women for dehumanization or both?

6. Discuss marriages of immigrant women with U.S. soldiers and to what extent these arrangements are successful or problematic.

7. Check out the Universal Declaration of Human Rights on the Internet and its civil and social provisions. Are there some rights spelled out in this document that Americans lack?

8. What lessons can be learned from abroad that are relevant to empowerment of women?

WEB DESTINATIONS

Amnesty International: www.amnesty.org

Captive Women Rescue: www.captivedaughters.org

Demanding human rights for women and families around the world: www.madre.org

Equality Now: www.equalitynow.org

Feminist Majority Foundation: www.feminist.org

Human Rights Watch: www.hrw.org

International Victimology web site: www.victimology.nl

Minnesota Restorative Justice: www.doc.state.mn.us

Restorative Justice Resources: www.restorativejustice.org

UN Universal Declaration of Human Rights: www.un.org

Women's Human Rights: www.whrnet.org

World Health Organization: www.who.org

REFERENCES

Afrol News (2005, September 5). Female genital mutilation: A vote-winner in Sierra Leone. Africa News Agency. *Afrol News*. Retrieved from www.afrol.com.

Amnesty International (1999). *Not part of my sentence: Violations of human rights of women in custody.* New York: Amnesty International.

Amnesty International (2001). *Broken bodies, shattered minds: Torture and ill treatment of women.* New York: Amnesty International.

Amnesty International (2005, May 31). *Nigeria: Unheard voices.* Amnesty International. Retrieved from http://web.amnesty.org/actforwomen.

Anderson, R. (2005, September 6). Home front casualties. *Seattle Weekly.* Retrieved from www.seattleweekly.com.

Anonymous (2005/1945). *A woman in Berlin: Eight weeks in the conquered city.* New York: Metropolitan Books.

Banister, J. (2004). *Shortage of girls in China today* 21(1): 19–45.

Bellamy, C. (2003, March 8). To the symposium on female genital mutilation in Berlin. UNICEF. Retrieved from http://www.unicef.org.

Bhuyan, R., Mell, M., Senturia, K., Sullivan, M., and Shiu-Thornton, S. (2005, August). "Women must endure according to their karma." *Journal of Interpersonal Violence* 20(8): 902–921.

Braithwaite, J. (2002). *Restorative justice and responsive regulation.* Oxford, U.K.: Oxford University Press.

Brownmiller, S. (1975). *Against our will: Men, women and rape.* New York: Bantam.

Brownmiller, S. (1993). Making female bodies the battlefield. *Newsweek*: 37.

Bui, H. (2003). Immigration context of wife abuse: A case of Vietnamese immigrants in the United States. In R. Muraskin (ed.), *It's a crime: Women and justice* (pp. 394–410). Upper Saddle River, N.J.: Prentice Hall.

Chesler, E., and Dunlop, J. (1995, September 29). Consensus on women's rights cleared the skies in China. *Christian Science Monitor*: 18.

Counts, D., Brown, J., and Campbell, H. (1992). *Sanctions and sanctuary: Cultural perspectives on the beating of wives.* Boulder, Col.: Westview Press.

Daye, R. (2004). *Political forgiveness: Lessons from South Africa.* Maryknoll, N.Y.: Orbis Books.

DeMause, L. (2002, Spring). The childhood origins of terrorism. *Journal of Psychohistory* 29(4): 340–348.

Dominelli, L. (2002). *Feminist social work theory and practice.* Hampshire, U.K.: Palgrave.

Dotinga, R. (2005, September 14). Wartime memoirs by women in vogue. *Christian Science Monitor*: 15.

Dow, M. (2004). *American gulag: Inside U.S. immigrant prisons.* Berkeley, Calif.: University of California Press.

Downie, A. (2005, July 20). A police station of their own. *Christian Science Monitor*: 15.

Ehrenreich, B., and Hochschild, A. (eds.) (2003). *Global woman: Nannies, maids, and sex workers in the new economy.* New York: Metropolitan Books.

Equality Now (2005, August). Pakistan: The Hudood ordinances—Denial of justice for rape. Equality Now. Retrieved from www.equalitynow.org.

Erez, E. (2000, April 10–17). Women as victims and survivors in the context of transnational crime. Paper presented at the 10th U.N. Congress on Crime Prevention and the Treatment of Offenders, Vienna, Austria.

Erez, E., and Bach, S. (2003). Immigration, domestic violence, and the military: The case of "military brides." *Violence Against Women* 9(9): 1093–1117.

Falcón, J. (2005). The Peruvian truth and reconciliation commission's treatment of sexual violence against women. *Human Rights Brief* 12(2): 1–4.

Farr, K. (2005). *Sex trafficking: The global market in women and children.* New York: Worth.

Farwell, N. (2004). War rape: New conceptualizations and responses. *Affilia* 19(4): 389–403.

Feminist Majority Foundation (2005, July 14). All-female African village thriving after 10 years. *Feminist Daily News Wire.* Retrieved from www.feminist.org/news.

Fried, S. T. (1997, Summer). Accountability and action: Monitoring U.N. commitments to the human rights of women. *Global Center News* 4: 4.

Friedman, T. (2005). *The world is flat: A brief history of the 21st century.* New York: Farrar, Straus and Giroux.

Gilfus, M. (2002). Women's experiences of abuse as a risk factor for incarceration. *National Electronic Network on Violence against Women.* Retrieved from www.vawnet.org.

Gittings, J. (2002, May 13). Growing sex imbalance shocks China. *The Guardian.* Retrieved from http://www.guardian.co.uk.

GlenMaye, L. (1997). Empowerment of women. In L. M. Gutiérrez, R. J. Parsons, and E. O. Cox (eds.), *Empowerment in social work practice* (pp. 29–51). Belmont, Calif.: Brooks/Cole.

Griswold, E. (2003, September). Where the Taliban roam. *Harpers:* 57–65.

Hentz, J. (2005). The impact of HIV on the rape crisis in the African Great Lakes region. *Human Rights Brief 12*(2): 12–15.

Hochschild, A. (2003). Love and gold. In B. Ehrenreich and A. Hochschild (eds.), *Global woman: Nannies, maids, and sex workers in the new economy* (pp. 15–30). New York: Metropolitan Books.

Human Rights Watch (2002a). Human Rights Watch world report: United States. Retrieved from www.hrw.org.

Human Rights Watch (2002b, July 1). International justice for women: The ICC marks a new era. Retrieved from www.hrw.org.

Human Rights Watch (2003). The international criminal court. Retrieved from www.hrw.org.

Ife, J. (2001). Human rights and social work: Towards rights-based practice. Cambridge, England: Cambridge University Press.

Kennedy, M. (2004, Spring). Cheaper than a cow. *Ms.:* 50–53.

Koch, S. (2003, May 15). Women, war, and peace. Paper presented at the May Institute, University of Northern Iowa, on Peace, Human Rights and U.S. Foreign Policy.

LaFraniere, S. (2005, August 11). Entrenched epidemic: Wife-beatings in Africa. *New York Times:* A1.

Landsberg, M. (2002, September 8). Afghan women remain victims of hope unfulfilled. *Toronto Star:* A2.

Lite, J. (2002, October 3). Report indicates gender-related violence is global. *Women's E News.* Retrieved from www.womensenews.org.

Lynch, C. (2004, November 26). Congress seeks to curb international court. *Washington Post:* p. A02.

Mason, R. (1995, June 1–4). An agenda for women's empowerment. *Quaker United Nations Office Briefing Paper:* 1.

McGeorge, N. (2003, May). Restorative justice and the E.U. *Around Europe.* Brussels, Belgium: Quaker Council for European Affairs.

NASW (2003). International policy on human rights. In *Social work speaks: National Association of Social Workers policy statements 2003–2006* (pp. 209–217). Washington, D.C.: NASW Press.

Pittaway, E. (2003). A court to defend those raped in war. *The Sydney Morning Herald.* Retrieved from www.smh.com.au.

Rehn, E., and Sirleaf, E. J. (2002). *Women, war and peace: The independent expert's assessment on the impact of armed conflict on women and women's role in peace-building.* New York: United Nations Development Fund for Women.

Rupert, J. (2005, March 29). Report from Pakistan: Pakistani women: A cruel repression. *Newsday.* Retrieved from http://web.lexis-nexis.com.

Russell, D. (2001a). AIDS as mass femicide: Focus on South Africa. In D. Russell and R. Harmes (eds.), *Femicide in global perspective* (pp. 110–111). New York: Teachers College Press.

Russell, D. (2001b). Defining femicide and related concepts. In D. Russell and R. Harmes (eds.), *Femicide in global perspective* (pp. 12–25). New York: Teachers College Press.

Snyder, C. S., Gabbard, W. J., May, D., and Zulic, N. (2006). On the battleground of women's bodies: Mass rape in Bosnia-Herzegovina. *Affilia: 21*(2), 184–195.

Steinem, G., and Morgan, R. (2002, spring). Female genital mutilation. *Ms.:* 42–44.

Stone, L., and James, C. (1995). Dowry, bride-burning, and female power in India. *Women's Studies International Forum 18*(2): 125–134.

Umbreit, M. (2000). *Family group conferencing: Implications for crime victims.* Office for Victims of Crime. Washington, D.C.: U.S. Department of Justice.

United Nations (1948). *Universal declaration of human rights*. Resolution 217A (III). New York: United Nations.

United Nations (1989). *Convention on the rights of the child* (U.N. Document A/res/44/23). New York: United Nations.

United Nations (2003a, January 16). Sierra Leone: Human Rights Watch details sexual atrocities in civil war. *UNWire*. Retrieved from www.unfoundation.org/unwire.

United Nations (2003b). *The world's women 2003*. United Nations Statistics Division. Retrieved from www.unstats.un.org/.

United Nations (2005, October 12). The promise of equality: Gender equity, reproductive health and the millennium development goals. *The State of World Population 2005*. New York: United Nations Population Fund.

United Nations Children's Fund (UNICEF). (2003). *The state of the world's children 2003*. New York: UNICEF.

United Nations Crime Commission acts on basic principles (2002). Restorative justice network. Retrieved from www.restorativejustice.org.

United Nations Development Fund for Women (UNIFEM) (2003, May 13). The lack of equal rights for Africans is a central cause of the rapid transmission of HIV/AIDS on the Continent. Retrieved from www.unifem.org.

United Nations Office for the Coordination of Humanitarian Affairs (2004). Our bodies—Their battle ground: Gender-based violence in conflict zones. *Integrated Regional Information Networks*. Retrieved from www.irinnews.org/webspecials.

van Wormer, K. (2004). Confronting oppression, restoring justice: From policy analysis to social action. Alexandria, Va.: Council on Social Work Education.

Watkinson, A. M. (2001). Human rights laws: Advocacy tools for a global civil society. *Canadian Social Work Review 18*(2): 267–286.

Wetzel, J. (1993). *The world of women: In pursuit of human rights*. London: Macmillan.

Wikipedia (2005, August). International Criminal Court. *Wikipedia, The Free Encyclopedia*. Retrieved from http://en.wikipedia.org.

Wind, A. (2000). Book credits women's shelters for saving men's lives. *Waterloo-Cedar Falls Courier*. Online at www.sonic.net~doretk.

Wing, A., and Merchan, S. (1993). Rape, ethnicity, and culture: Spirit injury from Bosnia to Black America. *Columbia Human Rights Law Review 25*(1): 1–46.

Women's Action (2005, June). Ethiopia: Abduction and rape. *Equality Now*. Retrieved from www.equalitynow.org.

World Health Organization (WHO) (2002). *World report on violence and health*. Geneva: WHO.

Zamichow, N., and Perry, T. (2003, June 25). Home is where the hurt is. *The Los Angeles Times*: A1.

PART FIVE

Women as Professionals

The three chapters of this part—on the woman police officer, the woman lawyer, and the woman who works in corrections—have many similarities. They examine the role behavior of women who are attempting to break into a male subculture, one that sees itself as reserved for males. Women lawyers appear to have had the greatest success in breaking into this man's world, but women probation and parole officers have also been widely accepted, both by fellow workers and by clients. Women police officers have had the most difficulty in breaking into the men's club of policing, but women correctional officers in men's prisons are not far behind in encountering barriers and obstacles created by male corrections staff. In addition to the lack of acceptance that women have experienced, sexual harassment, especially in policing and in men's prisons, has posed a real problem for women who are employed in these fields.

Racial discrimination has joined with gender and culture in revealing the oppression that women professionals experience. The African American woman who is a police officer experiences even less acceptance in police agencies than does the white woman who is a police officer. She frequently feels alienated from white male and female officers and often even from African American male officers. In law school, the African American woman may experience discrimination in areas ranging from acceptance to admittance to student study groups. Subsequent to law school, this pattern of racial discrimination extends to limited opportunities for African American women attorneys to practice in high-status, financially remunerative, and powerful positions.

CHAPTER

11 Women in Law Enforcement

Entry into the men's club of policing is difficult for a woman. The resistance to entering this male-dominated world seems to continue throughout a woman's career. The difficulty of finding acceptance may start on the first day in the academy and not end until retirement. The problematic nature of policing as a career for women further expresses itself in the appraisal process of new recruits, in supervisory attitudes and treatment, in attitudes of male line police officers, and in promotional opportunities and career advancement. Reluctance to accept a woman police officer extends also to citizens in the community.

Another expression of the problematic nature of policing for women involves the career adjustments women face to make it as police officers. Even though a number of studies reveal that female police officers are equally as competent as male police officers, policewomen typically feel that they must prove themselves over and over. Women police officers often feel that they must display and identify with a "masculine" role (competency, intelligence, and independence), but the danger is that this may result in their being typecast as pushy, unfeminine, and aggressive (Lord, 1995, p. 631). Women police officers also must decide whether they want to be respected as crime fighters and work with the men or become specialists in community-oriented policing, in juveniles, or in vice. Policewomen must further find ways to establish their own networks and support groups, because they have been excluded from the male-dominated police culture.

In addition, the majority of women acknowledge that they have experienced abuse and sexual harassment and that each woman police officer must decide how much is too much. Susan L. Webb (1994) defines **sexual harassment** as:

1. The behavior in question is sexual in nature.
2. The behavior is deliberate and/or repeated.
3. The behavior is not welcome or asked for and is not returned.
4. The more severe the behavior is, the fewer times it needs to be repeated before it can be reasonably defined as harassment, and the less responsibility the receiver has to speak up.
5. The less severe the behavior is, the more times it needs to be repeated, and the more responsibility the receiver has to speak up. (pp. 26–29)

Considering this difficulty, why do women want to join this exclusively male club? The first and obvious answer is the freedom to have the same privileges, rights, and responsibilities that men have (Schaper, 1997, p. 32). Pure economics is a second reason. The pay is good in most agencies, benefits are usually excellent, and it is a secure job once you have passed probation (Harrington, 2004, p. 2). A third reason, and perhaps even more important, many women enter policing because they have a lot of enthusiasm for and commitment to becoming police officers. They see policing as a career in which they can make a difference, or they may anticipate that policing is an exciting job. Similar to men entering policing, women want to put the uniform on and feel that adrenaline rush when the action goes down. Or they may be attempting to prove something, for example, that they can do this job just as well as men can.

A History of Women in Policing

The policewomen's movement can be traced to demands of benevolent groups for prison, jail, and police matrons. In the 1820s volunteer Quaker women, along with upper-middle-class women, blamed the poor living conditions of female inmates on "neglect and sexual exploitation by male keepers." For example, "Rachel Welch, one of a small number of women in Auburn Prison in New York, became pregnant while serving a punishment sentence in a solitary cell. As a result of a flogging by a male prison official, Welch died after childbirth" (Schulz, 1995, p. 10).

The pressure for reform that followed this scandalous event resulted in Auburn creating the position of prison matron to oversee women's quarters in 1832 and influenced the passing of the 1928 law requiring the separation of males and females in county prisons. New York City officials followed the Auburn example by responding to pressure from the American Female Moral Reform Society to hire six matrons for its two jails in 1845 (Schulz, 1995, pp. 10–11).

During the post–Civil War period, women again became concerned about the welfare of female prisoners, noting "overcrowding, harsh treatment, and sexual abuse by their male keepers" (Schulz, 1995, p. 11). The Women's Christian Temperance Union and the General Federation of Women's Clubs demanded an increased role for women in caring for women and children in police custody. These organizations helped create and finance the position of police matron in the 1880s, which was women's first entry into police departments, albeit as social workers.

New York was the first city to hire full-time police matrons in 1845 (Berg and Budnick, 1986). But in 1887 the Men's Prison Association expressed opposition to placing matrons in each station house in New York City. At this time, the "city detained 14,000 women prisoners and received 42,000 female lodgers for overnight shelter." The association based its objection "on lack of space for a matron, on the violent state of the women, and on their fear of a matron's physical inability to handle the women" (p. 314).

In the late nineteenth and early twentieth centuries, a number of social forces contributed to the appearance of women police officers outside correctional settings. The most significant of these social forces were the expansion of the frontier, the surge toward industrialization, the development of the steam engine, the extension of political democracy, and the development of new economic institutions. This was also an era of religious revivalism, utopian experiments, and increased social consciousness. People joined together to sponsor the temperance movement, to institute public education, and to establish humane management systems for the insane, deviant, and delinquent.

The experience of the female abolitionists, as well as such social problems as widespread poverty, breakdown of the family, child labor, and increases in juvenile delinquency and female-related crime, provided the catalyst for the appearance of a women's movement called the suffragettes. The primary goal of this movement was to eliminate some of the social ills besetting children and women. This movement also gave birth to what is called the "child-saving movement" and the development of the juvenile court and its *parens patriae* philosophy (Platt, 1969, p. 76). The entry of women into law enforcement in a social worker mode during this era was "due to the reformist zeal of the period, an acceptance of a limited and special role for women in law enforcement, and the efforts of a few dedicated progressive reformers" (Lord, 1995, p. 628).

Reformers began to push for the appointment of women with the skills to work in the streets with prostitutes, runaways, and juvenile delinquents (Feinman, 1986, p. 81). In 1905 Lola Baldwin, secretary to the protective group Travelers' Aid Society, was hired as a "safety worker" as part of the Lewis and Clark Exposition in Portland, Oregon. Hers was the first documented appointment of a woman with police power, and her duties were to protect girls and women from harassment as well as to stop girls and women from pursuing men. The city government decided to retain Baldwin as director of the Department of Public Safety for the Protection of Young Girls and Women after the exhibition ended (Heidensohn, 1992, p. 43).

> Neither she nor the police department wanted women to be called "policewomen," because neither wished to associate women with the concept or job of policemen. The women, called "operatives" or "safety workers," considered themselves social service workers. (Feinman, 1986, pp. 81–82)

In 1910, Alice Stebbins Wells was officially classified as a "policewoman" in Los Angeles, California. Her contributions to women in police were significant. She was hired at the rank of detective after she convinced the city that a sworn woman police officer could be effective. The publicity about her hiring caused other cities to hire women, and in 1915, she founded the International Association of Policewomen.

Although Alice Wells was pictured in newspapers as "a masculine individual, grasping a revolver, and dressed in unfeminine clothing," policewomen of her era did not consider themselves female versions of policemen, a concept they derogatorially termed "little men" (Schulz, 1995, p. 4). They perceived themselves to be superior to policemen in social class, education, and professionalism. They "embodied the concept of the policewoman-as-social worker . . . seeking to bring social services and order into the lives of women and children. . . ." At the same time they avoided "the trappings of police, opposing uniforms for themselves and choosing not to carry firearms even if permitted to do so" (p. 4). Despite this limited role, their acceptance was only marginal, and the demands for policewomen were almost always imposed on police executives from outside sources (pp. 2–5).

Frances Heidensohn's (1992) examination of this period concluded that a number of factors shaped the development of women policing in both the United States and Britain. First, this movement had a moral basis: The entrance of women in policing was "vigorously promoted by groups formed for moral protection, and sometimes feminist causes who did so to attain social purity, rescue, and welfare goals" (p. 52). Second, volunteers had an important role in the origins of women police officers. A group of women who sought to be police officers were willing to volunteer their services on patrol. Third, considerable proselytizing for women took place in policing; supporters of this movement, as well as the pioneers themselves, pursued their cause with missionary zeal. Fourth, policewomen's strongest opposition came from both rank-and-file and senior police officers. Fifth, the women's movement in policing advocated specialist work because it sought the right of women to work with women and children. Finally, women sought gender control, in that they wanted to protect their own sex and did not seek a mandate to police men (pp. 52–54).

Women's place in policing became more secure after the First World War. In 1922 there were 500 women officers; by 1932, there were more than 1,500. Then, partly due to the Great Depression, the number leveled off. In 1950 there were 2,600 policewomen and in 1960, 5,617 (Heidensohn, 1992, pp. 52–54). The number of women police officers was to nearly double in the decade of the 1960s due in part to the social experimentation of that period. Both the civil rights movement and the women's movement benefited from the spirit of the times, but it was the women's movement that fueled the demands of women to have equal opportunity and career advancements in police departments (Lord, 1995, p. 628).

The 1950s brought a different type of woman into policing (Schulz, 1993). These "second-generation" policewomen, who were often military veterans, were middle-class careerists. Having more education (most had at least some college) and higher in social-class orientation than their male peers, these women had more similarity with male police officers than did their predecessors. According to Schulz, "they formed a bridge between the upper-middle class, college-educated, feminist, progressive women who had served as policewomen before them and today's women officers, most of whom are comparable to the overwhelmingly working-class, high school educated men with whom they serve" (p. 7).

The demand for expanded roles in policing for women greatly increased after a 1961 lawsuit that allowed women police officers to compete in promotional examinations. The New York Police Department promoted its first female sergeant in 1964 (Schulz, 1995, pp. 2–5). In 1968 Indianapolis police officers Betty Blankenship and Elizabeth Coffal were the first women to put on a uniform, strap on a gun belt, and drive a marked police vehicle, answering police calls like their male counterparts (pp. 2–5).

The 1964 Civil Rights Act and the 1972 Equal Employment Opportunity Commission (EEOC) expanded the rules of state and civil service bodies and made it illegal to discriminate in employment. The EEOC rules, which pressured police agencies to change hiring practices and show why a woman or minority person is not qualified to become a police officer, had a major impact on the presence of women on the police employment lists.

On September 20, 1974, while attempting to arrest a bank robber, 24-year-old Gail Cobb became the first African American policewoman to die of gunshot wounds (Schulz, 1995, p. 140). Currently, the National Law Enforcement Officers Memorial has 111 female officers' names engraved on its wall, only seven of whom were killed before 1970 (National Law Enforcement Officers Memorial Fund, 1997). Box 11.1 reveals the evolving role of women in policing during the twentieth century.

BOX 11.1
Women in Law Enforcement

Gloria E. Myers's *Municipal Mother: Portland's Lola Greene Baldwin, America's First Policewoman* takes a detailed look at Baldwin's 17-year career. What makes this book so valuable is that Myers analyzes the social and historical factors that led to the appointment of policewomen in a number of cities in the United States and Canada in the early decades of the twentieth century. Baldwin's initial success, as well as her longevity (she remained in her position through the incumbency of six chiefs of police and five mayors), was not so much a story of police reform as the story of Progressive Reformers' concern about morality and sexual activity among girls and women.

Myers's book describes how issues of class, crime, and social control merged with concerns about leisure-time activities to create a climate leading to a new career for women—that of policewoman. She explains how Portland's upper-middle-class activist women used concerns about immorality among both women and men to forge alliances with social hygiene and temperance activists to alter societal expectations of police enforcement. It was this combination of interests in Portland and around the nation that led to positions for women in police departments.

Gayleen Hays, with Kathleen Moloney's autobiography *Policewoman One: My Twenty Years on the LAPD*, offers a candid street-wise autobiography that explores all aspects of Hays's professional and personal life. It traces her career from its beginnings in 1967 as a "policewoman" (not a police officer) to her retirement in October 1989. In 1972 when the department was forced to sexually integrate its workforce and eliminate separate and discriminatory job categories, Hays made the decision not to become a police officer. Thus, she chose to forgo the possibility of promotion and assignments to regular patrol or traffic duty. She felt that the image of a policewoman is different from that of a policeman. She comments that there are many situations "where it's better to have a nurturing female persona than that of a confrontational male."

(continued)

B O X **11.1** Continued

During her career, Hays worked prostitution as well as rape and child abuse and in almost every bureau of the Los Angeles Police Department. She even worked in an elite plainclothes unit whose duty was to pursue hard-core criminals. Hays frankly discusses her personal life throughout the book, including her three marriages, her atypical childhood, being sexually molested, and how these personal experiences affected her on the job. Nicknamed as a dinosaur, Hays was the last of a dying breed. When she left the force, her badge, "Policewoman #1," was retired. Today, only police officers are on the LAPD.

Hosansky and Sparling's *Working Vice* chronicles the career of Lieutenant Lucie J. Duvall in the Cleveland Police Department. In her current position she is head of the department's sex crime and child abuse unit. She was still working when the book was published. In the beginning of the book, we find a confident police lieutenant as she is put through a yearly firearms qualification exercise. She is comfortable with her work, the mechanics of her job, and the decisions she must make because of the responsible position

she holds. Using "flashback" sequences, the reader is taken through her career. When Lieutenant Duvall began her career in law enforcement during the early 1970s, she was part of a monumental time in the history of women in policing, because women were first hired to do the same job as male police officers. The book explores fully her devotion to her life's work. It follows her personal triumphs as well as hardships; it reveals other officers' positive and negative opinions of her police work.

Critical Thinking Questions: What is the value of looking at biographical sketches of the early women police officers? What can they teach us about the development of policing in the United States?

Sources: Gloria E. Myers, *A Municipal Mother: Portland's Lola Greene Baldwin, America's First Policewoman* (Corvallis, Ore.: Oregon State University Press, 1995); Gayleen Hays with Kathleen Moloney, *Policewoman One: My Twenty Years on the LAPD* (New York: Vilard Books, 1992); and Tamar Hosansky and Pat Sparling, *Working Vice: The Gritty True Story of Lt. Lucie J. Duvall* (New York: HarperCollins, 1992).

Barriers to Women in Policing

Penny Harrington and Kimberly A. Lonsway (2004), in examining the status of women in policing, list a number of barriers that women face in becoming a police officer.

- Women face damaging stereotypes, especially the one that women are not strong enough or aggressive enough for police work.
- Women also face discrimination in the hiring process; both the written examination and oral interview process can be used to keep women out of policing.
- Women are vulnerable to sexual harassment during both academy training and field training.
- Women police officers experience isolation, as they learn that they are not accepted as equally valued members of the organization.
- Women sometimes face a double standard in performance evaluations, in which they feel that they must outperform the men officers to be considered "as good"

as they are. The double standard can operate to the particular detriment of women of color, who are often viewed as "tokens" even more than white women are.

- Male officers usually receive the most highly valued assignments, which are dangerous or otherwise require a great deal of physical endurance. In contrast, women are assigned to less desirable assignments, including child abuse investigations, domestic violence units, and community relations, generally defined as "women work" within policing.
- Promotions have been more difficult for women to attain, because of the cumulative bias against women police officers. Only about 125 women serve as police chiefs.
- Women also face in policing the lack of family-friendly policies and programs, such as child care, pregnancy leave, and elder care.
- Sexual harassment and retaliation, as will be discussed later in this chapter, constitute one of the major barriers to women in policing (pp. 499–507).

Comparison of Male and Female Officers' Job Performance

One of the criticisms of women who want to enter policing is that they lack skills to perform well as police officers. In the 1970s, a large amount of research was done to evaluate the performance of women police officers. These studies were conducted for Washington, D.C.; New York City; Denver, Colorado; Newton, Massachusetts; Philadelphia, Pennsylvania; the California State Highway Patrol; and St. Louis County, Missouri (Lord, 1995, p. 632).

In those studies, as well as more recent ones, researchers consistently demonstrated that women can handle the crime-fighting, rescue, combat, peacekeeping, and social service aspects of police work as well as men, regardless of differences in biological constitution and socialization practices (Horne, 1980). A lingering question in the minds of many male officers is whether female officers can handle patrol duties as well as male officers. Although some gender differences were found, all but the second phase of the Philadelphia study found that men and women were equally capable of patrol work (Martin and Jurik, 1995, p. 55). These studies also generally indicate that "men are in no more danger with women as partners than with men as partners" (Feinman, 1986, p. 95).

Differences occurred between male and female police officers in how they performed on the job. Policewomen were typically seen as showing more restraint in using their firearms and in managing family disturbances; as being more sensitive to citizens' needs and using a more community-oriented policing style; and as using less sick time. Moreover, women were significantly less likely to be involved in employing excessive force and deadly force and in acts of corruption than were men officers (Harrington and Lonsway, 2004, pp. 499–507). Policemen generally had better shooting ability, had superior strength and agility, and required less assistance in making arrests (Lord, 1995, p. 632). The findings from the Philadelphia study also reported that women officers were assaulted more often, had more vehicle collisions, and sustained more injuries. Furthermore, some evidence exists that women have higher turnover rates than men in policing (Doerner, 1995, p. 205).

Gender, Race, and Culture

The themes of gender, race, and culture are critical to understanding the careers of women in policing. Policing, as the opening section of this chapter suggested, is an extremely biased, gender-oriented occupation. Sexual harassment is a problem that most women police officers confront in some way during their careers. Increased numbers of women police officers have brought this problem to the attention of the courts. Race is also a critical variable in policing. African American women tend to have much different experiences in policing from white women. African American policewomen often feel alienated from white male, white female, and even African American male police officers. Female officers tend to come from higher-class backgrounds than male police officers and to have earned higher educational achievements, but culture is a much more important variable in policing than is class. Police culture has typically excluded the female; it is a club for men, and women are not wanted.

Gender and Culture: Women Are Not Wanted—This Is a Man's Job

Policing has been one of the most resistant occupations to accept women (Belknap and Shelley, 1992, p. 47). Susan E. Martin described the initial resistance as "strong, organized, and sometimes life-threatening" (Martin, 1994, p. 389). Catherine Milton's 1992 study reported that policewomen were being used almost exclusively in clerical or juvenile functions, that they were required to have more education than men, that they were regulated by hiring quotas, and that they were allowed to compete for promotions or openings only in the women's bureau. Donna Schaper (1997) writes about her experience:

> For me, the myth that women are physically less able than men found a remarkable rebuff one day in San Francisco 20 years ago. The San Francisco police department was in the throes of a lawsuit that would allow women to become police officers. I was taking a group of teenagers on a tour of the police department when the officer guiding us said that the real reason women couldn't be on the force was that they could never pass basic training, which required carrying a 100-pound bag of sand in a straight line for 100 feet. Then, an 18-year-old horsewoman in our group spotted the sandbag in the weight-training room, hoisted it on her shoulders and carried it for the rest of the tour. (p. 32)

Women have made gains in policing, which Susan Martin (1989, p. 162) claims are related in large part to the "development of a substantial body of law requiring nondiscrimination on the basis of sex in terms and conditions of employment" (p. 315). As of 2001, women comprised only 12.7 percent of all sworn law enforcement positions in the United States (National Center for Women & Policing, 2002). For other key findings of this report, see Box 11.2.

BOX **11.2**

The Percentage of Sworn Women Police Officers, 2001

- Over the last ten years, the representation of women in large police agencies has slowly increased from 9 percent in 1990 to 12.7 percent in 2001—a gain of less than 4 percent.
- There is mounting evidence that the slow pace of increase in the representation of women in large police agencies has stalled or even possibly reversed. For example, the percentage of women in large police agencies was 14.3 percent in 1999, 13.0 percent in 2000, and 12.7 percent in 2001.
- Women currently hold only 7.3 percent of top command positions, 9.6 percent of supervisory positions, and 13.5 percent of line operation positions. Sworn women of color hold 1.6 percent of top command positions, 3.1 percent of supervisory positions, and 5.3 percent of line operations positions.
- More than half (55.9 percent) of the large police agencies surveyed reported no women in top command positions, and the vast majority (87.9 percent) reported

no women of color in their highest ranks. For small and rural agencies, 97.4 percent have no women in top command positions, and only 1 of the 235 agencies has a woman of color in their highest ranks.

- The percentage of women serving in corrections facilities is more than twice as high as the percentage of sworn women police personnel, 26.3 percent in corrections compared to 12.7 percent in sworn law enforcement positions.

Critical Thinking Questions: What is the significance of the statistic that the representation of women in large police departments has stalled or even perhaps reversed? Why do you think the percentage of women serving in corrections is more than twice as high as the percentage of sworn women police personnel?

Source: National Center for Women and Policing, *Equality Denied: The Status of Women in Policing: 2001* (Washington, D.C.: U.S. Government Printing Office, 2002), pp. 4, 9.

Larger police departments tend to hire more women than smaller departments. The Madison, Wisconsin, police department is an exception. This small university town boasts 31.9 percent women officers, the highest percentage of any department in the nation. For the top ten agencies with the largest percentage of sworn women officers, see Table 11.1.

The resistance toward women in policing must ultimately be viewed in terms of the patriarchal society. For the past three thousand years, society has been based on social, philosophical, and political systems in which men have controlled women. Men have used force, direct pressure, tradition, ritual, customs, law, and language to determine what roles women shall or shall not play. In this male-dominated social role, the female is everywhere subordinated to the male. In policing, women had the "audacity" to desire entrance to an all-male occupation, one that male officers perceived to demand dominance, aggressiveness, superiority, and power.

TABLE 11.1 **Top Ten Agencies with the Largest Percentage of Sworn Women Officers, 2001**

Agency	Total Sworn Officers	Total Sworn Women Officers	Percentage Sworn Women Officers	Percentage Sworn Women Top Command	Percentage Sworn Women Supervisory	Percentage Sworn Women of Color
Terrebonne Parish, Sheriff, La.	187	78	41.71	9.09	3.33	2.14
Madison Police, Wisc.	347	111	31.99	16.67	22.22	4.03
Lafayette Parish Sheriff, La.	251	71	28.29	9.09	20.00	4.38
Cook County Sheriff, Ill.	2,587	699	27.02	17.24	24.64	10.32
Detroit Police, Mich.	4,195	1,085	25.86	17.39	27.28	20.07
Boulder Police, Col.	176	45	25.57	12.50	4.55	0.57
Philadelphia Police, Penn.	6,990	1,682	24.06	7.74	9.60	15.64
Spartanburg Police, SC	139	31	22.30	0.00	21.43	7.91
Miami-Dade Police, Fla.	3,078	676	21.96	17.98	18.46	13.55
Douglas County Sheriff, Ga.	116	256	21.55	0.00	23.55	0.00

Source: National Center for Women and Policing, *Equality Denied: The Status of Women in Policing: 2001* (Washington, D.C.: U.S. Government Printing Office, 2002), p. 21 (Appendix B).

In addition to the cultural barrier of the wider society, it is thought that certain aspects of police work are unsuitable for women. First, it is believed that women are unsuitable for police work because "they cannot cope with danger, do not command authority, and should not be exposed to degradation." Second, there is the fear that the introduction of women "will undermine male solidarity, threaten their security, and their self-image" (Heidensohn, 1992, p. 200). This could be regarded as the "porcelain policeman" argument; that is, male police officers "are so fragile and delicate that they will feel threatened and undermined, their solidarity shattered, and their loyalty over-stretched by the presence of women" (Heidensohn, 1992, p. 216). Third, women officers must cope with norms that create a disadvantage in interacting with male officers. Swearing and sexual jokes, it is charged, are an inevitable part of police culture and women should not have to deal with this "seamy" aspect. Finally, the argument for the exclusion of women is made that their lower status (in comparison with male officers) creates problems in arrest situations with both male and female citizens (Martin, 1989, pp. 321–322).

The issue of women as tokenism in policing has received some attention. Rosabeth Moss Kanter (1976) claims that token women (whose numbers fall below 15 percent of the total population) perceive themselves to be highly visible, attracting disproportionate attention to themselves. This often results, asserts Kanter, in dysfunctional performance pressures (pp. 415–430). Joanne Belknap and Jill Shelley's (1992) research supported Kanter's theory regarding one aspect of tokenism—visibility—because they found that "the most consistent characteristic significantly related to policewomen's perceptions and experiences was the percentage of women in the department" (p. 47).

Martin's examination of women in policing (1979) found that women are considered only tokens for male police officers and "they face performance pressure, isolation from coworkers, entrapment in stereotypic roles, and tests of loyalty" (p. 314). She concluded that the future is not bright: "It is likely that the dynamics of tokenism will continue to operate, leaving policewomen with a number of difficult choices in the face of the expectation that they think like men, work like dogs, and act like ladies" (pp. 314–323).

Teresa Lynn Wertsch (1998) also examined the issue of women police officers and tokenism among one group of female police officers employed in a medium-sized Pacific Northwest city. Of the twenty-four female officers in that department, sixteen agreed to be interviewed. Wertsch found that tokenism, when combined with such factors as family commitments and organizational structures, plays a major role in determining upward mobility and in serving to reduce the frequency of women's promotion to supervisory positions in police departments (pp. 25–26). According to this study, stereotypical categorization of the token into specific roles also created dissatisfaction and frustration. Two women officers reveal this dissatisfaction in the following statements:

> The guys can view you as a sex object instead of a professional. It makes me try harder to put up more fronts and play more of the macho, boy role rather than accept that I am a female. It makes me nervous and uncomfortable. You can't be meek or mild, too quiet. You can't be too loud or boisterous because then you would be a dike, too masculine. "That's why she can do the job because she's a dike," so the men automatically put you in a male role. If you're not good looking and act very masculine, they'll give you the job because you're a dike.
>
> . . .
>
> I wish it didn't have to be this way, but you're either a bitch, a dike, or a slut. It makes me frustrated because I don't know which I am. I'm not gay. I'm not a slut. I would probably fall more into the bitch category, which is the one that I have decided I would rather be in. (pp. 35–36)

Lesbian police officers report experiencing greater barriers as a result of their gender (because men officers see policing as such a "macho" job) rather than their sexual orientation. Using data collected from two midwestern police departments, one emphasizing traditional crime control and the other community policing, Martin, Forest, and Jurif (2004) examined how the lesbians' sexual orientation affects their police performance in a culture in which gender, sexuality, and race are all important components. Whether they come out or hide their identity, it is necessary for lesbian officers to negotiate their identities while doing their jobs. In the department emphasizing traditional crime control, lesbians believed that sexism as well as homophobia created barriers to their success in policing. Officers in this department who chose to hide their identity found this to be a stressful experience, because they were especially fearful of losing the respect of coworkers once their sexual orientation became known. In the department emphasizing community policing, lesbian officers perceived that their greatest barriers related to gender rather than sexual orientation. Martin and colleagues found that lesbians of color in both departments had the most concern about disclosing their sexual identity (pp. 511, 519, 521, 523).

Community to Community: Changing Roles for Police Officers

The nationwide movement toward community policing, the newest trend in policing today, aims to build closer ties between police and residents through frequent and informal noncriminal contact. This approach emphasizes a spirit of cooperation, familiarity, trust, and appreciation between police and community residents. These traits have traditionally been associated with female gender roles and attributes (Martin, 2000, p. 260).

Yet as a masculine occupation, policing has overwhelmingly rejected "feminine" voices and virtues; indeed, the criminal justice and legal system has been traditionally viewed as operating with a uniquely masculine voice—a detached and impersonal one emphasizing the traditional over the relational (Martin, 1999). Accordingly, when the ideological preoccupation with masculinity in policing is considered, any behavior that suggests femininity, subjectivity, or weakness is suspect and questioned in police subcultures (Martin, 2000, p. 260).

Martin suggests that this movement in many departments toward community policing raised some interesting questions:

> . . . How can this alternative style [community policing] be accepted by the police, since for it to be adopted, "feminine" traits must be appropriated as masculine traits and reshaped to appear as powerful and desirable? What happens if some men only "pretend" to personify this new breed of officer, particularly if they think doing so is tied to promotion? Do women police officers bring a "different voice" to policing than their male counterparts? Can a more feminine style of policing be introduced in a way that both men and women will embrace this approach and not fear the consequences of "doing policing" in this transformed style? (Martin, 2000, p. 260)

Community policing has varying levels of commitment in those departments that claim to be focused toward the mission of community policing. It is not unusual for top command of departments to have much more commitment toward community policing than is true among line officers. Nevertheless, Martin's questions are a reminder that, at least in some community-oriented policing departments, negotiated role identities must take place with male officers, and it would appear that "feminine" traits will need to be more valued in policing than they have been in the past. What this means is that at least some departments will need to redefine what constitutes a "good" police officer and hence a "good" candidate for a position (Harrington and Lonsway, 2004, p. 507).

Sexual Harassment in the Police Culture

One of the most unbelievable accounts of sexual harassment is what Romona Arnold, the first female officer in the City of Seminole, Oklahoma, police department, experienced. This case, which was decided on July 10, 1985, documented that in 1977 Arnold's problems began when she was transferred to the midnight shift under the supervision of Lt. Herdlitchka. He informed her that "he did not believe in women officers." He not only refused to speak with her and was hostile toward her, but "he told her that he would harass her until she quit or was fired" (*Arnold v. City of Seminole,* 1985).

The sexual harassment became stationwide when "demeaning cartoons and pictures were posted for public view within the police station with the plaintiff's name written thereon." Her son was arrested and taken to jail in June 1979. The charges against him were eventually dropped "because it was determined that the arrest and detention of plaintiff's son were totally unjustified. Lt. Downing advised plaintiff that the arrest of plaintiff's son was pure harassment." Officers with less service and seniority were promoted over her. When the department obtained new vehicles, male officers got them. She was informed that "as a woman, she didn't know how to take care of it." The windows of her car were rolled down when it was raining so that her seats would become wet. Her name was removed from her mail shelf, and the shelf was eventually removed altogether. Her husband, "a fireman for the City of Seminole, was told that if his wife filed a discrimination complaint, both husband and plaintiff would be fired" (*Arnold v. City of Seminole,* 1985).

On February 25, 1983, perhaps the most serious of all events in this sad account of police deviancy took place. Arnold received a call from Tommy Gaines, a known drug and alcohol addict, who wanted to see her. "He said it would only take five minutes and that it was urgent. When she arrived, Gaines told her that 'the County' had tapped his phone and was taping conversations." He also said, "In exchange for a reduced sentence," he "was to try to set plaintiff up in an illegal drug transaction." He assured her "that the Seminole Sheriff's office and the city police were involved" (*Arnold v. City of Seminole,* 1985).

The court decision concluded that "the plaintiff suffers from sexual assault stress syndrome caused by the sexual harassment and discrimination detailed herein; in addition, she suffers from physiological problems induced by stress and anxiety." As a result, she "has been unable to return to work at the Seminole Police

Department essentially since January 1, 1984, due to the deterioration of her physical and mental health as outlined above."

Eighty plaintiffs have joined the growing class-action sexual harassment and discrimination lawsuit of *Tipton-Whittingham v. Los Angeles*. According to the *Los Angeles Times*, many of the Los Angeles Police Department's female officers felt that the 1994 inquiry into sexual harassment at the West Los Angeles Division was a failure of department leadership, because it did not follow through on this inquiry's recommendations. The inquiry reported sexist and racist remarks, male police officers who failed to back up female officers needing help, and so deeply ingrained mistreatment that policewomen had come to accept it as a part of life. The true scope of the problem will never be known because many female officers were reluctant to complain for fear of retaliation. As expressed by officer May Elizabeth Hatter, who has joined the Tipton-Whittingham case, "Management has thumbed its nose at this problem. . . . I had to prove myself every single day as a police officer. How can management just turn its back on me?" (Daum and Johns, 1994, p. 49).

There are a number of other tragic examples of sexual harassment. A two-week academy cadet was victimized when a firearms instructor approached her from behind, reached around, and grabbed her left breast as she was practicing. In repulsing the advance, she made it very clear that it was unwelcome and offensive. As a result, she failed her marksmanship test. This same instructor refused to send the cadet's broken firearm in for repair, claiming she could not shoot. He told the cadet the next day that she had "better learn to shoot" and called her "stupid" and "a dumb broad." Moreover, this same cadet was assaulted twice by a classmate who "pulled her against his body, and told her that he wanted to feel her body and that her body felt good" (*Watts v. New York City Police Dept.*, 1989).

A policewoman of color was working in the traffic division when she returned to her desk to find seven of her case files ripped and soda poured into her typewriter. She was harassed on other occasions when her personal vehicle was vandalized, including tires slashed, windshield wipers removed, and paint scratched. Furthermore, pornographic pictures were placed in her personal desk drawer and her male coworkers addressed her in sexist terms. Another disturbing incident involved items of her clothing, located in the officer's locker, which had a lime substance placed on them that caused severe burns to her back (*Andrews v. City of Philadelphia*, 1990).

A Caucasian policewoman in the same division was harassed with sexually foul and lascivious language. When she found sexual devices and pornographic magazines in her desk drawer, the males in the unit laughed at her. Officers also removed files from her desk, coworkers refused to help her with work, and she received obscene phone calls at her unlisted home phone number. After complaining to her supervisor about a case file removed from her desk, he warned her, "You know, you're no spring chicken. You have to expect this working with the guys" (*Andrews v. City of Philadelphia*, 1990).

A study done by R. Max Mendel and Elizabeth Shoenfelt (1991) demonstrates bias even in the appraisal process for new recruits. They surveyed a random sample of 226 police chiefs, serving populations over 80,000, to determine what administrative action they would use based on an actual arrest during which a male training officer was shot and after which his female trainee-partner was fired for cowardice. Mendel and Shoenfelt concluded that female trainees were significantly more likely than male trainees to be terminated for the same actions. This predisposition toward biased judgments of policewomen's performance not only questions disciplinary actions against female officers, but also contributes to why female officers are reluctant to report harassment.

Many of the harassment problems endured by female officers in large departments are likewise experienced by policewomen in small-town law enforcement, which makes up 85 percent of municipal departments in the United States. Curt R. Bartol and colleagues' (1992) study on stressors and problems in small-town police departments reported that 53 percent of female officers had been sexually harassed, predominantly by male supervisors; two respondents reported they had been sexually assaulted by male supervisors. Eighty-three percent felt that male supervisors frequently communicated negative attitudes about women in policing. One female officer wrote, "The most stressful factor is the belief that the attitude of male supervisors toward female police officers is not likely to change anytime in the near future or during my career as a law enforcement officer" (p. 240).

African American Women in Policing

Some evidence exists that African American women entering policing have to face a much different reception from African American males. The combination of the effects of race and gender expose African American women to multiple disadvantages, known as "double jeopardy" (Martin, 1994, pp. 383–384). According to some analysts, the African American's "unique social location at the intersection of different hierarchies has produced a distinct feminist consciousness different from that of white women." Martin continues, "White women have ample contact with white men and the potential for increased power by association with one of them. But they have limited their influence by internalizing an image of helplessness and allowing themselves to be 'put on a pedestal'" (p. 384). She concludes that "due to racism, black women have experienced far less protection and a far greater element of fear based on white hostility, physical separation, and intimidation" (p. 384).

Felkenes and Schroeder (1993) found that, during the police training academy experience, the dominant group of white male officers created and supported a culture that both implicitly and explicitly encouraged a wide range of discriminatory behaviors directed against minority women. It is no wonder, then, that minority women officers had higher rates of attrition and lower levels of satisfaction with the training. Subsequent to graduating from the academy, minority women officers continued to experience social discrimination, to face racist and sexist comments sent as computer messages from one patrol car to another, and to have to deal with the existence of openly racist and sexist cliques operating out of several bureaus in the Los Angeles Police Department.

Martin, in examining the interactive effects of race and gender in five large municipal police agencies, conducted in-depth interviews with 106 African American and European American officers and supervisors. One African American woman recounted:

> Males didn't want to work with females, and at times I was the only female or black on the shift so I had to do a lot to prove myself. I was at the precinct 10 days before I knew I had a partner 'cause . . . (the men) called in sick and I was put in the station. The other white guys called the man who was assigned to work with me the 11th day and told him to call in sick . . . he came anyway. (p. 390)

Martin's study also found that several African American women "observed differences in their treatment that reflect differences in the cultural images and employment experiences of black and white women" (p. 394). European American women, especially those who were physically attractive or attached to influential European American men, were more likely than African American women to be protected from street patrol by being given station house duty. When European American women were assigned to the streets, they were more likely than African American women to receive protection from both European American and African American males (p. 394).

This study also found that African American women's relationships to African American males were "strained by tensions and dilemmas associated with sexuality and competition for desirable assignments and promotions." Part of the explanation for these strained relationships was the competition "for position and promotions earmarked 'black' by affirmative action programs." Thus, within these five departments, African American women were, in a number of ways, the victims of "widespread racial stereotypes as well as outright racial harassment" (p. 394).

Success in a Difficult Career Path

Women must decide how they will cope with their jobs because they are, at best, accepted at the fringes of the male's culture of policing. At the extremes of adaptation, women can decide to become either defeminized or deprofessionalized. "Defeminized" women become superefficient and see themselves as as good as or better than their male colleagues. Their competence, then, serves to mask their femininity. In contrast to competing with male colleagues, "deprofessionalized" women accept subordinate status and concessions granted to them (Hochschild, 1973, pp. 79–82).

Martin, in applying these extremes of adaptation to twenty-eight women patrol officers in Washington, D.C., renamed the two polar positions calling them **"policeWOMEN"** and **"POLICEwomen."** POLICEwomen focus on law enforcement, rather than service. They show a high commitment to the job and even criticize fellow female officers. Similar to male police officers, they wish to do specialist work and be promoted. PoliceWOMEN, on the other hand, emphasize the feminine. By accepting the male's invitation to function as a nominal equal, they are actually functioning as assistants or junior partners. They usually receive treatment and exemptions from work tasks that are inappropriate for a "lady" (Martin, 1980, p. 315).

More recently, Brewer (1996) observed two primary groups of women police officers in the Royal Ulster Constabulary in Northern Ireland. The first he labeled "Hippolytes." These women "interactionally manage the question of gender identity by retaining for themselves as much of their femininity as the bureaucratic regimen and the situation allows, and they resist the adoption and performance of occupational traits that are masculine" (p. 241). Described as loners, they avoided participation in the police occupational culture and were not looked on as effective as police officers. The "Amazons" were the polar opposites of the Hippolytes. Brewer reported that these officers used "aggressive humour and all the interactional and conversational devices associated with being 'one of the boys.' Being one of the boys is the defining characteristic of the way the Amazon type handle the problem of their female gender in the masculine occupational culture of the police station" (p. 242).

Regardless of what roles they pursue, women who survive in policing usually develop a thick skin. Men officers frequently pick on female officers, and if they discover their tender points, then they intensify their ribbing. One woman officer, in acknowledging that those sensitive to abuse could not survive an eight-hour shift, revealed her means of adaptation: "I've got a skin like a table. Nothing bothers me. I just made up my mind that I had to take it and live with it and just move on from there and that's what I did. Truly, truly nothing bothers me jobwise" (Fletcher, 1995, p. 162).

Another successful coping technique that women officers use is the talents they have on the job. Many women use their verbal skills to deescalate confrontative or potentially violent situations. Jeanne McDowell (1992) puts it this way, "cool, calm and communicative, they [women officers] help put a lid on violence before it erupts" (p. 70). Another woman officer expressed the importance of verbal skills a little differently:

> So my theory is, you have to go in with your brain. I talk to people. And I talk to big guys and I talk to little guys and I talk to big women and I talk to little women. I talk to everybody. I think it comes in with this basic amount of respect for others as human beings. I don't take things personally. You can't. But a lot of people take things personally. As far as I'm concerned, the uniform walks into a situation all by itself. But it's not me. (Fletcher, 1995, p. 24)

Women, who are normally excluded from the culture of policing, must establish their own supportive and nourishing network if they intend to survive on the job. These networks may be in the departments in which they are employed or they may be statewide or national networks of associations of policewomen (Heidensohn, 1992, p. 197).

Because of their superior interpersonal relationship skills, policewomen appear to handle stress better than their male counterparts. According to Patricia Lunneborg (1989), 90 percent of the policewomen talked out their sources of stress, versus 45 percent of the policemen she surveyed (p. 99). Beermann and colleagues (cited in Blumenthal, 1994) also found that the "double burden" of the unequal division of domestic duties, particularly for those with children, did not result in more severe psychosocial or subjective health impairments. This extra burden, in fact, may be a source of stress relief as policewomen are forced to change roles from cop to mom. This allows them to leave the job behind, avoiding the "live to work" mentality that traps male officers as they become couch potatoes (resulting in withdrawal and numbing of emotions) or associate with other officers after work. Accordingly, "being married and having children is a protective factor against completed suicide for women—but not for men" (p. 3).

Women officers do experience the stressors of both low acceptance in the police agency and lack of access to the peer-group support structure of male officers. The importance of access to this peer-group support structure or police culture is that it helps to mitigate the strain of occupation-related stress by providing a forum within which individual officers can safely ventilate (Lord, 1995, p. 631). J. G. Wexler and V. Quinn's (1985) examination of the occupation-related stress experiences of women officers in a major metropolitan department in California found that women experienced a major stressor in attempting to demonstrate that they could be effective officers without compromising their femininity (pp. 98–105).

Many women police officers report that their jobs contribute to social and marriage problems. They claim that some men are too intimidated to date or marry a female cop (Kirschman, 1997, p. 203). They appear to be intimidated by assertive and self-confident women, whose work is a driving force in their lives, who sometimes are tougher and stronger than they are, and who are authority figures who strap on a gun to protect society and them. An officer reflects on her dating experiences:

> If you're a single woman cop and you meet a guy, it's a three-month thing. That's it. Three months. At first, they love the fact that you're a cop. Then you notice a change. What's the matter? They're intimidated, they're disturbed that you're capable and intelligent.
>
> Well, try to understand. They work nine to five. They go home. You go out on midnights. You put on a gun so you can protect people. That's intimidating. They think they can handle it. But that's bullshit. They can't handle it. They're gone after three months.
>
> Now I don't tell people what I do. (Fletcher, 1995, p. 187)

An Arizona State University study found the divorce rate of female officers to be twice that of the national average and three times that of male officers. In addition, female officers were almost twice as likely to be separated. Twenty-one percent felt that police work was definitely a factor in their divorce, and another 20 percent were undecided (testimony of Leanor Boulin Johnson, 1991).

Women officers also have a lower suicide rate than men officers. Explanations for this are that women are more likely than men to have stronger social supports; women seem to be more willing to seek professional help; and men are more humiliated by job-related life events, job loss, or problems. According to Susan Blumenthal (1996), former head of the Suicide Research Unit at the National Institute of Mental Health, "being married and having children is a protective factor against completed suicide for women but not men" (p. 3).

Policewomen generally are much less involved in deviancy than are policemen. For example, the Christopher Commission found that women officers handled suspects more successfully than men did as they are "less personally challenged by defiant suspects and feel less need to deal with immediate force or confrontational language" (Morrison, 1991, p. 84). Little evidence also exists that women officers are frequently involved in corruption. As Hunt (1990) suggests, an explanation for this might be that male officers tend to fear that "the moral woman would expose police involvement in corruption" (p. 14). Female officers, then, are likely to be excluded from both socializing events with male officers and from whatever corruption is taking place in the department.

Legal Protections

In terms of having a successful and satisfying police career, women police officers need protection from the sexual harassment that traditionally has been present in most police departments.

Four categories of law cover sexual harassment in the workplace: (1) the United States Civil Rights Act of 1964 and 1991; (2) state statutes on fair employment practices; (3) common tort and criminal law; and (4) Statute 42 United States Code Section 1983 (Civil Rights Act of 1871).

United States Civil Rights Act

The **Civil Rights Act of 1964** makes discrimination on the basis of race, color, religion, sex, or national origin illegal. Title VII of this act "prohibits employers from, among other things, discriminating on the basis of sex with respect to compensation, terms, conditions, or privileges of employment" (Rubin, 1995, p. 1).

Congress established the **Equal Employment Opportunity Commission** (EEOC) as the enforcing agency, but restricted its oversight to employers with fifteen employees or more and placed a back pay liability limitation of two years before the filing of charges (O'Linn, 1995, p. 2). In addition, Title VII did not apply to local governments, including police departments, until almost a decade later when Congress passed the Equal Opportunity Act of 1972 (Berg and Budnick, 1986, p. 314). Until then it was rare to see policewomen in a patrol function (Charles, 1982, p. 194).

By 1980, as a result of pressure from women's groups, the Equal Employment Opportunity Commission ruled that sexual harassment was a form of sex discrimination covered under Title VII and issued guidelines on discrimination because of gender (Petrocelli and Repa, 1994, pp. 1, 19). These guidelines did not have the force of law, but were acknowledged by the United States Supreme Court in its first ruling on sexual harassment, *Meritor Savings Bank, FSB v. Vinson et al.* Sixteen years after the *Meritor* decision, Congress passed the Civil Rights Act of 1991 to correct some inadequacies in the Civil Rights Act of 1964.

The new law made possible a jury trial if punitive damages are alleged. Punitive damages are available under Title VII, providing the employer acted with reckless indifference or malice to federally protected rights. The limits on punitives range from $50,000 to $300,000 depending on the size of the workforce. If an employee is successful, the Civil Rights Act provides redress of reinstatement and promotion, back pay and benefits, a limited amount of money damages, injunctive relief to prevent similar harassment from taking place in the future, and a portion of or all of attorney's fees.

Fair Employment Practices (FEP)

Legal definitions of sexual harassment, as well as laws governing the enforcement of sexual harassment laws, vary from state to state. Although some states have no laws at all, most state **Fair Employment Practices (FEP) agencies** have powers similar to the EEOC's to seek remedies. In addition, various states' FEP laws provide remedies for recovering substantial monetary damages for personal injuries without limitations; other states have no remedy. Moreover, states vary widely on the amount of compensation they allow for damages. Only about half the states allow for punitive damages. Several states require that an administrative claim be filed with the enforcing agency before relief can be pursued under the FEP laws in court. Finally, counties and cities often have their own laws prohibiting sexual harassment and administrative agencies (Petrocelli and Repa, 1994). A complainant may find better relief filing with a state agency, but research and possibly legal advice is required to seek the best avenue for a remedy.

Tort Laws and Criminal Charges

A tort claim in state court may be the best solution for some victims; indeed, it may be the only remedy for victims who work for a small agency, whose governing entity's aggregate employment is fewer than fifteen employees (O'Linn, 1995). A tort is a "breach of duty, other than a breach of contract, for which the offender will be subject to legal responsibility" (*The New Lexicon Webster's Encyclopedic Dictionary of the English Language,* 1992, p. 1402). Common law torts include assault, battery, intentional infliction of emotional distress, wrongful discharge, and defamation (O'Linn, 1995, p. 5).

Providing a wider range of remedies than those available under the Civil Rights Act and most states' FEP laws, torts include both compensatory damages for the emotional and physical distress suffered from the workplace harassment and the possibility of large punitive damages aimed at punishing the wrongdoer

(Petrocelli and Repa, 1994, pp. 2, 8). Unlike the Civil Rights Act, which pertains only to the employer, common tort actions can penalize the predator with punitive damages. The following are two examples of common tort claims based on sexual harassment: A woman who quit her job because of sexual harassment was entitled to unemployment benefits even though she voluntarily resigned. The court found that she had been subjected to severe sexual harassment and that any prudent person would have quit. She was awarded unemployment benefits and attorney's fees. The Court of Appeals in Atlanta ruled that a female who brought suit under Title VII against an employer for sexual harassment was properly permitted to bring state law tort claims. This woman was awarded $3,000 in back wages under Title VII, and a jury awarded her $10,000 for common law battery and $25,000 in compensatory damages for invasion of privacy under state law.

In addition to tort claims, criminal charges can be filed against the perpetrator for such actions as assault, battery, and sexual assault. As witnessed in the O. J. Simpson trials, filing criminal charges does not preclude taking civil action. In fact, the criminal action often precedes the civil one for the purpose of solidifying a claim or as a fact-finding measure.

Statute 42 United States Code Section 1983

Until the Civil Rights Act of 1991, there was more incentive to file under United States Code Section 1983 to obtain punitive damages and a jury trial. Unlike the Civil Rights Act of 1991, Section 1983 provides the opportunity to file for punitive damages against the offending party by establishing personal liability. Punitive damages allowed by Title VII are against the employer; Section 1983 can be against the predator (O'Linn, 1995). Section 1983 states:

> *Every person who, under color of any statute, ordinance, regulation, custom or usage, of any State . . . subjects, or causes to be subjected, any citizen of the United States . . . to the deprivation of any rights, privileges, or immunities secured by the constitution and laws, shall be liable to the party injured in an action at law."* (*42 United States Code Section 1983; O'Neal v. DeKalb County, 1988*)

Mildred K. O'Linn, an attorney who specializes in the representation of law enforcement personnel and agencies in civil litigation, reminds law enforcement officers that "Statute 42 of the United States Code Section 1983 provides for civil remedies if an individual acting under color of law violates the civil rights of another individual." She adds that "if you are a peace officer, you are acting under color of law whenever you are on duty or off duty if there is a strong enough nexus or connection made between whatever your actions were and the fact that you are a police officer. Simply put," she says, "you are still acting under color of law if you are using the powers of your office. Under that statute, if you violate an individual's civil rights as a police officer in the form of sexual harassment, you can be sued under Section 1983" (interviewed in 1997).

In *Monell v. New York City Department of Social Services*, the court concluded that "sexual harassment can violate the equal protection provisions of the Fourteenth Amendment, thus creating a basis for an award of damages under Section 1983" (*Carrero v. New York City Housing Authority*, 1989). In addition, Section 1983 offers incentives for attorneys because employers can also be sued as persons (deep-pocket theory), and attorney's fees are recoverable pursuant to 42 U.S.C. §1988 (*Monell v. New York City Department of Social Services*).

The Courts and Findings of Sexual Harassment

Harassment violations were first considered by the court in 1972 in *Anderson v. Methodist Evangelical Hospital*, which required employers to maintain a work atmosphere free from racial and ethnic intimidation and insult (O'Linn, 1993, pp. 4, 14). Since that time, sexual harassment law has been rapidly evolving as courts interpret federal, state, and local antidiscrimination statutes.

According to Sarah E. Burns (1995), the most important unresolved issues concern the amount and kind of proof required to establish certain elements of sexual harassment claims and the employer's liability for harassment by nonsupervisory personnel (p. 193). Other important aspects concern the application of the law to the factual circumstances of a specific case, the evaluation of the parties' claims and proof, and the determination of proper damages. Nonetheless, courts have shown their disdain for sexual harassment practices:

> *Sexual harassment which creates a hostile or offensive environment for members of one sex is every bit the arbitrary barrier to sexual equality at the work place that racial harassment is to racial equality. Surely, a requirement that a man or woman run a gauntlet of sexual abuse in return for the privilege of being allowed to work and make a living can be as demeaning and disconcerting as the harshest of racial epithets. (Henson v. Dundee, 1982)*

Sexual harassment has been categorized in two forms: (1) "quid pro quo" (something for something) harassment—sexual favors as a condition for receiving a tangible benefit, and (2) as a hostile work environment—an offensive environment that unreasonably interferes with the employee's job performance. The first two sections of the Equal Employment Opportunity Commission's definition of sexual harassment pertain to quid pro quo harassment; the last refers to hostile work environment.

Until the United States Supreme Court's ruling in *Meritor Savings Bank v. Vinson*, there was considerable debate in the lower courts as to whether harassment fell into the legal definitions of sexual discrimination (O'Linn, 1995). The Supreme Court concluded:

> *The EEOC Guidelines fully support the view that harassment leading to noneconomic injury can violate Title VII. . . . Since the Guidelines were issued, courts have uniformly held, and we agree, that a plaintiff may establish a violation of Title VII by proving that discrimination based on sex has created a hostile or abusive work environment. (Meritor Savings Bank, FSB v. Vinson, 1986)*

In addition the Supreme Court held that: "... The correct inquiry is whether respondent by her conduct indicated that the alleged sexual advances were unwelcome..." (*Henson v. Dundee*, 1982).

According to some critics, the unwelcome standard places the plaintiff on trial similar to a rape victim. A plaintiff is "routinely required to explain why, if she was being subjected to sexual harassment, consistent with her claim of unwelcomeness, she failed to complain, remained politely silent, appeared flattered, joked, or even affirmatively participated in reciprocal slurs" (Burns, 1995, p. 194). In essence, she becomes the accused having to defend her actions. The proof of unwelcomeness "is usually determined by the sufferer's testimony corroborated by evidence that either she behaved as if the conduct were 'unwelcome' to her or the conduct was the kind likely to be obviously unwelcome or both" (Burns, 1995, p. 195). Proving or refuting a claim of sexual harassment can be very difficult, a he said/she said paradox centering on who is the most creditable person.

The Reasonable Woman Standard

The Ninth Circuit in *Ellison v. Brady* in 1991 focused the severity and persuasiveness of sexual harassment on the perspective of the victim, applying the **"reasonable woman" standard:**

> *We hold that a female plaintiff states a prima facie case of hostile environment sexual harassment when she alleges conduct which a reasonable woman would consider sufficiently severe or pervasive to alter the conditions of employment and create an abusive working environment.* (Ellison v. Brady, 1991)

The circuit court felt that the "reasonable man" or "reasonable person" did not take into account the concerns women share. "For example, because women are disproportionately victims of rape and sexual assault, women have a stronger incentive to be concerned with sexual behavior than men" (*Ellison v. Brady*, 1991).

The decision of the Supreme Court in *Harris v. Forklift Systems, Inc.* two years later was its second on sexual harassment. The Court took the middle ground to resolve a conflict among the circuit courts, holding "that to be actionable under Title VII 'abusive work environment' harassment, the conduct need not seriously affect an employee's psychological well-being or lead to the employee to suffer injury" (O'Linn, 1995, p. 18). The Court did leave vague what standard the plaintiff needed to meet to prevail in such a claim (reasonable woman, reasonable victim, reasonable person standard). In using the test of an objectively reasonable employee, the Court did provide guidance, saying that the totality of the circumstances needed to be considered:

1. How often the conduct occurs;
2. How serious the conduct is;

332 PART FIVE / Women as Professionals

3. Whether the behavior physically threatens the victim, or stops at offensive comments; and
4. Whether the behavior unreasonably interferes with work performance; and
5. The victims must perceive the environment to be abrasive in order for the conduct to be considered illegal. (*Harris v. Forklift Systems, Inc.,* 1993)

Anita Bernstein (1997) argues in an article in *Harvard Law Review* that sexual harassment can be better explained using the concept of respect. She defended the legal virtues of a legal rule that affirms respect, saying that these virtues

> include the resonance of respect as a value among ordinary people, the history of inclusion based on human dignity that informs respect, the orientation of respect around the conduct of an agent (rather than the reaction of a complainant, the focus of current rules) and congruence with a tradition, found in many other areas of American law, of calling on citizens to render respect. (Bernstein, 1997, p. 446)

This standard of respect is actually being used to guide behavior in many businesses. For example, the 3M Corporation's "Appropriateness Test" raises the following questions: "Would I be embarrassed to discuss my language and behavior at work with my family? Would a newspaper account of my language and behavior at work embarrass me or my family? Would I be embarrassed to discuss my language and behavior at work with my supervisors and members of management?" ("The Appropriateness Test").

Rosemarie Skaine (1996) provides more in-depth questions for men to ask themselves to aid in assessing their behaviors:

> Would I mind if someone treated my wife, partner, girlfriend, mother, sister, or daughter this way? Would I mind if this person told my wife, partner, girlfriend, mother, sister, or daughter about what I was saying or doing? Would I do this if my wife, partner, girlfriend, mother, sister, or daughter were present? Would I mind if a reporter wanted to write about what I was doing? If I ask someone for a date and the answer is "no," do I keep asking? If someone asks me to stop a particular behavior, do I get angry and do more of the same instead of apologizing and stopping? Do I tell jokes or make "funny" remarks involving women and/or sexuality? (p. 401)

Issues of Women Working as Police Officers

The good news for women in policing is that they have made considerable progress. The bad news, as documented by the *2001 Status of Women in Policing Survey,* is that the number of sworn women police officers remains small and the pace of increase has stalled or even reversed in large agencies.

It is also discouraging that so few women are in command positions in police departments. As previously noted, over half of the large police agencies reported in the *2001 Status of Women in Policing Survey* (2002) that only 7.3 percent of sworn women officers hold top command positions. In small and rural agencies, fewer sworn women officers (3.4 percent) hold top command positions (p. 4).

In addition, the various studies have revealed how embedded sexism and racism are in policing. Martin found that racism divides white women from African American women and sexism divides African men officers from African women officers. Women of color, then, have the interactive effects of racism and sexism (Martin, 2004, p. 527). African American women continue to enter policing at higher rates than in the past, but few women of color have been hired in the majority of departments, and even in urban departments that have employed more women of color, few are promoted to supervisory status, with even fewer promoted to top command positions (p. 21).

The advent of community policing, especially in those departments that give more than lip service to community-oriented policing, has ushered in a new perspective on the police role that emphasizes cooperation and maintenance of connection with the community. The ideal community officer needs such "feminine" skills as caring, empathy, and connection that historically were unacceptable to male officers and continue to be challenged by many male officers. Yet as Martin has noted, for community policing to succeed, it will need to be repackaged so that adherents of traditional policing do not sabotage its potential for success. Thus, the success of community policing may greatly depend on reshaping unacceptable traits associated with femininity into acceptable traits associated with masculinity and "real police work" so that both men and women are able to deploy talents and skills in the gender-neutral realm of community policing (Martin, 1999, p. 95).

Summary

Policing has been reluctant to accept women police officers for several reasons. Law enforcement is perceived to be a man's job, and it is feared that its image of masculinity can be tarnished by the presence of women wearing police uniforms and carrying guns. The vulnerability of male police officers, so its defenders claim, is increased when men must depend on women for backup and support. There is also the concern that male camaraderie would be immeasurably harmed if a woman's presence interferes with men's talk in the locker room. In this age of sexual scandal, police supervisers are, of course, greatly concerned about the presence of women in the station house and on the street resulting in sexual alliances with married officers and contributing to the breakup of marriages of male officers.

Despite these concocted explanations for rejecting women as police officers, the most viable consideration is whether women can do the job. Research studies continue to indicate that female police officers have somewhat different skills from male police officers but that their competence is equal to that of male officers. These studies have specifically found that women can handle the crime-fighting, combat, rescue, peacekeeping, and social service aspects of police work as well as men. Studies have also found that men and women are equally capable of patrol work. In addition, there is strong evidence that men are in no greater danger with women as partners than they are with men as partners.

Yet the initial resistance to women entering this male-dominated world continues in too many departments. It is found in the appraisal process of new recruits, in supervisory attitudes and treatment, in attitudes of male line officers, and in promotional opportunities and career advancements. Policing may be gender resistant to women, but it is more resistant to an African American police officer. The effects of race and gender expose African American women police officers to "double jeopardy" (Martin, 1994, pp. 383–384). Particularly unfortunate is that African American policewomen not only experience the effects of race from white women and men, but their relationships with African American males on the police force are also often strained (p. 394).

The issue of sexual harassment affects women who work in the criminal justice system. It is a particular concern for women police officers, most of whom have experienced some form of sexual harassment at some point in their careers. The examination of sexual harassment in this chapter reveals that the term *sexual harassment* itself is multidimensional and has been expressed in various ways in law enforcement.

There is much that we do not know about sexual harassment in law enforcement. We do not know what the backgrounds of the offenders are. Are race and ethnicity factors? Are males from some groups more likely to harass women sexually than are males from other groups? Is education a factor? Are college-educated male officers more or less likely to victimize female officers? Is satisfaction in police work a factor? What is the relationship between job satisfaction and sexual harassment? Is emotional maturity a factor? How well adjusted are those who sexually victimize others?

Women police officers who have been pleased with their careers have generally pursued three adaptive strategies to the men's club they must deal with on a daily basis: First, they have attempted to be competent and do the best job possible. Second, on a departmental, state, or national level (and sometimes on all three), they have developed a supportive network with other women officers. Third, they have found positive reenforcements outside the job, such as family, friends, and hobbies, that permit them to balance the difficult experiences they often face on a daily basis.

KEY TERMS

Civil Rights Act of 1964
Equal Employment
    Opportunity Commission
Fair Employment Practices
    (FEP) agencies

lesbian police officers
policeWOMEN
POLICEwomen

"reasonable woman"
    standard
sexual harassment

CRITICAL THINKING QUESTIONS

1. You're a sergeant. A female officer takes you into her confidence to talk to you about male officers who are making vulgar comments about women. She tells you that she does not want to get anyone in trouble or to have the complaint followed up on. What should you do?

2. While attending a briefing, some officers start complaining about a female dispatcher. The male lieutenant responds, "That big-titted bitch is not going to dispatch on my shift." As a patrol officer, what would you do next?

3. You're an officer on the Special Weapons and Tractical Team (SWAT) when a female officer joins the team. She is only allowed to participate in drug raids by driving the support vehicle. The team leader will not help her with her gear and yells at her in front of the team for the smallest mistakes. After she endures a particularly vicious encounter with the team leader, you notice her vomiting behind the van, apparently traumatized by her harsh treatment. What should you do?

4. In your role of lieutenant, several female officers complain to you about three other female officers watching them in the locker room. They are very uncomfortable about this, and if you do not do something about it, they will start reporting for work late to avoid these officers. What would you recommend?

WEB DESTINATIONS

Statistics on women and men personnel in the criminal justice system can be found in: www.albany.edu/sourcebook.

The International Association of Women Police can be found at: http://www.iawp.org/

For the National Center for Women and Policing, *Equity Denied: the Status of Women in Policing 2001*, see: www.womenandpolicing.org

National Criminal Justice Reference Service, Policing in Europe. www.ncjrs.org/policing/fem635.htm

REFERENCES

42 United States Code Section 1983.

Andrews v. City of Philadelphia, 895 F.2d 1469 (3rd Cir. 1990).

Arnold v. City of Seminole, Okl. 614 F.Supp. 853 (D.C.Okl. 1985).

Bartol, C. R., Bergen, G. T., Seager Volckens, J., and Knoras, K. M. (1992, September 1). Women in small-town policing. *Criminal Justice and Behavior 19:* 240.

Belknap, J., and Shelly, J. K. (1992). The new lone ranger: Policewomen on patrol. *American Journal of Police 12*(2): 47–75.

Berg, B. L., and Budnick, K. J. (1986). Defeminization of women in law enforcement: A new twist in the traditional police personality. *Journal of Police Science and Administration 14:* 314.

Bernstein, A. (1997). Treating sexual harassment with respect. *Harvard Law Review 111:* 446.

Blumenthal, S. J. (1994). Cited in Suicide and gender. *American Foundation for Suicide Prevention.*

Brewer, J. D. (1991). Hercules, Hippolyte and the Amazons—or policemen in the RUC. *British Journal of Sociology 42*(2): 231–248.

Burns, S. E. (1995). Issues in workplace sexual harassment law and related social science research. *Author's Abstract Journal of Social Issues 51*(1): 193.

Carrero v. New York City Housing Authority, 890 F.2d 569 (2nd Cir. 1989).

Charles, M. T. (1982). Women in policing: The physical aspect. *Journal of Police Science and Administration 10:* 194.

Daum, J. M., and Johns, C. M. (1994, September). Police work from a woman's perspective. *The Police Chief*, p. 49.

Doerner, W. G. (1995). Officer retention patterns: An affirmative action concern for police agencies. *American Journal of Police 14:* 205.

Ellison v. Brady, 924 F.2d 872 (9th Cir. 1991): 878–879.

Feinman, C. (1986). *Women in the criminal justice system*, 2nd ed. (pp. 81–82, 95). New York: Praeger.

Felkenes, G. T., and Schroeder, J. R. (1993). A case study of minority women in policing. *Women and Criminal Justice 4:* 65–89.

Fletcher, C. (1995). *Breaking and entering: Women cops talk about life in the ultimate men's club* (pp. xi, 24, 162, 187). New York: HarperCollins.

Gallagher, G. P. (1996, November and December). When will the message about harassment be acted upon. *The Law Enforcement Trainer 11*(5): 21.

Harrington, P. E. (2000). Advice to women beginning a career in policing. *Women and Criminal Justice 14:* 1–13.

Harrington, P. E., and Lonsway, K. A. (2004). Current barriers and future prospects for women in policing. In Barbara Raffel Price and Natalie J. Sokoloff (eds.), *The criminal justice system and women: Offenders, prisoners, victims, and workers*, 3rd ed. (pp. 495–510). New York: McGraw-Hill.

Harris v. Forklift Systems, Inc., 114 S.Ct. 367 (1993).

Heidensohn, F. (1992). *Women in control? The role of women in law enforcement.* Oxford: Clarendon Press.

Henson v. Dundee, 682 F.2d 897 (1982), p. 902, as cited in *Meritor Savings Bank, FSB v. Vinson, et al.*, 477 U.S. 57 (1986), p. 67.

Hochschild, A. P. (1973). Making it: Marginality and obstacles to minority consciousness. *Annals of the New York Academy of Science 208:* 79–82.

Horne, P. (1980). *Women in Law Enforcement*, 2nd ed. (pp. xix–xx, 2–5, 10–11, 15–17, 23, 35–36, 52–55, 114, 140, 151, 192, 216). Springfield, Ill.: Charles C. Thomas.

Hunt, J. C. (1990). The logic of sexism among police. *Women and Criminal Justice 1:* 3–30.

Johnson, L. B. (1991, May 20). Testimony in hearing before the Select Committee on Children, Youth, and Families, House of Representatives (pp. 41–42). Washington, D.C.: U.S. Government Printing Office.

Kanter, R. M. (1976). The impact of hierarchical structures on the work behavior of women and men. *Social Problems 23:* 415–430.

Kirschman, Ellen. (1997). *I love a cop: What police families need to know* (p. 203). New York: Guilford.

Lord, L. K. (1995). Policewomen. In *The encyclopedia of police science*, 2nd ed. (pp. 627–636). William G. Bailey (ed.). New York: Garland Press. See also P. Horne. (1980). *Women in law enforcement*. Springfield, Ill.: Charles C. Thomas.

Lunneborg, P. W. (1989). *Women police officers current career profile* (p. 99). Springfield, Ill.: Charles C. Thomas.

Martin, S. E. (1994, August). "Outsider within" the station house: The impact of race and gender on black women police. *Social Problems 41:* 383–384, 389.

Martin, S. E. (1989). Female officers on the move? A status report on women in policing. In R. Dunham and G. Alpert (eds.), *Critical issues in policing: Contemporary readings* (pp. 313, 315, 321–322). Prospect Heights, Ill.: Waveland Press.

Martin, S. E. (1979). Policewomen and police*women:* Occupational role dilemmas and choices of female officers. *Journal of Police Science and Administration 7:* 314–323.

Martin, S. E. (1980). *Breaking and entering* (p. 315). Berkeley: University of California Press.

Martin, S. L. (1990). *Gender and community policing: Walking the talk.* Boston: Northeastern University Press.

Martin, S. L. (2000). Gender and policing. In Claire Renzetti and Lynne Goodstein (eds.), *Women, crime, and criminal justice: Original feminist readings.* Los Angeles: Roxbury Publishing Company.

Martin, S. L. (2004). The interactive effects of race and sex on women police officers. In Barbara Raffel Price and Natalie J. Sokoloff (eds.), *The criminal justice system and women: Offenders, prisoners, victims, and workers,* 3rd ed. (pp. 527–541). New York: McGraw-Hill.

Martin, S. L., Forest, K. B., and Jurik. N. C. (2004). Lesbians in policing: Perceptions and work experiences within the macho cop culture. In Barbara Raffel Price and Natalie J. Sokoloff (eds.), *The criminal justice system and women: Offenders, prisoners, victims, and workers,* 3rd ed. (pp. 511–525). New York: McGraw-Hill.

Martin, S. E., and Jurik, N. C. (1995). *Doing justice, doing gender* (p. 55). Thousand Oaks, Calif.: Sage Publications.

McDowell, J. (1992, February 17). Are women better cops? *Time:* 70, 72.

Mendel, R. M., and Shoenfelt, E. (1991, March 21). Gender bias in the evaluation of male and female police officer performance. Paper presented at the Annual Convention of the Southeastern Psychological Association, New Orleans.

Meritor Savings Bank, FSB v. Vinson, et al., 477 U.S. 57 (1986), p. 66.

Milton, C. (1972). *Women in policing.* Washington, D.C.: Police Foundation.

Monell v. New York City Department of Social Services, 436 U.S. 658 (1978).

Morrison, P. (1991, July 14). Women make better cops L.A. probers find. *Los Angeles Times.*

National Center for Women & Policing. (2002). *Equality denied: The status of women in policing: 2001.* Washington, D.C.: U.S. Government Printing Office.

National Law Enforcement Officers Memorial Fund, Inc. (1997). Law enforcement facts.

The new Lexicon Webster's encyclopedic dictionary of the English language (p. 1042), Deluxe ed. (1992). Danbury, Conn.: Lexicon Publications.

Newton, J. (1996, December 8). Harassment complaints continue to dog LAPD. *Los Angeles Times.*

O'Linn, M. K. (1995, January). Sexual harassment, handout prepared for the American Society of Law Enforcement Trainers Convention, Anchorage, Alaska, pp. 2, 4, 5, 14, 18.

O'Linn, Mildred K. Interviewed in 1997.

Petrocelli, W., and Repa B. K. (1994). *Sexual harassment on the job,* 2nd ed. (pp. 1, 2, 8, 19). Berkeley, Calif.: Nolo Press.

Platt, A. (1969). *The child savers* (p. 76). Chicago: University of Chicago Press.

Reaves, B. A. (1996). *Local police departments* (p. 1). Washington, D.C.: Bureau of Justice Statistics.

Rubin, P. N. (1995, October). Civil rights and criminal justice: Primer on sexual harassment. *National Institute of Justice: Research in action.* Washington, D.C.: U.S. Government Printing Office, p. 1.

Schaper, D. (1997, January 28). More women in uniform could be a force for peace. *Newsday:* 32.

Schulz, D. M. (1993). Policewomen in the 1950s: Paving the way for patrol. *Women and Criminal Justice 4:* 5–30.

Schulz, D. M. (1995). *From social worker to crimefighter: Women in United States municipal policing* (pp. 4, 10, 134, 135). Westport, Conn.: Praeger Publishers.

Schulz, D. M. (2004). Invisible no more: A social history of women in U.S. policing. In Barbara Raffel Price and Natalie J. Sokoloff (eds.), *The criminal justice system and women: Offenders, prisoners, victims, and workers*, 3rd ed. (pp. 483–493). New York: McGraw-Hill.

Skaine, R. (1996). *Power and gender: Issues in sexual dominance and harassment* (p. 401). Jefferson, N.C.: McFarland.

Status of women in policing: 1998. (1999). Washington, D.C.: National Center for Women & Policing.

3M Corporation. The Appropriateness Test.

U.S. Dept. of Justice, 1996 survey published in *American Police Beat 3* (October 1996): 24.

Watts v. New York City Police Dept., 724 F.Supp. 99 (S.D.N.Y., 1989).

Webb, S. L. (1991). Step forward: Sexual harassment in the workplace. What you need to know! *Master Media:* 26–29.

Webb, S. L. *The global impact of sexual harassment.* New York: Master Media Limited, 1994.

Wertsch, T. L. (1998). Walking the thin blue line: Policewomen and tokenism today. *Women and Criminal Justice 9:* 25–26.

Wexler, J. G., and Quinn, V. (1985). Considerations on the training and development of women sergeants. *Journal of Police Science and Administration 13:* 98–105.

12 Women in the Legal Profession

Women have made far more significant advances in the legal profession than in law enforcement (Rollins, 1996). Women now make up almost a third of the profession, and most law schools have an almost equal enrollment of both sexes (American Bar Association [ABA], 2003). In recognition of the contrast between women's accomplishments in law enforcement and law, a headline in *Working Woman* (1996) proclaimed, "Law and Order! Women Sit on the High Court, But on the Beat, It's a Man's World." Although this headline exaggerates women's success in breaking down the barriers in the practice of law, as we will see in this chapter women have made strides in this field that twenty to thirty years ago could only have been imagined.

Women have gravitated toward law in record numbers. Their rapid movement into the profession, in turn, has laid the groundwork for further possibilities. From the famous former prosecutors Marcia Clark and Janet Reno to Senator Hillary Rodham Clinton, a nationally prominent attorney in her own right, to Supreme Court Justices Sandra Day O'Connor (now retired) and Ruth Ginsburg, to law professors Lani Guinier and Anita Hill, to TV host, Nancy Grace, women lawyers are in the limelight. And for every one who has achieved national prominence, many more across the country are quietly making a contribution to law and, through law, to the whole society.

Because in the Anglo-Saxon tradition, the judiciary plays a recognizably powerful role, women's success here is of no small consequence. The "feminization of the legal profession," as Chen (2003) optimistically terms it, is occurring not only in the United States but in several Anglo-Saxon and European nations as well. In Canada, for example, women represent 53 percent of new entrants to the bar (The Law Society of Upper Canada, 2003). In the United Kingdom, 30 percent of all barristers (those who argue cases in court) and 40 percent of all solicitors are women (UK Department for Constitutional Affairs, 2005). This year about half of those called to the bar in the U.K. are women.

Irish law professor Ivana Bacik (2003), who participated in the first-ever report on women lawyers in Ireland, remarked on the dramatic increase in the numbers of women entering the legal profession in recent years; two-thirds of law students in Ireland, in fact, are women. Solicitors are 41 percent women while one-third of barristers (courtroom lawyers) are women and one-fifth of judges are women. The latter figure, as Bacik indicates, compares favorably with the number of judges in the United Kingdom, but not with France and Finland where the sex ratios for judges are about even.

In Norway, over half of law students are female. Women are well represented in the legal profession in Russia, where the practice of law is highly bureaucratized, and in countries like China, where they are likely to work in public service (Menkel-Meadow, 1995). The proportion of women lawyers is smallest in Japan and India where traditional sex roles remain very strong. In Germany, women flock into civil service jobs because family and maternity leaves are substantial; approximately one-third of the judges are women, accordingly.

Women's recent progress notwithstanding, the fact is that women are concentrated in the lowest echelons of the profession. The consistent pattern, as Menkel-Meadow (1995) suggests, is that women are "pulled" into work for which they are thought to have special talent, such as domestic relations, and "pushed" or kept out of high-status work, such as private commercial matters. Universally, women are underrepresented in litigation, even in egalitarian Norway, where they are overrepresented in the lower ranks of central government. In the United States, significantly, almost all paralegals are women.

Women's remarkable advances in the legal profession, in short, are cause for celebration but not complacency. In the law, as elsewhere, status and income disparities still exist. The strong differentiatials between male and female are reflected in the statistics that about half of new entrants to the bar are women but that women make up only 16 percent of partners in the nationally registered law firms, 33 percent of the American Bar Association's Board of Governors, and 17 percent of the federal bench (ABA, 2003).

What is true for women is true for minorities as well. Women of color are often isolated in law firms, and most leave before their seventh year. African American women gravitate toward work in the public sector and in small firms in big cities with a large African American clientele. Women of color now account for about 20 percent of entering law students but they remain underrepresented in the upper ranks of the profession (Rhode, 2001). This does not mean their contribution is to be discounted, however. Take, for example, the work of Yeshimebet Abebe. The granddaughter of a well-known African American and the daughter of a native of Ethiopia, Abebe exemplifies the adage, "Think globally, act locally." In 2003, Abebe's strong showing in a Waterloo, Iowa, mayoral election ultimately threw the election to a third candidate. Her education has been strikingly global (Jamison, 2003). After finishing law school, Abebe, who holds a master's degree in international law as well as a law degree, was the first American to receive full funding to study at the United Nations' University for Peace in Costa Rica. She has worked on the settlement of disputes through international tribunals and has spoken out internationally against human rights violations, including the racism of her U.S. milieu at home. Today Abebe continues her international work in human rights from her law office in Atlanta, Georgia (interviewed by van Wormer, October 7, 2005).

History of Women in Law

Women lawyers have come a long way, and most of the growth has occurred in the last ten to fifteen years. Besides Shakespeare's Portia who, disguised as a young man, brought a soft touch to the law in her famous "the quality of mercy is not strained" exhortation (Shakespeare, 1600/1970: 4.1.182), few literary or historical examples of women advocates in court exist. The first practicing lawyer in North America was Margaret Brent, who was asked by the governor of Maryland to be the executor of his estate. Brent became officially empowered by the Maryland legislature to serve as the governor's executor and lawyer and to settle claims by soldiers against his estate. So powerful was she in her day that colonists called her "Gentleman Brent" (Menkel-Meadow, 1995). After litigating 124 court cases on behalf of the governor's estate, Brent moved out of Maryland because she was denied the right to vote (Morello, 1986).

Not much was heard from women again on the issue for a long time, until the mid-1800s (Bernat, 1992). Before that time, women were prohibited from attending law school or otherwise qualifying to take the bar exam. Some evidence does exist that some women appeared before the local courts, especially out West to defend land claims. One such woman, an African American named Lucy Terry Prince, successfully defended a land claim before the U.S. Supreme Court before the Civil War (Morello, 1986).

During the 1830s and 1840s, women began to struggle for the right to own property and to work (Bernat, 1992). In Britain, women worked hard to reform marriage and divorce law and property rights. Under the principle of coverture, women could not own property in their own names or enter the legal profession (Menkel-Meadow, 1995). The professions were considered improper avenues for women because of their unique biological characteristics, which suited them to the home. Working-class women and the servant classes, of course, were under no such requirements to stay home. In both Britain and the United States, women's involvement in the abolitionist, suffrage, and temperance movements galvanized them to further ambitions.

The usual method of becoming a lawyer in the early days was through a clerkship under the auspices of a practicing attorney. Women who did study the law under this arrangement clerked with their husbands and fathers. The reasons that impelled women to enter law were somewhat different from those that drew women to corrections and law enforcement; pioneers in legal practice were not primarily reformers but were motivated more by practical and intellectual considerations (Feinman, 1994).

The first woman to be officially recognized as a lawyer in the United States was Arabella Babb Mansfield who was admitted to the Iowa State bar in 1869. The first female to graduate from a law school in the United States was Ada Kepley who graduated from the University of Chicago law school in 1870. In 1872, Charlotte E. Ray became the first black woman to formally enter the practice of law (Smith, 2000). She was admitted to the District of Columbia bar the same year she graduated from Howard Law School.

An ardent suffragist, Ada Kepley urged women to support temperance and seize political power. As long as discriminatory admissions policies continued, however, women could not get their hands on power. In eastern urban schools and at Ivy League colleges, women were denied admission well into the twentieth century (Bernat, 1992). The state laws were gradually changing, but in Britain, it was not until 1919 when the Sex Disqualification Removal Act was passed that the official barriers to women lawyers were lifted (Menkel-Meadow, 1995). Moreover, the legal profession continued to be exclusionary on the basis of class, race, ethnicity, and gender (Abel, 1995). The proliferation of the apprenticeship system kept "unsuitable" aspirants out. On the Continent, where the university was the entry route, women entered the legal profession earlier than they did in England, which relied on legal apprenticeship, as Abel indicates.

Admission to the bar presented a barrier to women in the United States. Before the summer of 1869, there was little hope that a woman would be permitted to practice law anywhere in the country (Friedman, 1993). Then, surprisingly, thanks to a progressive Iowa judge who was dedicated to women's equality, Arabella Mansfield was quietly admitted to the bar in Iowa. She never did practice law, however. One state away, in Illinois, Myra Bradwell (who studied law in her husband's law office) was seriously committed to a legal career. After performing brilliantly on the bar exam, Bradwell was still denied admission to the Illinois bar. Her appeal to the U.S. Supreme Court was denied not solely on the basis of gender, but also because as a married woman she could not sign contracts on behalf of her clients, a requirement for any lawyer. The Court's refusal to overturn Illinois's prohibition against women practicing law meant that women, by necessity, would be engaged in a state-by-state struggle for admission to the bar (Morello, 1986). Bradwell was to achieve her major impact on the legal field not through the practice of law but as editor of the highly influential *Chicago Legal Notes*.

It was not until 1918 that the American Bar Association began to accept women. Ultimately, it was the state legislatures, not the courts, that struck down the barriers to female practice. Women made up 1.1 percent of all lawyers in 1920, and between 1950 and 1970, women's percentage grew to a mere 3 or 4 percent.

Special mention should be made of the civil rights pioneer Constance Baker Motley, who as a young attorney represented Martin Luther King, Jr. and played a pivotal role in the civil rights movement (Neumeister, 2005). Earlier she had been a law clerk to Thurgood Marshall and through this connection she helped prepare some of the nation's most important civil rights cases, including the 1954 landmark case *Brown v. Board of Education* of Topeka, Kansas, in which the Supreme Court ruled that segregation in the public schools was unconstitutional. Motley died recently at the age of eighty-four.

This limited historical overview reveals a firm resistance to women's entry into the legal profession, as compared with their acceptance into social work, teaching, nursing, and even medicine. With regard to the latter, by 1971 women constituted 7 percent of American physicians, double their numbers in law (Menkel-Meadow, 1995). Although law is construed as masculine, perhaps thanks to its legacy of trial by combat, women could argue that their special qualities render them especially suited to caring for the sick.

The passage of **Title IX** of the Higher Education Act in 1972, which prohibited discrimination based on sex in the enrollment of students and hiring of faculty, was a landmark decision in terms of opening the doors to budding female attorneys (Martin and Jurik, 1996). Facing denial of federal funds if they continued to discriminate, law schools began admitting women applicants in unprecedented numbers and still do so today.

As women gained entry into law school in the 1970s, they continued to find many unexpected obstacles in their path. The reasons for the resistance to women in law can never be fully explained, but as Morello (1986) suggests, it is likely that it has to do with the law's close relationship to power in society. As in other male-dominated fields, such as the police or firefighting, many men felt that their masculinity and stature would be threatened if women were admitted to their ranks. The story of Flora Stuart (author van Wormer's sister), the first woman attorney to practice trial law in Bowling Green, Kentucky, typifies some of the difficulties women faced breaking into the profession in the 1970s. One of few women in her northern Kentucky Law School class, Stuart met tremendous resentment from professors (Hurst, 1977). Because of this coupled with the fact that some of the male law students refused to have anything to do with the women, Stuart helped found the Women Lawyer's Club, which was to grow dramatically over the following decade. How to dress professionally for court, to be confident and assertive without seeming aggressive or whiny, to be feminine without appearing flirtatious, and to persuade the members of a jury used to heeding male authority—all were dilemmas the women law students confronted that had to be resolved in the absence of role models or mentors.

Shortly after passing the bar exam, Stuart, as a young public defender was catapulted to early prominence with a case that was any feminist's dream: a young woman charged with manslaughter for performing an abortion on herself with a knitting needle.

"Miss Flora," as the judge called her, argued for her beautiful young client, the defendant, before a packed courtroom. Reporters from *Time* magazine and *Newsweek* were among those in attendance. Following a not-guilty verdict came guest appearances for the lawyer and her client on *Good Morning, America* and the *Phil Donahue Show*. Today, Stuart concentrates on personal injury cases; she has recently settled dozens of silicone breast implant lawsuits. She has what must be one of the few mother-daughter law firms in the country. In her words:

> *A second glance at the major law firms would immediately reveal the fact that the lead partners are mostly male. Women who join the firms now rarely move to the top. Finding a mother and daughter as a legal team is still rare, but it is not unusual to find a father and son duo practicing law together. Some attorneys (particularly from the earlier generation) still find it difficult to accept a female attorney as their full equal. Time will eventually melt away these extreme prejudices against our gender, but the battle is far from being won.*

Twenty-two years after I started my journey down the legal road, my daughter now practices law by my side. It is a different world from when I began. (Stuart, 2005, p. 1)

The contrast between the professional challenges that mother and daughter have known symbolizes the differences in the world a woman lawyer faced in the 1970s and the world of today. Unlike her mother, Natalie Stuart attended a law school in which almost half the students were female and was taught by female as well as male professors. On graduation, a place in an established law firm was ready for her. In her hometown, her mother had already blazed the trail. Not only is there no shock on people's faces today as the younger Stuart begins her opening statement before the "ladies and gentlemen of the jury," but the judge is likely to be a female, as is the opposing counsel.

A historical perspective is provided as well by the host of CNN Headline News' legal analysis show, Nancy Grace (2005) who recalls in her autobiography, *Objection!*, her early days as a prosecutor. In her words:

> *Sexism is alive and well in the courtroom. . . . One of the reasons I am writing this book is to propose remedies for the existing problems in our justice systems. Sexism is still an issue. It's the same way in the courtroom as it is in every other profession in this country: Women have to work twice as hard to be taken seriously and get the same job done as their male counterparts do. Lawyering is no different from any other profession in that way. There is one big difference in how it affects female lawyers, though. The prejudice against female lawyers has an impact on more than the individual—it affects her clients, her cases, and her causes. A case could be won or lost because of a sexual bias. Traditionally, juries love judges, because they look up to them and respect them. Whether that bias originates with the judge or the defense, the jury picks up on it.*
>
> *When I first came to the district attorney's office, there were very few female cops and lawyers—female judges were even harder to find. At the time, women were usually assigned to work juvenile cases, which are not jury trials and do not apply many of the standard rules of evidence. We were usually going after deadbeat dads, writing appeals, or acting as assistants to trial lawyers. Practically everybody involved in the actual trial of cases was a man—except the jury and, in many cases, the victim.*
>
> *I've been called "little lady," "young lady," "lady lawyer," and other not-so-nice names, right in front of juries by defense lawyers, experts, and judges—pretty much by everybody but the jury. (p. 163)*

Grace goes on to say that if a lawyer files a sexual harassment complaint or a motion for a hostile judge to recuse himself, it could seriously harm the case and all future cases before that judge or his cronies.

Law School Socialization

Given what law professor Patricia Williams terms the "clearly stated authority" of the law, that body of "hypnotically powerful rhetorical truths," as a female African American teacher of law she had to wrestle with the appropriate introduction of race, gender, class, and social policy into the law school curriculum (Williams, 1991, p. 10). She also had to confront the legacy of the institutional racism, sexism, and classism at her university. Williams's iconoclastic book, *The Alchemy of Race and Rights,* is the product of that struggle. Law school's mask of impersonality and "hyperauthenticity," as Williams suggests, is a cover for rigidity and prejudice. Being in law school is described by Williams as being on another planet, and being a law professor as being in another galaxy.

The traditional law school experience is sufficiently rigorous and formidable to be the subject of numerous films, novels, and nonfiction books. Because the dictates of the bar exam in each state to a large extent decree the nature of the education that law schools must offer, the law school experience is relatively comparable across the states.

In a painstakingly documented article published in the *University of Pennsylvania Law Review,* Guinier, Fine, Balin, Bartow, and Stachel (1994) presented a wealth of data on students, male and female, enrolled in law school. Entitled "Becoming Gentlemen: Women's Experience at One Ivy League Law School," this much-cited article convincingly presents the case that the law school experience of women differs markedly from that of their male peers. This study's findings are that women:

- despite having identical entry-level credentials to men are far less likely to excel academically;
- in their first year are much more highly critical than their male peers of the status quo, of legal education, and of themselves as students;
- as third-year students are far more complacent and less idealistic than they were earlier;
- enter law school with commitments to public interest law and justice and leave, like the men, with corporate ambitions;
- are alienated in class and report lower rates of class participation than men; and
- are inclined to complain of the change that has come over them and feel submerged in a foreign belief system. (pp. 1–2)

One of the most pervasive values of legal culture inculcated in law school is the belief in individuation through hierarchical stratification, according to Guinier and colleagues. Such practices as rigidly ranking students against each other and ranking faculty and deans as well as upper-level students above lower-level students within the law school trains students for later hierarchical relationships and a winner-take-all mentality. For female law school recruits, learning to think like a lawyer, as Guinier and her associates suggest, means learning to think and act like a man.

The narrative data collected by these authors add a poignancy to the findings. In interviews, women law students told of eating disorders, sleeping difficulties, crying (35 percent reported crying from stress compared to none of the men), and failure to learn in the intimidating environment of hostile questioning. As one third-year law student described her experience,

> *Just look at the way many professors here conduct their classes. They call on men predominantly. . . . I think if you look at the people in our class who have formed relationships with professors, they are very much the same men who all of us despise in class. The ones who feel they can monopolize the class time. (p. 51)*

Another woman concurs, "Women's sexuality becomes the focus for keeping us in place. If someone was rumored to be a woman who speaks too much, she was a lesbian" (p. 14). All the female students seem to echo the sentiment that human compassion is a negative trait in budding lawyers.

Stone (1997) echoes the sentiments of Guinier and her associates that U.S. law students generally succumb to peer pressure to abandon dreams of public interest work in favor of more lucrative and less altruistic forms of practice. The uncertainty and loss of confidence that women suffer in law school no doubt crush their resistance and lead to a turnabout in attitude. Compared to the American law school experience, however, the Australian equivalent, as Stone observes, is far less traumatic, and somewhat more hospitable to social welfare concerns. Female law students in Australia, therefore, are less demoralized than their American cousins and seemingly less malleable in the hands of their professors.

But the climate in American law schools is changing thanks to the influence of the influx of female students and women in positions of prominence on the faculty. Lani Guinier, who now teaches at Harvard Law School, has been instrumental in introducing more women-friendly approaches to teaching law (Zhao, 2004). Guinier's mission is to end the dominance of the Socratic Method, which demands quick responses and invites caustic treatment. Men are often better at giving quick, definitive answers under the intense pressure that this method creates. Guinier likens the Socratic Method to ritualized combat. The new teaching approach is built on teamwork and role-playing; the purpose is to redesign the classroom experience so that people with different learning styles can all thrive.

Patriarchal Nature of the World of Law

The world of law is decidedly and unequivocally masculine. It is not masculine in a physical sense but in a psychological sense. To have a "legal mind" is to be logical, or left-brain dominant. The law, in its Anglo-American format, is necessarily a site of conflict. It provides a means of dispute, notes Harrington (1994), but the means are combative.

A brief overview of the Anglo-Saxon **adversary system** will put the masculine, winner-take-all ethos of today's courtroom into historical perspective. "We are what we were," as the John Quincy Adams character in the 1998 movie *Amistad* so eloquently informed us. The origins of the adversary system hark back to trial by combat and before that and even more primitive, to trial by ordeal. Today the trial is the ordeal.

The rationale for our Anglo-American adversarial legal approach is found in its history. The history is one of ancient customs of judicial ordeal based on magical dogma. In the Middle Ages in England, the ordeals of fire, food, and poison required the accused to demonstrate the solicitude of some all-powerful spirit. With William the Conqueror, trial by battle was brought to the island. Eventually, no dispute existed that might not be submitted to the decision of the sword or club. Hired champions represented the interests of involved parties. According to Anne Strick (1977), trial by ordeal is alive and functioning in the United States; the judicial ordeal is now called the "adversary system" (p. 37).

The adversary model attempts to resolve differences through the opposition of two parties; the ultimate aim of cross-examination is to arrive at the truth (Gardner, 1982, p. 22). Whether this gladiatorial process is properly suited to the resolution of most family relations problems, such as divorce, or to provide justice to crime victims is another matter (Bazemore and Schiff, 2001).

The "hired champions" who fought in combat on behalf of the accused or accusing party were all men. Victory depended on physical strength and quickness. Law schools today are the training ground for success in the juridical ring. Through the harsh discipline of law school, the minds of the students are molded into marvelous instruments of control, or such is the aim. Law students are trained in verbal argumentation, "to make the worse appear the better cause" (see Aristophanes, 423 B.C.). Strategies that are compelling and victorious in the courtroom may one day suffice in the political arena as well. Lau (1983) viewed the patterns of legal thinking—the dichotomizing and aggressive argumentation—as having started far earlier than law school. In a comparison between the stereotypical masculine lawyer and the feminine social worker, Lau suggested that the characteristics might have a basis in dominant thought processes. The distinction may be biological, she contended, in that certain types of personalities are more attracted to certain types of professions. The qualities that make for a good lawyer are competitiveness; the ability to find creative solutions to problems and to persuade clients to take them; a willingness to take risks but knowing when to pull back and compromise; acting talent for convincing juries that the implausible is plausible; excellent short-term memory for quick mastery of the facts in a complicated case; sharp attention to detail while never losing sight of the big picture; and, above all, the versatility to work with people of diverse class and ethnic backgrounds. That these traits are not gender specific is revealed in the success of women attorneys in this competitive field today.

Legal Practice: Struggles in a Man's World

In her book, *Women Lawyers: Rewriting the Rules,* Mona Harrington (1994) followed women into the world of work. At the law office, women are torn between requirements of "the mind" and of "the body" and between the need to dress professionally and to be considered feminine at the same time. How to wear their hair is a minor crisis in itself. Harrington painted a picture of the legal landscape as cutthroat and highly competitive.

A fascinating biography of Hillary Clinton by Brock (1996), appropriately entitled *The Seduction of Hillary Rodham*, gives some idea of the pressures facing a young radical feminist trying to break into an established southern law firm:

> *The firm's secretaries, who resented having to work for a woman in the first place, made cruel comments about Hillary's appearance behind her back, to which she could not have been oblivious. The comments likely amplified her sense of alienation and rejection by the locals, whom she may accordingly have judged in her own mind all the more harshly as country bumpkins.*
>
> *   "At first, she didn't wear stockings and the old ladies at the firm were horrified," said Hillary's former Rose secretary from the late 1970s. "She was a comic figure as a lady lawyer. Her hair was fried into an orphan Annie perm. She had one large eyebrow across her forehead that looked like a giant caterpillar. We laughed until we cried. She tried to look good when she went to court, and she would put on some awful plastic jewelry. She'd be wearing high heels she couldn't walk in. There wasn't one stereotypically womanly or feminine thing about her." The office staff considered Hillary's weight problem an endless source of amusement as well. "She was on a perpetual diet," the secretary said. "She would show up for work with a big bag of lettuce and eat out of it all day." (p. 81)*

Even when women achieve conformity to the standardized legal norms, their patterns of interaction separate them from their male colleagues. In a content analysis of conversations between male lawyers and male clients, female lawyers and female clients, male lawyers and female clients, female lawyers and male clients, and same sex and mixed dyads of lawyer and lawyer, Bogoch (1997) was able to systematically measure gender differences in interaction. The setting was a legal aid office in Israel. What Bogoch found is that when clients related to female lawyers as women rather than as professionals, the women felt compelled to emphasize their legal role to the client. For example:

> *Lawyer to client: Look Madam, I am not a social worker. I'm a lawyer and I can't, I don't have time to hear this whole story from the beginning. (p. 10)*

Male lawyers in similar situations did not feel the need to define their professional roles; they simply deemed the client's remarks as irrelevant and returned to the task at hand. Occasionally, female attorneys did step out of their professional conception of themselves to relate to the life world of the clients; women lawyers especially granted legitimacy to the emotions of male clients.

Many women, noted Harrington (1994), shun chronic engagement in battle and gravitate toward areas of the law where they can work on deals, as between companies. The "macho" ethic of the office subjects women to subordinate roles. The emphasis among the male attorneys on winning as the ultimate value, and among prosecutors on browbeating witnesses, is distasteful to many women. Several of the African American women Harrington interviewed developed severe stress-related problems after working as tokens in big law firms.

A major stumbling block for women is the relentless work ethic and resistance to reduced or flexible schedules (Rhode, 2001). Salaried legal associates and partners are expected to work sixty- to seventy-hour weeks. Many of the large law firms in the East have an annual 2,000 **billable-hour quota.** This leaves no time for social life, family, or to "have a life." In the *ABA Journal's* 2000 poll, a third of the women doubted that it was realistic to combine the roles of lawyer, wife, and mother (Rhode, 2001). Twelve-hour days and weekend work are typical. Unpredictable deadlines, uneven workloads, and frequent travel pose further difficulties for those with family obligations. Although many of the largest law firms allow for flexible schedules, the message is, if you take that path you are not serious about your career. Accordingly, in the ABA poll of women attorneys, only 4 percent of respondents said they used part-time schedules. Part of the reason women can't take advantage of part-time schedules is that men are socialized not to take them. Due to the excessive demands of the work structure, there is a continual outmigration of women from the big firms, the "warrior-lawyer's habitat," and into routine, in-house positions, such as in the realty department of an investment firm. The cloister aspect of the in-house position effectively removes women from the power structure. Other possibilities, however, such as joining a small law firm with a civil rights focus or teaching on the faculty of a law school, do give women a voice and provide a network of lawyers who can recognize themselves as a class. We will consider women's influence on the legal system later in the chapter, but read the positive account in Box 12.1 of how one lawyer, Miryam Antunez de Mayolo, juggles motherhood and cases that many other attorneys probably would not touch.

B O X 12.1

Lawyer Juggles Motherhood, Cases

by Anelia Dimitrova

Miryam Antunez de Mayolo is a living proof of the American dream both in her profession and her personal life.

The immigration attorney and mother of seven-year-old triplets says that her story is very different from those of the immigrants she represents, but her reasons for coming to this country fourteen years ago were just as compelling.

Miryam left her native Peru to follow her husband, Philip Mauceri, a professor of political science at the University of Northern Iowa, to the U.S.

In the past seven years, Miryam has heard hundreds of immigrants stories, much less fortunate than hers. The 1998 University of Iowa Law School graduate believes that being

an immigration lawyer in the heart of the country is a noble calling.

"When you take into account that there are very few Spanish speaking immigration attorneys in the state of Iowa, and there is such a need for representation, practicing immigration law is tantamount to missionary work," she says over coffee and a cone at Cup of Joe's on a recent Tuesday morning. "I have to drive four and a half hours to get to immigration court."

Last month, Miryam moved her office to 315 West Second St., across the street from the premises she shared with attorney Ronnie Podolefsky. The transition has inspired Miryam to paint the house in colors reminiscent of paintings by Latin American artists. The ocean

(continued)

BOX **12.1** Continued

blue in her office reminds her of the Pacific Ocean where she used to surf while growing up in Lima. Surrounded by the pictures of her mother, Mari Teresa, and her father, Santiago, Miryam feels that she is continuing the family tradition while at the same time blazing her own path on American soil.

The cases she has worked on have enriched her life, Miryam says.

Her cases have caught the attention of local and statewide newspapers. The case of William Keleture, an assistant track coach in the Quad Cities, originally from the Sudan, is her most recent victory.

"He was almost on the plane, being deported to the Sudan, when I took the case," she says. "An attorney he had hired previously failed to do his job and did not file a brief in a timely fashion, so William was apprehended and taken into custody, regardless of the fact that he is married to an American citizen with whom he has a girl almost the same age as my children."

Last week, when the judge granted Keleture permanent residence, the emotion in the courtroom overwhelmed William and his wife.

"They were just in tears," says Miryam. "Even the journalist from the Quad-City Times who was there to cover the story was crying."

Immigration law is rather complex, says Miryam, because of the way it is drafted. "The power that the Department of Homeland Security has is unparalleled. After 9/11, things changed dramatically for the worst. People are so accustomed to their freedoms here that they don't really know or can't imagine that some of those freedoms are not enjoyed by immigrants who are placed in the removal proceedings. Sometimes, they are not even bondable, which I believe is unconstitutional because

everybody should have the right to be bonded out. We are not talking about criminal proceedings here since immigration court is an administrative body."

With all the hurdles immigrants face, coming to the U.S. continues to be a magnet for many.

"Most of the people I have represented throughout the years want to play by the rules and they just want what everybody else wants—a better future for their families and that's why they are here."

Motherhood has made Miryam a better lawyer, she admits. "When I represent someone who is going to be separated from his or her children, I know what is at stake," she adds.

Critical Thinking Questions: What is the nature of de Mayolo's contribution? How does this attorney's personal story impact her law practice?

Source: Cedar Falls Times, July 23, 2005, p. 1. Reprinted with permission of Anelia Dimitrova, editor.

In private correspondence to van Wormer (of August 18, 2005), de Mayolo described how her work relates to criminal law: "Criminal law intersects with immigration law quite often, since immigrants, even those who have been legally here for many years, and have spouses and children who are U.S. citizens, can be deported for committing even minor crimes. For instance, someone with a conviction for possession of cocaine will be deported, even if it's for personal use, even it's a first-time offense, regardless of the time he has spent in the U.S., regardless of the ties he has to this country, and regardless of the hardship that his deportation would pose to his family members. It is quite draconian." Then in a final paragraph she expresses her gratitude to the earlier generation of lawyers such as Flora Stuart who blazed the trail before her. "Every time I enter a courtroom, I am keenly aware that I have the privilege, because women like her [Stuart] had the guts to pave the path for me; and I am oh so thankful!"

Women on the Bench

The number of women on the bench in any generation is the product of the opportunities and experiences of women in law school and practice in earlier periods (Miller and Meloy, 2007). When women are restricted to law specialties handled in the back room rather than the courtroom, to legal research rather than litigation, they are effectively kept out of the eligibility pool for judgeships. They are also prevented from establishing the kind of reputation that could lead to judicial appointment.

At the 1998 conference in St. Louis of the National Association of Women Judges, an organization that has grown from 100 members in 1979 to more than 1,300 members today, current and former chief judges shared their stories. The stories typically concerned opposition to women in such positions of leadership by "in-your-face" male colleagues. Resistance to the female judges took many forms, ranging from locking one woman in her chamber room to inflicting verbal abuse on others (Lhotka, 1998).

In Milwaukee, also in 1998, the State Bar of Wisconsin honored the state's first 150 women lawyers, lawyers who broke through extraordinary legal and cultural barriers to achieve their right to practice law. Few of these women, however, went on to become judges. Not too many years ago, according to Janz (1998), the only robes women were permitted to wear were bathrobes.

Today, about 16 to 17 percent of Federal District Court Judges and U.S. Court of Appeal Judges are women (ABA, 2003). At the state level, women's numbers have risen to 28 percent. In just four years, between 1994 and 1998, the number of judges seated as state supreme court judges doubled (Rybak, 1998). Women are often assigned to jurisdictions that are traditionally considered the specialty of women, such as municipal or domestic courts in which, according to Feinman, women judges have little status and are provided few contacts so essential for those seeking a political career. Judges in domestic relations court (where many women judges work) do have wide discretion, but these courts—which handle matters such as divorce, child custody, and adoption arrangements—are at the lowest end of the judicial status totem pole. Although severely limited by court procedures and case law, not to mention mandatory sentencing laws, trial judges still possess an influence that extends beyond what they do in the courtroom. In the words of one Kentucky female circuit judge, "What you all do in the back halls and your informal conversations with male judges really has an influence on how they treat women in the courtroom" (Cross, 1999, 1B). Through such influence at equal status levels, women judges can help their male colleagues have greater sensitivity both for the kinds of pressure female attorneys face in the courtroom and for female victims and offenders who appear before the court. They also can help male judges have greater awareness when it comes to such matters as sexual harassment and job discrimination.

It is in the multijudge appellate courts, including state and federal supreme courts, however, where women can have the most impact. Here, as Feinman suggests, a woman can ask questions, raise issues, present data, and influence the progress of the discussion or debate. Therefore, it is significant that women are now being appointed to state and federal appellate courts in unprecedented numbers. One might expect that those women will help move public policy in the direction of greater sex equality. The need for adequate representation of women on the U.S. Supreme Court is, of course, essential.

But do women on the bench bring a different touch to justice? Does gender affect judicial decision making at all? Studies of judges' attitudes and observations seem to indicate that they do, and not only in the United States.

Among the research findings: Florida statewide samples of over 300 male and female judges revealed that women who dispense justice are more aware than their male counterparts of biased treatment of women in the courtroom (Stepnick and Orcutt, 1996); in-depth interviews with five female judges in an eastern state revealed that the women judges believe they are able to empathize more with victims than their male counterparts (Miller and Meloy, 2007). Young female judges have a heightened awareness of sexual harassment in the courtroom (Padavic and Orcutt, 1997); a New Zealand study revealed that female, compared to male, judges were twice as likely to believe that a female expert witness would be taken less seriously than a man and that the law reflected male interests and concerns predominantly (Bain, 1997); a Canadian study of decision making of women on the male-dominated Supreme Court of Canada found that the two women judges were more likely than the men on the court to be willing to "rock the boat" and write minority opinions (Tibbetts, 1999).

As more women take their place beside men in "courts of last resort," a new dynamic is emerging, according to an article in *The Christian Science Monitor* by Ryback (1998). "We do not feminize the bench, we humanize it," the California superior court judge is quoted as saying in this article (p. 1). Often focused on different issues from their male counterparts, women are subtly changing courthouse culture and the tenor of American jurisprudence. This fact is confirmed by the newly appointed female supreme court justice in Minnesota, Chief Justice Kathleen Blatz. A longtime supporter of children's issues, Blatz has a master's degree in social work as well as a law degree. Her self-description includes this accomplishment: "Loves to bake and is renowned for her peach cobbler" (p. 1).

Foust (2004) closely examined the personal style of women in public life in relation to their fulfillment of the cultural gender myth. Her discussion centers on the career and persona of Judge Judy Sheindlin, a TV judge who tries real cases and has been able to hold the attention of a wide audience. On the surface, Judge Judy's success is a paradox in that she is personally aggressive and sharp-spoken, yet popular with the American public and seen as a non-threatening. Foust explains Sheindlin's acceptability in terms of her role as **Tough Mother.** Like women of the early American Temperance Movement, Sheindlin may publicly speak in an aggressive way because society respects her moral authority. The Tough Mother emerges, as Faust explains, as an ideologically conservative, virtuous agent who employs practical advice to rescue a scene corrupted by morally lax citizens. Moreover, her persona plays into some of the public's worst victim blaming tendencies as she verbally assaults the people, usually poor and uneducated, who come before her. She scolds litigants for disrespect as well if they interrupt her or speak out of turn. Moreover, she often tells them they are lying and relies on intuition rather than the law in her rulings. Sheindlin's "take-no-prisoners" style taps into the public's growing resentment of people who are out to cheat the system or otherwise behave immorally. Foust's analysis draws our attention to the fact that a woman in law or politics who adopts a conservative, aggressive style may be less prone to criticism than her counterpart from the left wing who may invite the wrath of neoconservative elements and seem threatening to men (of a certain type).

Race, Class, Gender

To review one of the major assumptions of this book, the oppressions found in gender, class, and race are very much related to the careers of women lawyers.

Gender and Discrimination

Despite the generally favorable climate and the unprecedented opportunities for women in the law today, a legacy of discrimination remains. Although more women now hold faculty and administrative positions in law schools than in earlier decades, they are still accorded relatively low prestige if, as teachers, their main focus is on "women's issues" as opposed to business and corporation law (Feinman, 1994). Furthermore, female law students study case law from the male point of view; only men's opinions are cited. Legal issues that are important to women, such as marital rape, wife beating, and family law, meanwhile may be dealt with only superficially, as Feinman further suggests.

Survey results reported by MacCorquodale and Jensen (1993) indicate the depth and scope of gender bias in the legal profession. Males surveyed seemed relatively unaware of gender bias. Women were very aware of tokenism, preferential treatment by the judges and other lawyers, and inquiries addressed toward women to verify their professional status.

According to a survey of 220 female attorneys working in a midwestern city, many women reported that their gender helped them get hired (Rosenberg, Perlstadt, and Phillips, 1993). But respondents reported that discrimination existed in salary, promotion, and assignments. Approximately two-thirds of the women reported being addressed as "honey" or "dear" and receiving remarks about their appearance. Young women were especially susceptible. One-fourth of the lawyers reported being sexually harassed in the courtroom.

Rainmaking is a term that refers to the amount of business a member of a law firm can generate. More than anything else, rainmaking is the barometer of success in the legal world today. Critics complain that law is less driven by altruism and more driven by profit than it formerly was.

Still largely excluded from old boys' clubs, female lawyers are at a clear disadvantage, socially and professionally, compared to men. Legal experts explain that women's other obligations, such as family pressures, prevent them from entertaining or traveling (Deutsch, 1996). Women rarely participate in team sports or other male-type bonding activities. To help compensate for their lack of connections, some female lawyers are forming clubs, such as the Eleanor League of Detroit, members of which meet every month and routinely refer business to each other. In Miami, groups of minority and women lawyers have joined together to get greater representation on the South Florida bench (Haggman, 2003). While women and Cuban Americans have had success in being elected and appointed to the bench, African Americans and Caribbean Americans have been under-represented, and therefore the focus of the chapter of women lawyers is on this group. And in Chicago, women lawyers network over breakfast or lunch (Murphy, 2004). There is a bit of a sorority feeling at such events as women talk about things they don't discuss around men. At the national level, the National Association of Women Lawyers holds annual conferences that focus on issues relevant to career goals. Masters (2004) described a panel presentation at the Washington, D.C., gathering on the importance to women's success of an effective mentoring program and balanced working hours. Similar conferences are planned in major cities across the United States.

Also at the national level women are taking a very active role in annual meetings of the American Bar Association. They also have been instrumental collectively in establishing state and federal task forces on women and gender bias in the courts. Sexual harassment is a part of this bias, which is being thoroughly investigated.

Sexual Harassment

Following the Clarence Thomas–Anita Hill hearings, **sexual harassment** and discrimination claims filed with the Equal Employment Opportunities Commission increased 71 percent. Among the litigants were partners and associates in major law firms. Unwanted touching and other forms of sexual harassment were among the charges.

Like sexual demands on an unwilling wife, sexual harassment of women by male colleagues expresses the ancient rule that women should be sexually available to men. The existence of sexual harassment means that the woman who objects may put her career at risk; this form of activity reminds the professional woman that she is not really an equal (Harrington, 1994). Above all, sexual harassment is an abuse of power, sometimes by an older man inflicting unwanted attention on a younger, often unmarried woman. Typically, the harasser flatters himself that the woman enjoys his attentions. Most women are familiar with such examples of abuse of power in the form of sexual games and innuendos. Another form of harassment, *gender harassment*, is less obvious and less related to the perceived sexual attractiveness of a woman. Gender harassment entails *belittling* a woman as a woman, as a means of putting her down and preserving the status quo. Although prohibited under federal law by 1980, and by the Civil Rights Act before that, tradition decreed that sexual bantering and teasing were natural to relations between the sexes and that only male-bashing, prudish women would raise a fuss over teasing or "sweet talk."

The **Equal Employment Opportunity Commission (EEOC)** regulations passed in 1980 to protect the rights of minorities and women followed a survey that produced hard data on the extent of sexual harassment within the federal government. The two aspects of sexual harassment that were discussed in the previous chapter are quid pro quo, which implies a trade-off of sexual favors for job benefits, and the creation of a hostile work environment through offensive sexual conduct. These categories are the basis for sexual harassment suits. As Schultz (1988) notes, however, the law tends to equate workplace harassment with sexual pursuits, to the utter disregard of nonsexual forms of harassment. We need to attend to the larger social structures of workplace gender discrimination in which both sexual and not-so-sexual forms of harassment flourish (Schultz, 1998). Clearly, a greater commitment has to be made at the management level of law firms to encourage and provide an environment that is more receptive to women (Merlo and Pollock, 1995). Almost all law firms now have sexual harassment policies, which typically follow federal regulations prohibiting unwelcome sexual advances and conduct creating an intimidating, hostile, or offensive working environment. Yet recent surveys show that between almost half to two-thirds of female lawyers and somewhat fewer court personnel report experiencing or observing sexual harassment (Rhode, 2001). Sexual propositions, physical groping, and abusive comments remain a problem. As Rhode concludes in her report from the Commission on Women in the Profession, a lot of progress has been made over the last decade although more could be done in the future through training of supervisors and ensuring protection against retaliation. Stereotypical assumptions about gender, race, ethnicity, and sexual orientation are equally in need of attention.

Synergistic Nature of Race, Class, Gender, and Sexual Orientation

Race, class, and gender, as previously noted, are not simply additive forces; the effect of membership in more than one of these categories is **synergistic.** A woman, for example, who is both African American and working class inhabits a world in which the forces of gender, race, and class intersect with each other through the social and economic structure (Anderson and Collins, 1995).

The fact that approximately half of all African Americans grow up in poverty restricts their life chances; it also stigmatizes the members of that race as lazy and uneducated. We need to recognize that the intersection of race, class, and gender is not limited to those at the bottom of the social ladder. In the professions, especially prestigious professions such as law, one is expected to have the bearings of gentry. This includes a polished manner of speech and dressing like a lawyer in a subdued, not flashy, style of dress (Reidinger, 1996). A desirable attribute of a lawyer is the ability to bring business into the law firm. Bringing in poor clients charged with petty crimes may be considered a minus more than a plus.

In the legal profession, to be a person of color, lower class, and a woman is to have three strikes against you before you start. The path to law school is extremely difficult for persons without educational and financial advantages. The low-income college student must obtain loans and work his or her way through college. This ordinarily means less study time and a lower grade point average. The privileged student, on the other hand, has the luxury of study time and the lack of heavy financial debt. Then come the expensive crash courses in LSAT (Law Scholastic Aptitude Test), an exam that appears to be culturally and gender biased. Affirmative action programs help compensate for gender and racial discrimination in our society but not for class.

In her study, "The Plexiglass Ceiling: The Careers of Black Women Lawyers," Simpson (1996) examined the ways in which race and gender intersected to shape the career transitions of 238 African American women lawyers. Respondents worked in municipal and federal government predominantly, but also in private practice and law firms. Fifty-four percent had college-educated parents. Racism and sexism in law were first evidenced in law school. Of the respondents, 87 percent said discrimination was rampant. Alumni from a prestigious northeastern school recalled that the dean of students said that admitting blacks had lowered their academic standards. Ninety percent of respondents stated that they had been excluded from student study groups. This pattern of discrimination was further evidenced at the job entry level. Opportunities to practice in high status, powerful, and financially remunerative sectors of the profession were found to be few and far between for these African American attorneys.

In the University of Pennsylvania study described earlier (Guinier et al., 1994), attrition rates, or movement from job to job, were studied as an indirect gauge of career satisfaction. Almost 90 percent of the respondents moved from their first job to another entry-level position. Government lawyers showed the most stability. Respondents felt that "not being a white male" limited their chances of promotion tremendously. Questionnaire and interview results revealed that although affirmative action policies and programs dramatically increased the number of African American women lawyers, a "Plexiglass ceiling" limited their career choices.

A major economic obstacle confronts most law school graduates. Following law school, these graduates, like others, must pay for an expensive crash course to prepare for the bar exam and take a legal assistant job while awaiting bar exam results. Assuming favorable results, the newly admitted member of the bar may bear a debt of easily well over $100,000.

A major difference in the kind of specialty that women and minorities tend to choose occurs in the public interest arena (in which 4 percent of women compared to 1.7 percent of men choose to work). This arena includes legal aid and public and public defender work and, in general, work with the poor. Within the other branches of law, women are more likely than men to be willing to engage in pro bono legal work. The law firms do not reward their lawyers for performing work for the needy as a public service; only work done for billable hours is rewarded.

Income disparities between male and female lawyers are pronounced. Women lawyers' median weekly salary for full-time work is 76 percent of men's

(ABA, 2003). The disparities in pay are the most extreme in private practice, even when years of practice are accounted for. Also reported in an ABA survey was the lack of credibility women felt they had; about half reported being mistaken for an assistant (Compensation and Benefits for Law Offices, 2003).

In summary, given the structural conditions of the legal profession, it is very difficult for women of any ethnicity or background to assume positions of leadership or power within the profession. And yet, entering into the ranks of the powerful (whether through marriage or career) is the only way to have an impact. This is what is happening today, slowly and surely, as women acquire the language and tools of their successful brothers.

Mass Media Images

"The first thing we do, let's kill all the lawyers" (Shakespeare, 1590/1970 *King Henry VI, Part II*, 4.2.86). This sentiment from the sixteenth century is echoed today in newspaper articles, joke books, and comments by the general public concerning the alleged greed of attorneys. Whether or not everybody is suing everybody, this is often the public image. And it is true that the United States has the highest number of lawyers per capita of any country (the count is expected to climb to one million by 2000) and the greatest number of legal cases (Gubernick and Levine, 1996).

The low public image of lawyers is pervasive (Foust, 2004). Newspaper articles and magazine accounts decry (or proclaim) the unprecedented number of attorneys opting out of the profession. In Canada, too, many lawyers are dissatisfied with their work because of the long hours. In a recent study of ten large firms, a majority of the women and half of the men planned to leave the profession within five years (Schmitz, 2005).

American women of color have the lowest law firm retention rate of any group. One reason for this fact is the relative absence of mentoring for this group (Rhode, 2001). A related problem is that women of color are often confined to certain specialties for which race or ethnicity is viewed as an asset.

Despite growing tolerance toward gay and lesbian attorneys, those who are open about their sexual orientation too often risk isolation and denial of access to clients who might feel uncomfortable in their presence. Some lawyers in the ABA survey made it clear they did not want any gays or lesbians around. Women of color and lesbians reported overhearing racial slurs and homophobic jokes. Women in general reported being addressed by their first names when men are not. Commonly reported stereotypical assumptions that affect both the lawyers and their clients are that:

- Domestic violence victims are responsible for provoking, tolerating, or declining to report abuses;
- Rapes involving acquaintances are less harmful than "real" (i.e., stranger) rapes;

- Mothers who work full time or who have same-sex partners are less deserving of custody than fathers who are heterosexual or who have second wives willing to be full-time caretakers;
- Promiscuity is more serious for female juvenile offenders than for male offenders. (p. 22)

What has happened to the profession? As Gubernick and Levine (1996) suggest,

Law was once a respected profession. That was some compensation for the hard work and long hours. No longer. The antics and outrageous lawsuits launched and sometimes won by trial lawyers, and their corrupting influence on public life, have driven public regard for lawyers to new depths. (p. 75)

"No fee unless you win." This phrase, used in legal advertising to entice winning personal injury cases, sums up the contingency fee arrangement in a nutshell. Lawyers sue on behalf of injured clients when the claim is against a company or individual with assets. Lawyers collect 33 to 40 percent of the damages; usually such cases are settled out of court. If the case comes to court, as a civil case, the level of proof required is lower than that in a criminal case. The winning civil case against O. J. Simpson in the death of his wife illustrates how justice can be achieved monetarily when criminal justice cannot. The flaw in this system as it operates in the United States is that innocent people can be sued for damages and win, and yet still be socked with exorbitant legal expenses.

In the past, female attorneys concentrated on the divorce and family law, legal aid work, wills, and criminal law cases nobody wanted. Personal injury settlements were handled by men. Today, in states where lawyers advertise without restriction, assertive women can market their services through ads in telephone books, on the radio, and on television. Whether from reticence or complacency, however, few women have taken advantage of the possibilities for acquiring business through the use of the media.

In personal correspondence, Stuart (2005) recalls her success in marketing her services in the state of Kentucky:

Being somewhat of an anomaly and minority has had its advantages. My own firm, consisting of predominantly female attorneys, started many years ago and now includes my daughter. We describe ourselves as being the "family law firm that cares about people." What better way for an office of all females to express the compassion we have for our clients? I have even been known to shed a few tears with my clients (imagine a male attorney shedding tears). Our clients love it! (p. 2)

Television and Film Portrayals

We have been talking about the mass media. One of the main ways the general public forms impressions of a particular profession is through fictional accounts, especially through television portrayals. The first point that should be made about such portrayals is that they are far removed from legal reality. Typically these fictional accounts center on courtroom drama; never mind that the drama of trial is only an infinitesimal part of what lawyers do (Goldfarb, 2004). Even in criminal and civil law, most cases are settled out of court. And sensational cases are few.

Harrington (1994) conducted a study of Hollywood and television dramas involving women lawyers. One major theme during the plots in many of the shows is the women's attempt to maintain their feminine qualities in a world of power and intrigue. Harrington calls these the mind/body stories. The women who become too cold and calculating are sure to be punished in the end.

The plot of *Presumed Innocent* concerns the just deserts women victimizers of men receive. The movie begins with the murder of an attractive power-seeking prosecutor who, we learn as the plot unfolds, deserved her fate. The TV drama *L.A. Law* carried a similar warning to career women who manipulate men to get ahead. A tough, successful middle-aged attorney who has waged a successful sex-discrimination suit gets killed in a freak elevator accident.

Other images of women lawyers parallel yet contradict these images of women who successfully fight for justice through their clients, such as in *The Accused* and *The Client*. Similarly, lawyer heroines expose corruption in *Class Action* and *Music Box*, although at considerable personal cost. But on the whole, Harrington concludes, the ranks of the new heroines do not include a cadre of idealistic lawyers. Fictional lawyers, unlike their real-life counterparts, seem relatively unaware of both cultural biases in the legal system and the need for social change. Historically, the roles of female lawyers in the movies have been uncomplimentary to women and to lawyers, as Asinow (2002) suggests. In *I Am Sam*, for example, Michelle Pfeiffer's character is rude, disorganized, and unprofessional in her representation of a retarded man who is fighting to retain custody of his daughter.

A refreshing development is the casting of women in convincing professional roles such as the DA Helen Gamble, played by Lara Flynn Boyle, feminine as they come but hard as nails; or Camryn Manheim in the role of feisty attorney Ellenor Frutt, who fights for the underdog. The show was ABC's *The Practice* which premiered in the fall of 1998 (Graham, 1998). *The Practice* maintained its popularity for several years. Although it degenerated into "gimmicky sideshows" (Goldfarb, p. 5) before it came to an end, *The Practice* revealed some realistic attorney disagreements about the handling of tricky cases and portrayed women lawyers and judges intelligently during most of its protracted run. The new CBS production *Close to Home* presents Annabeth Chase as a young, attractive prosecutor of high ethical commitment, an advocate of victimized women. *Court TV* has brought real-life court cases to the public with some good results. Viewers can now watch real courtroom drama and gain insights about courtroom practices; the competence of women as defense attorneys and prosecutors shines through.

Strengths of Women Attorneys

How are women lawyers using their authority to help individual women? How are they advancing the equality of women generally?

To answer the first question, we can consider the work of the lawyers who described their careers for this chapter. Jones (2004) describes two law firms, one in

New York and one in Philadelphia, devoted exclusively to female clients and women's issues such as hormone-replacement and breast and uterine cancer diagnosis litigation. The clients, as Jones notes, find their women lawyers more understanding and empathic for such medical work. A New Orleans attorney sees much potential in marketing her business as a woman's firm; this firm offers a "grandmotherly" image and specializes in child custody cases.

In one type of criminal defense work, a woman has an advantage that raises serious ethical issues for feminists, and that is in representation of accused rapists, child molesters, and male batterers. Sociologist Cynthia Siemsen (2004) sought to discover how female defense attorneys balance feminist ideology against the defense of men accused of rape and similar anti-woman crimes. Most of the lawyers she interviewed who took such cases put the higher value on seeing that everyone gets a fair trial. The reason this is an ethical problem for women is that women are asked to use their gender as a strategy to strengthen the defense. When the defense attorney cross-examines the victim, members of the jury see one woman attacking another, and often blame the victim. Fortunately, women in private practice can usually decline to represent clients accused of rape, domestic violence, and the like, and many undoubtedly do so. But others, as Siemsen suggests, focus their attention on constitutional rights and manage their emotions accordingly.

Now to the second question: How are women lawyers advancing the equality of women generally? Whether the influx of women into the legal profession will transform the profession—feminize it—or whether the legal profession will transform women into clones of men who "think like a lawyer" is a hotly debated issue. Some theorists argue that women bring to the law a "different voice" that will enable such values as caring, empathy, and mediation to become more central to legal practice (see Anleu, 1992; Harrington, 1994; Jones, 2004; and Menkel-Meadow, 1995). Others proclaim that the bastion of the law is so imbued with male values such as value-free objectivity, abstract rights, and adversarial know-how that there is little scope for women to make a difference. Anleu refers to the former arguments as the "cultural feminist approach" and the latter as the "radical theorist approach." Both approaches offer a one-dimensional view of women, according to Anleu; women's differential locations within the settings need to be taken into account. Established female attorneys may thrive in their own law firms. Stuart (2005), in a semihumorous vein, provides the following account:

> My practice blossomed because women wanted a female attorney who could empathize with their plight—especially in divorce cases. Much to my surprise, men also began hiring me so they could have "a woman on their side." I later began handling bankruptcy cases in Federal Court and the creditors called me the "Bankruptcy Queen."
>
> Presently, we have established the only female law firm in our community. Through the years, some of my male clients have come up with such endearing names for me as "country child" (he wrote a poem for me). My favorite name was "pretty whipper snapper." Just this year, an opposing attorney with whom I was reviewing a case addressed me as "Listen Lady." (p. 2)

Let us now return to the question of whether women who enter law school lose their ideals through rigorous socialization or whether they emerge from their education with their principles unscathed. In truth, this is not an either-or proposition. As women or other minorities or working-class people enter the power structure, they can still hold onto their original values and goals. True, legal training socializes women to be advocates, to engage in gladiatorial-type contests for hire, and to be tough in negotiation. On the other hand, to paraphrase Audre Lorde (1984), acquiring the master's tools alone will never dismantle the master's house (p. 123). In other words, acquiring the legal knowledge and credentials may be a necessary but not sufficient condition for effecting social change. Real power and change, as Lorde argues, come with bonding (on the basis of race, class, and gender) and a militance in acknowledging rather than denying our differences. If we merge with the power structure, on the other hand, we will suffer a loss of identity. Borrowing Lorde's metaphor, we can conclude that only through acquiring the master's tools and gaining access to the power structure will we be able to dismantle the master's house. The risk is that in joining the rich and powerful, lawyers who set out to change the world will lose sight of their original goals.

Ronnie Podolefsky (1998), a feminist activist turned lawyer, has seen how economic pressures and materialism can divert even the most idealistic law students from their original course. See *Voices of Women and the Criminal Justice System* for an interview with Podolefsky, a specialist in employment discrimination and at the time of her writing, a member of the National Organization for Women board of directors. A recent interview with Flora Stuart is provided in the *Voices* booklet as well.

Significance of Women's Entrance into the Law

When women make their presence felt in a formerly all-male preserve, whether in the military, in prison, or in substance abuse treatment, the social climate changes: The effect is humanizing and even salutary (see Champion, 1998, p. 325). In an article entitled "Jurisprudence and Gender," Robin West (1998) argues that women bring to the legal culture a sense of literal connectedness with others and a linking between family and work that permeates the atmosphere. Jack and Jack (1989), in their study of the changing values of men and women lawyers, found the traditional male-female divide: men focusing on competition and winning, and women favoring cooperation and compromise; men reasoning formally and abstractly, and women reasoning contextually and holistically. As women intrude on an all-male preserve, such as a traditional law firm, the social climate changes. Conversations among colleagues are more personal than in male-only establishments. Personal experience and personal values relevant to legal work become integrated; the social norms shift to allow for ongoing conversations about one's family and recreational life (Harrington, 1994). The level of friendliness and intimacy at a cogender law office is palpable.

Another interesting effect of women's entry into legal work is revealed in Shore's (1997) study of the relationship of gender balance at work, family responsibilities, and workplace characteristics among male and female attorneys. Data for a survey of more than 500 male and female attorneys revealed that work-related drinking diminishes as contact with women peers becomes more frequent. The extent to which both men and women had household and child-related responsibilities after work also influenced the extent of workplace drinking.

Politically, women's presence in law has had an impact, even beyond their numbers. To gauge this impact, we have to look to the opposition. Conservative critics such as Weiss and Young (1996) inveigh on the courts and legislatures to resist efforts by feminists to limit individual rights under the guise of protecting women as a class. Weiss and Young's tirade about the "harm" feminist activists have done is oddly encouraging:

> In the past decade, feminist legal theory has become a formidable presence in many of America's top law schools. Feminist activism has also had a major impact on many areas of the law, including rape, self-defense, domestic violence, and such new legal categories as sexual harassment. However [the purpose of] the new agenda is to redistribute power from the "dominant class" (men) to the "subordinate class" (women), and such key concepts of Western jurisprudence as judicial neutrality and individual rights are declared to be patriarchal fictions designed to protect male privilege. (p. 1)

The writers further express their concern over the effects of feminist pressure regarding "loose and subjective" definitions of harassment and rape, "dangerous moves to eviscerate the presumption of innocence in sexual assault cases," and the "license to kill" that battered wives enjoy with regard to their allegedly abusive spouses (p. 1).

The impact of female activist lawyers, as Weiss and Young feared it would, has been pronounced. Consider the impact of Washington, D.C., attorney Brigida Benitez who worked for six years on affirmative action cases for the University of Michigan. When the Supreme Court finally settled the matter in June 2003, it marked the most important statement on affirmative action in a quarter of a century (Russell, 2005). The case involved a lawsuit by three white college applicants who claimed discrimination because race was considered in the application process. The Supreme Court upheld the university's policy to ensure diversity in the student body for the advantage of all students. *Hispanic Business* magazine singled out Benitez for her work on this once-in-a-lifetime case. Benitez was selected as Woman of the Year not only for her groundbreaking work but also her community pro bono service. As a Latina lawyer Benitez is a part of the minority of 3 percent of male and female lawyers who are Hispanic.

Law school, as Weiss and Young imply, is a powerful, transformative experience. Widely regarded as an ideological training ground, law school historically has been the domain of aggressive white males. Today, change is under way. Tightly enforced affirmative action programs at universities have resulted in an influx of minorities and women into the teaching arena. It is in this arena of law school that the feminist voice is increasingly heard.

What is the feminist legal theory to which Weiss and Young refer? And what is the nature of its impact? Sharyn Anleu (1995) describes feminist legal theory as a "transformative potential [that] derives from women's experiences of exclusion" (p. 395). These experiences create an outsider's critical perception, which engenders empathy for other subordinated and oppressed groups. In contrast to traditional legal theory, which stresses value neutrality, feminist theorists promote consciousness-raising as a central element in empowering the client. Through consciousness-raising, students are made aware of sexism, racism, and classism and of how some inequalities can be rectified through resourceful use of the law and courts. Feminist litigation is taught as one means of addressing human rights violations against women. Consistent with this perspective, law school professors and lawyers tend to recommend alternative, dispute resolution procedures, especially in family law and child welfare where the avoidance of adversarial conflict is an advantage to all parties. In regard to wife battering and rape, on the other hand, as Anleu indicates, women's groups tend to be adamant about the use of criminal penalties; they see little scope for mediation in light of inequalities in bargaining power between men and women.

One hope for the future is that the active involvement of women in the law and their keen interest in human rights issues based on gender and race will help galvanize the United States in the international arena. We are referring to international treaties, signed and unsigned, and to earlier statements by retired Supreme Court Justice Sandra Day O'Connor and current Justice Ruth Ginsburg that international law should be taken into consideration on issues such as the execution of mentally retarded persons and juveniles (*The Economist*, 2005). Furthermore, in this increasingly globalized century, input from women lawyers and judges who collectively have been subject to human rights violations may make their mark in helping to shape legislation to protect the rights of vulnerable populations.

Summary

The members of the first generation of women lawyers tended to be white, upper-middle- to upper-class, and the daughters or wives of lawyers, and they devoted all their energy to gaining the right to practice. They won tolerance rather than acceptance by playing conventional female roles and by being nonthreatening. Myra Bradwell, who worked toward legislative reform crucial to women, was an exception. The suffrage movement from the 1890s to 1920 and the postsuffrage era saw a little more legislative activity, but compared to other professions such as medicine or correctional administration, women have been largely excluded from the male legal power structure.

Thanks to federal laws from the 1960s, many of the traditional barriers against women's entry into the legal field, including law professorships, have been broken. Today, we are seeing a rise in a new class of professionals, women trained in knowledge of the law, who refuse to be treated as second-class citizens. The creation of specialized women's groups such as the Commission on Women in the Profession of the American Bar Association, the National Women's Lawyers Association, the National Association of Women Judges, and regional networking groups helps compensate for the reluctance of established attorneys to mentor new female recruits. Professional networking among women has helped to cata-pult some among their ranks to positions of national prominence and provide other women with the psychological support they need for professional growth. For all women in society, the gain is tremendous. For victims of crime, especially of sexual and physical abuse, for women seeking a divorce or needing to write a will, and for female offenders, female advocacy can provide a rare sense of protection. Male clients, similarly, can benefit from a warm, personal touch.

Discrimination against women in the legal profession persists nevertheless. In this chapter, we reviewed evidence that continues to show that our judicial arena retains its status as a battleground between opposing forces and still tends to be stratified by gender, race, and class and that women in law firms are less likely to become full partners during their careers, to earn as much money as their male peers, or to thrive in the highest-paid legal specialties. Moreover women, compared to men, express more dissatisfaction about their treatment in the courtroom and by other lawyers. Sexual harassment is the norm, especially for younger attorneys.

Despite the barriers erected to keep women out of the practice of law and, ultimately, lawmaking, many women have found a niche for themselves in this august and challenging field. Although only a small percentage of the female attorneys see themselves as social activists, those who do are developing new models for the practice of law and new arguments to guide their legal briefs. In short, in the practice of law, many women are finding fulfillment as they adopt the **"tools of the master"** for their clients' ends, perhaps not to "dismantle the mas-ter's house" as Lorde (1984) envisioned but, less drastically, to remodel and reno-vate it—and then to add some personal, finishing touches.

KEY TERMS

adversary system
billable-hour quota
Equal Employment
  Opportunity Commission
  (EEOC)

sexual harassment
synergistic

Title IX
"tools of the master"
Tough Mother

CRITICAL THINKING QUESTIONS

1. Consider the career path for women in the legal profession; to what extent have women been able to get their hands on power through the law?

2. Discuss male resistance to women's entry into this profession and the reasons for it.

3. Consider the title of Lani Guinier and colleagues' book, *Becoming Gentlemen*. What is the meaning of this title with regard to law students?

4. What does having a "legal mind" entail?

5. Is it accurate to portray the adversary system as trial by combat?

6. How does the quality of competitiveness make for a good lawyer given the present system?

7. What are some of the stumbling blocks that women lawyers face? How can these be overcome?

8. Explain how race, class, and gender are synergistic forces.

9. Discuss positive and negative media images of lawyers.

10. What are some major advantages that women lawyers have by virtue of their gender? And what are some liabilities?

11. One theme of the chapter relates to Audre Lorde's notion that adopting the "tools of the master" is not sufficient. What is the relevance here regarding receiving a law school education?

WEB DESTINATIONS

American Bar Association (ABA): www.abanet.org

Canadian Bar Association: www.cba.org

Legal information: www.law.com

National Association of Women Lawyers: www.abanet.org/nawl

Washington, D.C., Lawyers: www.dcbar.org

ABA Commission on Women: www.abanet.org/women

Australian Women Lawyers: www.womenlawyers.org/au

The Law Society of Upper Canada: www.lsuc.on.ca

British Bar Council: www.barcouncil.org

REFERENCES

Abel, R. (1995). Revisioning lawyers. In R. Abel and P. Lewis (eds.), *Lawyers in society: An overview* (pp. 1–38). Berkeley: University of California Press.

American Bar Association (ABA) (2003). *Current glance at women in the law.* Chicago, Ill.: Commission on Women in the Profession.

Anderson, M., and Collins, H. C. (1995). *Race, class, and gender,* 2nd ed. Belmont, Calif.: Wadsworth.

Anleu, S. L. (1992). Women in law: Theory, research, and practice. In B. R. Price and N. Sokoloff (eds.), *The criminal justice system: Offenders, victims, and workers* (pp. 359–371). New York: McGraw-Hill.

Anleu, S. L. (1992). Women in law: Theory, research, and practice. *The Australian and New Zealand Journal of Sociology 28:* 391–410.

Asinow, M. (2002). High crimes: A competent female lawyer emerges from the wreckage. *Picturing Justice: The On-Line Journal of Law and Popular Culture.* Retrieved from www.usfca.edu/pj/highcrimes.

Bacik, I. (2003). Women challenging "old boy" culture in the law. *Irish Independent.* Retrieved from http://0-web.lexis-nexis.com.

Bain, H. (1997, June 26). Discrimination widespread in judiciary, say women judges. *The Dominion* (Wellington, New Zealand): 3.

Bazemore, G., and Schiff, M. (2001). Understanding restorative community justice: What and why now? In G. Bazemore and M. Schiff (eds.), *Restoring Community Justice* (pp. 21–46). Cincinnati, Ohio: Anderson.

Bernat, F. P. (1992). Women in the legal profession. In I. Moyer (ed.), *The changing roles of women in the criminal justice system,* 2nd ed. (pp. 307–321). Prospect Heights, Ill.: Waveland.

Bogoch, B. (1997). Gendered lawyering: Difference and dominance in lawyer-client interaction. *Law and Society Review 31*(4): 677–712.

Brock, D. (1996). *The seduction of Hillary Rodham.* New York: Free Press.

Champion, D. (1998). *Criminal justice in the United States,* 2nd ed. Chicago: Nelson-Hall.

Chen, V. (2003, September 29). Women lawyers see cracks in the ceiling. *The American Lawyer 29* (39): 4.

Compensation and Benefits for Law Offices (CBLO) (2003). Are women lawyers now faring better? *LexisNexis Academic.* Retrieved from http://web.lexis-nexis.com.

Cook, B. B. (1983). The path to the bench: Ambitions and attitudes of women in the law. *Trial 19*(8): 48–57.

Cross, A. (1999, March 31). Women of the bench convene. *The Courier-Journal* (Louisville, Ken.), p. 1B.

Danner, N. (1998). Three strikes and it's women who are out: The hidden consequences for women of criminal justice policy reforms. In S. L. Miller (ed.), *Crime control and women: Feminist implication of criminal justice policy* (pp. 1–14). Thousand Oaks, Calif.: Sage.

Deutsch, C. (1996, June 2). Female lawyers join forces. *The Des Moines Register,* p. 1.

Dolan, M. (1995, July 13). Many lawyers sentenced to life of misery (from the *Los Angeles Times*). *Waterloo Courier,* p. 2a.

Economist (2005, June 11). The insidious wiles of foreign influence. *Economist,* 25–26.

Feinman, C. (1994). *Women in the criminal justice system,* 3rd ed. Westport, Conn.: Praeger.

Foust, C. (2004, Fall). A return to feminine public virtue: Judge Judy and the myth of the Tough Mother. *Women's Studies in Communication 27*(3): 269–294.

Friedman, J. M. (1993). *America's first woman lawyer: The biography of Myra Bradwell.* Buffalo, N.Y.: Prometheus Books.

Goldfarb, R. (2004). Lawyers on television. *Washington Lawyer.* Retrieved from www.dcbar.org. for_lawyers.

Gardner, R. (1982). *Family evaluation in child custody litigation.* Cresskill, N.J.: Creative Therapeutics.

Goldhaber, M. D. (1998, December 21). Women's numbers rise at the bigger law firms. *National Law Journal,* pp. A1, A11.

Grace, N. (2005). *Objection!: How high-priced defense attorneys, celebrity defendants and a 24/7 media have hijacked our criminal justice system.* New York: Hyperion.

Graham, J. (1998, August 26). For Manheim, practice is perfect. *USA Today,* p. 3D.

Gubernick, L., and Levine, J. (1996, November 4). Make lox, not law. *Forbes,* pp. 68–76.

Guinier, L., Fine, M., Balin, J., Bartow, A., and Stachel, D. L. (1994). Becoming gentlemen: Women's experiences at one Ivy League law school. *University of Pennsylvania Law Review 143*(1): 1–110.

Haggman, M. (2003, November 4). Bench is "sore spot": Educating members demystifying. *Broward Daily Business Review.* Retrieved from http://web.lexis-nexis.com.

Harrington, M. (1994). *Women lawyers: Rewriting the rules.* New York: Alfred A. Knopf.

Hunt, J. (1990). The logic of sexism among police. *Women and Criminal Justice 1*: 3–30.

Hurst, T. (1977, March 20). Bowling Green's only woman trial lawyer: "I wanted to change things." *Bowling Green Daily News*: 30.

Jack, R., and Jack, D. C. (1989). *Moral vision and professional decisions: The changing values of women and men lawyers.* New York: Cambridge University Press.

Jamison, T. (2003, October 14). Waterloo mayoral hopefuls tout qualifications at forum. *Waterloo-Cedar Falls Courier.* Retrieved from www.wcfcourier.com/articles.

Janz, W. (1998, October 28). Women lawyers had to overcome society's verdict. *Milwaukee Journal Sentinel*, p. 1.

Jones, L. (2004, July 20). Women to women. *National Law Journal*. Retrieved from www.law.com/jsp.

Lau, J. A. (1983). Lawyers vs. social workers: Is cerebral hemisphericity the culprit? *Child Welfare 62:* 21–29.

The Law Society of Upper Canada (2003). *Equity and diversity in the legal profession 2003.* Retrieved from www.lsuc.on.ca.

Lhotka, W. C. (1998, October 10). Women jurists discuss challenges from male colleagues. *St. Louis Post-Dispatch,* p. 8.

Lorde, A. (1984). *Sister outsider: Essays and speeches.* Trumansburg, N.Y.: Crossing Press.

MacCorquodale, P., and Jensen, G. (1993). Women in the law: Partners or tokens? *Gender and Society 7*(4): 582–593.

Martin, S. E., and Jurik, N. C. (1996). *Doing justice, doing gender: Women in law and criminal practice occupations.* Thousand Oaks, Calif.: Sage.

Masters, L. (2004, April 26). What women [lawyers] want—and need. *Legal Times:* 18.

Miller, S., and Meloy, M. (2007). Women on the bench: Mavericks, peacemakers, or something else? In R. Muraskin (ed.), *It's a crime: women and justice,* 4th ed. (pp. 679–722). Upper Saddle River, N.J.: Prentice Hall.

Mauro, T. (1998, August 5). Report: Minorities not reaching top legal levels. *USA Today,* p. 3A.

Menkel-Meadow, C. (1995). Feminization of the legal profession: The comparative sociology of women lawyers. In R. L. Abel and P. S. Lewis (eds.), *Lawyers in society: An overview* (pp. 221–280). Berkeley: University of California Press.

Merlo, A., and Pollock, J. (1995). *Women, law, and social control.* New York: Macmillan.

Morello, K. B. (1986). *The invisible bar: The woman lawyer in America 1968 to the present.* New York: Random House.

Murphy, L. (2004, March 29). Female general counsel give women the biz; Sisterhood kicks in when projects are doled out. *Crain Chicago Business.* Retrieved from http://web.lexis-nexis.com.

Neumeister, L. (2005, September, 29). Civil rights pioneer Constance Baker Motley dies. *USA Today:* 3A.

Padavic, I., and Orcutt, J. D. (1997). Perceptions of sexual harassment in the Florida legal system: A comparison of dominance and spillover explanations. *Gender and Society 11*(5): 682–699.

Palmer, N. (1991). Feminist practice with survivors of sexual trauma and incest. In M. Bricker-Jenkins, N. R. Hooyman, and N. Gottlieb (eds.), *Feminist practice in clinical settings* (pp. 63–82). Newbury Park, Calif.: Sage.

Podolefsky, R. (1998, November 30). Women in law. Presentation at University of Northern Iowa Department of Social Work, Cedar Falls, Iowa.

Reidinger, P. (1996). Dressing like a lawyer: Whether in a law office or courtroom, what you wear may be almost as important as what you say. *American Bar Association Journal 82:* 78–81.

Rhode, D. L. (1995, July 31). Career progress, yes: Equality, not quite yet. *The National Law Journal 17*(48): A21–A22.

Rhode, D. L. (2001). The unfinished agenda: Women and the legal profession. The commission on women in the profession. Retrieved from www.amazon.com/exec.

Rollins, J. H. (1996). *Women's minds/women's bodies: The psychology of women in a biosocial context.* Englewood Cliffs, N.J.: Prentice-Hall.

Rosenberg, J., Perlstadt, H., and Phillips, W. R. (1993). Now that we are here: Discrimination, disparagement, and harassment at work and the experience of women lawyers. *Gender and Society 7:* 415–433.

Russell, J. (2005, April). The case of a lifetime: A victory for affirmative action puts attorney Brigida Benitez in the winner's circle. *Hispanic Business:* 22–25.

Rybak, D. C. (1998, March 12). Minnesota gets a new benchmark. *The Christian Science Monitor,* p. 1.

Scanzoni, L., and Scanzoni, I. (1998). *Men, women and change: A sociology of marriage and family,* 3rd ed. New York: McGraw-Hill.

Schmitz, C. (2005, August 19). Objection! Lawyers lament poor public image. *Montreal Gazette.* Retrieved from www.freerepublic.com.

Schultz, V. (1998, May 25). Sex is the least of it: Let's focus harassment law on work, not sex. *The Nation:* 11–13.

Sheindlin, J. (1996). *Don't pee on my leg and tell me it's raining: America's toughest family court judge speaks out.* New York: HarperCollins.

Shore, E. R. (1997). The relationship of gender balance at work, family responsibilities and workplace characteristics to drinking among male and female attorneys. *Journal of Studies on Alcohol 58:* 297–313.

Siemsen, C. (2004). *Emotional trials: The moral dilemmas of women criminal defense attorneys.* Hanover, N.H.: Northeastern University Press.

Simpson, G. (1996). The Plexiglass ceiling: The careers of black women lawyers. *Career Development Quarterly 45*(2): 173–188.

Smith, J. (ed.) (2000). *Rebels in law: Voices in history of black women lawyers.* Ann Arbor, Mich.: University of Michigan Press.

Skaine, R. (1996). *Power and gender: Issues in sexual dominance and harassment.* Jefferson, N.C.: McFarland.

Stepnick, A., and Orcutt, J. D. (1996). Conflicting testimony: Judges' and attorneys' perceptions of gender bias in legal settings. *Sex Roles: A Journal of Research 34*(7–8): 567–579.

Stone, A. (1997). Women, law school, and student commitment to the public interest. In J. Cooper and L. G. Trubek (eds.), *Education for justice: Social values and legal education* (pp. 56–87). Aldershot, England: Ashgate.

Strick, A. (1977). *Injustice for all: How our adversary system of law victimizes us and subverts true justice.* London: Penguin.

Stuart, F. (2005, December). Personal reminiscence, unpublished communication with van Wormer.

Tibbetts, J. (1999, January 21). Gender colours judges' views: Study calls women on Supreme Court outsiders. *The Ottawa Citizen,* p. 4A.

UK Department for Constitutional Affairs (2005, May). *The legal profession: Entry, retention, and competition.* UK government report. Retrieved from www.dca.gov.uk.

Weiss, M., and Young, C. (1996, June 19). *Feminist jurisprudence: Equal rights or new paternalism? Policy analysis.* Washington, D.C.: Cato Institute.

West, R. (1998). Jurisprudence and gender. *University of Chicago Law Review 55*(1): 1–73.

Williams, P. J. (1991). *The alchemy of race and rights.* Cambridge: Harvard University Press.

Woodman, S. (1995, November/December). On the run from the law. *Ms.:* 38–42.

Working Woman. (1996, November/December). Law and order: Women sit on the high court, but on the beat, it's a man's world. *Working Woman 21*(11): 53.

Zhao, Y. (2004, November 7). Beyond "sweetie": Women's place in professional schools is merrier. *New York Times Ed. Life:* 20–22.

CHAPTER

13 Women in Corrections

Prisons have few friends. They have been described as dark, dingy, deteriorating, and depressive dungeons where the senses are deprived and the human spirit is destroyed by endless monotony and regimentation. Because this description is often all too accurate, dissatisfaction with prisons is widespread. Small cages, stone walls, and multitiered cellblocks make them seem oppressive and unfit for human habitation. They are too frequently the scene of brutality, violence, and racial unrest. Furthermore, although these institutions purport to cure offenders of crime, their record in that area has not been encouraging (Morris, 1974, p. ix). Few would share the vision of the Reverend James Finey, chaplain at Ohio Penitentiary in 1851:

> Could we all be put on prison-fare for the space of two or three generations, the world would ultimately be the better for it. Indeed, should society changes places with prisoners . . . taking to itself the regularity, temperance, and sobriety of a good prison, the goals of peace, light, and Christianity would be furthered . . . Taking the world and the next together . . . the prisoner has the advantage. (Nagel, 1974, p. 1)

The reasonable person might ask: Why would women ever want to subject themselves to working in such a toxic environment? Women work in prisons for the same reasons that women become police officers. The pay is reasonably good, particularly with overtime; the job provides security; jobs are available; and they feel that they can do some good. But the fact is that women work in corrections in many capacities. They are employed as probation and parole officers and supervisors; residential counselors and supervisors in community-based corrections; correctional counselors; jail officers; correctional officers; and correctional administrators, including wardens and superintendents. As women have received resistance in policing and law practice, so has the world of corrections, especially institutional corrections, been reluctant to receive women within the walls of prisons.

One of the problems of examining the careers of women who work in corrections is that so little research has been done in this area, with the exception of the female correctional officer who is working in a prison for male inmates. Accordingly, the major emphasis of this chapter is women who are correctional officers in men's prisons, but, based largely on Bartollas's experiences and observations, the other women working in corrections will receive some attention.

History of Women in Corrections

The history of women in probation and parole goes back to the early part of the twentieth century when there was an ever-increasing demand in juvenile probation for trained social workers to serve as probation officers. These social workers, trained under the medical model, began to treat juvenile probationers as disturbed children who needed psychiatric therapy. The philosophy and administration of probation thus retained the older concern with helping children adjust to their environment and added a new concern with helping them resolve their emotional problems. In addition to a greater interest in treating children's problems, twentieth-century probation theory also included the idea of more responsibility for the delivery of services to probationers, a greater consciousness of standards, and a desire to upgrade the probation officer and restore the volunteer to probation services.

This history of providing rehabilitative services was part of the rising *parens patriae* movement in juvenile justice and was also influenced by the Progressive reformers who were committed to the "child-saving" crusade (Platt, 1976). It sought out those who could provide treatment services to children and, not surprisingly, were willing to turn to women who had been trained as social workers. Aftercare in juvenile justice took longer to develop than juvenile probation, but, it too was treatment oriented and remained so until the 1980s. As a result, women were also welcomed in aftercare services. Thus, although women in policing and law careers encountered opposition and resistance, women interested in juvenile probation experienced far more receptivity.

With their greater acceptance in juvenile probation, the way was paved for the receptivity of women in adult probation and parole as well. Indeed, as revealed later in this chapter, it was only in the late 1970s and 1980s that the rehabilitative emphasis in adult probation and parole changed to a "get-tough" approach in which individuals were held accountable for their actions.

Women in community-based residential corrections programs also benefited from the reintegrative philosophy developed in the late 1960s and early 1970s. At that time the spirit was one of reform. The area of mental health had undergone a period of deinstitutionalization in the 1960s, during which greater numbers of mental patients were kept in the community rather than placed in large institutions. The turbulence brought on by the Vietnam War, urban riots, and disturbances on college campuses as well as the widespread questioning of traditional values by youth countercultures fostered a receptivity to new solutions. The bloody prison riots that erupted between 1971 and 1973 also helped support the conclusion that there must be a better way.

Federal funding, finally, provided the catalyst that linked correctional reform with social and political realities, thereby creating a huge array of community-based programs throughout the United States. For example, from the inception of the Law Enforcement Assistance Administration (LEAA) in 1967 through July 1975, $23,837,512 of the Safe Street Act federal monies was matched with $12,300,710 from state and local funds for grants devoted solely to residential aftercare programs for adults. Thus, guided by reintegrative philosophy, advocated by a number of blue-ribbon commissions, and supported by federal dollars, community-based programs sprouted in nearly every state. Jobs were available in these programs. Ex-offenders were hired in some programs, and women also received an acceptance that was denied them in more security-oriented institutional contexts.

Community-based corrections began to decline in popularity even more than it had gained public approval. In the mid-1970s, as the mood of the nation suddenly changed to a "get-tough-with-criminals" approach, publication of official statistics and media coverage of street crime convinced the public that the crime problem had gotten out of hand. By then women were firmly entrenched as part of the landscape of community-based corrections.

Some women in residential programs worked in programs for women, as either line staff or counselors. Others were employed in facilities that were co-correctional, serving both a male and a female population, and some were able to attain jobs as counselors for male-only residential programs. By the late 1970s, it was not unusual, especially in privately administered facilities, to find women who were directors of residential facilities. Debby Lidster, director of the Talbert Halfway House of Women, in discussing her career in community-based programming, gives some good advice to new counselors (quoted in Bartollas, 1981):

> To work with these women, you need to know where they're coming from—where they dope out and where they're picking up their tricks. You also have to know what they're talking about. If someone comes to you and says "I'm using half a tea a day or eight and two shot," you better know about it. Unless you take the time to learn, you'll show your ignorance, and if you show your ignorance, you won't communicate. (p. 119)

Despite the greater receptivity of women in probation and parole and residential programs, the path of acceptance in jails and prisons was certainly different. The history of women in institutions, as previously stated, can be traced to demands by benevolent groups outside the criminal justice system for prison, jail, and police matrons. In the 1820s, volunteer Quaker women, joined by upper-middle-class women, were motivated to reform female inmates and blamed their poor living conditions on neglect and sexual exploitation by male keepers.

From 1825 to 1873, reformers achieved occasional success in acquiring matrons for women. Eliza Farnham, a feminist and head matron of the women's section of Sing Sing from 1844 to 1848, was one such success. She adopted the reform program of Elizabeth Gurney Fry, which was to make the environment of the prison more like a home and interaction between staff and inmates more like a family. Farnham upheld the conviction that environmental conditions caused criminal behavior and, therefore, that a change in the environment would change behavior. She ended the silence system, as she grouped the women together for the purpose of educational instruction. She also established a library of secular books. In teaching the women to read and write, she instructed them in U.S. history, geography, astronomy, physiology, and personal hygiene. She expected the women to work and encouraged them to become involved with handicrafts. She had the women's wing of the prison decorated with maps, pictures, flowers, and lamps, and she had a piano brought in to provide music. Yet Farnham was not reluctant to employ discipline if it was needed, and solitary confinement was applied for recalcitrant inmates (Feinman, 1994, pp. 43–44).

Farnham was replaced in 1848 for being too liberal, but this did not stop reformers from lobbying for the better treatment of women in corrections. Eventually, reformers were able to convince a male legislature to establish a separate women's prison and to hire women superintendents and matrons. The first prison for women staffed by women opened in Indiana in 1873. By 1913, other reformatories had opened in Framingham, Massachusetts; Bedford Hill, New York; and Clinton, New Jersey. In 1932, the House of Detention for Women opened in New York City, representing the first separate jail for women (Feinman, 1994, p. 44).

Until the 1970s, women were hired strictly to work in prisons for women. Working in male prisons was not viewed as a job for a woman. Still, there were several positions of responsibility for women in male and female corrections. For example, Kate Barnard was the Commissioner of Corrections for Oklahoma from 1907 to 1915, Katherine B. Davis was the Commissioner of Corrections for New York City between 1914 and 1918, and Clara Waters served as the warden of Oklahoma State Reformatory in 1927 (Merlo and Pollock, 1995, p. 98). See Box 13.1 for the

BOX **13.1**

Mary Belle Harris: A Pioneer in Corrections

By her mid-twenties, Mary Belle Harris had gained a bachelor's degree in music, a master's degree in Latin and classics, and a Ph.D. in Sanskrit and Indo-European linguistics at the University of Chicago. In a journey that encompassed teaching Latin in schools in Kentucky and Chicago, working at the famous Hull House, playing the organ in various locales, and even publishing her musical compositions, her corrections career began in 1914 as a superintendent at the Workhouse in New York City. She then held positions as superintendent, State Reformatory for Women at Clinton, New Jersey; assistant director of the section on reformatories and detention homes for the U.S. War Department, and superintentent at/of the State Home for Girls in Trenton, New Jersey. In 1925, she was appointed the superintendent at the recently authorized Federal Institution for Women planned for Alderson, West Virginia.

In the period from 1925 to 1941, Harris championed rehabilitation at Alderson in a way that few had before or have since her time. Instead of the traditional prison structures, she insisted that this new federal facility be built with attractive red-brick Georgian Colonial buildings arranged around quadrangles, and that the women inmates be housed in cottages. She emphasized innovations, opportunity, and program options. Inmates were offered varied educational and vocational programs, extensive physical activities, a system of inmate self-government, exposure to music and other arts, a library, and typing equipment. They were even permitted to engage in charity affairs to benifit needy persons outside the prison.

There are shadows on the Harris legend for her implementation of racial segregation at Alderson and elsewhere, her fostering of sex-role stereotypes of her day, her tendency to exaggerate in her observations, and her frequent use and perhaps abuse of power. Nevertheless, beyond these shadows, she traveled where few women in corrections had gone before.

Critical Thinking Questions: How can an individual champion rehabilitation on the one hand and favor segregation on the other? Did the changes she made in corrections work accomplish her goal of better relating the prison as an institution to outside society?

Source: Joseph W. Rogers, "Mary Belle Harris: Warden and Rehabilitation Pioneer," *Women & Criminal Justice* (2000): 5–27.

career of Mary Belle Harris, one of the most distinguished figures in twentieth-century corrections.

Women Probation Officers

Probation is the most widely used judicial disposition for dealing with juvenile and adult offenders. Persons sentenced to probation are subject to conditions imposed by the court and are permitted to remain in the community under the supervision of a probation officer. Conditions of probation vary from jurisdiction to jurisdiction and from individual to individual, but they include some elements of payment of fines, restitution to victims, community service, periodic imprisonment, enrollment in drug or alcohol abuse programs, gainful employment, and cooperation with a citizen volunteer.

Probation emerged from a treatment model in the early part of the twentieth century. It was spearheaded by white, women **probation officers** who had been trained as social workers. This emphasis on rehabilitative services was altered somewhat in the late 1960s and early 1970s, as a reintegrative philosophy became widely accepted in probation services across the United States. Many women probation officers became deeply involved in providing services to probationers to help them adjust to community living. Box 13.2 presents an example of how one woman probation officer influenced the life of a client.

In the 1980s and 1990s, the goals of probation swung to risk assessment and increased surveillance models. In an attempt to convince the public, as well as policy makers, that probation could be "tougher" on criminals, probation administrators began to emphasize a number of strategies that would better ensure public acceptance of probation. The most widely used of these strategies have been the combination of probation and incarceration, financial restitution and community service programs, classification systems, intensive probation, and electronic monitoring and house arrest.

This change in goals in adult probation has adversely affected job morale and involvement. The demise of ideology contributed in large measure to the increased rates of burnout for both women and men adult probation officers. Yet, beyond dealing with the demise of ideology and the increased burnout rates, there are probably at least three reasons that women probation officers do not usually experience the rejection and harassment that they have faced in policing jobs and, to a lesser degree, in law careers. First, male probation and parole officers have not developed a culture, which is found in the men's club of policing and the "good old boys' network" in large law firms. Second, there is a long history of treatment in probation and even parole, and professionally training social workers, including both women and men, have been welcomed with open arms to be line probation officers and supervisors. Third, probation, especially, has never been known as a male occupation and, accordingly, male probation officers do not usually see a problem with women being hired in the office.

G. Wunder's (1969) survey of West German male and female probation officers revealed that female officers believed that their work with male clients was successful

BOX **13.2**

Probation Can Make a Difference

One success story I had as a probation officer was a seventeen-year-old black girl who had been arrested on first-degree robbery and prostitution charges. She had never been referred before. What it came down to was there were two juvenile girls with two adult males who were their boyfriends, and they were in a bar trying to shake down this white guy. The girls got him up to their apartment, and they were going to get it on with him. Then their boyfriends came up and were real mad because he was with their women. The white guy said, "Take anything," and they took some money he had in his car. The robbery charge was dropped, but there was a finding of fact on the prostitution charge. She was placed on supervision until her eighteenth birthday. When I got her, the first thing we did was go out to the hospital's family practice center to have her checked and placed on birth control. But she was already pregnant. The majority of time we spent together was concentrated on job, education, getting ready for the baby, and independent living skills. It wasn't a traditional probation case. We spent a lot of time together,

getting ready for the future. Her mother was dead and her father was in the mental health institute. Several older sisters were already on ADC, weren't married, and were not models by any means. So, I felt like I'm the one she counted on. I took her to the hospital when she had her baby and was with her during delivery. It was a neat experience. She asked me to be the godmother for her baby. She's very motivated to make something out of herself. She is now nineteen, has her own car, and keeps an apartment fairly well. She has either gone to school or worked since before she had the baby. With what she has had to work with, it's amazing she is doing so well.

Critical Thinking Questions: Do you believe that this quality of intervention frequently takes place with either juvenile or adult probation officers? If you do not, why not? Is this type of intervention within the job of a probation officer?

Source: Interview by Linda Dippold Bartollas in 1985 in the Midwest.

because they were able "to establish contact rapidly and to communicate effectively." Both male and female officers in this study acknowledged that female offenders were substantially more difficult to work with than male offenders. Younger female officers also believed that younger male clients had difficulty in accepting the authority of a woman, and the majority of female officers agreed that male sex offenders were inappropriate clients for supervision by a woman (pp. 91–107).

Another study of female probation officers to sexual assault felons in a metropolitan Ohio county in the years 1978 to 1981 found that male probation officers made more serious sentencing recommendations for sexual assault offenders than did female officers (Walsh, 1984). When given thirteen different criminal acts to consider, male officers ranked rape as the most serious and female officers ranked it eighth. Equally as surprising, female officers tended to view rape as a victim-precipitated crime, but male officers did not. Perhaps even more noteworthy, the average sex offender processed by male officers received about six more months of imprisonment than those offenders processed by female officers (Walsh and Anthony, 1984, pp. 371–388).

Anderson and Spanier's (1980) study of juvenile probation officers in Pennsylvania found that officers with a higher level of education were less likely to label acts as delinquent than were officers with less education and that officers who were treatment and service oriented were less likely to label juvenile acts as delinquent than were those officers who responded to lawyer role models. Consistent with the first two findings, those officers who made rehabilitative recommendations were less likely to label acts as delinquent than were those officers who did not (pp. 505–514).

A 1995 study examined the role of gender in determining the offense seriousness by male and female probation officers in England and Wales. In a review of 169 presentence reports, it was found that the officer's gender was an insignificant factor in terms of the degree to which officers considered aggravating and mitigating circumstances in determining the seriousness of the offense (Nash, 1995, pp. 250–258).

Michelle Hayes (1989) examined whether female probation officers in England and Wales were held back as a consequence of their socially ascribed gender roles or because of indirect discrimination by the probation services. They concluded that what restricted promotion and management as choices for women were the women's philosophical disagreements about the present style of probation service management (pp. 12–17).

Slate, Wells, and Johnson's study (2003) measured the effects of stress on probation officers in a southern state, especially in the deterioration of the probation officer's physical health. The sample population (635 officers) was made up of 52 percent women and 48 percent male officers, with 61 percent married. Respondents identified the most influential stressors to be inadequate salary, lack of promotional opportunities, belief that courts are too lenient on offenders, excessive paperwork, frustration with the criminal justice system, its ineffectiveness, expectations to do too much in too little time, lack of recognition, inadequate support from the agency, and lack of community resources.

In sum, some preliminary understanding has been developed concerning the female probation and parole officer's role expectation and performance and gender inequality in probation and parole services. Yet this understanding only scratches the surface of perceiving the challenges and obstacles of probation and parole for women officers, the comparison of rates of burnout between men and women officers, the effect of the "get-tough" crusade on work attitudes of women officers, the similarities and differences between how women and men officers handle clients and the sentences they recommend, and the actual dynamics of gender equality or inequality in probation and parole services.

Women Jail Officers

During the 1980s and 1990s, there was a dramatic increase in the number of women correctional officers working in U.S. jails (Pogrebin and Poole, 1997). In 1995, women constituted a larger percentage of correctional officers in jails (24.2 percent) than they did in either state (18 percent) or federal (11 percent) correctional institutions (Maguire and Pastore, 1996, pp. 91, 94).

Despite recent advances in employment in this nation's jails, women have not been welcomed in the jail setting. As Pogrebin and Poole (1997, p. 41) expressed it, the jail job "is perceived to be a highly sex-typed male job requiring qualities of dominance, authoritativeness, and aggressiveness. Female qualities of nurturing, sensitivity, and understanding are thought by many male jail officers to be unnecessary and even problematic." It is not surprising, then, that Pogrebin and Poole found from their semistructured interviews with 108 women deputies that women experience problems stemming from sexism and sexual harassment by their male coworkers.

Belknap's (1991) study of thirty-five **women correctional officers** working in a large metropolitan jail also revealed that women experienced discrimination and sexual harassment. Of this sample, 40 percent indicated that they chose a career in corrections because they wanted to become police officers; 40 percent responded that they were attracted to the money and benefits. In their support for gender equality, 94 percent of the respondents further indicated that they believed that men and women were equal and that they should receive more opportunities. But when asked about their advancement opportunities, 89 percent of these officers believed that they fared poorly compared with male officers. In this study, 31 percent of the women reported that sexual harassment had been an issue for them while working in the jail. White women (45 percent) were more likely than African American women (13 percent) to report sexual harassment, and younger women (47 percent) were more likely to report sexual harassment than older women (13 percent). In addition, these women correctional officers believed that their behavior toward inmates was more respectful than that of men but that their actions were devalued in comparison to the men's more aggressive approaches.

M. I. Caldwaladr's study (1993) of all conditions took place in a modern urban Canadian jail that housed 150 men awaiting trial or bail. This institution was designed to accommodate women correctional officers—inmates' shower stalls and toilets were enclosed and separate change facilities existed for female correctional officers. In-depth interviews were conducted with twenty-one female officers, who reported that they performed the job with a less aggressive style than male officers. They said that they were more likely than the men to rely on verbal skills and intuition to get the inmates to cooperate and to talk out problems. Male officers relied more heavily on internal disciplinary procedures. The female respondents did indicate that male officers believed female officers performed the day to day tasks of the job, but at the same time the male officers expressed the concern that female officers would not be able to back them up in a crisis situation. Most of the women officers reported that they did not personally experience unwanted touching or suggestions. They did go on to describe other forms of harassment from male peers, such as threats, unfounded graphic sexual rumor about individual women, and daily doses of demeaning remarks from peers, supervisors, and inmates. But these women officers decided not to complain because in their view the costs of complaining would outweigh the benefits.

Stohr, Mays, Beck, and Kelley's (1998) study of sexual harassment incidents in seven women's jails revealed that 22 percent reported that they had been victims of sexual harassment. In explaining the low level of harassment victimization compared with that in other correctional settings, these researchers concluded that it was probably significant that women were in a majority and occupied some of the midlevel management positions. This is so because it provides "support for the hypothesis that harassment will be reduced as women achieved more situational and achieved power in the criminal justice workplace" (pp. 147–148).

Women Wardens

Women have been **superintendents of women's correctional institutions** since late in the nineteenth century, but today increasing numbers of women are seeking for and being appointed wardens of men's prisons.

Early in the chapter, we discussed Eliza W. B. Farnham, head matron at New York's Sing Sing Prison, and the reforms that she instituted between 1844 and 1848. The first women administrator in U.S. corrections actually preceded Farnham, for Mary Weed was named principal keeper of the Walnut Street Jail in Philadelphia in 1793.

Other early leaders in women's corrections were Clara Barton, who served as superintendent of the Massachusetts Reformatory Prison for Women at Framingham in 1882; Kate Barnard, who was elected to be the first Commissioner of Charities and Corrections in Oklahoma in 1907 and served for two terms; Katherine Davis, who was superintendent of the Bedford Hills prison from 1901 to 1914; Kate Richards O'Hare, who was first an inmate sentenced for violation of the Federal Espionage Act and then, following her pardon, eventually became assistant director of the California Department of Penology; Mable Walker Willebrandt, who oversaw the administration of federal prisons from 1921 to 1929; and Dr. Miriam Van Waters, superintendent of the Massachusetts Reformatory for Women from 1932 to 1957 (Morton, 1992, pp. 76–82).

More recently, Elaine Hunt was appointed Louisiana corrections commissioner in 1972, but she died four years later before she could implement many of her reforms. In the 1980s, Ward Murphy in Maine, Ali Klein in New Jersey, and Ruth L. Rushen in California became directors of state systems. In 1990, Alaska, North Dakota, South Dakota, and Puerto Rico had women commissioners of adult corrections, a record number. In 1992, Kathleen M. Hawk was appointed director of the Federal Bureau of Prisons and became the sixth director of the Bureau of Prisons since its establishment in 1930. Women have also made some inroads in terms of administrators of male institutions, but the road has not been easy. By 1997, women represented about 10 percent of wardens and superintendents of the 900 statewide correctional facilities for men (Marks, 1997, p. 1). Camille Graham Camp was one groundbreaker who in 1977 became warden of the Maximum Security Center in South Carolina. She was responsible for the state's most violent inmates and was the first woman to head such a facility (Morton, 1992, p. 86).

Women have found an early and still present reception as superintendents of women's prisons, and a number of women have been appointed as chief administrators of aspects of or even total correctional systems. But to be appointed as warden of a prison for men has been a much more inaccessible career goal. Part of the difficulty is that women's acceptance in men's institutions has been extremely problematic. It is still believed, particularly by the old-timers, that women do not belong in a men's prison. On a different level, promotions to warden generally require a stint as assistant warden of operations of a men's prison. It is no simple matter for a woman correctional officer or woman correctional counselor to overcome the barriers to gender equality and to receive the promotion to head of security or assistant warden of operations of a men's prison. Old-timers, especially, charge that women may be there because the courts insist on it, but that does not mean that we have to trust institutional security to a *woman*.

Pamela K. Withrow (1992), who has served as warden in more than one men's prison, talks about her journey up the career ladder of corrections. In the midst of optimism in Michigan concerning the hiring of women in corrections, she notes that this movement took a backward step in 1987, when an inmate raped and murdered a female officer at the State Prison of Southern Michigan. In the early 1990s, she states that optimism was much less for women in the corrections profession. Women, she adds, continue to experience resistance from male coworkers, and the perception is still alive that prisons are too dangerous for women to work in. She contends, based on her conversations with a number of women corrections workers in Michigan, that women stay in corrections for a number of reasons. They like the interaction with others, especially the opportunity to work as a team; the wages and benefits; the opportunity to test their physical and mental abilities; the challenge of working with staff and inmates; and the fact that the job is fun and never monotonous (p. 90). Women also feel that they bring certain advantages to correctional institutions:

- A women's body language is nonthreatening.
- Being a woman reduces the number of critical incidents because women have to stop and think before getting physical. A low-key approach sometimes best controls a situation.
- Women can calm down hot situations. Male staff sometimes can't or won't back down.
- Women often hear things others present do not because they have good listening skills. Sharing these perceptions may help improve operations.
- Women can benefit from affirmative action, where available.
- Women receive a certain amount of respect simply because of their gender.
- Women are not as concerned with dominance and destructive power games.
- When a woman supervisor does make herself heard, staff really hear.
- Women more often are able to see inmates as people. (pp. 91–92)

Kathleen M. Hawk (1992), former director of the U.S. Bureau of Prisons, adds, "I recognize that many women have suffered trials in the field of corrections over the years and that their perseverance certainly opened many doors for my generation." But she claims that in her years in the profession, being a woman "has been nothing but a plus" (p. 132).

Tekla Dennison Miller (1996), a former warden and author of *The Warden Wore Pink*, gives another twist to women's acceptance: "You have to be terribly strong, not just to deal with the offender population, but also to deal with the negative attitudes of the employees. Many people say it's changed, but it's still there."

The Reverend Jannie Poullard, the first woman warden of New York City's Brooklyn House of Detention and the J. A. Thomas Center on Riker's Island, claims that women are still held to a higher standard and still must work harder to gain equal recognition. She says, "If they're males, it's automatically assumed they're responsible, in charge, and can manage males or females." But "a woman, on the other hand, no matter how qualified she is, always has to prove she can do the job equally as well" (Marks, 1997, p. 1).

A sexual harassment suit settled on November 30, 1997, revealed that the sexual harassment present so widely in law enforcement and in men's prisons with women's correctional officers can also affect women who are wardens. In this suit filed by Linda George, a former associate warden, she charged chief deputy warden Augustine Infante with touching her breasts in front of a prison Equal Employment Opportunity investigator, grabbing her by an ankle, following her off prison grounds in a manner "somewhat like stalking" and telling her she had "the hottest seat in the prison." The settlement on this suit was $6.57 million; including $2 million in damages, $1.8 million paid to private defense attorneys, $1.7 million in fees and expenses to plaintiff attorney, and $353,955 already awarded to Linda George (Wisely, 1998, p. 15).

In sum, the success of some women administrators and wardens of men's prisons has been impressive, and a convincing argument can be made that men's prisons need the talents and skills that women bring to the leadership of prisons. Morton, who has recently completed a national study of women wardens, adds: "They tend to be reform oriented. They all talk about changes they've made to make things better for their staff and to find additional programming for the inmates. Morton also contributes that this has been the traditional role women have played in the criminal justice system, but they rarely had the authority to implement their ideas (Marks, 1997, p. 1). Nevertheless, the number of women wardens will be limited until women gain greater acceptance as correctional officers and correctional counselors in men's prisons and are promoted to supervisory and administrative positions in greater numbers. It is this career path from which wardens are chosen by central offices.

The Correctional Counselor

The **correctional counselor** is the basic treatment officer in many adult correctional institutions. Counselors generally agree that they should serve four functions in adult correctional institutions, as:

1. A social change agent who is involved with opening up a closed and coercive system;

2. A resource developer who provides the link between community and institutional services;
3. A therapist who helps prisoners relate successfully to the community; and
4. An advocate who ensures to the greatest possible extent that inmates are not deprived of their rights. (Ivey, 1974, pp. 137–138)

Expectations of counselors range from the professional role they studied in college to the formal job description of the federal and state correctional systems to the role that institutional staff and inmates expect them to assume. The expectations of security staff and inmates are well documented in *Voices of Women* selections that tell how it feels to be a female employee in a male correctional institution. The personal narratives reflect the lack of authority and status that both male and female corrections counselors have in correctional settings. Counselors may bring the concept that they are professionals to the prison, but it does not take them long in a maximum-security facility to realize that they have no formal authority at all and little informal power or status. Because they have no formal authority to deal with institutional problems, they can only make inquiries or recommendations to those in line positions. For example, if a resident has no sheets, a counselor cannot order the appropriate correctional officer to distribute them. If a resident wants to enter an educational program, a counselor often does not have the power to authorize his enrollment.

The low status of the counselor is directly related to his or her marginal position in the prison environment. Security is the number one priority of every prison. When security breaks down, everything stops, including treatment programs; nor do counselors meet with inmates during a period of lockdown, or deadlock. Although a counselor may be given information in confidence, he or she is expected by the authorities to immediately report any breach of security to a custody officer. The counselor who is informed by an inmate that he smoked a joint the previous night is expected to find the source of the marijuana, to ascertain whether there is any more in the institution, and to pass this information on to one of the custody staff.

Counselors in maximum-security institutions work in a violent atmosphere. Inmates generally assault only other inmates, but sometimes they strike out against staff. Many counselors now have their offices in a cellhouse rather than in the administration building, and those who still do have an office "up front" must usually spend most of their workweek in the cellhouse. Thus, counselors are placed in a vulnerable position, and they know that if a riot occurs, they may be taken hostage, injured, raped, or killed.

Stages in Counselors' Correctional Careers

Correctional counselors generally go through several stages in their careers. These stages were developed during training sessions with correctional counselors at the Illinois Corrections Training Academy during 1980. The following stages are more characteristic of male than female correctional counselors. Women do not appear to react as strongly to manipulation by inmates as do men.

1. Counselors initially come into the institution full of enthusiasm, for they are hopeful that they can make a valuable contribution to offenders' lives.
2. This euphoric state quickly gives way to confusion as counselors become aware of the practical realities of the job. Inmates create much of the confusion, for they are constantly putting pressure on new counselors. They are also attempting to manipulate or intimidate the neophyte who is not yet familiar with the rules and regulations that determine eligibility for such a program.
3. This third stage occurs when counselors feel let down or manipulated by inmates. When new counselors see that their reputations with other staff members have suffered because of inmate manipulation, they frequently adopt a more inflexible, punitive approach to their clients.
4. At this stage, counselors swing back to a more moderate position. Although they may not be as accommodating as they were when they first came into the institution, they become more flexible than at any time in the preceding six months or so. Counselors who maintain the punitive, inflexible stance of the third stage are frequently transferred, or at least encouraged to transfer, to other correctional facilities.
5. During this final stage, counselors settle down and try to do the best job they can for their clients. Yet, because they have become realists, they know that they are working for the system and so do not want to jeopardize their reputation by going overboard for offenders. They also are aware that many wardens and assistant wardens started out as counselors and they therefore realize the possibility of upward mobility. Thus, with some their anticipation of a successful career in corrections, along with a growing awareness of their importance to the organization, results in good morale and the desire to stay on the job.

The male correctional counselor may feel marginal to the hostile world of the men's prison, but the women's correctional officers feel even more marginal. Lynn Zimmer (1989) paints a picture of the correctional world facing the woman who desires to be a correctional officer, but, as Ms. Loos's letter clearly reveals, the same scenario faces women correctional counselors:

> *Today, almost two decades after the integration process began, women in corrections continue to work in a generally hostile environment where they face opposition, discrimination, and harassment. These are problems the law has helped to create through its failure to mandate equality for male and female workers. They remain problems that the courts may be unable to resolve. Prison administrators themselves have been reluctant to confront them, perhaps still hoping that the courts will yet exclude women altogether from correctional employment in men's prisons. There is little ground for such a hope as the courts have, in recent years, moved toward a narrowing of male-female distinctions even as they have resisted their elimination. What most prison administrators have not done is look for ways to reduce inequality within the restrictions established by the courts. Without such an affirmative effort by prison administrators, there is little reason to be optimistic about the potential for substantial improvement in women's working conditions. (p. 56)*

In sum, the double marginality of the environment of the men's prison for the female correctional counselor makes it difficult for her to feel overly positive about her job. It is even more difficult for her to gain the respect of staff and inmates so that she would be considered for higher administrative responsibilities.

The Female Correctional Officer

The basic role expectation of the correctional officer is that he or she is to prevent escapes, riots, and disruptive inmate behavior. But this function is accomplished in various ways, depending on whether the correctional officer is assigned to a maximum-, medium-, or minimum-security institution.

In maximum-security and most medium-security cellhouses, the correctional officer is required to open and close the steel-barred door allowing entrance and exit; to conduct an inmate count several times a day; to distribute medicine, mail, and laundry; to supervise maintenance activities; and to answer the telephone. The guard must see that inmates are fed, either in the cellhouse or in the central dining facility, to which they must be escorted. The inmates' daily showers must also be supervised. If violations of rules occur, the cellhouse guard must write disciplinary tickets. During the day shift, the majority of the correctional officers are assigned to guard work areas, such as the metal factory, the furniture factory, the yard gang, the canteen, or another prison industry.

Correctional officers in maximum-security institutions also guard the towers and gates. Although faced with loneliness, often uncomfortable temperatures, and boredom, the guard in the tower must nevertheless keep inmates under constant surveillance. If a problem arises in the yard, the guard on the tower must resolve it. If an inmate attacks another prisoner or a correctional officer or dashes for the wall, the use of deadly force may be necessary.

The correctional officer at the gate is expected to search, check, and stamp the hands of all outsiders as they come into the prison. There are several gates in most maximum-security prisons, and a guard is assigned to each. Inmates are required to have a pass and to be "patted down" at each gate. Protected from the violence of prison life, the gate guard is also in the advantageous position of being highly visible to administrators and to outsiders. Thus, when promotions are made, the gate guard often has an advantage over those in the cellhouse and on the tower.

Officers in segregation units have many of the same responsibilities as officers in cellhouses, but they have the additional task of guarding inmates considered more disruptive than those in the general prison population. The job of these officers is more difficult today than ever before, for disruptive inmates no longer can be denied their constitutional rights. Nor is it wise to use brutality against inmates, because they can be awarded damages in a civil suit against their keepers. Thus, in view of the limitations placed on correctional officers, the pandemonium that exists in many of these units is not surprising.

Toxic Environment

The prison environment for both male and female correctional officers is toxic. Several studies have revealed that the arrival of female correctional officers has met with considerable resistance from male correctional officers (Peterson, 1982; Zimmer, 1986, pp. 156–159; Owen, 1985). Horne (1985) has stated this very strongly:

> Negative male attitudes towards women in corrections have been the most significant factor in hindering the advancement of female CO's. No solid proof supports this male bias against female CO's, but none is needed, since males run the corrections agencies. The feeling was, and still is, among the majority of male officers, that "prison work is a man's work." (p. 51)

However, Lawrence and Mahan's (1998) study of men and women officers working in men's prisons in a Midwestern state found that women officers did not face the resistance suggested by previous studies, but the resistance came chiefly from more experienced men officers. These researchers did note that this continued resistance is likely to provide an obstacle to the advancement and promotion of women officers in men's prisons.

Warden Pamela K. Withrow's (1992) conversation with women's correctional officers revealed a number of disadvantages women saw in working in men's prisons:

- Women often are not taken seriously. They have to work harder and do more before being able to increase staff respect for their abilities. This means having to prove themselves over and over every day—not only their abilities, but personal worth.
- If a woman is seen as an affirmative action appointment and makes a statement or gives an order, eyes may shift to supervisory men present for confirmation, even if the woman outranks them.
- Women are always on display. This visibility is not an advantage when a woman makes an error.
- Stereotypes live. Women get asked to type, take notes, or check punctuation and grammar even when they are custody staff.
- Informal networking—golf outings, fishing, hunting, and other traditionally male pursuits—excludes women.
- Tokenism is aggravating. Women may be assigned to the control center or the front desk so they will be visible to important visitors.
- In a tense, noisy situation, a woman's voice may not be audible or may lack the power to command.
- Sexual harassment and abuse of gender is widespread and difficult to combat, especially if the victim does not want to be seen as a snitch.
- Instead of sharing information, male coworkers let women figure things out for themselves and seem to hope they won't.
- When women want to be included, it seems they have to choose between using profanity or professional language. They also have to choose between

conduct that may violate personal standards (such as barhopping) or seeming to be aloof. . . .

■ There is pressure for women to seek advancement whether that is their goal or not. Also there is pressure to attend social functions that sometimes verges on sexual harassment.

■ Women sometimes must develop multiple personae. A woman feels like an actress as the day progresses.

■ Women and men have communication styles that often do not mesh, making the work harder than it already is.

■ Male staff sometimes use "PMS" as an explanation for any action by a woman they don't like or agree with.

■ Less-qualified male staff will sometimes complain that women get promoted over them because of their gender. (p. 92)

Jurik (1985), in an examination of barriers confronting women employed as correctional officers in a state department of corrections in the western United States, found that several organizational barriers have prevented greater acceptance of women correctional officers. One organizational problem is that the reforms initiated by the department created the perception of increased danger in the prison environment. This perception has contributed to the feeling that women are unreliable in such a violent setting. These fears about women's unreliability seem to be rooted in three popular beliefs about women: (1) the "greater physical weaknesses" of women make them incapable of functioning in dangerous situations; (2) the "mental weaknesses" of women prevents them from handling the strain of working in the prison; and (3) the sexual identity and behavior of female officers cast the fear that they will become emotionally involved with inmates (pp. 378–379).

Walters (1993) surveyed correctional officers at four facilities concerning their attitudes toward their jobs. As part of this study, male correctional officers were asked about their attitudes toward working with women correctional officers. The variables that were found to be significantly related to a "pro-woman" correctional officer attitude were the quality of the working relationship with women officers, custody orientation, job satisfaction, educational level, and prison type. But no significant relationships were found between a pro-woman correctional officer attitude and race, length of service, security level, rank, marital status, stress, or age of male respondents.

Crouch and Alpert (1982) studied occupational socialization among prison guards in three recruit classes trained at the Texas Department of Corrections between mid-June and the end of July 1979. They point out that research generally indicates that guards have an increased aggressive or punitive attitude toward inmates over time. However, when the variable of sex was examined, it was found that "women guards become much more tolerant and nonpunitive over time, while their male counterparts become increasingly punitive and aggressive" (pp. 169–170).

Gross, Larson, Urban, and Zupan (1994), in a study comparing work-related stress in male and female correctional officers, found that there were statistically significant differences between gender and stress outcomes for male and female correctional officers. Women were more likely to be absent more frequently and to have taken sick leave more often than men, but the latter finding, especially, may be due in part to greater family responsibilities.

Carlson, Anson, and George (2003) administered the Maslach Burnout Inventory to 277 correctional officers within a maximum security prison for men. Women correctional officers revealed a greater sense of job-related personal achievement and accomplishments than men officers did. But both groups were found to have similar degrees of emotional exhaustion and depersonalization.

A female correctional officer in a men's prison usually finds that the stress of working in a violent environment is coupled with conflict with male coworkers. But even assuming that problems with male coworkers can be resolved, the role confusion or uncertainty of the job may cause her to seek out or be assigned to low-contact positions (Zimmer, 1986). This, in turn, results in dead-end work assignments or limited promotional possibilities (Jurik, 1985).

Jenne and Kersting (1996) compared how male and female correctional officers deal with volatile inmate situations with male inmates. They found that female officers usually respond to aggressive incidents in the same manner as male correctional officers. Indeed, in some cases, female correctional officers even handle some encounters more aggressively than male correctional officers do. Jenne and Kersting claim that these results debunk the assumption or notion that women are incapable of handling situations that require an aggressive response.

Jurik and Halemba (1984) compared the job satisfaction of male and female correctional officers working at the same prison facility in a western state. They found that female correctional officers tended to be more highly educated than male correctional officers, come from more professional backgrounds, and have a much greater likelihood to be divorced or separated. In contrast, the majority of male correctional officers had previous law enforcement or military experience, but none of the female correctional officers had military experience and only about a third had previous police experience. But despite such demographic differences, Jurik and Halemba discovered that "women exhibited largely the same attitudes toward their work as did male officers," but that "female respondents, more often than men, cited intrinsic reasons for employment in corrections" (p. 564).

Britton (1997) examined the relationship between race and sex and perceptions of the work environment among correctional officers. Using data collected from the correctional officer sub-sample (N = 2,979) of the 1992 administration of the Prison Social Climate Survey, she found that sex and race played a role in shaping officers' perceptions of the work environment, that these differences between groups were not necessarily accounted for by job or institutional characteristics and did not reduce over time, and that there were factors that mediated this relationship between race and sex and workplace perceptions. With minority male officers, their greater efficacy in working with inmates seemed to be an important factor in creating lower levels of job stress, while white female officers' higher levels of overall job satisfaction were accounted for largely because of a more positive evaluation of the quality of supervision.

Privacy–Equal Employment Dilemma

Affirmative action measures have resulted in more minority officers, with the result that the percentage of racial minorities among officers is now equal in many states to that of the minority population of the state. But it was not until the enactment of equal employment legislation—specifically Title VII, which prohibited sex discrimination in hiring by state and local governments—that doors began to open for women in men's prisons.

Three criticisms have been directed toward women working as correctional officers in men's prisons: First, women are not fit for the job; for example, they are not strong enough, are too easily corrupted by inmates, or are poor backup for other officers in trouble. Second, women are a disruptive influence; that is, inmates will not follow their orders or will fight for their attention. Third, the presence of women violates inmate privacy, especially when women are working in shower areas or conducting strip searches of inmates (Hawkins and Alpert, 1989, p. 359).

Dothard v. Rawlinson (1977) and *Gunther v. Iowa State Men's Reformatory* (1979) have been the most important U.S. Supreme Court cases examining whether women are qualified to work in men's prisons. The former was an Alabama lawsuit filed by Diane Rawlinson, a recent college graduate in correctional psychology who was denied a job as a correctional officer because she was five pounds below the minimum weight requirement. Her class-action suit challenged the state's height and weight requirement; the suit also charged that a department of corrections' regulation preventing female officers from "continual close proximity" to prisoners in maximum-security prisons for men (known as the no-contact rule) was discriminatory. The Supreme Court, in a 5–4 decision, overturned a lower court decision that had invalidated the no-contact rule. The Court was unwilling to let women work in maximum-security prisons for men in Alabama because of the danger of sexual attack and because the extra vulnerability of women to attack would weaken security and endanger other prison employees.

However, in *Gunther v. Iowa,* the Court dismissed security issues as a reason for limiting women's employment as guards in that state. The *Gunther* decision defined that job requirements to strip search male inmates or witness them in showers constituted an attempt to prevent women from working as correctional officers.

These and other cases demonstrate that the courts have generally established procedures that both guarantee women the right to employment and protect inmate privacy as much as possible. In the *Forts v. Ward* decision (1978), the circuit court held that "equal job opportunity must in some measure give way to the right of privacy" (p. 1099). The background of this case was that female inmates at the Bedford Hills Correctional Facility in New York contended that their right to privacy was violated because male correctional officers were assigned to duties in hospital and housing units. As a result, the women inmates argued, male correctional officers were able to observe them while they were sleeping, showering, dressing, undressing, and using the toilet facilities. In the *Torres v. Wisconsin* decision (1988), prison officials used the bona fide occupational qualification (BFOQ) defense for restricting male correctional officers from working in the living units of a women's prison. The case went through two appeals processes, but eventually the rights of female inmates were determined to take precedence over the equal employment rights of male correctional officers (Maschke, 1996, p. 32).

Departments of corrections can maintain inmates' right to privacy by administrative policies preventing women from doing some types of searches, such as strip searches. The installation of modesty half-screens, fogged windows that permit figures to be seen, or privacy doors on toilet stalls offer another solution to privacy issues. Security does not have to be sacrificed, and these modifications can be made to the physical environment at little cost.

Comparison of How Female and Male Correctional Officers Do Their Jobs

Several studies have compared male and female correctional officers (Alpert, 1984, pp. 441–455; Peterson, 1982). They have generally found that men and women do not differ in the quality of their job performance. This does not mean that they are equal in all tasks. Although men may be able to handle physical assault better than women, women may more effectively defuse an incident before violence erupts (Peterson, 1982). Leo L. Meyer, a former warden in the Illinois correctional system, describes the role of women officers in a male medium-security institution (quoted in Bartollas, 1981):

> We probably have more female officers than any other correctional center because of the transfers from mental health. Two are lieutenants, and one of them just passed the NRA [National Rifle Association] test for instructor in firearms. I think she is the first woman in history to do this. A female who wants to be a warden has a real good opportunity. I say one thing about females, they're dependable and they seem to try harder. In terms of qualifying for their firearms test: Their scores are better than some men, and many have never shot a gun before. (p. 300)

Various studies have found that women correctional officers are more treatment oriented than are their male counterparts (Jurik and Halemba, 1984; Crouch, 1985). Women also tend to supervise inmates with a more personal interaction style than men officers. For example, women will frequently ask inmates to perform certain tasks, rather than commanding them to do so (Pollock, 1995, p. 107). Zimmer (1986) adds that inmates claim that women officers explain orders more fully, while male officers tend to bark orders and resent any attempt by inmates to get a fuller explanation.

Issues of Women Working as Correctional Officers

Women correctional officers face the same issue as discussed previously that women police officers do: whether the better strategy in this male-dominated area is to adopt a gender-neutral approach (same behavior by women and men) or gendered approach to policing (different behavior by women and by men—each having value). The debate among feminists is similar in correctional work to that in police work. Gender-neutral guarding of inmates appears to be favored among the majority of women corrections officers because "equal" should mean the "the same as" rather than "different but just as good as" (Schulz, 2004, p. 491).

Another issue quite different from those that women police officers confront is the widely prevalent sexual abuse of female inmates women correctional officers in women's prisons must address. As reported in an earlier chapter, this is a serious issue for correctional administrators, but on a much more personal level some women correctional officers certainly would have awareness of and possibly have witnessed this sexual exploitation. No study has been done on women correctional officers' responses to what must be an extremely disturbing experience, but the continued denial of or acceptance of such exploitation has serious ethical and moral issues for women officers.

Women correctional officers, especially in men's prisons, must deal with many levels of sexual and gender harassment. F. J. Till (1980) identified five levels of gender and sexual harassment that she reported from least to most severe. *Gender harassment*, the first level, involves putting down one's sex (usually women). Examples would be informing new officers or seasoned officers that "women aren't strong enough to control male prisoners" or that "women are too emotional to work with male offenders." *Seductive behavior* involves sexual advances or requests by the harasser to discuss the victim's dating or sexual life. This also takes place on a regular basis, but the more likely occurrences are sexual rumors circulated by male correctional officers. *Sexual bribery*, Till's third level of sexual harassment, involves the victim's being promised some type of reward, such as a job or a promotion, if she complies with the harasser's sexual request. This probably takes place to a lesser degree than in the private sector with women correctional officers because promotions and desirable job opportunities are more limited. All the evidence further suggests that *sexual coercion* and *outright sexual assaults and sexual abuse*, Till's fourth and fifth levels, infrequently take place in adult corrections facilities with women correctional officers.

Britton's recent book, *At Work in the Iron Cage*, proposes that the prison is a gendered organization (2003):

> . . . By arguing that the prison qua organization is gendered, I mean that rather than existing as a neutral bureaucratic entity, the prison was formed in and through a matrix of gender, race, class, and sexuality, and that it reproduces individuals, ideas, and inequalities along all these dimensions. As it is gendered, the prison is also raced and classed and sexualized. Though one may choose to emphasize a single dimension for analytical purposes, they never operate in exclusion from one another. Individuals possess these characteristics, of course, and they shape and confirm notions about their own "essential self," as well as the selves of others, through their work. Jobs are not generic slots in the organizational hierarchy but instead contain embedded assumptions about who the ideal worker is. The veracity of these assumptions is confirmed through policies and practices that privilege and reproduce this ideal. (p. 216)

Summary

This chapter examined the role of women working in corrections. Although the empirical examination of women probation and parole officers, women jailers, correctional counselors, and even wardens of men's prisons is thin, every indication is that women continue to experience the problems faced throughout policing careers and legal professions. These problems are particularly highlighted with women who attempt to become correctional officers in men's prisons. Consistent with the men's club in policing, women correctional officers face the time-worn "truth" that women do not belong in a men's prison. Women correctional officers have faced stiff resistance and, at times, physical intimidation and sexual harassment. But some women correctional officers, as with women correctional counselors and correctional administrators, have survived and even thrived in men's prisons.

What is fortunate about women's survival in corrections is the impact that they can bring to the toxicity of correctional environments. The early entrance of women in probation and parole had a considerable impact on humanizing the profession. It can be argued that much of the ideology of probation and parole throughout most of the twentieth century is attributable to the influence of its early women leaders. In some sense, this same tendency seems to be occurring in correctional systems that employ women wardens. There seems to be a consistent difference in how women and men correctional staff approach inmates, handle problems, defuse violence, and respond to crises. These disparities, over time, can make major differences in the quality of institutional life.

KEY TERMS

correctional counselor
probation

probation officer
women correctional officers

superintendent of women's
correctional institutions

CRITICAL THINKING QUESTIONS

1. How would the roles of the female probation officer, the female working in a jail, the female correctional officer, and the female warden or superintendent differ from males working in these positions?

2. Which position in corrections would be most difficult for women? Why?

3. Which position do you believe would be most fulfilling? Why?

4. Why do women choose to work in maximum-security prisons for men? Why not work only in women's prisons?

WEB DESTINATIONS

This site gives details on the career of a correctional officer: http:///www.jobbankusa.com/ohb/ohb156.htm1

This California Correctional Officers Association site is for anyone considering a career as a correctional officer: http:///www.susanvillenews.com/co.htm1

This article surveys recent innovations in definitions of the attitudes and role behavior of prison guards: http:///www.oicj.org/public/story.cfm?story=9FD2986A-F6AC-11D3-AA 9E-00CO4F4309AD4

REFERENCES

Alpert, G. P. (1984). The needs of the judiciary and misapplications of social research: The case of female guards in men's prisons. *Criminology 22:* 441–455.

Anderson, E., and Spanier, G. (1980). Treatment of delinquent youth: The influence of the juvenile probation officer's perceptions of self and work. *Criminology 17:* 505–514.

Bartollas, C. (1981). *Introduction to corrections.* New York: Harper and Row.

Belknap, J. (1991). Women in conflict: An analysis of women correctional officers. *Women and Criminal Justice 2:* 89–115.

Britton, D. M. (1997) Perceptions of the work environment among correctional officers: Do race and sex matter? *Criminology 35:* 85–105.

Britton, D. M. (2003). *At work in the iron cage: The prison as gendered organization.* New York: New York University Press.

Cadwaladr, M. I. (1993) Breaking into jail: Women working in a men's jail. M.A. thesis, Department of Sociology and Anthropology. The University of British Columbia.

Carlson, J. R., Anson, R. H., and George, T. (2003). Correctional officer burnout and stress: Does gender matter? *The Prison Journal 83:* 277–288.

Crouch, B. M., and Alpert, G. P. (1982). Sex and occupational socialization among prison guards: A longitudinal study. *Criminal Justice and Behavior 9:* 159–176.

Dothard v. Rawlinson, 433 U.S. 321, 1977.

Feinman, C. (1994). *Women in the criminal justice system,* 3rd ed. Westport, Conn.: Praeger.

Forts v. Ward, 471 F.Supp. 1095 (S.D.N.Y. 1978).

Gross, G. R., Larson, S. J. Urban, G. D., and Zupan, L. L. (1994). Gender differences in occupational stress among correctional officers. *American Journal of Criminal Justice 18:* 219–234.

Gunther v. Iowa State Men's Reformatory F.2d 1079 (8th Cir., 1979).

Hawk, K. M. (1992, August). BOP programming administrator sees opportunities for women. *Corrections Today 19:* 32, 34.

Hawkins, R., and Alpert, G. P. (1989). *American prison systems: Punishment and justice.* Englewood Cliffs, N.J. Prentice-Hall.

Hayes, M. (1989). Promotion and management: What choices for women? *Probation Journal 36:* 12–17.

Horne, P. (1985). Female corrections officers: A status report. *Federal Probation 49:* 46–54.

Ivey, A. E. (1974). Adapting systems to people. *Personnel and Guidance Journal 53:* 137–138.

Jenne, D. L., and Kersting, R. C. (1996). Aggression and women correctional officers in male prisons. *Prison Journal 76:* 442–460.

Jurik, N. C., and Halemba, G. J. (1984, Autumn). Gender, working conditions and the job satisfaction of women in a non-traditional occupation: Female correctional officers in men's prisons. *The Sociological Quarterly 25:* 551–566.

Jurik, N. C. (1985). An officer and a lady: Organizational barriers to women working as correctional officers in men's prisons. *Social Problems 32:* 375–388.

Lawrence, R., and Mahan, S. (1998). Women correctional officers in men's prisons: Acceptance and perceived job performance. *Women and Criminal Justice 9:* 63–83.

Lidster, D. (1979, March). Personal interview.

Maguire, K., and Pastore, A. (eds.). (1996). *Sourcebook of criminal justice statitics 1995.* Washington, D.C.: U.S. Government Printing Office.

Marks, A. (1997, April 23). Women break into some of the toughest men's prisons. *Christian Science Monitor:* 1.

Maschke, K. J. (1996). Gender in the prison setting: The privacy-equal employment dilemma. *Women and Criminal Justice 7:* 23–42.

Merlo, A. V., and Pollock, J. M. (1995). *Women, law, and social control.* Boston: Allyn & Bacon.

Miller, T. D. (1996). *The warden wore pink.* Brunswick, Minn.: Biddle Publishing.

Morris, N. (1974). *The future of imprisonment.* Chicago: University of Chicago Press.

Morton, J. B. (1992). Looking back on 200 years of valuable contributions. *Corrections Today 18:* 76–87.

Nagel, W. G. (1974). *An American archipelago: The United States Bureau of Prisons.* Hacksensack, N.J.: National Council on Crime and Delinquency.

Nash, M. (1995). Aggravation, mitigation and the gender of probation officers. *Howard Journal of Criminal Justice 34:* 250–258.

Owen, B. (1985). Race and gender relations among prison workers. *Crime and Delinquency 31:* 147–158.

Peterson, C. B. (1982). Doing time with the boys: An analysis of women correctional officers in all-male facilities. In B. R. Price and N. J. Sokoloff (eds.), *The criminal justice system and women.* New York: Clark Boardman.

Platt, A. (1976). *The child savers,* 2nd ed. Chicago: University of Chicago Press.

Pogrebin, M. R., and Poole, E. D. (1997, March). The sexualized work environment: A look at women jail officers. *The Prison Journal 77:* 41–57.

Pollock, J. M. (1995). Women in corrections: Custody or the "caring ethic." In A. V. Merlo and J. M. Pollock (eds.), *Women, law and social control* (pp. 97–116). Needham Heights, Mass.: Allyn & Bacon.

Rogers, J. W. (2000). Mary Belle Harris: Warden and rehabilitation pioneer. *Women and Criminal Justice 11:* 5–27.

Schulz, D. W. (2004). Invisible no more: A social history of women in U.S. policing. In B. R. Price and N. J. Sokoloff (eds.), *The criminal justice system and women* (pp. 483–493). New York: McGraw-Hill.

Slate, R. N., Wells, T. L., and Johnson, W. W. (2003). Operating the manager's door: State probation officer stress and perceptions of participation in workplace decision making. *Crime and Delinquency.*

Stohr, M. K., Mays, G. L., Beck, A. C., and Kelley, T. (1998). Sexual harassment in women's jails. *Journal of Contemporary Criminal Justice 14:* 135–155.

Till, F. J. (1980). Sexual harassment: A report on the sexual harassment of students. *Report of the National Advisory Council on women's educational programs.* Washington, D.C.: U.S. Government Printing Office.

Torres v. Wisconsin Department of Health & Social Services, 838 F.2d 944 (7th Cir. 1988).

Walsh, A. (1984). Gender-based differences. *Criminology 22:* 371–388.

Walters, S. (1993). Changing the guard: Male correctional officers' attitudes toward women as co-workers. *Journal of Offender Rehabilitation 20:* 47–60.

Wisely, W. (1998). $6.5 million spent in California sexual harassment suit. *Corrections Today 60:* 15.

Withrow, P. K. (1992, August). Workplace reality: Women staff tell it like it is. *Corrections Today:* 88–92.

Wunder, G. (1969). Zur Situation der Bew Ahrungshelfer: Algemeines zur Arbeitssituation der Bew, *Bewahrungshilfe-Germany 16:* 91–107.

Zimmer, L. (1989). Solving women's employment problems in corrections: Shifting the burden to administrators. *Women and Criminal Justice 1:* 55–75.

Zimmer, L. (1986). *Women guarding men.* Chicago: University of Chicago Press.

CHAPTER

14 Summary and New Directions for the Future

We have examined six feminist themes in this text. First, we applied an analysis based on gender, class, sexual orientation, age, and race/ethnicity to examine the experiences of women offenders, victims, and practitioners in the criminal justice system. Second, we considered the effects of the multiple oppressions of gender, class/ethnicity, sexual orientation, and age. Third, we focused on the social construction of knowledge and how the role of women has been influenced by male-oriented social constructionism, exposing a number of myths concerning female offenders, victims, and practitioners. Fourth, this text heavily emphasized social context, especially the social context of patriarchal society. We examined how, on a micro-level, women have developed subcultures within the wider society to escape its oppressiveness. Fifth, we looked at the broader theme of globalization in that women are part of larger systems of interaction, and the international perspective portrays this. Sixth and last, the theme of empowerment received some emphasis in nearly every chapter. These six themes, as well as other insights of this text, have been presented with the goal of enabling the reader to experience paradigm shifts concerning the role and treatment of women offenders by the criminal justice system.

Theme of Gender, Class, Race/Ethnicity, Sexual Orientation, and Age

The fundamental theme of this book is that women, especially troublesome ones, are subjected to various forms of discrimination, exploitation, and criminalization. The women who are most likely to experience such oppressions also are poor and from minority groups. With female delinquents, it is their sexual behavior that brings them to the attention of juvenile authorities. It can be argued that much of the state's response is a criminalization of young women's survival strategies (Schaffner, 1998).

Gender is further related to the themes of domination and subordination. Women in a patriarchal society experience inequality of many resources but chiefly of status and power. Placed in subordinate categories, they become more vulnerable to victimization. Wife battering, incestuous attacks of female adolescents by fathers or father substitutes, and rape are crimes of domination against women that take place in situations of inequality.

Class can be another form of exploitation experienced by females. It can increase the likelihood of entrance into homelessness, unemployment, drug use, survival sex and prostitution, and even more serious delinquent and criminal acts. In adolescence, lower-class girls are high risks to have unsatisfactory experiences at school, to lack educational goals beyond high school, to experience higher rates of physical and sexual abuse, to deal with pregnancy and motherhood, to be involved in drug and alcohol dependency, to confront the risk of AIDS, and to lack supportive networks at home. Lower-class adult women are more likely to be victimized than are middle- and upper-class ones and to be subjected to domestic abuse. Equally important, lower-class women are less likely to receive the benefits of chivalry.

Racial oppression of women further receives documentation throughout this text. Both minority girls and women are often forced by their minority status and poverty to deal early and regularly with problems of abuse, drugs, and violence. In addition, they are likely to be attracted to gang membership.

Some evidence also supports the belief that girls and women of color enjoy the benefits of chivalry much less than do white girls. They tend to be viewed as more dangerous to society and to require jail incarceration and long-term institutionalization.

Moreover, there is evidence that African American rape victims are reluctant to go to rape crisis centers or to report their rapes to the police. A large part of this reluctance relates to larger needs and concerns in their lives, including poverty, homelessness, unemployment, difficulties in feeding their children, racism, and fear of the police.

Theme of Multiple Oppressions of Gender, Class, Race/Ethnicity, Sexual Orientation, and Age

The tendency is to think about gender, class, and race in such a way that they are each examined and the total effect is equated to be the sum of each on offenders, victims, and workers in the justice system. Spelman notes that "it isn't easy to think about gender, race/ethnicity, and class in ways that don't obscure or underplay their effects on each other" (Spelman, 1989, p. 115). As a result, what has been most typically done is to focus on gender and sexism and then to ponder about how gender and racism are related to race and racism and to class and classism, but, as Spelman observes, this "obscures the way in which race and class identity may be intertwined with gender identity" (Spelman, 1989, pp. 112, 115). Lewis (1977) has added that because feminist theories of women's inequality "focused" exclusively on the effects of racism, this has been of "limited applicability to minority women subjected to the constraints of both racism and sexism" (p. 339). In Chapter 6, which examined women in prison, it was seen that it is not possible to separate the violence and discrimination against women based on their gender from issues of race, class, and ethnicity. These effects are exacerbated if women are African American or Latina and even more if they are living in poverty.

Kathleen Daly (1993) summarizes this argument by saying "that unless you consider all the key relations of inequality—class, race, gender (and also age and sexuality)—you have considered none" (p. 65). She added that "unless you consider the inseparability of these relations in one person, you do not understand what we are saying" (p. 65). What all this suggests is that both female delinquents and adult women suffer the consequences of multiple oppression as more than some form of simply additive experience and that the whole of gender, race, and class is greater than its individual parts.

Theme of Male-Oriented Social Construction of Knowledge

The major theoretical works on crime have been written by male criminologists about men and boys. Alarmingly gender blind, they added females as a type of footnote. Clearly, from the very beginning, the study of crime and the justice process has been shaped by male experiences and understanding of the social world (Daly and Chesney-Lind, 1988).

In the debate that has taken place between *sex*, which is a biologically based category, and *gender*, which refers to the socially constructed meanings that are associated with each sex, it has been argued that the claimed difference between women and men represents a political and social decision rather than a distinction given in nature (Rothenberg, 1998, p. 9).

The feminist movement, in offering a framework for viewing male-on-female violence, was to turn the conceptualization of rape upside down. For the first time, sexual assault was redefined from the victim's perspective. Rape was seen as the violence it is. Through the efforts of the antirape movement, it would soon become clear that such violence against women was one more mechanism for male social control (Schechter, 1982).

Such feminists as Brownmiller and Griffin helped conceive of rape not in either-or terms but as a series of acts along a continuum. Far from being an isolated event that could be rooted out from the society at large, the crime of rape was now seen as only the logical extension of what was already there. Brownmiller defined rape as "a conscious process of intimidation by which all men keep all women in a state of fear" (Brownmiller, 1975, p. 5).

In considering the crime of rape, a number of rape myths were examined and refuted. These included:

- Most rape claims are false; women feel guilty about sex and redefine the situation later.
- Rape happens only to bad women such as prostitutes.

- Unconsciously women want to be raped.
- Most rape is committed by a stranger down a dark alley.
- When women say no, they mean yes.
- Women's wearing of seductive clothes causes rape.
- Rapes are impulsive acts committed by men who are unable to control their passions.
- Rapes are black-on-white crimes.
- Rape is caused by male deviance and pathology.

Importance of Social Context

In Chapter 1 began a theme that ran throughout the book: U.S. society and many others have been affected by gender in the distribution of power, wealth, and opportunities. What is so disturbing about the social construction of gender is that males have assumed the power and control over women. This is what the term *patriarchal society* ultimately means. Women who live in such a society will be subordinate to the males.

For the past three thousand years, the power of patriarchy has been pervasive. It "has influenced our basic ideas about human nature and about our relation to the universe—'man's' nature and 'his' relations to the universe, in physical language" (Capra, 1988, pp. 29–30). It is a system that only recently has been challenged and whose doctrine seemed to be so universally accepted that it seems to be one of the laws of nature (p. 29).

The laws of society have represented one of the means by which women have been oppressed under patriarchy. The belief that women had to be protected from the sordid nature of life led to restricting them from working and earning a living on an equal basis with men, keeping them from owning property for much of the history of this nation, excluding them from jury duty, and punishing in a severe way those who violated what a woman should be.

The sexual harassment of women has emerged in the context of their employment in legal and criminal justice agencies. This context has been promoted by the cultures of the "men's club" of policing, the "good old boys" of law agencies, and male esprit de corps in correctional institutions and probation and parole agencies.

The kinds of violence that take place in intimate relationships also reveals the importance of social context in this nation. In understanding the violence of intimate relationships, including wife and partner abuse, marital rape, and child abuse, the issues of authority and control by men over women must be carefully explored. Indeed, a man's right to chastise his wife was affirmed in the doctrine of the church as well as in early Roman law and English common law. Even into the twentieth century, domestic violence was considered a private matter, not one for intervention by the state.

An examination of women offenders in correctional institutions reveals the sad story of one form of social injustice after another. Race, gender, and class intersect in the women's prison. One could easily make the argument that the antifeminist and antiwelfare movements are being played out in the prisons of the United States. The war on drugs has taken its toll on poor minority women and on their children, who are destined to grow up in foster homes while their mothers serve their time. The new "get-tough-on-crime" laws have brought their effect to bear disproportionately on persons without political and legal leverage in society.

Rape is a tool of dominance, power, and control. Rape in some situations, such as in war or by gangs, is an act of male bonding. Historically little sensitivity has been shown toward rape victims. In past centuries, a man who wanted a woman raped her and brought her into his tribe (Flowers, 1987). In our most recent past, the rape victim's behavior before the claim of rape, her behavior during the sexual encounter, and her relationship to the perpetrator all were often taken into consideration by legal officials in deciding whether a "real" rape occurred. Indeed, until the 1970s, the law in most states recognized that a rape occurred only when a man forced a woman to have sex under the threat of injury, when she had resisted strenuously, and there was outside corroboration. As part of the misfortune of rape, a woman who engaged in sex outside marriage, even against her will, was considered a "fallen" woman and was frequently blamed for her own victimization (Donat and D'Emilio, 1992).

Subcultures also become important in shaping behaviors of offenders, victims, and workers in the justice system. In the subcultures of some college campuses, men socialized into these subcultures regard sex in terms of gaining possession of a woman. According to Schwartz and DeKeseredy (1997), "the frustration caused by a reference-group-anchored sex drive often results in predatory sexual conduct" (p. 35).

The subculture of males in law has traditionally resulted in women being concentrated in the lowest echelons of the profession. Recently, women have made remarkable advances in the legal profession, but in the law, as elsewhere, status and income disparities still exist. The subculture of males in both policing and corrections has resisted the entrance and acceptance of women. Law enforcement, according to the perspective of the policing subculture, is a men's club and women are not wanted. Correctional staffs, especially in men's prisons, have been quick to say that women do not belong in men's prisons and have provided stiff and consistent opposition to the acceptance of female correctional officers.

Chapter 10 especially examines the victimization of women globally. The sad plight of women as victims internationally receives attention. We have much to be concerned about regarding the victimization of women in the United States, but when globalization is examined, we become painfully aware of the necessity of paradigm shifts in how women are treated in every culture and in every society.

Empowerment of Women Involved with the Justice System

In searching for solutions, this text has drawn on empowerment at all levels—personal, interpersonal, economic, educational, and political. For example, the rape reform and domestic violence intervention movements have made progress on several fronts: the legal one, women's group counseling centers, rape crisis centers, women's shelters, and other crisis intervention programs for victims. Police officers also have become more sensitized to the feelings of women who have been sexually abused. Women's entry into policing, corrections, and the law has had a tremendous impact on those fields, bringing a feminist perspective to issues of women and violence. The close relationship between substance abuse and women offending has encouraged a wide variety of treatment programs for women who have substance abuse problems.

Future Trends

Many trends and events of the twentieth century transformed the criminal justice system and the roles of women within it. Broadly, these events have been expressed as chivalry for white women of a certain class; harsh punishments for African female offenders; first a stress on rehabilitation and then a cynicism toward rehabilitation; a war on drugs and on drug users; and a conservative backlash against women on welfare and women convicted of crime.

There is a truism that says we can't know where we are going until we know where we have been. What we learn from the past is that the pendulum swings in one direction, then comes back to swing the other way. So how long will it take to reverse the present conservative trend?

We can say one thing for certain: Things may have to get worse before they get better. In all probability, this will mean more executions, harsher drug laws, more lethal weapons for the police, fewer rights for prisoners, and more politicians securing public support by capitalizing on the public's fear of crime, a fear largely generated in the mass media. Another truth worth pursuing is that changes at any level of the system will have repercussions throughout the system as a whole.

Over the past decades, the most significant change that portends well for the future is the increasing diversity of the population. This diversity is slowly being reflected in law, the legislatures, and the judiciary. Feminist women have worked for legal reform with some notable successes. Among these are the criminalizing of marital rape in many states and reforms in rape law, such as shielding the past sexual history of victims and removing corroboration requirements. The filing of lawsuits against state departments of corrections has improved career opportunities for women and minority staff as well as vocational training options for female inmates. As increasing numbers of women are appointed to the bench and join prosecution teams, we can expect to see greater protection for victims and prison inmates (another kind of victim) in the future.

The greatest single factor in producing social change and humanizing the criminal justice system at the turn of a new century, in short, may well be the voice of female authority. As women gain in political influence, areas for anticipated change relevant to criminal justice are:

- swifter punishments for male batterers; greater protection for battered women, legally and economically
- more protection for incest victims and less stress on reunification of violent and sexually abusive families
- legislation to provide extensive counseling services to child rape victims to prevent traumatization
- further improvements in rates of conviction of rapists as a result of advances in DNA testing and enhanced victims' rights
- less litigation and increased use of alternative forms of conflict resolution, such as mediation and conferencing between opposing parties
- greater focus on substance abuse, mental health, and medical treatment needs of female offenders
- increased funding for child halfway-house parenting programs for offenders
- as an alternative to imprisonment, much greater use of intensive community supervision programs
- within prison, strict rules restricting male guard access to female inmates
- improved educational and vocational opportunities for women in prison
- an end to mandatory minimum sentences and a return to an individualized approach to justice
- changes in the laws meting out harsh sentences to women convicted as conspirators due to their close associations with drug dealers
- a reversal in "welfare reform" laws so that women will have and be able to maintain more independence from men, if they so desire

Much more research is needed to explore the link between women's victimization in society—sexually, economically, and personally—and their criminality. Research is also needed to show how substance abuse and other addictive behavior figure into the equation.

REFERENCES

Britton, Dana M. (2002). *At work in the iron cage: The prison as gendered organization*. New York: New York University Press.

Brownmiller, S. (1975). *Against our will: Men, women, and rape*. New York: Bantam.

Clark, M. D. (1998, June). Strength-based practice: The ABC's of working with adolescents who don't want to work with you. *Federal Probation 62*(1): 46–53.

Daly, K. (1993). Class-race-gender: Sloganeering in search of meaning. *Social Justice 20*: 56–71.

Daly, K., and Chesney-Lind, M. (1988). Feminism and criminology. *Justice Quarterly 5*: 497–538.

Donat, P., and D'Emilio, J. (1992). A feminist redefinition of rape and sexual assault: Historical foundations and change. *Journal of Social Issues 48*: 9–20.

Flowers, R. B. (1987). *Women and criminality: The woman as victim, offender, and practitioner.* New York: Greenwood Press.

Lewis, D. K. (1977). A response to inequality: Black women, racism, and sexism. *Signs: Journal of Women in Culture and Society 3:* 339.

Rothenberg, P. S. (1998). *Race, class, and gender in the United States: An integrated theory,* 4th ed. New York: St. Martin's Press.

Schaffer, L. (1998, November). Female juvenile delinquency: Sexual solutions and gender bias in juvenile justice. Paper presented to the Annual Meeting of the American Society of Criminology in Washington, D.C.

Schechter, S. (1982). *Women and male violence.* New York: Macmillan.

Schwartz, M. D., and DeKeseredy, W. S. (1997). *Sexual assault on the college campus: The role of male peer support.* Thousand Oaks, Calif.: Sage.

Spelman, E. V. (1989). *Inessential woman.* Boston: Beacon Press.

INDEX